ACUTE CARE PSYCHIATRY

Diagnosis & Treatment

ACUTE CARE PSYCHIATRY

Diagnosis & Treatment

Edited by

LLOYD I. SEDERER, M.D.
Associate Professor of Clinical Psychiatry
Harvard Medical School
Boston, Massachusetts
Medical Director
McLean Hospital
Belmont, Massachusetts

ANTHONY J. ROTHSCHILD, M.D.
Professor of Psychiatry
Director of Clinical Research
Department of Psychiatry
University of Massachusetts Medical Center
Worcester, Massachusetts

Williams & Wilkins
A WAVERLY COMPANY

BALTIMORE • PHILADELPHIA • LONDON • PARIS • BANGKOK
BUENOS AIRES • HONG KONG • MUNICH • SYDNEY • TOKYO • WROCLAW

Managing Editor: Joyce A. Murphy
Marketing Manager: Daniell Griffin
Production Coordinator: Carol Eckhart
Copy Editor: Christiane Odyniec
Designer: Paul Fry
Illustration Planner: Wayne Hubbel
Typesetter: Peirce Graphic Services, Inc.
Printer and Binder: Edwards Brothers

**WM
141
A189
1997**

Copyright © 1997, Williams & Wilkins

351 West Camden Street
Baltimore, Maryland 21201–2436 USA

Rose Tree Corporate Center
1400 North Providence Road
Building II, Suite 5025
Media, Pennsylvania 19063-2043 USA

Accurate indications, adverse reactions and dosage schedules for drugs are provided in this book, but it is possible that they may change. The reader is urged to review the package information data of the manufacturers of the medications mentioned.

Printed in the United States of America

Library of Congress Cataloging-in-Publication Data

Acute care psychiatry : diagnosis and treatment / edited by Lloyd I. Sederer, Anthony J. Rothschild.
    p.   cm.
  Includes bibliographical references and index.
  ISBN 0-683-30006-7
  1. Crisis intervention (Psychiatry)   I. Sederer, Lloyd I.   II. Rothschild, Anthony J.
  [DNLM: 1. Mental Disorders—diagnosis.   2. Mental Disorders—therapy.
  3. Acute Disease—rehabilitation.   4. Psychiatry—methods.   WM 141 A189 1997]
  RC480.6.A27   1997
  616.89—dc21
  DNLM/DLC
  for Library of Congress   96-39069
                                           CIP

The publishers have made every effort to trace the copyright holders for borrowed material. If they have inadvertently overlooked any, they will be pleased to make the necessary arrangements at the first opportunity.

To purchase additional copies of this book, call our customer service department at **(800) 638-0672** or fax orders to **(800) 447-8438.** For other book services, including chapter reprints and large quantity sales, ask for the Special Sales department.

Canadian customers should call **(800) 665-1148,** or fax **(800) 665-0103.** For all other calls originating outside of the United States, please call **(410) 528-4223** or fax us at **(410) 528-8550.**

Visit Williams & Wilkins on the Internet: http://www.wwilkins.com or contact our customer service department at **custserv@wwilkins.com.** Williams & Wilkins customer service representatives are available from 8:30 am to 6:00 pm, EST, Monday through Friday, for telephone access.

97 98 99 00 01
1 2 3 4 5 6 7 8 9 10

*To the staff, trainees, and patients of McLean Hospital who have helped
to transform the provision of acute care from an idea to a reality.*
—LIS

*In memory of my father, Ernest Rothschild
To all my colleagues at McLean Hospital
and
the University of Massachusetts Medical School,
Department of Psychiatry.
To my patients.
Thank you.
—AJR*

Contributors

Stuart A. Anfang, M.D.
Staff Psychiatrist
Baystate Medical Center
Springfield, Massachusetts
Assistant Professor of Psychiatry
Tufts University School of Medicine
Boston, Massachusetts

Michael J. Bennett, M.D.
Associate Clinical Professor of Psychiatry
Harvard Medical School
Boston, Massachusetts

Elizabeth G. Brenner, L.I.C.S.W.
Program Director
Family and Home Consultation Service
Choave Health Management
Stoneham, Massachusetts

Franca Centorrino, M.D.
Instructor in Psychiatry
Harvard Medical School
Boston, Massachusetts
Assistant in Psychiatry
McLean Hospital
Belmont, Massachusetts

James A. Chu, M.D.
Clinical Director
Trauma and Dissociative Disorders Program
McLean Hospital
Belmont, Massachusetts
Assistant Professor of Psychiatry
Harvard Medical School
Boston, Massachusetts

John F. Clarkin, Ph.D.
Professor
Department of Psychology
The New York Hospital
Cornell Medical Center
White Plains, New York

Joseph T. Coyle, M.D.
Chairman
Consolidated Department of Psychiatry
Harvard Medical School
Boston, Massachusetts

Barbara Dickey, Ph.D.
Director, Department of Mental Health Services
　　Research
McLean Hospital
Belmont, Massachusetts
Associate Professor
Department of Psychiatry
Harvard Medical School
Boston, Massachusetts

Lisa Beth Dixon, M.D.
Assistant Professor
Department of Psychiatry
University of Maryland
Baltimore, Maryland

James M. Ellison, M.D., M.P.H.
Chief, Mental Health Department
Robert H. Ebert Burlington Health Center
Harvard Pilgrim Health Care
Burlington, Massachusetts
Associate Clinical Professor of Psychiatry
Harvard Medical School
Boston, Massachusetts

David Fassler, M.D.
C.E.O., Choate Health Management, Inc.
Clinical Associate Professor
Department of Psychiatry
University of Vermont College of Medicine
Burlington, Vermont

Glen O. Gabbard, M.D.
Callaway Distinguished Professor of
Psychoanalysis and Education
Karl Menninger School of Psychiatry
The Menninger Clinic
Topeka, Kansas
Clinical Professor of Psychiatry
University of Kansas School of Medicine
Wichita, Kansas

Ira D. Glick, M.D.
Professor of Psychiatry
Stanford University School of Medicine
Director of Inpatient & Partial
Hospitalization Services
Stanford University Hospital
Stanford, California

Rachel Lipson Glick, M.D.
Clinical Assistant Professor
Department of Psychiatry
University of Michigan Medical School
Ann Arbor, Michigan

Tana A. Grady, M.D.
Assistant Professor
Department of Psychiatry and Behavioral Sciences
Director of Residency Education
Duke University Medical Center
Durham, North Carolina

Thomas G. Gutheil, M.D.
Professor of Psychiatry
Harvard Medical School
Co-Director, Program in Psychiatry and The Law
Massachusetts Mental Health Center
Boston, Massachusetts

Gail Hanson-Mayer, R.N., C.S., M.P.H.
Senior Vice President for Operations
Choate Health Management, Inc.
Stoneham, Massachusetts

Patricia A. Harney, Ph.D.
Licensed Clinical Psychologist
Boston Regional Medical Center
Stoneham, Massachusetts
Research Psychologist
Victims of Violence Program
Cambridge Hospital
Cambridge, Massachusetts

Gordon Harper, M.D.
Associate Professor of Psychiatry
Harvard Medical School
Director, Inpatient Psychiatry
Children's Hospital
Boston, Massachusetts

James Hilliard, Esq.
Connor and Hilliard
Walpole, Massachusetts

Douglas H. Hughes, M.D.
Administrative Chief of Psychiatry
Boston Veteran's Administration Medical Center
Lecturer, Harvard Medical School
Boston, Massachusetts

Susan Kemker, M.D.
Assistant Professor of Psychiatry
Department of Psychiatry
Albert Einstein College of Medicine
Bronx, New York

Howard D. Kibel, M.D.
Professor of Psychiatry
New York Medical College
Director of Group Psychotherapy
Psychiatric Institute
Westchester County Medical Center
Valhalla, New York

Trude Kleinschmidt, M.D.
Medical Director
Clinical Evaluation Center
McLean Hospital
Belmont, Massachusetts
Instructor in Psychiatry
Harvard Medical School
Boston, Massachusetts

Jeremy A. Lazarus, M.D.
Assistant Clinical Professor
Department of Psychiatry
University of Colorado Health Sciences Center
Denver, Colorado

Margaret T. Lee, Ph.D.
Brandeis University
Heller School/Institute for Health Policy
Waltham, Massachusetts

Stephen L. Pinals, M.D.
Instructor in Psychiatry
University Hospitals of Cleveland
Case Western Reserve University Medical School
Cleveland, Ohio

Michelle Riba, M.D.
Clinical Assistant Professor
Director, Resident and Fellow Education
Department of Psychiatry
University of Michigan Medical Center
Ann Arbor, Michigan

Anthony J. Rothschild, M.D.
Professor of Psychiatry
Director of Clinical Research, Department of
    Psychiatry
University of Massachusetts Medical Center
Worcester, Massachusetts

Kathy M. Sanders, M.D.
Director, Acute Psychiatry Service
Massachusetts General Hospital
Instructor in Psychiatry
Harvard Medical School
Boston, Massachusetts

Andrew Satlin, M.D.
Director of Geriatric Psychiatry
Department of Psychiatry
McLean Hospital
Belmont, Massachusetts
Assistant Professor of Psychiatry
Harvard Medical School
Boston, Massachusetts

Jack E. Scott, Sc.D.
Research Assistant Professor
Department of Psychiatry
University of Maryland at Baltimore
Baltimore, Maryland

Lloyd I. Sederer, M.D.
Associate Professor of Clinical Psychiatry
Harvard Medical School
Boston, Massachusetts
Medical Director
McLean Hospital
Belmont, Massachusetts

Mauricio Tohen, M.D., Dr.P.H.
Associate Professor of Psychiatry
Harvard Medical School
Associate Professor of Epidemiology
Harvard School of Public Health

Joseph Triebwasser
New York, New York

Roger Weiss, M.D.
Associate Professor of Psychiatry
Harvard Medical School
Boston, Massachusetts
Clinical Director
Alcohol and Drug Abuse Program
McLean Hospital
Belmont, Massachusetts

Carlos A. Zarate, Jr., M.D.
Director
Bipolar and Psychotic Disorders Outpatient
    Services
McLean Hospital
Belmont, Massachusetts
Instructor in Psychiatry
Harvard Medical School
Boston, Massachusetts

Gwen Zornberg, M.D., M.S.
Instructor of Psychiatry
Harvard Medical School
Boston, Massachusetts
Assistant Psychiatrist
McLean Hospital
Belmont, Massachusetts

Contents

Contributors *vii*

Introduction *xv*
  Lloyd I. Sederer

Section I: PSYCHIATRIC ASSESSMENT AND INTERVENTION

1 The Four Questions 3
  Lloyd I. Sederer

2 Suicide Risk Assessment 15
  Anthony J. Rothschild

3 Risk Assessment—Violence 29
  Douglas Hughes

4 Psychiatric Triage, Crisis Intervention, and Disposition 47
  Trude Kleinschmidt and Kathy Sanders

5 Acute Psychiatric Disorders in Primary Care 67
  Michelle Riba and Rachel Glick

Section II: ACUTE CARE

PART A: SPECIFIC DISORDERS

6 Depression 83
  Tana A. Grady, Lloyd I. Sederer, and Anthony J. Rothschild

7 Panic and Obsessive-Compulsive Disorders 123
  Patricia A. Harney and James M. Ellison

8 Mania 141
  Mauricio Tohen

9 Schizophrenia 167
  Lloyd I. Sederer and Franca Centorrino

10 Trauma and Dissociative Disorders 195
  James A. Chu

11   Substance-Related Disorders   221
          Gwen Zornberg and Roger Weiss

12   Disorders of the Geriatric Population   249
          Stephen L. Pinals and Andrew Satlin

13   Disorders of Childhood and Adolescence   277
          Gordon Harper

14   Borderline and Antisocial Personality Disorders   293
          Joseph Triebwasser and Lloyd I. Sederer

P A R T B: SPECIFIC INTERVENTIONS AND TREATMENTS

15   Case Management   323
          Lisa Dixon and Jack Scott

16   Family Support and Intervention   337
          Ira D. Glick and John F. Clarkin

17   Focal Psychotherapy   355
          Michael J. Bennett

18   Group Psychotherapy   375
          Susan Kemker and Howard D. Kibel

19   Home-Based Care   391
          David Fassler, Gail Hanson-Mayer, and Elizabeth G. Brenner

Section III: ADMINISTRATIVE ASPECTS OF ACUTE CARE PSYCHIATRY

20   The Medical Record in the Acute Care Setting   415
          Thomas G. Gutheil

          Appendix 20A: Contents of the Psychiatric Record in Acute Care
          Settings   426

21   Legal Issues in Acute Care Psychiatry   431
          Stuart A. Anfang and James T. Hilliard

22   Treatment Guidelines and Algorithms in Acute Care Psychiatry   457
          Carlos A. Zarate, Jr.

23   The Salience of Neuroscience in the Education of Psychiatrists   469
          Joseph T. Coyle

24   Training Residents in Psychodynamic Psychiatry   481
          Glen O. Gabbard

25   Ethical Issues in Acute Care   493
          Jeremy A. Lazarus

26 Assessing Quality of Care in Clinical Practice   503
Barbara Dickey and Lloyd T. Sederer

   Appendix 26A: Consumer-Oriented Mental Health Report Card: Final
   Report of the MHSIP Task Force, April 1996   516

   Appendix 26B: PERMS 1.0: Performance Measures for Managed Behavioral
   Healthcare Programs Produced by the Quality Improvement and Clinical
   Services Committee of the American Managed Behavioral Healthcare
   Association, July 1995   534

   Appendix 26C: BASIS-32™ Behavior and Symptom Identification Scale   538

   Appendix 26D: Perceptions of Care   541

27 Professional Satisfaction and Compensation   543
Lloyd I. Sederer and Margaret T. Lee

Index   533

Introduction

Revolution is not new to psychiatry. The revolution in the financing, management, and delivery of psychiatric services that has consumed psychiatry in the United States throughout this decade is but one of a series of profound reorganizations in the conception and provision of clinical care. The enormous impact of the current revolution on professional practice, professional lives, and patient care should not be minimized by any panoramic view. Rather, this perspective of ongoing revolutions is offered because of the importance of acknowledging that, in science, the only constant is change, and the incorporation of new ideas and methods is both vitalizing and inevitable.

Two hundred years ago, immediately following the French and American revolutions, psychiatry saw its first clinical revolution. Moral therapy was introduced in France and rapidly spread throughout Europe to the United States. Humane care, coupled with carefully structured and purposeful asylum life (usually in a rural or suburban setting), served as the underlying principles of moral therapy and fostered the birth of mental hospitals throughout the 19th century.

The second revolution in psychiatry occurred early in the 20th century when Freud abandoned the seduction theory (that actual sexual trauma was at the root of neuroses) and turned his attention to the unconscious. Much of psychiatric practice moved from the mental hospital to the consulting room, where psychoanalytic treatment aimed to bring ego to where id had ruled and turn neurotic misery into ordinary unhappiness. Dynamic psychiatry exploded in Europe and was imported to the United States, first by the exchange of ideas and then by the Diaspora of eastern European analysts who fled from the impending holocaust. By the 1950s, psychoanalytic theory and practice had become the prevailing treatment philosophy in psychiatry, the chairman [sic] of almost every department of psychiatry was an analyst, and psychiatric training was considered incomplete without a personal analysis. Dynamic psychiatry reigned supreme until about 25 years ago. Today its irreplaceable contributions are in peril as the juggernaut of cost control threatens to delete depth psychology, long-term psychotherapy, and psychoanalysis from insurance reimbursement, therapeutic practice, and clinical training.

The third revolution began gathering momentum after World War II. The war had demanded techniques of crisis stabilization, front-line (community) services, and group and milieu treatment. More importantly, however, safe and effective pharmaceutical agents for the treatment of major mental disorders were introduced. Before the war, psychiatry's pharmacopoeia included sedatives and chemical agents to induce shock; the remainder of the biologic interventions were electroconvulsive therapy and lobotomy. By the 1970s, psychiatrists had available to them lithium, two classes of antidepressants, the neuroleptics, and anxiolytics. The third revolution gained in credibility, proponents, and federal financial support. During the 1970s and 1980s, an intense struggle existed between dynamic and biologic psychiatrists for intellectual hegemony and for control of services, training, and departments of psychiatry. Some readers will recall the acrimony of that struggle and some of its casualties. By the 1990s, psychiatry had entered the decade of the brain.

Arnold Relman, former editor of the *New England Journal of Medicine*, was referring to the fourth revolution when he stated that the 1980s represented the revolt of the payers. Despite unprecedented growth in medical services—or perhaps because of it—the increasing costs of health care, which appeared to be unrestrained, were alarming. Business and government, the principal payers, feared that medical costs would erode competitiveness and profits or actually bankrupt the Social Security trust account. The fact that tens of millions of Americans were either uninsured or underinsured emphasized that the United States was spending more than any other country on earth, yet was the only industrialized Western country without universal health care. The payers revolted. Thus the fourth revolution began, extant throughout medicine, but most severely felt by psychiatry. This revolution has become known as managed care.

Managed care, at worst, seeks to curtail and shift costs; at best, it is a philosophy of population-based care with accountability for clinical outcomes. The economic revolution that embroils medicine today began with aggressive utilization review conducted by proprietary corporations whose mandate was profit. This was the first wave of managed care. Clinicians, patients, and families had reason to fear that clinical care would be subordinated to corporate profits. Rationing decisions were driven disproportionately by business interests, rather than by clinically informed and ethically based guidelines. Considerable distrust now exists about managed care, and rightfully so. However, the economic revolution that fostered the emergence of managed care has not, and will not, disappear. Resources have become increasingly scarce. Today, treatment interventions must meet the standard of cost-effectiveness. Variance in practice will increasingly give way to practice guidelines and scientifically based algorithms. Focused, intermittent psychotherapy and ongoing pharmacotherapy may allow affordable, universal access to care for persons with most major mental disorders and for the conflicts and deficits that exist with great prevalence in this and every other country.

Although this revolution has been fueled by economics and competition, managed care should not be viewed as merely a matter of money, despite the enormous capital that has transferred hands in a very few years. We are witnessing a revolution in the financing and delivery of health care that insists that clinical care be population based and judged by outcome, accessibility, cost-effectiveness, and patient satisfaction. In short order, managed care corporations themselves will be subjected to the same expectations they first espoused: only cost-effective, necessary, and accountable services will be allowed. The financial margins for proprietary managed care corporations are shrinking, and their value is diminishing in a health-care system that ultimately requires only patients and providers. Like every other preceding revolution, the contributions of managed care will be incorporated into clinical practice and its excesses and redundancies will be eradicated.

This text is a product of the economic revolution in health care. Its predecessor (*Inpatient Psychiatry: Diagnosis and Treatment*), through three editions, addressed acute care rendered in a hospital setting. This is no longer the case. Acute care of the major mental disorders is now provided in a host of intensive treatment environments: intensive outpatient treatment (more than two visits per week), home care, partial hospital, respite care, acute residential care, and the inpatient unit that is rapidly becoming the ICU of psychiatric services. Unlike inpatient treatment, acute care is provided within what has been termed a continuum of care. Not every patient goes through every level of care; in fact, few go through more than two levels of care. But any patient may enter the continuum at any level of care and move from less-intensive to more-intensive care and vice versa when clinically warranted.

Acute care is more critically reliant on accurate assessment than was inpatient treatment alone. The safety of the inpatient unit (whether locked or staff secure) previously allowed for a greater margin of error in assessing suicidal risk or danger of violence. The constant observation of many professionals on an inpatient unit permitted greater data collection to establish a diagnosis and assess the effects of treatment. This text on acute care emphasizes the importance of assessment. Clinicians will no longer use inpatient units on a routine basis; they will need to hone their assessment skills to work effectively with acutely ill patients. Consequently, the first section of this text principally focuses on assessment, and the first chapter, "The Four Questions," offers a method for assessing the acutely ill patient.

This section continues with chapters on the risk assessment of suicide and violence. Assessment is the foundation for the next chapter, "Psychiatric Triage, Crisis Intervention, and Disposition," a critical subject in the provision of acute care in a managed care environment. This section concludes with the chapter, "Acute Psychiatric Disorders in Primary Care." As care is increasingly managed and psychiatric services are better integrated with general medical and surgical care, primary care physicians will increasingly confront acutely ill psychiatric patients in their offices. These physicians will need guidance in assessing and safely managing and referring these patients.

The four questions discussed in the first chapter serve to organize the beginning of each chapter in the second section of the text, entitled "Acute Care." This section has two parts. The first part concentrates on the disorders most commonly encountered (recognizing that some conditions had to be excluded) in acute care: depression, panic and obsessive-compulsive disorders, mania, schizophrenia, trauma and dissociative disorders, substance-related disorders, disorders of the geriatric population, disorders of childhood and adolescence, and borderline and antisocial personality disorders. Each chapter uses the same structure to guide the reader in understanding diagnosis and treatment and to help unify a multiauthored text. The chapters have the following design: definition of the disorder; *Diagnostic and Statistical Manual*, 4th edition, diagnosis; epidemiology; the four questions (what are the [1] descriptive and differential diagnoses, [2] ego defenses and character style, [3] formulation, and [4] focal problem?); biologic evaluation; assessing the level of care; treatment; controversies; and course and prognosis.

The second part of the section on acute care focuses on specific interventions and treatments characteristic of acute care psychiatry. Chapters on case management, family support and intervention, focal psychotherapy, group psychotherapy, and home-based care offer the reader discussions on a variety of critical approaches and techniques that are essential to acute care psychiatry.

The third section of the text addresses administrative aspects of acute care psychiatry. In this era of managed health care, which still carries forward the regulatory world that preceded it, no system of care can run smoothly and effectively, demonstrate the desired outcomes of its services, train the next generation of clinicians, be paid, stay out of court, successfully grapple with the ethical dilemmas of practice, and offer professional satisfac-

tion to its staff unless the clinical services are thoughtfully administered.

The duty to faithfully care for patients is now hitched to a second and compelling duty—serving as stewards of a just system of care that must attend to the needs of an entire community of patients. Acute care psychiatry is (1) the accurate diagnosis and formulation of the symptoms, signs, and painful experiences that patients present, (2) the provision of the most worthwhile treatments in the least-restrictive, cost-effective sites of service, and (3) the ability to prove that the care provided brings clinical improvement in a manner that meets the patient's definition of satisfaction and is also cost-effective. The goals of acute care are safety, symptom stabilization and containment, diagnosis and formulation, alliance with the patient and family (or significant others), and initiation of the process of clinical recompensation, which will continue in ambulatory care. More than ever, the skills of clinicians and clinical leaders will be tested. That is the challenge and the gratification awaiting those who commit themselves to acute care. The editors and authors of this text hope that our writings make that commitment a bit easier.

L.I.S.

Section I

PSYCHIATRIC ASSESSMENT AND INTERVENTION

Chapter 1   The Four Questions
Chapter 2   Suicide Risk Assessment
Chapter 3   Risk Assessment—Violence
Chapter 4   Psychiatric Triage, Crisis Intervention, and Disposition
Chapter 5   Acute Psychiatric Disorders in Primary Care

Chapter 1

The Four Questions

Lloyd I. Sederer

The provision of psychiatric care to acutely ill patients has become increasingly exacting. Accurate diagnosis and safe and effective treatments must be rendered rapidly and as inexpensively as possible, which increases the risk of error and hence requires highly developed clinical acumen. Moreover, the payers and the public are restive; they demand access, information, accountability, confidentiality, dignity, and good outcome. If these demands are not met, they will take their business elsewhere (in a buyer's market) or litigate or both.

Fortunately, in psychiatry, the reliability and validity of the diagnostic system (the *Diagnostic and Statistical Manual*, 4th edition) and the efficacy of the treatments have achieved remarkable levels of performance (1). In fact, psychiatric treatments of major mental disorders are as effective or more effective than those of other medical specialties (2).

The science of diagnosis and treatment—nosology and epidemiology notwithstanding—will always be rendered through the medium of practice. Successful practice, in turn, rests on knowledge, skill development, and experience. This chapter describes four critical areas of knowledge and skill acquisition for the clinician who seeks to make the experience of acute care psychiatry a successful one.

THE FOUR QUESTIONS

Four critical areas of assessment can be used as the structure and foundation of the clinical encounter with an acutely ill patient. When used effectively, the clinician's ability to understand and articulate these key areas will optimize alliance, intervention, and outcome; provide necessary documentation for the medical chart and malpractice prevention (risk management); and meet the increasing demands of payers and regulators (3). These four questions are as follows:

1. What is the patient's descriptive diagnosis and the attendant differential diagnosis?
2. What are the ego defenses principally

used by the patient at the time of the examination and what is the character diagnosis of the patient?

3. What current stresses have affected what intrinsic vulnerabilities (biologic and psychological) to render the presenting symptom picture? This is the formulation of the case.

4. What problem(s) must be addressed to restore safety and/or equilibrium to enable the patient to leave acute care? Harper called this the "focal problem" (4).

The remainder of this chapter describes each area of inquiry and provides case examples of their practice. First, however, the conceptual approach that underlies psychiatric thinking, and thereby shapes its actions, is examined.

AN ORGANIZING MODEL FOR PSYCHIATRY

The field of psychiatry presents an overwhelming volume of clinical data, hypothetical notions, and theoretical constructs. "Dopamine mingles with denial and serotonin with symbiosis. Defenses and divorce appear as meaningful, and influential, as gamma amino butyric acid and the endorphins. Urban drift, ego-deficits, and ventricular enlargement may be found rubbing conceptual shoulders" (5). To effectively use such a broad database and such comprehensive and diverse constructs, clinical psychiatry has amalgamated its biologic, psychological, and social perspectives into what has been referred to as the biopsychosocial model (6, 7).

The biologic perspective draws on a disease orientation and a medical model. Each individual may be host to a discrete pathogen or a disease process, or may be the bearer of an inherited genetic maladaption or vulnerability. Observable signs, reportable symptoms, and a distinct pathogenesis, course, and prognosis define each disorder. Treatment is directed at remedying or arresting the disease and restoring, to the extent possible, premorbid functioning.

The psychological perspective is drawn from a very different cast of mind. Developmental traumas or neglects, disturbed relationships, learned maladaptive thoughts and behaviors, and intrapsychic deficits and conflicts are the ingredients of personality disorder and human agony. Diagnosis is based on observable behavior and inferred psychic structure. Etiology also must be inferred because psychogenic processes will never fulfill Koch's postulates. From a psychological perspective, treatment is rooted in the doctor-patient relationship, which differs from the medical model in which this relationship may be seen as enabling to treatment but never the curative factor. Finally, treatment is aimed at adaptation and psychological growth rather than cure or remediation.

By stepping out of and beyond the individual's biology and psychology, we may enter the social perspective. Context matters. Environmental disturbances and dislocations are the agents that undo a fragile equilibrium and induce symptomatology. Family crises, economic misfortunes, government failures, emigration, war, and catastrophe are the genesis of disorder. Intervention, not treatment, is directed at the environment, not the person. There is no illness, only socially induced distress and decompensation.

In the biopsychosocial model, these three perspectives (disease, person, and social situation) converge and conceptually complement one another. Destiny is multidetermined. Although this model falls short of being considered a unifying paradigm, it does provide a diverse and coherent framework for clinical inquiry and therapeutic action (8).

Question 1: What is the Patient's Descriptive Diagnosis and the Attendant Differential Diagnosis?

Descriptive diagnosis is built on objective signs and symptoms and an observable history and course of a disorder. The term diagnosis is derived from the Greek words for "two" (*di*) and "to know" (*gnosis*); based on this derivation, diagnosis requires a knowledge of the difference between two entities. In effect, diagnosis is the process of differentiating one disorder from another. Differential diagnosis is the process of putting forward the best guess (hypothesis) about which disorder is principally responsible for the patient's malady. Also, in differential diagnosis, other disorders are considered as alternative explanations for the illness.

The American Psychiatric Association published the first edition of the *Diagnostic and Statistical Manual: Mental Disorders* (DSM-I) in 1952 and the fourth edition in 1994. An official nomenclature has been evolving for more than 40 years. With the past two editions, a foundation of empirical evidence became the watchword for the nomenclature. For example, DSM-IV was developed through a lengthy process of comprehensive literature reviews, re-analyses of existing data sets, and field trials. Psychiatric diagnosis has become a reliable, criterion-based science.

The clinical usefulness of diagnosis for mental disorders is indisputable. The first question that must be asked when a patient presents with a mental disorder is, "What is the diagnosis?" The more acute the disorder (in symptomatology or in risk to the patient or others), the more critical the diagnosis. The corollary to the first question is, "What is the differential diagnosis?" This question aims to ensure that the diagnosis has not been reached prematurely or erroneously, as an accurate diagnosis is crucial in selecting effective treatment and in forecasting course and prognosis.

DSM-IV provides three axes for diagnostic consideration. The third axis (Axis III), which is used for encoding general medical conditions, is extremely important in understanding the patient's presentation and in managing his or her care. However, this axis does not code for psychiatric disorders and hence will not be considered in this text. Axis I encompasses the clinical disorders or, put another way, "psychiatry's illnesses." A patient may present signs and symptoms of more than one Axis I disorder. Axis II, which encompasses the personality disorders and mental retardation, may include more than one personality disorder. It also may be used to indicate persistent and prominent maladaptive personality features that do not fully meet criteria for the diagnosis of a personality disorder. For example, a patient may show features of a histrionic personality but may not meet the diagnostic criteria for the disorder. In recording diagnoses, the clinician should include all that apply but emphasize the primary disorder that warrants priority intervention.

Axis II disorders of personality also are included in the descriptive and differential diagnoses. An Axis II disorder should be distinguished from the patient's ego defenses (see below in the section on question 2). There will be some, perhaps considerable, overlap between the characteristic behaviors, affects, and defenses that constitute a personality disorder (Axis II) and the specific defense mechanisms used by a patient. The critical distinction, however, is that DSM-IV is descriptive and amotivational. Axis II of the DSM-IV enables the clinician to define a behavioral profile of a long-standing disorder of personality. The DSM does not allow for a depiction of the underlying structure and dynamics of personality. An Axis II diagnosis does not offer an operational definition of the patient's ego defenses. These defenses are critical to the patient's efforts to adapt. It is essential that the clinician understands these defenses if he or she is to engage the patient effectively in an alliance and enhance opportunities for therapeutic success. For example, a patient diagnosed with a borderline personality disorder would have met five or more of the behavioral criteria listed in DSM-IV. However, it would not be apparent (from the DSM) at the clinical interview that the patient was primarily using the defenses of idealization and devaluation unless question 2 was asked and answered.

□ **C A S E   E X A M P L E**

A 57-year-old university professor sought urgent consultation for symptoms of a severely depressed mood that had been unremitting for more than 1 month. She cried every day, was besieged by guilty preoccupation, and could not concentrate adequately to perform her work. Her sleep was interrupted with early morning awakening and she was fatigued throughout the day. She described herself as "lifeless" and could barely mobilize any energy or interest in her family or her work, which was contrary to her usual state of mind. As her mood and symptoms worsened, without relief, she began to believe that she could not be helped, that she was a burden to others, and that her family would be better off if she were dead. There were no indications of psychotic thinking. Although she had experienced brief blue periods (which remitted spontaneously) after two normal pregnancies, she had no history of mental disorder.

Her family history was positive for a mood disorder in the maternal lineage and for alcoholism in the paternal lineage. She was agreeably married, achieved considerable success professionally, and maintained strong and lasting friendships. Psychologically, this patient showed obsessional traits of dutiful, methodical work; high standards for herself and others; an overdeveloped conscience; and limited emotional range. Medically, she was in good health and was taking no medications. Menopause had occurred 5 years earlier.

The patient's research was threatened because of shrinking federal funding. In the past year, the patient's mother had died unexpectedly of an aggressive malignancy.

To answer question 1, the following can be postulated. The patient's likely diagnosis on Axis I is that of a mood disorder, specifically major depressive disorder, severe, without psychosis. The principal differential diagnoses are those of bereavement or a mood disorder due to a general medical condition (in her case undiagnosed). The patient's history supports obsessional personality traits, but there is no evidence of obsessive-compulsive personality disorder. In working with this patient, it will be essential to differentiate bereavement from depression and to rule out any undiagnosed medical disorder that may be masquerading as depression. Once the diagnosis of major depressive disorder is established, treatment with antidepressant medication and psychotherapy can be initiated promptly, with very good likelihood of success. Educating the patient (and her family) and giving the patient as much control and responsibility over her care as she can tolerate will capitalize on her character traits and facilitate an alliance.

Question 2: What Are the Ego Defenses Principally Used by the Patient at the Time of the Examination and What Is the Character Diagnosis of the Patient?

The assessment of the patient is further advanced by this question. Although psychoanalytic experience would be useful, clinicians must learn to develop the capability to assess ego and character early in training and hone this skill through clinical practice and supervision.

The ego is a hypothetical construct that has been critical in the history and development of psychology and psychoanalysis in the Western world. Early psychoanalytic theoreticians identified the ego as one of three mental structures, namely, the ego, id, and superego. Over time, the ego came to be understood as a group of mental functions essential for psychological equilibrium and adaptation. These functions are subject to disturbances that can result in symptoms and subjective distress. The principal functions of the ego are discussed below (9).

Relationship to Reality

This function is composed of reality testing and a "sense of reality." Reality testing is the capacity to correctly appraise the external world. Failure to do so results in impairment in reality testing; when pronounced, this failure produces psychosis. A sense of reality refers to an individual's experience of the world, its very appear-

ance, and familiarity. Together, reality testing and a sense of reality are basic to adaptation.

Regulation and Control of Drives

Drives are the urges, wishes, and needs experienced from within. Control and regulation allow drives to be delayed and internal demands to be less overwhelming. Without this function, civilization or sublimation could not be realized.

Object Relations

The capacity to establish and maintain attachments with others is the function that has been termed object relations. Contemporary psychodynamic thinking has focused especially on object relationships as primary human motivators and sources of pleasure.

Thought Processes

Perception, memory, concentration, judgment, planning, detection of differences, and abstraction are all examples of thought processes. Disturbances in thought, consequently, can be manifold.

Ego Defenses (or Defense Mechanisms)

Defense mechanisms are ". . . automatic psychological processes that protect the individual against anxiety and from the awareness of internal or external dangers of stressors" (1, p. 751). The defense mechanisms mediate internal and external conflicts, enhance adaptation, and are used by individuals to satisfy internal needs and reconcile them to external reality. The more effective the defensive adaptation, the more likely that success can be achieved in relationships (love), work, and play. In fact, defenses have been categorized according to their level of adaptation (10). Moreover, DSM-IV proposes for study a scale that would hierarchically categorize defensive functioning by levels. These levels, which are listed below, can be useful as a tool for clinicians assessing the defensive organization of the patient under evaluation (1, pp. 751–753).

- High adaptive level: anticipation, affiliation, altruism, humor, self-assertion, self-observation, sublimation, suppression.
- Mental inhibitions (compromise formation) level: displacement, dissociation, intellectualization, isolation of affect, reaction formation, repression, undoing.
- Minor image-distorting level: devaluation, idealization, omnipotence.
- Disavowal level: denial, projection, rationalization.
- Major image-distorting level: autistic fantasy, projective identification, splitting of self-image or image of others.
- Action level: acting out, apathetic withdrawal, help-rejecting complaining, passive aggression.
- Level of defensive dysregulation: delusional projection, psychotic denial, psychotic distortion.

Character diagnosis, unlike descriptive diagnosis, is based on an assessment of these ego defense mechanisms and an appreciation of the psychological development of the individual. Kernberg's work perhaps best exemplifies this area of assessment (11, 12). Kernberg developed his classification of character along a continuum of levels of psychological organization ranging from higher to intermediate to lower levels of character "pathology." In this schema, he did not address the most disturbed end of the spectrum as seen in psychotic characters, nor the more developed character formations as seen in high functioning, neurotic personalities or in "normality." Obsessional and high functioning hysterical characters are examples of higher level characters, and borderline patients are typical of the lower level of character pathology.

Kernberg classified levels of character pathology by examining four psychic domains: the defensive operations of the ego, superego development, instinctual development, and internalized object relationships. Examples of defense mechanisms were provided above, although Kernberg's examples differ somewhat. He regarded higher level characters to use repression (with intellectualization, rationalization, undoing, and higher levels of projection) as the principal defensive operation. Instinctual wishes can be sublimated by higher level characters. Intermediate level characters also use repression, but with a faulty defensive barrier so that impulses are partially expressed, as in passive aggressive maneuvers. Splitting is the predominant defense at the lower level of organization with its related defenses of projective identification, idealization, and devaluation. Impulses are poorly contained by these defenses; consequently, aggressive and sexual drives and behaviors break through.

Higher level characters show well-developed although somewhat stern superegos (the superego is a theoretical construct that encompasses the functions of morality, conscience, and guilt). A component of the superego, the ego ideal, is the structure that addresses aspiration and self-esteem. Intermediate characters show evidence of more punitive and rigid superegos and less capacity for guilt. Lower level characters have impaired superego functioning, with limited capacity for guilt and concern, and tend to project aspects of a highly punitive, judgmental conscience onto others.

The instinctual development of higher level characters demonstrates appropriately inhibited (or channeled) aggressive drives and genital levels of sexuality. Regression from genital sexuality to pregenital needs, especially dependency, is typical of intermediate level characters. Lower level characters show pronounced pregenital aggression and poorly contained sexual drives.

From a psychodynamic perspective, object relations refers to the internalized identifications and introjections (less developed, less internalized identifications) of the emotionally valued people in a person's life that form the basis for a sense of identity. From an interpersonal perspective, these internalized identifications and introjections can be assessed by examining the nature, duration, and gratification of an individual's relationships with other people. Higher level characters possess a stable sense of self and have only limited conflicts and experience of deprivation in relationships. They are capable of experiencing a wide range of feeling with others and of showing concern for others. Intermediate characters have the capacity for enduring relationships with others but these are suffused with conflict and suffering. Their sense of self is intact but also subject to internal conflict. Lower level characters show severely disturbed object relations without a sense of self or object constancy. As a consequence, they feel terrorized by doubts of the predictability of anything. Moreover, their relationships tend to be intensely dependent (and angry) and marked by rapidly shifting views of the self and others as all good or all bad.

The second question thus asks clinicians to assess the person in addition to the illness. What is the nature of this person's established psychological organization (his or her character diagnosis) and what are the primary defenses used at the time of the examination?

□ CASE EXAMPLE

A 24-year-old man was brought by his girlfriend to the emergency department of a hospital in the middle of the night after impulsively taking an unknown amount of acetaminophen. His history revealed that he episodically abused alcohol and cocaine and had overdosed before. His relationships with friends, women, and coworkers were characterized by brief, intense attachments followed by angry disappointments with vindictive and self-destructive behaviors. His parents no longer welcomed him at home, and he left a trail of angered employers, making job opportunities increasingly limited. His distrust of others was paramount at the time he presented to the emergency department; he did not want help and was persuaded that "... if you trust anyone, they will suck you dry." He reported that he had been mistreated by his boss and that his girlfriend was inadequate in caring for him. His family history was significant for alcoholism, impulsivity, and antisocial behavior.

This patient showed lower level character pathology with instinctual (impulse) dyscontrol (especially aggressive acting out), alternating idealized and disappointed/devalued relationships, instability in his sense of self and others with consequent impairment in relationships and work, limited capacity for concern or guilt, projection of responsibility for his difficulties (he blames others), and a markedly handicapped capacity to adapt to the realities of everyday life. At the time of examination, his defensive functioning was principally projective, with disavowal. He did not see himself as the agent of his destiny and had an internalized view of others as both responsible for his difficulties and inadequate to his needs. He used splitting and the derivative defense of devaluation. On an action level, he resorted to acting out.

In working with this patient (after any medical danger is past), the clinician will need to proceed with caution. The patient will mistrust any effort to help or could easily switch and imagine that the clinician will be the one to save him. Therapeutic modesty and appropriate insistence that the patient be responsible for the future of his treatment will be essential. However, care must be taken not to be excessively confrontational because the patient already expects to be unfairly judged and punished. The patient's impulsivity, substance misuse, and self-destructiveness makes psychopharmacologic intervention a high risk. Prognosis will be guarded, especially if substance misuse continues (or becomes dependence) or if his relationships, such as they are, become more punitive or frankly paranoid.

Question 3: What Current Stresses Have Affected What Intrinsic Vulnerabilities (Biologic and Psychological) to Render the Presenting Symptom Picture?

This is the formulation of the case that should not be seen as a rarefied search for an ultimate understanding of a patient. Rather, the formulation should be a working hypothesis, with frequent additions, deletions, and revisions as the clinician better understands the patient. The purpose of the formulation is to put the patient's current presentation in perspective

(for the patient, the family, and the treatment team) and to better inform treatment planning. In fulfilling these purposes, the formulation becomes a practical tool to enhance alliance and treatment planning (13, 14).

An effort to understand, "Why now?" is central to every formulation. To answer this question, the clinician will need to search for both the underlying vulnerabilities (biologic and psychological) intrinsic to the patient and the current stresses and conflicts that converge on those vulnerabilities to unleash the distress, symptomatology, and disability that have brought the patient to acute care.

The formulation begins with the precipitating event that may be psychological, environmental, or biologic (organic). Regardless of its nature, the event must have the power to disequilibrate the individual. What is it about the event that gives it such power? For example, why does the anniversary of the death of the patient's mother induce a symptomatic reaction? Why does the vacation of a therapist prompt suicidal ideation in a previously compensated patient? Why has the prescription by the patient's internist of a beta blocker for hypertension induced severe depressive symptoms? Why has a postpartum state prompted manic symptoms requiring locked-door containment? The clinician's search for and understanding of the precipitating event should not stop until the power of the purported precipitant is adequate to explain the decompensation.

☐ CASE EXAMPLE

A 54-year-old mentally retarded man with a known seizure disorder was transferred from a community residence to an emergency triage site after a rather abrupt onset of disruptive, aggressive behavior and two tonic-clonic seizures. Because of his highly agitated behavior in the emergency department, he was admitted to the hospital. At the time of his admission, the counseling staff at the community residence could not explain why the patient had decompensated from his previously stable condition. They did mention, however, that approximately 1 month before this emergency admission the patient had been given a new roommate.

After admission, several lengthy telephone conversations with the inpatient psychiatrist, the residence director, and the mental health center psychiatrist who prescribed medications for this patient revealed the following. After the patient's new roommate arrived, the patient became more restless and preoccupied. An appointment was made with the outpatient psychiatrist, who drew a Dilantin blood level; that level was slightly higher than the therapeutic range. The psychiatrist then lowered the patient's anticonvulsant dose to bring him into the therapeutic range. No other medication changes were made. Within 1 week, the patient developed the severe symptoms and seizure activity described above.

For this patient, a novel and challenging social stressor (a new roommate) triggered a medication review. The result of that review was to treat the patient's laboratory value, not the patient. As a consequence, the patient's anticonvulsant level fell below the therapeutic range. Mental status and neurologic instability ensued. The precipitant to acute care was an unnecessary change in anticonvulsant medication in a seizure-disordered man, perhaps because the residential staff was having

difficulty helping the patient adapt to a new roommate. Restoration of the higher dose of Dilantin stabilized the patient's neurologic condition, and he returned to his residence.

The formulation is further developed by a hypothesis that asks, what psychological purpose or function does the symptomatology serve? This does not suggest a consciously calculated or manipulative design on the patient's part (although there are times when this is the case). Instead, clinicians seek to comprehend the psychological utility of the decompensation. Typically, the patient is not aware that his or her illness can serve a purpose. Psychic equilibrium and interpersonal conflicts and communications generally are managed out of the patient's awareness. What needs are satisfied through the symptoms? What impulses or affects are contained through the defenses used, even if they are painful and transiently disabling? What object relations (critical human ties) are maintained through the presenting illness? What guilty feelings or overbearing conscience is assuaged? What is communicated to key persons in the patient's life (especially therapist or psychiatrist) through the distress and help-seeking behavior?

□ **C A S E E X A M P L E**

A middle-aged physician was brought by his spouse for acute care from a distant state. The spouse indicated that the patient had been self-prescribing a variety of psychoactive substances and had been abusing alcohol. Efforts to engage this physician in an effective treatment had been unsuccessful despite mandatory requirements by his state licensing board.

Notably, the patient's history revealed that his father, also a physician, reportedly had been physically and emotionally abusive to him as a child. The patient's use of psychoactive substances and alcohol blunted overwhelming affects that were flooding him and simultaneously elicited help from a maternal figure—in this case, his wife.

Because of his early trauma, the patient could neither trust nor put himself in the hands of another physician. By fleeing to a distant state, he was eluding a commitment to a treatment relationship with his doctor while simultaneously achieving the attention of a maternal figure.

Question 4: What Problem(s) Must Be Addressed to Restore Safety and/or Equilibrium to Enable the Patient to Leave Acute Care?

Harper called this the "focal problem" (4). The focal problem stands between the patient and discharge to a less-intense level of care (for more detailed information, see Chapter 13). In answering question 4, the clinician translates understanding (formulation) into action. By addressing this question, a specific problem (or problems) is identified: what must be changed for the patient to graduate successfully from acute care? Precise, achievable goals derive from knowing the focal problem and inviting the patient into the treatment process. By identifying the focal problem in language understandable to the patient, mutually understood goals are established that form the basis of an effective treatment alliance. The focal problem also can be understood by families, significant others, and payers and can be translated readily into short-term goals for treatment planning and documentation.

Harper has emphasized a collateral question: "Where (literally) are most patients with this problem?" (4, p. 32). If the answer is not an acute care setting, then the clinician has not answered question 4 specifically enough. For example, auditory hallucinations and paranoid delusions are commonplace in the severely and persistently psychotic ill. However, most of these patients are not in acute care; hence, hallucinations and delusions typically are not a focal problem. An example of a focal problem would be medication noncompliance resulting in acute hallucinations and personal neglect, brought about by the hospitalization of the patient's mother (the caretaker), who is not available.

The focal problem is different from a focal conflict. Focal conflicts are concepts well known to the field of brief or focused psychotherapy (see Chapter 17) (15, 16). A focal conflict depicts, for example, the internal tension the patient experiences between a desire and a prohibition, or between reality and fantasy. However, the focal conflict does not expressly identify in problem-solving, everyday language what must be done to enable the patient to return to a life outside the medical care system. The focal conflict empathically explains the patient's pain and shapes the themes of psychotherapy. The focal problem generates the explicit goals needed to focus acute care interventions.

□ CASE EXAMPLE

The physician discussed in the case example of question 3 was detoxified, over 48 hours, so that he could bring adequate cognitive capacities to bear on his dilemma. The focal problem then could be identified and addressed with the patient and his wife. The focal problem was not addiction, although he did have an addictive disorder. The problem was his flight from any caregiver (or authority) who could gain power, therapeutic or otherwise, over him. His wife's willingness to bring him out of state, ostensibly for greater confidentiality (although he was known to his medical board), colluded in his flight. The focal problem was his fear of entrusting himself into effective, local care and facing the emotional demands this would place on both husband and wife. Acute care treatment, therefore, focused on securing a responsible caregiver in his area, helping the couple understand the purpose(s) served by their flight, and not beginning a process of care, distant from their home, that could not endure. The patient and wife were able to return home within days.

□ **C A S E   E X A M P L E**

A 23-year-old woman was brought to the emergency department by her therapist after she resumed severe cutting and head-banging behavior. She had a history of profound self-abuse and had spent much of her adolescence in hospital care. With effective long-term treatment, principally psychotherapy, her self-destructive behaviors abated and she began to function well in the work place. Her disturbed behaviors resumed on the day that she heard that her uncle, the man who sexually abused her as a child, died in a car accident.

Flooded with rage, guilt, and shame, the patient was able, with the help of her therapist and friends, to contain briefly her self-destructive behaviors. Those behaviors again erupted when she heard that her family wanted her to attend the uncle's funeral.

The patient's focal problem was the expectation by her family that she provide the pretense of normality at her uncle's funeral. To do so would subvert her psychological and moral integrity and threaten to undo the work of her therapy, which had emphasized the critical importance of her protecting herself. Faced with the conflict between responding to her family's needs and her own, which were so contrary, she decompensated into symptomatic behavior. The focal problem could only be resolved by recognizing the destabilizing impact of the funeral and its meaning to the patient, and providing the therapeutic support the patient needed to defend herself appropriately against the exploitative needs of others.

CONCLUSIONS

As the end of the 20th century approaches, many advancements have been made in psychiatry. A highly reliable nosology has been established, along with the capacity to effectively diagnose the mental disorders that afflict a sizable proportion of the population. Moreover, psychiatric treatments are highly effective and are becoming more so as neuroscience and health services research introduce new treatments and better inform treatment choices. The provision of acute care for psychiatric patients has also been distinguished by improved diagnostics and treatment efficacy. Clinicians can make a significant difference for patients and, by extension, for their families and all others who are affected by the ravages of mental illness.

This chapter has offered a method for the assessment of the acutely ill patient. Assessment begins with an accurate descriptive diagnosis and differential diagnosis but cannot stop there. There must be an understanding of the person with the illness and how that person's ego defenses work in a time of crisis. The formulation then is developed to answer the question, "Why has this disorder emerged now?" The precipitating event should be assessed to uncover the reason for its power to destabilize the person's equilibrium—either its biologic power or psychological power (meaning) or both. Other questions to be answered include the following: What does the symptomatology do for the patient? What needs are satisfied? What conflicts are mollified? What purpose does the disorder serve in the patient's internal and external world? Finally, as precisely as possible, the focal problem—that which stands between the patient and recompensation and between the patient and discharge from acute care— must be posited.

By understanding the four questions, an effective alliance based on accurate diagnosis and empathic formulation can be established. This understanding allows clinicians to target their biologic, psychological, and social interventions effectively. The outcomes for patients, families, employers, and payers then can be remarkable. The gratification for clinicians is in seeing our patients benefit from our labors.

REFERENCES

1. The diagnostic and statistical manual. 4th ed. Washington, DC: American Psychiatric Press, 1994.
2. National Institute of Mental Health. Health care reform for Americans with severe mental illness: report of the National Advisory Mental Health Council. Washington, DC: NIMH, March 1993.
3. Sederer LI, Dickey B. Outcomes assessment in clinical practice. Baltimore: Williams & Wilkins, 1996.
4. Harper G. Focal inpatient treatment planning. J Am Acad Child Adolesc Psychiatry 1989;28:31–37.
5. Sederer LI. An organizing model for those entering the field of psychiatry. J Psychiatr Educ 1988;12:71–81.
6. Engel GL. The biopsychosocial model and the education of health professionals. Ann NY Acad Sci 1978;310:169–181.
7. Engel GL. The clinical application of the biopsychosocial model. Am J Psychiatry 1980;137:535–544.
8. Kuhn TS. The structure of scientific revolutions. 2nd ed. Chicago: University of Chicago Press, 1970.
9. Moore BE, Fine BD. A glossary of psychoanalytic terms and concepts. 2nd ed. New York: The American Psychoanalytic Association, 1968.
10. Vaillant GE. Adaptation to life. Boston: Little, Brown & Co., 1977.
11. Kernberg OF. Borderline conditions and pathological narcissism. New York: Jason Aronson, 1975.
12. Kernberg OF. A psychoanalytic classification of character pathology. J Am Psychoanal Assoc 1970;18:800–822.
13. Perry S, Cooper AM, Michels R. The psychodynamic formulation: its purpose, structure and clinical application. Am J Psychiatry 1987;144:545–550.
14. Melchiode GA. The psychodynamic formulation: how and why. Gen Hosp Psychiatry 1988;10:41–45.
15. Mann J. Time limited psychotherapy. Cambridge: Harvard University Press, 1973.
16. Budman SH. Forms of brief psychotherapy. New York: Guilford Press, 1981.

Chapter 2

Suicide Risk Assessment

Anthony J. Rothschild

INTRODUCTION

Scope of the Problem

Suicide, a major preventable cause of death, is a significant public health problem in the United States that creates deep distress in surviving family and friends. During the past century, the suicide rate in the United States has averaged 12.5 deaths per 100,000. Suicide is the eighth leading cause of death for the general population and is the third leading cause of death for persons aged 15 to 24 in the United States (1, 2). Suicide, which is one of the leading causes of death among younger age groups, is almost entirely preventable.

The risk of suicide in the United States increases as a function of age, with the highest rates of suicide seen in elderly men (3). However, when the relationship between age and suicide is examined over the past two decades, the percentage of deaths due to suicides for persons 15 to 25 years of age has increased, whereas the percentage of total suicide deaths for per-

sons older than 44 years of age has decreased (4). From 1950 to 1980, rates for suicide among white males age 15 to 19 increased by 305%; among males age 20 to 24, rates increased by 196% (4).

Higher rates of suicide have been reported in the baby boom cohort (5, 6), although cohorts born since World War II have been healthier and were raised during a time of economic prosperity. Klerman and Weissman (6) have postulated that the large baby boom birth cohort may result in increased competition for scarce resources, resulting in higher unemployment, lower earnings, and decreased access to educational opportunity. The higher rates of suicide also have paralleled important temporal, social, and economic events, including changes in family structure, shifts in gender roles, increase in women entering the work force, changes in decisions to marry, increase in access to lethal weapons, and the effects of increased media exposure on violence (6).

Suicide rates have been shown to be higher in men than in women; however, females make three times as many attempts as males. Differences in methods of suicide when analyzed by gender are apparent. Males choose violent means (e.g., firearms, explosives, hanging) to commit suicide more frequently than females, who often choose more nonviolent means (e.g., drug overdose) (2). Although rates of suicide increase with age in both women and men, the peak rate in women is often 10 years earlier than in men (7).

Problem of Prediction

Although suicide is a major preventable cause of death and considerable progress has been made in identifying high-risk groups, the demographic data are far too general to be of practical use. Demographic data can identify large groups with greater than average risk (e.g., persons who are single, widowed, or divorced); however, data identify large numbers of people who are never at risk (8). Although statistical methods can identify subgroups of patients with unusually high rates of subsequent suicide, the base rate of suicide is so low that even a predictive test with high specificity and sensitivity will still include far too many false-positives for practical use (9).

However, despite weak predictive value, clinical studies do provide the clinician with useful information. In the evaluation of a particular patient for suicidal ideation, the clinician should assess how closely the patient resembles the profile of a described high-risk population. An adequate evaluation requires that the clinician assess the degree of the patient's suicidal intent in the present and project what it is likely to be in the immediate future. In addition, the clinician should judge the quality of the controls, both internal and environmental, that are available to the patient to act against the suicidal intent. The objective risk factors (outlined below) are important guides, but the clinician's ability to elicit the patient's thoughts and feelings in the clinical interview is crucial.

Patients Needing Special Evaluation for Suicide

Patients can exhibit suicidal ideation or intent to the clinician in a variety of ways. Some patients who present for evaluation may be recent survivors of a suicide attempt. Other patients may present with the chief complaint of suicidal thoughts or urges. Some patients will present with other complaints but will admit to suicidal thoughts during the evaluation. Finally, some patients (often brought for evaluation by family members or friends) will deny suicidal ideation or intent but are behaving in a way that demonstrates suicide potential or are creating concern among those living with or observing the patient.

All patients with a major psychiatric disorder should be asked about suicidal ideation as a routine part of the mental status examination. Patients at risk for suicide will not be detected unless the clinician inquires about suicidal ideation and suicidal behaviors. Although this may seem obvious, many clinicians do not routinely ask about self-destructive behaviors or previous suicide attempts, which are among the most powerful predictors of future suicidal behavior. The failure to ask may be due to a misconception that asking about suicidal ideation will encourage a patient to contemplate suicide when he or she had not done so previously. Patients with suicidal ideation are often relieved to be able to discuss their suicidal ideas with a clinician and to have these ideas explained in the context of their psychiatric illness. Patients are often reassured by hearing that suicidal feelings and ideas are not uncommon for psychiatrically ill patients and that they often are resolved with treatment.

Several types of patients require special attention. Patients suffering from a mood disorder (15% lifetime risk of suicide), panic disorder (7–15% lifetime risk of suicide), schizophrenia (10% lifetime risk of suicide), alcoholism (3% lifetime risk of suicide), and borderline personality disorder (7% lifetime risk of suicide) are at particular risk (see section on psychiatric disorders below). Other states potentially leading to suicide include deliria (such as delirium tremens) or toxic states (such as LSD or phencyclidine [PCP] intoxication) in which the patient may respond to hallucinations or delusional ideas that can lead to suicide. Other situations requiring special attention include patients suffering from terminal illness or chronic pain who experience significant demoralization or hopelessness. Other conditions that can increase suicide risk include physical illness; psychopathology in the family and social milieu, including significant life stress and crisis; a family history of psychiatric illness and particularly a family history of suicide; and the presence of firearms in the home (particularly for adolescents).

Difficulties for the Clinician

The evaluation of suicidal patients may be complicated by the fact that such patients can evoke strong countertransference feelings in the clinician. When the clinician likes or identifies with the patient, he or she may be tempted to deny serious risk of suicide. The clinician then may reassure the patient that everything will be fine or attempt to talk the patient out of his or her suicidal feelings. This can make it difficult for the patient to fully express feelings and can deny the patient proper evaluation and treatment. Conversely,

some patients (particularly those with histories of multiple suicide gestures) may arouse anger or aversion in the clinician. This, too, can make objective assessment difficult or can result in the clinician prescribing interventions that are more punitive than therapeutic. Many suicidal patients will provoke anxiety in the clinician because of the awareness that an error in management could have catastrophic consequences. Thus, clinicians should be aware of their feelings and be alert to their countertransference reactions when evaluating suicidal patients and should not let these reactions interfere with the clinical evaluation.

INTERVIEWING THE SUICIDAL PATIENT

General Approach

The diagnostic interview is a critical element in suicide prevention. Rapport needs to be established with the patient before direct questions about suicide can be asked. The clinician should remain calm and uncritical, proceeding from more general questions to the specific. An empathic approach using sensitive and thorough questioning conveys to the patient that someone cares and that they are not alone and isolated in their suffering (many patients who have attempted suicide express feelings of isolation and that no one cares). Patients who have survived serious suicide attempts frequently report that they felt that there was no one they could turn to for help. Thus, the clinician can play a critical role in enabling the patient to see that there can be relief from suffering and abatement of symptoms without resorting to self-harm.

Patients can be questioned about suicidal ideation and feelings of hopelessness and despair. The clinician then can explain that it is not uncommon for patients who are depressed to feel that life is not worth living or to consider suicide. Questions such as, "Have you ever felt so bad that you would prefer not to go on living?" or "Have things been so bad that you have had thoughts of hurting yourself?" can elicit important information in a sensitive manner. Specific information should be obtained regarding frequency of suicidal feelings, length of each episode, alleviation of suicidal feelings, and methods of suicide that have been considered. It may be useful to ask patients to describe their suicidal fantasy and to verbalize their expectations as to what would happen to them and to their families and friends after their death. Very concrete plans, such as wishing to be reunited with a deceased loved one, putting one's affairs in order, and feeling that "others would be better if I were dead" are often ominous signs.

Although bringing family and friends into the clinical interview can be useful, the patient may find it difficult to divulge suicidal ideas and motives unless given the opportunity to talk to the clinician alone. Clinicians should not attempt to talk patients out of their suicidal thinking; this approach can be perceived by the patient as a lack of empathy or a lack of permission to discuss their suicidal thinking.

All suicidal threats should be taken seriously, even if they seem manipulative. Any patient who conveys a sense of hopelessness must be questioned about suicide. Studies have found that suicidal intent is correlated more highly with hopelessness than with depression (10), and that hopelessness is a strong, long-term predictor of future suicides (11). Patients who have been depressed and suddenly improve also should be asked about suicide. Patients contemplating suicide are often ambivalent regarding taking a fatal step. The ambivalent patient who is contemplating suicide often is quite agitated and anxious. However, after making the decision to commit suicide, the patient may become calmer because the ambivalence is resolved. Thus, inexplicable improvement in a patient who has been depressed or hopeless may stem from having made a decision to commit suicide.

Patients who have a history of frequent accidents also should be asked about current life problems, alcohol and drug use, depression, and self-destructive thoughts. If a patient who is being evaluated for potential self-destructive behavior or suicidal intent wishes to leave the clinical setting before the completion of the evaluation, the patient should be detained until the evaluation is completed.

All obtained data, clinical reasoning, and therapeutic interventions should be carefully documented in the patient's record. In a recent study of 50 patients who were identified by systematic research evaluations as having attempted suicide and as having a current major depressive episode, clinicians (including psychiatrists) who performed routine intake and discharge assessments failed to document adequately the presence of a lifetime history of suicide attempts in 24% of cases on admission and in 28% of cases in the discharge summary (12). Furthermore, the physician's discharge summary did not document the presence of recent suicidal ideation or planning in 38% of patients (12).

Goals of the Evaluation

The patient should be evaluated for ideas, wishes, and motives indicative of suicidal thinking. The degree to which the patient intends to act on his or her suicidal thoughts and the dynamic meanings and motivation for suicide should be explored. The presence or absence of a suicidal plan should be noted. Whether the planned means of suicide are available to the patient (e.g., pills or firearms) and whether the patient knows how to use them should be explored. Whether the means are potentially lethal and whether the patient has made any provision for being saved should be noted. The presence or absence of overt suicidal/self-destructive behavior should be ascertained. The patient's physiologic, cognitive, and affective states should be noted, particularly whether the patient is depressed, demoralized, hopeless, psychotic, or intoxicated.

The patient's coping potential, environmental supports, and alliance with the therapist also should be evaluated. Does the patient have future plans and are they realistic? Has the patient recently put his or her affairs in order? Can the patient resist the suicidal impulses? If the patient has been psychotic or extremely impulsive in the past, the clinician should assume that the patient will not have effective controls against suicide.

Environmental supports also should be assessed. Are there family members available to watch and supervise medication? The clinician also should assess whether the patient's risk of suicide is likely to increase in the immediate future. The factors to consider in forecasting worsening (or improvement) in suicidality include the natural history of the patient's psychiatric illness, the likelihood that treatment will be effective, and the patient's personal and demographic risk factors. It is critical to assess the strength of the patient's personal relationships and the therapeutic relationship (alliance) between patient and clinician. Many individuals who are depressed and hopeless and wish to end their lives are dissuaded by thoughts of children, parents, and friends who care or of a therapist with whom they have a positive alliance. Patients who have ended relationships and connections and who do not have a relationship or alliance with anyone (including the clinician) are at greatest risk for suicide. Finally, the patient's personal and demographic risk factors for suicide should be determined (see below).

PERSONAL AND DEMOGRAPHIC RISK FACTORS FOR SUICIDE

Psychiatric Disorder

Mood Disorders

More than 90% of patients who attempt suicide suffer from a major psychiatric disorder. The lifetime risk of suicide in patients with mood disorders is 15%. Suicidal ideation is a serious complication of major depressive disorder (MDD) (13, 14) and may predate a completed suicide (9, 15–19). The risk of suicide is particularly high in patients suffering from psychotic (delusional) depression in which the potentially dangerous combination of a dysphoric mood state and nihilistic delusions are present simultaneously (20). The likelihood of suicide within 1 year of MDD is increased when the patient exhibits panic attacks, psychic anxiety, anhedonia, or alcohol abuse. The likelihood of suicide during the ensuing 1 to 5 years is increased when the patient exhibits increased hopelessness (11), suicidal ideation, or a history of suicide attempts.

Panic Disorders

Recent studies suggest that patients with panic disorder have an increased risk of suicidal behavior (21). The suicide does not necessarily occur during a frank panic attack. In these patients, suicide is more highly correlated with having a more severe form of the illness, having comorbid mood and substance use disorders, experiencing demoralization, or experiencing a significant loss.

Schizophrenia

Fifteen percent of patients with schizophrenia commit suicide (22–24). The risk is greatest for those schizophrenic patients who feel hopeless, fear mental disintegration, have made previous suicide attempts, have a chronic relapsing course to their illness, and are not compliant with treatment (22, 24–27). Most schizophrenic patients who commit suicide are unemployed young males who had been at a high level of functioning before the onset of the illness. The co-occurrence of alcohol or drug abuse in patients with schizophrenia also contributes to suicide risk (22, 26, 28–31). Suicide potential also can be increased by the patient's recognition of his or her deterioration during a postpsychotic, depressed phase of the schizophrenic illness (24, 29, 32, 33).

Alcohol and Substance Abuse

Alcohol and substance abuse represent major risk factors for suicide in both alcoholic and nonalcoholic populations. Between 5% and 27% of all deaths of alcoholics are caused by suicide (34, 35), with a lifetime risk of suicide estimated to be 15% (14, 34–36). Alcohol use typically is associated with 25–50% of completed suicides (34, 37–41); its contribution is second only to that made by affective disorders. In contrast to affective disorders, in which suicide is more likely to occur early in the disease (42), suicide in patients suffering from alcohol dependence is likely to occur late in the disease. Suicide in alcoholics often is related to rejection, interpersonal loss, or the onset of medical complications of the illness (34–37, 40, 41, 43).

Alcohol and drug abuse are frequently complications of other psychiatric disorders, including affective and anxiety disorders, schizophrenia, and personality disorders (44). It is estimated that 60–70% of alcoholic patients have an additional psychiatric diagnosis (34, 35). In drug abusers, the incidence of suicide is 20 times greater than that for the general population and often represents a "solution" to the anxiety or mood disturbance associated with a masked, comorbid psychiatric disorder. Therefore, the clinician's ability to reduce the incidence of suicide in chemically dependent persons is associated with accurate diagnosis and appropriate treatment of the substance abuse and any other comorbid psychiatric disorder (34, 35, 45).

Borderline Personality Disorder

Although patients with borderline personality disorder often engage in self-destructive behavior without lethal intent, a substantial number (at least 5–10%) do eventually commit suicide (46, 47). The presence of a concurrent major mood disorder and/or substance abuse increases the risk of suicide in these patients (46). Suicidal behavior in adults also is associated with the diagnosis of antisocial personality disorder. An estimated 5% of patients with antisocial personality disorder die by suicide, and as many as 46% attempt suicide (36, 46). Antisocial personality disorder and criminality have been reported as predictors of recurrent suicide attempts (46). Fifty percent of these attempts are preceded by a crisis in a significant relationship, involve a nonviolent method, and can be seen as an effort to change the behavior of others (48). Five percent of patients suffering from antisocial personality who complete suicide also may suffer from a concurrent affective disorder, substance abuse, and/or other personality traits or environmental stressors that increase their risk for suicide (46).

History of Attempts and Threats

A history of suicide attempts and threats is a strong risk factor. Patients with a history of attempting suicide have demonstrated their ability to overcome any personal, religious, or societal inhibitions to take their own lives or an inability to withstand suicidal impulses or both. Several studies have shown that a history of suicidal behavior is one of the best predictors of future suicidal behavior (9, 49, 50). Up to 40% of people who eventually commit suicide have made a prior suicide attempt (37, 51). Moreover, there is a 32% increase in relative risk associated with each prior attempt (52). The risk of suicide is highest in the year following a suicide attempt (51), although an additional 10% of persons make an attempt to commit suicide in the following 10 years (53).

Age

As discussed previously, the risk of suicide increases as a function of age, with the highest rate of suicide seen in elderly men (3). Suicide is uncommon (but on the increase) before adolescence. The suicide rate among adolescents and young adults has increased significantly in recent years.

Gender

Men commit suicide more frequently than women (see above), although women make more frequent suicide attempts than men. In general, males choose more violent means to commit suicide than females. Unpublished evidence suggests that the distinction between men and women

in the use of violent means to commit suicide is disappearing in the United States.

Social Factors

Suicide is more common in people who are single, separated, divorced, or widowed. Married couples with children are at a decreased risk for suicide, and this risk decreases further with increased numbers of children (54). The loss of a spouse increases risk; the risk for suicide is greatest during the first year after the loss and extends for 4 years thereafter (55). People who live alone and those who have failed in a love relationship in the past year are also at increased risk.

Occupational Factors

The unemployed and unskilled are at increased risk for suicide. In a study that compared unemployment rates with suicide rates in eight countries, Boor (56) observed that suicide rate and unemployment correlated positively in many countries. This correlation held true for both men and women. This finding differs from earlier studies that revealed higher rates for men than for women during times of economic adversity; however, the more recent data may reflect the fact that more women are employed or are entering professions. In general, studies have shown that the unemployment rate among those who commit suicide is greater than 50% (57). Among professionals, a sense of failure in a particular role is a risk factor, (e.g., demotion or the anticipation of economic, social, or financial losses).

Health Factors

Patients who suffer from a medical illness are at increased risk for suicide. In 11 studies in which the frequency of medical illness in a series of suicides was examined in the United States, Great Britain, Sweden, and South Africa, a mean of 43% of persons who committed suicide across the studies (range, 20–70%) were judged to be suffering from a medical illness at the time of death (58). Suicide risk is especially increased by terminal illnesses such as acquired immune deficiency syndrome (AIDS) (59), Huntington's chorea (60), cancer (61), and chronic diseases such as rheumatoid arthritis (62) or spinal cord injury (63). As noted earlier, the risk may be related more to depression and hopelessness than to the terminal illness.

Akathisia

Akathisia, a syndrome marked by distinctly unpleasant symptoms of motor restlessness and anxiety, may increase the risk of suicide. Drake and Ehrlich (30) reported impulsive suicide attempts associated with akathisia secondary to neuroleptic treatment in two patients with no previous history of suicidal ideation despite histories of severe psychosis. In both cases, suicidal ideation appeared suddenly, concurrent with the development of the akathisia, and disappeared when the akathisia was treated. Shaw et al. (64) reported a case of suicidal and homicidal ideation with akathisia in a double-blind neuroleptic cross-over study. Shear et al. (65) described two patients who committed suicide after the development of akathisia secondary to depot fluphenazine treatment. Similar observations have been reported in depressed patients who developed akathisia during treatment with antidepressants (66, 67). It is unclear whether a common pharmacologic basis for akathisia and suicidal ideation exists, although it has been postulated that suicidal ideation and suicide occur secondary to the emotional distress of

akathisia (30, 65, 66, 68). Clinicians should be alert to the development of akathisia, particularly in patients with a history of suicidal ideation or attempts. If akathisia occurs, a reduction in dosage of the akathisia-inducing medication or treatment of the akathisia (e.g., with low-dose propranolol) is warranted.

Family History

A family history of suicide increases the risk for suicide attempts (69). This increased risk appears to be independent of psychiatric diagnosis. It remains unclear whether there is a disease-based genetic risk for suicide that runs in families or a psychological explanation (e.g., a family history may create a sense of permission for suicide in other family members, an identification with the dead family member, or the psychological sequelae of having had a family member suicide). A positive family history for a mood disorder is significant in helping to diagnose a potential underlying mood disorder in the suicidal patient.

Access to Lethal Means

The access to lethal means may be an independent risk factor for suicide. In a study of suicides occurring at home, Kellermann et al. (70) found that the presence of one or more guns in the home was associated with an increased risk of suicide. This finding confirms earlier work by Brent et al. (44), which found that guns were more likely to be present in the homes of adolescent suicide victims than in the homes of demographically similar suicidal inpatients (44). Remarkably, the risk of suicide is present in households that own guns whether or not there is a previous history of mental illness in the household (70).

CHOICE OF TREATMENT AND DISPOSITION

General Comments

The disposition of choice will depend on the clinician's overall impression of the patient's risk for immediate or ongoing suicide, as well as the patient's psychiatric treatment needs and medical stability. The immediate risk of suicide and the risk of worsening suicidality (in the near future) is determined by the clinical assessment. A safe outcome is more likely when the treatment plan rests on a solid foundation of data and assessment. The risks and benefits of each possible treatment alternative must be weighed. The patient and family/significant others should be involved in the treatment planning process whenever possible. The latter may contribute useful information in the formulation of a treatment plan and may play a role in the prescribed treatment plan. When a patient lacks the capacity to participate in treatment planning, the clinician must make judgments about the most appropriate treatment plan. Also, involving any treating clinicians (including prescribing physician) in the follow-up treatment plan is very important.

Although "contracts" between the suicidal patient and the clinician have been considered useful, such "contracts" have no legal standing. They play a role only if used as part of a comprehensive evaluation and treatment plan. Contracts can give clinicians a false sense of security (i.e., "the patient signed a contract") and may circumvent a thorough suicide assessment. The principal focus of the treatment relationship should be to form an alliance, which does not have to be in writing to be effective. As noted earlier, documenting the nature of the alliance is essential and may serve as a better risk management tool than a written contract.

Choosing a Disposition

The possible dispositions, in ascending order of restrictiveness, include sending the patient home, with outpatient follow-up; partial hospital care; acute residential care; voluntary admission to inpatient care; and involuntary hospitalization.

Patients who are not acutely suicidal and who are at low risk for immediate worsening can be sent home; however, realistic plans for follow-up care must be made. Patients should not be sent home if they are likely to be alone. Patients who are sent home should have an emergency number to call or should be instructed to return to the emergency room if their suicidal feelings become more severe.

The inpatient unit, which is especially effective in the treatment of acute suicidality, offers safety, support, and hope. Hospitalization acts both to prevent the suicide and to allow aggressive treatment of the patient's psychiatric illness. Optimally, the patient will agree to hospitalization voluntarily. A patient who is judged to be severely suicidal but refuses treatment requires involuntary hospitalization. Application for involuntary admission is made according to the state law.

Partial hospital care is indicated for those patients who do not require the safety and support of an inpatient unit but are not able to return home and be treated only in an ambulatory setting. Some patients may require partial hospital care with residential living, particularly those who are not yet ready to live at home or do not have family or significant supports in the community. Other patients may be able to return home and participate in partial hospital care simultaneously. For the suicidal patient, partial hospital care often is an effective stepdown from an inpatient unit.

In general, if suicide has been attempted, a short inpatient hospital stay is indicated unless the following factors are present: the attempt was of low risk, the patient is being treated by a clinician who knows the patient well, and the clinician agrees to follow-up and concurs that discharge is reasonable. If a serious attempt has been made, inpatient treatment is necessary. Patients who are seriously depressed should be hospitalized, especially if their illness is worsening or not responding to treatment. Patients who are intoxicated should be kept for observation until sober and then reevaluated. Psychotic patients who are suicidal generally should be hospitalized.

Psychopharmacologic Interventions

Prevention of suicidal behavior rests on the appropriate treatment of the underlying psychiatric disorder. Therefore, somatic therapies for the adult suicidal patient generally are aimed at treating the underlying, primary disorder. When treating the suicidal patient, the potential lethality of the specific medication prescribed should be taken into account. For many patients, the prescription of medication can offer hope that their symptoms will improve, which is important to the suicidal patient. The physician should avoid oversupplying patients with potentially dangerous amounts of medication. A careful approach to the suicidal patient should begin with a review of the adequacy of previous medication trials and the patient's history of compliance. For particularly toxic medications when taken in overdose (e.g., tricyclic antidepressants), the physician should prescribe relatively small amounts. Because the physician will be reevaluating the suicidal patient more frequently than a nonsuicidal patient, additional supplies of medication can be given at follow-up appointments.

Whereas the response rate of depressed outpatients to antidepressants is approximately 65–80% (71, 72), the response generally will take several weeks. Although starting antidepressants in depressed suicidal individuals as soon as possible is critical, delay in the effectiveness of the antidepressants must be anticipated.

Thus, nonpharmacologic interventions are crucial in the treatment of the depressed suicidal patient to keep them alive until the antidepressant medication begins to act. Newer agents, such as the selective serotonin reuptake inhibitors (SSRIs), offer advantages in suicidal depressed patients because of their margin of safety in overdose compared with the older classes of antidepressants such as the tricyclics (72, 73).

Psychotic Depression

Patients with psychotic depression have a suicide risk 5 times higher than nonpsychotic depressed patients (74). Robins (75) reported that 19% of 134 subjects who committed suicide also had been psychotic. Patients with psychotic depression are frequently psychologically guarded and hence not forthcoming about their thoughts (76), making the assessment for true suicide risk difficult. The most effective treatments for psychotic depression are either the combination of an antidepressant plus a neuroleptic, or electroconvulsive therapy (ECT) (20, 77). When using medications, the neuroleptic usually is started first and the antidepressant added after a few days. As with nonpsychotic depressed patients, the response to the medications can take several weeks.

Schizophrenia

Over the course of a lifetime, between 20% and 40% of schizophrenic patients will attempt suicide and between 9% and 13% will succeed (78). Frequently, patients with schizophrenia take their own lives because of hopelessness, despair, or depression associated with the painful recognition of the nature of their illness and its prognosis (78). The majority of schizophrenic suicides occur in outpatients, often soon after hospital discharge. In schizophrenic patients whose increased agitation or psychosis contribute to the suicidal ideation, adequate treatment with antipsychotic medication is essential. In general, suicidal schizophrenic patients are more likely to be depressed than nonsuicidal schizophrenic patients. The belief that antidepressant treatment for the symptoms of depression in schizophrenic patients could result in an exacerbation of the schizophrenic condition is not well supported in the literature. At times, the schizophrenic patient's distress can be increased secondary to undesirable side effects from the neuroleptic medications (e.g., akathisia, see above). Thus, patients with schizophrenia need to be monitored closely for undesirable side effects from medication. At times, a shift in the chemical class of the antipsychotic may be necessary if side effects are problematic.

Recent studies suggest that atypical antipsychotic medications may be more effective than standard neuroleptics in treating suicidal schizophrenic patients. A study of treatment-resistant patients with schizophrenia (78) demonstrated that improvements in depression and hopelessness in schizophrenic patients receiving clozapine therapy compared with placebo resulted in an 86% reduction in suicide attempts. The fact that clozapine is more effective than standard neuroleptics (e.g.,

chlorpromazine) in treatment-resistant schizophrenia (79) makes this drug particularly useful for those schizophrenics at greatest risk for suicide.

Alcohol and Substance Abuse

Because alcohol and drug abuse are commonly associated with suicide (see above), there is no substitute for treatment programs aimed at abstinence. However, patients with alcohol and drug abuse often suffer from other psychiatric illnesses that are associated with an increased risk of suicide (e.g., depression). Pharmacotherapy for the underlying psychiatric disorder should be initiated along with treatment programs designed to promote abstinence.

Borderline Personality Disorder

Patients with borderline personality disorder with impulsivity, unstable and intense interpersonal relationships, inappropriate and intense anger, identity disturbance, affective instability, self-destructive acts, and a chronic sense of emptiness generally are not good responders to psychopharmacologic interventions. However, medications may alleviate certain troubling symptoms. Soloff et al. (80) reported that haloperidol produced significant improvement in depression, anxiety, hostility, paranoid ideation, and psychotic thinking in borderline patients, whereas amitriptyline was minimally effective. Goldberg et al. (81) also described a therapeutic benefit from thiothixene compared with placebo in treating selected symptoms of borderline personality disorder. Cowdry and Gardner (82) reported that carbamazepine was effective in decreasing the self-destructive behavior of borderline patients when compared with other drug regimens. Other studies (83) have argued that neuroleptics should be reserved only for borderline patients with sustained and severe symptoms to avoid unnecessary risks and harmful side effects. Further studies are needed to address the usefulness of medications in reducing suicidality in patients with borderline personality disorder.

CONCLUSIONS

The proper identification, assessment, and treatment of psychiatric disorders is critical to the prevention of suicide. The clinician must be able to detect risk factors for suicidal behavior and strengthen protective factors in his or her patients. By playing a key role in the clinical management of patients at high risk for suicide, the clinician should provide support and hope, use psychiatric consultation and hospitalization appropriately, and carefully attend to the patient's environment and support systems. Through these efforts, the rates of this tragic yet preventable cause of death can be diminished.

REFERENCES

1. Cross CK, Hirschfeld RMA. Epidemiology of disorders in adulthood: suicide. In: Michels R, Cavenar J, Brodie HKH, et al., eds. Psychiatry. Philadelphia: JB Lippincott, 1985.
2. National Center for Health Statistics. Vital statistics of the United States: deaths for selected causes. Tables 290, 292. Rockville, MD: Health Resources Administration, 1989.
3. Schaffer D, Garland A, Gould M, et al. Preventing teenage suicide: a critical review. J Am Acad Child Adolesc Psychiatry 1988;27:675–687.
4. Rosenberg ML, Smith JC, Davidson LE, et al. The emergence of youth suicide: an epidemiologic analysis and public health perspective. Ann Rev Public Health 1987;8:417–440.
5. Holinger PC, Offer D, Ostrov E. Suicide and homicide in the United States: an epidemiologic study of violent death, population
6. Klerman GL, Weissman MM. Increasing rates of depression. JAMA 1989;261:2229–2235.
7. Sainsbury P. Suicide and attempted suicide. In: Kisker K, Meyer J-E, Muller C, et al., eds. Psychiatrie der gegenwart. Berlin: Springer-Verlag, 1975.
8. Murphy GE. Clinical identification of suicidal risk. Arch Gen Psychiatry 1972;27:356–359.
9. Pokorny AD. Prediction of suicide in psychiatric patients: report of a prospective study. Arch Gen Psychiatry 1983;40:249–257.
10. Minkoff K, Bergman E, Beck AT, et al. Hopelessness, depression, and attempted suicide. Am J Psychiatry 1973;130:455–459.
11. Beck AT, Steer RA, Kovacs M, et al. Hopelessness and eventual suicide: a 10-year prospective study of patients hospitalized with suicidal ideation. Am J Psychiatry 1985;142:559–563.
12. Malone KM, Scanto K, Corbitt EM, et al. Clinical assessment versus research methods in the assessment of suicidal behavior. Am J Psychiatry 1995;152:1601–1607.
13. Avery D, Winokur G. Suicide, attempted suicide and relapse rates in depression. Arch Gen Psychiatry 1978;35:749–753.
14. Guze SB, Robins E. Suicide and primary affective disorders. Br J Psychiatry 1970;117:437–438.
15. Rosen DH. The serious suicide attempt: epidemiological and follow-up study of 886 patients. Am J Psychiatry 1970;127:64–70.
16. Nordentoft M, Breum L, Munck LK, et al. High mortality by natural and unnatural causes: a 10 year follow-up study of patients admitted to a poisoning treatment center after suicide attempts. Br Med J 1993;306:1637–1641.
17. Nordentoft M, Breum L, Munck LK, et al. Attempted suicide. Are affective disorders missed? Br Med J 1993;307:866. Reply.
18. Hawton K, Fagg J, Platt S, et al. Factors associated with suicide after parasuicide in young people. Br Med J 1993;306:1641–1644.
19. Morgan G. Long term risks after attempted suicide: identifying risk factors should help to reduce subsequent suicide. Br Med J 1993;306:1626–1627.
20. Schatzberg AF, Rothschild AJ. Psychotic (delusional) major depression: should it be included as a distinct syndrome in DSM-IV? Am J Psychiatry 1992;149:733–745.
21. Weissman MM, Klerman GL, Markowitz JS, et al. Suicidal ideation and suicide attempts in panic disorder and attacks. N Engl J Med 1989;321:1209–1214.

changes, and the potential for prediction. Am J Psychiatry 1987;144:215–219.

22. Johns C, Stanley M, Stanley B. Suicide in schizophrenia. Ann NY Acad Sci 1986;487:294–300.

23. Roy A. Suicide in chronic schizophrenia. Br J Psychiatry 1982;141:171–177.

24. Roy A. Suicide in schizophrenia. In: Roy A, ed. Suicide. Baltimore: Williams & Wilkins, 1986.

25. Brent DA, Kupfer DJ, Brometeg EJ, et al. The assessment and treatment of patients at risk for suicide. In: Francis AJ, Hales RE, eds. Psychiatry update: American Psychiatric Association annual review. Washington, DC: American Psychiatric Press, 1988;7.

26. Drake RE, Gates C, Cotton PG, et al. Suicide among schizophrenics: who is at risk? J Nerv Ment Dis 1984;172:613–617.

27. Virkkunen M. Attitude to psychiatric treatment before suicide in schizophrenia and paranoid psychosis. Br J Psychiatry 1976;128:47–49.

28. Alterman AI, Ayre FR, Williford WO. Diagnostic validation of conjoint schizophrenia and alcoholism. J Clin Psychiatry 1984;45:300–303.

29. Drake RE, Cotton PG. Depression, hopelessness and suicide in chronic schizophrenia. Br J Psychiatry 1986;148:554–559.

30. Drake RE, Ehrlich J. Suicide attempts associated with akathisia. Am J Psychiatry 1985;142:499–501.

31. Negrete JC, Knapp WP, Douglas DE, et al. Cannabis effects the severity of schizophrenic symptoms: results of a clinical survey. Psychol Med 1986;16:515–520.

32. Johnson DA. Studies of depressive symptoms in schizophrenia. I: the prevalence of depression and its possible causes. Br J Psychiatry 1980;138:89–101.

33. McGlashan TH, Carpenter T. Post psychotic depression in schizophrenia. Arch Gen Psychiatry 1976;33:231–239.

34. Francis RJ, Franklin J, Flavin DK. Suicide and alcoholism. Ann NY Acad Sci 1986;487:316–326.

35. Murphy GE. Suicide in alcoholism. In: Roy A, ed. Suicide. Baltimore: Williams & Wilkins, 1986.

36. Miles C. Conditions predisposing to suicide: a review. J Nerv Ment Dis 1977;164:231–246.

37. Barraclough B, Bunch J, Nelson B, et al. One hundred cases of suicide: clinical aspects. Br J Psychiatry 1974;125:355–373.

38. Dorpat T, Ripley H. A study of suicide in the Seattle area. Compr Psychiatry 1960;1:349–359.

39. Hagnell O, Lanke J, Rorsman B. Suicide rates in the Lundby study: mental illness as a risk factor for suicide. Neuropsychobiology 1981;7:248–253.

40. Robins E, Murphy GE, Wilkinson RM, et al. Some clinical considerations in the prevention of suicide based on a study of 134 successful suicides. Am J Public Health 1959;49:888–898.

41. Robins E. The final months: a study of the lives of 134 persons who committed suicide. New York: Oxford University Press, 1981.

42. Khuri R, Alliskal HS. Suicide prevention: the necessity of treating contributory psychiatric disorders. Psychiatr Clin North Am 1983;6:193–207.

43. Rich CL, Fowler RC, Fogarty LA, et al. San Diego suicide study: III. relationships between diagnoses and stressors. Arch Gen Psychiatry 1988;45:589–592.

44. Brent DA, Perper JA, Goldstein CE, et al. Risk factors for adolescent suicide: a comparison of adolescent suicide victims with suicidal inpatients. Arch Gen Psychiatry 1988;45:581–588.

45. Schuckit MA. Alcoholism and affective disorder: diagnostic confusion. In: Goodwin DW, Erikson CF, eds. Alcoholism and affective disorders: clinical, genetic, and biochemical Studies. New York: SP Medical & Scientific Books, 1979.

46. Francis A. Personality and suicide. Ann NY Acad Sci 1986;487:281–293.

47. Francis A, Blumenthal SJ. Personality disorders and characteristics in youth suicide. In: Alcohol, Drug Abuse, and Mental Health Administration. Report of the Secretary's Task Force on Youth Suicide: risk factors for youth suicide. DHHS publication no. ADM-89–1622. Washington, DC: US Government Printing Office, 1989;2.

48. Blumenthal SJ. Suicide: a guide to risk factors, assessment, and treatment of suicidal patients. Med Clin North Am 1988;72:937–971.

49. Fawcett J, Scheftner W, Clark D, et al. Clinical predictors of suicide in patients with major affective disorders: a controlled prospective study. Am J Psychiatry 1987;144:35–40.

50. Appleby L. Suicide in psychiatric patients: risk and prevention. Br J Psychiatry 1992;161:749–758.

51. Garzotto N, Buglass D, Holding T, et al. Aspects of suicide and parasuicide. Acta Psychiatr Scand 1977;56:204–214.

52. Leon AC, Friedman RA, Sweeney JA, et al. Statistical issues in the identification of risk factors for suicidal behavior: the application of survival analysis. Psychiatry Res 1990;31:99–108.

53. Cullberg J, Wasserman D, Seransson CJ. Who commits suicide after a suicide attempt? Acta Psychiatr Scand 1988;77:598–603.

54. Durkheim E. Suicide: a study in sociology. Translated by Spalding JA, Simpson G. New York: Free Press, 1966.

55. MacMahon B, Pugh TF. Suicide in the widowed. Am J Epidemiol 1965;81:23–31.

56. Boor M. Relationships between unemployment rates and suicide rates in 8 countries: 1962–1967. Psychol Rep 1980;47:1095–1101.

57. Buda M, Tsuang MT. The epidemiology of suicide: implications for clinical practice. In: Bloomenthal SJ, Kupfer DJ, eds. Suicide over the life cycle: risk factors, assessment, and treatment of suicidal patients. Washington, DC: American Psychiatric Press, 1990.

58. MacKenzie TB, Popkin MK. Medical illness and suicide. In: Blumenthal SJ, Kupfer DJ, eds. Suicide over the life cycle: risk factors, assessment, and treatment of suicidal patients. Washington, DC: American Psychiatric Press, 1990.

59. Marzook PM, Tierney H, Tardiff K, et al. Increased risk of suicide in persons with AIDS. JAMA 1988;259:1333–1337.

60. Chandler JH, Reed TE, DeJong RN. Huntington's chorea in Michigan. Neurology 1960;10:148–153.

61. Louhivuori KA, Hakama M. Risk of suicide among cancer patients. Am J Epidemiol 1979;109:59–65.

62. Dorpat TL, Anderson WF, Ripley HS. The relationship of physical illness to suicide. In: Resneck HLP, ed. Suicidal behaviors: diagnosis and management. Boston: Little, Brown & Co., 1968.

63. Wilcox NE, Stauffer ES. Follow-up of 423 consecutive patients admitted to the Spinal Cord Center, Rancho Los Amigos Hospital, 1 January–31 December, 1967. Paraplegia 1972;10:115–112.

64. Shaw ED, Mann JJ, Weiden PJ, et al. A case of suicidal and homicidal ideation and akathisia in a double-blind neuroleptic crossover study. J Clin Psychopharmacol 1986;6:196–197.

65. Shear MK, Francis A, Weiden P. Suicide associated with akathisia and depot fluphenazine treatment. J Clin Psychopharmacol 1983;3:235–236.

66. Rothschild AJ, Locke CA. Re-exposure to fluoxetine after serious suicide attempts by three patients: the role of akathisia. J Clin Psychiatry 1991;52:491–493.

67. Wirshing WC, Van Putten T, Rosenberg J, et al. Fluoxetine, akathisia, and suicidality: is there a causal connection? Arch Gen Psychiatry 1992;49:580–581.

68. Weiden P. Akathisia from prochlorperazine. JAMA 1985;253:635. Letter.

69. Adam KS. Attempted suicide. Psychiatric Clin North Am 1985;8:183–201.

70. Kellerman AL, Rivara FP, Somes G, et al. Suicide in the home in relationship to gun ownership. N Engl J Med 1992;327:467–472.

71. Chan CH, Janicak PG, Davis JM, et al. Response of psychotic and nonpsychotic depressed patients to tricyclic antidepressants. J Clin Psychiatry 1987;48:197–200.

72. Baldessarini RJ. Current status of antidepressants: clinical pharmacology and therapy. J Clin Psychiatry 1989;50:117–126.

73. Grimsley SR, Jann MW. Paroxetine, sertraline and fluvoxamine: new selective serotonin reuptake inhibitors. Clin Pharmacol 1992;11:930–957.

74. Roose SP, Glassman AH, Walsh TB, et al. Depressions, delusions and suicide. Am J Psychiatry 1983;140:1159–1162.

75. Robins E. Psychosis and suicide. Biol Psychiatry 1986;21:665–672.

76. Rothschild AJ, Schatzberg AF. Diagnosis and treatment of psychotic (delusional) depression. In: Grunhaus L, Greyden JF, eds. Severe depressive disorders. Washington, DC: American Psychiatric Press, 1994:195–207.

77. Rothschild AJ. Management of psychotic treatment — resistant depression. Psychiatr Clin North Am 1996;19:237–252.

78. Meltzer HY, Okayli G. Reduction of suicidality during clozapine treatment of neuroleptic-resistant schizophrenia: impact of risk-benefit assessment. Am J Psychiatry 1995;52:183–190.

79. Kane J, Honigfeld G, Singer J, et al. Clozapine for the treatment-resistant schizophrenic: a double-blind comparison with chlorpromazine. Arch Gen Psychiatry 1988;45:789–796.

80. Soloff PH, George A, Nathan S, et al. Progress in pharmacotherapy of borderline disorders: a double-blind study of amitriptyline, haloperidol and placebo. Arch Gen Psychiatry 1986;43:691–700.

81. Goldberg SC, Schulz SC, Schulz PM. Borderline and schizotypal personality disorders treated with low-dose of thiothixene vs. placebo. Arch Gen Psychiatry 1986;43:680–686.

82. Cowdry RW, Gardner DC. Pharmacotherapy of borderline personality disorder. Arch Gen Psychiatry 1986;45:111–119.

83. Gunderson JG. Pharmacotherapy for patients with borderline personality disorder. Arch Gen Psychiatry 1986;43:698–700.

Chapter 3

Risk Assessment—Violence

Douglas Hughes

INTRODUCTION

General Review of Statistics

The assessment of violence is a major challenge for psychiatry in the United States and throughout the world. There are distinct differences in rates and types of violence in different countries. In the developed world, the United States is not the leading country in all forms of violence. In particular, sexual assaults are significantly higher in other countries; the incidence of sexual assaults is approximately 20% higher in Australia, nearly 50% higher in England, and roughly 300% higher in Canada. However, the rate of aggravated assaults in the United States is three times greater than that of Canada and 37 times greater than that of Australia. The homicide rate in the United States is more than four times greater than in Australia and Canada and nine times greater than in England (1).

Although violence is multifactorial in origin, variables such as guns and alcohol correlate positively to the incidence of violence worldwide. Easier access to firearms is often associated with higher homicide rates (1). Alcohol, including the type of alcohol consumed, has been studied in relationship to violence. One international study found that nations with a preference for beer consumption have a higher incidence of assaults and domestic violence than countries that predominantly prefer wine. The study concluded that beer-drinking countries like the United States, Britain, Australia, and Germany may have a corresponding bravado culture, in which drinking large quantities of beer and getting into fights is socially sanctioned. Countries prone to wine consumption (e.g., Italy, France, Greece, and Spain) correspondingly tend to be less aggressive (2).

In the United States, the Federal Bureau of Investigation states that one American is murdered every 21 minutes and that roughly 25,000 murders occur each year (3). Nonlethal assaults are much more frequent than homicides; hence, violence affects an even greater number of Americans. Twelve percent of murder victims are related to their perpetrators, whereas another 34% are acquainted with their murderers (3). A 1993 poll found that 34% of adults reported seeing a man beating his wife or girlfriend and that nearly 33% of women seen in medical emergency rooms have injuries or symptoms of physical abuse (4).

A significant correlation has been demonstrated between major mental illness and violence (5). As Torrey stated, "There is a statistical significant relationship between serious mental illness and violent behavior, and while violence committed by seriously mentally ill individuals makes only trivial contribution to the overall level of violence in society . . . they make a highly significant contribution to specific segments of our society" (6). In particular, family members have been found to be at greater risk for assaults by the violent mentally ill. Roughly 11% of mentally ill people have physically harmed another person, often a family member (7). One study found that 27% of released male and female patients reported at least one violent act within 4 months of their discharge from an inpatient psychiatric hospital (8).

The study of violence is multifaceted and includes sociocultural, political, clinical, neurologic, and/or psychological factors. Violence is a function of many social and biologic systems and is only one part of a much larger area of study that encompasses the whole ecology of human behavior (9).

Because the etiology of violence is so complex, a comprehensive review of the topic is beyond the scope of this chapter. However, a number of clinical studies on violence are discussed, as well as the prediction of violence, acute management, medication for violence, staff and trainee experience with the violent client, documentation and legal issues, and interventions and dispositions for aggressive patients.

REVIEW OF CLINICAL STUDIES

Mental Illnesses (Epidemiologic Catchment Area Study)

Political pressure from Congress or their constituents can adversely influence the support of research on violence. One example is the vigorous lobbying efforts of the National Rifle Association (NRA) for the elimination of the National Center for Injury Prevention and Control, which conducts epidemiologic research on firearm-related injuries (10).

In 1983, the federal government conducted a major study on violence, the Epidemiologic Catchment Area (ECA) Survey, which examined a large cross-section of subjects in cities throughout the United States. This survey found that individuals diagnosed with a major mental illness, substance abuse, or both have significantly higher rates of violence than the general population (11). For example, schizophrenics are nine times more likely to have been in a fight in the past year, are eight times more likely to have physically abused their children, and are nearly 22 times more likely to have used a weapon (11).

The ECA results indicating that the incidence of violence among the seriously mentally ill is much higher than that of the general population have been confirmed in subsequent studies in the United States and abroad. A Swedish study found that men with major mental illness were more than four times more likely to have been convicted of a violent crime than those without a psychiatric diagnosis. The corresponding figure for women was 27% (12).

Definition, Assumptions, and National Comparisons

In addition to being more likely perpetrators of violence, the severely mentally ill also may be at greater risk of being victims of violence. Hillard et al. (13) studied more than 5000 consecutive psychiatric emergency patients and found that the rate of accidental death was 2.5 times greater than that of the general population and the rate of homicidal death was nearly twice the expected rate.

Why is the violence in the United States more lethal in character than other countries? One illuminating study compared violence in the United States with Canada by reviewing statistics in the cities of Seattle and Vancouver. Comparison data showed fairly similar rates of robbery, burglary, and assault in both cities but found that the frequency of assaults involving guns was seven times higher in Seattle. Not surprisingly, the relative risk from homicide was also significantly higher in Seattle. The investigators concluded that restricting access to handguns may reduce the rate of homicide (14). The differences in the level of violence in these two countries may be related to the assessment and treatment of potential offenders. Torrey et al. (15) conducted a study comparing the United States with British Columbia and found the Canadian mental health system to be superior because of single-source funding, a stronger mandate to treat such patients, and a more comprehensive approach to providing care.

Psychiatry as a science must continually retest its clinical assumptions. If the assumptions about violence are flawed, the research results may be invalid. A possible case in point is that the study of outpatient schizophrenic men was very small ($n = 31$). Conventional wisdom says that the less psychotic a schizophrenic patient, the less violent he or she is likely to be. These investigators found the opposite to be true—patients who were the most intact cognitively were the most likely to be violent (16).

Special Populations

The following list of at-risk populations for the perpetration of and victimization by assault is by no means complete. Certain segments of our population, such as women and children, are at greater risk of assault. Juveniles, ages 10–16 years, experience high rates of assault. Some surveys have found that nearly 25% of juveniles experience some form of an assault each year. Moreover, at least 1% of U.S. children require medical attention for injuries from assault (17). Juveniles also are more likely to be assailants. Studies of youths who commit murders find that as many as 96% were seen to have psychopathology, but only 17% ever received treatment for a mental disorder or behavioral problem (18).

Women are another group more likely to be victims of violence. Each year, approximately 4% of married women are severely beaten and approximately 10% are raped at least once during their marriage (19). It is also possible that women are becoming more violent (20). A study of female patients seen in a psychiatric emergency service found that male and female patients did not differ significantly in frequency and seriousness of violence, but they did differ on who the combatant was and where the violence took place (21). Another study found that women who committed homicides were 70 times more likely to be diagnosed with antisocial personality or substance abuse with either a personality disorder or schizophrenia (22).

In addition to gender, certain symptoms such as auditory hallucinations and defense mechanisms may also be particularly helpful to clinicians in identifying patients at risk of becoming violent. A study of patients who had command auditory hallucinations found 73% compliance with the voice when the commands were less dangerous, but 46% reported at least partial compliance with more dangerous commands (23). Defense mechanisms as indicators of the risk of violence have also been studied. According to Apter et al. (24), the use of displacement differentiated violent from nonviolent patients. Repression tended to turn aggression inward, and projection and denial turned aggression outward.

PREDICTING VIOLENCE

Demographic Variables

Although numerous demographic data on violence exist, the best demographic predictor is a history of violent behavior (25). A study of persons convicted of homicide found that male perpetrators of these crimes were 10 times more likely to commit more than one murder compared with the general population. This rate increased to a staggering 150 times more likely to commit murder if, in addition to a previous homicide, at least four previous violent crimes were committed (26). Other demographic predictors included a history of violence in the family of origin (violent groups have significantly more physical aggression expressed in the home), high levels of anxiety and aggression at the time of evaluation, and a diagnosis of schizophrenia (as a DSM diagnostic group, schizophrenics have one of the highest percentages of inflicting injury in an assault) (25). Other demographic variables include youth, male gender, and a history of criminal behav-

ior (27). Homeless persons are 40 times more likely than the general population to commit violent crimes, the most common being assault, robbery, and attempted murder (28). In addition, certain behaviors such as confusion, irritability, boisterousness, physical threats, verbal threats, and attacks on objects have been found to be more predictive of violent acts. One study found that these behaviors predicted a total of 85% of violent acts committed (29).

Violence before and after discharge has also been investigated. In one study, 44% of the patient sample had been violent before admission, with 18% committing serious level-one (physical contact) violence and 26% committing level-two (threatening without physical contact) violence. Ten weeks after discharge, the incidence remained nearly the same with 13% committing level-one violence and 24% committing level-two violence. Also, 80% of victims were friends or family of the patient and 20% were strangers (30).

Cultural norms may affect the victim's definition of violence. In a cross-cultural study of Anglo-American and Mexican-American women, the Anglo-American women perceived more types of behavior as being abusive and exhibited a less tolerant attitude toward domestic violence than did the Mexican-American women (31).

Pregnancy and the recent birth of a child is a risk factor for domestic violence. Studies have shown that domestic violence begins or escalates during pregnancy (32). Also, demographics for violence exist in very small and specific groups such as parental hostage takers. According to a small study, the risks for violence among this group include recent birth of a child, substance abuse, a family history of domestic violence, and an acute escalation of events due to hostility to police involvement (33).

New risk factors are continually being investigated for violence. For example, research on serotonin level and its correlation to violent behavior indicates that a central serotonin deficit exists in alcoholics, arsonists, and impulsive and violent offenders (34, 35).

Prediction Validity of Violence

As noted, demographic data may be used to predict violence for populations as a whole (and possibly for subpopulations), but may not allow for the prediction of violence in the individual. Although debate on this point continues, the majority of research confirms, and the American Psychiatric Association clearly states, that "psychiatrists have no special knowledge or ability with which to predict dangerous behavior. Studies have shown that even with patients in which there is a history of violent acts, predictions of future violence will be wrong for two out of every three patients" (36). Predictions of self-violence/suicide also appear to be equally difficult (37).

Despite evidence to the contrary, it may be possible to predict more accurately violent behavior in certain subsets of patients or in particular settings. In the context of emergency civil commitment, one study found that psychiatric emergency clinicians could predict violence within the first 72 hours in 66% of their patients (38). Other researchers contend that these studies are flawed and that ". . . the reported accuracy of clinical predictions of assaultive behavior is markedly affected by the choice of sampling strategy, comparison group, outcome measures, and follow-up period. Including seclusion and violent threats in the outcome variable appears to lead to deceptive findings" (39).

ASSESSMENT OF VIOLENCE

Patient Presentation

In general, the potential for violence underlies most crisis situations. The trained clinician needs to make an initial assessment of violence potential within minutes of seeing the patient. Common sense antecedents to violence include patients who are agitated, have had restrictions placed on their behavior, or have been provoked by other patients or family members (40). Not surprisingly, several studies have found that patients brought in by police suffered from more severe forms of mental illness and were more likely to be assaultive or threatening both before admission and during assessment in the psychiatric emergency service (41, 42). Family members, friends, therapists, and even the police who accompany the patient often can provide useful information on the patient's potentially dangerous behavior. If the clinician is evaluating a patient in the community, as many outreach teams do, a police escort may provide the needed security (43).

Weapons Concerns

During the initial assessment, the clinician should always consider the possibility that the patient may be carrying a weapon. Studies have found that 4–17% of patients carry weapons into psychiatric emergency services (44, 45). In trying to identify the personal characteristics of patients who bring guns into a clinical setting, most studies conclude that this is a heterogeneous group and that clinicians cannot predict accurately who may be armed (46). Conversely, other investigations have concluded that whereas most patients did not differ significantly from the control group, male patients with a history of substance abuse were at greater risk to carry weapons (45).

The patient most likely to be searched for weapons in the hospital setting is usually a young, homeless, unemployed male. A clinician's intuitive cues may be important criteria in formulating the decision to search for weapons (47).

Unfortunately, literature on evaluating or handling an agitated patient in private offices is sorely lacking. Based on experience in other clinical settings, the clinician should be cognizant of escape routes and dangerous objects that may be used as weapons (48). Inpatient studies may be applicable, and one such study found that 3% of patients used weapons and that the most common weapon used was furniture. This may also be true for violence in private offices (49).

The presence of weapons may be an even greater concern if the initial evaluation takes place in the patient's home. Increasingly, home evaluations are performed by psychiatric outreach crisis workers. Again, the concern is the high prevalence of guns found in homes. Research shows that 10% of Americans have guns in their homes, that 29% of those who own guns keep them loaded, and that 21% keep the loaded guns in an unlocked area (50).

Rapid Assessment

It is important to understand the dynamics underlying violent behavior. Primarily, the violent patient is frightened. At the outset, the clinician needs to assess quickly why the patient feels threatened and then to proceed in an appropriate manner (51). Personal interactions are often useless, and emergency interventions such as restraints are needed.

When faced with an emergency situation, the expedient assessment of a patient's potential for violence is essential. As stated previously, this assessment is based primarily on contextual cues that are immediately available in most clinical instances. Important signs can be noted in a patient's posture (relaxed or agitated), manner (cooperative or threatening), appearance (sober or intoxicated), speech (normal volume or loud), cognition (thoughts organized or psychotic), and mode of arrival (self, police, therapist) (52).

Measured Assessment

The assessment of violence should be seen as an evaluation of risk rather than as a prediction of dangerousness. Demographic risk factors of violence, present and past psychiatric history (including substance abuse), mental status examination, and a medical assessment are all important in the measured assessment of aggression.

The initial inquiries to the patient should be sympathetic, focused on building rapport, and deal directly with safety and violence. The questions of violent impulses, weapons, and homicidal ideation should be asked very early in the evaluation because the answers to these questions determine whether the clinician has the legal right to retain the patient should an attempt be made to leave before the assessment is complete. Some clinicians fear that direct questions regarding violence may prompt the patient to act out; however, the opposite result is probably the case. Patients often feel relieved and understood when their aggression is directly questioned (52). The history of violence and the possession of weapons are important in this formulation of violence. It is important to arrive at a DSM-IV diagnosis in all five axes. Although violent patients were more likely to be hospitalized than nonviolent patients, clinical variables such as diagnosis and overall severity of psychiatric impairment were more important determinants than violent behavior in predicting hospitalization decisions (53).

A mental status examination is an important tool in this assessment. All patients need to be questioned about current aggressive thoughts and homicidal ideation. The prevalence of aggressive thoughts and homicidal ideation in certain settings may be as high as 17% (54, 55). Suicide assessment is also important in the assessment of violence. Possibly one third of all homicidal patients also have concurrent suicidal ideation (54, 55). Hallucinations are an important consideration in assessment. Psychotic patients with auditory hallucinations were found to be at greater risk for violence. Some studies have found command hallucinations to be more dangerous (23). Clinicians may find that mental status examinations are better predictors of nonviolence than violence. A study by McNiel and Binder (56) found that patients whose mental status was characterized by low levels of hostility-suspiciousness and high levels of anxiety-depression were significantly more likely to be classified correctly as being at low risk for violence.

Medical evaluations are important in assessing violent behavior. Medical conditions such as delirium or intoxication can contribute to violence. Basic medical screening, such as taking vital signs, reviewing physical symptoms, and obtaining a history of substance abuse, is mandatory. If the basic medical screen reveals concerns, such as elevated vital signs, then a routine blood test (complete blood count, electrolytes, and toxicology screens), physical examination, and possible further medical consultations may be considered.

Toxicology screens are also an important diagnostic tool in assessing aggression. Both acute intoxication and withdrawal can produce violent behavior. Because these tests are frequently ordered, toxicology screens will be reviewed here. A positive or negative toxicology screen is only helpful if the clinician knows what substances are present on the screen. Comprehensive screens usually have 40 substances, whereas inhouse screens may have as few as 2 or 3 substances.

Toxicology screens can be performed on serum, urine, or gastric samples. Serum samples, the most frequently ordered, allow determination of quantitative drug results. A urine screen, however, detects in a more sensitive manner many additional substances that may contribute to aggressive behavior such as cocaine, amphetamines, and narcotics. Yield and accuracy improve when both urine and serum samples are submitted for analysis (52, 57).

The effectiveness of drug screens, unfortunately, is diminished by their limitations. Many substances, including lithium and volatile hydrocarbons, are not routinely measured and require specific tests. Even when general categories are tested, specific members of that category may not be included in the assay. For example, most toxicology screens test for benzodiazepines, yet few newer agents such as alprazolam (Xanax; Upjohn, Kalamazoo, MI) are detected. Also, a high margin of error exists for drug screens; experts recommend confirmation by retesting and interpretation of results in light of an individual's clinical history and interview (58, 59).

ACUTE MANAGEMENT OF THE VIOLENT PATIENT

Private Office Setting

All office support staff should be instructed on the management of aggressive/threatening patients. The receptionist is often the first person a potentially violent patient will encounter. Support staff should respond to the agitated patient in a calm manner and, if possible, excuse themselves quickly. If that is not possible, the receptionist should alert the therapist to the emergency situation without alarming the patient (60). This can be achieved by establishing a prearranged code such as, "A client is here to see you. The front office next to the bathroom is free" (60). The therapist may then ask the receptionist a yes or no question to assess the level of risk further. If appropriate, the therapist may decide to call the police before seeing the client. In the private office situation, the best approach in an escalating patient encounter might be to emphasize negotiation and collaboration rather than to attempt to gain control (61). If support staff are unavailable or the patient's aggressive behavior surfaces during the session, the following guidelines of possible interventions may prove helpful and should be used sequentially:

a. Encourage the patient to express his or her feelings in words.

b. Reinforce the patient's own coping skills and internal controls.

c. Tell the patient that aggressive behavior is unsettling and request that he or she respect limits such as lowering the voice or remaining seated.

d. Encourage the patient to leave the office and to reschedule the appointment.

e. Leave the office and call the police.

f. Ask the police to transport the patient to the nearest emergency room for an evaluation and possible psychiatric hospitalization.

Institutional Setting

More options exist in an institution, and the safety of the staff is probably more secure than in private offices. Acute management depends on the state of the patient's aggression. If the patient is agitated and threatening and violence appears imminent, the range of interventions given below might be helpful. If the patient's aggressive behavior is escalating rapidly, the clinician may want to move through these initial steps quickly or skip immediately to the most appropriate step. If the patient arrives actively violent or becomes so in the assessment, the clinician should go to the restraint step immediately (62).

The range of possible interventions for aggressive patients in an institutional setting is as follows.

a. Encourage the patient to express his or her feelings in words.

b. Reinforce the patient's own coping skills and internal controls.

c. Tell the patient that the aggressive behavior is unsettling and request that he or she respect limits.

d. Offer medications.

e. Tell the patient that if limits are not respected and behavior continues to be aggressive, restraints may have to be used.

f. Use physical restraints.

Clearly, therapists need to plan for violent behavior in their offices or work environment so that untoward events can be prevented.

MEDICATION MANAGEMENT OF HOSTILITY

The following review of newer psychiatric medications that may be particularly helpful in controlling aggressive behavior is not a general overview of the psychopharmacology of violent patients. The U.S. Drug Enforcement Administration (DEA) has not approved drugs specifically for the treatment of violent behavior. However, medication has been approved for numerous DSM-IV psychiatric diagnoses that frequently occur with or have been found to exacerbate violent behavior. These include some antipsychotics, mood stabilizers, antidepressants, and benzodiazepines.

Acute psychopharmacologic treatment of violent behavior includes both the administration of medications that immediately help resolve aggressive actions and the rapid introduction of medications that may take several weeks to reach maximum effectiveness. In this era of managed care, clinicians may need to broaden their definition of acute management to include the time frame of a 2- to 3-week intensive outpatient treatment plan.

Antipsychotics

As a class, antipsychotics are generally reserved for patients with psychotic symptoms. Neuroleptic medication is also indicated for patients suffering from certain character disorders or from substance abuse who are acutely and severely agitated. The acute benefit of an antipsychotic medication is sedation, often a side effect, especially when administered intramuscularly. If violent behavior is driven or exacerbated by psychosis, clearly both symptoms (i.e., psychotic and violent behavior) might improve by using an antipsychotic.

Although the sedative side effects may be beneficial immediately in controlling aggression, an underlying thought disorder will require 2 to 3 weeks to improve. Aggressive parenteral administration has not been found to shorten this time delay (63).

However, if the crisis is being contained or if the escalating aggressive and psychotic behavior is identified early enough, this wait may be managed through outpatient treatment.

Interesting data suggest that the newer antipsychotic risperidone may be beneficial in decreasing hostility (64). The rationale is that, "Atypical antipsychotics are believed to curb hostility as a specific effect, via their combined action on the serotonergic and dopaminergic systems. Typical neuroleptics primarily block the dopamine receptors, leading to reductions in hostility that are only secondary to their effect on psychotic symptoms such as delusions and hallucinations" (65).

Success has also been noted in the use of risperidone to treat psychotic adolescents (66). An advantage of risperidone is that many patients do not report feeling drowsy, which may translate into better compliance. A drawback is that it is not yet available in an intramuscular injection, leaving only the parenteral route. Risperidone has the same properties and mechanisms of action as clozapine, another new and effective neuroleptic; however, clozapine requires frequent blood work to monitor for agranulocytosis.

Akathisia, a side effect of antipsychotic medication, especially in young males, may result in motor restlessness and lead to aggressive behavior. If not recognized as akathisia, higher doses will potentially worsen the behavior (67). Doses for aggressive and psychotic adult males are as follows:

a. Haldol, 5–10 mg orally or by intramuscular injection. This dose may be repeated in 1 hour if the patient is still agitated.

b. Risperidone, 1–2 mg orally. This dose may also be repeated in 1 hour if needed.

Mood Stabilizers

The mood stabilizers, including lithium and carbamazepine, have long been known to be effective in controlling aggression related to manic excitement (68). Valproate has been found to be an effective treatment for controlling behavioral agitation in dementia among elderly patients, with few side effects (69). Valproate is as effective as lithium for controlling mania and can have a more timely onset; specifically, as high as 54% of patients with rapid cycling bipolar disorder respond acutely (70). Because hypomanic and manic patients can exhibit aggressive behavior, a rapidly acting mood stabilizer can be a distinct benefit, and psychiatric emergency services are increasingly using valproate (71). However, the mood stabilizers, although efficacious, do not compare with the neuroleptics, which are much more rapidly sedating.

Before initiating either lithium or valproate, base laboratory tests should be conducted to determine the status of the kidney, liver, and thyroid. Doses for the aggressive and hypomanic or manic male are as follows: start lithium at 300 mg twice a day, follow blood levels, and increase dose until blood levels between 0.6 and 1.0 mEq/L are reached; start valproate at 125 mg twice a day, follow blood levels, and increase dose until blood levels are between 50 and 100 μg/mL.

Antidepressants

Numerous studies have associated deficiency or dysregulation of serotonin with violent, impulsive, and self-destructive behavior (72, 73). With the selective serotonin reuptake inhibitors (SSRIs) being safer in overdoses than the tricyclic antidepressants, and with the serotonin agents also possibly conferring some antiaggressive property, the SSRI are preferred in treating violent and depressed patients. As with the antipsychotics, these medications can take 2 to 3 weeks to reach therapeutic levels.

Starting doses for aggressive and depressed patients are as follows: fluoxetine (20 mg), sertraline (50 mg), and paroxetine (20 mg).

Benzodiazepines

In the literature, confusion still exists about the effectiveness of benzodiazepines in treating aggressive behavior (68). Several investigations have noted increased levels of aggressive behavior, and other studies report paradoxical induction of rage with benzodiazepine use (68). The use of this medication is further complicated by the fact that many patients prone to violence may be substance abusers or be at risk of becoming substance abusers and benzodiazepines can be habit-forming. Despite this debate, many clinicians use benzodiazepines, frequently with antipsychotics, to help sedate very violent patients.

STAFF AND TRAINEES EXPERIENCE WITH VIOLENCE

Assessing Risks for Assaults

In evaluating the risk of violence among staff and clinical trainees, a survey of emergency departments in 127 teaching hospitals found that 32% of the staff reported near daily verbal threats from patients, and 18% reported being threatened by a patient with a weapon in the past year (74). Nurses and male doctors were at the greatest risk of assault, whereas receptionists were at the least risk (75). Studies of mental health professionals found that 14% of this group had been assaulted by a patient during their careers and that 36% had been threatened with physical violence. Psychiatrists had been threatened twice as often and assaulted four times more than other mental health professionals (76). Rates for psychiatrists being assaulted at least once in their careers was 42% (77). Male psychiatrists were injured at a rate 50% higher than female psychiatrists (78).

Trainees, younger psychiatrists, and psychiatrists more recently out of residency may be more likely to be injured by patients (78). One small study of three training sites found that 56% of psychiatric residents had been assaulted and that 54% had encountered a weapon in the emergency room setting. The study concluded that trainees were often exposed to dangerous situations, although serious injury was rare (79). Sexual harassment from patients occurred at rates of 25%, especially for female, minority, and gay physicians (80).

The type of weapon used by patients also was investigated. One study showed that patients used their fists in 25% of cases, guns in 24%, chairs in 23%, ashtrays in 12%, knives in 11%, and tables in 4% (81). Precipitants of violence were attributed at the following rates in the cases studied: 24% for conflict in the therapy, 22% for paranoid ideation, and 10% for transference. Interestingly, 40% of assaults had no known precipitant (81).

The therapist was only able to predict the actual assault in 9.4% of cases (76). Further, stress induced by exposure to violence may lead to impaired staff performance and adoption of behaviors that make the recurrence of violence more likely (82).

Avoiding High-Risk Situations

Training appears to decrease assaults and injuries among staff significantly (83). The Occupational Safety and Health Administration (OSHA) has become very active in protecting hospital staff from patient assaults, requiring hospitals to reduce the risk of violence or face fines of up to $70,000. Hospitals are expected to develop written policies for crisis prevention and management and provide mandatory training in crisis prevention techniques and restraints. Training for nonprofessional employees was viewed as equally important as the training of professional staff (84).

One study characterized staff members' limit-setting styles into six categories: belittlement, platitudes, solution without options, solution with options, affective involvement without options, and affective involvement with options (85). The first three styles all generated patient anger. Of the remaining three styles, success depended on the diagnosis of the patient. For the impulsive patient, only one limit-setting style, affective involvement with options, kept anger at a low level.

Assisting Staff Members Who Have Been Assaulted

It is important to assist staff members who have been assaulted. Because they may be too embarrassed or stunned to ask for assistance, a clear policy is needed to address the steps to be taken. Immediately after the assault, the staff member should be taken to a medical emergency room for attention. Even apparent minor injuries may turn out to be more severe later. Next, a timely debriefing with the assaulted staff member should take place with a supervisor. Later, a general staff meeting should be held to review and reeducate the whole staff regarding the specific violent incident and violence in general. Staff members who have been assaulted by patients may eventually require a variety of services, such as trauma/crisis counseling, legal advice, and possibly information regarding insurance and worker's compensation benefits (86). Some hospitals are establishing assaulted staff action programs to debrief assault victims and help readjust staff members to the work environment (87).

DOCUMENTATION AND LEGAL CONCERNS

Good Documentation

Good documentation is important and should include a previous history of violence, current substance abuse, and lethal means available. Information gathered from significant others and therapists also should be included. Certain diagnoses— such as major depression, anxiety disorders, bipolar disorder, and symptoms such as hopelessness—also need to be

noted in the chart. In documenting data on aggressive patients, treatment preferences should be noted, particularly if the potentially violent patient is being sent home to fearful family members instead of being hospitalized.

With large numbers of interviews, the clinician may rely on shorthand, such as "neg. H.I." for negative homicidal ideation. If such a system is used, however, the shorthand should be understood by others reading the chart. Structured evaluation forms are helpful in providing good clinical care and consistent documentation (Fig. 3.1).

Better alternatives are check lists that are standard for the service or practice and have space for the explanation of why a patient would be returned to the community with a known risk factor. Putting a suicide checklist beside the homicide list reminds the clinician of the potential overlap in these aggressive behaviors.

If the clinician fails to document important information concerning violence and there is an adverse outcome, a jury may conclude that this information was

		Suicide		Homicide		
		Yes	No	Yes	No	N/A
(Fill out for all. Circle applicable headings.)						
a.	Previous history of suicide/homocide	☐	☐	☐	☐	☐
b.	Means available (e.g., guns, pills)	☐	☐	☐	☐	☐
c.	Acutely intoxicated	☐	☐	☐	☐	☐
d.	Major depression or schizophrenia present	☐	☐	☐	☐	☐
e.	Anxiety/panic disorder present	☐	☐	☐	☐	☐
f.	Note written/threats made	☐	☐	☐	☐	☐
g.	Family/friends agree with aftercare	☐	☐	☐	☐	☐
h.	Therapist involved in aftercare	☐	☐	☐	☐	☐
i.	Hopelessness present (suicide)	☐	☐	—	—	☐
j.	Victims notified (homicide)	—	—	☐	☐	☐
k.	Domestic violence and/or sexual abuse history	☐	☐	☐	☐	☐

FIGURE 3.1.   Histed suicide and homicide evaluation questions. Reprinted from New Dimensions in Mental Health Services, 1995.

not obtained and, therefore, that negligence occurred. In short, good clinical documentation is good for both the patient and the health care provider.

Legal Issues

Two court decisions, one state and one federal, have a direct bearing on violence assessments: Tarasoff v. Regents of the University of California-California Supreme Court (1974) and McCabe v. City of Lynn-Federal District Court of Massachusetts (1995).

In Tarasoff, the court's ruling established that a clinician has a legal responsibility to reasonably protect society from the violent behavior of his or her patients (88). This responsibility can be discharged by the clinician by therapeutically resolving the violent behavior (this includes hospitalization) or, failing that, by interventions warning the potential victim(s) and notifying the appropriate police department(s).

As a result of this ruling, many clinicians tended to be clinically cautious and used involuntary evaluations and hospitalizations to protect society from their clients' violent behavior.

In the second case, a federal district judge ruled that the involuntary evaluation of a patient amounted to a civil rights violation. The judge disagreed with the psychiatrist's clinical assessment that the patient could not take care of himself and might possibly harm himself. By viewing this case as an infringement of civil rights, malpractice insurance and the clinics/hospitals would not cover financial damages. Clinicians had to pay multimillion-dollar settlements out of their own pockets. The message from the legal system is that before a clinician takes away an individual's civil rights by hospitalization or forced evaluation, the clinician should be sure that the danger to self or others is imminent. This message cautions against the practice of defensive psychiatry by overhospitalizing patients with questionable harm to self or others.

INTERVENTIONS AND DISPOSITIONS

Insurance and Managed Care

The assessment and treatment of violence are affected by the changes that are occurring in the health care industry. The focus of managed care has increasingly shifted from treating severely mentally ill patients on an inpatient basis to treating these patients outside the hospital setting (89–91). Interventions and dispositions of violent patients have always been challenging, and managed care and the changes in the health care industry make this even more so. Only a small percentage of persons with psychiatric disorders (including violence-prone patients) receive treatment, and many of those who do receive treatment may not be getting the ideal treatment (92). The individual and social costs associated with the lack of treatment or undertreatment of violent patients are probably substantial (93).

Home Setting

Because family members are the most likely victims of violent patients (94), the clinician needs to include or at least consider the family setting to which the potentially violent patient is returning. The objective and subjective burdens violent patients can put on their caregivers and families can be profound and need to be considered before returning the patient home and to outpatient treatment (95).

The actual incidence of violence in mentally ill relatives that reside at home varies from 5% to 38%. "The impact of fear, anxiety, and tension on the family is much higher, because overt or subtle threats and intimidation are far more common than frank violence, and can be as damaging as violence itself. Violence demolishes and disorganizes the whole family and tends to isolate both patients and family from the supports they need to provide a healthy setting for healing" (96).

The clinician needs to consider who might need help in the home environment. The profiles of the female and male victims of violence are similar. Both male and female victims of battering might need help with alcohol problems and depression (97).

Outpatient Treatment

Consumer surveys indicate that the vast majority of those who receive psychotherapy find it helpful in managing their lives. Longer treatments were reported to be the most helpful (98). The continued trend toward limited or denied visits with managed care can substantially affect treatment, with 18% of the U.S. population currently enrolled (in California, more than 35%) (99). Research has shown that the best treatment for the violence-prone patient is consistent medical care with medication and comprehensive social services (36).

Preventive therapy also may be possible. One study found that individuals who are predisposed to adult criminal behavior by virtue of demonstration antisocial behavior in adolescence may be protected from further criminal behavior by timely initiation of certain forms of therapy (100).

Hospitalization

If outpatient interventions have not decreased the likelihood of violence, a psychiatric hospitalization may be needed. Research has shown that when a patient with a major mental illness who has either a history of violence or is in current danger of committing violence presents to a psychiatric emergency service, he or she will be admitted 83–89% of the time (101).

One study of the decision to hospitalize found that among first year psychiatric residents, the rates for emergency patient hospitalization declined from an initial admission rate of 33% to a year-end rate of 19%. "For residents in the early training phase, various clinical features, including psychosis, thought disorder, schizophrenic diagnosis, dangerousness, and overall symptoms, were associated with higher rates of patient hospitalization. By the end of training, only dangerousness and overall symptoms remained significantly related to the hospitalization decision" (102). Not surprisingly, the length of stay in a psychiatric hospital is affected by violence. One study found that schizophrenic patients who assaulted someone soon after admission were more likely to have extended stays in the hospital (103).

Protective Custody

If a patient arrives intoxicated and violent with no other psychiatric diagnosis, some psychiatric emergency services will use police protective custody as a solution. If a patient has been violent, this procedure can create an ethical dilemma: is the initiation of arrest and prosecution ever an acceptable response for a clinician (104)? Although there is an active debate about the advantages and disadvantages of this course of action, at this time not enough has been written on the topic to venture a strong recommendation. Clearly, the clinician involved needs to individualize these decisions. However, calling the police is always indicated when the patient's violent behavior immediately threatens a clinician's safety or when the behavior exceeds the security capabilities of the hospital or clinic.

CONCLUSION

In summary, violence in the United States has reached staggering dimensions. Reviews of clinical studies show that major mental illness and/or substance abuse is positively correlated with higher rates of physical aggression. Therefore, the acute risk assessment of violent behavior in the mentally ill is a crucially important role for all clinicians. In all evaluations for violence, the clinician needs to be cognizant that the patient may be carrying or have access to a weapon. Moreover, other demographic and descriptive data need to be gathered and considered in the acute assessment. Because the preponderance of scientific research indicates that violence is not predictable, clinicians need to continue to compensate by overpredicting for violent behavior.

The acute management of the violent patient can require limit-setting techniques, physical restraints, and aggressive medicating of coexisting psychiatric disorders. Risperidone and valproate are two new and effective medications that may have secondary benefits in controlling hostility and aggression.

Because mental health clinicians are at risk of being assaulted by certain patients and because crisis prevention techniques help decrease assaults, staff education in this area is important. Finally, intelligent, not voluminous, documentation is vital for good patient care and clinical risk management.

REFERENCES

1. Carter P. Violence from the grave to the cradle. Financial Post Magazine 1995;Sept:23–40.
2. Reuters. Beer vs wine: violence level found to differ. Boston Globe 1994;Aug 24:2.
3. Anonymous. As easy as buying a toothbrush. Lancet 1993;341:1375–1376. Abstract.
4. Anonymous. Emergency department response to domestic violence. MMWR 1993;42(32):617–620. Abstract.
5. Robins LN, Regier DA, eds. Psychiatric disorders in America: epidemiologic catchment area study. New York: Free Press, 1991.
6. Torrey EF. In reply. Psychiatric Services 1995;46:407–408. Letter.
7. Steinwachs DM, Kasper JD, Skinner EA. Family perspectives on meeting the needs for care of severely mentally ill relatives: a national survey. Arlington, VA: National Alliance for the Mentally Ill, 1992.
8. Monahan J. Mental disorder and violent behavior. Am Psychol 1990;147:746–750.
9. Bronfenbrenner U. The ecology of human development. Cambridge, MA: Harvard University Press, 1979.
10. Moran M. Federal agency that studies injuries and their prevention becomes target of groups opposed to gun control. Psychiatric News 1995;Dec 2:11.
11. Swanson JW, Holzer CE, Ganju VK, et al. Violence and psychiatric disorder in the community: evidence from the epidemiologic catchment area surveys. Hosp Community Psychiatry 1990;41:761–770.
12. Anonymous. Serious mentally ill do have higher rates of violence, Torrey reports. Psychiatric News 1993;Nov 19:5, 21.
13. Hillard JR, Zung WWK, Ramm D, et al. Accidental and homicidal death in a psychiatric emergency room population. Hosp Community Psychiatry 1985;36:640–643.
14. Sloan JH, Kellerman AL, Reay DT, et al. Handgun regulations, crime, assaults, and homicide: a tale of two cities. N Engl J Med 1988;319:1256–1262.
15. Torrey EF, Bigelow DA, Sladen-Dow N. Quality and cost of services for seriously mentally ill individuals in British Columbia and the United States. Hosp Community Psychiatry 1993;44:943–950.
16. Lapierre D, Braun CMJ, Hodgins S, et al. Neuropsychological correlates of violence in schizophrenia. Schizophr Bull 1995;21:253–262.
17. Hudson L. Study says juvenile violence is underestimated. Medical Herald 1994;Dec:16.

18. Anonymous. Youths who become murderers often victims of failed system. Psychiatric News 1995;Dec 2:5.
19. Goodwin J. Family violence: principles of intervention and prevention. Hosp Community Psychiatry 1995;36:1074–1079.
20. Inamdar SG, Darrell E, Lewis DO, et al. Hospitalized adolescents: trends in violence. Paper presented at the American Psychiatric Association 138th annual meeting, Dallas, 1985.
21. Newhill CE, Mulvey EP, Lidz CW. Characteristics of violence in the community by female patients seen in a psychiatric emergency service. Psychiatric Services 1995;46:785–789.
22. Eronen M. Mental disorders and homicidal behavior in female subjects. Am J Psychiatry 1995;152:1216–1218.
23. Juninger J. Command hallucinations and the prediction of dangerousness. Psychiatric Services 1995;46:911–914.
24. Apter A, Plutchik R, Sevy S, et al. Defense mechanisms in risk of suicide and risk of violence. Am J Psychiatry 1989;146:1027–1030.
25. Blomhoff S, Seim S, Friis S. Can prediction of violence among psychiatric inpatients be improved? Hosp Community Psychiatry 1990;41:771–775.
26. Tiihonen J, Hakola P, Nevalainen A, et al. Risk of homicidal behavior among persons convicted of homicide. Forensic Sci Int 1995;21;72:43–48.
27. Calicchia JA, Moncata SJ, Santostefano S. Cognitive control differences in violent juvenile inpatients. J Clin Psychol 1993;49:731–740.
28. Martell DA, Rosner R, Harmon RB. Base-rate estimates of criminal behavior by homeless mentally ill persons in New York City. Psychiatric Services 1995;46:596–601.
29. Yager J. Predicting violent outbursts in inpatients. Journal Watch 1995;Nov:77.
30. Anonymous. Violence among mentally ill found to be concentrated among those with comorbid substance abuse disorders. Psychiatric News 1995;Dec 2:8.
31. Torres S. A comparison of wife abuse between two cultures: perceptions, attitudes, nature, and extent. Issues Ment Health Nurs 1991;12:113–131.
32. Bewley CA, Gibbs A. Violence in pregnancy. Midwifery 1991;7:107–112.
33. Kennedy HG, Dyer DE. Parental hostage takers. Br J Psychiatry 1992;160:410–412.
34. Virkkunen M, Rawlings R, Takula R, et al. CSF biochemistries, glucose metabolism, and diurnal activity rhythms in alcoholic, violent offenders, fire setters, and healthy volunteers. Arch Gen Psychiatry 1994;51:20–27.
35. Virkkunen M, Kallio E, Rawlings R, et al. Personality profiles and state aggressiveness in Finnish alcoholic, violent offenders, fire setters and healthy volunteers. Arch Gen Psychiatry 1994;51:28–33.
36. Anonymous. Violence and mental illness. APA Fact Sheet 1994;Nov:1–4.
37. Hughes DH. Can the clinician predict suicide? Psychiatric Services 1995;46:449–451.
38. McNiel DE, Binder RL. Predictive validity of judgments of dangerousness in emergency civil commitment. Am J Psychiatry 1987;144:197–200.
39. Apperson LJ, Mulvey EP, Lidz CW. Short-term clinical prediction of assaultive behavior: artifacts of research methods. Am J Psychiatry 1993;150:1374–1379.
40. Powell G, Caan W, Crow M. What events precede violent incidents in psychiatric hospitals? Br J Psychiatry 1994;165:107–112.
41. McNiel DE, Hatcher E, Zeiner H, et al. Characteristics of persons referred by police to the psychiatric emergency room. Hosp Community Psychiatry 1991;42:425–427.
42. Kneebone P, Rogers J, Hafner RJ. Characteristics of police referrals to a psychiatric emergency unit in Australia. Psychiatric Services 1995;46:620–622.
43. Lamb HR, Shaner R, Elliott DM, et al. Outcome for psychiatric emergency patients seen by an outreach police-mental health team. Psychiatric Services 1995;46:1267–1271.
44. Goetz R, Bloom J, Chenrell S, et al. Weapons possession by patients in a university emergency department. Ann Emerg Med 1991;20:8–10.
45. McNiel DE, Binder RL. Patients who bring weapons to the psychiatric emergency room. J Clin Psychiatry 1987;48:230–233.
46. Anderson AA, Ghali AY, Bansil RK. Weapon carrying among patients in a psychiatric emergency room. Hosp Community Psychiatry 1989;40:845–847.
47. Privitera MR, Springer MO, Perlmutter RA. To search or not to search. Is there a clinical profile of a patient harboring a weapon? Gen Hosp Psychiatry 1986;8:442–447.
48. Schuster JM. Psychiatric consultation in the general hospital emergency department. Psychiatric Services 1995;46:555–557.
49. Hunter ME, Love CC. Types of weapons and patterns of use in a forensic hospital. Hosp Community Psychiatry 1993;44:1082–1085.
50. Anonymous. Firearms training: safe storage. Focus 1995;Jan 6:3.
51. Rada RT. The violent patient: rapid assessment and management. Psychosomatics 1981;22:101–109.
52. Hughes D. Assessment of the potential for violence. Psychiatric Annals 1994;24:1–6.
53. McNiel DE, Myers RS, Zeiner HK, et al.

The role of violence in decisions about hospitalization from the psychiatric emergency room. Am J Psychiatry 1992;149:207–212.

54. Feinstein R, Plutchik R. Violence and suicide risk assessment in the psychiatric emergency room. Compr Psychiatry 1990;31:337–343.

55. Hoffman DP, Dubovsky SL. Depression and suicide assessment. Emerg Med Clin North Am 1991;9:107–121.

56. McNiel DE, Binder RL. Correlates of accuracy in the assessment of psychiatric inpatients' risk of violence. Am J Psychiatry 1995;152:901–906.

57. Haddad LM, Roberts JR. A general approach to the emergency management of poisoning. In: Haddad LM, Roberts JR, eds. Poisoning and drug overdose. Philadelphia: Harcourt, Brace & Jovanovich, 1990:2–22.

58. Hoyt DW, Finnigan RE, Nee T, et al. Drug testing in the workplace: are methods legally defensible? JAMA 1987;258:504–509.

59. Hughes D. Medical causes of anxiety: a guide to recognition. In: Ellison J, ed. Integrative treatment of anxiety disorders. Washington, DC: APA Press, 1996:249–274.

60. Edelman SE. Managing the violent patient in a community mental health center. Hosp Community Psychiatry 1978;29:460–462.

61. Harris D, Morrison EF. Managing violence without coercion. Arch Psychiatr Nurs 1995;9:203–210.

62. Hyman SE. The violent patient. In: Hyman SE, ed. Manual of psychiatric emergencies. 3rd ed. Boston: Little, Brown & Co., 1984:21–28.

63. Baldessarini RJ. Drugs and the treatment of psychiatric disorders. In: Gilman AG, Rall TW, Nies AS, et al., eds. Goodman and Gilman's the pharmacological basis of therapeutics. 8th ed. Elmsford: Pergamon Press, 1990:383–435.

64. Czobor P, Volavka J, Meibach RC. Effect of risperidone on hostility in schizophrenia. J Clin Psychopharmacol 1995;15:243–249.

65. Anonymous. Risperidone and hostility. Psychiatric Drug Alerts 1995;9:73–74.

66. Fras I, Major L. Clinical experience with risperidone. J Am Acad Child Adolesc Psychiatry 1995;34:833. Letter.

67. Siris SG. Three cases of akathisia and "acting out." J Clin Psychiatry 1985;46:395–397.

68. Yudofsky SC, Silver JM, Schneider SE. Pharmacologic treatment of aggression. Psychiatric Annals 1987;17:397–404.

69. Lott AD, McElroy SL, Keys MA. Valproate in the treatment of behavioral agitation in elderly patients with dementia. J Neuropsychiatry Clin Neurosci 1995;7:314–319.

70. Calabrese JR, Markovitz PJ, Kimmel SE, et al. Spectrum of efficacy of valproate in 78 rapid-cycling bipolar patients. J Clin Psychopharmacol 1992;12(Suppl):53–56.

71. Forster P, King J. Definitive treatment of patients with serious mental disorders in an emergency service, part II. Hosp Community Psychiatry 1994;45:1177–1178.

72. Mehlman PT, Highley JD, Fucher I, et al. Low CSF 5-HIAA concentrations and severe aggression and impaired impulse control in nonhuman primates. Am J Psychiatry 1994;151:1485–1491.

73. Garza-Treviño ES. Neurobiological factors in aggressive behavior. Hosp Community Psychiatry 1994;45:690–699.

74. Lavoie F, Carter G, Danal D, et al. Emergency department violence in United States teaching hospitals. Ann Emerg Med 1988;17:1227–1233.

75. Cembrowicz SP, Shepherd JP. Violence in the accident and emergency department. Med Sci Law 1992;32:118–122.

76. Bernstein HA. Survey of threats and assaults directed toward psychotherapists. Am J Psychother 1981;35:542–549.

77. Madden DJ, Lion JR, Penna MW. Assaults on psychiatrists by patients. Am J Psychiatry 1976;133:422–425.

78. Carmel H, Hunter M. Psychiatrists injured by patient attack. Bull Am Acad Psychiatry Law 1991;19:309–16.

79. Black KJ, Compton WM, Wetzel M, et al. Assaults by patients on psychiatric residents at three training sites. Hosp Community Psychiatry 1994;45:706–710.

80. Bianchi A. Trying patients. Harvard Magazine 1995;Jan/Feb:18–19.

81. Hatti S, Dubin WR, Weiss KJ. A study of circumstances surrounding patient assaults on psychiatrists. Hosp Community Psychiatry 1982;33:660–661.

82. Whittington R, Wykes T. An observational study of associations between nurse behavior and violence in psychiatric hospitals. J Psychiatr Ment Health Nurs 1994;1:85–92.

83. Infantino JA, Musingo S-Y. Assaults and injuries among staff with and without training in aggression control techniques. Hosp Community Psychiatry 1985;36:1312–1314.

84. Appelbaum PS, Dimieri RJ. Protecting staff from assaults by patients: OSHA steps in. Psychiatric Services 1995;46:333–334, 338.

85. Lancee WJ, Gallop R, McCay E, et al. The relationship between nurses' limit-setting styles and anger in psychiatric inpatients. Psychiatric Services 1995;46:609–613.

86. Engel F, Marsh S. Helping the employee victim of violence in hospitals. Hosp Community Psychiatry 1986;37:159–162.

87. Flannery RB Jr, Fulton P, Tausch J, et al. A program to help staff cope with psychological

sequelae of assaults by patients. Hosp Community Psychiatry 1991;42:935–938.

88. Beck JC. The potentially violent patient: legal duties, clinical practice and risk management. Psychiatric Annals 1987;17:695–699.

89. Stroup TS, Dorwart RA. Impact of a managed mental health program on Medicaid recipients with severe mental illness. Psychiatric Services 1995;46:885–889.

90. Koran LM. Psychiatrists' patients. Psychiatric Services 1995;46:873.

91. Hughes D. Trends and treatment models in emergency psychiatry. Hosp Community Psychiatry 1993;44:927–928.

92. Landerman LR, Burns BJ, Swartz MS, et al. The relationship between insurance coverage and psychiatric disorder in predicting use of mental health services. Am J Psychiatry 1994;151:1785–1790.

93. Hankin JR, Steinwachs DM, Regier DA, et al. Use of general medical care services by persons with mental disorders. Arch Gen Psychiatry 1982;39:225–231.

94. Anonymous. Family member most likely victim of violent psychiatric patient. Clin Psychiatry News 1986;14:5.

95. Jones SL, Roth D, Jones PK. Effect of demographic and behavioral variables on burden of caregivers of chronic mentally ill persons. Psychiatric Services 1995;46:141–145.

96. Hyde AP. The management of violence in mentally ill people who live at home. Psychiatric Times 1994;Oct:44–47.

97. Bergman BK, Brismar BG. Do not forget the battered male! A comparative study of family and non-family violence victims. Scand J Soc Med 1992;20:179–183.

98. Anonymous. Consumer reports survey finds most people are helped by psychotherapy: longer treatment best. Psychiatric Services 1995;46:1304.

99. Duffy JF. Total HMO enrollment continues to rise. Psychiatric Times 1995;Jun: 62–63.

100. Raine A, Venables PH, Williams M. High autonomic arousal and electrodermal orienting at age 15 years as protective factors against criminal behavior at age 29 years. Am J Psychiatry 1995;152:1595–1600.

101. Rabinowitz J, Slyuzberg M, Salamon I, et al. A method for understanding admission decision making in a psychiatric emergency room. Psychiatric Services 1995;46:1055–1060.

102. Fichtner CG, Flaherty JA. Decision to hospitalize: a longitudinal study of psychiatric residents. Academic Psychiatry 1993;17:130–137.

103. Greenfield TK, McNiel DE, Binder RL. Violent behavior and length of psychiatric hospitalization. Hosp Community Psychiatry 1989;40:809–814.

104. Rachlin S. The prosecution of violent psychiatric inpatients: one respectable intervention. Bull Am Acad Psychiatry Law 1994;22:239–247.

Chapter 4

Psychiatric Triage, Crisis Intervention, and Disposition

Trude Kleinschmidt and Kathy Sanders

INTRODUCTION

Directors of psychiatric emergency, evaluation, and triage services in urban and suburban settings see psychiatrically ill patients in crisis. Emergency and evaluation services are viewed as much more than a gateway (1) to the mental health system; these services function as sites for psychiatric back-up, crisis intervention, and triage decisions about disposition. Moreover, in this era of cost containment, emergency and evaluation centers will be increasingly central in the allocation of scarce clinical resources.

The day-to-day experience of frontline emergency and triage staff members has been likened to working in a field hospital in the middle of a war, i.e., casualties arrive at an ever-increasing pace. Managed care and limits on government reimbursement require that patients be triaged more accurately and efficiently. Because resources have been sharply curtailed, more care must be provided with what often seems like fewer means.

Psychiatric emergency services have been expanded to include everything from extended treatment in secure holding beds to community outreach programs. The Community Mental Health Centers Act, passed in 1963, was critical in this expansion and requires the inclusion of psychiatric emergency treatment in all federally funded community mental health centers (2). Some deinstitutionalized psychiatric patients now use emergency services as their primary source of care (3). In fact, emergency staffs function increasingly as the bridge between the public and private sector, providing coordination and consultation to multiservice treatments. Because the effectiveness of treatment depends on integrated care, emergency triage services are becoming linchpins in the provision of all psychiatric services.

The demand for and practice of brief interventions in psychiatry is also increasing (3). More than in other medical specialties, success in psychiatric work depends on an interactive process; evaluation, stabilization, and efficient triage requires a precise understanding of the patient and his or her environment. Every intervention initiated in the first hours of treatment relies on an accurate assessment of the case. From this evaluation comes the formulation—the best hypothesis about the current crisis situation set in a historical context. The formulation provides the basis of negotiating treatment with the patient, treater, family, and payer.

In addition to an accurate formulation, success in crisis and triage services depends on establishing an alliance with the patient and family, which can be achieved through empathy, understanding (formulation), and a recognition and use of the patient's strengths. When interventions are effective, the progression of an illness can be prevented, and disrupted social systems can be stabilized and restored.

The decisions of clinicians working in these settings can enhance prevention and provide early intervention and effective treatment. However, the tools for measuring clinical outcomes in crisis intervention and disposition are just being developed. Outcomes research will be crucial to the development of rational triage services, and early detection of patients at high risk and tertiary prevention (i.e., reducing the severity and ongoing disability associated with a disorder) will be important (4).

This chapter reviews the current status of psychiatric evaluation, triage, crisis intervention, and disposition. Case examples from hospital emergency services illustrate each area of clinical activity.

EVALUATION

Although a crisis and a psychiatric emergency may differ in the immediacy of the intervention, both require an evaluation (5). The approach to a patient in a crisis or an emergency situation has three aspects: evaluating and alleviating the symptoms present during the patient's acute disorder (tertiary prevention), providing continu-

ity of patient care, and monitoring the course of the patient's symptoms during the crisis (4–6). The evaluation also may lead to a primary intervention by identifying a patient at risk for the development of a disorder. For example, posttraumatic stress disorder may be prevented after a traumatic event by proper treatment. Crisis intervention also may serve as a secondary prevention by intervening early enough in the evolution of an illness (e.g., major depression) to alter its duration and course (4).

Successful intervention, therefore, hinges on an accurate and thorough assessment of the patient in crisis. As described in Chapter 1, the four key assessment questions "can be used as the structure and foundation of the clinical encounter with an acutely ill patient . . . [and] the clinician's ability to understand and articulate these key areas will optimize alliance, intervention, and outcome."

These questions are the tools that help to locate the patient in the context of the current crisis and to make effective interventions. The answers allow clinicians to understand the current state of the patient's attachment to important others, which can influence psychosocial and biological vulnerabilities; to determine which biologic vulnerabilities are chronic and which are currently activated; to understand and support the patient's strengths; to consult and bolster the patient's system of care, not replace it; and to involve the patient and his or her support system in developing the treatment plan.

In psychiatric crisis and emergency care, the essential questions of a psychiatric evaluation are as follows:

- What is the working diagnosis?
- What is the risk of harm to self or others?
- What is/are the contributing medical illness(es)?
- What is the formulation of the problem?

Establishing a Working Diagnosis

The working diagnosis for a patient in crisis derives from the symptomatic presentation, the essentials of the history, and the mental status examination.

Symptomatic Presentation

The symptoms of a patient in crisis can range from autistic withdrawal to significant agitation. An acute confusional state must be differentiated from dementia. Does the patient have an exacerbation of a long-standing personality disorder with high risk for substance abuse or self-destructive behavior? Whether a visit to the emergency department is deemed urgent or emergent often depends on a patient's symptoms and not on the diagnosis (2).

Essentials of the History

A patient's history focuses on the question, "Why now?" For example, disrupted attachments are often the context for a patient's noncompliance with medication and eventual crisis. Although the first interview with a patient in crisis is often complicated by the limitation of time and the degree of the patient's distress, it is important to let the patient tell his or her story as much as possible (7).

Mental Status Examination

When done systematically and carefully, this examination provides one of the most powerful tools in the assessment of patients in crisis (8). Until a more developed examination can be accomplished, a rapid but concerted scan of only the patient's level of arousal, skin color, clarity of speech, and capacity to ambulate is an effective way to

begin to triage patients within the emergency service. The Mini-Mental State Exam (MMSE) is a brief and useful screening cognitive examination but does not substitute for a full mental status examination (7).

Risk Assessment: Suicide and Dangerousness

The assessment of risk is a crucial element in the evaluation that must be performed on all crisis patients (see Chapters 2 and 3). Risk can be broadly defined as the interaction of motivation and opportunity. Consequently, risk changes over an individual's lifetime. Although it is not possible to predict scientifically which individuals will commit suicide or violence toward others, groups of patients at higher risk can be identified.

Suicide Assessment

This is an essential skill for a psychiatrist seeing patients in an emergency setting. Most of the 250,000 patients who attempt suicide each year in the United States have been seen in an emergency department of a general hospital (9, 10). Studies indicate that most patients who commit suicide have had contact with nonpsychiatric physicians shortly before their death (9, 10).

Suicide studies typically indicate which patients are at higher-than-average lifetime risk for suicide rather than identify short-term risk factors that could be treated (11). The best prospective study of predictors of imminent (within 1 year) suicide (12) included 948 patients from a multicenter study (569 patients with unipolar depression; 185 patients with bipolar type 1; 114 patients with bipolar type II; and 80 patients with schizoaffective disorder). In this study, 13 patients committed suicide during the first year of the study, and 32 patients committed suicide during the 10 years of the study. The following predictors of imminent suicide were identified:

- Severe psychic anxiety,
- Severe anhedonia,
- Global insomnia,
- Difficulty in concentration,
- Indecision,
- Acute alcohol abuse,
- Panic attacks,
- Absence of responsibility for children, and
- Current episode of cycling affective illness.

This study concluded that targeting anxiety and panic symptoms in depressed patients was extremely important as a preventive intervention; another study confirmed this finding for medication-induced akathisia (13).

Violence Assessment

This is another crucial skill for every psychiatrist and clinician working with crisis patients (see Chapter 3). Violent acts represent the culmination of highly individual biologic, psychological, and behavioral processes. Although mental health professionals are limited in their ability to predict violence in any given patient, harmful acts toward others rarely occur without warning. Identifiable, individual-specific variables interact with the environment to greatly increase the risk for violence. Identification of these triggers and of any early warning signs should be a joint enterprise and a fundamental part of the assessment (8).

The accurate assessment of the risk of violence over hours, days, or weeks is based on understanding the confluence of several

factors, including the internal (mental status changes) and external (environmental/situational) variables that have contributed to violence in the past, the presence of any of these variables in the present, active substance abuse, and the role of the patient's psychiatric illness in past violent behavior.

The assessment of the risk of violence over seconds to minutes focuses on the clinician paying attention to the physical here and now of the patient. Parks (14) provides the following visible inventory:

- Posture consisting of sitting on the edge of the chair and gripping the armrests.
- Motor tension evident from clenched fist or jaw.
- Speech that is increasingly loud, strident, or profane.
- Increased motor restlessness evidenced by pacing.
- Angry or irritable affect.
- Increased startle reflex.
- Inability or unwillingness to follow directions.
- Agitated, intoxicated, or paranoid state.
- Violent acts in the very recent past.

As part of the assessment, during the evaluation of the violent patient, the clinician should take any necessary precautions to feel safe. If clinicians ignore their fear, everyone is placed at risk—staff members are at risk for injury or assault, and the patient is at risk for inadequate care because the clinician's denial compromises a thorough evaluation (15).

Contributing Medical Illness

Considerable literature exists on the medical evaluation of emergency psychiatric patients and on the importance of differentiating medical from psychiatric illness (16, 17). Medical clearance standards (see triage section below) continue to wrestle with which psychiatric patients are at higher risk for irreversible harm if medical screening fails to detect coexisting medical illness (18).

The psychiatrist evaluating a crisis patient must consider several factors: the psychiatric illness may be the result of an underlying medical condition, the psychiatric illness may be exacerbated by an underlying medical condition, or the psychiatric illness may be masking an underlying medical condition (17). It is essential that the psychiatrist be alert for signs and symptoms of medical illness and screen for organicity using the mental status examination (17). Elderly, demented, and psychotic patients as well as patients with human immunodeficiency virus (HIV) are known to be at high risk for medical illness (17). The evaluating physician must be especially attentive when a thorough examination of the patient is difficult for some reason (e.g., when the patient is a repeat user of crisis services, or help-rejecting, or identified as a VIP).

Formulation

The formulation provides the critical link between assessment and triage. The formulation is an understanding of the interaction between the current difficulties and the patient's biopsychosocial vulnerabilities; it also represents the best hypothesis about the current crisis (see Chapter 1). In addition to shaping appropriate interventions, the formulation offers the patient a clear and concise view of the present crisis as it connects with any past difficulties in language that is free of jargon. In this way, the alliance is fostered and the patient is invited to think about his or her problems from a different perspective (19).

Key Dimensions of the Formulation

In addition to the diagnosis, assessment of risk, and contributing medical illness, the formulation includes the following elements.

LOCATING THE CURRENT CRISIS IN THE OVERALL COURSE OF THE PATIENT'S ILLNESS

A knowledge of the longitudinal course of the illness enables the clinician to educate the patient, family, treater, and payer about the progression and prognosis of a disorder. For example, a significant percentage of patients diagnosed with borderline personality disorder kill themselves within 5 years of the original diagnosis; therefore, early intervention may significantly reduce morbidity and mortality. Another example is Post's work (20) about the transduction of stress following a first break of affective illness, which may have been triggered by a significant loss. He suggests that early, aggressive biopsychosocial treatment may prevent or ameliorate future recurrence of the disorder.

DETERMINING THE STATUS OF CURRENT ATTACHMENTS

The importance of loss as a triggering event for a crisis is well known (19), but the status of the patient's current relationships is equally important. The patient's social life often shapes his or her sense of well-being. In patients with alcohol dependence, for example, social disruption with its attendant alteration in well-being may increase their vulnerability to a disturbance in mood, with significant consequences (21).

UNDERSTANDING THE PROBLEM FROM THE PATIENT'S PERSPECTIVE

This key element of the formulation is often the starting point of an evaluation. By inviting the patient to tell his or her story, the problem is heard from the patient's perspective. Without this information, the clinician and the patient cannot develop a formulation of the problem that the patient can recognize and use.

UNDERSTANDING THE DYNAMIC FORMULATION

The dynamic formulation is informed by a psychological model that is not represented on any of the five axes of the *Diagnostic and Statistical Manual* (22). It typically consists of an analysis of the ego defenses, character structure (including superego and drive development), and the nature of the object relations (including an understanding of the internalized objects that constitute a sense of self) (see Chapter 1). Understanding the dynamic structure of the crisis helps the clinician bolster the patient's weakened defenses and ally empathically with the patient. It may also provide an opportunity for growth and change.

□ **CASE EXAMPLE**

A 28-year-old woman was sent by the case manager at her residential program to the emergency service of a hospital for evaluation of dysphoria and impulses to cut and burn herself. She revealed a recurrent thought over the past several days to overdose on her medication. She denied current suicidal intent but stated, "It could end up that way."

The patient was well known to the psychiatrist and social worker on call. Both had worked with her over the years, for brief periods, typically when she presented in crisis. Her history was remarkable for stormy relationships with family and treaters, numerous failed medication trials, impulsive self-mutilative behaviors, and two suicide attempts (both by overdose, one requiring significant medical intervention). Her parents were openly disappointed with both the treatment and the patient. The patient had recently begun to lament her fate.

The patient's therapist of several years was on vacation and was also to begin maternity leave in 3 months. The patient was bland in her discussion of these facts. Before the therapist's vacation, she had confronted the patient for not pushing herself to find a job.

In her discussion, the patient focused on her older sister's anger and disappointment when the patient abruptly reneged on her offer to baby-sit. The patient blamed her sister for not understanding the nature of her mood disorder. Curiously, the patient expressed hope that she would be able to attend her volunteer job the next day, if she were not hospitalized.

There were several challenges in working with this patient. Given the patient's anger, mistrust, and somewhat inappropriate affect, an undisclosed overdose should be considered. The fact that she was well known made it easier to make certain assumptions during the evaluation (e.g., pushing her to take more responsibility for her treatment would likely make her feel further misunderstood and criticized). An invitation to explore her own anger and disappointment with her progress—sharpened by her therapist's vacation, pregnancy, and maternity leave—might be more useful. A review of the ways in which the patient might derive a sense of accomplishment if she stayed out of the hospital and met her responsibilities could also be considered. Given her sense of abandonment and hopelessness, a family meeting might be an important step.

PSYCHIATRIC TRIAGE

Psychiatric triage is the process of rapidly determining the patient's level of acuity and the proper site for further assessment and management. The levels of acuity are routine, urgent, and emergent. The acuity determines whether the patient can be evaluated safely over the telephone, in routine outpatient care, through the use of mobile outreach, at a crisis center, or within the emergency department of a general hospital (2, 23–28). The factors involved in level of acuity assessment include:

1. Risk for suicide or violence.
2. Attendant substance abuse.
3. Comorbid or presenting medical problems.
4. Commitability.
   a. Voluntary or involuntary.
   b. Competency.

Local emergency departments within community or academic medical centers serve to contain and evaluate patients safely, provide crisis intervention services, perform admission screenings, set up intensive outpatient services, and initiate psychotropic medication (3, 29, 30). A general hospital emergency department is the best site for safe containment when medical assessment is needed during the crisis assessment and disposition of patients. Life-threatening, psychiatric symptoms require an emergency department or psychiatric hospital for evaluation and management. Patients who are motivated for treatment and who manifest mild to moderate psychopathology are triaged to a nonmedical crisis center, intensive outpatient services, and mobile or telephone outreach. The standard of practice seeks to use the least restrictive environment for any given level of symptomatology (31).

□ C A S E   E X A M P L E

A 55-year-old bipolar patient living with her daughter was sporadically compliant with her usual medications of valproic acid and lithium carbonate. For the past 3 days, she stopped taking her medications and became increasingly irritable and argumentative. When she threw household objects at her daughter, the daughter threatened to call the police. This prompted the patient to take a dose of her usual medications and voluntarily come to the emergency department. By the time the patient arrived, she had calmed considerably. However, because of the recent escalation of irritability and violence in the home and a questionable commitment to remain compliant with her medication, the patient was urged to remain in a crisis (respite) bed for the next 24–48 hours to ensure medication compliance and to establish clinical stability. Commitment and involuntary hospitalization were averted.

Medical clearance is part of crisis assessment and triage (8, 16, 17, 32, 33). Patients who are chronically mentally ill will experience new-onset medical problems just as any other patient populations do (17, 34–36). Additionally, acute mental status changes in the absence of significant psychosocial stressors suggest an underlying medical disorder (37, 38). There is no formula for medical clearance (8, 39,

TABLE 4.1. Life-threatening and Treatable Causes of Acute Mental Status Changes (Mnemonic: WWHHHHIMPS)

Withdrawal from barbiturates
Wernicke's encephalopathy
Hypoxia and hypoperfusion of the brain
Hypertensive crisis
Hypoglycemia
Hyper/hypothermia
Intracranial bleeding/mass
Meningitis/encephalitis
Poisoning
Status epilepticus

Adapted from Wise MG, Rundell JR. Concise guide to consultation psychiatry. Washington, DC: APA Press, 1988, and from Tesar GE. The agitated patient. Part II: pharmacologic treatment. Hosp Community Psychiatry 1993;44:627–629.

40). Hegarty et al. (18) analyzed data on 3000 emergency psychiatric evaluations that included medical clearance during a 6-month period. The study concluded that healthy adults younger than 55 years of age with known psychopathology, no evidence of substance abuse, normal vital signs, and no focal findings on a general physical examination may be safely referred (or admitted) to any psychiatric facility. When a patient presents with new mental status changes, no previous psychiatric history, abnormal vital signs, abnormal physical examination, or intoxication, a more comprehensive laboratory and medical evaluation is indicated. The clinician first must rapidly rule out any life-threatening cause. The mnemonic, WWHHHHIMPS (Table 4.1), is a useful tool for medical clearance. A more exhaustive list of organic causes of acute mental status changes can be summed up with the mnemonic, VINDICTIVE MAD (Table 4.2).

In general, toxicology screening of blood and/or urine, serum electrolytes, blood counts, and enzymes are not indicated unless specific history or clinical findings point to drug or alcohol abuse, overdose, or medical problems.

□ **CASE EXAMPLE**

A 45-year-old man was brought to the emergency department by hospital security after his orthopedic surgeon became concerned by his provocative suicidal statements during a routine appointment for a chronic arthritic condition. The patient was fully alert, oriented, and articulate about his condition and rights while denying suicidal ideas or intent. He was observed to have a normal gait. On examination, the patient smelled of stale alcohol but was so articulate and seemingly clear headed that the examiner did not consider him intoxicated. The patient vehemently denied drinking that day and vociferously wanted to leave; he argued the illegality of holding him against his will because he was not suicidal. The odor of alcohol, however, prompted the emergency department psychiatrist to order a blood alcohol level (BAL). The BAL was 3200 (1000 = legally intoxicated). The clinician was relieved to have held the patient in the department. Once the patient was no longer intoxicated, an accurate assessment of his mental status and suicide risk could be performed.

TABLE 4.2. Organic Causes of Acute Mental Status Changes (Including Mood, Psychotic, Anxiety, and Dissociative Disorders) (Mnemonic: VINDICTIVE MAD)

Vascular	Hypertensive encephalopathy, cerebral arteriosclerosis, intracranial hemorrhage or thromboses, microemboli from various sources (e.g., atrial fibrillation or endocarditic valve), circulatory collapse, vasculitis, collagen vascular diseases, sarcoid, hyperviscosity syndrome, polyarteritis nodosa, throbotic thrombocytopenic purpura, disseminated intravascular coagulation
Infectious	Encephalitis, bacterial or viral meningitis, sepsis, general paresis, malaria, HIV, lyme disease, fungal meningitis, parasitic infection, mumps, brain abscess, Behçet's disease
Neoplastic	Space-occupying lesions (e.g., glioma, meningioma, metastasis, necrosis), paraneoplastic syndromes, carcinomatous meningitis, carcinoid syndrome
Degenerative	Senile and presenile dementias (e.g., Alzheimer's disease, Pick's disease), Parkinsonism, Huntington's chorea, Creutzfeld-Jacob disease, Wilson's disease, multiple sclerosis
Intoxication	Chronic intoxication or withdrawal from sedative-hypnotic drugs (e.g., bromides, opiates, tranquilizers, barbiturates, benzodiazepines, anticholinergics, anesthetics, anticonvulsants), carbon monoxide poisoning, burn inhalation, neuroleptic malignant syndrome
Congenital	Aneurysm, epilepsy, postictal states, complex partial seizures, status epilepticus
Traumatic	Postconcussive syndrome, subdural and epidural hematomas, cerebral contusion, blunt or penetrating cerebral trauma, shock states, multiple organ failure, heat stroke, fat emboli, postoperative syndromes
Intraventricular	Bleed, hydrocephalus (including normal pressure)
Vitamin deficiency	Wernicke-Korsakoff (thiamine), pellagra (niacin), pernicious anemia (B_{12})
Endocrine-Metabolic	Diabetic coma or shock, uremia, myxedema, hypothyroidism, hyperthyroidism, parathyroid dysfunction, hypoglycemia, hepatic or renal failure, porphyria, severe electrolyte or acid/base disturbances, Cushing's disease, Addison's disease, sleep apnea, carcinoid, Whipple's disease
Medications and Metals	Heavy metals (e.g., lead, mercury, arsenic, manganese, thallium), antiarrhythmics, antibiotics, anticholinergics, anticonvulsants, antihypertensives, antivirals, barbiturates, beta blockers, histamine blockers, digitalis, dopamine agonists, GABA agonists, immunosuppressives, lithium, narcotic analgesics, nonsteroidal antiinflammatory drugs, steroids, sympathomimetics
Anoxia	Hypoxia and anoxia secondary to pulmonary or cardiac failure, anesthesia, anemia
Depression—other	Depressive pseudodementia, conversion, hysteria, catatonia, somatoform, dissociative, malingering, transient global amnesia

Adapted from Popkin MK, Tucker GJ. "Secondary" and drug-induced mood, anxiety, psychotic, catatonic, and personality disorders: a review of the literature. J Neuropsychiatry 1992;4:369–385; Ludwig AM. Principles of clinical psychiatry. New York: The Free Press, 1980; and Cassem NH, ed. Handbook of general hospital psychiatry. 3rd ed. St. Louis: Mosby-Year Book, 1991.

CRISIS INTERVENTION

A crisis is a serious life event that stresses a person beyond the limits of their usual coping. In 1968 (as quoted by Jacobson), Caplan, one of the originators of crisis theory, defined it as follows:

"A crisis is provoked when a person faces an obstacle to important life goals that is, for a time, insurmountable through the utilization of customary methods of problem-solving. A period of disorganization ensues, a period of upset, during which many different abortive attempts at solution are made. Eventually some kind of adaptation is achieved which may or may not be in the best interest of that person or his fellows" (41).

Crisis theory posits that emotional homeostasis is disrupted by biologic, intrapsychic, and environmental factors (42). The life stress may cause a person to seek mental health services, either in an office or in an emergency department, even if that person has no underlying psychiatric illness (8).

Crisis intervention is a method of intense and focused engagement (43). The goals are relief from the acute distress, restoration to the patient's baseline, prevention of the evolution or progression of a psychiatric illness, and achievement of a sense of mastery (8, 42, 43).

Therefore, crisis intervention involves tasks different from evaluation and triage. The intervention generally is geared toward stabilizing the acute situation in two ways—internally (through symptom relief and the development of a new perspective on the crisis) and externally (by involving family, treaters, and others in the crisis, which provides an opportunity to change and/or strengthen ongoing relationships and treatment).

Effective intervention with an individual in a crisis depends on two factors: making an alliance by understanding the nature of the problem from the patient's perspective, and negotiating the formulation and treatment plan with the patient, family, treaters, and payer.

Alliance: Finding the Patient from His or Her Perspective

As Gerson and Bassuk (2) noted, Caplan described the ways in which people in crisis can provoke disorganized reactions in others, including their treaters, resulting in a clinician's attempt to manage a patient's treatment without inviting the aid of family or outside treaters.

The paramount clinical goal is to establish an alliance, the critical variable that predicts good outcome, because compliance with treatment principally rests on the working alliance (44). Although the relationship established in a crisis setting is not psychotherapy, the interaction is therapeutic and depends on the active involvement of patient and treater.

To establish a working relationship, the clinician must articulate the presenting problem from the patient's perspective. The goal is to understand what prompted the patient to seek help (42).

Locating and admiring the patient's real strengths is crucial to the alliance and is essential for a good outcome. The clinician should speak to the patient's best efforts to manage the situation. The work in a crisis setting should always be in the direction of support and clarification, rather than exploration and interpretation (19).

Initiation of medication may be useful in relieving the patient's symptoms, increasing the patient's sense of internal control and organization, and thereby bolstering the alliance (45). The evaluating psychiatrist first must assess whether the current crisis was heralded by misuse of medication or an adverse drug reaction before considering the addition of a medication to the treatment plan (29).

Finally, the status and quality of the patient's attachments must be assessed. Any recent loss or change in an important relationship should be identified. The most common cause of acute emotional disturbance is the loss of an important other through death, separation, divorce, rejection, or abandonment (5). Loss of an important attachment (person, pet, job, or status) is commonly associated with a reduction in clarity of thought and ability to solve problems. The intensity and duration of the emotional arousal typically determines whether coping mechanisms will be overwhelmed (46). Seeking support from other people, generally not professionals, helps lower the intensity of that arousal. By assessing the status of the patient's attachments, the crisis clinician can determine whether the patient is likely to have needed coping supports.

Negotiating the Formulation and Plan

The involvement of the patient, family, treater, and payer is essential to stabilizing the situation. The formulation and plan inform and direct the clinicians who receive the patient at the next level of care. The treatment plan will be effective only if it derives from an agreed on view of the crisis and its resolution. Realistic goals that identify what is achievable and at what rate must be set collaboratively. Clinicians should try to address how the patient hoped to be helped and capitalize on the patient's internal resources and external supports.

☐ CASE EXAMPLE

A 37-year-old married engineer was held for observation at the evaluation service of a hospital after referring to suicidal preoccupation in a session with her psychiatrist. She had worked with this psychiatrist for the past 3 months, following the departure of her previous psychiatrist whom she saw for 11 years. The patient initially refused to have her husband participate in the interview, and efforts to engage her were met with angry and agitated refusals to answer any questions.

The history as obtained from the outpatient treater revealed that the patient had been treated for the past 12 years for schizoaffective disorder, which was well controlled with an antidepressant and neuroleptic. The pa-

tient recently had met and married a colleague who knew little about her psychiatric history. The patient and her husband were eager to begin a family, and the patient was adamant that she would not take medication while trying to conceive. She had reviewed this with her psychiatrist without her husband's involvement. Her doctor recommended a slow tapering off of the neuroleptic with careful monitoring for any recurrence of symptoms. He emphasized the importance of bringing her husband into this process, but was met with significant resistance. She abruptly discontinued her medication 10 days before the crisis evaluation.

The patient admitted to hearing voices at the time of the interview but would not be specific about the content of her thoughts. She was tearful and distressed but denied any intention of harming herself. She stated angrily that she would resume medication, "If it will get me out of here." She admitted to feelings of hopelessness and despair about the possibility of getting pregnant. She was considering terminating with her new psychiatrist, whom she felt had "panicked," and she did not see the need to involve her husband in the decision about medication or her disposition.

The crisis team agreed to the patient's plan, in which she return home, with two stipulations: daily contact by telephone or in person and the ongoing involvement of her husband, with whom she would have to discuss her history and her current symptoms. After an emergency meeting with her husband and treater, the patient was able to discuss with her therapist her fears about becoming a mother and about her husband's panicked reaction when she began to reveal the ex-

TABLE 4.3. Level of Care for Acute Psychiatric Presentation

None
Self-help
Outpatient
Intensive outpatient/case management
Day treatment/evening care
Partial hospitalization
Residential/respite
Observation/holding admission
Voluntary inpatient hospitalization
Involuntary hospitalization

tent and severity of her history. Without a formulation of this couple's limited communication, the problem could be seen erroneously as an issue of noncompliance with medication, rather than as a family crisis.

DISPOSITION

The central factors in disposition include:

- Dangerousness,
- Severity of psychiatric and medical pathology,
- Substance abuse,
- Compliance,
- Liability,
- Resources, and
- Insurance coverage.

Disposition options range in progressively restrictive levels from no further intervention through involuntary inpatient hospitalization (Table 4.3). Each disposition level is selected from a knowledge of the patient's coping skills, motivation for treatment, compliance, therapeutic alliance, social supports, living arrangements, and insurance benefits. When a patient has low motivation for seeking care, crisis intervention attempts to form an alliance to engage the patient in the least restrictive level of care for the presenting acuity.

Outpatient Care

This level of care refers to the many modalities used in the symptom resolution of a particular episode of emotional distress and mental illness. The variety of outpatient approaches includes psychopharmacology and many psychosocial treatments such as cognitive behavioral therapy, individual psychotherapy (e.g., dynamic, supportive, insight oriented), and couples, family, or group therapies (47–49). For some patients, regular appointments can be made and treatment established in a contractual fashion. When the patient is new to the mental health system, crisis resolution starts with time-limited and problem-oriented interventions. The goals of outpatient care include stabilization of symptoms to prevent further decompensation and enhancement of social and family supports to prevent regression. An outpatient disposition requires a voluntary and motivated patient, with adequate social supports, whose symptoms are likely to respond to specific interventions.

Intensive Outpatient and/or Case Management

This level of care manages rapidly changing symptoms that require frequent contact to stabilize the patient in a less restrictive environment. The more intensive interventions used may include increased frequency of regular outpatient therapies; the addition of group, couples, or family therapy; and/or rapid access to medication consultation. Patients in crisis may have an established outpatient treatment but require specific interventions of a more frequent or intense focus to stabilize existing care (50).

Case management coordinates mental health services within a larger system of care (51). The aim of assertive outreach or coordination of services is to reach patients before further decompensation and to maintain the patient in an outpatient setting. If the patient requires inpatient care, the case manager quickly establishes outpatient follow-up and maintains continuity of treatment. The tools of case management for patients in crisis include telephone outreach, mobile or home visits, same-day psychopharmacology consultation, arrangement of insurance benefits or housing, and financial assistance (52–58). The goals are early detection and rapid and assertive interventions to control progression of the crisis or avert relapse. Crisis case management requires a voluntary and motivated patient.

☐ CASE EXAMPLE

A 37-year-old man with chronic schizoaffective illness lived in a group home and was part of an Assertive Community Treatment (ACT) service. The group home had recently undergone a change in management staff, and half of the front-line staff had not been rehired. One layed-off staff member had developed a friendly and supportive relationship with the patient. The news of her departure was very difficult for the patient; he began to withdraw and refused to take medication. The patient's case manager was called and came to the group home that same day. Crisis intervention focused on the loss and changes in staff. The patient was able to resume medication, and his illness did not progress to a more serious decompensation.

Day Treatment or Evening Care

These programs provide structured activities and skills training to support recovery from a recent decompensation. Patients in these programs usually have been stabilized by administration of medications, and the immediate crisis has passed. The goal is to consolidate therapeutic gains through social skills training and structured activities. Skilled tasks help the patient improve concentration, work, or relational capacities. Professional supervision ensures a progressive improvement while a patient is consolidating gains. If improvement is not maintained, early intervention can be used to prevent deterioration. Day/evening treatment is effective with chronically ill patients who have been hospitalized recently or are likely to be rehospitalized if functioning does not improve. These patients require social supports adequate for independent overnight functioning.

Partial Hospitalization

Partial hospitalization is used for patients who require almost daily monitoring of medication changes and intensive therapeutic activities and who are not at high risk for dangerous behavior. Adequate social supports are required to allow the patient to live outside a hospital. Although this level of care is often used as a step down from inpatient level of care, patients are admitted directly from outpatient care. The goals are to continue intensive inpatient care in a less-restrictive environment or to prevent inpatient care. Partial hospitalization services include rapid medication changes with adequate medical observation; active individual, group, and family intervention; and structure to prevent regression. Partial hospitalization requires a voluntary patient who is motivated to participate in outpatient treatment and has adequate social supports at home in the evenings or at night.

Residential/Respite Care

This level of care is a nonmedical, group setting that provides 24-hour care for patients who are in acute crisis (59–61). Active psychiatric and medical services are provided in a protected, structured environment with adequate staff to facilitate crisis resolution and disposition planning. This level of care is used for patients who need respite from a current living situation or have inadequate social supports required for outpatient treatment. The goal of respite care is to prevent the need for hospital level of care. Residential respite provides a short-term, structured living situation under the observation of 24-hour staff until comprehensive outpatient treatment can be achieved safely. Patients must be voluntary and motivated and must not warrant commitment. No serious, acute medical problems must complicate the current psychiatric symptomatology. Social supports must be too limited to care for the patient at home, and the respite must provide the likelihood of preventing hospitalization.

□ **C ASE E XAMPLE**

A 49-year-old bipolar woman arrived in Boston from New York to take a "pleasure trip" to Nova Scotia. The patient had not informed her group home staff about her impulsive decision to take a trip nor had she packed her medications, which included valproate, resperidone, and clonazepam. Police found her wandering in the Boston Common, talking intrusively to passersby. The police took her to a hospital emergency department where she was frightened and hypomanic. She was considered uninsured because her Medicaid benefit was from New York. Because she recognized her decompensation and was motivated to get help, she was a good candidate for the crisis bed program. She agreed, went to the crisis bed, resumed her usual medications, and returned to New York after 3 days.

Observation or Holding Beds

Inpatient hospital beds are used for patients requiring stabilization in less than 24 hours (62). The hospital environment allows a patient to be medically and psychiatrically monitored for a longer period than is feasible in an emergency department. Rapid stabilization and comprehensive disposition planning are the focus of the ultrashort stay. The goals include medical and psychiatric observation, containment of disruptive behaviors, and treatment and disposition planning. Unclear medical, substance abuse, and psychiatric issues prevent more rapid disposition planning. The patient may or may not be voluntary. Triage to an observation bed anticipates that the crisis will resolve within 24 hours.

Hospital

This level of care is used to contain, diagnose, and manage severe psychiatric pathology with or without medical complications (63–66). Behavioral control must warrant this restrictive level of care. The goals are safe containment and intensive (daily) medical and/or psychiatric assessment and intervention. The patient is expected to benefit from acute care and continue in outpatient treatment. Patients are either voluntary or involuntary, are at imminent risk of harm without this level of care, or have severe symptoms that require daily medical and psychiatric monitoring and management.

☐ **C ASE E XAMPLE**

A 20-year-old college student had become withdrawn and despondent after failing a crucial premed course. His dormitory house master had noticed the withdrawal and commented on it to the student, who became quite angry. When the student did not appear for breakfast the next morning, the house master looked for him. He was found unconscious, in bed, with an empty bottle of over-the-counter sleeping pills. He was rushed to the emergency department and required 2 days of intensive care medical management. A psychiatric consultant was called to assess for psychiatric disposition. The student was minimally communicative and refused to discuss the stress of school. He reported his disappointment that he had not been successful in overdosing. He endorsed, directly or indirectly, many neurovegetative symptoms of major depression, but the psychiatrist could not determine whether the affective illness had psychotic features. Because of the serious overdose, persistent suicidal ideation, and lack of ability to voluntarily engage in treatment, the patient was committed to a psychiatric hospital.

Triage of Special Populations

The unpredictability of a crisis and the fact that no two cases are alike are the most challenging aspects of emergency psychiatry. There are no routine patients. All patients require a thorough assessment of personal skills, defenses, resources, and supports. A brief discussion of special populations encountered in the emergency department follows.

Patients who have legal charges pending or who have been brought by the police from jail or prison to the emergency department because of acute mental status changes present problems when hospital level of care is required. Every local mental health system should have a protocol for handling the psychiatric problems of the incarcerated patient. If the inmate has not been arraigned, court proceedings will be needed before hospitalization can proceed. Otherwise, the inmate remains in the custody of the police. It is crucial to know the procedures for suicide precautions in a particular jail or prison to determine whether a safe disposition can be achieved. When a patient undergoes a psychiatric evaluation in preparation for a court hearing, the emergency clinician must focus on current symptoms rather than attempt a forensic evaluation. "Fit for duty" evaluations associated with disability applications or problems related to the work place also have no place in emergency psychiatry.

Patients with weapons require special precautions and a well-trained security staff. Clinicians should be aware of available security measures (e.g., panic buttons) and should not hesitate to use them or call security during the evaluation of a threatening or historically violent patient.

Repeat users of crisis services often evoke negative countertransference among staff. Although the population is heterogenous, the staff's attitude toward these patients may lead to less-attentive evaluations and premature clinical dismissal. Repeaters are likely to be psychotic, variably compliant with taking medication, and substance abusers. This combination of symptoms increases impulsivity, hostility, and management problems during the crisis. Case management services and/or treatment protocols can help guide staff members when these patients appear for acute care (8, 67, 68).

Homelessness is a reality of modern society. The high comorbidity of substance abuse and mental illness in this population makes disposition and treatment plans particularly challenging (69). Each homeless individual is unique, and listening to the patient's reality will make it easier to establish a treatment plan with a greater likelihood of compliance and success.

Domestic violence is a common yet underrecognized societal problem (70, 71). Clinical sensitivity to domestic violence encourages a woman to break her silence and share the pain, fear, and humiliation of victimization. Directing the patient to resources for respite, counsel, and legal help begins a vital process. Domestic violence is a continuum of behaviors that typically evolves over a long period. The recovery process is generally characterized by progress and setbacks. Patience and support of the patient's efforts to access needed resources will be necessary, especially when violence is severe and persistent or when the legal system is involved.

The acute psychiatric evaluation of children is compounded by the often limited availability of child and adolescent mental health resources (72, 73). Prolonged waits in the emergency department are common as clinicians sort out the focus of psychopathology, legal concerns, level of care needed, and limitations of insurance benefits. When possible, ready access to child psychiatrists and social services for consultation and help with disposition should be available to the front-line crisis staff.

Geriatric patients require diligent medical clearance, competency evaluation, and medication to manage behavioral disturbances. Families who seek crisis services are often exhausted by the care and supervision required for an aging or dementing family member. Careful attention to case management and home services is necessary for avoiding unnecessary hospitalization (74, 75).

CONTROVERSIES IN PSYCHIATRIC CRISIS/TRIAGE SERVICES

Cost: Can We Afford What We Want? Do We Want What We Can Afford?

Emergency and evaluation services are typically the most expensive services in a hospital; moreover, revenue is low. Even the diversion of patients from inpatient to less-intensive and less-expensive levels of care is expensive (76).

The emergency sign at the hospital's entrance obligates that institution to provide care to whomever comes in the door. Increasingly, this includes the homeless, uninsured, and chronically disabled, especially given the ever-widening gulf between the services available in the public and private sectors (1, 3, 30). The ability of the emergency service to provide continuous care and to hold patients under observation status has been extremely important to managed care companies. Emergency psychiatry may increasingly be practiced outside the emergency department as mobile crisis units make community outreach a reality.

Psychiatric emergency services are expanding in the delivery of mental health; as these services increase, demand also increases (1, 2, 29). The diversification and expansion of emergency services is expensive, however. Society may want emergency services but may find the available budgets too limited.

Emergency Outcome Research: Identifying Stress Hardiness

In the new economics of health-care delivery, a major solution to the problem of dwindling resources and competing needs is to maximize efficiency (77). Cutting cost, however, is the denominator of that solution; the numerator is treatment effectiveness.

Outcome research is critical to assessing the efficacy of treatment. Clinicians in emergency and evaluation services should know who is most at risk and who might respond to less-intensive interventions when triage decisions are made.

Studies in the management of stress have begun to identify a group of persons, termed stress hardy, who seem to tolerate or master repeatedly serious misfortune and threats to their psychological and physical equilibrium. These individuals have a fortitude or resilience that helps them rebound or emerge stronger, with a sense of mastery and control. Better identification of these individuals and their responses to stress might lead to information about the other group, those who suffer psychological scarring and stricture following a crisis, and might result in more effective treatment.

Resources will continue to be curtailed. Creative ways to allocate limited resources must be developed, and an empiric system of care shaped by outcome research must be built.

CONCLUSIONS

The essential task of psychiatric evaluation and triage is to engage the individual, family (or significant other), treater, and payer. Emergency mental health clinicians are reconceptualizing their interventions to function more like catalysts to the system of care. The reality of spiraling costs and limited resources has forced all those involved in crisis care to reckon with the impact of economics.

As the demand for emergency service increases, new opportunities arise. The psychiatric emergency service is increasingly a training site that offers a unique experience (29). The curriculum for a rotation in emergency psychiatry includes such topics as risk assessment and triage, establishment of an alliance, pharmacologic management of agitation, differential diagnosis of acute change in mental status, and treatment of the violent patient. Exposure to varied forms of brief treatment is increasingly needed (and sought) by trainees who must develop skills to work with individuals, couples, and families in crisis.

Finally, the interface between primary medical care and psychiatry is profoundly evident in the emergency department. The emergency service is the back-up to primary care and witnesses the limitations of medical practice. Mastering this interface (and maintaining a patient focus) will be crucial to the transformation in medicine and medical economics that is dominating psychiatry.

REFERENCES

1. Ellison JM, Wharff EA. More than a gateway: the role of the emergency psychiatry service in the community mental health network. Hosp Community Psychiatry 1985;36:180–185.
2. Gerson S, Bassuk E. Psychiatric emergencies: an overview. Am J Psychiatry 1980;137:1–11.

3. Hillard JR. The past and future of psychiatric emergency services in the U.S. Hosp Community Psychiatry 1994;45:541–543.

4. Greenfield SF, Shore MF. Prevention of psychiatric disorders. Harvard Rev Psychiatry 1995;3:115–129.

5. Puskar KR, Obus NL. Management of the psychiatric emergency. Nurse Pract 1989;14:9–26.

6. Finch SJ, Burgess PM, Herrman HE. People with acute psychiatric illness. Aust J Public Health 1991;15:122–129.

7. Folstein MF, Folstein SE, McHugh PR. Mini-mental state: a practical method for grading the cognitive state of patients for the clinician. J Psychiatr Res 1975;12:189–198.

8. Hyman SE, Tesar GE. Manual of psychiatric emergencies. Boston: Little, Brown & Co., 1994.

9. Kelly MJ. Suicide assessment in the emergency department. Forum Risk Management Foundation of the Harvard Medical Institutions Inc. 1993;14:5–6.

10. Hirshfeld RMA. Algorithm for the evaluation and treatment of suicidal patients. Prim Psychiatry 1996;3:26–29.

11. Forster P. Accurate assessment of short-term suicide risk in a crisis. Psychiatr Ann 1994;24:571–578.

12. Fawcett J, Clark DC, Busch KA. Assessing and treating the patient at risk for suicide. Psychiatr Ann 1993;23:244–255.

13. Rothschild AJ, Locke CA. Reexposure to fluoxetine after serious suicide attempt by three patients: the role of akathisia. J Clin Psychiatry 1991;52:491–493.

14. Parks J. Violence. In: Manual of clinical emergency psychiatry. Washington, DC: American Psychiatric Press, 1990:148–149.

15. McCarthy EA. Resolution of the psychiatric emergency in the emergency department. Psychiatr Clin North Am 1983;6:281–292.

16. Tintinalli JE, Peacock FW, Wright MA. Emergency medical evaluation of psychiatric patients. Ann Emerg Med 1994;23:859–862.

17. Buckley RA. Differentiating medical and psychiatric illness. Psychiatr Ann 1994; 24:584–591.

18. Hegarty JD, Julian JN, Sanders KM, et al. The MGH Medical Clearance Project: clearance of low medical risk psychiatric admissions. American Psychiatric Association Annual Meeting, 1995. Abstract.

19. Glick RA, Meyerson AT. The use of psychoanalytic concepts in crisis intervention. Int J Psychoanal Psychother 1980–81;8:171–188.

20. Post RM. Transduction of psychosocial stress into the neurobiology of recurrent affective disorder. Am J Psychiatry 1992;149:999–1010.

21. Duberstein PR, Conwell Y, Cain ED. Interpersonal stressors, substance abuse, and suicide. J Nerv Ment Dis 1993;181:80–85.

22. American Psychiatric Association. Diagnostic and statistical manual of mental disorders. 4th ed. Washington DC: American Psychiatric Association, 1994.

23. Murdach AD. Decision making in psychiatric emergencies. Health Soc Work 1987; Fall:267–272.

24. Wood KA, Khuri R. Temporal aspects of emergency room psychiatric evaluations. J Nerv Ment Dis 1988;176:161–166.

25. Slagg NB. Characteristics of emergency room patients that predict hospitalization or disposition to alternative treatments. Hosp Community Psychiatry 1993;44:252–256.

26. Sanguineti VR, Samuel SE, Schwartz SL, et al. Retrospective study of 2,200 involuntary psychiatric admissions and readmissions. Am J Psychiatry 1996;153:392–396.

27. McNiel DE, Myers RS, Zeiner HK, et al. The role of violence in decisions about hospitalization from the psychiatric emergency room. Am J Psychiatry 1992;149:207–212.

28. Chang MM. Clinician-entered computerized psychiatric triage records. Hosp Community Psychiatry 1987;38:652–656.

29. Ellison JM, Hughes DH, White KA. An emergency psychiatry update. Hosp Community Psychiatry 1989;40:250–260.

30. Curry JL. The care of psychiatric patients in the emergency department. J Emerg Nurs 1993;19:396–407.

31. Puryear DA. Proposed standards in emergency psychiatry. Hosp Community Psychiatry 1992;43:14–15.

32. Chandler JD, Gerndt JE. The role of the medical evaluation in psychiatric inpatients. Psychosomatics 1988;29:410–416.

33. Thienhaus OJ. Rational physical evaluation in the emergency room. Hosp Community Psychiatry 1992;43:311–312.

34. Bartsch DA, Shern DL, Feinberg LE, et al. Screening CMHC outpatients for physical illness. Hosp Community Psychiatry 1990;41:786–790.

35. Carlson RJ, Nayar N, Suh M. Physical disorders among emergency psychiatric patients. Can J Psychiatry 1981;26:65–67.

36. Honig A, Tan ES, Weenink A, et al. Utility of a symptom checklist for detecting physical disease in chronic psychiatric patients. Hosp Community Psychiatry 1991;42:531–533.

37. Henneman PL, Mendoza R, Lewis RJ. Prospective evaluation of emergency department medical clearance. Ann Emerg Med 1994;24:672–677.

38. Popkin MK, Tucker GJ. "Secondary" and drug-induced mood, anxiety, psychotic, catatonic, and personality disorders: a review of

the literature. J Neuropsychiatry 1992;
4:369–385.

39. Riba M, Hale M. Medical clearance: fact or fiction in the hospital emergency room. Psychosomatics 1990;31:400–404.

40. White AJ, Barraclough B. Benefits and problems of routine laboratory investigations in adult psychiatric admissions. Br J Psychiatry 1989;155:65–72.

41. Jacobson GF, Strickler M, Morley WE. Generic and individual approaches to crisis intervention. Am J Public Health 1968;58:338–343.

42. Ewing CP. Crisis intervention as psychotherapy. New York: Oxford University Press, 1978:3–29.

43. Lambert M. Psychiatric crisis intervention in the general emergency service of a veterans affairs hospital. Psychiatric Services 1995;46:283–284.

44. Henry WP, Schacht TE, Strupp HH. Patient and therapist introject, interpersonal process, and differential psychotherapy outcome. J Consult Clin Psychol 1990;58:768–774.

45. Rosenberg RC. The therapeutic alliance and the psychiatric emergency room crisis as opportunity. Psychiatr Ann 1994;24:610–614.

46. Caplan G. Loss, stress and mental health. Community Ment Health J 1990;26:27–48.

47. Solomon P, Gordon B. Outpatient compliance of psychiatric emergency room patients by presenting problems. Psychiatr Q 1988;59:271–283.

48. Glenister DA. A therapeutic group for clients with acute mental health problems. J Adv Nurs 1993;18:1968–1974.

49. Scheidlinger S. An overview of nine decades of group psychotherapy. Hosp Community Psychiatry 1994;45:217–225.

50. Merson S, Tyrer P, Onyett S, et al. Early intervention in psychiatric emergencies: a controlled clinical trial. Lancet 1992; 339:1311–1314.

51. Sledge WH, Astrachan B, Thompson K, et al. Case management in psychiatry: an analysis of tasks. Am J Psychiatry 1995;152:1259–1265.

52. Levinson D, Hershko S, Cohen Y. Prevention of hospitalization by a community intensive mental health care unit. Isr J Psychiatry Relat Sci 1991;28:40–52.

53. Tufnell G, Bouras N, Watson JP, et al. Home assessment and treatment in a community psychiatric service. Acta Psychiatr Scand 1985;72:20–28.

54. Reynolds I, Jones JE, Berry DW, et al. A crisis team for the mentally ill: the effect on patients, relatives, and admissions. Med J Aust 1990;152:646–651.

55. Zealberg JJ, Santos AB, Fisher RK. Benefits of mobile crisis programs. Hosp Community Psychiatry 1993;44:16–17.

56. Zealberg JJ, Christie SD, Puckett JA, et al. A mobile crisis program: collaboration between emergency psychiatric services and police. Hosp Community Psychiatry 1992;43:612–615.

57. Dixon L, Friedman N, Lehman A. Compliance of homeless mentally ill persons with assertive community treatment. Hosp Community Psychiatry 1993;44:581–583.

58. Bengelsdorf H, Alden DC. A mobile crisis unit in the psychiatric emergency room. Hosp Community Psychiatry 1987;38:662–665.

59. Stroul BA. Residential crisis services: a review. Hosp Community Psychiatry 1988;39:1095–1099.

60. Britton JG, Mattson-Melcher DM. The crisis home: sheltering patients in emotional crisis. J Psychosoc Nurs 1985;23:18–23.

61. Schweitzer R, Dubey DR. Scattered-site crisis beds: an alternative to hospitalization for children and adolescents. Hosp Community Psychiatry 1994;45:351–354.

62. Breslow RE, Klinger BI, Erickson BJ. Crisis hospitalization on a psychiatric emergency service. Gen Hosp Psychiatry 1993;15:307–315.

63. Gabbard GO. Comparative indications for brief and extended hospitalization. In: Review of psychiatry. Washington, DC: American Psychiatric Press, 1992;11:503–517.

64. Sederer LI. Brief hospitalization. In: Review of psychiatry. Washington, DC: American Psychiatric Press, 1992;11:518–534.

65. Faulkner LR, McFarland BH, Bloom JD. An empirical study of emergency commitment. Am J Psychiatry 1989;146:182–186.

66. Way BB, Evans ME, Banks SM. Factors predicting referral to inpatient or outpatient treatment from psychiatric emergency services. Hosp Community Psychiatry 1992;43:703–708.

67. Sullivan PF, Bulik CM, Forman SD, et al. Characteristics of repeat users of a psychiatric emergency service. Hosp Community Psychiatry 1993;44:376–380.

68. Ellison JM, Blum N, Barsky AJ. Frequent repeaters in a psychiatric emergency service. Hosp Community Psychiatry 1989;40:958–961.

69. Bierer MF, Tesar GE. Homelessness and psychiatric emergencies. In: Manual of psychiatric emergencies. Boston: Little, Brown & Co., 1994:96–103.

70. Sugg NK, Inui T. Primary care physicians' response to domestic violence. JAMA 1992;267:3157–3160.

71. Sassetti MR. Domestic violence. Prim Care 1993;20:289–305.

72. Kalogerakis MG. Emergency evaluation of adolescents. Hosp Community Psychiatry 1992;43:617–621.

73. Ruffin JE, Spencer HR, Abel A, et al. Crisis stabilization services for children and adolescents: a brokerage model to reduce admissions to state psychiatric facilities. Community Ment Health J 1993;29:433–439.

74. Waxman HM, Carner EA, Dubin W, et al. Geriatric psychiatry in the emergency department: characteristics of geriatric and non-

geriatric admissions. J Am Geriatr Soc 1982;30:427–432.

75. Jenike MA, Cremens MC. Geriatric emergencies. In: Manual of psychiatric emergencies. Boston: Brown, Little & Co., 1994:60–72.

76. Bengelsdorf H, Church JO, Kaye RA, et al. The cost effectiveness of crisis intervention. J Nerv Ment Dis 1993;181:757–762.

77. Clark RE. Searching for cost-effective mental health care. Harvard Rev Psychiatry 1996;4:45–48.

Chapter 5

Acute Psychiatric Disorders in Primary Care

Michelle Riba and Rachel Glick

A new patient arrives in the primary care office and refuses to check in with the receptionist. He starts pacing and is talking loudly and rudely to no one in particular. The other patients in the waiting room— a pregnant woman and her 5-year-old daughter and an elderly couple—look very worried. It is clear to the receptionist that this may be escalating into a potentially dangerous situation.

Mental health clinicians are all too familiar with encountering such behavioral problems on locked psychiatric hospital wards or in emergency departments where there are other trained staff members to help deal with security and safety issues. In a less-intensive, ambulatory setting, clinicians may be caught off guard and not expect to see psychiatric emergencies. In fact, until the psychiatric problem becomes more fully developed, it may not be diagnosed and therefore not managed.

This chapter discusses four important neurobehavioral problems that should not be missed in the primary care office—agitation, acute delirium, acute psychosis, and suicide. We focus on proper assessment as well as diagnosis and management and stress safety. Finally, we offer recommendations on how to be prepared optimally for such emergencies.

AGITATION AND VIOLENCE

Definition

Agitation is a state of increased mental and motor activity. Agitated patients may be threatening in verbal and/or physical ways and can quickly become violent.

Diagnosis and Overview

Various patient populations are predisposed or at risk for agitation and/or violence. History, demographics, and underlying medical and psychiatric diagnoses are the keys to assessment. Violence is often part of the clinical picture of agitation and is discussed in additional detail in Chapter 3.

History

It is important and useful to know if and under what circumstances the patient previously has been agitated or violent. Prior violence is the best predictor of future violence. Family or other informants sometimes can provide that information if the patient is unwilling or unable to help. A formal psychiatric history, including psychiatric hospitalizations or if the patient has been a victim of violence or abuse, is important to obtain.

Demographics

Factors associated with violence include (but are not limited to) age, sex, and socioeconomic factors.

Young males, particularly those between the ages of 15 and 24, are at demographic risk for violence. Other contributing variables include poverty, disenfranchisement from majority or other groups, feelings of racial or other types of prejudice, and lack of social supports.

Diagnoses Associated with Agitation and Violence

Delirium is often associated with neurobehavioral problems such as agitation and assaultiveness. Substance abuse (especially withdrawal or intoxicated states) and psychosis (whatever the underlying cause) may be associated with agitation and violence.

Primary cerebral disorders such as dementia, seizure disorders, and strokes and those disorders affecting global, frontal, or temporal areas are associated with unpredictability, agitation, frustration, and violence.

Personality disorders, particularly antisocial, paranoid, and borderline person-

TABLE 5.1. Signs or Signals of Impending Attack

Loud, angry, or profane speech

Hyperactivity—pacing or any increased motor activity

Intoxication

Increased muscle tension such as clenching of the jaw or fists

Rigid posture

Poor eye contact

Increased autonomic symptoms (diaphoresis of the palms or forehead, red face, tachycardia, widened pupils)

Angry, hostile, or irritable affect

Picking up objects as if they could be thrown

Slamming doors, chairs, or other objects

Suspiciousness

Verbal or physical threats

Blocking the door or other escape route

The clinician feels a sense of danger

ality disorders, may be linked with aggressiveness and hostility. Mood states, such as major depression and bipolar disorder, manic, often are associated with agitated behavior.

Assessment

In an office setting, there may be clues about violence from the moment the patient enters the reception area. There is often a period of increasing tension, felt by those in the presence of the patient. Accompanying family members may look troubled and frightened. Some specific clues to assess agitation and impending violence are presented in Table 5.1.

In evaluating agitated or threatening patients, clinicians must decide if they feel safe enough to proceed with the examination. If a clinician does not feel safe, he or she should get help and transfer the patient to a facility where restraint and seclusion are available, such as a hospital emergency department.

If the patient can be calmed with verbal intervention, the clinician may then proceed to assess the patient further.

1. A screening mental status examination (MSE) must be performed. The clinician will probably already have noted something about the patient's appearance (including eye contact), behavior, psychomotor symptoms, speech, and thought processes. The patient should be asked about mood/affect (e.g., anger), thought content (suicidality or homicidality, paranoid thinking, delusions, or hallucinations), cognition and motivation, insight, and judgment.

2. If the patient appears intoxicated, a Breathalyzer and blood or urine toxicology screens may be used to determine if substances are involved. On physical examination, evidence of head injury, an acute abdomen, and other sequelae of trauma (e.g., contusions from a fall) should be sought. Disposition or other management strategies should never be discussed with an intoxicated patient. The patient should be kept safe and in a quiet but observed area.

3. If the patient is psychotic, it is very important to know if this is new onset psychosis or a chronic psychiatric problem. If the patient is older, the new onset psychosis may be a symptom of a medical (including neurologic) problem. Agitation may be a symptom of an acute psychiatric problem, of an acute medical problem, or both.

4. Fluctuating levels of consciousness and confusion on the cognitive section of the MSE suggest delirium. Questions about orientation (date, time, place, person); remote, recent, and immediate memory; concentration (serial 100s, serial 20s; months of year backward); drawing the face of a clock; and a written command that the patient is asked to follow are all useful.

5. If it is determined that there is no apparent psychiatric explanation for the patient's agitation and threatening behavior, the patient should be told that such behavior will not be tolerated in the office (see below).

Management/Treatment

If the psychiatric issues are unclear, a formal consultation from a knowledgeable colleague should be obtained. A "curbside consult" may be an initial step. The clinician may also want to present the case formally to a consultant for recommendations. If the patient is willing, he or she should see the consulting psychiatrist. The patient should be informed that the clinician is trying to be maximally helpful by getting input from another physician.

Almost any object can be turned into a weapon by an agitated or aggressive patient. Often, the patient holding the weapon is just as scared as the clinician. To secure safety for all, the patient should be convinced to give up the weapon without feeling overpowered or that he or she is losing control. Other suggestions include the following:

1. Move very slowly, cautiously, and deliberately. Do not startle the patient.
2. Keep talking in a calm, reassuring, and natural tone of voice. A scared or angry tone could cause the patient to become more frightened.
3. Try to make and keep eye contact with the patient. Looking in other directions may make the patient feel that he or she cannot trust the clinician.
4. Assume the patient is in control and tell him or her so.
5. Instead of directly asking the patient to give up the weapon, ask why he or she feels the need for a weapon. It should be

explained to the patient how frightened the clinician feels and that it is hard to listen or help when feeling so threatened. This can prompt the patient to give up the weapon voluntarily.

6. If the patient is prepared to surrender the weapon, do not take it directly. Often people are injured when weapons change hands. Instead, ask the patient to leave the weapon on a table, chair, or floor where it can be removed safely by security personnel.

7. Do not escalate the patient's potential for violence. Do not threaten verbally. Do not try to physically overpower or disarm the patient.

8. If the patient refuses to surrender the weapon, leave the situation as quickly as possible and get assistance. Panic/security buttons strategically yet inconspicuously placed in the examination room or corridors can be invaluable when escape is not possible.

It may be difficult or impossible to continue caring for a patient when the clinician or other staff members feel threatened. Patients can be banned from an office or clinic as long as they are not abandoned clinically. A clinician may discharge the duty to treat the patient by sending a registered letter apprising him or her of why termination will be necessary and providing alternative sites for medical care. The advice from a consulting physician (see above) can be used when deciding how to best discharge the duty to treat. The clinician's reasoning, any consultations, and planning should always be documented.

Threats against a clinician, his or her family, or staff members and their families should be taken seriously. Consider, with consultation, referring the threat to the local law enforcement agency. Threats from psychotic patients or those with borderline (and other) personality disorders need to be evaluated regarding whether they can be handled clinically or should be referred to law enforcement authorities.

□ **CASE EXAMPLE**

Mr. S is 25 years old with intermittent use of alcohol and cocaine. He is currently receiving disability due to back pain from a work-related injury that occurred 2 months ago. His boss had asked him to climb a ladder and he slipped. He asks for a prescription for Tylenol no. 3, but by your computation, the refill that you gave him over the telephone last week should have been adequate. He tells you how much pain he is in, but there is no focal neurologic change on examination. You suspect that he is seeking narcotics. You notice that his breath smells of alcohol and his pulse and blood pressure are slightly elevated. As he begins to realize that you may not give him a refill, he becomes angry and threatens to sue you for incompetence. He gets off the examination table and begins pacing. He asks you how you would feel if you could not work and people would not help you with the pain. He also starts talking about getting even with his boss for causing the injury. You sense that there might be imminent danger. You ask him to remain in the room while you check on some of his previous laboratory work. Once out of the room, you ask the receptionist to call the police. The police arrive, the patient quiets quickly, and the police escort him to a nearby emergency department where he is treated for alcohol and narcotic abuse and withdrawal.

ACUTE DELIRIUM

Definition

Delirium is an acute state of fluctuating cerebral dysfunction. Delirium typically is transient and reversible. Onset of delirium may be acute or subacute. A wide range of mental status abnormalities may occur, including the following:

- Decreased or impaired attention.
- Changes in level of consciousness.
- Disturbances in orientation.
- Agitation or decreased psychomotor activity.
- Disturbances in the sleep-wake cycle.
- Cognitive impairment in memory, concentration, thinking, and perception; fearfulness and increased startle reactions.
- Poor judgment.

Diagnosis/Overview

Delirium is a medical emergency that requires accurate diagnosis and intervention. The causes of delirium are extensive. In general, the causes fall into the following broad medical or neurologic categories (see Chapter 12) (1).

1. Neurologic disorders

   a. Meningitis or encephalitis

   b. Intracranial bleeding or hypoperfusion

   c. Drug- or alcohol-induced encephalopathy or withdrawal (e.g., Wernicke's encephalopathy, delirium tremens)

   d. Central nervous system traumas, tumor, and infection

2. Medical disorders

   a. Metabolic (e.g., hypoglycemia or hyperglycemia)

   b. Hypoxia

   c. Toxins, drugs, heavy metals

   d. Infections

   e. Endocrinopathies

Almost any medication, prescribed or over the counter, can induce delirium. Patients in an acute delirium are not reliable historians. It is best to enlist the help of family members to retrieve any and all of the patient's pill bottles to try to reconstruct what has been ingested.

Assessment

In the outpatient setting, an altered, fluctuating mental status may be the first clue that there is a serious underlying medical problem.

□ **C A S E E X A M P L E**

A 76-year-old woman in previous good health was brought by her daughter because, "Mother is just not acting like herself. She had been sleeping more than usual in the daytime and not sleeping at night. Sometimes she appears like her usual self, and sometimes she appears frightened. She seems confused. All this started about 3 days ago."

Populations at Risk

The very young and the very old are at risk for delirium, but anyone can become delirious. In the outpatient setting, the clinician is most likely to see the following:

1. Young children with very high fevers (infection).
2. Elderly patients in general, particularly those who

a. are taking multiple medications,

b. have decreased metabolic capacity,

c. have visual or auditory deficits,

d. have had recent major surgery (e.g., hip fracture, heart bypass),

e. have an underlying infection (e.g., urinary tract infection), and

f. have an underlying dementia.

3. Patients who abuse or are dependent on drugs or alcohol and are prone to withdrawal states.
4. Patients with acquired immune deficiency syndrome (AIDS).

Clinical Features

1. Fluctuating MSE.
2. Anxiety, irritability, restlessness, sleep-wake cycle irregularities.
3. Attention and concentration difficulties (distractibility).
4. Altered immediate and recent memory.
5. Disorientation (first to date, then place, finally to person).
6. Altered perceptions.
7. Labile emotions (e.g., anger, sadness, anxiety).

Evaluation

To make the diagnosis, the clinician should do the following:

1. Obtain vital signs and perform a focused physical examination.
2. Elicit a good history from the family (and the patient if he or she is able to cooperate), including a good chronology of the symptoms.
3. Determine the medications/drugs/alcohol used and the quantities ingested.
4. Determine what changes in mental status have occurred.

5. Suspect an underlying medical or neurologic cause for the delirium.
6. Consider laboratory, lumbar puncture, imaging, and electroencephalograph (EEG) testing.

Management/Treatment

Safety is the primary concern. Delirious patients often are confused, anxious, or frightened. They may be a danger to themselves or others.

Proper evaluation of delirium should be accomplished in a hospital setting. Transport to the hospital from the office generally is best done via ambulance (rather than in the family car). Under no circumstances should the patient drive.

If the patient refuses hospitalization, the patient's competency to understand the risks and benefits of receiving care should be evaluated. Although competency technically is a legal decision, the clinician and the family may need to determine what is in the patient's best interest.

Avoid medications, if possible, in the initial stage of management. If a tranquilizer is needed, low-dose haloperidol (0.5–1 mg by mouth) is recommended. The intramuscular route is often dangerous when the patient has a fluctuating mental status because the syringe may prompt the patient to become agitated. Benzodiazepines may further disinhibit delirious patients; an exception is the patient in an acute withdrawal state (e.g., alcohol withdrawal).

The clinician should attempt to reassure and educate the patient and family, who are frightened and do not know what to expect. It should be explained that there is a medical cause for the delirium that must be medically evaluated. If the patient is suspicious, he or she should be told that the clinician understands and wants to try to help because feeling that way is confusing and uncomfortable.

Mrs. R brings her daughter, Jane, for an urgent appointment. Jane is 19 years old and home from college on spring break. Since last evening, Jane has been behaving strangely. She seemed confused before falling asleep last night and did not sleep well. This morning she was tearful, angry, and at one point seemed to be hallucinating, according to her mother. She has no history of psychiatric problems; her mother does not think she uses drugs. Jane is sleepy and difficult to arouse. Once the examination is begun, she becomes agitated, appears frightened, and then tries to bite the clinician. With the assistance of the nurse and with Mrs. R standing by and reassuring Jane, the clinician takes the patient's vital signs and finds a temperature of 101.4°F. Although she is difficult to examine, she seems to have a stiff neck. It is arranged that the patient be immediately transferred by ambulance to the emergency department for work-up and treatment of presumed meningitis. While she awaits transfer, a staff member remains in the room to observe the patient's behavior and assure that she is safe. The clinician explains delirium to Jane's mother and stresses the need for hospital evaluation and treatment. Mrs. R is also told that because delirious patients are unpredictable, it will be safer for Jane to go to the hospital by ambulance.

ACUTE PSYCHOSIS

Definition

Psychosis is a symptom, not a diagnosis. Psychosis refers to a break with reality and may include hallucinations, delusions, dis-organized thinking, or paranoia. There are many causes for psychosis. Whatever the cause, acute psychosis requires medical/psychiatric evaluation and treatment.

Diagnosis/Overview

A history should be obtained from the patient, family, and friends. Patients often minimize, forget, or are unable to link evolving changes in behavior, perception, or thinking to the current problem.

The cause of acute psychosis should be presumed to be medical until proven otherwise. Medical causes fall into two categories: life-threatening and non–life-threatening.

1. Life-threatening causes of psychosis.

    a. Central nervous system infection (e.g., meningitis, encephalitis).

    b. Encephalopathy (e.g., drug induced [Wernicke's], hypertension).

    c. Metabolic (e.g., hypoglycemia, hypercalcemia).

    d. Hypoxia.

    e. Intracranial hypoperfusion or bleeding.

    f. Drug intoxication or withdrawal.

2. Non–life-threatening causes of psychosis.

    a. Medical

        1. Industrial exposures (e.g., carbon tetrachloride).

        2. Toxic reaction to prescribed medications (e.g., steroids).

        3. Nutritional deficiencies (e.g., vitamin B_{12}).

        4. Metabolic, neurologic disorders (e.g., Huntington's disease).

5. Drug withdrawal or intoxication (e.g., LSD, PCP).

b. Psychiatric

1. Schizophrenia or schizophreniform disorder.

2. Mood disorders (psychotic depression, bipolar disorder, manic).

3. Schizoaffective disorder.

Assessment

Safety is a primary concern. Before evaluating the patient, it should be decided if the evaluation can be done in the office setting or requires a more secure environment, such as a hospital emergency department. If a transfer is indicated, voluntary versus involuntary hospitalization should be determined (see below).

The office evaluation of acute psychosis includes the following:

1. Vital signs.
2. Physical examination, including neurologic examination and inspection for evidence of trauma.
3. MSE.

a. Appearance—disheveled or inappropriate grooming (e.g., wearing a cotton, short-sleeved shirt and no overcoat on a cold, winter morning).

b. Behavior—uncooperative, hostile, or aggressive interactions.

c. Psychomotor agitation.

d. Speech—poverty of words, disorganized or nonsensical ideas, neologisms, increased rate, long pauses, blocking.

e. Mood, may vary—irritable, angry, depressed, frightened.

f. Affect—facial expressions inappropriate to stated mood, behavior, or circumstances.

g. Thought process—looseness of association, flight of ideas, tangentiality, grandiose ideas, blocking.

h. Thought content—delusions; perceptual abnormalities such as auditory, visual, olfactory, or tactile hallucinations (auditory hallucinations are more common in primary psychiatric disorders; if visual, olfactory, or tactile hallucinations are present, suspicions of underlying medical or neurologic abnormalities should be raised); paranoia; suicidal or homicidal ideation, intent, or plan; ideas of reference or influence.

i. Cognition—should be evaluated for orientation to time, place, person. Memory—immediate, recent, and remote may be altered by certain psychotic illnesses. Concentration—usually altered; Proverbs—concrete (unable to abstract); Judgment—usually impaired; Insight—often limited.

4. Laboratory Tests

In the office setting, the following should be ordered if possible.

a. Complete blood count including differential with mean corpuscular volume.

b. Glucose level.

c. Urine or blood drug screen, alcohol level.

d. Urinalysis.

e. Electrolytes, blood urea nitrogen, creatinine.

Other tests to consider, depending on the patient's presentation, history, and circumstances, include the following.

a. Electrocardiogram (ECG).

b. Chest radiograph.

c. Calcium, magnesium levels.

d. Thyroid function tests (TSH and T_4).

e. EEG (sleep deprived, nasopharyngeal leads).

f. Computed tomography (CT) or magnetic resonance imaging (MRI) of the head.

g. Liver function tests.

h. Human immunodeficiency virus (HIV); serum test for syphilis.

i. Lumbar puncture.

j. Erythrocyte sedimentation rate.

k. Vitamin B_{12}, folate levels, heavy metal screen, ceruloplasmin, ammonia level, cortisol level.

l. Arterial blood gas.

m. Neuropsychologic testing.

5. Safety in the Office

a. The patient should never be left unattended. If family members are available, they should sit in the room with the clinician and the patient.

b. The staff should know when the clinician is with a psychotic patient—they may need to call the police or be ready to assist with a show of force.

c. Things should be kept simple and calm for the patient. Repetitive, intrusive questions should not be asked. The clinician should tell the patient what he or she is doing, especially during the physical examination. Sudden moves should be avoided if possible. If the patient refuses part of the physical examination or a blood test, it should be explained to the patient and family why examination needs to be done.

Management/Treatment

When the diagnosis is acute psychosis, the clinician then must determine whether to continue management in the outpatient setting or whether the patient needs a more secure setting—a hospital emergency department, an admission to a medical hospital service, or admission to a psychiatry hospital service.

Determine the Setting for Further Management

Acutely psychotic patients may be a danger to themselves or others. If the patient is agitated or paranoid, he or she should be transferred via ambulance to a hospital emergency department for further evaluation. The patient will probably need to be committed for this evaluation.

If the psychotic patient is suicidal, homicidal, or has engaged in dangerous behavior and there is no life-threatening medical problem, it may be best to transfer the patient to a locked psychiatric facility for behavioral control. Any further medical work-up for the cause of the psychosis can be done on the psychiatric unit.

If the patient is calm and cooperative and the family is supportive and reliable, further work-up of the cause of the psychosis may be possible in the outpatient setting. Regardless of the cause of the psychosis, antipsychotic medication is the treatment of choice. Haloperidol (or its equivalent) may be used; doses range from 2 to 10 mg/day, depending especially on age. A liquid preparation is more rapidly absorbed and causes less suspicions in paranoid patients. In patients at higher risk for dystonic reactions from antipsychotic medications (younger men, particularly African-Americans), anticholinergic prophylaxis is indicated. Benztropine, 1 mg by mouth, twice a day, is useful.

Management of Psychosis in the Primary Care Setting:

PSYCHOSIS SECONDARY TO A MEDICAL CAUSE

If the medical cause is determined and treated, the psychosis may resolve with time, recur, or become chronic. When treatment with antipsychotic medication must be continued, the patient's informed consent must be obtained. It is important to inform the family of the psychiatric problem and the need for medication. The patient should be examined for extrapyramidal symptoms before starting an antipsychotic medication and then be reexamined every 3 months while taking the medication.

PRIMARY PSYCHOSIS DUE TO A PSYCHIATRIC DISORDER

It should be determined if the primary care office is the optimal setting for long-term treatment of a primary psychotic disorder. A factor to consider is whether the office can accommodate the patient's needs to integrate psychosocial treatments. Will the patient need groups, training, or day treatment opportunities? Is a case manager needed? Are there any payment/insurance limitations?

Additionally, as noted earlier, informed consent must be obtained from the patient for taking antipsychotic medication. Diagnosis, treatment, course, prognosis, and prevention should be discussed with the patient and family. Their questions, as well as questions from the patient, should be encouraged.

□ **CASE EXAMPLE**

Mr. V is a 35-year-old attorney with diabetes. His wife brings him to the office because he is upset and agitated. When asked what is wrong, he makes little sense and talks rapidly about the end of the world in a confusing manner. Mr. V has no psychiatric history and no known substance abuse. He has had insulin-dependent diabetes for a number of years, but recently has had more difficulty controlling his glucose level. His wife thinks he may have increased his insulin in the past few days. A finger-stick test is performed, and his blood glucose level is only 38. He is given intravenous dextrose in the office while both his wife and a nurse observe him. During the next 30 minutes, his mental status returns to normal.

SUICIDE

Assessment of the Suicidal Patient in Primary Care

Seventy-five percent of all patients who commit suicide visit their primary care physician within 3 months of killing themselves. Fifty percent of patients who attempt or complete suicide have seen a physician during the prior week. For these reasons, among others, it is critical for primary care providers to understand and recognize the warning signs and symptoms of suicidal ideation, intent, and plan.

It is never wrong to ask a patient if he or she has been thinking about suicide. Asking the question does not put the thought into someone's head. Patients with major depression or bipolar disorder, psychotic disorders, borderline personality disorders, delirium, substance or alcohol abuse or dependence, recent losses such as death of a spouse, recent stressors (related to work, finances, relationships, or medical condition), availability of a weapon, and history of suicide attempts are associated with increased suicide rates.

What questions should a patient who has been contemplating suicide or has actually tried be asked? We recommend the following:

1. How often are you thinking about suicide? Once a year (on an anniversary) or every day?
2. What method are you considering? Has it been well thought out and planned? If so, are the weapons readily available (e.g., guns, pills, rope)?
3. Have you arranged for your finances? Have legal papers been drawn up and arranged?
4. Who have you confided in?
5. Have you practiced the plan? Is the plan possible?
6. (If the patient has suicidal ideation) Do you want to go through with it or would you like to get help? Do you have any hope?
7. Have any written notes telling loved ones about your plans or reasons?
8. Have you visualized your funeral? Who would be there?
9. Have you thought about the impact on friends, family? If so, what are these feelings?
10. Do you really want to die?

For those patients who have suicidal ideation but would like help and do not wish to die, further assessment may be done in the primary care office setting. Referral to a mental health professional should be considered in all cases. Assessment of the suicidal ideation should include evaluation of the primary psychiatric diagnosis as well as stressors and losses that have contributed to the current problem. A focus should be on the treatment of the underlying psychiatric problem and ways to enlist support from family and friends during the treatment.

Although patients who have made a suicide attempt or who have clear intent or plan may confide in their primary care provider, the patient should still be referred to a mental health professional for further assessment and treatment. The primary care provider should convey that the patient is not being abandoned, but that more expert help is needed. The primary care provider should also determine if the patient will be transferred voluntarily to an emergency setting or will need to go involuntarily. All states have commitment laws that allow licensed physicians to have patients evaluated (for a specific time) if the patient is a danger to himself or herself or others or gravely disabled due to a mental disorder.

Primary Care Treatment

Should the primary care provider decide to treat the patient, options may consist of the following.

1. Talk with the patient's family or friends about their ability to stay with the patient until the suicidal feelings improve. Focus on their comfort level with this responsibility and on the patient's ability to depend on others for help.
2. Inform family members that weapons or lethal materials, such as guns, pills, and alcohol, should be removed from the patient's home (or wherever the patient will be staying).
3. Contract for safety. Some health care providers try to make arrangements with patients to follow a plan if suicidal impulses or thoughts begin to overwhelm them. Such arrangements may consist of calling friends or family, calling the physician, having the patient go to the emergency department, and taking a prescribed medication that might be useful (e.g., benzodiazepines or antipsychotics). Although such contracts alone should not reassure the clinician that the patient will be safe,

and they certainly are not legally binding, some patients are able to adhere to them. Some patients tend not to regress (as much) and are better in control with such safety contracts. The authors do not use safety contracts, but they are mentioned here because some primary care practitioners find such plans helpful for familiar patients.

4. Attempt the following when patients call on the telephone and state their suicide intent, plan, or attempt.

> a. Get the patient's telephone number and address. If the patient refuses to say where he or she is calling from, try to stay on the telephone. Write a note to a colleague/staff member in your office to call the police and have them trace the call or send a car or ambulance to the patient's home.

> b. Keep the patient talking.

> c. Ask to speak to a family member or friend who may be in the house with the patient.

5. Ask for help. Many local hospital emergency departments or community mental health centers have professionals on call to help with treatment options for suicidal patients. They can help guide the clinician in matters such as state commitment procedures, resources such as outreach teams, and availability of psychiatric facilities in the area.

□ **C ASE E XAMPLE**

Ms. N is a 42-year-old woman who has been treated for asthma and hypertension for 13 years. She has no psychiatric history. She called the office this morning requesting an emergency appointment, saying her asthma is much worse. When the clinician greets her, she begins to cry and says she has just learned that her husband is having an affair and also that she has lost her job. She says she thinks the emotional stress is worsening her asthma. After discussing adjustments in her asthma medication, she is asked about her mood and how she is coping with the stress. She again begins to cry and says, "I don't know how I am going to go on." When asked if she has had thoughts of suicide, she says, "I'm so embarrassed. I have thought about killing myself to stop the pain." By exploring her suicidal thoughts in detail, it is learned that she has no plans or intent and that both her religious beliefs and her children prevent her from committing suicide. She has many symptoms of depression. At the clinician's suggestion, she agrees to a consultation with a psychiatrist to determine if antidepressants are necessary. The clinician also encourages the patient to call the office if her suicidal urges get worse. She states that she will.

□ **C ASE E XAMPLE**

Mr. M is a 65-year-old, recently retired, widowed man who has been referred for routine medical care. According to his records, he has no active medical issues and no psychiatric history. He appears depressed, and his daughter who has accompanied him says she is worried about how sad he has seemed since retiring. After the daughter leaves the room, the patient is asked about suicidal thoughts and says, "I don't want to talk about it." He refuses to answer any questions about his safety. Because the clinician does not know the patient, there is concern about suicide risk. While the patient is dressing, the clinician again speaks with the daughter and asks if she is concerned about her father's suicide risk. She seems relieved by the question and states that she has been worried. She also says that her father will not talk to a psychiatrist. Whenever she has suggested it, he gets very angry; the week before he had thrown a glass at her when she asked. It is arranged for an ambulance and the police to stand by while the clinician tells Mr. M that an evaluation by a psychiatrist has been arranged, even if it needs to be against his will. The patient becomes agitated and begins to yell obscenities at his daughter and the clinician. The police are necessary to escort him to the ambulance. He is transferred to a psychiatric emergency center for further evaluation.

CONCLUSION

In the primary care setting, acute behavioral changes can be frightening to the clinician, staff members, the patient, and others who observe the situation. This chapter has outlined a general approach to handling patients with psychiatric emergencies that can arise in the office setting: agitation, delirium, acute psychosis, and suicide. For the interested reader, other texts offer further information on these subjects (2–5).

The most important things to do when a patient presents with one of these problems are (a) to ensure the safety of the patient and all others and (b) to look for an underlying medical cause for the symptoms. This approach, coupled with appropriate use of psychiatric consultation, will allow the clinician to manage acute psychiatric disorders more safely and effectively in primary care.

REFERENCES

1. Wise MG, Brandt GT. Delirium. In: Yudofsky S, Hales R, eds. The American Psychiatric Press textbook of neuropsychiatry. 2nd ed. Washington, DC: American Psychiatric Press, 1992.
2. Hyman SE, Tesar GE. Manual of psychiatric emergencies. 3rd ed. Boston: Little, Brown, & Co., 1994.
3. Kaplan HI, Sadock, BJ. Pocket handbook of emergency psychiatric medicine. Baltimore: Williams & Wilkins, 1993.
4. Hilliard JR. Manual of clinical emergency psychiatry. Washington, DC: American Psychiatric Press, 1990.
5. Blumenreich PE, Lewis S. Managing the violent patient: a clinician's guide. New York: Bruner/Mazel Publishers, 1993.

Section II

ACUTE CARE

Part A: SPECIFIC DISORDERS
Chapter 6   Depression
Chapter 7   Panic and Obsessive-Compulsive Disorders
Chapter 8   Mania
Chapter 9   Schizophrenia
Chapter 10   Trauma and Dissociative Disorders
Chapter 11   Substance-Related Disorders
Chapter 12   Disorders of the Geriatric Population
Chapter 13   Disorders of Childhood and Adolescence
Chapter 14   Borderline and Antisocial Personality
              Disorders

Part B: SPECIFIC INTERVENTIONS
        AND TREATMENTS
Chapter 15   Case Management
Chapter 16   Family Support and Intervention
Chapter 17   Focal Psychotherapy
Chapter 18   Group Psychotherapy
Chapter 19   Home-Based Care

Chapter 6

Depression

Tana A. Grady, Lloyd I. Sederer, and Anthony J. Rothschild

DEFINITION

Depression is the most common major psychiatric disorder. More than 15% of all adults will experience a depressive episode at some point in their lives (1, 2). Depression is widely found among medically and surgically ill patients in ambulatory and hospital settings (3). Individuals with depression will frequently present to primary care ambulatory settings and subsequently be referred to mental health professionals (see Chapter 5). Severe depression associated with suicidal thoughts and/or behaviors is the most common cause for psychiatric hospitalization (4).

The central feature of major depressive disorder is a subjective experience of significant sadness (depressed mood) or a pervasive loss of interest and pleasure in the individual's usual activities (anhedonia). Irritability or anxiety may be the predominant mood disturbance in some cases, whereas agitation may be the major complaint in other cases. A feeling of lowered self-esteem is common, as are feelings of helplessness. Depressed patients are fre-

quently preoccupied (often obsessed) with work, family, finances, and their health and approach these matters with marked pessimism and hopelessness. Guilty feelings for past or current acts are also frequently found in patients with major depressive disorder. The combination of hopelessness, pessimism, low self-esteem, and guilt may prompt morbid and/or suicidal thoughts.

Many patients will experience insomnia, anorexia (loss of appetite), and significant weight reduction with their mood disturbance; however, a subset of patients experiences increased sleep (hypersomnia), increased appetite (hyperphagia), and weight gain. Patients with the latter symptoms have the atypical subtype of major depressive illness; this group is usually young women with mild to moderate mood disturbance who are exquisitely sensitive to interpersonal rejection (5, 6).

Sleep disturbances include difficulty falling asleep, difficulty remaining asleep, and/or early morning awakening (initial, middle, and terminal insomnia). Psychomotor disturbances may also be present. Some patients may have an increase in psychomotor activity and are described as having agitation. Patients with an agitated depression may demonstrate pacing, hand-wringing, nail-biting, and incessant smoking or talking. Other depressed patients exhibit decreased psychomotor activity and are considered psychomotor retarded. These patients typically complain of lethargy and fatigue. Objectively, their body movements are slowed and limited. Moreover, their speech is impoverished, monotonous, and increasingly latent. In some severely psychomotor retarded patients with depression, a clinical syndrome approaching catatonia may occur. In these cases, the patient is virtually mute and has no spontaneous movement (7). Catatonic patients show very little interest in eating or taking care of their bodily needs.

Additional signs and symptoms associated with depression include decreased libido, poor concentration, and feelings of guilt. Cognitive changes may also occur, including slowed thinking and indecision. These symptoms frequently result in significant impairment of social and occupational functioning.

Many depressed patients verbalize multiple somatic complaints. Gastrointestinal disturbances, headaches, backache, and urinary difficulties are common. Depressed patients with a mild preexisting medical condition will often present with an exacerbation of that symptom, and those patients from diverse ethnic backgrounds (e.g., African Americans and Asian Americans) will frequently have somatic complaints rather than mood disturbances (8). Appropriate diagnosis and treatment of major depression has become increasingly important with regard to decreasing the morbidity and mortality of various chronic medical illnesses, including diabetes mellitus and coronary artery disease (9–11).

Disturbances in reality functioning may also occur and are classified as major depressive disorder with psychosis. These patients frequently have "mood congruent" delusions and/or hallucinations that are consonant with their sense of self-reproach or pessimism. For example, patients with psychotic depression may describe somatic delusions of "worms eating their bodies" or have highly critical or persecutory auditory hallucinations.

In addition to the atypical and psychotic subtypes of major depressive disorder, the *Diagnostic and Statistical Manual of Mental Disorders* (DSM-IV) describes a number of other depressive subtypes, including major depressive disorder with a seasonal pattern and major depressive disorder with postpartum onset (12). Seasonal affective disorder is characterized by recurrent depressed mood associated with hypersomnia, overeating, and carbohydrate craving and a predictable annual onset in the fall/winter with remission in the spring/summer (or vice versa) (13). The prevalence of this subgroup has not yet been determined (14).

Postpartum depression is characterized by the presence of a major depressive episode in women 1 week to several months postpartum. This subtype must be distinguished from the nonpathologic, postpartum "blues," which is experienced by up to 70% of postpartum women. The "blues" are believed to be secondary to rapid hormonal fluctuations that occur during parturition and immediately postpartum. Postpartum depression, however, is a more severe illness, with a 10% prevalence in the general population and an estimated 20% prevalence in women with a history of a major depressive episode (15). Appropriate pharmacologic treatment with antidepressant medication alone or in combination with psychotherapeutic modalities is indicated for women with postpartum depression.

DIAGNOSIS

The DSM-IV provides criteria for the diagnosis of major depressive disorder and its various subtypes (12). Major depressive disorder is classified under mood disorders, with bipolar I and II disorders, dysthymia, cyclothymia, and mood disorders due to general medical conditions. In addition to either depressed mood or loss of interest or pleasure, the patient must have at least four other neurovegetative signs or symptoms of at least 2 weeks.

Exclusionary criteria for major depressive disorder include the presence of direct physiologic effects of a psychoactive substance or a general medical condition that may be contributing to the symptom presentation, normal bereavement, or mixed manic episode. In the case of major depressive disorder with psychotic features, the clinician must also exclude the following: the presence of delusions or hallucinations in the absence of prominent mood symptoms and the presence of a psychotic disorder (e.g., schizophrenia, schizophreniform disorder, delusional disorder, or psychotic disorder not otherwise specified).

Dysthymia is also included in DSM-IV among the Axis I mood disorders. This represents an old condition previously known as neurotic depression. Clinically, dysthymia may present as a low-grade depression of at least 2 years (12, 16). Multicenter collaborative research studies indicate that 25% of patients seen in clinics and university hospitals and diagnosed as having major depression also demonstrate a history of dysthymia. Those with both major depression and dysthymia are said to suffer from "double depression" (17, 18). Furthermore, the longer the duration of the chronic low-grade depression, the greater the probability of relapse into major depression and of consequent chronicity (19).

DSM-IV also provides criteria for the diagnosis of major depression with melancholia (12). The indicators for melancholic depression include lack of reactivity to pleasurable stimuli, loss of interest in activities, diurnal mood variation (AM worse than PM), early morning awakening, and significant anorexia and psychomotor disturbances. Patients with melancholic depression appear to be significantly different in their symptom profiles and are often refractory to nonbiologic treatments (20).

EPIDEMIOLOGY

It has been estimated that more than 15% of adults are at risk of developing clinical depression during their lives (1, 2). If dysthymia is included, the risk for depression in the course of a lifetime appears to increase to 20–30%. Because only a small portion of patients with clinical depression seek medical or psychiatric care, the high number of unreported cases may result in falsely low figures (1).

Incidence

The incidence of a disorder is the rate of new cases in a given population in 1 year. Epidemiologic findings from multicenter collaborative research on depression suggest a progressive increase in the rates of depression in successive birth cohorts throughout the 20th century. Furthermore, each birth cohort evidenced an earlier age of onset and a decrease in the magnitude of the female-to-male ratio (21).

Prevalence

A cumulative prevalence rate of major depression across the five sites in the Epidemiological Catchment Area (ECA) study averaged 1.5% in the 2 weeks before subject interview. A 4.4% lifetime prevalence rate of major depressive disorder was demonstrated in this study (1). The National Comorbidity Study (NCS) reported a 17.1% lifetime prevalence and 10.3% 1-year prevalence of major depressive disorder (2).

Age, Gender, and Race

Depression may occur at any age. Evidence from ECA data, however, demonstrates 27 years as a mean age of onset for major depression (1). Any major psychiatric disorder (excluding dementia and delirium) with an initial onset after the age of 35 years is likely to be depression.

Depressive disorders are approximately twice as prevalent in women as they are in men (1, 2). This finding appears to be true of the range of depressive disorders and is especially the case for less severe forms of depression. Weissman and Klerman (22) demonstrated that the prevalence differences between men and women are accurate findings (without methodologic error or significant differences in health-seeking behavior). They also demonstrated that the differences in prevalence appear to be multifactorial, with biologic (either genetic or endocrinologic) and psychosocial influences (a woman's needs to balance multiple roles in today's society) playing important roles (22).

Data from the ECA study, NCS study, and smaller community and clinical samples have not demonstrated any difference in the prevalence of major depression across racial or ethnic lines. However, major depressive disorder may have differences in clinical presentation across cultures. For example, several ethnic groups tend to have a more somatic presentation of major depression (8).

Socioeconomic and Marital Status

At one time, bipolar disorder was considered to be a condition of the upper and middle classes (23). Recent epidemiologic research, however, has found no highly valid or reliable data to support the theory that depression is found principally in any one socioeconomic stratum.

Several authors have hypothesized that the status disadvantage of a married woman is related to her vulnerability to depression (24–26). Their data indicate that married women show higher rates of depression than married men, and that unmarried women show a lower rate of psychiatric disorder than unmarried men. Evidence also suggests that the stress of marital separation and/or divorce may be related to increased rates of depressive illness (27).

THE FOUR QUESTIONS

Descriptive and Differential Diagnosis

The differential diagnosis of depression requires a thorough knowledge of both psychiatric and medical disorders that can appear to resemble depressive syndromes. Failure to distinguish a medical condition with depressive symptoms will result not only in the patient's failure to respond to treatment for the ersatz depression, but will also allow the other medical disorder to progress without diagnosis and appropriate, specific treatment. The failure to distinguish major depressive illness from a variety of other psychiatric disorders will result in lack of specificity of treatment with the potential for an adverse effect on course and prognosis.

A variety of psychiatric disorders may

appear to be major depressive disorder. Dysthymia resembles depression, but the signs and symptoms are not as severe. Recent studies have shown the usefulness of antidepressant agents in treating this disorder, although this remains somewhat controversial (28). Patients with dysthymia can develop a major depressive episode. As noted previously, dysthymia with superimposed major depression has been referred to as double depression (17, 18).

Cyclothymia is a chronic mood disorder in which the patient demonstrates fluctuating mood disturbance alternating between episodes of low-level depressed mood and hypomania. Like dysthymia, the periods of depression do not meet criteria for a clinical depression. Hypomania, by definition, is less severe than mania.

Patients with personality disorders may demonstrate depressive features. For example, patients with obsessive-compulsive and dependent personality disorder may show signs of depression when their self-esteem is low or when a loss has occurred. Moreover, patients with borderline personality disorder may have marked mood swings in the context of a number of other symptoms. In all cases of personality disorders, the basis for making the diagnosis of major depression is the presence of the DSM-IV constellation of mood and physical symptoms.

In patients with psychotic depression, the mood disturbance usually precedes the onset of psychotic symptoms, which are only present in the context of a mood disturbance. In patients with schizophrenia, psychotic symptoms are of a longer duration and usually occur before any mood disturbance. Premorbid and family histories help to differentiate patients with schizophrenia from those with delusional depression. Finally, schizophrenia can only be diagnosed when persistent psychotic symptoms last for more than 6 months.

Schizoaffective disorder may be a subset of the mood disorders, although the diagnosis remains classified as a psychotic disorder (29). Family history, acute treatment with lithium or other mood stabilizers, and long-term outcome all support the characterization of this syndrome as a mood disorder.

DSM-IV added the category of bipolar II disorder to the mood disorders. Bipolar II disorder is characterized by the presence of hypomanic and major depressive episodes. Because of the implications for treatment, clinicians must assess for hypomanic symptoms in patients with major depressive disorder. In addition to the individual's personal history, a family history of bipolar disorder may also provide a clue to the possible diagnosis of bipolar II disorder. Women appear to be at increased risk for bipolar II disorder compared with bipolar I disorder, in which an equal prevalence exists between sexes.

Individuals who have suffered the death of a family member or intimate friend demonstrate a normal human response called bereavement (30). The symptoms of bereavement may be indistinguishable from those of depression. Sadness and neurovegetative disturbances are common. Unlike depression, bereavement does not tend to be associated with worthlessness and self-reproach.

Depressive symptoms are common among patients who abuse alcohol and other psychoactive drugs that can depress the central nervous system (e.g., narcotics, tranquilizers, and hypnotics). The diagnosis of primary depression in a patient with alcohol or substance abuse should be strongly considered in the presence of one or more of the following conditions: positive family history of depres-

TABLE 6.1.   Some Organic Causes of Depression

Neurologic disorders
   Parkinson's disease
   Huntington's disease
   Multiple sclerosis
   Primary degenerative dementia
   Postconcussion syndromes
   Chronic subdural hematoma
Metabolic abnormalities and endocrinopathies
   Hyper or hypothyroidism diabetes
   Hyponatremia
   Hypokalemia
   Pernicious amenia
   Pellagra
   Hyperparathyroidism
   Uremia
   Cushing's disease
   Addison's disease
   Hepatic disease
   Wernicke-Korsakoff syndrome
Neoplastic disease
   Pancreatic carcinoma
   Primary cerebral tumor
   Cerebral metastasis
Drugs and poisons
   Alcohol
   Amphetamines
   Cocaine
   Barbiturates
   Opiates
   Antihypertensives
   Sedatives
   Digitalis
   Steroids
   Oral contraceptives
   Lead poisoning
   Other heavy metals
Infectious diseases
   Tuberculosis
   Central nervous system syphilis
   Mononucleosis
   Hepatitis
   Encephalitis
   Postencephalitic states
Other medical conditions
   Acquired immune deficiency syndrome
   Cardiovascular disease (e.g., coronary artery disease, hypertension)
   Systemic lupus erythematosus
   Fibromyalgia
   Postpartum syndromes

TABLE 6.2.   Guidelines for the Laboratory and Radiologic Diagnosis of Depression

Recommended baseline laboratory studies
  Complete blood count with differential
  Electrolytes
  Chemistry panel including glucose, blood urea nitrogen/creatinine, liver function tests, calcium, and
    phosphorus
  Comprehensive serum and/or urine toxic screen, particularly if substance use/abuse is suspected
  Thyroid-stimulating hormone and thyroxine, especially when considering lithium treatment or if
    thyroid problem suspected
  Electrocardiogram, in patients with cardiac disease, taking cardiotoxic medication, and/or older than
    40 yr
  Beta human chorionic gonadotropin, in female patients of child-bearing age
Special laboratory studies
  Serum B_{12} and folate
  Erythrocyte sedimentation rate
  Antinuclear antibody
  Serum ceruloplasmin
  Tuberculosis skin test
  Lumbar puncture
Radiologic studies (only if neurologic disorder suspected or if moderate to severe cognitive deficits are
    present)
  Computed tomography and/or magnetic resonance imaging
  Single photon emission computed tomography or positron emission tomography
Diagnostic studies
  Dexamethasone suppression test
  Thyroid stimulating test
  Polysomnography

sion, personal history of depression, onset of substance abuse after depressive symptoms, and worsening of depressive symptoms after weeks of abstinence. When present, untreated depression is associated with higher rates of relapse into addictive behaviors (31).

Psychiatrists should rule out any medical problem that may be masquerading as major depression. The presence of a powerful precipitating psychosocial event or history of depression should not bias clinicians against considering an underlying medical condition as the potential cause of the current depressive episode.

Table 6.1 lists medical conditions that may commonly present as major depressive disorder. Many endocrinologic disorders, including hypothyroidism or hyperthyroidism and Cushing's syndrome, will present with depressive symptoms. Patients with diabetes mellitus also appear to be at increased risk for major depression that, if untreated, can increase the morbidity from diabetes mellitus (9). Fibromyalgia (a nonarticular pain syndrome) and systemic lupus erythematosus are two common rheumatologic disorders that can present with symptoms of major depression. These disorders, particularly fibromyalgia, are seen more frequently in female patients; therefore, female patients should be screened for these disorders when presenting with depressive symptoms. Cardiovascular diseases such as hypertension and coronary artery disease are associated with major depression. Cardiovascular disorders should be ruled out because, like diabetes mellitus, a concurrent major depression may increase the morbidity and mortality from these illnesses (10, 11). A careful history with additional information from family members, a full review of systems, a physical and neurologic examination, and appropriate laboratory tests (Table 6.2) will assist the clinician in ruling out the presence of a medical condition.

Ego Defenses and Character Style

One of the symptoms typically associated with major depressive disorder is low self-esteem. A reduction in self-esteem is frequently associated with the defense mechanisms of devaluation, help-rejecting complaining, and passive aggression.

Cluster C personality traits or disorders (avoidant, dependent, and obsessive-compulsive) are most frequent in patients with major depressive disorder. Patients with personality traits in this cluster tend to be anxious, fearful, and/or depressed. The patient's Axis I condition should be assessed independently before diagnosing an Axis II disorder. Frequently, patients who appear to have features of a personality disorder during a major depressive episode will not demonstrate those traits on recovery from the mood disorder.

Over time, clinicians have become aware that certain personality types appear prone to depression. Obsessive-compulsive and dependent personality traits, for example, are frequently found in the premorbid personality evaluation of depressed patients. Empiric work, however, has questioned these clinical impressions. Assessment of personality cannot be accurately accomplished when the patient is in a depressed state (32). Although modest evidence exists for obsessive and dependent character constellations in major depressive disorder, the data are strongest for the premorbid trait of introversion (33). No evidence suggests that a specific personality constellation (or pathology) exists for subjects who will develop a unipolar mood disorder.

Formulation

Biologic

Biochemical hypotheses of the etiology of depression have centered on disturbances in central nervous system neurotransmitters (34, 35). Monoamines (norepinephrine and serotonin) are the primary neurotransmitters implicated in classic biochemical hypotheses of major depressive illness.

The original amine hypothesis was derived from clinical research with a number of centrally active medications. Experiments with reserpine demonstrated that norepinephrine and serotonin are depleted by this drug. The monoamine oxidase inhibitor (MAOI) isoniazid was shown to increase central nervous system catecholamines. The tricyclic antidepressants (TCAs) delayed inactivation of neurotransmitters via reuptake blockade. Lithium produced an increase in the reuptake of catecholamines, thereby decreasing the availability of these transmitters. Electroconvulsive therapy (ECT) demonstrated an increase in norepinephrine levels.

The original amine hypothesis of depression posits a deficiency of monoamines (norepinephrine and serotonin) in the neural synaptic junction. Antidepressants were thought to alleviate depression by correcting this deficiency, which they achieve by inhibiting uptake or decreasing catabolism once uptake has occurred (36, 37). More recent investigations of specific neurotransmitters in mood disorders do not fully support the original monoamine hypothesis of depressive illness. For example, depressed patients who are depleted of catecholamines (38) or tryptophan (39) do not uniformly demonstrate an increase in depressive symptoms. Thus, alternatives to this hypothesis have been considered, including activation of the norepinephrine system. In fact, normal or elevated plasma and/or cerebrospinal fluid (CSF) levels of norepinephrine and its metabolites have been observed in depressed patients (40–42). Moreover, decreases in CSF and plasma 3-methoxy-4-hydroxyphenylglycol (MHPG), a norepinephrine metabolite, have been seen in patients who successfully respond to antidepressant treatment (43, 44). No definitive explanation has been found for the disparate biochemical findings of earlier or more recent studies. Conceivably, the discrepancy may be secondary to the design and/or methodology of the investigations or to biologic differences in subgroups of depressed patients.

Evidence suggests that other neurotransmitter systems may also play a role in depression. Acetylcholine has been posited as an etiologic agent based on data that procholinergic agents can induce depression (45, 46). Decreased CSF and plasma gamma-aminobutyric acid (GABA) levels have been observed in depressed patients (47, 48), which has led to speculation about its potential role in depression (49). Evidence supports an antidepressant effect of the GABA agonist, progabide (50, 51), and various benzodiazepines, such as alprazolam, which facilitate GABA neurotransmission (49).

Another focus of research has been on receptor sensitivity. Findings point to a decrease in the number of postsynaptic B-adrenergic receptors by almost all antidepressants. The decrease in receptors has been termed "downregulation"; interestingly, drugs that increase postsynaptic receptors (e.g., reserpine, propranolol) can induce depression (52, 53). Both hypotheses of the etiology of depression may apply: disturbances in norepinephrine and serotonin could be etiologic and could be corrected by antidepressants, but this could be achieved by a process that involves downregulation of synaptic receptors, perhaps presynaptically and postsynaptically (54, 55).

Genetic hypotheses about major depressive illness have drawn their data from studies of twins, families, and adoptions. The heterogeneity of major depressive illness makes progress in this specific area rather limited in contrast to bipolar I disorder, which is believed to be genetically more homogenous. Nevertheless, concordance rates for mood disorder (unipolar and bipolar I) in monozygotic twins are estimated to be 75%, whereas concordance rates for dizygotic twins are 20% (which approximates the morbidity risk among siblings) (56–58). Monozygotic twins reared apart show a concordance equal to monozygotes reared together. No studies report one twin developing mood disorder and the other twin developing schizophrenia. Data that separate unipolar from bipolar disorders among twins reveal a concordance for unipolar depression of 41% in monozygotic twins and 13% in dizygotic twins (58).

Family studies of major depressive disorder indicate that first-degree relatives have a morbidity risk of approximately 15%. Male first-degree relatives have a risk rate of 11%, compared with 18% for female first-degree relatives. Morbidity risk for affective disorder among parents is 13%, among siblings 15%, and among children 20% (59–62).

Adoption studies have attempted to control for nongenetic familial factors. Cadoret (63) studied the adopted children of normal and affectively disordered (unipolar and bipolar) biologic parents and found that the risk rate for adopted children of affectively disordered biologic parents was 38%. The normal controls had a risk rate of 7%.

Although the mode of transmission of affective disorder remains to be established, these findings strongly support a genetic factor in the etiology of unipolar depression. The data also indicate that affective disorders are genetically distinct from schizophrenia.

Other areas under investigation with regard to potential biologic hypotheses of major depression are neuroendocrinology and circadian rhythms, including neurohormonal hypotheses that focus on the regulation and functional properties of neurohormones within the hypothalamic-pituitary-adrenal (HPA) and hypothalamic-pituitary-thyroid axes. Early investigations in this area resulted in the development of the dexamethasone suppression test (DST) and thyrotropin releasing hormone stimulation test as possible laboratory tools in the diagnosis of depression. Although these tests offer scientific results, their usefulness is questionable in today's cost-conscious market. This is particularly true because the results of either test will generally not alter the clinician's assessment or treatment plan.

Alterations in the sleep-wake cycle associated with depression and recent findings of possible effects of temperature regulation on mood have resulted in investigations of circadian rhythm disturbances as possible etiologic factors in depression (14). Sleep deprivation and phase advance treatments have been found to be transiently effective in depressed patients (64). This work in circadian rhythms has resulted in increased interest in the role of melatonin in the etiology and possible treatment of mood disorders. Premenstrual dysphoric disorder (65) and rapid cycling bipolar disorder (66) are the two areas in which melatonin has been most studied. Further systematic investigation

of the role of melatonin in the etiology of major depressive illness is warranted.

Extensive research has been conducted in sleep physiology and its potential relationship to depression (67). Some consistent abnormalities in sleep electroencephalograms (polysomnograms) among depressed patients include shortened rapid eye movement (REM) latency and increased REM duration and density (i.e., number of rapid eye movements per REM period). Finally, work has recently been done on the utility of various sleep parameters in monitoring antidepressant treatment and in predicting relapse after biologic treatment has been stopped (68, 69).

Psychological

Abraham (70) was the first to psychodynamically link grief and melancholy. He stated that normal mourning or grief becomes melancholy, or depression, when anger and hostility accompany love for the lost object. Freud, in his famous paper on mourning and melancholia, advanced Abraham's ideas (71). In addition to ambivalent feelings toward the lost object, Freud considered melancholia as a "disturbance of self-regard." The melancholic, unlike the mourner, suffers a loss of self-respect. Furthermore, mourning was described as occurring only in response to a realistically lost object, whereas melancholia could occur in reaction to the unconsciously perceived or imagined loss of an object.

In melancholia, the anger experienced toward the real or imagined loss of the loved object is hypothetically turned on the self. This "retroflexed rage" is a well-known psychodynamic formulation of melancholy (72). It helps to explain the self-reproach and loss of self-esteem seen in depression as well as the melancholic's need for punishment. Hostility directed toward the self rather than toward the lost object has epidemiologic support in the inverse relationship seen between suicide and homicide (73, 74). Furthermore, one clinical study demonstrated that depressed patients show less expressed anger than do normal controls (75).

The universality of the retroflexed rage hypothesis is, however, brought into question by the existence of a clearly identified group of "hostile depressives who show concomitant anger and depression" (76). Weissman et al. (77) demonstrated coexistent hostility and depression in certain patients. Finally, the expression of hostility by depressed patients toward the lost object does not correlate with clinical improvement and may even result in a worsening of depression (78).

As psychoanalytic theory evolved and the ego became more the locus of study, depression was seen as a disorder of esteem (79). Mourning was not truly for the lost object, but for the mourner's loss of self-esteem. The lost person or object was understood as symbolic of the individual's lost self-esteem.

Klein (80) posits that a capacity for depression exists in all of us. She postulated the "normal depressive position" as the stage of life from 6 to 12 months. In this stage, the infant experiences a fall from the omnipotence of early infancy to the stage of being separate, dependent, and vulnerable.

The relationship between separation in early life and depression has also been considered. Bowlby (81) hypothesized that an interruption in the normal course of development, by separation or loss, produces "anxious attachment." Spitz (82) studied normal infants after 6 months of age who had been separated from their mothers and placed in foundling homes. He described a triphasic reaction of protest, despair, and finally detachment, which he called anaclitic depression.

A number of studies have tried to clarify the role of separation in acute-onset adult depressive states, suggesting that although separation events are common precipitants in depressive disorders, separation is not a specific nor sufficient cause for depression (83–85).

Beck et al.'s (86–88) behavioral model of depression is built on a cognition of negative expectations. Beck considered hopelessness and helplessness to be central to the experience of depression. His hypothesis is that the depressive mood succeeds, not precedes, a set of cognitive processes involving a negative self-conception, negative interpretations of one's life events, and a pessimistic view of the future. Helplessness and hopelessness can only ensue in view of these cognitive expectations. His cognitive psychotherapy for depression, which has demonstrated efficacy, is aimed at altering cognition. Although cognitive treatment is effective, it cannot be established that maladaptive attitudes actually cause depression rather than exist as a symptom of the disorder (89, 90).

The clinician should be theoretically broad based when working with a depressed patient. Anyone may develop depression; no single psychodynamic process, personality type, stressful life event, or developmental experience is unique to depressive states.

Social

Social models of depression stress that adaptiveness and helplessness are learned. If—as cognitive behaviorists suggest—depression is a learned form of helplessness, it is important to look for role models of helplessness within the family. Further, disruptions in the family early in the individual's life and, more specifically, disturbances in early parent-child relationships can leave a person vulnerable to depression.

Events in a person's life show a clear relationship to the development of depression (91–94). Major losses—including death, divorce, loss of health, and loss of money—are frequently associated with depression. These stressful life events may, in some persons, be a necessary cause but have not been shown to be a sufficient cause for depression.

The clinician should question the depressed patient about any current environmental stressors. Areas that must be assessed include the patient's living and work environments and interpersonal relationships (spouse, friends, and family). The multiple roles that women frequently balance in today's society may play a contributing role in the increased prevalence of depression in women. Women with major depressive disorder will often emphasize the numerous tasks for which they feel primarily responsible, including family and occupational tasks and community service roles. The clinician must assess and be empathic about the difficulty of balancing these roles.

In summary, major depression is a complex condition that is caused by a combination of factors. Clinicians must comprehensively evaluate the possible biologic, psychological, and social factors that may be instrumental in the patient's depressive disorder.

Focal Problem

The primary focal problem in patients with major depressive disorder is safety. The clinician must inquire directly about any active suicidal ideation or self-destructive behaviors and evaluate for a history of suicidal thoughts and/or attempts. Moreover, the clinician should determine the patient's degree of intent for self-harm and any means to do so, based on the stated plan. For example, if the patient describes a plan of suicide via a self-inflicted gunshot wound, the clinician must ask about the availability of firearms. The degree of safety will affect the level of

psychiatric care and the management strategies used.

Depressive disorders should be understood as illnesses by the patient and his or her family members, friends, and coworkers. Psychoeducation is valuable training for patients with major depressive illness and can enhance the patient and his or her family's willingness to comply with the treatment recommendations.

BIOLOGIC EVALUATION

The biologic evaluation is the first step for any patient who presents with depression. The clinician must feel confident that an underlying medical condition that may cause depression has been ruled out before proceeding with the conventional methods for treating major depressive disorder. The disorders to consider are listed in Table 6.1.

History

A detailed history of the patient's chief complaint and current illness must be obtained. The recording of significant medical and psychiatric illnesses, including any medications or treatment that the patient has undergone or is currently taking, is essential. A family history, with particular emphasis on inheritable medical and psychiatric disorders, is part of the comprehensive history. The person's habits, including use of tobacco and psychoactive substances as well as dietary habits, must also be included.

Clinicians should inquire about a history of sexual or physical abuse because many victims of abuse have depressive symptomatology in association with post-traumatic stress disorder. Additionally, particularly in emergency department settings, clinicians should ask directly about family violence (95, 96).

In taking the history, the physician must be alert to any information regarding recent prescribed or nonprescribed drug ingestion or ingestion of any toxic substances. A history of infection, abnormal neurologic activity, or any medical treatment must be sought.

The patient's account should be augmented by collaborative information from the family and significant others if possible. Any person who has witnessed the patient's unique behavior or who has pertinent knowledge about the events before the evaluation should be contacted.

In the mental status examination, the clinician must search for any signs of an altered sensorium, prominent cognitive deficits, or psychosis. Suicide assessment is essential in all patients. A mini-mental status examination may be administered to help document cognitive impairment and discriminate between dementia and pseudodementia. A thorough review of systems must be taken. A history of depression only suggests that the current episode is a recurrence, and this presumption is unfair to any patient. Although the odds favor such a conclusion, the clinician must consider that an autonomous medical disorder may be masquerading as depression.

Physical Examination

A physical examination must be completed to complement the history. Careful attention must be paid to the patient's vital signs and to the neurologic examination.

Laboratory, Radiologic, and Diagnostic Studies (Table 6.2)

Neuroendocrine Studies

A disturbance in HPA functioning has been demonstrated in a significant number of patients with major depressive disorder (97). The most specific and documented measure of HPA axis activity is the DST, which was one of the first laboratory studies developed to help in the diagnosis of depression.

In recent years, the overall usefulness of the DST has been investigated extensively (98, 99). The average sensitivity (those with illness who will have a positive test) of the DST is 40–50% in major depression. For very severe, melancholic depressions, particularly those associated with psychosis, the sensitivity is 60–70%. The specificity (those without illness who will have a negative test) of the DST ranges from 70–90%. Several factors have contributed to false-positive test results, including use of various drugs (e.g., barbiturates, carbamazepine, phenytoin, alcohol, antidepressants), recent alcohol withdrawal (3–4 weeks), endocrinopathies (e.g., Cushing's syndrome, pregnancy, diabetes mellitus), and other medical conditions (e.g., infections, cancer, low body weight—malnutrition/anorexia nervosa, advanced renal or hepatic disease) (98).

The DST may prove to be most useful as a predictor of response. Those patients who have nonsuppression and fail to revert to the suppressed state during treatment are more likely to relapse than those depressed patients whose DST became normal. For those DST nonsuppressors who fail to revert, continuation of medication appears to be indicated. Thus, clinicians need to weigh all the data regarding the clinical utility and limited cost-effectiveness of the DST and to use this test only in selected cases.

The thyrotropin releasing hormone stimulation test is another neuroendocrine study that has been used in the evaluation of depression. This test has not been as widely used, which may be related to the somewhat complicated and costly nature of the procedure. Its overall clinical usefulness and cost-effectiveness remain in question.

Sleep Studies

As mentioned previously, sleep physiology has been an important focus of the research on depression. Polysomnography may be of some diagnostic use in major depression. Consistent findings are shortened REM latency and increased REM duration and density (67). Studies continue to examine the role of polysomnography in diagnosis, treatment response, and recurrence of major depression (67–69). Although these investigations have intrinsic scientific value and may provide more insight into the biologic etiology of major depressive disorder, it is not clear that the polysomnogram will alter the course of treatment of a patient with major depressive illness.

Psychological Testing

Psychological testing can be very helpful in the differential diagnosis of depression. The Bender-Gestalt and WAIS-R tests can be highly discriminant of organic deficits and can help rule in or out a dementia. Psychological testing can also uncover the presence of well-guarded psychotic thought processes that, if present, may call for the addition of antipsychotic medication.

ASSESSING LEVEL OF CARE

The patient's potential for self-harm (or harm to others) is the primary issue in deciding the appropriate level of care. The clinician should inquire directly about current suicidal ideation or self-destructive behaviors. A history of suicidal thoughts and/or attempts is frequently an important clue in the assessment of suicidal risk (see Chapter 2). For example, an actively suicidal, depressed patient who has a history of a suicide attempt by overdose and a current plan and intent of hanging would be at great risk and warrant care in a secure setting.

Another important variable in the level of care decision is the patient's ability for self-care and/or the presence of an intact support system. The clinician must assess the patient's current general health status (including appetite and eating and sleep behaviors), energy level, and motivation. When the patient cannot take care of the usual activities of daily living and has no intact family support system, an inpatient admission may be warranted. However, if the patient has a spouse or another family member who is aware of and understands the underlying illness and is comfortable managing the patient in his or her own living environment, it may be possible to manage an acute depressive episode in an intensive ambulatory or partial hospital setting.

Finally, the presence of unstable, comorbid medical illness and/or psychoactive substance abuse, in combination with a moderate to severe major depressive episode, may warrant a more intensive level of care.

TREATMENT

Psychopharmacologic Management

Psychopharmacologic treatment of major depressive disorder is an essential aspect of caring for the acutely depressed patient. Moreover, significant medical morbidity and mortality are likely in patients with untreated severe depressions.

During the past 50 years, remarkable advances have been made in the biologic treatment of depressive illness. In fact, 70–85% of patients with major depressive disorders will demonstrate significant im-

TABLE 6.3.   Dose Ranges of Antidepressants

Generic name	Brand names	Usual therapeutic dose range (mg/day)[a]
Tricyclics		
Amitriptyline	Elavil, Endep	150–300
Desipramine	Norpramin, Pertofrane	150–300
Imipramine	Tofranil, Janimine, Sk-Pramine	150–300
Nortriptyline	Pamelor, Aventyl	50–150
Heterocyclics		
Amoxapine	Asendin	150–450
Maprotiline	Ludiomil	150–200
Trazodone	Desyrel	150–300
MAOIs		
Phenelzine	Nardil	45–90
Tranylcypromine	Parnate	30–50
SSRIs		
Fluoxetine	Prozac	20–80
Paroxetine	Paxil	20–50
Sertraline	Zoloft	50–200
Other		
Bupropion	Wellbutrin	200–450
Venlafaxine	Effexor	75–375
Nefazodone	Serzone	300–500

MAOIs, monoamine oxidase inhibitors; SSRIs, serotonin reuptake inhibitors.
[a]Dose ranges are approximate. Many patients will respond at relatively low doses (even below ranges given above); others may require higher dosages.

provement with a carefully chosen and administered biologic therapy regimen (100, 101). The past 10 years have seen a resurgence of psychopharmacologic development with the advent of selective serotonin reuptake inhibitors (SSRIs) and other "new" antidepressant agents. These newer agents, with an improved side effect profile, were developed specifically to treat depression. This development is unlike the prior serendipity in the "discovery" of TCAs and MAOIs. Before the development of newer classes of antidepressant agents, the antidepressant of choice for major depressive disorder without psychosis was one of the TCAs. However, the more tolerable side effect profile of newer agents, safety in medically ill patients, and the lack of lethality in overdose have resulted in the routine use of the newer

agents as first-line antidepressants. Table 6.3 provides a summary of commonly used antidepressants. Some controversy still exists due to conflicting reports about whether the newer agents are as effective for acutely and severely ill depressed patients compared with those treated in ambulatory care settings (102).

In general, a clinical trial of an antidepressant medication lasts at least 4–6 weeks. If no clinical response is seen at 6 weeks, a variety of alternatives exist. One option is to switch from one antidepressant to another in the same or a different class. Another alternative is to attempt potentiation of the original antidepressant with a second agent. Lithium carbonate, L-triiodothyronine, estrogen, bromocriptine, and pindolol are agents that have been used for antidepressant augmentation. These potentiation attempts are effective in only a portion of patients (103–109).

A variety of options are available for those patients with nonpsychotic major depression who do not respond to either antidepressants alone or antidepressants with augmentation. The MAOIs are a class of second-line agents. Although proven to be as effective as TCAs in the treatment of depression, these agents carry a number of serious side effects and dietary restrictions that have limited their use, particularly by nonpsychiatric physicians. Additionally, lithium alone, "heterocyclics" (trazodone, maprotiline, amoxapine), and psychostimulants have been found to be useful in some patients with major depression without psychosis. SSRIs are also rapidly becoming first-line agents for patients with moderate to severe major depression. Since the use of SSRIs began, several other "new" antidepressants have been released including venlafaxine (which blocks the reuptake of both serotonin and norepinephrine) and nefazodone (a serotonergic antidepressant with 5-HT_2 receptor blockade). These agents have been demonstrated to have efficacy equal to traditional antidepressants with a generally more tolerable side effect profile (110, 111).

Some severely ill patients or patients in whom multiple medication trials have failed may proceed directly to a second-line agent or to ECT. Studies suggest that patients with a more atypical presentation of their depression (hypersomnia, hyperphagia, and/or rejection sensitivity) may respond better to MAOIs than to tricyclics (5, 112). Anecdotal reports also indicate that patients with the atypical subtype of depression may preferentially respond to SSRIs. Finally, for patients who are unable to tolerate antidepressant medication and who present with life-threatening illness, the immediate use of ECT will be indicated.

Patients who present with depression and a history of at least one hypomanic or manic episode have bipolar depression. Although lithium is less likely to provide antidepressant action than a TCA (50% improvement is reported in 1-month trials), it should be considered in this population for several reasons. First, the use of antidepressants in depressed patients with bipolar disorder puts them at risk of developing antidepressant-induced mania or rapid mood cycling during acute treatment (113). Second, patients who do not immediately develop mania are at greater risk for developing a rapid cycling of moods during the maintenance phase of treatment (114). Virtually all antidepressants have been demonstrated to have the potential for induction of mania. Of the available antidepressant agents, bupropion, tranylcypromine, and fluoxetine may be less likely to induce a switch into mania or may limit the severity of the manic episode compared with other agents (115, 116). Finally, if the patient responds to lithium, this medication may provide acute and prophylactic treatment against recurrences of depression and hypomania/mania. In fact, lithium can be used concurrently with antidepressant agents in patients with bipolar depression to decrease the likelihood of a switch into mania. Earlier studies suggest that bipolar patients are more responsive to MAOIs than to other antidepressants (117). The combination of lithium and carbamazepine may also be considered as potential first-line treatments for bipolar depression (118). The use of divalproex sodium or sodium valproate has recently gained Food and Drug Administration approval and has many desirable attributes in the treatment of bipolar patients (see Chapter 8). Failure to respond to pharmacologic treatment, inability to tolerate these agents, or life-threatening illness are indications for the use of ECT in patients with bipolar depression.

Because patients with psychotic (delusional) depression do not demonstrate a significant response to standard tricyclic agents alone (119), a different treatment approach is required. Antipsychotic medications in combination with antidepressants show better results than either agent alone (120). ECT is also highly effective for psychotic depression. It has a more rapid onset of action and may be better tolerated by some patients (particularly the elderly) than the combination of medications.

TCAs

The TCAs are broad-action drugs that block the reuptake of both norepinephrine and serotonin, but with primary effects on the norepinephrine system. Unfortunately, the side effect profile of the TCAs remains suboptimal because of considerable anticholinergic and cardiovascular side effects, weight gain, and sedation. These side effects often lead to poor compliance. In general, the older tertiary amine tricyclics (e.g., amitriptyline, imipramine) have more side effects than the secondary amine tricyclics (e.g., desipramine, nortriptyline).

The prescription of TCAs requires gradual titration of the patient's dose until a therapeutic dose is achieved (Table 6.3). For most TCAs the usual starting dose is 25 or 50 mg at bedtime with gradual increases by 25- or 50-mg increments to a dose range of approximately 150–300 mg/day (with the exception of nortriptyline, which is usually half these amounts). Most patients will not be able to tolerate the therapeutic dose without gradual titration. This is different from some of the newer agents, such as the SSRIs (see below) for which the starting dose for many patients is also the therapeutic dose.

An important disadvantage of the TCAs is their toxicity when taken in overdose. A dose of 1500 mg or more of most of the TCAs is lethal if taken in overdose; thus, a 7- to 10-day supply or more of a TCA could be fatal (101). When initiating TCA or any antidepressant treatment, it is generally advisable to prescribe small amounts until the patient is better, because the risk of suicide in depression is present until the depressed mood abates. Although the somatic complaints of low energy level and sleep disturbance improve early during recovery from depression, the depressed mood—which is correlated with risk for suicide—is often the last symptom to improve (121).

Heterocyclic Antidepressants

Heterocyclic antidepressants (e.g., amoxapine, maprotiline, trazodone) were introduced in the United States in the early 1980s in an attempt to provide antidepressants with better side effect profiles than the TCAs. The mechanism of action (and the efficacy) of the heterocyclics is similar to the TCAs and, in general, they exhibit fewer TCA-like side effects.

Maprotiline has not been used widely because of concerns regarding a higher rate of seizures (122). Amoxapine, although an antidepressant, is converted by the liver to the neuroleptic loxapine, and patients taking amoxapine exhibit antidopaminergic side effects such as galactorrhea, pseudo-Parkinsonism, and tardive dyskinesia (123). Trazodone is a very sedating antidepressant that can produce acute dizziness and fainting when taken on an empty stomach (particularly in high dosages). Its sedative properties are sometimes useful as a sleeping pill when

TABLE 6.4. Side Effect Profiles of Antidepressant Medications

Drug	Central nervous system			Cardiovascular		Other	
	Anticholinergic†	Drowsiness	Insomnia/agitation	Orthostatic hypotension	Cardiac arrhythmia	Gastrointestinal distress	Weight gain (>6 kg)
Amitriptyline	4+	4+	0	4+	3+	0	4+
Desipramine	1+	1+	1+	2+	2+	0	1+
Doxepin	3+	4+	0	2+	2+	0	3+
Imipramine	3+	3+	1+	4+	3+	1+	3+
Nortriptyline	1+	1+	0	2+	2+	0	1+
Protriptyline	2+	1+	1+	2+	2+	0	0
Trimipramine	1+	4+	0	2+	2+	0	3+
Amoxapine	2+	2+	2+	2+	3+	0	1+
Maprotiline	2+	4+	0	0	1+	0	2+
Trazodone	0	4+	0	1+	1+	1+	1+
Bupropion	0	0	2+	0	1+	1+	0
Fluoxetine	0	0	2+	0	0	3+	0
Paroxetine	0	0	2+	0	0	3+	0
Sertraline	0	0	2+	0	0	3+	0
MAOIs	1	1+	2+	2+	0	1+	2+
Nefazodone	0	2+	0	1+	0	1+	0
Venlafaxine	0	1+	1+	0	0	3+	0

From: Rothschild AJ. Adherence to antidepressant therapy. Fed Pract 1996; April 13 (Suppl):16.
0, absent or rare; 1+ to 2+, in between; 3+ to 4+, relatively common.
† Dry mouth, blurred vision, urinary hesitancy, constipation.
MAOIs, monoamine oxidase inhibitors.

combined with nonsedating antidepressants such as the SSRIs.

MAOIs

The MAOIs, like the TCAs, are an older class of antidepressant medication. A little more than a decade ago, MAOIs were generally the second-line agents (after the TCAs) for the treatment of depression. Their use has declined in recent years because of the advantages of the newer antidepressant agents. MAOIs are generally reserved for patients who have not responded to TCAs and SSRIs.

MAOIs can have activating side effects and can cause insomnia at night with considerable sedation during the day (124). Patients prescribed MAOIs are susceptible to hypertensive crises from drug-drug or food-drug interactions (125). Patients taking MAOIs require special tyramine-free diets in which foods with high levels of tyramine are avoided. However, on a day-to-day basis, the most problematic side effect with MAOIs is typically orthostatic hypotension.

WHAT ARE THE MECHANISMS OF ACTION THAT PRODUCE ANTIDEPRESSANT SIDE EFFECTS?

Side effects from antidepressants occur because of the blockade of neuronal receptors. Examples include blockade of the α_1-adrenergic receptor, the histamine (H_1) receptor, and the muscarinic receptor.

Blockade of the α_1-adrenergic receptor potentially induces postural hypotension, dizziness, and reflex tachycardia (126). Blockade of the histamine receptor can result in sedation, weight gain, and hypotension (126). Blockade of the muscarinic receptor can result in anticholinergic side effects such as dry mouth, constipation, blurry vision, urinary retention, memory dysfunction, and sinus tachycardia (126). The TCAs, heterocyclics, and MAOIs block postsynaptic receptors to a moderate to great extent, whereas the newer agents (such as the SSRIs) have very little effect on these receptors (126–128). This explains why, in vivo, the newer agents do not cause the side effects commonly seen with the TCAs and MAOIs; this is also a major reason for their wide acceptance and frequent use among psychiatric and nonpsychiatric physicians. Table 6.4 provides a summary of antidepressant side effects.

Bupropion

Bupropion is a newer agent whose specific mechanism of action has not been elucidated. In double-blind studies it is comparable in efficacy to TCAs (129, 130). Bupropion has a low incidence of anticholinergic side effects (131), orthostatic hypotension (132), and effects on cardiac conduction (133). This agent can occasionally be activating. It is reported to have a fourfold higher incidence of grand mal seizures compared with TCAs (125). The rate of grand mal seizures in patients taking bupropion increases if the total daily dose of bupropion is greater than 450 mg/day or if any single dose is greater than 150 mg (125). For this reason, it is recommended that bupropion be prescribed in divided doses (e.g., twice or three times a day) with no single dose greater than 150 mg.

SSRIs

The SSRIs are a new and widely prescribed class of antidepressants. The SSRIs inhibit free synaptic serotonin reuptake and (in contrast to the TCAs) have negligible effects on norepinephrine and dopamine uptake (126, 128, 134). When compared with the TCAs in double-blind studies, the SSRIs have been found to be equally effective but better tolerated than the TCAs (101, 135). The distinct advantages of the SSRIs (compared with TCAs) are their low potential for seizures and safety when taken in overdose (101, 135).

The dose ranges of the SSRIs are shown in Table 6.3. The vast majority of patients with major depression will respond at the starting dose or in the midrange. High doses of SSRIs (although often well tolerated by patients) are usually not required, although trials of standard doses of up to 6–8 weeks may be needed (136, 137).

Fluoxetine

In 1988, fluoxetine became the first SSRI available in the United States. Fluoxetine has few of the tricyclic-like side effects and tends not to cause weight gain. It can be given in once a day dosing and has a wide margin of safety in overdose (101). The common side effects of fluoxetine include nausea, anxiety, nervousness, and insomnia (125). There have also been reports of akathisia (a side effect more commonly seen with antipsychotic medications), which has been proposed as a possible explanation for the occasional emergence of suicidal ideation during fluoxetine treatment (138–140). Akathisia often responds to low doses of propranolol (138, 139). Side effects tend to be dose related and may respond to a reduction in dosage.

Sertraline

Early in 1992, sertraline became the second SSRI on the market in the United States. It has some similarities to fluoxetine and some differences, particularly in its pharmacokinetics and drug-drug interactions. Similar to fluoxetine, sertraline is a highly selective SSRI equal in efficacy to the TCAs, but with few tricyclic-like side effects (135). Unlike fluoxetine, the metabolite of sertraline, N-desmethylsertraline, is substantially less active than the parent compound (sertraline) (141, 142). The half-lives of sertraline and its metabolite are considerably shorter than the half-lives of fluoxetine and its equipotent metabolite norfluoxetine (143). Thus, sertraline reaches a steady-state plasma level of active drug faster and has a shorter washout period than fluoxetine.

Sertraline can be given once a day because it has a mean half-life of 26 hours (143). A steady-state plasma level of the active drug is achieved in approximately 1 week (143, 144). The most common side effects of sertraline include nausea, diarrhea, loose stools, tremor, and insomnia (106). These side effects tend to be dose related and may respond to a reduction in dosage. Similar to fluoxetine, sertraline is associated with significantly less anticholinergic, antihistaminic, and cardiovascular side effects than the TCAs. Patients taking large overdoses have survived without sequelae (135).

Paroxetine

Paroxetine became available in the United States in 1993. Paroxetine has no active metabolites and a mean half-life of approximately 24 hours; steady-state plasma levels are reached in approximately 1 week (similar to sertraline) (145). The recommended dose range is 20–50 mg/day, although the recommended maximum dose in the geriatric population is 40 mg/day. The most commonly reported side effects of paroxetine include nausea, somnolence, insomnia, dizziness, headache, dry mouth, constipation, and tremor (125). Paroxe-

TABLE 6.5. Pharmacokinetic Profiles of the Serotonin Reuptake Inhibitors

	Fluoxetine	Paroxetine	Sertraline
Half-life	2–3 days	24 hr	26 hr
Metabolite activity	Equal	Essentially inactive	Substantially less
Half-life of metabolite	7–9 days	—	2–4 days
Washout period	35–45 days	7 days	7 days
Steady state	35–45 days	7 days	7 days

tine exhibits some affinity for the muscarinic cholinergic receptor; in multicenter studies, paroxetine caused mild anticholinergic side effects such as dry mouth and constipation (146, 147).

Differences Among the SSRIs

Side Effects

Large double-blind studies comparing SSRI side effects have not been performed. Clinical experience suggests that some patients may tolerate one SSRI when they could not tolerate another. In an open study, Brown and Harrison (148) reported that 75% of patients who could not tolerate fluoxetine were able to tolerate sertraline (148). A double-blind study reported that patients taking fluoxetine tended to have a higher incidence of activating side effects (e.g., agitation, anxiety) than patients who received sertraline (149).

Pharmacokinetic Profiles

The pharmacokinetic profiles of three SSRIs are shown in Table 6.5 (143, 145, 150). Fluoxetine has a longer washout period and takes a longer time to achieve a steady-state plasma level than paroxetine or sertraline because of the long half-life of its equipotent metabolite norfluoxetine. Long washout periods may be significant when the physician wants the

medication to leave the patient's body quickly (e.g., when mania is induced or side effects become unbearable, when pregnancy is discovered, when concurrent medical problems develop, or when other medications must be added).

Drug-Drug Interactions

All SSRIs are metabolized extensively in the liver by the cytochrome P-450 microsomal enzyme system. However, differences exist among the three SSRIs in the degree to which they inhibit the P450IID6 isoenzyme system. This system metabolizes a variety of medications used in psychiatric, neurologic, and general medical practice. Inhibition occurs at therapeutic doses of the SSRIs and consequently can produce drug interactions of clinical significance (151). Fluoxetine, its equipotent metabolite norfluoxetine, and paroxetine are significantly more potent inhibitors of cytochrome P450IID6 than sertraline and its principal metabolite N-desmethylsertraline. These differences are evident in vitro (152, 153) and in vivo (154, 155).

The cytochrome P450IID6 isoenzyme is important in the metabolism of many commonly prescribed medications including TCAs, antiarrhythmics (e.g., quinidine), haloperidol, some benzodiazepines, codeine, and dextromethorphan (the ingredient found in over-the-counter medications such as Dristan, Comtrex, Tylenol

Cold and Flu, Robitussin DM, and Benylin DM).

The inhibitory effects of SSRIs on the cytochrome P-450 isoenzymes may slow the metabolism or inhibit the clearance of affected drugs and thereby produce higher plasma concentrations. Thus, it may be necessary to lower the dosage of affected drugs when therapy with fluoxetine or paroxetine is initiated or start with a lower dose of the affected drug when it is added to an ongoing regimen of an SSRI. Likewise, when the SSRI is withdrawn from therapy, it may be necessary to increase the dose of the coadministered drug.

Several clinical reports suggest that the addition of an SSRI to TCA therapy can convert a nonresponder to a responder (156–158). However, caution should be exercised when combining TCAs with certain SSRIs, particularly fluoxetine (155) and paroxetine (159). Inhibition of the cytochrome P450IID6 isoenzyme by these SSRIs has been shown to cause elevated plasma desipramine concentrations and may result in subsequent toxicity (132–136).

The SSRIs should not be given concomitantly with MAOIs because the combination can result in the potentially fatal serotonin syndrome (160). The symptoms of the serotonin syndrome include hyperthermia, muscle rigidity, and autonomic hyperactivity. The syndrome can progress to coma and death. It is also important not to prescribe SSRIs and MAOIs in temporal proximity. When switching from an MAOI to any of the SSRIs, a washout period of 2 weeks is recommended. When switching from an SSRI to an MAOI, a washout period of 2 weeks is recommended for sertraline and paroxetine; a 5-week washout period is recommended when switching from fluoxetine to an MAOI (Table 6.5).

Venlafaxine

Venlafaxine became available in the United States in 1994. In animal model studies, venlafaxine blocks the reuptake of norepinephrine, serotonin, and dopamine (161). In vitro studies demonstrate that it appears to lack anticholinergic, antihistaminergic, and antiadrenergic activity. In multicentered trials, the side effects of venlafaxine versus placebo were nausea (35% versus 10%), somnolence (24% versus 10%), dizziness (18% versus 6%), dry mouth (22% versus 11%), and sweating (12% versus 2%) (162). Venlafaxine treatment is associated with sustained increases in blood pressure; therefore, it is advisable to check the patient's blood pressure before and after the prescription of venlafaxine (163). An increased pulse rate has also been reported with venlafaxine (164).

The half-life of venlafaxine is 3–5 hours and its active metabolite, o-Desmethylvenlafaxine, has a half-life of 9–11 hours. This short half-life requires that it be prescribed in divided doses (164). Venlafaxine may be useful in treatment-resistant, unipolar depressed patients (165).

Nefazodone

Nefazodone was released in 1995. It is a weak inhibitor of neuronal serotonin uptake and a potent $5-HT_2$-receptor antagonist (166). Nefazodone has been shown to be as effective as imipramine for the treatment of major depression (166–168). Side effects include somnolence, dizziness, orthostatic hypotension, asthenia, dry mouth, nausea, constipation, headache, and blurred and impaired vision (166). As with trazodone, to which it is chemically related, sedation may limit patient acceptance. Twice daily dosing is recommended because of the short half-lives of the parent compound and its active metabolites (169). The recommended initial dose is 200 mg/day, administered as 100 mg twice a day, although many patients may require a smaller starting dose. The optimal therapeutic range is 300–500 mg/day; the maximum recommended total daily dose is 600 mg/day (169).

Because nefazodone is a potent inhibitor of the cytochrome P4503A4 isoenzyme, its concomitant use with terfenadine or astemizole is contraindicated (169). When using nefazodone with alprazolam or triazolam, which are also metabolized by cytochrome P4503A4, a dosage reduction of the benzodiazepine is recommended (169).

Augmentation Strategies

The addition of lithium carbonate or thyroid hormone (T_3) to an antidepressant is a popular strategy for treatment of nonresponders or partial responders to antidepressants (122, 123, 125, 126, 170, 171). Although clinical experience suggests that T_3 augmentation is less efficacious than lithium carbonate, a recent double-blind, placebo-controlled study reported that lithium carbonate and T_3 were equally effective (and both were more effective than placebo) when added to TCA treatment (107).

Sexual Dysfunction

Decreased libido and sexual satisfaction have been associated with depression in unmedicated individuals (172, 173) and with almost all the antidepressant medications currently prescribed (174). Thus, it is important to ask about sexual dysfunction in depressed patients before prescribing an antidepressant.

Several options exist for the physician if sexual dysfunction occurs as a side effect of antidepressant medication. First, a lower dose of the antidepressant should be considered to perhaps alleviate the sexual dysfunction. If a dosage reduction is not advisable or is unsuccessful, the addition of cyproheptadine (175–177), bethanacol (178–180), amantadine (181), yohimbine (182), or the use of buspirone (183) or bupropion (184) should be considered. A switch to another antidepressant (185, 186) or delaying the intake of the antidepressant until after coitus (187) may also be considered. One of the authors (A.J.R.) recently reported that a weekend "drug holiday," in which the patient stops taking sertraline or paroxetine for the weekend, often provides relief from sexual dysfunction side effects without a recurrence of depressive symptoms (188).

General Comments

RATE OF RESPONSE

When evaluating the response of patients to antidepressants, it is important to remember that the symptoms of depression resolve gradually (usually over several weeks). The dysphoric mood state is typically the last symptom of depression to improve. Consequently, the patient may report improvement in energy level, sleep disturbance, or somatic complaints; the physician may observe that the patient smiles for the first time and has improved cognitive processes. However, the patient reports that he or she still feels lousy or that "the medication is not working." If the physician observes signs of improvement in depression (or the patient's family reports improvement), it is important to continue the antidepressant currently prescribed because the early signs of improvement may predict a full response.

Although it is possible for patients to experience significant improvement in the symptoms of major depression within the first week, this is not common. In fact, if the patient contacts the physician immediately after the antidepressant is prescribed and profusely thanks the physician for starting the antidepressant, two things should be considered: the patient is bipolar and has switched into hypomania or mania, or it is a placebo effect. Although the occurrence of mania with antidepressant therapy is not always predictable, a thorough patient and family history for bipolar disorder before starting medications may reveal a bipolar diathesis. If a placebo effect is a possibility, the patient should be encouraged to continue to take the medication, but the physician should not be surprised if in 7–10 days the patient reports that the medication "has stopped working."

PRESENCE OF ANXIETY

Anxiety is a common symptom in major depression (189). Although the patient may be very distressed by the anxiety, the physician should not be distracted from recognizing any central symptoms of depression. However, it is often difficult to distinguish whether the patient is suffering primarily from a mood disorder (e.g., major depression) or primarily from an anxiety disorder (e.g., generalized anxiety disorder). Distinguishing differences between these two diagnostic possibilities include the following. First, patients with major depression more commonly exhibit anhedonia (loss of interest or pleasure in usual activities), fatigue, weight/appearance changes, sad affect, and excessive guilt. Second, whereas patients with anxiety and patients with mood disorders both frequently have difficulty falling asleep, patients with major depression ex-

hibit early morning awakening (waking up at 3:00 or 4:00 AM and not being able to fall back to sleep); patients with anxiety disorder usually do not exhibit early morning awakening once asleep.

To the degree to which anxiety is symptomatic of the major depressive episode, an antidepressant will help alleviate this symptom. In contrast, an anxiolytic medication (e.g., buspirone, benzodiazepines) will alleviate only anxiety symptoms without an effect on the many other symptoms of depression (e.g., anhedonia, suicidal ideation), resulting in inadequate treatment of depression.

SEDATING VERSUS NONSEDATING ANTIDEPRESSANTS

Some physicians have been reluctant to prescribe SSRIs in patients with a significant degree of insomnia because the SSRIs are not sedating. However, the SSRIs (like all antidepressants) can be effective in alleviating the insomnia associated with depression. Although it is true that the prescription of a very sedating antidepressant (such as amitriptyline or trazodone) will result in a depressed patient with insomnia initially sleeping better, it is important to remember that insomnia is only one symptom of depression. Moreover, it is unlikely that a starting dose of 50 mg of amitriptyline or trazodone will treat adequately symptoms of hopelessness, poor energy, anhedonia, and suicidal ideation. Doses of 150–300 mg/day of amitriptyline or trazodone are in the therapeutic range. These doses of sedating antidepressants often create the problem of next-day oversedation.

Although the SSRIs are often effective in alleviating the sleep disturbance seen in major depression, at times they do not relieve this problem or actually cause insomnia as a side effect. Some studies suggest that fluoxetine (190) and paroxetine (191) can produce disruptions in sleep, whereas similar alterations have not been observed following treatment with sertraline (192). If a sleep disturbance persists or develops during SSRI treatment, adding a low dose of a sedating antidepressant as a sleeping medication (e.g., trazodone) to the SSRI is often effective (193).

Antidepressant Overdose

TCAs are the third most common cause of drug-related death (following alcohol-drug combinations and heroin) (194). TCAs also rank fourth in overdoses seen in emergency departments (195). A total of 70–80% of patients who take TCA overdoses do not reach the hospital alive (196). For these reasons, the newer agents offer an important advantage in their wider margin of safety in overdose.

ECT

ECT is the oldest and one of the most effective somatic therapies currently available in psychiatric practice. Depressed patients account for approximately 80% of patients treated with ECT today. With the advent of effective and better-tolerated medications, ECT is usually reserved for (1) patients who do not respond to medication, (2) patients who are unable to tolerate the side effects of pharmacotherapy, (3) patients with a history of response to ECT, and (4) patients who need a rapid and definitive intervention because of the life-threatening nature of their illness (e.g., catatonia, high suicide risk). Mania and psychotic illness account for the 20% of patients who are treated with ECT for other than depressive illness (197, 198).

Psychotic depression may represent a condition in which ECT would be indicated as a first-line treatment. The elderly, who frequently present with more severe depression with complicating psychosis, may not be able to tolerate the multiple medications required for adequate treatment. ECT may also be safer in pregnant patients because of the risk of exposing the fetus to psychoactive agents.

The literature reports an overall response rate of 75–85% for ECT in the treatment of depression (199). Although attempts to establish positive predictors of response to ECT have produced inconsistent results, failure to respond to therapeutic trials of antidepressants may be the best predictor of nonresponse to ECT and to early relapse from this treatment. Prudic et al. (200) argue that the long-held view that approximately 85% of nonpsychotic depressed patients in whom antidepressant treatment failed will respond to ECT is no longer accurate. Previous studies on outcome with ECT were uncontrolled or did not compare patients in whom medications failed or who had inadequate drug trials. Patients, at varying treatment sites, who previously did not respond to one or more adequate antidepressant trials appear to be less likely to respond to ECT than patients who had no history of medication resistance. Specific resistance to certain agents (e.g., tricyclics and maprotiline, nomifensine) predicted poorer response to ECT; resistance to SSRIs and MAOIs did not demonstrate a significant predictive effect (200–202).

Mandel et al. (203) reported prediction of response to ECT on the basis of clinical symptomatology. A positive response to ECT has been associated with delusions (somatic or paranoid), sudden onset of symptoms, guilt, mood lability, fluctuating course, and a prior response to ECT. Solan et al. (204) studied psychotic and nonpsychotic depressed patients and did not find the presence of psychosis to be generally predictive of response to ECT. However, they did report a significant difference in response within the psychotic group based on the content of delusions (i.e., those with nihilistic delusions demonstrated better outcome than those with paranoid delusions) (204). Concomitant personality pathology (especially borderline, hypochondriacal, and dependent features) augurs a poor response to ECT.

More than 100 different hypotheses have been proposed to explain the mechanism of therapeutic action of ECT (205). Because ECT effectively treats both depression and mania, it is difficult to attribute its therapeutic effect to any one neurochemical. Animal studies indicate that norepinephrine, serotonin, and dopamine are increased by ECT, suggesting a common mechanism with the antidepressants (206). One notable exception is the 5-HT2 receptor, whose activity in animals is increased with ECT but decreased by antidepressants. The recent finding that response to medication predicts response to ECT supports the view that similar mechanisms of action exist (205).

In debilitated, elderly, ill, and most medication-intolerant patients, ECT can be used with remarkable safety when measures are taken to monitor and manage any concomitant medical disorder. In fact, there may be no absolute contraindications to ECT (198, 199, 207–209). However, the risk-benefit analysis (and intracranial pressure) must be carefully considered if there is a space-occupying lesion (e.g., tumor, subdural). A history of stroke or myocardial infarction within 1 month of beginning ECT is also associated with increased risk.

The workup for ECT proceeds along two lines. First, informed consent must be obtained from the patient or guardian (210). Informed consent is the written version of the establishment of a trusting, working alliance with the patient and his or her family. The second part of the workup is the medical evaluation that includes the following:

1. Medical history and review of systems.
2. Physical examination.
3. Complete blood count (CBC), urine analysis, blood urea nitrogen (BUN), glucose, and serum glutamic-oxaloacetic transaminase (SGOT).
4. Electrocardiogram (ECG)

In addition, the patient's psychotropic medication regimen must be reviewed carefully. Benzodiazepines should be avoided because they raise seizure threshold, as do barbiturates. If evening or morning sedation is needed, hydroxyzine may be used. Tricyclic antidepressants can cause arrhythmias, intraventricular conduction abnormalities, and hypotension. However, a comparison of ECT with and without tricyclics did not reveal a significant difference in cardiac complications (211, 212). MAOIs carry the risk of an intensified sympathetic nervous system; however, ECT has also been used in combination with MAOIs without a significant increase in adverse events (213). The SSRIs can usually be combined safely with ECT. Although a limited number of case reports have raised the question of prolonged seizures, initial studies combining fluoxetine with ECT did not find a significant effect on seizure threshold (214). Case reports on bupropion suggest that it may lengthen seizure duration (215). Among the mood stabilizers, lithium has been associated with delirium when combined with ECT; the anticonvulsant, antiepileptic drugs raise seizure threshold (214). In general, any medication that was not effective before

ECT should be considered for withdrawal before commencing a series of ECT treatments. Initiating new medications during a course of ECT should be kept to a minimum, but can be done when necessary or if the addition of an new agent will hasten recovery.

ECT can be administered unilaterally or bilaterally. Unilateral, nondominant hemisphere treatment is associated with less post-ECT cognitive difficulties and usually does not increase the number of treatments needed (216).

Generally, 6–12 treatments are given in a series, although some patients may require more to obtain relief. Patients are premedicated with intramuscular atropine or intravenous glycopyrrolate to reduce secretions and to minimize vagal cardiac dysrhythmias (217). Intravenous methohexital, a rapid-acting barbiturate, is used for anesthesia, and intravenous succinylcholine is used for muscular relaxation. The electrical stimulus is administered once the effects of the medication have been established, and oxygenation is achieved via an airway. Optimal dosage of the electrical stimulus is a moderate suprathreshold dose of electricity, which is typically estimated by a number of techniques.

After completion of the seizure, oxygenation is resumed, and the patient is carefully monitored. Most patients are up and about 1 hour after the treatment is completed. Adverse effects commonly reported with ECT include headache and muscle spasms, which are usually ameliorated with symptomatic treatment. Cognitive changes include postictal confusion and anterograde and retrograde amnesia for events surrounding the course of ECT. The amnesia is almost always transient and resolves within 30–60 days after completion of treatment.

Considerable misinformation and mystery surround ECT. Patients and their families may be reassured by an open and honest discussion of this procedure with the treating clinician. Several books and videos are available and should be recommended or provided to receptive patients and families. ECT is a safe and highly effective treatment for major depression. All clinicians should be familiar with this treatment and when it should be prescribed; it may be the remedy for many patients who cannot be treated by other methods.

Alliance and Psychotherapeutic Management

Individual psychotherapy has a very important place in the treatment of the depressed patient. Somatic treatments and psychotherapy complement each other in specific ways. Medications or ECT are efficacious in treating the neurovegetative symptoms (e.g., eating, sleeping, motor, and cognitive disturbances), whereas psychotherapy acts as a specific and effective treatment for the interpersonal and social disturbances that accompany depression (e.g., isolation, dependence, constricted or hostile communication, rumination, and decreased work performance) (90, 218–220). Evidence also suggests that the combination of psychotherapy and pharmacotherapy is more effective than either treatment modality alone and is definitely superior to placebo (220).

One of three psychotherapeutic approaches may be taken in the treatment of patients with major depressive disorder. These techniques are psychodynamic, cognitive behavioral, or interpersonal (221, 222). The selection of a specific psychotherapeutic technique should be based on an individual patient's presentation and preferences.

Conventional principles of dynamic, exploratory, or reconstructive psychotherapy, which entails a nondirective, interpretative therapeutic posture, are not appropriate for the acutely depressed patient. Nondirective, exploratory psychotherapy unduly stresses the severely depressed person and reinforces an unconscious view of unavailable, uncaring, and rejecting caregivers. Thus, psychodynamic techniques are generally not the best initial therapeutic approach to the severely depressed patient, although a psychodynamic understanding of the patient may be invaluable.

Instead, psychotherapy for the acutely ill depressed patient aims to be supportive and restitutive. The therapist should be active and persistent in inquiry, flexible in scheduling, friendly in demeanor, and interested in contact with relatives. Defenses are reinforced, and areas of adaptive functioning are sought and encouraged. Restitutive psychotherapy involves empathic listening, because the depressed patient wants to share his or her grief. The therapist must be able to bear the patient's pain; extra time may be needed for this affect to emerge, especially in view of the depressed patient's psychomotor retardation. The therapist should not be too warm or too funny. The depressed patient feels unworthy of excessive warmth and tends to withdraw and feel worse when this is offered. Excessive humor on the part of the therapist denies the patient his or her suffering and is devaluing.

The therapist must convey a sense of hope to the depressed patient, but not in the form of simple reassurance or universal optimism. The therapist must seek out and understand the patient's underlying fears and anxieties. For example, the fear that depression is an illness that will last forever was understood in one patient to be a fear of becoming like his mother, who became depressed and remained ill for a lifetime. Only when the therapist understands these underlying concerns can the patient be responded to, reassured, and given hope.

Aside from establishing clear safety measures to prevent the depressed patient from self-harm, the clinician should avoid taking responsibility for decisions the patient must make. Most important decisions can be deferred until the patient has obtained some significant improvement in depression.

Dependent needs are pronounced yet generally unacceptable to the depressed person, who anticipates that these needs will not be satisfied. Anger, conscious and unconscious, may develop as dependent needs are perceived as being unmet. The depressed patient also often seeks nurturance through suffering. The therapist can never fully satisfy the patient's dependent needs, and anger can soon occupy the therapeutic relationship, particularly if the therapist appropriately avoids taking unnecessary control of the patient's life. Anger in the transference needs to be allowed and can spontaneously lead to anger toward other important people and losses that the patient has experienced. The direct expression of hostility, in therapy or with important others, has not had a reliable result in clinical improvement (73, 74). Working through in this area (typically done through outpatient follow-up) promotes patient autonomy and helps to curtail any helplessness and suffering that is pathologically aimed at securing caring.

Countertransference feelings can become quite powerful in the treatment of depressed and suicidal patients (223). When the therapist feels guilty (often over feelings of anger at the patient), there is reason to suspect covert aggression on the part of the patient. For example, when the patient subtly makes overwhelming or impossible demands, the therapist first becomes helpless, then guilty. Boredom and impatience may also be felt in the countertransference when the patient somehow elicits rejection from the therapist. Although the therapist may understand that the patient is unconsciously driving away the desperately needed source of nurturance, careful self-inspection, supervision, or consultation may be needed to assist the therapist in dealing with these complicated countertransference processes.

As short-term, restitutive therapy progresses, the therapist and patient begin to plan for follow-up care. Continued psychotherapy, in conjunction with appropriate family work and psychopharmacologic treatment, will improve long-term course and prognosis (224–226).

Family Support, Education, and Intervention

Most spouses and families of depressed patients welcome contact from the treating clinician. Families often feel left out, unrecognized, and uncared for, often because the identified patient generally has been the focus of previous professional contact. An effective alliance with the patient's spouse, significant other, or family is critical in several ways. Additional collaborative history may be essential diagnostically, and distortions shaped by the patient's illness can be corrected. Contact with the family also promotes a clearer exploration and identification of stressors. Furthermore, an effective alliance with the family enlists their support for treatment and reduces the possibility of their resisting treatment for reasons intrinsic to the family's psychopathology or need to maintain its current equilibrium,

which may be dependent on one person being ill. Effective family intervention can positively influence treatment compliance, which correlates with outcome (see Chapter 16) (224–226).

Throughout the family contact, the therapist should adopt a stance of listening, calming, and educating. Families are often immersed in the distress of the depressed person and can be emotionally and financially drained by the illness. Many families do not understand depression and can view symptoms as willful. When a family feels heard and empathically responded to, they are more likely to listen to the therapist.

On the basis of the evaluation, a recommendation for continued family contact or formal marital or family therapy is made, when indicated. Indications include marital distress, which is very common in depression (227); family psychopathology that rests, at least in part, on the patient occupying a sick role; or an impasse in the development of the family (e.g., children leaving home) that appears associated with the patient's depression.

Many family members have concerns about the genetic transmission of depression. A parent may worry about what might have been conveyed to a child, and a child may worry about his or her vulnerability to depression. If family members do not raise these concerns spontaneously, the clinician can address these frequent questions and concerns in a family meeting, thus encouraging their expression.

Genetic factors in the etiology of depression can be reviewed candidly with family members. The risk of developing a depression in first-degree relatives of an affected patient is estimated to be 15%. A child with one parent with depressive illness has a 26% risk, and a child with both parents affected has a 43% risk. Concordance is 13% for dizygotic twins and 41% for monozygotic twins (228).

CONTROVERSIES IN THE TREATMENT OF DEPRESSION

Use of ECT

Although ECT has been demonstrated to be a safe and effective treatment for major depression, its use in clinical practice remains controversial. For example, ECT is often underused in medically ill and/or geriatric patients with major depression because of unfounded concerns about its risks. As previously noted in this chapter, ECT is a more rapid and generally safer treatment in this population.

ECT also may be underused in the treatment of patients with less clear-cut diagnoses. For example, victims of trauma may exhibit depressed mood, sleep disturbance, isolative behavior, sexual dysfunction, and self-destructive/suicidal ideation or behavior, in addition to symptoms characteristic of posttraumatic stress disorder (e.g., flashbacks, intrusive phenomena, hypervigilance, and startle response). In the absence of a known history of trauma, the clinician may make a diagnosis of chronic major depression. Such patients often undergo complex medication trials and ultimately may be referred for ECT. The use of ECT in this population can divide members of a multidisciplinary treatment team: some argue that the mood disturbance is secondary to the trauma history and that a primary psychotherapeutic approach (with adjunctive medications) is the best treatment option. Staff members may also object to the use of ECT because of the nature of the procedure (i.e., having something done to the patient while he or she is anesthetized), which may be reminiscent of earlier traumatic experience. Moreover, some team members argue that the transient cognitive deficits observed with ECT may interfere with the patient's capacity to use individual and milieu psychotherapy.

ECT is a safe and effective treatment that should be considered for severe, persistent, or life-threatening major depression. Clinicians should carefully evaluate patients who present with symptoms of major depression and use the best treatment modality based on the individual patient's clinical picture, not on myth, misinformation, or prejudice.

Polypharmacy

The recent trend toward polypharmacy (i.e., simultaneous use of more than one antidepressant agent in a given patient) is another controversy in the acute care of the depressed patient. Patients with treatment-resistant depression often receive complex pharmacotherapeutic regimens in an effort either to produce a response or augment a partial response. Complicated regimens are controversial because of the increased risk of adverse reactions and interactions, the potential for reduced patient compliance, and the increased financial costs.

Although empiric trials documenting the efficacy of various combination treatments are still needed, such treatment is not unreasonable provided that clinicians have thoroughly investigated and discussed alternatives with their patients.

Managed Care

The economic climate of health care and its global effect on psychiatric treatment have become increasingly apparent. Inpatient treatment of depressive illness has been reduced dramatically, secondary to improved early recognition of mood disorders, enhanced pharmacologic management strategies in outpatient settings, and use of alternative acute care settings. Hospitalization has been principally limited to patients who are dangerous to themselves. For those hospitalized, discharge typically occurs before the action of the antidepressant medications can be achieved.

The rapid turnover of patients associated with managed care creates controversy and concern among clinical staff members and trainees. No patient, for economic or other reasons, should be released from a secure setting until the staff members have judged that it is safe for the patient to leave. Effective alliance, evidence of hope, reliable social supports, and continuity of therapeutic care can permit acutely ill, depressed patients to avoid hospital level of care or to leave the hospital in a very short time.

COURSE AND PROGNOSIS

Eighty-five percent or more of patients with major depressive disorder will improve from a specific, carefully chosen biopsychosocial treatment plan. Untreated depressions have been reported to remit spontaneously in 6–9 months (229). Treated depressions can respond in weeks to months. Predictors of recovery from depression include acute onset and severe illness in patients who have no chronic history of depression (230).

Ten to fifteen percent of depressed patients will have a chronic course. Statistically significant increases in relapse rates are associated with underlying chronic depression and three or more previous episodes of affective disorder (230). The multiaxial (biopsychosocial) perspective is helpful in understanding a chronic course. Depression involves an interplay between biology, person, and environ-

ment. Patients with personality disorders and those with limited social resources (e.g., family, money, access to medical care) are apt to have a poorer course and a worse prognosis. Patients treated with a combination of drugs and psychotherapy will have a better prognosis, perhaps because of the interplay between personality and social axes (220, 222, 227, 231).

Fifty percent of patients who have one episode of depression will have a second, recurrent episode. Patients with two or more episodes show increased risk as the number of episodes increases. The recurrent nature of major depressive disorder emphasizes the importance of maintenance treatment. Frank et al. (232) conducted a longitudinal study that reviewed several maintenance therapies, including interpersonal therapy alone and in combination with imipramine treatment, imipramine alone, and placebo alone. Their findings strongly support the long-term use of maintenance antidepressant therapy in patients with recurrent depression.

The course and prognosis of depression is, of course, affected by suicide. Bipolar patients show a lifetime suicide rate of approximately 15%. Unipolar patients (including patients whose conditions are chronic) show higher rates (233–235). In effect, more than 15–20% of patients with depressive disorders will take their own lives. The optimism for treating depression must be tempered by caution, concern, and careful assessment and management of suicidal behavior (See Chapter 2).

REFERENCES

1. Regier DA, Narrow WE, Rae DS, et al. The de facto US mental and addictive disorders service system: epidemiological catchment area prospective 1 year prevalence rates of disorders and services. Arch Gen Psychiatry 1993;50:85–94.
2. Kessler RC, McGonagle KA, Zhao S, et al.

Lifetime and 12-month prevalence of DSM-III-R psychiatric disorders in the United States. Arch Gen Psychiatry 1994;51:8–19.

3. Wells KB, Burnam MA, Rogers W, et al. The course of depression in adult outpatients: results from the medical outcomes study. Arch Gen Psychiatry 1992;49:788–794.

4. Williams RA. Special report on the depressive illnesses. Washington, DC: U.S. Department of Health, Education and Welfare, November 1970.

5. Aarons SF, Frances AJ, et al. Atypical depression: a review of diagnosis and treatment. Hosp Community Psychiatry 1985;36:275–282.

6. Silberman EK, Sullivan JL. Atypical depression. Psychiatr Clin North Am 1984;7:535–547.

7. Gelenberg AJ. The catatonic syndrome. Lancet 1976;1:1339–1341.

8. Jones-Webb RJ, Snowden LR. Symptoms of depression among blacks and whites. Am J Public Health 1993;83:240–244.

9. Goodnick PJ, Henry JH, Buki VMV. Treatment of depression in patients with diabetes mellitus. J Clin Psychiatry 1995;56:4.

10. Frasure-Smith N, Lesperance F, Talajic M. Depression following myocardial infarction. Impact on 6-month survival. JAMA 1993;270:1819–1825.

11. Frasure-Smith N, Lesperance F, Talajic M. Depression and 18-month prognosis after myocardial infarction. Circulation 1995;91:999–1005.

12. American Psychiatric Association. Diagnostic and statistical manual of mental disorders. 4th ed. Washington, DC: American Psychiatric Press, 1994.

13. Rosenthal NE, Sack DA, et al. Seasonal affective disorder. Arch Gen Psychiatry 1984;41:72–80.

14. Schwartz PJ, Brown C, Wehr TA, et al. Winter seasonal affective disorder: a follow-up study of the first 59 patients of the National Institute of Mental Health seasonal studies program. Am J Psychiatry 1996;1028–1036.

15. Stowe ZN, Nemeroff CB. Women at risk for post-partum onset major depression. Am J Obstet Gynecol 1995;173:639–645.

16. Clark DA, Beck AT, Beck JS. Symptom differences in major depression, dysthymia, panic disorder and generalized anxiety disorder. Am J Psychiatry 1994;151:205–209.

17. Keller MB, Shapiro RW. Double depression. Am J Psychiatry 1982;139:438–442.

18. Keller MB, Lavori PW, et al. Double depression: two year follow-up. Am J Psychiatry 1983;140:689–694.

19. Akiskal HS. Dysthymic disorder: psychopathology of proposed chronic depressive subtypes. Am J Psychiatry 1983;140:11–20.

20. Brown RP, Sweeney JP, et al. Involutional melancholia revisited. Am J Psychiatry 1984;141:24–28.

21. Klerman GL, Lavori PW, et al. Birth-cohort trends in rates of major depressive disorder among relatives of patients with affective disorder. Arch Gen Psychiatry 1985;42:689–693.

22. Weissman MM, Klerman GL. Sex differences and the epidemiology of depression, Arch Gen Psychiatry 1977;34:98–111.

23. Faris RE, Dunham HW. Mental disorders in urban areas. Chicago: University of Chicago Press, 1939.

24. Tucker JS, Friedmand HS, Wingard DL, et al. Marital history at midlife as a predictor of longevity: alternative explanations to the protective effect of marriage. Health Psychol 1996;15:94–101.

25. Radloff L. Sex differences in depression. The effects of occupation and marital status. Sex Roles 1975;1:249–269.

26. Weissman MM, Paykel ES. The depressed woman: a study of social relationships. Chicago: University of Chicago Press, 1974.

27. Kiecolt-Glaser JK, Glaser R. Psychosocial moderators of immune function. Ann Behav Med 1987;9:16–20.

28. Koscis JH, Frances AJ. A critical discussion of DSM-III dysthymic disorder. Am J Psychiatry 1987;144:1534–1542.

29. Pope HG, Lipinski JF, et al. Schizoaffective disorder: an invalid diagnosis? A comparison of schizoaffective disorder, schizophrenia and affective disorder. Am J Psychiatry 1980;137:921–927.

30. Lindemann E. Symptomatology and management of acute grief. Am J Psychiatry 1944;101:141–148.

31. Hatsukami D, Pickens RW. Post-treatment depression in an alcohol and drug abuse population. Am J Psychiatry 1982;139:1563–1566.

32. Hirschfeld RMA, Klerman GL, et al. Assessing personality: affects of the depressive state on trait measurement. Am J Psychiatry 1983;140:695–699.

33. Akiskal HS, Hirschfeld RMA, et al. The relationship of personality to affective disorders. Arch Gen Psychiatry 1983;40:801–810.

34. Goodwin FK, Bunney WE. A psychobiological approach to affective illness. Psychiatr Ann 1973;3:19.

35. Schildkraut JT. The catecholamine hypothesis of affective disorders: a review of supporting evidence. Am J Psychiatry 1965;122:509–522.

36. Maas JW. Biogenic amines and depression. Biochemical and pharmacological separations

of two types of depression. Arch Gen Psychiatry 1975;32:1357–1361.

37. Baldessarini RJ. Biogenic amine hypotheses in affective disorders. Arch Gen Psychiatry 1975;32:1087–1093.

38. Miller HL, Delgado PL, Salomon RM, et al. Clinical and biochemical effects of catecholamine depletion on antidepressant-induced remission of depression. Arch Gen Psychiatry 1996;53:117–128.

39. Delgado PL, Charney DS, Price LH, et al. Serotonin function and the mechanism of antidepressant action: reversal of antidepressant-induced remission by rapid depletion of plasma tryptophan. Arch Gen Psychiatry 1990;47:411–418.

40. Siever LJ, Davis KL. Overview: toward a dysregulation hypothesis of depression. Am J Psychiatry 1985;142:1017–1031.

41. Lake CR, Pickar D, Ziegler MG, et al. High plasma norepinephrine levels in patients with major affective disorder. Am J Psychiatry 1982;139:1315–1318.

42. Koslow JH, Maas JW, Bauder CL, et al. CSF and urinary biogenic amines and metabolites in depression and mania: a controlled, univariate analysis. Arch Gen Psychiatry 1985;42:1181–1185.

43. Linnoila M, Karoum F, Calil HM, et al. Alteration of norepinephrine metabolism with desipramine and zimelidine in depressed patients. Arch Gen Psychiatry 1982;39:1025–1028.

44. Nyback HV, Walters JR, Aghajanian GK, et al. Tricyclic antidepressants: effect on the firing rate of brain noradrenergic neurons. Eur J Pharmacol 1975;32:302–312.

45. Janowsky DS, Risch SC, Parker D, et al. Increased vulnerability to cholinergic stimulation in affective disorder patients. Psychopharmacol Bull 1980;16:29–31.

46. Snyder SH. Cholinergic mechanisms in affective disorders. N Engl J Med 1984;311:254–255.

47. Berrettini WH, Nurnberger JI, Hare TA, et al. Plasma and CSF GABA in affective illness. Br J Psychiatry 1982;141:483–487.

48. Gold BI, Bowers MJ Jr, Roth RH, et al. GABA levels in CSF of patients with psychiatric disorders. Am J Psychiatry 1980;137:362–364.

49. Morselli PL, Bossi L, Henry JF, et al. On the therapeutic action of SL 76–002, a new GABA-mimetic agent: preliminary observations in neuropsychiatric disorders. Brain Research Bulletin 1980;5(Suppl 2):411–414.

50. Thaker GK, Moran M, Tamminga CA. GABA-mimetics: a new class of antidepressant agents. Arch Gen Psychiatry 1990;47:287–288.

51. Petty F, Trivedi MH, Fulton M, et al. Benzodiazepines as antidepressants: does GABA play a role in depression? Biol Psychiatry 1995;38:578–591.

52. Sulser F. Mode of action of antidepressant drugs. J Clin Psychiatry 1983;44:14–20.

53. Richelson EL. The new antidepressants: structures, pharmacokinetics, pharmacodynamics and proposed mechanisms of action. Psychopharmacol Bull 1984;20:213–223.

54. Hyman SE, Nestler EJ. Initiation and adaptation: a paradigm for understanding psychotropic drug action. Am J Psychiatry 1996;153:151–162.

55. Baron FM, Ogden AM, Siegel BW, et al. Rapid down-regulation of beta-adrenoreceptors by co-administration of desipramine and fluoxetine. Eur J Pharmacol 1988;154:125–134.

56. Rosanoff AJ, Handy LM, Plesset IR. The etiology of manic-depressive syndromes with special reference to their occurrence to twins. Am J Psychiatry 1935;91:725–762.

57. Allen MG, Cohen S, Pollin W, et al. Affective illness in veteran twins: a diagnostic review. Am J Psychiatry 1974;131:1234–1239.

58. Kendler KS, Eaves LJ, Walters EE, et al. The identification and validation of distinct depressive syndromes in a population-based sample of female twins. Arch Gen Psychiatry 1996;53:391–399.

59. Perris C. A study of bipolar (manic-depressive) and unipolar recurrent depressive psychoses. Acta Psychiatr Scand Suppl 1966;194:1–189.

60. Gershon E, Mark A, Cohen N, et al. Transmitted factors in the morbid risk of affective disorders: a controlled study. J Psychiatr Res 1975;12:283–299.

61. James NM, Chapman CJ. A genetic study of bipolar affective disorder. Br J Psychiatry 1975;126:449–456.

62. Tsuang MT, Winokur G, Crowe R. Morbidity risks of schizophrenia and affective disorders among first degree relatives of patients with schizophrenia, mania, depression and surgical conditions. Br J Psychiatry 1980;137:497–504.

63. Cadoret RJ. Evidence for genetic inheritance of primary affective disorders in adoptees. Am J Psychiatry 1978;135:463–466.

64. Sack DA, Nurnberger J, et al. Potentiation of antidepressant medications by phase advance of the sleep-wake cycle. Am J Psychiatry 1985;142:606–608.

65. Parry BL, Berga SL, Kripke DF, et al. Altered waveform of plasma nocturnal melatonin secretion in premenstrual depression. Arch Gen Psychiatry 1990;47:1139–1146.

66. Leibenluft E. Women with bipolar illness:

clinical and research issues. Am J Psychiatry 1996;153:163–173.

67. Reynolds CF, Kupfer DJ. Sleep research in affective illness: state of the art circa 1987. Sleep 1987;10:199–215.

68. Grunhaus L, Tiongco D, Roehrich H, et al. Serial monitoring of antidepressant response to electroconvulsive therapy with sleep EEG recordings and dexamethasone suppression tests. Biol Psychiatry 1985;20:805–808.

69. Rush AJ, Erman MK, Giles DE, et al. Polysomnographic findings in recently drug-free and clinically remitted depressed patients. Arch Gen Psychiatry 1986;43:878–884.

70. Abraham K. Notes on the psychoanalytical investigation and treatment of manic-depressive insanity and allied conditions: the selected papers of Karl Abraham. London: Hogarth Press, 1927.

71. Freud S. Mourning and melancholia. In: Strachey J, ed. Standard Edition (14) London: Horgarth Press (1917), 1958.

72. Fenichel O. Depression and mania. The psychoanalytic theory of neurosis. New York: Norton, 1945.

73. Kendell R. Relationship between aggression and depression: epidemiological implications of a hypothesis. Arch Gen Psychiatry 1970;22:308–318.

74. Henry A, Short J. Suicide and homicide. Chicago: Free Press, Glencoe, IL, 1954.

75. Friedman A. Hostility factors and clinical improvement in depressed patients. Arch Gen Psychiatry 1970;524–537.

76. Paykel E. Classification of depressed patients: a cluster analysis of derived grouping. Br J Psychiatry 1971;118:275–288.

77. Weissman M, Fox K, et al. Hostility and depression associated with suicide attempts. Am J Psychiatry 1973;130:450–455.

78. Klerman G, Gershon E. Imipramine effects upon hostility in depression. J Nerv Ment Dis 1970;150:127–132.

79. Bibring E. The mechanism of depression. In: Greenacre P, ed. Affective disorders. New York: International Universities Press, 1953.

80. Klein M. A contribution to the psychogenesis of manic-depressive states. In: Contributions to psychoanalysis. London: Hogarth Press, 1945:228–310.

81. Bowlby J. The process of mourning. Int J Psychoanal 1961;42:317–340.

82. Spitz RA. Anaclitic depression. The psychoanalytic study of the child. New York: International Universities Press, 1946;2.

83. Leff M, Roatch J, et al. Environmental factors preceding the onset of severe depressions. Psychiatry 1970;33:293–311.

84. Paykel E. Myers J, et al. Life events and depression. Arch Gen Psychiatry 1970;21:753–760.

85. Clayton P, Halikas J, et al. The depression of widowhood. Br J Psychiatry 1972;120:71–77.

86. Beck AT. Depressive neurosis. In: Areti S, Brody EB, eds. American handbook of psychiatry. 2nd ed. New York: Basic Books, 1974;3:61–90.

87. Rush AJ, Beck AT, et al. Comparative efficacy of cognitive therapy and pharmacotherapy in the treatment of depressed outpatients. Cognit Ther Res 1977;1:17–37.

88. Kovacs M, Bect AT. Maladaptive cognitive structures in depression. Am J Psychiatry 1978;135:525–533.

89. Silverman JS, Silverman JA, et al. Do maladaptive attitudes cause depression? Arch Gen Psychiatry 1984;41:28–30.

90. Simons AD, Garfield SL, et al. The process of change in cognitive therapy and pharmacotherapy for depression. Arch Gen Psychiatry 1984;41:45–51.

91. Ilfeld FW. Current social stressors and symptoms of depression. Am J Psychiatry 1988;134:161–166.

92. Lloyd C. Life events and depressive disorder reviewed. Part 2: events as precipitating factors. Arch Gen Psychiatry 1980;37:541–548.

93. Paykel ES. Life stress, depression and attempted suicide. J Hum Stress 1976;2:3–12.

94. Fava GA, Munari F, Pavan L, et al. Life events and depression: a replication. J Affect Dis 1981;3:159–165.

95. Alpert EJ. Violence in intimate relationships and the practicing internist: New disease or new agenda? Ann Intern Med 1995;123:774–781.

96. Abbott J, Johnson R, Koziol-McLain J, et al. Domestic violence against women. Incidence and prevalence in an emergency department population. JAMA 1995;273:1763–1767.

97. Gold PW, Goodwin FK, Chrousos GP. Clinical and biochemical manifestations of depression: relation to the neurobiology of stress. N Engl J Med 1988;319:413–420.

98. APA Task Force on Laboratory Tests in Psychiatry. The dexamethasone suppression test: an overview of its current status in psychiatry. Am J Psychiatry 1987;144:1253–1262.

99. Arana GW, Baldessarini RJ, Ornsteen M. The dexamethasone suppression test for diagnosis and prognosis in psychiatry. Arch Gen Psychiatry 1985;42:1193–1204.

100. Chan CH, Janicak PG, Davis JM, et al. Response of psychotic and nonpsychotic depressed patients to tricyclic antidepressants. J Clin Psychiatry 1987;48:197–200.

101. Baldessarini RJ. Current status of antidepressants: clinical pharmacology and therapy. J Clin Psychiatry 1989;50:117–126.

102. Roose SP, Glassman AH, Attia E, et al. Comparative efficacy of selective serotonin reuptake inhibitors and tricyclics in the treatment of melancholia. Am J Psychiatry 1994;151:1735–1739.

103. Goodwin FK, Prange AJ. Potentiation of antidepressant effects by L-triiodothyronin in tricyclic non-responders. Am J Psychiatry 1982;139:34–38.

104. Schwarcz G, Halaris A, et al. Normal thyroid function in desipramine non-responders converted to responders by the addition of L-triiodothyronine. Am J Psychiatry 1984;141:1614–1616.

105. Gelenberg A, ed. For the treatment-resistant depressed woman: estrogen? Biol Therapies Psychiatry 1989;12:1, 4.

106. Fava M, Rosenbausm JF, McGrath PJ, et al. Lithium and tricyclic augmentation of fluoxetine treatment for resistant major depression: a double-blind, controlled study. Am J Psychiatry 1994;151:1372–1374.

107. Joffe RT, Singer W, Levitt A, et al. A placebo controlled comparison of lithium and tri-iodothyronine augmentation of tricyclic antidepressants in unipolar refractory depression. Arch Gen Psychiatry 1993;50:387–393.

108. McGrath PJ, Quitkin FM, Klein DF. Bromocriptine treatment of relapses seen during selective serotonin reuptake inhibitor treatment of depression. J Clin Psychopharmacol 1995;15:289–291.

109. Artigas F, Perez V, Alvarez E. Pindolol induced a rapid improvement of depressed patients treated with serotonin reuptake inhibitors. Arch Gen Psychiatry 1994;51:248–251.

110. Feighner JP, Boyer WF, Herbstein J. New antidepressants. Psychiatry Lett 1988;6:1–4.

111. Cooper GL. The safety of fluoxetine: an update. Br J Psychiatry 1988;153(Suppl 3): 77–86.

112. Liebowitz MR, Quitkin FM, Stewart JW, et al. Antidepressant specificity in atypical depression. Arch Gen Psychiatry 1988;45:129–137.

113. Wehr TA, Goodwin FK. Do antidepressants cause mania? Psychopharmacol Bull 1987;23:61–65.

114. Wehr TA, Goodwin FK. Can antidepressant cause mania and worsen course of affective illness? Am J Psychiatry 1987;144:1403–1411.

115. Fogelson DL, Bystritsky A, Pasnau R. Bupropion in the treatment of bipolar disorders: the same old story? J Clin Psychiatry 1992;53:443–446.

116. Sachs GS, Lafer B, Stoll AL, et al. A double-blind trial of bupropion versus desipramine for bipolar depression. J Clin Psychiatry 1994;55:391–393.

117. Prien RF, Kupfer DJ, et al. Drug treatment in the prevention of recurrences in unipolar and bipolar affective disorders. Arch Gen Psychiatry 1984;41:1096–1104.

118. Kramlinger KG, Post RM. The addition of lithium to carbamazepine. Arch Gen Psychiatry 1989;46:794–800.

119. Chan CH, Janicak PG, Davis JM, et al. Response of psychotic and nonpsychotic depressed patients to tricyclic antidepressants. J Clin Psychiatry 1987;48:197–200.

120. Spiker DG, Weiss JC, et al. The pharmacological treatment of delusional depression. Am J Psychiatry 1985;142:430–436.

121. Fawcett J, Scheftner W, Clark D, et al. Clinical predictors of suicide in patients with major affective disorders: a controlled prospective study. Am J Psychiatry 1987;144:35–40.

122. Dessain EC, Schatzberg AF, Woods BT, et al. Maprotiline treatment in depression: a perspective on seizures. Arch Gen Psychiatry 1986;43:86–90.

123. Cohen B, Harris P, Altesman R. Amoxapine: neuroleptic as well as antidepressant? Am J Psychiatry 1982;139:1165–1167.

124. Teicher MH, Cohen BM, Baldessarini RJ, et al. Severe daytime somnolence in patients treated with an MAOI. Am J Psychiatry 1988;145:1552–1556.

125. Physician's desk reference. 48th ed. Oradell, NJ: Medical Economics Company, 1994.

126. Richelson E. Synaptic pharmacology of antidepressants: an update. McLean Hosp J 1988;13:67–88.

127. Koe BK. Preclinical pharmacology of sertraline: a potent and specific inhibitor of serotonin reuptake. J Clin Psychiatry 1990;51(Suppl B):12–17.

128. Tulloch IF, Johnson AM. The pharmacologic profile of paroxetine, a new selective serotonin reuptake inhibitor. J Clin Psychiatry 1992;53(Suppl 2):7–12.

129. Feighner JP, Hendrickson G, Miller L, et al. Double-blind comparison of doxepin versus bupropion in outpatients with a major depressive disorder. J Clin Psychopharmacol 1986;6:27–32.

130. Mendels J, Amin MM, Chouinard G, et al. A comparative study of bupropion and amitriptyline in depressed outpatients. J Clin Psychiatry 1983;44:118–120.

131. Lineberry CG, Johnston A, Raymond RN, et al. A fixed-dose efficacy study of bupropion and placebo in depressed outpatients. J Clin Psychiatry 1990;51:194–199.

132. Farid FF, Wenger TL, Tsai SY, et al. Use of bupropion in patients who exhibit orthostatic hypotension on tricyclic antidepressants. J Clin Psychiatry 1983;44:170–173.

133. Wenger TL, Cohn JB, Bustrack J. Comparison of the effects of bupropion and amitriptyline on cardiac conduction in depressed patients. J Clin Psychiatry 1983;44:174–175.

134. Heym J, Koe K. Pharmacology of sertraline: a review. J Clin Psychiatry 1988;48(Suppl 8): 40–45.

135. Grimsley SR, Jann MW. Paroxetine, sertraline and fluvoxamine: new selective serotonin reuptake inhibitors. Clin Pharmacy 1992;11:930–957.

136. Stoll AL, Pope HG, McElroy SL. High dose fluoxetine: safety and efficacy in 27 cases. J Clin Psychopharmacol 1991;11:225–226.

137. Schweitzer E, Rickels K, Amsterdam JD. What constitutes an adequate antidepressant trial for fluoxetine? J Clin Psychiatry 1990;51:8–11.

138. Lipinski JF Jr, Mallya G, Zimmerman P, et al. Fluoxetine-induced akathisia: clinical and theoretical implications. J Clin Psychiatry 1989;50:339–342.

139. Rothschild AJ, Locke CA. Reexposure to fluoxetine after serious suicide attempts by three patients: the role of akathisia. J Clin Psychiatry 1991;52:491–493.

140. Wirshing WC, VanPutten T, Rosenberg J, et al. Fluoxetine, akathisia and suicidality: is there a causal connection? Arch Gen Psychiatry 1992;49:580–581.

141. Koe BE, Weissman A, Welsh WM, et al. Sertraline 15, 45-N-methyl-4(3,4 dichlorophenyl)-1,2,3,4-tetrahydro-1-naphthylamine, a new uptake inhibitor with selectivity for serotonin. J Pharm Exp Ther 1983;226:686–700.

142. Leonard BE. Pharmacological effects of serotonin reuptake inhibitors. J Clin Psychiatry 1988;49(Suppl 8):12–17.

143. Doogan DP, Caillard V. Sertraline: a new antidepressant. J Clin Psychiatry 1988;49(Suppl):46–51.

144. Ronfeld RA, Shaw GL, Termaine LM. Distribution and pharmacokinetics of the selective 5-HT blocker sertraline in man, rat and dog. Psychopharmacol 1988;96(Suppl):269. Abstract.

145. DeVane CL. Pharmacokinetics of the selective serotonin reuptake inhibitors. J Clin Psychiatry 1992;53(Suppl 2):13–20.

146. Thomas DR, Nelson DR, Johnson AM. Biochemical effects of the antidepressant paroxetine, a specific 5-hydroxytryptamine uptake inhibitor. Psychopharmacology 1987;93:193–200.

147. Boyer WF, Blumhardt CL. The safety profile of paroxetine. J Clin Psychiatry 1992;53(Suppl 2):61–66.

148. Brown WA, Harrison W. Are patients who are intolerant to one SSRI intolerant to another? Psychopharmacol Bull 1992;28:253–256.

149. Aguglia E, Casacchia M, Cassano GB, et al. Double-blind study of the efficacy and safety of sertraline versus fluoxetine in major depression. Int Clin Psychopharmacol 1993;8:197–202.

150. Rickels K, Schweitzer E. Clinical overview of serotonin reuptake inhibitors. J Clin Psychiatry 1990;51(Suppl B):9–12.

151. Ciraulo DA, Shader RI. Fluoxetine drug-drug interactions. J Clin Psychopharmacol 1990;10:48–50, 213–217.

152. Preskorn S. Recent pharmacologic advances in antidepressant therapy for the elderly. Am J Med 1993;94(Suppl 5A):2–12.

153. Crewe HK, Lennard MS, Tucker GT, et al. The effect of selective serotonin re-uptake inhibitors on cytochrome P4502D6 (CYP2D6) activity in human liver microsomes. Br J Clin Pharmacol 1992;34:262–265.

154. Brøsen K, Hansen JG, Nielsen KK, et al. Inhibition by paroxetine of desipramine metabolism in extensive but not in poor metabolizers of sparteine. Eur J Clin Pharmacol 1993;44:349–355.

155. Preskorn SH, Alderman J, Chung M, et al. Pharmacokinetics of desipramine coadministered with sertraline or fluoxetine. J Clin Psychopharmacol 1994;14:90–98.

156. Weilburg JB, Rosenbaum JF, Biederman J. Fluoxetine added to non-MAOI antidepressants converts nonresponders to responders: a preliminary report. J Clin Psychiatry 1989;50:447–449.

157. Weilburg JB, Rosenbaum JF, Meltzer-Brody S, et al. Tricyclic augmentation of fluoxetine. Ann Clin Psychiatry 1991;3:209–213.

158. Seth R, Jennings AL, Bindman J, et al. Combination treatment with noradrenalin and serotonin reuptake inhibitors in resistant depression. Br J Psychiatry 1992;161:562–565.

159. Alderman J, Greenblatt DJ, Allison J, et al. Desipramine pharmacokinetics with the selective serotonin reuptake inhibitors (SSRIs) paroxetine or sertraline. Poster presented at the American Psychiatric Association Sequicentennial Celebration, Philadelphia, Pennsylvania, May 21–26, 1994.

160. Sternbach H. The serotonin syndrome. Am J Psychiatry 1991;148:705–713.

161. Muth EA, Haskins JT, Moyer JA, et al. An-

tidepressant biochemical profile of the novel bicyclic compound Wy-45,030, an ethyl cyclohexanol derivative. Biochem Pharmacol 1986;35:4493–4497.

162. Montgomery SA. Venlafaxine: a new dimension in antidepressant pharmacotherapy. J Clin Psychiatry 1993;54:119–126.

163. Manufacturer's prescribing information, 1994. In: Physician's desk reference. 49th ed. Oradell, NJ: Medical Economics Company, 1995.

164. Schweizer E, Weise C, Clary C, et al. Placebo-controlled trial of venlafaxine for the treatment of major depression. J Clin Psychopharmacol 1991;2:233–236.

165. Nierenberg A, Feighner JP, Rudolph R, et al. Venlafaxine for treatment-resistant unipolar depression. J Clin Psychopharmacol 1994;14:419–423.

166. Fontaine R. Novel serotonergic mechanisms and clinical experience with nefazodone. Clin Neuropharmacol 1992:15(Suppl 1):99.

167. Rickels K, Schweizer E, Clary C, et al. Nefazodone and imipramine in major depression: a placebo-controlled trial. Br J Psychiatry 1994;164:802–805.

168. Fontaine R, Ontiveros A, Elie R, et al. A double-blind comparison of nefazodone, imipramine, and placebo in major depression. J Clin Psychiatry 1994;55:234–241.

169. Prescribing information. Serzone (nefazodone hydrochloride) tablets. Princeton, NJ: Bristol-Myers Squibb Company, December 1994.

170. deMontigny C, Grunberg F, Mayer A, et al. Lithium induces rapid relief of depression in tricyclic antidepressant drug non-responders. Br J Psychiatry 1981;138:252–256.

171. Prange AJ Jr, Wilson IL, Breese GR, et al. Hormonal alteration of imipramine response: a review. In: Sachar EJ, ed. Hormone, behavior and psychopathology. New York: Raven Press, 1976:41–67.

172. Mathew RJ, Weinman ML. Sexual dysfunction in depression. Arch Sex Behav 1982;11:323–328.

173. Howell SR, Reynolds CF, Thase ME, et al. Assessment of sexual function, interest and activity in depressed men. J Affect Dis 1987;13:61–66.

174. Segraves RT. Overview of sexual dysfunction complicating the treatment of depression. J Clin Psychiatry Monograph 1992;10:4–10.

175. Steele TE, Howell EF. Cyproheptadine for imipramine-induced anorgasmia. J Clin Psychopharmacol 1986;6:326–327. Letter.

176. Sovner R. Treatment of tricyclic antidepressant-induced orgasmic inhibition with cyproheptadine. J Clin Psychopharmacol 1984;4:169. Letter.

177. McCormick S, Olin J, Brotman AW. Reversal of fluoxetine-induced anorgasmia by cyproheptadine in two patients. J Clin Psychiatry 1990;51:383–384.

178. Yager J. Bethanechol chloride can reverse erectile and ejaculatory dysfunction induced by tricyclic antidepressants and mazindol: case report. J Clin Psychiatry 1986;47:210–211.

179. Gross MD. Reversal by bethanechol of sexual dysfunction caused by anticholinergic antidepressants. Am J Psychiatry 1982;139:1193–1194.

180. Segraves RT. Reversal by bethanechol of imipramine-induced ejaculatory dysfunction. Am J Psychiatry 1987;144:1243–1244. Letter.

181. Balogh S, Hendricks SE, Kang J. Treatment of fluoxetine-induced anorgasmia with amantadine. J Clin Psychiatry 1992;53:212–213. Letter.

182. Price J, Grunhaus LJ. Treatment of clomipramine-induced anorgasmia with yohimbine: a case report. J Clin Psychiatry 1990;51:32–33.

183. Norden MJ. Buspirone treatment of sexual dysfunction associated with selective serotonin re-uptake inhibitors. Depression 1994;2:109–112.

184. Labbate LA, Pollack MH. Treatment of fluoxetine-induced sexual dysfunction with bupropion: a case study. Ann Clin Psychiatry 1994;6:13–15.

185. Walker PW, Cole JO, Gardner EA, et al. Improvement in fluoxetine-associated sexual dysfunction in patients switched to bupropion. J Clin Psychiatry 1993;54:459–465.

186. Feiger A, Kiev A, Shrivastava RK, et al. Nefazodone versus sertraline in outpatients with major depression: focus on efficacy, tolerability, and effects on sexual function and satisfaction. J Clin Psychiatry 1996;57(Suppl 2):53–62.

187. Olivera AA. Sexual dysfunction due to clomipramine and sertraline: nonpharmacological resolution. J Sex Educ Ther 1994;20:119–112.

188. Rothschild AJ. Selective serotonin reuptake inhibitor-induced sexual dysfunction: efficacy of a drug holiday. Am J Psychiatry 1995;152:1514–1516.

189. Coryell W. Anxiety secondary to depression. Psychiatr Clin North Am 1990;13:685–698.

190. Nicholson AN, Pascoe PA. Studies on the modulation of the sleep-wakefulness continuum in man by fluoxetine, a 5-HT uptake inhibitor. Neuropharmacology 1988;27:597–602.

191. Oswald I, Adam K. Effects of paroxetine on human sleep. Br J Clin Pharmacol 1986;22:97–99.

192. Winokur A, Lexon N, Allen K, et al. Sertraline administered for eight weeks to depressed patients did not alter sleep architecture: a preliminary report. New Research Program and Abstracts, American Psychiatric Association Annual Meeting NR 212, 1994:110.

193. Nierenberg AA, Adler LA, Peselow E, et al. Trazodone for antidepressant-associated insomnia. Am J Psychiatry 1994;151:1069–1072.

194. Beaumont G. The toxicity of antidepressants. Br J Psychiatry 1989;154:454–458.

195. Callahan M. Epidemiology of fatal tricyclic antidepressant ingestion: implications for management. Ann Emerg Med 1985;14:1–9.

196. Kulig K. Management of poisoning associated with newer antidepressant agents. Ann Emerg Med 1986;15:1039–1045.

197. Rudorfer MV, Henry ME, Sackeim HA. Electroconvulsive therapy. In: Tasman A, Kay J, Lieberman JA, eds. Psychiatry. Philadelphia: WB Saunders. (In Press).

198. Weiner RD, Fink M, Hammersly DW, et al. The practice of electroconvulsive therapy: recommendations for treatment, training and privileging. A task force report of the American Psychiatric Association. Washington, DC: American Psychiatric Press, 1990.

199. Crowe RR. Electroconvulsive therapy: a current perspective. N Engl J Med 1984;311:163 –167.

200. Prudic J, Haskett RF, Mulsant B, et al. Resistance to antidepressant medications and short term clinical response to ECT. Am J Psychiatry 1996;153:985–992.

201. Kindler S, Shapira B, Hadjez J, et al. Factors influencing response to bilateral electroconvulsive therapy in major depression. Convul Ther 1991;7:245–254.

202. Prudic J, Sackheim HA, Devanand DP. Medication resistance and clinical response to electroconvulsive therapy. Psychiatry Res 1990;31:287–296.

203. Mandel MR, Welch CR, et al. Prediction of response to ECT in tricyclic-intolerant or tricyclic-resistant depressed patients. McLean Hosp J 1977;2:203–209.

204. Solan WJ, Khan A, Avery DH, et al. Psychotic and nonpsychotic depression: comparison of response to ECT. J Clin Psychiatry 1988;49:97–99.

205. Sackeim HA. Central issues regarding the mechanisms of action of electroconvulsive therapy: directions for future research. Psychopharmacol Bull 1994;30:281–308.

206. Fochtmann LJ. Animal studies of electroconvulsive therapy: foundations for future research. Psychopharmacol Bull 1994;10:321–444.

207. Maltbie AA, Wingfield MS, Volow MR, et al. Electroconvulsive therapy in the presence of brain tumor: case reports and an evaluation of risk. J Nerv Ment Dis 1980;168:400–405.

208. Fried D, Mann JJ. Electroconvulsive treatment of a patient with known intracranial tumor. Biol Psychiatry 1988;23:176–180.

209. Greenberg LB, Mofson R, Fink M. Prospective electroconvulsive therapy in a delusional depressed patient with a frontal meningioma: a case report. Br J Psychiatry 1988;153:105–107.

210. Culver CM, Ferrell RB, et al. ECT and special problems of informed consent. Am J Psychiatry 1980;137:586–591.

211. Azar I, Lear E. Cardiovascular effects of electroconvulsive therapy in patients taking tricyclic antidepressants. Anesth Analg 1984;63:1140.

212. Drop LJ, Welch CA. Anesthesia for electroconvulsive therapy in patients with major cardiovascular risk factors. Convul Ther 1989;5:88–101.

213. Remick RA, Jewesson P, Ford RWJ. Monoamine oxidase inhibitors in general anesthesia: a reevaluation. Convul Ther 1987;3:196–203.

214. Kellner CH, Nixon DW, Berstein HJ. ECT-drug interactions: a review. Psychopharmacol Bull 1991;27:595–609.

215. Rudorfer MV, Manji HK, Potter WZ. Bupropion, ECT, and dopaminergic overdrive. Am J Psychiatry 1991;8:1101–1102.

216. Sackeim HA, Prudic J, Devanand DP, et al. Effects of stimulus intensity and electrode placement on the efficacy and cognitive effects of electroconvulsive therapy. N Engl J Med 1993;328:839–846.

217. Bouckoms AJ, Welch CA, Drop LJ, et al. Atropine in electroconvulsive therapy. Convul Ther 1989;5:48–55.

218. Weissman MM, Prusoff BA, et al. The efficacy of drugs and psychotherapy in the treatment of acute depressive episodes. Am J Psychiatry 1979;136:555–558.

219. Weissman MM, Klerman GL, et al. Treatment effects on the social adjustment of depressed patients. Arch Gen Psychiatry 1974;30:771–778.

220. Conte HR, Plutchik R, Wild KV, et al. Combined psychotherapy and pharmacotherapy for depression: a systematic analysis of the evidence. Arch Gen Psychiatry 1986;43:471–479.

221. Karasu TB. Toward a clinical model of psy-

chotherapy for depression: systematic comparison of three psychotherapies. Am J Psychiatry 1990;147:133–147.

222. Clarkin JF, Pilkonis PA, Magruder KM. Psychotherapy of depression: implications for reform of the health care system. Arch Gen Psychiatry 1996;53:717–723.

223. Maltsberger JT, Buie DH. Countertransference hate in the treatment of suicidal patients. Arch Gen Psychiatry 1974;30:625–633.

224. Kupfer DJ, Frank E, Perel JM, et al. Five-year outcome for maintenance therapies in recurrent depression. Arch Gen Psychiatry 1992;49:769–773.

225. Clarkin JF, Glick ID, Haas GL. A randomized clinical trial of inpatient family intervention. Part 5: results for affective disorders. J Affect Dis 1990;18:17–28.

226. Glick ID, Burti L, Minakawa K, et al. Effectiveness of psychiatric care. Part 2: outcome for the family after hospital treatment for major affective disorder. Ann Clin Psychiatry 1991;3:187–198.

227. Friedman AS. Interaction of drug therapy with marital therapy in depressive patients. Arch Gen Psychiatry 1975;32:619–637.

228. Tsuang MT, Winokur G, Crowe R. Morbidity risks of schizophrenia and affective disorders among first-degree relatives of patients with schizophrenia, mania, depression and surgical conditions. Br J Psychiatry 1980;137:497–504.

229. Robins E, Guze SB. Classification in affective disorders. In: Williams TA, Katz MM, eds. Recent advances in the psychobiology of the depressive illnesses. Washington, DC: US Government Printing Office, 1972.

230. Keller MB, Shapiro RW, et al. Recovery in major depressive disorder. Arch Gen Psychiatry 1982;39:905–910.

231. Simons AD, Murphy GE, Levine JL. Cognitive therapy and pharmacotherapy for depression: sustained improvement over one year. Arch Gen Psychiatry 1986;43:43–48.

232. Frank E, Kupfer DJ, Perel JM. Early recurrence in unipolar depression. Arch Gen Psychiatry 1989;46:397–400.

233. Miles CP. Conditions predisposing to suicide: a review. J Nerv Ment Dis 1977;164:231–246.

234. Nordentoft M, Breum L, Munck LK, et al. Attempted suicide: are affective disorders missed? Br Med J 1993;307:866.

235. Schatzberg AF, Rothschild AJ. Psychotic (delusional) major depression: should it be included as a distinct syndrome in DSM-IV? Am J Psychiatry 1992;149:733–745.

Chapter 7

Panic and Obsessive-Compulsive Disorders

Patricia A. Harney and James M. Ellison

DEFINITION

Anxiety Disorders and the Sense of Control

Who has not experienced the pangs of anxiety that accompany a real or imagined disaster? Anxiety is a universal and normative experience, yet it also appears in destructive and powerful guises. For many individuals, anxiety's combination of mental and somatic symptoms becomes an internal enemy that threatens normal functioning. This chapter focuses on two common and distinctive anxiety disorders, panic disorder (PD) and obsessive-compulsive disorder (OCD), to illustrate a continuum of biologically based, maladaptive responses to feared or actual loss of control. Individuals predisposed to suffer PD experience and fear the loss of bodily control. Those with OCD, by contrast, experience a sense that their mind is out of control and resort to ritualized thoughts and actions to bind anxiety.

Acute care becomes necessary when anxiety symptoms threaten to overwhelm an individual's preexisting balance of internal and external supports. For PD or OCD patients, previously successful defenses break down, leading to a sense that body and/or mind are out of control. The specific crisis that leads a patient to seek treatment often involves a frustrating impasse, a self-destructive action, or a loss of external supports that has occurred in relation to one or more identifiable stressors. Acute diagnosis is based on the individual's presenting signs and symptoms, understood within the context of personal history, supports, and the acute stressor. Acute treatment does not attempt the definitive cure of an anxiety disorder; rather, acute interventions rely on the identification of specific target problem(s) and the formulation of a corresponding treatment plan. For patients with PD or OCD, the distress of acute anxiety often is relieved by helping a patient mobilize internal resources, limit self-destructive action, and reengage or build external supports. External supports include treatment that is provided at an appropriate level of containment and support. The possible treatment choices include psychotherapy, pharmacotherapy, partial hospitalization, or inpatient care.

DIAGNOSIS

A panic attack is an overwhelming and acute event, experienced in both mind and body. DSM-IV defines a panic attack as developing within approximately 10 minutes, with an escalation of four or more of the following: (*a*) palpitations, pounding heart, or accelerated heart rate; (*b*) sweating; (*c*) trembling or shaking; (*d*) shortness of breath or the sensation of being smothered; (*e*) feelings of choking; (*f*) chest pain or dizziness; (*g*) nausea or abdominal distress; (*h*) derealization; (*i*) fear of losing control or going crazy; (*j*) fear of dying; (*k*) paresthesias; and (*l*) chills or hot flashes (1). For an individual with PD, these symptoms recur without warning. The central experience of PD is repeated loss of control, primarily physical, combined with a fearful anticipation of recurrence of the panic. Avoidant behavior originally aimed at limiting attacks or their consequences can progress to the severe avoidance that characterizes agoraphobia.

Individuals with OCD experience a cognitive rather than somatic loss of control. Their symptoms are repetitive and persistent thoughts, impulses, or images termed obsessions that are experienced as ego-dystonic and cause significant anxiety. The accompanying compulsive behaviors, which can include both repetitive actions or forced mental acts, are believed to represent attempts to limit obsessive thoughts or their feared consequences. Two central diagnostic features are the recognition that the obsessions or compulsions are excessive or unreasonable and that they consume a significant portion of, or significantly interfere with, a person's time or routine. Thus, a central feature of OCD is the distressing experience of repetitive, uncontrollable thoughts, associated with anxious attempts to regain control by means of rigidly defined, time-consuming, mental or physical behaviors (1).

EPIDEMIOLOGY

Approximately 25% of the U.S. population admits to having experienced anxiety at some point in their lives (2). Panic attacks are not uncommon; recent investigations found that 15% of the general U.S. population has experienced at least one panic attack in their lifetimes (3). Current estimates indicate that approximately 1.5% of the general population qualify for a diagnosis of PD (1); women are twice as likely as men to have this disorder (4). The prevalence of PD is similar among African-Americans, Mexican-Americans, and white Americans (5, 6). Educational level is correlated inversely with the occurrence of PD. Individuals with less than 12 years of education are almost 4 times more likely to experience panic attacks and 10 times more likely to suffer from PD than individuals with a college education (3).

The acute assessment of a patient with PD must consider the rate of comorbid mood, other anxiety, personality, and substance abuse disorders. One longitudinal study on the course of PD found that 45% of patients had a lifetime history of major depressive disorder (including 11% with a concurrent episode of major depression), 57% had a comorbid anxiety disorder, and 40% met criteria for a personality disorder (primarily from the "anxious" Cluster C of DSM-IV) (7). Among a group of male inpatient alcoholics, 13% had experienced PD (8). The onset of PD preceded or coincided with the onset of alcoholism in approximately 50% of these subjects. Estimates are that 33–50% of PD patients meet criteria for concurrent agoraphobia (2, 3).

Current estimates of OCD place its prevalence at 2% of the U.S. population (9). An international investigation found similar rates in seven different regions worldwide (10). Although OCD may be slightly more frequent among women (9, 10), the gender-associated differential prevalence is much smaller than that for PD. In the Epidemiological Catchment Area (ECA) study, African-American respondents had significantly lower rates of OCD than did non-Hispanic white American respondents (4). Unemployed persons were more likely than employed individuals to suffer from OCD, and the disorder was much more frequent among divorced or separated individuals (9).

Other mental illnesses may occur with OCD. Among the ECA subjects, 31.7% of individuals with OCD also suffered from a major depressive episode, 13.8% suffered from PD, and 24.1% suffered from alcohol abuse at some point in their lives (9). The majority of individuals with major depression or alcohol abuse developed these disorders after the onset of OCD.

THE FOUR QUESTIONS

Descriptive and Differential Diagnosis

Differential diagnosis, the process by which a specific disorder is diagnosed while other similar conditions are ruled out, is critical to focused and effective acute care. When assessing patients with PD or OCD symptoms, the clinician must consider not only the other syndromes that resemble these disorders, but the possible presence of one or more comorbid anxiety, mood, or medical disorders that would complicate treatment.

In addition to PD and OCD, the DSM-IV includes the following syndromes within the category of anxiety disorders: acute stress disorder, agoraphobia without history of PD, generalized anxiety disorder, posttraumatic stress disorder, specific phobia, social phobia, anxiety disorder due to a medical condition, substance-induced anxiety disorder, and anxiety disorder not otherwise specified. A related syndrome from the adjustment disorder category, adjustment disorder with anxiety, is differentiated from the primary anxiety disorders by its clear relationship to acute stress and time-limited symptoms.

All anxiety disorders have in common the subjective experience of anxiety or fear, although some OCD patients appear to feel little overt anxiety as long as they are able to experience their obsessions or perform their compulsions. Anxiety disorders differ in the extent to which anxiety or fear become generalized over time and in relation to external events. Generalized anxiety disorder (GAD), for instance, may lack a "precipitating event" and may involve worry about several different aspects of life, whereas acute stress disorder may be clearly related to a particular experience and may be associated with specific worries. GAD symptoms might intensify or wax and wane over time, whereas acute stress disorder symptoms might decrease over a brief period. Specific phobia is a fear of a particular stimulus; exposure to the stimulus results in a near-immediate experience of intense anxiety. Agoraphobia involves the fear of panic-like symptoms; individuals who suffer from this disorder often severely restrict their lives to avoid the onset of distressing symptoms. Social phobia involves the fear of social situations that may result in embarrassment; individuals with social phobia typically avoid situations that may evoke anxiety (1). In differentiating these disorders from PD and OCD, clinicians should consider the patient's baseline level of functioning, any identifiable internal or external stressors (including loss of supports), any preexisting pattern of anxiety, and the mental and physical behaviors associated with the anxiety.

Anxiety as a nonspecific symptom can also accompany a range of medical disorders. The acute care clinician should take care not to overlook the syndrome of anxiety disorder due to a general medical condition. Prominent medical disorders with panic-like anxiety include diabetes mellitus with hypoglycemia, agitation, and restlessness; hyperthyroidism with cardiac symptoms, motor restlessness, and psychic anxiety; primary cardiac disorders, especially arrhythmias, with palpitations and anxiety (11); and limbic seizures with alterations of autonomic function and affect. Substance-related anxiety symptoms can occur with the ingestion of excessive caffeine or other stimulants or with a reduction in alcohol use or sedative-hypnotic medications (12). Antipsychotic medications and some antidepressants can produce a syndrome of restless legs and anxiety, termed akathisia.

Clinicians should conduct or request a thorough medical examination to rule out metabolic, endocrine, cardiorespiratory, neurologic, or toxic anxiety contributions to symptoms (12). Such an examination should include the patient's personal and family history and a focused physical examination that measures vital signs and searches for stigmata of substance abuse. Patients should be questioned carefully about their use of prescription or illicit substances, including stimulating herbal or homeopathic preparations. Toxic screens should be requested as appropriate, with recognition of their limitations.

In clinical practice that requires the needs of a previously unfamiliar patient to be deciphered quickly, assessment is complicated further by comorbidity with complex syndromal concatenations. Primary anxiety disorders can be interlaced with other disorders that worsen anxiety or develop as a consequence of anxiety. For example, a male with a history of panic attacks experienced a worsening of symptoms when his primary care physician prescribed a stimulating decongestant to relieve congestion from an upper respiratory infection. When insomnia and increased restlessness resulted in an excessive use of alcohol, he and his family became alarmed, and he abruptly stopped drinking. By the time he presented at the emergency room in acute alcohol withdrawal, a thorough inquiry was needed to understand all the components of his anxiety.

Because somatic fears and preoccupations are present in many anxiety disorders, determining the presence of PD or OCD in somatically preoccupied patients presents a diagnostic challenge. In general, the presence of compulsive physical behaviors or mental acts distinguishes OCD from other anxiety disorders (13), and the presence or fear of panic attacks suggests the presence of PD. A patient who complains of a persistent fear of cancer may be understood to suffer from OCD if the intrusive thoughts about cancer are accompanied by checking behaviors (e.g., checking of lymph nodes).

The range of possible compulsions is nearly unlimited, and many patients are only partly aware of the extent of their compulsions. A careful inquiry should seek to identify the patient's principal, repetitive, anxiety-binding maneuvers. The typology of "core features" of OCD developed by Rasmussen and Eisen (13) is a useful framework for identifying various OCD subsyndromes. This typology also may provide clues about the likelihood of a comorbid anxiety or tic disorder. Individuals who persistently obsess about a "one-in-a-million" calamity are particularly likely to appear very anxious and to suffer from a comorbid anxiety disorder. Those whose symptoms are organized around perfectionism and balancing (e.g., making sure objects on a desk are arranged in an even and symmetrical manner) appear less anxious and are more likely to suffer from tic disorders (13, 14). Whether these subtypes are useful in predicting differential treatment response has not been established and requires further study.

Neuropsychiatric Components of PD and OCD

PD and OCD are considered to have strong neuropsychiatric roots, although no biologic test is available for practical diagnostic use. Data supporting biologic hypotheses for PD and OCD derive from a variety of sources, including familial, biochemical, and neuroimaging studies. Popp et al. (15) have reviewed this area in more detail. The neuropsychiatric data on PD and OCD need not suggest the primacy of biologic treatments.

Familial studies suggest a 10-fold increase in PD (41% vs. 4% in controls) among the first-degree relatives of PD subjects (16). A sample of monozygotic twin pairs were concordant for PD five times as frequently as they were for GAD (17). Perhaps the most convincing line of evidence demonstrating the biologic nature of PD, however, derives successful efforts to reproduce attacks in susceptible individuals under controlled laboratory conditions by means of biochemical probes. Intravenous infusion of DL-lactate solution (18), inhalation of air enriched with CO_2, and oral administration of caffeine or yohimbine are well studied

means of inducing panic symptoms (19). Positron emission tomography (PET) scans of PD patients' brains during lactate-induced attacks or anticipatory states suggest specific dysfunctional areas of the limbic system (20, 21). Animal studies also suggest the importance of locus ceruleus noradrenergic activity in panic (22).

Familial studies on OCD also demonstrate an unexpectedly high prevalence among first-degree relatives of identified patients (20–25% affected with the disorder). Concordance among monozygotic twin pairs is greater than in dizygotic twin pairs (23). Neuropsychiatric investigations of OCD have focused on the importance of serotonergic neurotransmission. The strongest evidence in support of a serotonergic mechanism is the consistent observation of positive clinical effects produced by serotonergic antidepressants (24, 25). Less consistent data derive from studies of pharmacologic probes (26) and from PET scan findings of a dysfunctional prefrontal cortex/basal ganglia/thalamic circuit (27).

Psychodynamic and Interpersonal Components of PD and OCD

Traditional psychodynamic perspectives on PD and OCD regard these disorders as expressions of disavowed, repressed, or denied affects that are barred from an individual's conscious experience and replaced by symptoms of anxiety (28, 29). PD has been viewed as a consequence of loss and unresolved separation anxiety (29, 30). A study investigating the relationship between psychosocial stress and the onset of PD reported that PD patients experienced a significantly greater number of stressful events in the year before illness onset than did control subjects

(31). A study on twins revealed that adult women who experienced the death of or separation from a parent before age 17 were significantly more likely to suffer from PD than women who did not have similar experiences (32). Separation anxiety may be a persistent, if unconscious, concern of PD patients. Support for this hypothesis is provided by a study that compared the thematic content of dreams reported by panic and nonpanic subjects. The dreams of panic patients were significantly more likely to contain themes of separation anxiety and covert hostility than those of nonpanic patients (28). The disturbing emergence of these themes into consciousness during a panic attack provides a psychodynamic explanation of the PD patient's subjective experience of impending disaster or imminent loss of control (33).

Although repression or denial of unacceptable affects may limit the experience and expression of anxiety, reliance on these defenses can also generate additional negative affects. Anticipatory anxiety (fear of the next panic attack) is a cardinal feature of PD; moreover, the repeated experience of panic attacks may foster a generalized sense of helplessness. Loss of self-esteem results when hopelessness and loss of a sense of mastery in the world occur (34). The avoidance of anxiety can lead PD patients to restrict their emotional experience in general (34).

According to classical psychoanalytic theory, OCD originates in early life when issues of autonomy and control are paramount (24, 35). According to this view, hostile impulses emerge toward parents who intrude on the developing self. These unacceptable impulses are warded off by obsessive and compulsive defenses that include magical thinking (as manifested in mental rituals or ritualistic behavior) and doing and undoing. Although this formulation regards compulsive rituals as expressions of unconscious rage and enables clinicians to be aware of patient's conscious or unconscious anger, current research strongly suggests that OCD is most practically understood as a neuropsychiatric disorder (36) with affective and relational consequences that help to determine treatment choices.

Compulsive rituals cause individuals to feel a loss of control over their will and behavior; OCD patients often describe the feelings of shame that derive from hiding ritualistic behaviors and from actually failing to fulfill necessary obligations as a result of time-consuming symptoms. The reactions of significant others can adversely affect the patient and the course of the disorder. Conversely, family members' accommodation of a patient's obsessive-compulsive symptoms can produce secondary emotional stress in them that may undermine the patient's social support network (37). Negative attitudes held by family members can have a poor effect on patient symptoms (38).

Contrary to common belief, obsessive-compulsive personality disorder (OCPD) does not commonly co-occur with OCD. Results from empiric investigations suggest that the rate of OCPD among OCD patients is approximately 6% (35). Unlike OCD, OCPD is characterized by persistent perfectionism and rigidity in social and occupational functioning. DSM-IV designates the following characteristics as possible manifestations of this personality disorder: preoccupation with details, order, and organization to the extent that the main point of the activity is lost; perfectionism that hinders task completion; overinvolvement in work with consequent neglect of relationships; excessive conscientiousness and rigidity in moral structure; tendency to hoard useless items; difficulty working collaboratively with others; stinginess; and stubbornness (1). Also unlike OCD, OCPD has not been found to respond specifically to pharmacotherapy; instead, psychodynamically oriented psychotherapy has been suggested as the treatment of choice (35).

Formulation

To understand the symptoms of acute panic or obsessive-compulsive anxiety, clinicians should consider the impact of current stressors on an individual's specific biopsychosocial vulnerabilities. A challenge to the individual's level of control in a given situation frequently exacerbates PD or OCD symptoms. Stresses that may threaten a person's sense of control include a threat to employment, the onset of a physical illness, or the disruption of an interpersonal relationship. Limited internal coping skills and/or external supports render an individual more vulnerable.

Although many individuals seek evaluation for anxiety-related symptoms, relatively few present in an acute crisis necessitating intervention beyond outpatient psychotherapy and pharmacotherapy. The following case example illustrates how individual vulnerabilities interacted with psychosocial factors, resulting in a need for more intensive acute intervention.

□ **C A S E   E X A M P L E**

Ms. B, a 30-year-old woman, had attended individual psychotherapy sessions with an exploratory and insight-oriented focus for approximately 1 year. She had marital problems and was the child of an alcoholic. In the course of her psychotherapy, Ms. B recognized the correspondence between the behaviors of her alcoholic husband and her alcoholic father, whose death had bereaved her during her childhood. When she confronted her husband about his alcohol abuse, he denied any difficulties and refused to limit his intake of alcohol. Soon afterward, the couple argued more frequently, and Ms. B experienced the onset of panic attacks. Eight months after Ms. B first confronted her husband, he moved out of their home. At that time, her anxiety symptoms worsened to the extent that she could no longer attend work regularly. Eventually, she requested a medical leave. Her psychotherapist referred her to a psychiatrist, who prescribed a low dose of lorazepam. Although medication provided limited relief, Ms. B's panic attacks increased in both frequency and intensity after her husband filed for divorce. When she developed suicidal thoughts, her psychotherapist referred her for emergency evaluation, requesting inpatient admission.

Ms. B's progressive loss of control over her life was paralleled by loss of control over her physiologic responses. A perceived need for hospital care occurred when the threat of divorce and loss of external supports led to intolerable hopelessness.

The Focal Problem

Ms. B's path to the hospital demonstrates how the experience of feeling out of control can result in a need for intensive containment. Perhaps, however, hospitalization could have been averted with early treatment that addressed her internal resources (strengths and vulnerabilities), the precipitating stressors, and alternate environmental supports. Progressive loss of control was her central experience. Psychotherapy with behavioral training (e.g., relaxation training or exposure with response prevention) might have restored her sense of stability. Support for her marital difficulties might have come from attendance at Al-Anon meetings or involvement of her husband in psychotherapy sessions for couples. Also, the use of a medication with more specific antipanic effects likely could have helped arrest the progression of her symptoms.

The approach of Harper (39) of focusing on acute stressors and supports rather than simply on diagnosis has been termed formulation of the focal problem. He recommends that the clinician identify the circumstances that differentiate one patient from others with the same diagnosis. The clinician should ask, for example, "Why is this patient with PD in the emergency room when other individuals with PD are not?" Because the focal problem involves the failure of internal and/or external resources, the clinician should seek ways to help the patient resolve immobilization, limit self-destructive activity, promote self-constructive behaviors, and engage social supports. In broadest terms, the goal of acute care is the resolution of the focal problem.

This approach to treatment planning is easily adapted to the acute assessment of an anxious patient in crisis. The focal problem brings the person to assessment at a particular time; its resolution should alleviate the acute crisis, although further assessment or treatment may be valuable in achieving longer-term goals. In Ms. B's case, the focal problem of her crisis could be stated as "suicidal ideation and escalating panic attacks precipitated by the threat of divorce." Her internal resources were compromised by her illness (PD), a dependent personality style, and her limited capacity to bear separation anxiety. Her external supports were compromised by

the limited focus of her psychotherapy on her anxiety symptoms, the nonspecific pharmacotherapy regimen, and the financial and relational losses associated with her medical leave from work. Intensive treatment of her anxiety, guided by the formulation of a focal problem and an emphasis on reestablishing her sense of control, could provide her with anxiety management behavioral techniques, control her panic pharmacologically, mobilize her back into work, and reconnect her with essential financial and social supports.

ASSESSING LEVEL OF CARE

The appropriate level of treatment is determined, as illustrated in the care of Ms. B, on the basis of a patient's focal problem, internal resources, psychosocial supports, and acute change in functioning. When available, the effects of past and current treatment interventions provide important information for treatment planning. Occasionally, no treatment beyond a reassuring assessment is the appropriate intervention. Treatment, however, usually requires outpatient psychotherapy and/or pharmacotherapy, partial hospitalization, or occasionally inpatient hospitalization.

In contrast to depression, in which suicidal or psychotic behaviors may make inpatient care necessary, hospitalization of patients with anxiety disorders more typically occurs when patients become unable to care for basic survival needs. In these patients, the recurrence of panic attacks has become overwhelming or all available time is consumed in the performance of compulsive behaviors. Suicide is a possible risk in either PD or OCD, but the crisis is more frequently functional paralysis.

When acute risk of harm to self or

other is identified, treatment must offer protection. The presence of suicidal or homicidal ideation alone, however, does not determine whether an actual risk is present. PD patients, for example, often fear imminent death. OCD patients can harbor a fear that they will kill themselves or another person. Therefore, the emergency clinician must consider whether a rapid increase in support to the patient might improve his or her ability to manage suicidal or homicidal ideation. Ms. B felt so completely alone in her distress that she feared she might impulsively and violently harm herself, despite a wish to remain alive. Because she possessed significant internal resources (e.g., the capacity to form a therapeutic alliance), some external supports (a home and a job to which she could return), and no history of impulsive, self-destructive actions, Ms. B was able to bypass inpatient care and enter directly into a partial hospitalization program. The rapid implementation of this plan helped to contain Ms. B's anxiety and alleviate her functional paralysis. She received individual and group psychotherapy and met with a psychopharmacologist for medication reassessment. Ms. B felt less isolated and was able to use therapeutic support to practice anxiety management techniques. With increased social support and reduced anxiety, Ms. B was able to plan a strategy to cope with her financial stress. A greater sense of mastery enabled her to return to outpatient psychotherapy and to experience safely and integrate her feelings about divorce. Attendance at Al-Anon meetings provided additional support.

TREATMENT

The acute treatment of anxiety disorders is targeted toward identifying and enhancing a person's internal resources and external supports to restore a sense of control and to alleviate the reaction to an acute stressor. To achieve these goals, pharmacotherapy, psychoeducation, and psychotherapy (e.g., individual, couples, family, or group) can be prescribed according to the needs of each patient. The treatments reviewed in this section may be undertaken in inpatient, outpatient, or partial hospital settings. The patient's length of stay in an acute care setting will affect the particular treatment goals that can be accomplished, however, and certain treatment combinations may be appropriate to ensure a more graceful transition between various levels of care. For example, a patient might begin a 10-week outpatient therapy group during a 1-week inpatient admission to allow for continued support while he or she copes with transitions to a lesser level of care.

Psychopharmacologic Management

The pharmacotherapy of an acutely anxious patient should be organized to maximize autonomy, giving the patient as much control as possible. To this end, the clinician can emphasize, from the start, that the use of medications is voluntary and that the most frequent side effects, should they occur, are usually mild and reversible. Patients frequently ask whether medications will be required permanently, and the clinician can respond reassuringly that a significant number of patients are able to taper or discontinue medications after acute symptoms are adequately controlled. The involvement of family members in psychoeducational discussions may be particularly important in PD and OCD because familial support and understanding can help patients with these disorders to control their anxieties about medications. Although a recommendation of pharmacotherapy during the initial evaluation is a common practice, some highly anxious patients may comply more wholeheartedly if the initial visit is devoted to history-taking, alliance-building, psychoeducation, and a discussion of the full range of treatment options. Differential diagnostic considerations can be reviewed, discussions with other relevant care givers can occur, and appropriate laboratory results and medical records can be obtained before the follow-up visit when pharmacotherapy can be initiated. Pharmacotherapy initiated during a follow-up visit often conveys that the clinician better understands the nature and extent of the patient's difficulties. This is especially important with the somatically preoccupied individual who may be convinced that a serious and life-threatening physical condition was overlooked as the result of a clinician's hasty psychiatric diagnosis.

Panic Disorder

The pharmacotherapy of PD, which includes a broad range of options previously reviewed elsewhere (40), will be summarized briefly in this chapter with an emphasis on acute care. Patients who present with extreme or intolerable distress can be treated initially with a high-potency benzodiazepine (e.g., alprazolam or clonazepam) to alleviate symptoms rapidly. This practice provides prompt relief, often within hours, yet carries an important potential drawback. Patients who experience symptom relief and desire to discontinue their medication often find it more difficult to discontinue a benzodiazepine than an antidepressant. Rebound interdose anxiety, especially pronounced with the shorter-acting alprazolam, may be partly responsible for patients' difficulties

in tapering a benzodiazepine because the symptoms of withdrawal resemble panic. Some cognitive behavior therapists prefer that patients receiving combined therapy use a nonbenzodiazepine medication, if any at all, to avoid an extreme blockade of the anxiety response that must be elicited under controlled conditions during the process of behavioral treatment. Briefly, a benzodiazepine may help a PD patient regain control more quickly over his or her symptoms, but it may reduce the eventual achievement of a sense of mastery due to rebound anxiety and potential interference with cognitive behavior therapy (CBT).

When benzodiazepines are used, alprazolam therapy can be initiated at a dosage of 0.5 mg twice a day and titrated rapidly to within the 2–6 mg/day range. Divided dosing (three to four times a day) is often necessary to avoid interdose rebound anxiety. Because clonazepam is slower to reach a steady-state serum level, care must be taken to avoid titrating the dose upward too quickly. The dose range for clonazepam of 1–4 mg/day is adequate for the majority of patients. Twice-daily dosing usually is adequate to maintain a steady anxiolytic effect.

Antidepressants, in contrast, can take longer to work and often are associated with unpleasant physical side effects; however, they are effective antipanic agents, with the exception of bupropion and probably trazodone. Imipramine has been well studied and achieves effects comparable to those of alprazolam. Other tricyclic antidepressants (TCAs) may be preferred for specific patients on the basis of their side effect profiles. Desipramine, for example, has less pronounced anticholinergic effects than imipramine, and dosage should be started at a low level, even as low as imipramine at 10–25 mg/day, to allow the patient's accommodation to side effects. Autonomy can be enhanced by permitting the patient to increase the daily dosage as desired within a predefined range. Final effective doses often are low compared with those required in the treatment of depression, but studies correlating blood levels with treatment response indicate that antidepression dosage levels may be necessary (41).

Currently, many clinicians begin treatment of PD with one of the serotonin reuptake inhibitors (SRIs). Studies suggest the effectiveness of fluvoxamine, fluoxetine, sertraline, and paroxetine, and anecdotal reports exist for venlafaxine and nefazodone. As with the TCAs, the patient's acceptance of treatment and sense of control can be supported by starting with a low dose and allowing the patient to titrate within predefined limits. The following dosages are recommended: fluvoxamine can be started at 50 mg/day, fluoxetine at 5 to 10 mg/day, sertraline at 25 mg/day, paroxetine at 10 mg/day, venlafaxine at 12.5 mg/day, and nefazodone at 25–50 mg/day. When restlessness or akathisia are prominent reactions or when greater acute relief of anxiety is essential, the temporary use of an adjunctive high-potency benzodiazepine can help a patient tolerate the initial weeks of antidepressant treatment. As with TCA treatment, the final treatment SRI dose can range from relatively low doses to full antidepression levels.

The monoamine oxidase inhibitors (MAOIs) are recognized as highly effective antipanic agents, but are rarely the first-line choice in view of the availability of other effective medications with more acceptable side effect profiles. MAOIs should be considered as a treatment option in patients refractory to the other classes of antipanic medications. Other interventions in treatment-resistant PD patients include the augmentation of a TCA, SRI, or high-potency benzodiazepine with propranolol, buspirone, lithium, or valproic acid (40).

PD follows a chronic course in many patients, suggesting that repeated episodes of therapy or prolonged maintenance treatment will be necessary for some. The issues relevant to long-term treatment with antidepressants or high-potency benzodiazepines are an ongoing area of discussion (42, 43). Many patients discontinue TCAs because of the side effects, particularly overstimulation, weight gain, and anticholinergic effects (42). Long-term follow-up data on the antipanic use of serotonergic antidepressants are not yet available. Although many patients and clinicians fear long-term use of benzodiazepines because of their alleged addictive potential, abuse is a risk primarily among individuals who abuse other drugs (44); in fact, with many patients doses decrease over the continuation of treatment (43).

Discontinuation of high-potency benzodiazepines should be handled carefully because of the similarity between withdrawal symptoms and panic. In a study of PD patients who were taking alprazolam at an average daily dose greater than 5 mg/day for an average of 7 months, a 1-month tapering schedule succeeded in only 4 of 18 patients. An additional four patients successfully stopped taking alprazolam over several months (45). Concurrent cognitive behavior psychotherapy may facilitate PD patients' discontinuation of a benzodiazpine (46).

Obsessive-Compulsive Disorder

The pharmacotherapy of OCD, reviewed recently by Sherman et al. (47), is based primarily on the use of serotonergic antidepressants. Whereas medicating OCD is often an uncomplicated process, several important differences exist between this process and the treatment of PD. Although many clinicians believe that doses higher than those given for antidepression are needed to achieve the optimal response in OCD, this point is controversial (25). Furthermore, trials of medication often must be relatively prolonged (e.g., 10–12 weeks) to avoid discarding a potentially effective regimen (48). An SRI trial with fluoxetine, sertraline, fluvoxamine, or paroxetine is often the initial choice. When this treatment is ineffective, a switch to clomipramine may be successful. Some clinicians find it helpful to combine an SRI with clomipramine (24), although careful consideration then must be given to the danger of producing a toxic clomipramine level through SRI inhibition of the cytochrome P-450 enzyme system.

In patients who fail to respond to fluoxetine monotherapy, the addition of the 5-HT agonist buspirone, at a dosage of 10 mg, three times a day, has been reported as helpful (49). Buspirone augmentation is recommended on the basis of anecdotal evidence for patients resistant to the antiobsessional effects of other medications; however, controlled trials of augmentation have shown mixed results (25). Fenfluramine, a medication that increases serotonin release and blocks its presynaptic uptake, enhanced treatment effectiveness at doses ranging from 20 to 60 mg/day in seven treatment-resistant OCD patients (50). Further studies must address the acute and long-term risks of fenfluramine, given evidence of neurotoxicity in animals (25). A study of a group of patients who derived benefit from the addition of a neuroleptic to fluvoxamine (51) suggests the possibility that some patients who demonstrate schizotypal personality traits or the presence of tics may benefit from the addition of a neuroleptic to their serotonergic antidepressant.

Like PD, OCD is a long-term disorder that produces intermittent symptomatic episodes in most patients. The first goal of pharmacotherapy is to establish relief of acute symptoms. Patients can then consider the value of maintenance treatment.

Alliance, Psychotherapeutic Management, and Family Support and Education

Among the various psychotherapies recommended for PD, CBT approaches have been researched most fully. Psychoeducation, relaxation training, cognitive restructuring, and exposure therapy each can have a role in treatment. One psychotherapeutic approach directed specifically at PD symptom abatement, panic control treatment, has been developed by Barlow (52). In panic control treatment, instruction in anxiety-reducing techniques is combined with exposure of the patient to feared somatic experiences. When successful, this treatment fosters a sense of mastery over previously fear-inducing sensations. Panic control treatment was found to be more effective than general relaxation techniques in a controlled treatment outcome study (52). This treatment also has impressive long-term benefits. In a 2-year follow-up study (53), patients who received panic control treatment were significantly more likely to remain panic free than patients who used nonspecific relaxation techniques.

Several studies have examined the relative effects of pharmacotherapy and CBT on PD. In one investigation, patients were randomly assigned to one of three treatment conditions—fluvoxamine, CBT, or placebo—and those patients who received fluvoxamine had greater symptom improvement than patients in the CBT or placebo groups (54). More recent studies have demonstrated that combined treatment approaches are more effective than the application of any single treatment. In a study of patients with PD and agoraphobia, those who received fluvoxamine and exposure in vivo treatment showed significantly greater symptom reduction than patients who received either treatment alone (55). CBT may enhance the long-term benefits of treatment and facilitate discontinuation of medication. One study found that patients who received CBT in addition to alprazolam were significantly less likely to use alprazolam again after discontinuation (56).

Although no known well-designed, controlled investigations have compared the efficacy of psychodynamically oriented psychotherapy with CBT for PD, the latter generally is considered to be the non-pharmacotherapeutic treatment of choice because of the empiric evidence of its efficacy (53, 57). Several researchers have noted that the unconscious meaning of particular psychosocial stressors may play a role in the etiology of panic (29), which raises questions about the potential benefit of psychodynamic treatment for PD. Gabbard (29) suggests that dynamic treatment may be useful for patients who are especially psychologically minded or are opposed to medications or behavior therapy.

Psychodynamic treatment may be helpful, particularly when panic attacks occur in an individual with a personality disorder. A recent case report describes a 23-year-old woman with PD who was treated solely with psychodynamically oriented psychotherapy. Within 2 months of individual treatment, twice weekly, the panic attacks ceased (58). The investigators hypothesize that the panic attacks resolved when the patient could tolerate and express in the therapeutic relationship feelings of rage that previously had been split off. The ability to tolerate and express these feelings may have enhanced the patient's sense of mastery and control as well as an understanding of the precipitants that triggered the panic attacks. The

length of time over which these attacks resolved (8 weeks) does not differ significantly from the treatment duration often used in studies of CBT. Moreover, the treatment aspects that may have facilitated change in this patient's PD (e.g., understanding the precipitants to panic, accepting and tolerating the feelings) may be similar to the basic goals of CBT. In this case, psychodynamic psychotherapy continued beyond the resolution of PD to facilitate characterologic change.

The most successful form of CBT for OCD is exposure with response prevention. Some investigators believe that pharmacotherapy can further enhance treatment response (59). Exposure treatment involves having the person with OCD make contact with the feared stimulus (e.g., dirt, mud). The person is then prevented from engaging in compulsive behavior and thus develops a tolerance for the anxiety provoked by the stimulus. With practice, the stimulus no longer produces the same degree of anxiety. This form of treatment also has impressive long-term benefits; follow-up studies have found that the majority of patients maintain a reduction in symptoms for several years (36).

Although exposure with response prevention may be the most effective single tool for altering the symptoms of OCD, other interventions contribute to a successful treatment. Thorough education about OCD and CBT may be necessary to increase patient's confidence in a successful outcome, despite a very painful process. Engaging family members in the treatment also may increase patient compliance, particularly during in vivo practice sessions when a therapist may not be present (59). Sherman et al. (47) also recommended a discussion of "relapse prevention" in the course of psychoeducation. These authors noted that it may be especially helpful for OCD individuals, who may have "black-or-white" cognitive styles, to learn to regard relapses as "slips" that do not connote ultimate failure.

Compared with PD, OCD is regarded as more clearly linked with a pathologic neuropsychiatric diathesis, although the pathophysiology of this disorder is not yet fully established. Because intrapsychic conflicts and disturbing affects are considered less central to the etiology of OCD, psychodynamically oriented psychotherapy is not regarded as a primary treatment modality for OCD (36). Dynamic psychotherapy may be helpful to individuals who suffer from OCD if the treatment goal is something other than relief from obsessive-compulsive symptoms. Moreover, psychodynamically oriented treatment may be useful to individuals with OCPD. Because OCPD is not particularly amenable to pharmacotherapy or behavior therapy (35), the syndrome may be etiologically distinct from OCD.

Although the treatment of PD and OCD appears to be most effective when both psychotherapy and pharmacotherapy are included, clinicians should recognize that the addition of a treatment modality is not equivalent to its integration into a treatment plan. As mentioned previously, several studies indicate that the long-term benefits of combined treatment are significantly greater than psychotherapy or pharmacotherapy alone. However, patient ability or desire to engage in a combined treatment approach varies. Some patients may consider pharmacotherapy alone to be more expedient, and the reduction of symptoms can lessen such a patient's motivation to engage in the psychotherapeutic work that would reduce risk of relapse following a medication taper. Other patients may be significantly less interested in medication and desire a strict course of behavioral treatment, yet may be unable to

make progress until the intensity of their anxiety has diminished. Ongoing psychoeducation, active collaboration between pharmacologist and psychotherapist, and supportive attention to individual fears should increase a patient's ability to benefit from a combined treatment approach.

CONTROVERSIES IN THE CARE OF PD AND OCD

Two controversies in the treatment of PD and OCD will be discussed. First, clinicians frequently dispute whether a cognitive behavior or a pharmacotherapeutic intervention is more effective. Second, both clinicians and patients often ask whether long-term dangers attend the prolonged use of pharmacotherapeutic agents.

The choice between behavioral and pharmacotherapeutic interventions may be more of an imagined than real dilemma. Considerable data support the efficacy of each treatment approach independently, and the combination may confer additional benefits, as noted previously. Pharmacotherapy of PD or OCD typically establishes a more rapid response but may be accompanied by side effects and an increased risk of relapse after discontinuation. CBT is slower to take effect but may enhance a patient's sense of control and autonomy. In clinical practice, many patients prefer to simplify treatment and reduce the initial investment of their resources by starting with either medication or psychotherapy, but not both. The psychotherapist who offers CBT, however, should incorporate a psychoeducational discussion of pharmacotherapy, and a pharmacotherapist should inform patients about the nature and availability of CBT. Many pharmacotherapists may encourage a patient to avoid withdrawal from potentially stressful circumstances and may support self-paced exposure through instruction in a relaxation technique. The decision regarding the initial choices of approaches rests especially with a patient's preferences and available treatment programs.

The controversy regarding long-term treatment risks takes on a different character when reframed in the context of the chronicity of PD and OCD. When untreated, each disorder confers significant morbidity and even disability. PD has been linked with increased rates of suicide (2) and increased use of medical services (60). Relapse rates after discontinuation of pharmacotherapy, although probably lower when adjunctive CBT is offered, are nonetheless significant (see below). Clinicians should consider the risk/benefit balance between treated and untreated anxiety, rather than simply the problem of long-term treatment and the consequent avoidance of medication.

COURSE AND PROGNOSIS

Although short-term pharmacotherapy of PD is effective in reducing symptoms, the longer-term course of PD typically is marked by relapse and recurrence. Data suggest that 30–75% of acutely treated patients experience continued panic attacks and/or phobic avoidance, whereas longitudinal studies find persistent anxiety symptoms in 50–80% patients (40). Relapse rates after discontinuation of antidepressants can exceed 50% (61), and the rates of relapse are thought to be even greater after discontinuation of benzodiazepine (62). These statistics support the findings of long-term follow-up of PD patients indicating that 50–78% of patients received continued pharmacotherapy after acute treatment (40).

As with PD, OCD has a relapsing course. Approximately 50% of patients will respond to acute pharmacotherapy, but the relapse rate is high. One study, observed relapse within 7 weeks of clomipramine discontinuation in nearly 90% of successfully treated OCD patients (63). Relapse rates have been lower in controlled studies of combined pharmacotherapy with CBT (64, 65), again suggesting the importance of a combined approach when feasible.

CONCLUSION

PD and OCD can evoke enormous distress, morbidity, and dysfunction. Central to the acute manifestations of each disorder is the feeling of being out of control, physically and mentally. Many individuals with anxiety disorders do not seek treatment, but acute intervention often becomes necessary when disruption creates an imbalance between an individual's internal resources and external supports. An acute stressor often precipitates the disruption by emphasizing the loss of control.

In such cases, acute treatment should be guided by a careful formulation of a focal problem. The goal of acute treatment is to restore the individual's equilibrium by bolstering internal resources and/or creating additional external supports. Acute care can be provided in various levels of care, often combining verbal with pharmacotherapeutic interventions. When rapid, focused, and effective care is offered during a time of crisis, anxious individuals can increase their ability to cope and improve their sense of physical and mental control.

REFERENCES

1. American Psychiatric Association. Diagnostic and statistical manual of mental disorders. 4th ed. Washington, DC: American Psychiatric Association, 1994.

2. Weissman MM. Panic disorder: epidemiology and genetics. In: Wolfe BE, Maser JD, eds. Treatment of panic disorder: a consensus development conference. Washington, DC: American Psychiatric Press, 1994.

3. Eaton WW, Kessler RC, Wittchen HU, et al. Panic and panic disorder in the United States. Am J Psychiatry 1994;151:413–420.

4. Reiger DA, Boyd JH, Burke JD, et al. One-month prevalence of mental disorders in the United States: based on five epidemiologic catchment area sites. Arch Gen Psychiatry 1988;45:977–986.

5. Horwath E, Johnson J, Hornig CD. Epidemiology of panic disorder in African-Americans. Am J Psychiatry 1993;150:465–469.

6. Karno M, Golding JM, Burnam MA, et al. Anxiety disorders among Mexican Americans and non-Hispanic whites in Los Angeles. J Nerv Ment Dis 1989;177:202–209.

7. Pollack MH, Otto MW, Sachs GS, et al. Anxiety psychopathology predictive of outcome in patients with panic disorder and depression treated with imipramine, alprazolam and placebo. J Affect Dis 1990;30:273–281.

8. Johannessen DJ, Cowley DS, Walker RD, et al. Prevalence, onset, and clinical recognition of panic states in hospitalized male alcoholics. Am J Psychiatry 1989;146:1201–1203.

9. Karno M, Golding JM, Sorenson SB, et al. The epidemiology of obsessive-compulsive disorder in five US communities. Arch Gen Psychiatry 1988;45:450–457.

10. Weissman MM, Bland RC, Canino GJ, et al. The cross national epidemiology of obsessive compulsive disorder. J Clin Psychiatry 1994;55:5–10.

11. Walker JI. The anxious patient. In: Walker JI, ed. Psychiatric emergencies: intervention and resolution. Philadelphia: JB Lippincott, 1983.

12. Pfaelzer C, Ellison JM, Popp S. Panic disorder: pharmacotherapy in integrative treatment. In: Ellison JM, ed. Integrative treatment of anxiety disorders. Washington, DC: American Psychiatric Press, 1996.

13. Rasmussen SA Eisen JL. The epidemiology and differential diagnosis of obsessive compulsive disorder. J Clin Psychiatry 1992;53(Suppl):4–10.

14. Baer L. Factor analysis of symptom subtypes of obsessive-compulsive disorder and their relation to personality and tic disorders. J Clin Psychiatry 1994;55:11–23.

15. Popp S, Ellison JM, Reeves P. Neuropsychiatry of the anxiety disorders. In: Ellison JM, Weinstein CS, Hodel-Malinofsky T, eds. The psychotherapist's guide to neuropsychiatry: diagnostic and treatment issues. Washington, DC: American Psychiatric Press, 1994.

16. Crowe RR, Noyes R, Pauls DL, et al. A family study of panic disorder. Arch Gen Psychiatry 1983;40:1065–1069.

17. Uhde TW, Nemiah JC. Anxiety disorders [anxiety and phobic neuroses]. In: Kaplan HI, Sadock BJ, eds. Comprehensive textbook of psychiatry. 5th ed. Baltimore: Williams & Wilkins, 1989.

18. Cowley DS, Arana GW. The diagnostic utility of lactate sensitivity in panic disorder. Arch Gen Psychiatry 1990;47:277–284.

19. Nutt D, Lawson C. Panic attacks: a neurochemical overview of models and mechanisms. Br J Psychiatry 1992;160:165–178.

20. Reiman EM, Raichle ME, Robins E, et al. Neuroanatomical correlates of a lactate-induced anxiety attack. Arch Gen Psychiatry 1989;46:493–500.

21. Reiman EM, Fusselman MJ, Fox PT, et al. Neuroanatomical correlates of anticipatory anxiety. Science 1989;243:1071–1074.

22. Charney DS, Woods SW, Nagy LM, et al. Noradrenergic function in panic disorder. J Clin Psychiatry 1990;51(Suppl):5–11.

23. Baxter LR Jr, Schartz JM, Guze BH, et al. PET imaging in obsessive compulsive disorder with and without depression. J Clin Psychiatry 1990;51(Suppl):61–69.

24. Zetin M, Kramer MA. Obsessive-compulsive disorder. Hosp Community Psychiatry 1992;43:689–699.

25. Goodman WK, McDougle CJ, Price LH. Pharmacotherapy of obsessive compulsive disorder. J Clin Psychiatry 1992;53(Suppl):29–37.

26. Barr LC, Goodman WK, Price LH, et al. The serotonin hypothesis of obsessive compulsive disorder: implications of pharmacologic challenge studies. J Clin Psychiatry 1992;53(Suppl):17–28.

27. Baxter LR. Positron emission tomography studies of cerebral glucose metabolism in obsessive compulsive disorder. J Clin Psychiatry 1994;55(Suppl):54–59.

28. Free NK, Winget CN, Whitman RM. Separation anxiety in panic disorder. Am J Psychiatry 1993;150:595–599.

29. Gabbard GO. Psychodynamics of panic disorder and social phobia. Bull Menninger Clin 1992;56(Suppl):A3–A13.

30. Klein DF. Anxiety reconceptualized. In: Klein DF, Rabkin JG, eds. Anxiety: new research and changing concepts. New York: Raven Press, 1981.

31. Roy-Byrne PP, Geraci M, Uhde YW. Life events and the onset of panic disorder. Am J Psychiatry 1986;143:1424–1427.

32. Kendler KS, Neale MC, Kessler RC, et al. Childhood parental loss and adult psychopathology in women: a twin study per-

spective. Arch Gen Psychiatry 1992; 42:109–116.

33. Bellak L, Small L. Panic—endogenous and exogenous. In: Bellak L, Small L, eds. Emergency psychotherapy and brief psychotherapy. 2nd ed. New York: Grune & Stratton, 1978.

34. Zeitlin SB, McNally RJ. Alexithymia and anxiety sensitivity in panic disorder and obsessive-compulsive disorder. Am J Psychiatry 1993;150:658–660.

35. Jenike MA. Psychotherapy of obsessive-compulsive disorder. In: Jenike MA, Baer L, Minichiello WE, eds. Obsessive-compulsive disorders: theory and management. 2nd ed. Littleton: Year Book, 1990.

36. Geist JH. An integrated approach to treatment of obsessive compulsive disorder. J Clin Psychiatry 1992;53:38–41.

37. Calvocoressi L, Lewis B, Harris M, et al. Family accommodation in obsessive-compulsive disorder. Am J Psychiatry 1995;152:441–443.

38. Skeketee G. Social support and treatment outcome of obsessive compulsive disorder at 9-month follow-up. Behav Psychother 1993;21:81–95.

39. Harper G. Focal inpatient treatment planning. J Am Acad Child Adolesc Psychiatry 1989;28:31–37.

40. Rosenbaum JF, Pollock RA, Jordan SK, et al. The pharmacotherapy of panic disorder. Bull Menninger Clin 1996;60(Suppl):A54–A75.

41. Mavissakalian MR, Perel JM. Imipramine treatment of panic disorder with agoraphobia: dose ranging and plasma level-response relationships. Am J Psychiatry 1995;152:673–682.

42. Noyes R, Perry P. Maintenance treatment with antidepressants in panic disorder. J Clin Psychiatry 1990;51(Suppl):24–30.

43. Davidson JRT. Continuation treatment of panic disorder with high-potency benzodiazepines. J Clin Psychiatry 1990;51:12(Suppl):31–37.

44. Schweizer E, Rickels K, Uhlenhuth EH. Issues in the long-term treatment of anxiety disorders. In: Bloom FE, Kupfer DJ, eds. Psychopharmacology: the fourth generation of progress. New York: Raven Press, 1994.

45. Fyer AJ, Liebowitz MR, Gorman JM, et al. Discontinuation of alprazolam treatment in panic patients. Am J Psychiatry 1987;144:303–308.

46. Otto M, Pollack M, Sachs G, et al. Discontinuation of benzodiazepine treatment: efficacy of cognitive-behavior therapy for patients with panic disorder. Am J Psychiatry 1993;150:1485–1490.

47. Sherman A, Ellison JM, Iwamoto S. Obsessive-compulsive disorder: integration of cognitive-behavior therapy with pharmacotherapy. In: Ellison JM, ed. Integrative treatment of anxiety disorders. Washington, DC: American Psychiatric Press, 1996.

48. Jenike MA. Management of patients with treatment-resistant obsessive-compulsive disorder. In: Pato MT, Zohar J, eds. Current treatments of obsessive disorder. Washington, DC: American Psychiatric Press, 1991.

49. Markovitz PJ, Stagno SJ, Calabrese JR. Buspirone augmentation of fluoxetine in obsessive-compulsive disorder. Am J Psychiatry 1990;147:798–800.

50. Hollander E, DeCaria CM, Schneier FR, et al. Fenfluramine augmentation of serotonin reuptake blockade antiobsessional treatment. J Clin Psychiatry 1990;51:119–123.

51. McDougle CJ, Goodman WK, Price LH, et al. Neuroleptic addition in fluvoxamine-refractory obsessive-compulsive disorder. Am J Psychiatry 1990;147:652–654.

52. Barlow DH. Cognitive-behavioral approaches to panic disorder and social phobia. Bull Menninger Clin 1992;56(Suppl):A14–A28.

53. Craske MG, Brown TA, Barlow DH. Behavioral treatment of panic disorder: a two-year follow-up. Behav Ther 1991;22:289–304.

54. Black DW, Wesner R, Owers Bowers W, et al. A comparison of fluvoxamine, cognitive therapy and placebo in the treatment of panic disorder. Arch Gen Psychiatry 1993;50:44–50.

55. DeBauers E, van Balkon AJLM, Lange A, et al. Treatment of panic disorder with agoraphobia: comparison of fluvoxamine, placebo, and psychological panic management combined with exposure and of exposure in vivo alone. Am J Psychiatry 1995;152:683–691.

56. Bruce TJ, Spiegel DA, Gregg SF, et al. Predictors of alprazolam discontinuation with and without cognitive behavior therapy in panic disorder. Am J Psychiatry 1995;152:1156–1160.

57. Craske MG. An integrated treatment approach to panic disorder. Bull Menninger Clin 1996;60(Suppl):A87–A104.

58. Milrod B, Busch FN, Hollander E, et al. A 23-year-old woman with panic disorder treated with psychodynamic psychotherapy. Am J Psychiatry 1996;153:698–703.

59. Jenike MA, Rauch SL. Managing the patient with treatment-resistant obsessive compulsive disorder: current strategies. J Clin Psychiatry 1994;55:11–17.

60. Katon W, Von Korff M, Lin E, et al. Distressed high utilizers of medical care: DSM-III-R diagnoses and treatment needs. Gen Hosp Psychiatry 1990;12:355–362.

61. Mavissakalian M, Perel J. Clinical experiments in maintenance and discontinuation of

imipramine therapy in panic disorder with agoraphobia. Arch Gen Psychiatry 1992;49:318–323.

62. Noyes R, Garvey MJ, Cook B, et al. Controlled discontinuation of benzodiazepine for patients with panic disorder. Am J Psychiatry 1991;148:517–523.

63. Pato MT, Zohar-Kadouch R, Zohar J, et al. Return of symptoms after discontinuation of clomipramine in patients with obsessive-compulsive disorder. Am J Psychiatry 1988;145:1521–1525.

64. Cottraux J, Mollard E, Bouvard M, et al. A controlled study of fluvoxamine and exposure in obsessive-compulsive disorder. Clin Psychopharmacol 1990;5:17–30.

65. Marks IM, Lelliott P, Basoglu M, et al. Clomipramine, self-exposure and therapist-aided exposure for obsessive-compulsive rituals. Br J Psychiatry 1988;152:522–534.

Chapter 8

Mania

Mauricio Tohen

DEFINITION

More than 2000 years ago, Aretaeus of Cappadocia first described the condition of mania (1). Hippocrates also provided early descriptions of manic symptomatology (2). More recently, Kraepelin (3) systematically described manic depressive illness and carefully noted its difference from dementia praecox (schizophrenia). Kraepelin underlined the differences between the courses of the two conditions, with manic depression having an episodic course interspersed with occasional euthymia and, generally, a better prognosis. Kraepelin described three types of manic depressive illness—pure manic, depressed, or mixed.

In the United States, the first edition of the *Diagnostic and Statistical Manual of Mental Disorders* (DSM-I) was published in 1952 (4) and it contained the strong psychobiologic influence of Adolf Meyer. In DSM-I, two types of manic depressive illness were described: manic depressive reaction manic type, and manic depressive reaction other, which included mixed mania. Psychotic features were not mentioned; as a result, patients with psychotic mania were classified within the schizophrenic spectrum (4). In 1968, when DSM-II was published, the term manic depressive reaction was changed to manic depressive illness. It was classified as a major affective disorder and was grouped under the affective psychoses, acknowledging the presence of psychotic symptoms as part of manic depressive illness (5).

DSM-III was published in 1980 (6). The term manic depressive illness was changed to bipolar disorder that, together with unipolar disorder, were part of the mood disorders. For the first time, operational diagnostic criteria were established that allowed clear definitions of the manic, depressive, and mixed subtypes. In addition, cyclothymia was classified as a mood disorder as opposed to a previously classified personality disorder.

DIAGNOSIS

The publication of DSM-IV represents a number of improvements over earlier editions (7). First, a duration criterion of 1 week was introduced to establish the diagnosis of bipolar disorder. The duration criterion was part of the DSM-III classification but was eliminated in the revised edition (8). The 1-week duration criterion, however, is not necessary if hospitalization occurs.

In DSM-IV, the definition of mixed episodes became more clearly operationalized. A mixed episode is characterized by the fulfillment of both manic and major depressive episode criteria occurring concurrently nearly every day for at least 1 week. Another improvement of DSM-IV includes a clear definition for hypomania that specifies that the duration of mood change should be present for at least 4 days and that a change in functioning should be observed by others. In addition, DSM-IV establishes criteria for bipolar II disorder, which is defined as separate episodes of hypomania and major depressive disorder.

In DSM-IV, an acute manic episode is described as a distinct period of abnormal and persistently elevated expansive or irritable mood lasting at least 1 week or requiring hospitalization (7). In addition, three or more of a number of symptoms must be persistent to a significant degree and four or more if mood is irritable. Symptoms of a manic episode include:

1. Inflated self-esteem or grandiosity.
2. Decreased need to sleep.
3. Pressured speech or increased talkativeness.
4. Racing thoughts or flight of ideas.
5. Distractibility.
6. Increased goal-directed activity or psychomotor agitation at school or work.
7. Excessive involvement in pleasurable activities with a high degree of harmful consequences.

In addition to these symptoms, the mood disturbance cannot be secondary to a general medical condition or to illicit drugs or medications. If the manic episode is precipitated by antidepressant drugs, it is not classified as bipolar disorder. Also, the episode must be sufficiently severe to cause functional impairment or require hospitalization to prevent harm to self or others.

DSM-IV allows the classification of bipolar disorder according to cross-sectional features, including the presence or absence of psychotic symptoms that are either mood congruent or mood incongruent. In one study that supported the difference between the two types of psychotic features (9), patients with mood incongruent psychotic features had a worse outcome, defined as an increased risk of relapse. Another finding was that Schneiderian first-rank symptoms were also predictors of poor outcome. This finding supported the importance of obtaining a detailed mental status examination, because the identification of certain symptoms will predict a poor outcome. Additional specifiers of bipolar disorder include melancholic, atypical, and catatonic features.

Another improvement of DSM-IV over previous editions includes the classification of bipolar disorder according to its longitudinal pattern and the concept of course modifiers. The longitudinal pattern of bipolar disorder can be classified as single episode either with or without full interepisode recovery. The concept of a single episode type is also present in DSM-IV. The importance of identifying a subgroup of single episode only has clear implications for maintenance treatment. Factors that have been identified as predicting a single episode type include absence of family history of bipolar illness, absence of psychotic features, and absence of comorbid substance use disorder (SUD) (10, 11). DSM-IV allows for different options in terms of longitudinal pattern, including single episode with no cyclothymic course, single episode superimposed on a cyclothymic course, recurrent with or without full interepisode recovery, and recurrent with or without full interepisode recovery that may or not be superimposed on a cyclothymic disorder.

DSM-IV also introduces the concept of course specifiers allowing for three options: rapid cycling, seasonal pattern, and postpartum onset. The rapid cycling concept was first introduced by Kraepelin (3). It was operationalized by Dunner et al. (12), who described rapid cycling as a subgroup of patients experiencing four or more affective episodes per year. Their definition was adopted by DSM-IV, and the term rapid cycling was used even if manic episodes were induced by antidepressants.

EPIDEMIOLOGY

Epidemiology is the study of the causes and distribution of illnesses (13). To understand the determinants of an illness accurately, the first step is to consider its prevalence in a community and/or clinical setting. The proper identification of a case is a major concern in psychiatric epidemiology. Although epidemiologic studies have been conducted for many years, the lack of precise tools to identify cases has hampered the validity of such studies (14). Improvement in case identification began with the development of structured diagnostic interviews. The Schedule for Affective Disorders and Schizophrenia (SADS) was the first widely used structured diagnostic interview (15). The SADS is an instrument designed to be administered by clinicians; therefore, its use is limited in large population-based epidemiologic studies due to the need for clinically trained interviewers. The Diagnostic Interview Schedule (DIS) was designed to enable nonclinical interviewers to administer the instrument in large population-based studies (16). This diagnostic interview was used in the National Institute of Mental Health (NIMH) Epidemiologic Catchment Area (ECA) Study (17). More recently, the Composite International Diagnostic Interview (CIDI) was used in the National Comorbidity Survey (NCS) (18).

The first population-based study conducted in the United States that used a structured diagnostic interview was the New Haven Community Sample (19). This study used the SADS and identified a prevalence of bipolar disorder of 0.8%. The prevalence varied across different socioeconomic classes, from 0.9% in lower social classes to 4.6% in upper middle social classes. The ECA study obtained prevalence rates for bipolar II and bipolar I conditions as well as for specific manic symptoms. The most prevalent manic symptoms identified in the ECA study were hyperactivity (9.3%), decreased need to sleep (7.52%), and distractibility (7.2%). In contrast, elevated or irritable mood was present in 2.7% of the population. The lifetime prevalence for bipolar disorder was 0.8–1.0%. The number of individuals suffering from the condition at any point in time (point prevalence) was 0.4%. The NCS, which studied a probability sample in all 48 contiguous states, estimated a lifetime prevalence of 1.6% (20).

The ECA study also provided data on psychiatric comorbidity. Bipolar disorder had the highest prevalence of comorbid SUD with a 60.7% lifetime prevalence, three times higher than that of depression. The ECA study presented data on the utilization of health and mental services. In a 1-year period, 79.2% of all bipolar patients received treatment in a medical outpatient setting, 38.5% in a psychiatric outpatient setting, 29.5% in a medical in-

McLEAN HOSPITAL MULTI-DISCIPLINARY TREATMENT PLAN BIPOLAR AND PSYCHOTIC DISORDERS

_____
PATIENT NAME

PATIENT STRENGTHS/ASSETS: ( ) Financial Resources, ( ) Supportive Family/Friends, ( ) Stable Outpatient Treatment Program,
( ) Stable Living Situation, ( ) Stable Work/School Situation, ( ) Other _____

DSM-IV DIAG: ( ) Bipolar Manic, ( ) Bipolar Depressed, ( ) Schizoaffective, ( ) Bipolar Mixed, ( ) Schizophrenia _____ Type, ( ) Psychotic Disorder, NOS,
( ) Organic Delusional Disorder, ( ) Other _____

CHARACTERIZED BY:	GOAL #	SHORT TERM GOALS: PATIENT WILL:
( ) Sleep disturbance	1	Sleep _____ hours per night _____ days
( ) Poor reality testing	2	Eat _____% of 3 meals per day x _____ days
( ) Hallucinations	3	Report decreased paranoia, hallucinations/delusions
( ) Paranoid delusions	4	Perform ADL's without prompting _____% of time
( ) Grandiose thoughts	5	Identify and talk about stressors/strengths by
( ) Cognitive impairment, distractibility	6	Demonstrate improved concentration by attendance in groups over _____ days
( ) Depressed mood	7	Be compliant with prescribed medications by
( ) Denial	8	Not threaten others or act on self destructive thoughts
( ) Impaired judgment	9	Talk about pros/cons of living situation by
( ) Agitation, irritability	10	Identify/discuss behaviors that interfere in living situation by
( ) Aggressive thoughts/gestures	11	Identify current/past leisure activities/interests by
( ) Suicidal thoughts/gestures	12	Arrange living situation by
( ) Inability to care for self	13	Arrange Outpatient Treatment by
( ) Organic Impairment	14	Detox in _____ days
Complicated By:	15	Obtain AA, NA, RR sponsor by and arrange meetings by
( ) Unstable work situation, (unemployed)	16	Identify relapse prevention plan by
( ) Impaired family relationship	17	Report to Nursing/MD staff significant changes in symptoms
( ) Unstable living situation	18	Cooperate with prescribed meds, tests, consults
( ) Drug abuse	19	Other:
( ) Unstable medical condition		

LONG-TERM GOALS: AT DISCHARGE THE PATIENT WILL:
( ) Report a decrease in psychotic symptoms
( ) Manage activities of daily living with less supervision
( ) Manage self-destructive/homicidal feelings
( ) Manage in less restrictive setting
( ) Have an adequate aftercare plan
( ) Other

ANTICIPATED DISCHARGE DATE

McLEAN HOSPITAL MULTI-DISCIPLINARY TREATMENT PLAN BIPOLAR AND PSYCHOTIC DISORDERS

PATIENT NAME

Treatment Interventions: Bipolar and Psychotic Disorders

Goal #

PHYSICIAN   **MD**   **CASE MANAGER**

Assess and prescribe level of observation and privileges

PRESCRIBE, MONITOR AND TITRATE:

Medical Consult for:_____

( ) Drug Levels_____
( ) Lab Tests_____
( ) Other:_____

( ) Mood Stabilizer_____
( ) Antipsychotic medication_____
( ) Antidepressant medication_____
( ) Education about risks/benefits of meds
( ) ECT_____

THERAPY_____ **X WEEK:**_____ **X MIN. FOCUSING ON:**

( ) Impulse control
( ) Denial
( ) Abstinence from addictive
      substances
( ) Education about disease process
( ) Aftercare planning

( ) Behavioral change
( ) Cognitive restructuring
( ) Reality orientation
( ) Conflict Resolution
( ) Safety Issues
( ) Other:_____

NURSING   **RN**

See Standard of Care for: Bipolar Disorder, Manic, Schizophrenia
or Schizophreniform or Schizoaffective Disorder

Implement protocols for: ( ) CPI   ( ) Falls   ( ) Lithium   ( ) Valproate   ( ) Patient who is Suspicious   ( ) Motor-Activity Disturbance
( ) Antiparkinsonian Drug   ( ) Antipsychotic   ( ) ECT   ( )Hygiene/Grooming   ( ) Other:_____

SOCIAL WORKER/CASE MANAGER

( ) Contact family for additional information
( ) Arrange meeting with family/significant others to provide education, support about ( ) illness, ( ) aftercare resources,
      ( ) need for follow-up therapy, meds, ( ) self-help groups
( ) Assess patient for appropriate entitlements
( ) Liaison with ( ) outpatient agencies/MD's, ( ) Residential Treatment, ( ) partial hospitalization program
( ) Work with patient to ( ) Arrange outpatient treatment program, ( ) provide resource material for leisure time activities
( ) Assess for potential abuse/neglect by_____ contact_____
( ) Evaluate symptoms and monitor level of functioning in group activities
( ) Explore options through 1:1 vocational counseling
( ) ADL assessment to determine capacity for independent living
( ) Assess and explore leisure time options through 1:1 or group activities
( ) Work with patient on structured daily routine through 1:1 or group activities
( ) Other:_____

Participation by ( ) patient ( ) family ( ) other:_____   Patient unable to participate. Reason_____   X

Anticipated Discharge Plan: Psychopharm with/at_____   Residential Treatment at_____; Partial Hospitalization_____
week at_____; Outpatient Therapy with at_____

THE ABOVE STAFF HAVE PARTICIPATED IN THE DEVELOPMENT OF THIS TREATMENT PLAN

_____MD   DATE:_____

FIGURE 8.1. Format of a treatment plan for bipolar disorder patients used at McLean Hospital.

patient setting, and 9.6% in a psychiatric inpatient setting. A total of 60% of all bipolar disorder subjects received some mental or medical service.

Recently, a shift in the diagnoses of patients admitted to psychiatric hospitals has occurred. A study addressing different diagnostic groups hospitalized during a 5-year period showed an increase in the prevalence of affective disorders, whereas schizophrenia was diagnosed less frequently (21). Possible explanations may include a change in diagnostic criteria or perhaps a true incidence change. Another cause may be a treatment-oriented diagnostic bias in which a clinician's diagnosis is based on categories that can use newly available pharmacologic treatments. In this case, the availability of lithium salts in the early 1970s probably caused a shift toward diagnosing patients with affective psychosis. A similar phenomenon may have occurred in the late 1980s, when fluoxetine first became available. In a study conducted at McLean Hospital, a higher frequency was seen in the diagnosis of obsessive-compulsive disorder after fluoxetine became available (22). In a third example, concurrent with the availability of treatments for mixed mania (e.g., divalproex and carbamazepine), the diagnosis of mixed mania increased in hospitalized patients (23).

Incidence data refer to newly diagnosed individuals. Incidence can be estimated for a certain period. For instance, the annual incidence rate represents the number of individuals who are diagnosed for the first time within 1 year. For bipolar disorder in the ECA study, the annual incidence rate was 0.5%.

Studies outside North America have reported similar prevalence rates for bipolar disorder (14). For instance, in an Italian sample, Faravelli et al. (24) reported a prevalence of 0.65% for males and 1.86% for females. In contrast, a Puerto Rican sample reported a prevalence of 0.7% for males and 0.4% for females (25).

FOUR QUESTIONS

Descriptive and Differential Diagnosis

DSM-IV has a descriptive approach to diagnosis and clear operational criteria. The differential diagnosis of bipolar disorder varies depending on age. In recent years, the onset of bipolar disorder has appeared at younger ages. Weissman et al. (26) have suggested that the younger age of onset in bipolar disorders may be related to the increased use of illicit drugs in the community. In children and adolescents, the differential diagnosis should include attention deficit hyperactivity disorder (ADHD), in which symptoms overlap with those of bipolar disorder. In the differential diagnosis between bipolar disorder and ADHD, a decreased need to sleep is seen in bipolar disorder; in ADHD, sleep is impaired by problems of falling asleep and waking up during the night, accompanied by tiredness. Family history of bipolar disorder also supports the diagnosis. The co-occurrence of both diagnoses should also be considered.

In the adult bipolar patient, the differential diagnosis should consider nonaffective psychosis, including schizophrenia and schizoaffective disorder. In bipolar II disorder, the differential diagnosis should include Axis II conditions, especially borderline personality disorder and narcissistic personality disorder. Medical conditions that need to be ruled out include hyperthyroidism and acquired immune deficiency syndrome (AIDS)-related neurobehavioral changes.

Within bipolar disorder, the differential diagnosis between the euphoric, mixed, and depressed subtype is not trivial because the pharmacologic treatment for each subtype is different. In DSM-IV, mixed mania requires that full criteria are met for mania and depression, lasting at least 1 week, nearly every day, and are of sufficient severity to cause significant impairment in occupational functioning. However, a number of investigators have suggested different definitions for mixed mania (27, 28). The episode needs to be accurately classified for the clinician to determine the right pharmacologic treatment. In the case of a euphoric mania, pharmacologic choices include lithium carbonate or divalproex (valproate sodium plus valproic acid). For mixed mania, however, the literature shows superiority of divalproex over lithium (29, 30). Agitated depression can be a challenging differential diagnosis to establish vis-a-vis dysphoric mania. Clearly, the treatment of agitated depression would be different from that of mixed or euphoric mania.

Ego Defenses and Character Style

The psychoanalytic literature provides a number of explanations for the development of manic symptomatology secondary to ego defenses. Unfortunately, such theoretical considerations are difficult to document through empiric research (2). Although different character styles have been described for bipolar disorder (2), the specification of a character style in the presence of an acute mania episode is difficult to establish. Conversely, the comorbidity of personality disorders in patients with bipolar illness is well established and has been identified as a predictor of both poor and good outcomes in bipolar disorder (31). Further research is needed to clarify these controversial findings.

Formulation

In all psychiatric disorders, the formulation must include the patient's strengths, diagnostic features, treatment interventions, and short- and long-term goals. The treatment interventions should match the goals and should be specific to discipline (e.g., physician, social worker, or nurse). Special consideration should be given to the establishment of the aftercare plan. Figure 8.1 illustrates the format of a treatment plan for bipolar disorder patients used at McLean Hospital.

For the patient with bipolar disorder, the treatment goals should include treatment of acute symptoms, prevention of recurrences, assurance of treatment compliance, and improvement of quality of life.

Post (32) proposed a useful paradigm into which a biopsychosocial formulation of bipolar disorder appears to be a good fit. He suggested that bipolar disorder represents a kindling phenomenon. Kindling (also known as sensitization) is a phenomenon that occurs in laboratory rodents when continuous stimulation is applied to their brains to cause seizures. With repeated stimulation, the rodent will eventually have seizures without the need of the external stimulation. Post suggested that the course in bipolar disorder reflects a kindling effect.

The kindling phenomenon may explain the finding by numerous investigators that the incidence of previous episodes is one of the best predictors of future relapses (28, 33, 34). It also explains why drugs with antikindling effects, such as divalproex and carbamazepine, are beneficial in the treatment of bipolar disorder. Furthermore, it also may explain some of the inconsistencies regarding the cause-and-effect association between life events and relapse in bipolar disorder. Studies that have assessed life events at the onset of the illness have found a cause-and-effect association with relapse (2). In contrast, those studies that have looked at life events in patients with multiple episodes have not found a cause-and-effect association with relapse (2). In other words, at the onset of the illness, the additional variable (in this case, the life event) is necessary to have a relapse. Later, as the frequency of the episodes increases, the individual could have relapses even in the absence of life events. Of course, the frequency of life events in multiple-episode patients might actually increase, but the cause-and-effect association is no longer clear (32).

The kindling phenomenon also has provided a paradigm regarding the association between the use of illicit drugs such as cocaine and the increased risk of relapse. In animal studies, the kindling effects of cocaine have been demonstrated, thus explaining why a number of studies have identified the use of illicit drugs as a predictor of relapse (28, 32, 35–37). Alcohol withdrawal also may represent a kindling phenomenon that explains why patients with comorbid substance abuse require a longer recovery time (10). Malcolm et al. (38) reported preliminary data about the possible efficacy of carbamazepine in the treatment of alcohol withdrawal syndrome, suggesting that carbamazepine's antikindling effects were responsible for the improvement. In the formulation of a case, the effects of illicit drugs in the course of the illness need to be considered. Close attention to the prevention of substance use is essential. Another study emphasized the use of antikindling agents and cognitive educational therapy groups for dual-diagnosis patients (39).

In the formulation of a treatment plan for bipolar disorder, the clinician must address the importance of the prevention of stressful life events. This prevention may have an effect on patients who have experienced one or two episodes, but may have far less of an effect on patients who have experienced multiple episodes. Therefore, psychotherapy of first-episode patients should emphasize the prevention of stressful life events; multiple-episode patients may benefit from psychotherapy that addresses the prevention of stressors and focuses on rebuilding skills through rehabilitation.

Focal Problems

The determination of when to transfer a patient to the next level of care is likely to be conducted within a managed care framework. Mental health providers are required to provide the best quality of care at the least possible cost, which in most cases means in a less-restrictive level of care. Managed care reviewers consider the need for acute care based on behavioral changes. In bipolar disorder, the behaviors that necessitate an intensive level of care include risk of harm to self or others. The level of functioning of a patient may also be more important than the specific symptomatology.

Managed care emphasizes a focus on customer (patient) satisfaction, including the pharmacologic treatment, addressing not only efficacy but also tolerability. Patient outcome and effectiveness of treatment are the primary goals of care. Efficacy, in terms of symptom amelioration, is no longer the sole criterion to determine outcome, which now includes cost-effectiveness and patient satisfaction.

BIOLOGIC EVALUATION

Laboratory Tests

A patient having an acute episode of mania should receive a complete psychiatric and medical examination. The latter should include a physical examination. A toxicology screen should be considered when history or symptoms warrant the detection of prescribed or illicit drugs.

Laboratory examinations include a complete blood cell count, chemistry, and thyroid function tests. An electrocardiogram (ECG) should be performed in individuals older than age 45. A medical evaluation should be conducted to rule out possible physical conditions that may mimic a manic episode, such as hyperthyroidism, and to diagnose any medical comorbidity that would affect diagnosis, treatment, and course of illness. In addition, baseline laboratory tests should be obtained before the prescription of antimanic drugs (see section below on specific drugs).

Brain Imaging and Electroencephalogram

The value of magnetic resonance imaging (MRI) in the assessment of the bipolar patient remains unclear. Brain imaging was evaluated as part of the McLean/Harvard First Episode Mania Study (40). Findings included the presence of white hyperintensities in temporal lobes in manic patients but not in nonaffective psychotic patients. Replications of this finding may prove useful in the differential diagnosis of mania from nonaffective psychoses.

The value of the electroencephalogram (EEG) also remains unclear. A number of studies have identified an abnormal EEG as a predictor of response to treatment with anticonvulsants. Stoll et al. (41) found that an abnormal EEG was a predictor of response to divalproex in bipolar disorder patients.

ASSESSING LEVEL OF CARE

In an era of cost-containment and managed care, continuous review of the appropriateness of the level of care is needed. When the severity of illness in a manic patient is evaluated, some symptoms are more relevant than others in assessing the need for a high-intensity level of care. Impulsivity, risk of harm to self or others, or psychosis leading to impaired judgment determine the need for an intensive level of care. In fact, impulsive behavior is more important in assessing level of care than is the degree of the bizarreness of delusions. In addition, level of functioning may be as important or more important than any specific symptomatology short of imminent dangerousness.

TREATMENT

The American Psychiatric Association (APA) recently published practice guidelines for the treatment of bipolar disorder (42) that emphasize the need to establish and maintain a therapeutic alliance. Considering that 90% of bipolar patients will eventually have another episode of illness, the need for a long-term, supportive therapeutic relationship is essential. The relationship between the clinician and the patient should be conceptualized as a partnership that can identify significant life events and stressors. The therapeutic alliance will also need to identify subsyndromal or interepisodal symptoms that are predictors of relapse (28, 43). It should be maintained with the family as well. The APA's guidelines also emphasize the importance of ongoing education on bipolar disorder for the patient, family, and significant others (Fig. 8.1).

Alliance and Psychotherapeutic Management

Treatment Compliance

Noncompliance has been reported as a major predictor of relapse in bipolar disorder (2). Noncompliance of self-administered, long-term pharmacologic treatment for all medical conditions has been estimated at approximately 50% (44). Noncompliance is also more likely to occur in episodic conditions in which the short-term disadvantages of adverse effects are believed by many patients to outweigh the long-term benefits of relapse prevention. A study by Bosco and Rush (45) estimated that 46% of patients taking lithium carbonate were noncompliant. Similar information is not yet available regarding compliance with divalproex or carbamazepine. Another identified predictor of noncompliance in bipolar disorder is the presence of comorbid substance use (2). In the McLean/Harvard First Episode Mania Study, a higher degree of noncompliance was found in patients suffering from comorbid SUD (10). The loss of perceived benefits of hypomania has also been reported as a predictor of noncompliance, including loss of creativity and feelings of loss of attractiveness (46, 47).

Management of Noncompliance

Psychoeducation about the illness and focused psychotherapy have been suggested as effective approaches to manage noncompliance. Cochran (48) reported an improvement in treatment compliance after 6 weeks of individual, cognitive therapy intervention. Group psychotherapy has also been reported to enhance treatment compliance (49).

Noncompliance appears to be a particular problem in patients after their first episode. Winokur et al. (50) reported that 2 years after their first episode, 57% of patients were not following treatment recommendations compared with a similar population of multi-episode patients with noncompliance of 27%.

A practical way to address noncompliance is the simplification of pharmacologic treatment. Greenberg et al. (51) found that in a variety of medical conditions, noncompliance ranged as high as 58% when medication was prescribed four times a day, compared with only 27% when single-dose medication was prescribed.

Another intervention recommended by the APA in the psychiatric management of bipolar patients is psychoeducation regarding understanding of the psychosocial losses secondary to bipolar illness. In many cases, bipolar disorder has major effects in the functioning of patients. Acute exacerbations of the illness affect the occupational and social life of the patient, and chronicity impairs overall functioning. Issues related to genetic counseling also need to be addressed to aid in understanding and compliance. Denial of illness and medication noncompliance may be related to the inability to confront the implications of having the illness on one's progeny.

Family Support, Education, and Intervention

Unstable marital relationships are not unusual in patients with bipolar disorder. The spouse of a bipolar patient is often the target of the patient's mood and stability. Approximately 60% of these patients are divorced (52). The management of bipolar patients should include meetings with the spouse or, in cases of children or young adults, meetings with the parents.

The Therapeutic Milieu

The therapeutic milieu of patients suffering from a manic episode should provide an adequate structure that will reduce the level of stimulation. In severe cases, impulsive behaviors need to be contained with pharmacologic or physical interventions. As much as possible, physical restraints should be avoided unless the patient or others are at imminent risk of physical harm. Once the clinical condition improves, the therapeutic milieu should provide a supportive environment. As soon as the patient is able to move to the next level of care, referral to self-support groups should be emphasized. Such support groups (e.g., the Depressive and Manic Depressive Association [DMDA] or those provided by the National Alliance of the Mentally Ill [NAMI]) provide comfort and education to the patient and family.

Pharmacologic Management

Lithium

Lithium was the first drug to be reported to have antimanic effects (53). Lithium salts were first prescribed in the 19th century to treat psychotic agitation (54). The approval by the Food and Drug Administration (FDA) took 20 years after the first report by Cade (53), in part due to the number of cases of severe intoxication and death due to its use as table salt by impaired individuals (55).

The efficacy of lithium monotherapy in the treatment of acute mania has been clearly documented with seven double-blind, placebo-controlled trials conducted between 1954 and 1972 with a total of 162 patients (56). In addition, a number of double-blind studies have proven the efficacy of lithium as a maintenance treatment (57).

Before a patient begins taking lithium, thyroid (TSH) and renal (creatinine) function tests should be performed. An ECG is also required in patients older than 45 years of age. In cases of abnormalities in thyroid or renal function, a medical consultation is necessary before prescribing lithium.

Administration of Lithium

Lithium lasts in the body from 18 to 36 hours. Although it can be prescribed in multiple dosing, single dosing is preferable. Recent reports suggest that single dosing might decrease urinary adverse effects, such as polyuria and polydipsia, and perhaps the risk of glomerulosclerosis and renal interstitial fibrosis (58, 59). Another advantage of single dosing is an increase in medication compliance (44). Lithium should be taken with meals to diminish gastrointestinal adverse effects. The recommended blood levels are 0.8–1.0 mEq/L (60). Dosing is typically started at 600 mg per day and modified according to blood levels. Blood levels should be drawn 12 hours after the last dose has been administered.

Blood monitoring after the patient is stable includes lithium blood levels every 3–6 months; TSH and creatinine blood levels should be obtained at least twice a year. In individuals older than age 45, an annual ECG is recommended.

In view of the recent need to decrease hospital lengths of stay, a major drawback of lithium is the delayed onset of action (estimated to be approximately 10–14 days). In addition, its narrow therapeutic index causes limitations in its use in acutely agitated, uncooperative, metabolically unstable patients (61, 62). Typically, patients with acute mania are treated with antipsychotic agents until symptoms diminish; then lithium salts are added to stabilize the mania (62). This approach cannot be abbreviated and can lead to an increase in hospital stay.

Although the frequency of serious adverse effects is rare, mild adverse effects appear to be common (56, 62). Kidney damage, long regarded as the most serious adverse effect, is relatively rare. The most frequent adverse effects of lithium include polyuria and polydipsia, which can be present in up to 50% of patients (2). Increased 24-hour urine output has been reported in 20% of patients (56). Nephrogenic diabetes insipidus secondary to increased levels of antigenic hormone has also been reported. However, irreversible renal insufficiency is rare. Quarterly monitoring of serum creatinine is recommended (56). In 10% of cases, reversible enlargement of the thyroid gland has been reported. Another adverse effect, neurocognitive impairment, is especially common in the elderly and in neurocognitively impaired individuals, documented by neuropsychological assessment (63). It is also a principal reason for noncompliance (2). Dermatologic side effects are also common.

Lithium interacts with other drugs. Increases in lithium blood levels may occur with the use of nonsteroidal antiinflammatory drugs and with certain antihypertensive drugs, such as angiotensin converting enzyme (ACE) inhibitors.

Divalproex

Divalproex is the other drug approved by the FDA for the treatment of acute mania. It was approved in Europe in the mid 1960s. Lambert et al. (64) reported an open trial suggesting mood stabilizing properties of valpromide, which is an amide of valproic acid. The first placebo control study of the use of valproate in mania was conducted by Pope et al. (65). The inclusion criteria of this study required a history of lack of response to lithium or inability to tolerate lithium's adverse effects. The study used divalproex, which is a combination of valproic acid and sodium valproate. Divalproex was statistically significantly superior to placebo, with a decrease of symptoms of mania within 4 days of obtaining valproate therapeutic levels. This study provided evidence that patients who do not respond or cannot tolerate lithium have a good response to divalproex.

The second double-blind placebo control study of divalproex was conducted by Bowden et al. (30) and included placebo, lithium, and divalproex treatment arms. It did not require a previous lack of response to lithium. The study showed equal efficacy between lithium and divalproex, and both drugs were statistically significantly superior to placebo. Divalproex was also equally effective in subjects who had previously responded poorly to lithium and those who had a previous good response to lithium. Unlike lithium (which was less effective), divalproex was also effective in those patients with mixed symptoms. Furthermore, there appeared to be higher patient satisfaction with the use of divalproex, with only 6% reporting intolerance to the drug compared with 11% for those taking lithium. The recommended blood level for divalproex is 50—120 ng/mL.

To summarize, it appears that lithium and divalproex are equally effective in the treatment of pure mania, but divalproex is superior in patients with mixed symptoms and those who could not tolerate or had failed to respond to lithium. Thus, the literature suggests a broader-spectrum efficacy and superior patient satisfaction for divalproex.

Divalproex Oral Loading Technique

Studies conducted at the University of Cincinnati have reported good efficacy and tolerance for the use of oral loading (20 mg/kg/day) in acutely agitated manic patients, with a response within 3–5 days (66–68). A recent report by McElroy et al. (68) reported a randomized comparison of the divalproex oral loading (20 mg/kg/day) versus haloperidol (0.2 mg/kg/day). The study found that the divalproex oral loading and haloperidol were equally effective in the reduction of manic and psychotic symptoms within 3 days. The only difference between the two treatments, not surprisingly, was a higher degree of extrapyramidal adverse effects with the use of haloperidol. Importantly, the study included only psychotic manic patients, suggesting that the treatment of psychotic mania is as effective with a neuroleptic as it is with divalproex.

Adverse Effect Profile and Safety of Divalproex

In a review conducted by Schmidt (69), the most common adverse effect of valproate used in monotherapy and in combination with other anticonvulsants was drowsiness (1.4% and 14.4%, respectively). In combination with other drugs, other common adverse effects were anorexia (4.2%), hair loss (4%), and nausea (3.2%). Gastrointestinal adverse effects may be associated with an increase in gastric motility and pepsinogenic secretion; the use of the enteric coded preparation (divalproex) is useful in reducing this side effect. Nausea may be reduced if the drug is taken with meals.

H_2 receptor agonists, such as ranitidine or cimetidine, can be helpful. Pancreatitis has been described in 30 isolated cases by Asconape et al. (70). The latter review concluded that pancreatitis was not dose related, but was associated predominantly with younger age. It usually developed during the initial months after treatment initiation, with up to 75% of cases reporting pancreatitis after the first month of treatment. Notably, one third of patients were receiving other anticonvulsants. The outcome in the vast majority of cases was good, with 85% of patients suffering from mild to moderate pancreatitis and recovering after valproate discontinuation; three cases had a fatal outcome.

Discontinuation of valproate is recommended for consideration when vomiting and severe abdominal pain occur. Monitoring amylase levels in an asymptomatic patient is not justified in light of reports of mild amylase elevations in asymptomatic patients (71). Rechallenging patients who have experienced pancreatitis is not recommended.

Liver Toxicity

Liver toxicity is a rare but recognized adverse effect associated with valproate (71). There are two types of hepatotoxic reactions. The most common is an asymptomatic, transient, dose-related elevation of liver enzymes. The incidence of liver enzyme elevation ranges between 2.4% and 44%, with higher rates in patients taking multiple drugs. The second reaction type is an idiosyncratic irreversible hepatic failure that is rare, non–dose-related, and usually appears in the first 6 months of treatment.

Elevation of liver enzymes does not appear to be a good predictor of valproate-associated hepatic failure. By 1981, 43 deaths from hepatotoxicity had been reported world-wide. In 1986, Scheffner (72) documented 100 fatalities world-wide: 90% occurred in individuals younger than 20 years of age, and 95% of cases occurred within the first 6 months of treatment. In 1987, Dreifuss et al. (73) reviewed all hepatotoxic cases reported in the United States from 1978 to 1984. The study concluded that children younger than 2 years of age, who were receiving other antiepileptic drugs, and who had other medical problems were most likely to develop hepatotoxicity. Dreifuss and Langer (74) concluded that monitoring liver enzymes was not a good predictor of the development of serious hepatotoxicity. They recommend monitoring the clinical parameters of liver dysfunction such as nausea, vomiting, malaise, and anorexia. In a follow-up study that reported the U.S. experience from 1985 to 1986, Dreifuss et al. (73) found a five-fold decrease in the incidence of hepatic fatalities despite the increased number of valproate prescriptions. Evidently, physicians were not prescribing for high-risk patients.

It has been estimated that in patients from 3 to 10 years old, the risk of fatal hepatotoxicity is 1 in every 7000. The Physician's Desk Reference (PDR) recommends monitoring liver enzymes in patients receiving valproate. Baseline liver function tests should be obtained before treatment initiation and at intervals thereafter, especially in the first 6 months. The frequency of monitoring liver enzymes remains controversial. Some investigators suggest quarterly monitoring, whereas others suggest none. Dreifuss et al. (75) suggest that a significant elevation of liver enzymes in the early course of treatment should lead to treatment discontinuation, considering that most fatalities secondary to liver toxicity have been described within the first 3 months of treatment.

Quality assurance guidelines include liver enzymes at baseline, 2 weeks, months 2 and 3, and quarterly thereafter. For clinical and risk management purposes, it is recommended that clear operational criteria be established regarding frequency of monitoring and discontinuation of treatment. For example, the guidelines could include treatment discontinuation if liver enzymes increase twofold to threefold. Mildly elevated liver enzymes secondary to hepatitis or alcohol intoxication should not result in divalproex contraindication; instead, laboratory and clinical monitoring should be implemented.

Weight gain secondary to divalproex has been reported in 3–20% of patients and appears to be secondary to increased appetite. Management can include diet and exercise.

Another adverse effect with divalproex in 3% of cases is alopecia, which is usually transient, mild, and dose related. Hurd et al. (76) reported a good response of hair regrowth with the use of zinc, 22.5 mg/day.

Blood dyscrasias, especially thrombocytopenia, have been reported secondary to valproate (77). In a study of 1200 patients treated with valproate, no cases of thrombocytopenia, agranulocytosis, or aplastic anemia were documented (78). Only mild leukopenia (0.02% prevalence) was detected, a prevalence seen in a similar population exposed to desipramine. Complete blood cell counts are recommended at baseline, 2 weeks, 3 and 6 months, and biannually thereafter.

Other Treatments

Other treatments include the use of approved drugs without the indication to treat mania. In this category, carbamazepine is used most frequently (56, 79), and open studies have reported mixed results in terms of its maintenance efficacy

(80–82). Carbamazepine has a low acceptability by patients due to its adverse effect profile (83, 84). The most common adverse effects include sedation, confusion, nausea, rash, and blood dyscrasias (56, 78). Carbamazepine also increases its own metabolism and reduces blood levels of other drugs (56).

Electroconvulsive Treatment

Although the primary indication for electroconvulsive treatment (ECT) is major depression, it has also been used in the treatment of acute mania. Predictors of response in acute mania include greater severity of manic and depressive symptoms at baseline (85). Reports of the use of ECT in mania go back more than 50 years (86). A recent publication by Mukherjee (87) reviewed the use of ECT in the past 50 years and found that 313 of 400 patients (78%) treated with ECT experienced significant clinical improvement. Two contemporary, prospective, random-assignment, control studies discussed the use of ECT in mania. The first study compared ECT with lithium and allowed the use of concomitant neuroleptics (85). This study showed equal efficacy when ECT was compared with lithium. The second study compared ECT with a combination of lithium and haloperidol (88). This study had four treatment arms: lithium plus haloperidol, bilateral ECT, right unilateral ECT, and left unilateral ECT. The superiority of ECT over the lithium/haloperidol combination was demonstrated. To date, no comparative study has been conducted comparing ECT with valproate. However, in one study, patients who had not responded to carbamazepine were responsive to ECT (89).

Most studies have shown that the average number of ECT treatments ranges from 4.4 to 11 (87). Mukherjee's review (87) of ECT suggested that the effectiveness of unilateral ECT in mania may be limited and that bilateral treatments may be necessary. Another factor to be considered is the placement of the electrodes, because longer interelectrode distances (e.g., the d'Elia placement) may be more effective than the shorter interelectrode distances (Lancaster placement). A study conducted by Small et al. (90) found that patients with mania were more likely to be switched to bilateral ECT if they initially received right unilateral ECT.

To summarize, it is estimated that 80% of manic patients treated with ECT will have significant clinical improvement, including those patients who fail to respond to lithium or neuroleptics (87). Although the use of ECT for maintenance treatment has received less attention, a recent European study using once-a-month administration of unilateral or bilateral ECT showed promising results as a maintenance treatment (91). Neurocognitive impairment remains a concern in the use of ECT. Although improvement in neurocognition has been documented after the clinical condition improves, neurocognitive impairment follows immediately after the administration of the treatment and can affect the patient's quality of life (92). Before ECT can be recommended as a first-line treatment for mania, more studies are needed, especially regarding its use as a maintenance treatment.

Maintenance Psychopharmacologic Treatment

Considering that 90% of bipolar patients have two or more episodes, the psychia-

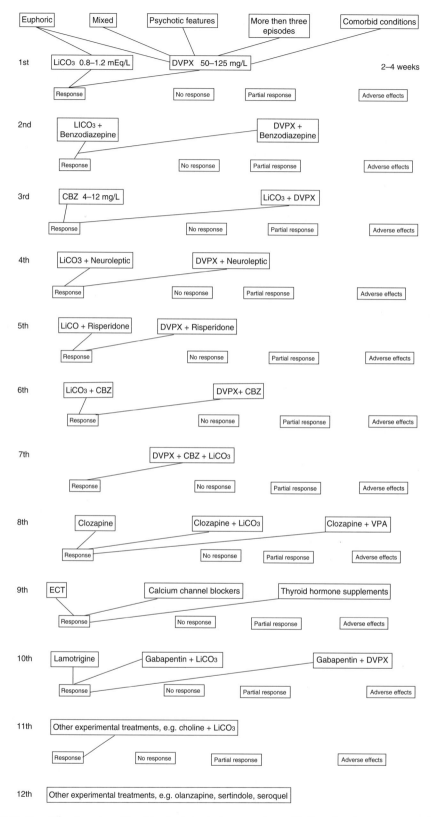

FIGURE 8.2. The American Psychiatric Association practice guidelines for the treatment of bipolar disorder.

trist's choice of pharmacologic agent should consider acute and maintenance treatment. A number of studies have proven the prophylactic efficacy of lithium carbonate (56, 62). A U.S. multi-site maintenance study comparing divalproex, lithium, and placebo has been completed, but the results have not been published. A number of open studies have suggested the prophylactic efficacy of divalproex and its derivatives (93). A randomized nonblinded maintenance study comparing valpromide with lithium carbonate showed equal prophylactic efficacy (94). A total of 150 patients were studied; 42 of those taking lithium relapsed, and 39 of those taking valpromide relapsed. Superior patient satisfaction with the use of valpromide was also noted. Patients were allowed to switch from one treatment to the other. Four elected to switch from valpromide to lithium, and 10 switched from lithium to valpromide (6 were due to adverse effects).

The pharmacologic treatment of mania has changed dramatically in the past 2 years. The group at McLean Hospital has been documenting prescribing practices using a pharmacoepidemiologic approach (71, 23). Changes in medications prescribed to patients admitted to McLean Hospital during the past 7 years have been documented. In 1987, the most prescribed drug in patients with bipolar disorder was lithium (87%), the second most prescribed drug was carbamazepine (30%), and the third most prescribed drug was valproate (20%). In the following 6 years, the prescription of lithium decreased, the prescription of valproate increased, and the prescription of carbamazepine remained approximately 10%. In 1994, valproate became the most prescribed drug. The change in prescribing practices occurred not only in patients with multiple hospitaliza-

tions, but also in first-episode patients (10). Valproate has become the most prescribed drug for multiple-episode patients, who are likely to be treatment resistant, and for patients suffering from their first episode of mania.

Pharmacologic Treatment Algorithm

The use of algorithms in the treatment of different psychiatric disorders is receiving increased attention (95, 96). Based on clinical experience and reports in the literature, a treatment algorithm for acute mania has been developed. As shown in Figure 8.2, the presence of a number of specific clinical features supports the use of the divalproex as a first-line agent. These features include the presence of mixed mood and psychotic symptoms, occurrence of more than three previous episodes, and the presence of other comorbid conditions. From the point of view of efficacy, there appears to be no difference between lithium and divalproex for first-episode mania. However, the faster onset of action and greater patient satisfaction (due to its more benign adverse effect profile) would favor the use of the divalproex over lithium carbonate.

Treatment can be enhanced with the use of benzodiazepines. The use of lorazepam in the treatment of acute mania has become a common practice due to its pharmacokinetic properties, which include fast onset of action, relatively short half-life, and availability as an intramuscular medication. Benzodiazepines may also have some antimanic properties (97). If no response to lithium or divalproex is seen, carbamazepine can be used as the next treatment of choice or, alternatively, a combination of divalproex and lithium that may be synergistic (12). The next step would be a neuroleptic drug plus divalproex or lithium (56, 62). Use of risperidone should also be considered. However, risperidone has been reported to possibly cause exacerbation of manic symptoms in schizoaffective bipolar patients who are not taking mood stabilizers (98). Other studies on risperidone have reported antimanic effects when combined with mood stabilizers (99). The next step would be a combination of carbamazepine and the other mood stabilizers. Synergistic effects have also been reported with lithium and carbamazepine (100). Synergistic effects have been reported with a combination of divalproex and carbamazepine (101, 102). In a study of 24 patients who had been treated with divalproex and carbamazepine (102), 12 of 15 patients with bipolar disorder had a good response, and no patient's condition worsened. In seven of the good response patients, the response was described as moderate; in five patients, the response was significant. Eight patients responded poorly to both drugs when used separately. Nevertheless, when this combination is used, close monitoring of blood levels is needed. Carbamazepine may decrease blood levels of divalproex due to its enzyme inducing effects and may also increase blood levels of 4-en-valproate, which is a toxic monounsaturated metabolite of valproate. In addition, valproate increases the blood level of 10–11 epoxide, which is a toxic metabolite of carbamazepine. When the valproate/carbamazepine combination is used, monitoring of blood levels should occur every 2 to 3 months or every time a dose is changed (102).

Patients who do not respond to divalproex, lithium, carbamazepine, or their combinations should be considered candidates for clozapine (103). One study showed that the response to clozapine in bipolar patients in whom mood stabilizers had failed was moderate to significant in 75% of patients (104). In addition, experience with maintenance clozapine was equally positive (96). Clozapine monotherapy may be an effective treatment for bipolar disorder, suggesting that clozapine may have mood stabilizing properties (96).

Other treatments that should be considered include ECT, calcium channel blockers, and thyroid hormone supplements. Recently released anticonvulsant drugs also appear promising in the treatment of bipolar disorder. Recent anecdotal reports on the use of lamotrigine and gabapentin in the treatment of bipolar disorder have prompted the initiation of clinical trials. Lamotrigine, which was recently approved as an adjunctive treatment for partial complex seizures, has affinity with glutamate receptors. Preliminary studies suggest therapeutic benefit, especially in the depressed phase of bipolar disorder (105). Recent reports have also suggested that gabapentin in combination with divalproex or lithium may be an effective antimanic treatment. The adverse effect profile of gabapentin appears to be quite benign, and blood monitoring is not needed. Finally, new atypical antipsychotic drugs such as olanzapine, sertindole, and quetiapine may prove to have mood stabilizing effects, considering their similarity to clozapine. Notably, they do not carry the risk of agranulocytosis. Thus, these agents may further strengthen the pharmacologic methodology for the treatment of bipolar disorder.

THE DECISION TO TRANSFER TO THE NEXT LEVEL OF CARE

An important aspect of case management is the need to avoid unnecessary delays in moving from one level of care to the other. A system that has proven to be helpful in the Bipolar and Psychotic Disorders Program at McLean Hospital is the "continuity-of-care" model. The same clinical team follows the patient from one level of care to the other, thereby avoiding reformulations, redundancies, and disruption in care. With a continuity-of-care model, poor communication among treaters is eliminated. It also offers a clear case ownership and accountability.

Shortening of length of stay has become the rule in psychiatric care. Shorter lengths of stay have forced clinicians to reevaluate different treatment modalities. Treatments must have proven efficacy, rapid onset of action, high tolerability, and high patient satisfaction. Managed care has enabled clinicians to conceptualize episodes of care as opposed to the provision of treatments in separate levels of care. The treatment of a manic patient becomes a longitudinal rather than a cross-sectional intervention. The clinician needs to consider the best treatment possible to rapidly "move out" and "keep out" a patient from an inpatient level of care. The reduction of length of stay is effective as long as the treatment does not increase the risk of relapse and rehospitalizations.

CONTROVERSIES IN THE CARE OF MANIA

The selection of the first-line antimanic treatment may represent a controversy in the treatment of acute mania. The FDA has approved two drugs for the treatment of acute mania—lithium and divalproex. From the standpoint of efficacy, no difference between the two drugs is apparent in the treatment of classic mania; however, a number of factors indicate the superiority of divalproex over lithium, particularly in the treatment of mixed mania (30). Studies have also shown that divalproex is superior to lithium in terms of a faster onset of action (68, 106, 107). Another advantage of divalproex is the lack of neurocognitive impairment, which leads to superior patient satisfaction and medication compliance (108).

Other controversies in the treatment of bipolar disorder include the need for lifelong maintenance treatment. Most clinicians would agree that the literature strongly supports continuous maintenance treatment in patients who have experienced at least two manic episodes. The need for indefinite maintenance treatment after a first episode appears to be less definite. One factor to consider is a 90% outcome of two or more episodes in all bipolar patients, indicating that the odds of having a single episode are 1 to 9. Another factor is that the median time between the first and the second episode is 4.3 years. In a first-episode study conducted at McLean/Harvard, only 60% of patients had experienced their second episode after a 4-year follow-up, suggesting that more episodes will likely occur at longer follow-ups (36). Therefore, the decision to stop maintenance treatment after a first episode of mania should be made after 4 years of remission. Other aspects that will help in the decision to continue maintenance treatment include the presence of subsyndromal or interepisode symptoms that have been identified as predictors of relapse (28, 109). In other words, the presence of interepisode symptoms would favor a continuation maintenance treatment. Family history of multiple episodes is also a predictor of relapse. The McLean/Harvard study found that the presence of bipolar illness in relatives is a strong predictor of relapse in first-episode probands (31). Discontinuing treatment not only increases the risk of an immediate relapse, but more importantly, may worsen the long-term outcome of the illness as proposed by the kindling paradigm (32). The decision to stop maintenance treatment should always be discussed within the framework of a partnership. The clinician should provide the patient (and family) with the relevant information, and the final decision should be made by the patient.

COURSE AND PROGNOSIS

Bipolar disorder is a lifelong condition. Follow-up studies have shown that multiple recurrences have a deteriorative effect on quality of life, level of functioning, and treatment response (28, 57, 84, 110). The Medical Practice Information Demonstration Project estimated that without treatment, a 25 year-old woman with bipolar disorder would have a decrease of life expectancy of 9.2 years and a decrease in productivity of 4.2 years (111). With optimal treatment, this patient will regain 6.4 years of life expectancy and 10.2 years of life productivity. This study highlights the importance of timely diagnosis and appropriate psychiatric treatment.

The importance of obtaining longitudinal information in psychiatric disorders was first emphasized by Kraepelin (3). In a review published in 1979, Zis and Goodwin (112) concluded that nonsystematic sampling and differences in diagnostic and outcome criteria accounted for most of the difference in outcome studies. A number of contemporary studies have shed more light on the outcome of bipolar illness (34, 113).

Predictors of Recovery and Relapse

The NIMH collaborative study (113) found that polarity of the index episode predicted speed of recovery. Patients who presented with pure mania had a shorter time to recovery compared with those patients with mixed mania. Another study, conducted at McLean and that consisted of 75 patients hospitalized with an episode of mania, found that the presence of comorbid alcohol abuse/dependence predicted a shorter time in remission (28, 35). Other factors identified as predictors of poor outcome included the presence of psychotic features. Furthermore, the type of psychotic features also affected the outcome (9). The study found that the presence of mood incongruent psychotic features, especially the presence of first-rank symptoms, predicted a shorter time in remission. In addition, the presence of interepisode symptoms at 6 months predicted a shorter time in remission. Similar findings on the presence of subsyndromal symptoms predicting poor outcome have been reported by Keller et al. (113). Another predictor of poor outcome, both in the collaborative study and the McLean study, was the presence of previous episodes. In the McLean study, the presence of depressive symptoms also predicted a shorter time in remission (28). This study also provided information suggesting that as the frequency of episodes increases, the severity of interepisode symptoms increases. This suggests that with each additional episode, there is an increased risk of a less complete recovery.

Zis and Goodwin (112) suggest that the discrepancies among studies is related to the inclusion of both first- and multiple-episode patients. In bipolar illness, in which many patients experience a deteriorating course and in which changes are likely to occur at the onset of the illness, patients should undergo follow-up from the onset of their illness.

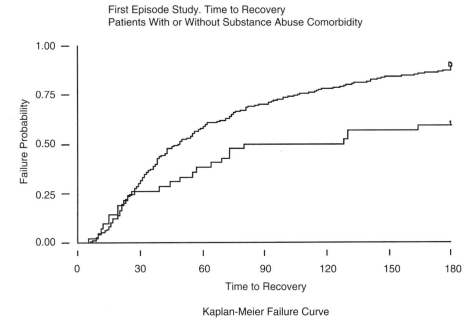

First Episode Study. Time to Recovery
Patients With or Without Substance Abuse Comorbidity

Kaplan-Meier Failure Curve

FIGURE 8.3.   First episode study. Time to recovery. Patients with or without substance abuse comorbidity.

At McLean, first-episode studies are being conducted (9, 10, 35). In a previous first-episode study, the presence of comorbid SUD and psychotic features predicted a poor outcome (28). In a 4-year follow-up of this first-episode sample, 40% of patients had not relapsed. Importantly, Kraepelin (3) documented that the mean length between the first and the second episode is 4.3 years. An 11-year follow-up of the same cohort is currently being conducted. In 1989, the McLean/Harvard First Episode Psychosis Project was started, and more than 250 patients have undergone follow-up (9, 36). One finding was the relatively low (17%) prevalence of SUD, which was much less than the 60% reported in multiple-episode samples. In addition, the presence of SUD predicted a longer time to recovery, as seen in Figure 8.3. By 6 months, 90% of those patients without comorbid SUD had recovered compared with only 60% of those with comorbid substance use conditions. Furthermore, time in remission was decreased in those with comorbid SUD. By 2 years, 80% of those patients without SUD remained in remission compared with only 60% of those without comorbid SUD. Another finding at 2-year follow-up was the higher rate of noncompliance in patients with comorbid SUD; 50% of those with comorbid SUD had stopped medication compared with only 18% of those without SUD comorbidity.

Conclusions

Bipolar disorder is a major public health concern because of its prevalence and consequent utilization of medical services. Most patients with acute manic episodes require inpatient care. The clinician can best improve the utilization of medical resources by decreasing the length of inpatient treatment and by preventing rehospitalizations. The appropriate use of pharmacologic treatments coupled with psychosocial therapies focusing on psychoeducation and alliance offers patients with bipolar disorder the best opportunity for a good outcome.

REFERENCES

1. Adams F, ed. The extant works of Aretaeus, the Cappadocian. London: The Sydenham Society, 1856.
2. Goodwin FK, Jamison KR. Manic-depressive illness. New York: Oxford University Press, 1990.
3. Kraepelin E. Manic-depressive insanity and paranoia. Barclay RM, translator. Robertson GM, ed. Edinburgh: Livingstone, 1921.
4. American Psychiatric Association. Diagnostic and statistical manual of mental disorders. 1st ed. Washington, DC: American Psychiatric Association, 1952.
5. American Psychiatric Association. Diagnostic and statistical manual of mental disorders. 2nd ed. Washington, DC: American Psychiatric Association, 1968.
6. American Psychiatric Association. Diagnostic and statistical manual of mental disorders. 3rd ed. Washington, DC: American Psychiatric Association, 1980.
7. American Psychiatric Association. Diagnostic and statistical manual of mental disorders. 4th ed. Washington, DC: American Psychiatric Association, 1994.
8. American Psychiatric Association. Diagnostic and statistical manual of mental disorders. 3rd ed. Washington, DC: American Psychiatric Association, 1987.
9. Tohen M, Tsuang MT, Goodwin DC. Prediction of outcome in mania by mood-incongruent psychotic features. Am J Psychiatry 1992;149:1580–1584.
10. Tohen M, Zarate C, Zarate S, et al. The McLean/Harvard First Episode Mania Project: pharmacologic treatment and outcome. Psychiatr Ann 1996;26:1–5.
11. Zarate CA Jr, Cohen BM, Tohen M, et al. The McLean first-episode family study. Presented at Second Annual Harvard Research Day, March 19, 1994.
12. Dunner DL, Stallone F, Fieve RR. Lithium carbonate and affective disorders. Part V: a double blind study of prophylaxis of depression in bipolar illness. Arch Gen Psychiatry 1976;33:117–120.
13. Tohen M, Bromet E. Epidemiology. In: Tasman K, Lieberman J, eds. Psychiatry. Philadelphia: WB Saunders, 1996.
14. Tohen M, Goodwin FK. Epidemiology of bipolar disorder. In: Tsuang M, Tohen M, Zahner G, eds. Psychiatric Epidemiology. New York: John Wiley & Sons, 1995:301–316.
15. Endicott J, Spitzer RL. A diagnostic interview: the schedule for affective disorders and schizophrenia. Arch Gen Psychiatry 1978;35:837–844.
16. Robins LN, Helzer JE, Croughan J, et al. The NIMH Diagnostic Interview Schedule: version II. Rockville, MD: Center for Epidemiologic Studies, 1979.
17. Regier DA, Myers JK, Kramer M, et al. The NIMH Epidemiologic Catchment Area Program: historical context, major objectives, and study population characteristics. Arch Gen Psychiatry 1984;41:934–941.
18. Kessler RC, Sonnega A, Bromet E, et al. Post-traumatic stress disorder in the National Comorbidity Survey. Arch Gen Psychiatry 1995;52:1048–1060.
19. Weissman MM, Myers JK, Harding PS. Psychiatric disorders in the U.S. urban community: 1975–1976. Am J Psychiatry 1978;135:459–462.
20. Kessler RC, McGonigle KA, Zhao S, et al. Lifetime and 12 month prevalence of DSM-III-R psychiatric disorders in the United States: results from the National Comorbidity Study. Arch Gen Psychiatry 1994;51:8–19.
21. Stoll AL, Banov M, Kolbrener M, et al. Antidepressant-associated mania. A controlled comparison with spontaneous mania. Am J Psychiatry 1994;151:1642–1645.
22. Stoll AL, Tohen M, Baldessarini RJ. Increasing diagnostic frequency of obsessive-compulsive disorder. Am J Psychiatry 1992;149:638–640.
23. Zarate CA Jr, Tohen M, Baraibar G, et al. Prescribing trends of antidepressants in bipolar depression. J Clin Psychiatry 1995;56:260–264.
24. Faravelli C, Degg'Innocenti BG, Aiazzi L, et al. Epidemiology of anxiety disorders. A community survey in Florence. J Affect Disord 1990;20:135–141.
25. Canino GJ, Bird HR, Shrout PE, et al. The prevalence of specific psychiatric disorders in Puerto Rico. Arch Gen Psychiatry 1987;44:727–735.
26. Weissman MM, Merikangas KR, Risch NJ. Comorbidity and co-transmission of alcoholism, anxiety and depression. Psychol Med 1994;24:69–80.
27. McElroy SL, Keck PE Jr, Bennet JA. Valproate as a loading treatment in acute mania. Neuropsychobiology 1993;27:146–149.
28. Tohen M, Waternaux CM, Tsuang MT. Outcome in mania. A four-year prospective follow-up of 75 patients utilizing survival analysis. Arch Gen Psychiatry 1990;47:1106–1111.

29. McElroy SL, Keck PE Jr, Pope JG, et al. Valproate in the treatment of rapid-cycling bipolar disorder. J Clin Psychopharmacol 1988;8:275–279.

30. Bowden CL, Brugger AM, Swann AC. Efficacy of divalproex vs. lithium and placebo in the treatment of mania. JAMA 1994; 271:918–924.

31. Zarate C, Tohen M. Axis II comorbidity in bipolar disorder. New York: Marcel Dekker (In press).

32. Post PM. Transduction of psychosocial stress into the neurobiology of treatment of affective disorders. Am J Psychiatry 1992;149:999–1010.

33. Keller MB, Shapiro RW, Lavori PW, et al. Relapse in major depressive disorder: analysis with the life table. Arch Gen Psychiatry 1982;39:911–915.

34. Harrow M, Goldberg JF, Grossman LS, et al. Outcome in manic disorders: a naturalistic follow-up study. Arch Gen Psychiatry 1990;47:665–671.

35. Tohen M, Waternaux CM, Tsuang MT, et al. Four-year follow-up of 24 first-episode manic patients. J Affect Disord 1990;19:79–86.

36. Tohen M, Greenfield S, Weiss R. Outcome of mania and comorbid substance use disorder. Harvard Rev Psychiatry (In press).

37. Harrow M, Goldberg JG, Grossman LS, et al. Outcome in manic disorders: a naturalistic follow-up study. Arch Gen Psychiatry 1990;47:665–671.

38. Malcolm R, Ballenger JC, Stugis ET, et al. Double-blind control trial comparing carbamazepine to oxazepam treatment of alcohol withdrawal. Am J Psychiatry 1989;146:617–621.

39. Weiss RD, Greenfield S, Tohen M, et al. Medication adherence in bipolar substance abusers. APA Annual Meeting, New York, May 4–9, 1996.

40. Renshaw PF, Yurgelun-Todd DA, Tohen M, et al. Temporal lobe proton magnetic resonance spectroscopy of first episode psychosis. Am J Psychiatry 1995;152:444–446.

41. Stoll AL, Mayer PV, Kolbrener M, et al. Neurological factors predict a favorable valproate response in bipolar and schizoaffective disorder. J Clin Psychopharmacol 1994;14:311–313.

42. Hirshfeld RMA, Clayton PJ, Cohen I, et al. Practice guideline for the treatment of patients with bipolar disorder. Am J Psychiatry 1994;151(Suppl):1–31.

43. Keller MB, Klerman GL, Lavori PW, et al. Treatment received by depressed patients. Mania 1982;248:1848–1855.

44. Sackett DL, Haynes RB, Guyatt GH, et al. Helping patients follow the treatments you prescribe. In: Clinical epidemiology: a basic science for clinical medicine. 2nd ed. Boston, MA: Little, Brown & Co., 1991:249–281.

45. Bosco MR, Rush AJ. Compliance with pharmacology in mood disorders. Psychiatr Ann 1995;25:269–279.

46. Jamison KR, Gerner RH, Goodwin FK. Patient and physician attitudes toward lithium: relationship to compliance. Arch Gen Psychiatry 1979;36:866–869.

47. Van Putten T. Why do patients with manic-depressive illness stop their lithium? Compr Psychiatry 1975;16:179–183.

48. Cochran SD. Preventing medical noncompliance in the outpatient treatment of bipolar affective disorders. J Consult Clin Psychol 1984;52:873–878.

49. VanGent EM, Zwart FM. Psychoeducation of partners of bipolar manic patients. J Affect Disord 1991;21:15–18.

50. Winokur G, Coryell W, Keller M, et al. A prospective follow-up of patients with bipolar and primary unipolar affective disorder. Arch Gen Psychiatry 1993;50:457–465.

51. Greenberg PE, Finklestein SN, Berndt ER. Economic consequences of illness in the work place. Sloan Management Review 1995:Summer.

52. DeNour AK. Psychosocial aspects of the management of mania. In: Belmaker RH, VanPraag HM, eds. Mania: an evolving concept. New York: Spectrum Publications, 1980:349–365.

53. Cade JFJ. Lithium salts in the treatment of psychotic excitement. Med J Aust 1949;36:349–352.

54. Hammond WA. The treatment of insanity. In: A treatise on the disease of the nervous system. New York: Appleton and Co., 1871:325–384.

55. Talbot JH. Use of lithium salts as a substitute for sodium chloride. Arch Int Med 1950;85:1–10.

56. Baldessarini RJ, Tondo L, Suppes P, et al. Pharmacological treatment of bipolar disorder throughout the life cycle in mood disorders across the life span. Shulman KI, Tohen M, Kutcher MT, eds. New York: John Wiley & Sons, 1996.

57. Prien W, Potter WZ. NIMH workshop report on treatment of bipolar disorder. Psychopharmacol Bull 1990;26:409–427.

58. Hettner O, Posen UJ, Ladefoged J, et al. Lithium: long term effects on the kidney, a prospective follow-up study ten years after kidney biopsy. Br J Psychiatry 1991;158:53–58.

59. Plenge P, Stensgaard A, Jensen HV, et al. 24 hour lithium concentration in human brain

studies by Li-7 magnetic resonance spectroscopy. Biol Psychiatry 1994;36:511–516.

60. Gelenberg AJ, Kane JM, Keller MB, et al. Comparison of standard and low serum levels of lithium for maintenance treatment of bipolar disorder. N Engl J Med 1989;321:1489–1493.

61. Jefferson JW, Griest JH. Lithium in psychiatry: a review. CNS Drugs 1994;1:448–464.

62. Baldessarini RJ. Chemotherapy in psychiatry. 3rd ed. Cambridge, MA: Harvard University Press (In press).

63. Kocis JH, Shaw ED, Stokes PE, et al. Neuropsychologic effects of lithium discontinuation. J Clin Psychopharmacol 1993;13:268–276.

64. Lambert PA, Caraz G, Borselli S, et al. Action neuro-psychotrope d'un nouvel antiepileptique: le depamide. Ann Med Psychol 1966;1:707–710.

65. Pope HG Jr, McElroy SL, Keck PE, et al. Valproate in the treatment of acute mania: a placebo-controlled study. Arch Gen Psychiatry 1991;48:62–68.

66. McElroy SL, Keck PE Jr, Bennett JA. Valproate as a loading treatment in acute mania. Neuropsychobiology 1993;27:146–149.

67. Keck PE, McElroy SL, Kmetz GF, et al. Clinical features of mania in adulthood. Mood disorders across the life span. In: Shulman KI, Tohen M, Kutcher SP, eds. New York: Wiley-Liss, 1996:265–279.

68. McElroy SL, Keck PE, Stanton SP, et al. A randomized comparison of divalproex oral loading versus haloperidol in the initial treatment of acute psychotic mania. J Clin Psychiatry 1996;57:142–146.

69. Schmidt D. Adverse effects of valproate. Epilepsia 1984;25(Suppl 1):44–49.

70. Asconape JJ, Penry JK, Dreifuss FE, et al. Valproate-associated pancreatitis. Epilepsia 1993;34:177–183.

71. Tohen M. The adverse effect profile and safety of divalproex. Rev Contemp Pharmacother 1995;6:587–595.

72. Scheffner D. Fatal liver failure in children on valproate. Lancet 1986;2:511.

73. Dreifuss FE, Santilli N, Langer DH, et al. Valproic acid hepatic fatalities: a retrospective review. Neurology 1987;37:379–385.

74. Dreifuss FE, Langer DH. Side effects of valproate. Am J Med 1988;(Suppl 1A):34–41.

75. Dreifuss FE, Langer DH, Moline KA, et al. Valproic acid hepatic fatalities. Part II: US experience since 1984. Neurology 1989;39:201–207.

76. Hurd RW, van Rinsvelt HA, Wilder BJ, et al. Selenium, zinc and copper changes with valproic acid: possible relation to drug side effects. Neurology 1984;34:1393–1395.

77. Dreifuss FE. Adverse effects of antiepileptic drug. In: Ward AA Jr, Penry JK, Purpura D, eds. Epilepsy. New York: Raven Press, 1983:249–266.

78. Tohen M, Castillo J, Baldessarini RJ, et al. Blood dyscrasias with carbamazepine and valproate: a pharmacoepidemiological study of 2,228 cases at risk. Am J Psychiatry 1995;152:413–418.

79. Ballenger JC, Post RM. Carbamazepine in manic depressive illness: a new treatment. Am J Psychiatry 1980;137:782–790.

80. Klien E, Beatal E, Lerer B, et al. Carbamazepine and haloperidol v. placebo and haloperidol in excited psychoses: a controlled study. Arch Gen Psychiatry 1984;41:165–170.

81. Post PM, Uhde TW, Roy-Byrne PP, et al. Correlates of antimanic responses to carbamazepine. Psychiatry Res 1987;21:71–83.

82. Frankenburg F, Tohen M, Cohen BM, et al. Long-term response to carbamazepine: a retrospective study. J Clin Psychopharmacol 1985;8:130–132.

83. Denikoff KD, Meglathery SB, Post RM, et al. Efficacy of carbamazepine compared with other agents: a clinical practice survey. J Clin Psychiatry 1994;55:70–76.

84. Prien RF, Gelenberg AJ. Alternatives to lithium for preventive treatment of bipolar disorder. Am J Psychiatry 1989;146:840–848.

85. Small JG, Klapper MH, Kellams JJ, et al. Electroconvulsive treatment compared with lithium in the management of manic states. Arch Gen Psychiatry 1988;45:727–732.

86. Smith LH, Hughes J, Hastings DW, et al. Electroshock treatment in the psychoses. Am J Psychiatry 1942;98:558–561.

87. Mukherjee S. Mechanisms of the antimanic effect of electroconvulsive therapy. Convulsive Ther 1989;5:227–243.

88. Mukherjee S, Sackeim HA, Lee C. Unilateral ECT in the treatment of manic episodes. Convulsive Ther 1988;4:74–89.

89. Stromgren LS. Electroconvulsive therapy in Aarhus, Denmark, in 1984: its application in nondepressive disorders. Convulsive Ther 1988;4:306–313.

90. Small JG, Small IF, Milstein V, et al. Manic symptoms: an indication for bilateral ECT. Biol Psychiatry 1985;20:125–134.

91. Vanelle JM, Carvalho JP, Olie HL. Evidence of the efficacy of maintenance electroconvulsive therapy in rapid cycling bipolars. J Eur Coll Neuropharmacol 1996;5:229.

92. Small JG, Klapper MH, Kellams JJ, et al. Electroconvulsive therapy compared with lithium in the management of manic states. Arch Gen Psychiatry 1986;45:727–732.

93. Calabrese JR, Woyshville MJ. Diagnosis and

treatment of rapid-cycling bipolar disorder. Dir Psychiatry 1994;14:1–8.

94. Lambert PA, Venaud G. Etude comparative du valpromide versus lithium dans la prophylaxie des troubles thymiques. Nervure Journal de Psychiatrie 1992;7:1–9.

95. Suppes T, Calabrese JR, Mitchell PB, et al. Algorithms for the treatment of bipolar, manic-depressive illness. Psychopharmacol Bull 1995;31:469–474.

96. Zarate CA, Daniel DG, Kinon BJ, et al. Algorithms for the treatment of schizophrenia. Psychopharmacol Bull 1995;31:461–467.

97. Chouinard G. Clonazepam in acute and maintenance treatment of bipolar affective disorder. J Clin Psychiatry 1987;48(Suppl):29–36.

98. Dwight MM, Keck PE Jr, Stanton SP, et al. Antidepressant activity and mania associated with risperidone treatment of schizoaffective disorder. Lancet 1994;344:554–555.

99. Tohen M, Zarate CA Jr, Centorrino F. Risperidone in the treatment of mania. J Clin Psychiatry 1996;57:1–6.

100. Lipinski JF, Pope HG Jr. Possible synergistic action between carbamazepine and lithium carbonate in the treatment of three acutely manic patients. Am J Psychiatry 1990;139:948–949.

101. Keller TA, Pazzaglia PJ, Post RM. Synergy of carbamazepine and valproic acid in affective illness: case report and review of the literature. J Clin Psychopharmacol 1992;12:276–281.

102. Tohen M, Castillo J, Pope H, et al. Concomitant use of valproate and carbamazepine in bipolar and schizo-affective disorder. J Clin Psychiatry 1994;14:67–70.

103. Calabrese JR, Delucchi GA. Spectrum of valproate in 55 patients with rapid-cycling bipolar disorder. Am J Psychiatry 1990;147:275–279.

104. Banov MD, Zarate C, Tohen M, et al. Clozapine therapy in refractory affective disorders: polarity predicts response in long-term follow-up. J Clin Psychiatry 1994;55:295–300.

105. Weisler R, Risner M, Ascher J, et al. Use of lamotrigine in the treatment of bipolar disorder. New Research Program and Abstracts of the 146th annual meeting of the American Psychiatric Association, Philadelphia, Pennsylvania, May 1994. Abstract no. NR611.

106. Keck PE Jr, McElroy SL, Strakowski SM, et al. Pharmacologic treatment of schizoaffective disorder. Psychopharmacology 1994;114:529–538.

107. McElroy SL, Keck PE, Stanton SP, et al. A randomized comparison of divalproex oral loading versus haloperidol in the initial treatment of acute psychotic mania. J Clin Psychiatry 1996;57:142–146.

108. Trimble MR, Thompson PJ. Sodium valproate and cognitive function. Epilepsia 1984;25(Suppl 1):60–64.

109. Keller MB, Shapiro RW, Lavori RW, et al. Relapse in major depressive disorder: analysis with the life table. Arch Gen Psychiatry 1982;39:911–915.

110. Dion GL, Tohen M, Anthony W, et al. Symptom and functioning of patients with bipolar disorder six months after hospitalization. Hosp Community Psychiatry 1988;39:652–657.

111. The Medical Practice Information Demonstration Project. 1979:42.

112. Zis AP, Goodwin FK. Major affective disorders as a recurrent illness: a critical review. Arch Gen Psychiatry 1979;6:835–839.

113. Keller MB, Lavori PW, Rice J, et al. Differential outcome of pure manic, mixed/cycling, and pure depressive episodes in patients with bipolar illness. JAMA 1986;255:3138–3142.

Chapter 9

Schizophrenia

Lloyd I. Sederer and Franca Centorrino

DEFINITION

A defining feature of schizophrenia is the presence of psychotic symptomatology. Psychosis refers to a gross impairment in reality testing and of ego boundaries. For some patients, psychosis also involves delusions, hallucinations, disorganized thinking and speech, or disorganized or bizarre behavior. By its nature, psychosis compromises adaptive capacities; consequently, psychotic patients suffer from a diminution in functioning.

Schizophrenia is a disorder that persists for at least 6 months and evidences at least 1 month of acute symptomatology in the form of delusions, hallucinations, disorganized speech, grossly disorganized or catatonic behavior, or negative symptoms such as lack of motivation or will, affective blunting, and impoverished speech. No symptom is pathognomonic of schizophrenia. Occupational and social functioning typically become impaired over time (1).

The term dementia praecox was introduced in 1852 by Morel to denote a disorder of early dementia (2). Morel described the case of a boy who developed a thought disorder in early adolescence. At the end of that century, Kraepelin proposed that dementia praecox be diagnosed in psychotic patients whose illness had an early onset and a chronic and deteriorating course (3). Kraepelin was determined to demonstrate that mental disorders were distinct from one another and could be differentiated by differing symptom presentations, causes, course, and prognosis. Dementia praecox, he argued, was different from circular insanity (manic-depressive or bipolar disorder; see Chapter 8).

The term schizophrenia was introduced by Bleuler early in the 20th century (4). The term literally meant "split soul" and portrayed a mind divided against itself. Bleuler, who was able to follow a hospital population over an extended period, did not believe that all cases of schizophrenia (or dementia praecox) followed a deteriorating or pernicious course. Bleuler's diagnostic criteria have become known as the four As, which he regarded as the primary disturbances in schizophrenia. He considered hallucinations and delusions as accessory or secondary symptoms. The four As are as follows:

1. Autism: a tendency to withdraw from reality into fantasy.
2. Association: a loosening of thoughts or associations.
3. Affect: affects (or feelings) that are split off or inappropriate to the circumstances.
4. Ambivalence: profoundly mixed or contradictory feelings or attitudes that can become severe enough to immobilize the patient.

Schneider offered a phenomenologic perspective on schizophrenia (5). His work emphasized the internal experience of the patient. Schneider posited first-rank symptoms that he believed to be specific to schizophrenia. Although no support for the specificity of these symptoms exists, they occur commonly in schizophrenia and are clinically important (6). The first-rank symptoms are audible thoughts (auditory hallucinations that echo or speak thoughts aloud), voices debating or disagreeing, voices commenting, somatic passivity (the experience of sensations imposed on one's body by an outside force), thought withdrawal (thoughts are withdrawn or taken out of one's mind by an outside force), thought insertion, thought broadcasting (thoughts are experienced as broadcast or disseminated to the world), made impulses (a compelling impulse that is experienced as not one's own), made acts (actions and will are experienced as under the control of an outside force), and delusional perception (patients perceive an object in the environment, ascribe idiosyncratic value to it, and develop the perception into a delusion; e.g., a person the patient meets is ascribed great power and then becomes a demonic figure whom the patient fears).

Although the *Diagnostic and Statistical Manual*, 4th edition (DSM-IV) now holds the standard criteria for the diagnosis of schizophrenia, a varied perspective, as offered above, can broaden the clinician's understanding of the patient's experience and his or her course and prognosis.

DIAGNOSIS

DSM-IV defines schizophrenia as a disorder of at least 6 months' duration, with 1 month (DSM-IIIR only required 1 week) of two or more active-phase symptoms: delusions, hallucinations, disorganized speech, grossly disorganized or catatonic behavior, and negative symptoms (see above) (1). The diagnostic subtypes of schizophrenia defined in DSM-IV are paranoid, disorganized, catatonic, undifferentiated, and residual.

The six criteria for the DSM-IV diagnosis of schizophrenia are as follows:

1. Criterion A. This criterion defines the characteristic symptoms of the illness, two of which must be present for 1 month (less if treated) in the acute phase. These symptoms are listed above. Only one symptom is required if the delusions are bizarre or if auditory hallucinations are keeping up a running commentary or are conversing with each other.
2. Criterion B. This criterion emphasizes social/occupational dysfunction. Work, school, interpersonal relations, or self-care must have deteriorated from the patient's premorbid state for a significant period since the onset of the illness.
3. Criterion C. The disorder must have a duration of at least 6 months, which may include prodromal or residual periods.
4. Criterion D. Schizoaffective and mood disorders must be excluded.
5. Criterion E. The disorder must not be due to the effects of a substance (e.g.,

abused drug or medication) or due to a general medical condition.

6. Criterion F. When the patient has a history of autistic disorder (or other pervasive developmental disorders), an additional diagnosis of schizophrenia is made only when prominent hallucinations or delusions are present for at least 1 month.

The subtypes of schizophrenia will be discussed below (see Descriptive and Differential Diagnosis). The course specifiers in DSM-IV can be applied after 1 year has elapsed since the onset of the acute-phase symptoms. The specifiers are episodic with interepisodic residual symptoms; with prominent negative symptoms; episodic with no interepisodic residual symptoms; continuous; single episode in full remission; and other or unspecified pattern.

EPIDEMIOLOGY

Prevalence refers to the number of cases, reported by percentage or per 1000 persons, in a given population at a given time. The lifetime prevalence for schizophrenia has been estimated to range from 1.0–1.9%, and the 1-month point prevalence has been estimated to be 0.7% (7, 8). The incidence of a disorder is the number of new cases annually in a given population. The incidence of schizophrenia in the United States has been estimated to be 0.05%, although worldwide studies suggest a somewhat lower rate (9, 10). Although these prevalence rates are lower than many of the other disorders described in this text, the proportion of schizophrenic patients who receive care and the substantial morbidity of this disorder result in very great personal, public health, and economic problems.

A consistent finding in schizophrenia is the inverse relationship between this disorder and social class (11, 12). Two theories prevail that attempt to explain the higher rates of schizophrenia in lower socioeconomic status groups. The social causation model identifies the increased stresses of the lower class as a risk factor in the illness. The selection-drift model posits that schizophrenics are either prevented from achieving greater socioeconomic advantage (selection) or have drifted to the lower echelons of society because of the often catastrophic consequences of their illness (13–15).

Although the prevalence of schizophrenia has been regarded as equal between the sexes, more recent work indicates a higher rate of utilization of services by males, suggesting that morbidity may be greater in males than in females (16, 17). The onset of the illness occurs typically in adolescence or early adulthood (more so for males than females), and the disorder is most prevalent in persons aged 15 to 50 years (7, 8). Risk rates are higher for nonmarried than married persons, and females are more likely to be married than males (12, 18). World Health Organization (WHO) studies indicate comparable incidence rates for schizophrenia in various cultures (19). Pregnancy and birth complications have been increasingly identified as risk factors for schizophrenia (20).

THE FOUR QUESTIONS
Descriptive and Differential Diagnosis

The subtypes of schizophrenia are defined by the predominant clinical symptoms that the patient exhibits. Catatonic type refers to motor immobility or excessive motor activity that is either purposeless or unrelated to the external world, extreme negativism or mutism, posturing, or echolalia or echopraxia (mimicking words or actions). Paranoid type refers to a preoccu-

TABLE 9.1.   General Medical and Substance Induced Conditions in the Differential Diagnosis of Schizophrenia

Toxins—exogenous
   Amphetamines
   Cocaine
   Psychomimetics
      Lysergic acid diethylamide (LSD)
      Phencyclidine (PCP)
   Mescaline
   Alcohol
      Alcoholic hallucinosis
      Alcohol withdrawal states, including delirium tremens (DTs)
   Barbiturates
      Barbiturate intoxication
      Barbiturate withdrawal
   Steroids
   Anticholinergics
Infections
   Viral encephalitis; herpes meningitis; viral or bacterial meningitis; syphilis (lues); subacute bacterial endocarditis (SBE)
Metabolic—endocrine
   Thyroid
      Hyperthyroidism
      Hypothyroidism
   Adrenal disease
      Addison's disease
      Cushing's disease
   Porphyria
   Electrolyte imbalances
Space–occupying lesions
   Tumors
      Primary tumors
      Metastases (e.g., lung, breast)
   Subdural hematoma
   Brain abscess
Nutritional deficiencies
   Niacine: pellagra
   Thiamine: Wernicke-Korsakoff's syndrome
Vascular abnormalities
   Collagen disorders
   Aneurysm
   Intracranial hemorrhage
Cerebral hypoxia
   Secondary to severe anemia
   Secondary to decreased cardiac output
Miscellaneous
   Complex partial seizures: temporal lobe epilepsy
   Wilson's disease
   Huntington's chorea
   Normal pressure hydrocephalus

pation with delusions or persistent auditory hallucinations and the relative absence of disorganized speech, behavior, or flat affect. The disorganized type shows disorganized speech, behavior, and flat or inappropriate affect. The undifferentiated type evidences symptoms that meet Criterion A (noted earlier) but does not meet symptomatic criteria of catatonia, paranoia, or disorganization. The residual type is used when at least one episode of schizophrenia has occurred, but the current presentation lacks prominent, positive psychotic symptoms. Continuing evidence for negative symptoms or attenuated Criterion A symptoms must also be present.

Schizophrenia must be differentiated from a psychotic disorder due to a general medical condition. Table 9.1 lists medical disorders that can present with psychotic and cognitive disturbances that may be confused with schizophrenia. The diagnosis of a general medical condition causing psychosis is made when the delusions or hallucinations are the direct physiologic consequence of the medical condition. Substance-induced psychotic disorder must also be differentiated from schizophrenia (Table 9.1). This diagnosis is made when a substance is determined to be the cause of the psychotic symptom.

Mood disorder with psychotic features, as distinguished from schizophrenia, is diagnosed when psychotic symptoms occur only during periods of mood disturbance. Schizoaffective disorder is diagnosed when mood disturbance occurs simultaneously with the active phase of schizophrenia and is present for a substantial portion of the total duration of the disorder, and when hallucinations or delusions are present for at least 2 weeks in the absence of mood symptoms.

Schizophreniform disorder is diagnosed on the basis of duration. Schizophrenia is only diagnosed after 6 months; schizo-phreniform disorder can be diagnosed after 1 month (and does not require a deterioration in functioning). Delusional disorder is diagnosed when delusions exist in the absence of other symptoms of schizophrenia (e.g., hallucinations, negative symptoms).

Ego Defenses and Character Style

Early ego psychology theory considered schizophrenics to suffer from an inborn ego defect that rendered them easily overwhelmed by internal drives and affects (21). Object relations theorists (especially Klein, Fairbairn, Guntrip, and Winnicott) also subscribed to constitutional deficits in ego capacities to regulate and control drives, relate to other people, understand and adapt to reality, and perform cognitively. Harry Stack Sullivan, perhaps the most influential American psychiatrist of the interpersonal school, argued that mental illness was the product of a failure in interpersonal relationships from birth onward (22, 23). Although his etiologic propositions have dimmed in influence, his contributions to understanding psychotic experience and to working interpersonally with schizophrenic patients should not be overlooked.

Schizophrenic patients, when psychotic, typically use the defenses of profound or psychotic denial, projection, and severe distortion. When compensated, these defenses may persist but in a more flexible form, thereby allowing some perspective on the illness when the patient is not in the acute phase.

Schizotypal patients have a personality disorder characterized by pervasive social and interpersonal deficits. They are profoundly uncomfortable in close relationships and seek emotional distance. They also show eccentric behavior and cognitive and perceptual distortions (e.g., ideas of reference, odd beliefs, perceptual illusions). Schizotypal patients may represent a position on a continuum from this severe personality disorder to schizophreniform disorder to the various subtypes of schizophrenia.

Formulation

Schizophrenic patients suffer from profound problems of identity. A defective sense of self and disturbed interpersonal boundaries often make it difficult for these patients to differentiate themselves from others. They can experience themselves as either merged with others or utterly alone. The clinician seeking to establish a working alliance with a schizophrenic patient must bear in mind the patient's fears of fusion and, alternately, the patient's alienation and estrangement. Vulnerability and dependency, characteristics of the schizophrenic patient, are caused by limited ego capacities. Dependency, however, is a difficult feeling for schizophrenic patients to bear because of fear of closeness and an already compromised self-regard. Finally, anger and aggression are especially difficult affects because of boundary disturbances and weak ego controls. Anger, therefore, is typically unmodulated and can appear as unrestrained rage or may be denied and result in passivity and apathy (24).

The psychosocial history should consider early development and explore for evidence of compromised ego functioning in school and relationships. The patient's educational, social, and occupational history should assess strengths and limitations. Past psychiatric treatment should be examined with special attention to the successes and failures of relationships with prior treaters. Premorbid functioning will familiarize the clinician with the patient's

adaptive capacities and inform prognostic considerations. The patient's premorbid defensive operations should be evaluated as extensively as possible. Before he or she psychologically turned to the acute defenses of denial, projection, and distortion used in psychosis, the clinician should determine whether the patient used withdrawal, reaction formation, intellectualization, denial, somatization, acting-out, or other defensive operations (1, 25).

The formulation lends meaning to the patient's decompensation by depicting the stresses that were instrumental to the onset of the acute illness. Details of the stresses and losses in the patient's life should be sought; this information is best understood in terms of the limitations in ego functioning, boundaries, affect regulation, and interpersonal distance that characterize schizophrenic psychopathology.

An assessment of the home and social environment is also crucial. Family studies have demonstrated that environments that are critical, hostile, or include an emotionally overinvolved relative result in higher relapse rates for schizophrenic patients (26–29). WHO studies indicate that schizophrenics in non-Western, traditional societies, where families and communities are more tolerant of psychopathology, have a better outcome than those seen in Western, industrialized cultures (30). Establishing an alliance and educating the family will be critical to the ongoing care and course of the disorder.

Focal Problem

Suicidal or combative behavior is always the first priority in the care of any patient, including the patient with acute psychosis. A careful risk assessment for suicide (see Chapter 2) and for behavior dangerous to others (see Chapter 3) should be performed for all psychotic patients. Acute care, including hospital level of care, must aim to protect the patient and others. Psychotic patients may be at risk for combative behavior when they are fearful of others and believe that they may be injured. These patients should be reassured that staff members do not mean to harm them and that they can keep themselves in control. Paranoid patients require distance and should be allowed their privacy. Confrontation is generally not an effective approach with these patients. A focal problem that can contribute to aggressiveness in psychotic patients is withdrawal from nicotine. Many patients with schizophrenia smoke. Nicotine may serve as a tranquilizer, and its sudden withdrawal (as can occur with emergency, residential, or inpatient settings) can prompt aggressive behavior. Use of nicotine replacement (by patch or gum) or cigarette breaks should be considered in the acute care of nicotine-dependent patients.

The focal problem, the immediate difficulty that has precipitated acute care, must be addressed for the patient to leave the acute care setting. For first-break psychotic illness, the focal problem may be elusive. Although an insidious deterioration in functioning may have occurred over a number of years, a specific stressor usually precedes the acute decompensation. More important, however, are the focal problems that must be addressed to allow the patient to leave acute care with a treatment plan acceptable to the patient and family. The absence of an adequate living situation or a family that cannot understand or tolerate the patient's illness are key focal problems for the acute treatment of a patient early in the course of the disease.

Clinicians working with schizophrenic patients with an established history recognize the three problems most commonly associated with relapse: failure to attend outpatient treatment, failure to take medications, and use and abuse of alcohol and nonprescribed legal and illegal drugs. These three problems are not distinct; in fact, they often co-occur.

Although the immediate interventions of acute care involve detoxification from any substances of abuse and the resumption of pharmacotherapy, clinicians would be short-sighted if they did not address the motives and needs of the patient that led to the treatment failure. To form an alliance with the patient, and to enhance the likelihood of treatment compliance, the clinician must work to understand why the patient did not follow through with treatment or continued to use destabilizing substances. Patients can often explain their noncompliance and, at times, these are problems to which the clinician can respond. For example, akathisia is a common reason for noncompliance with high-potency neuroleptics, as is excess sedation for noncompliance with low-potency agents. Denial of illness and consequent treatment noncompliance may be due to the profoundly disturbing impact of acknowledging a schizophrenic illness. Patients with any chronic illness require time and support to adjust to living with a severe and debilitating illness, particularly if relatively good premorbid functioning was enjoyed. Schizophrenic patients often report the use of alcohol and other drugs to reduce social anxiety and to enable contact with other people; this may be true especially for adolescent and young adult patients. For some patients, these drugs provide the only pleasure they can derive. Acute care will not be optimal for the patient and family, and will not be cost-effective over time, unless the needs and motives of patients are recognized and inform treatment planning.

BIOLOGIC EVALUATION

The psychotic symptoms seen in schizophrenic patients may also occur in a wide range of psychiatric and medical illnesses. The evaluation of acute psychosis should include a careful history and mental status examination. For hospitalized patients, and for other acute care patients when the history or presenting problems raise concerns, a physical examination and laboratory tests to rule out physical illness or drug-induced psychosis should be performed. The index of suspicion for a medical or drug-related problem should be high when the patient evidences variation in level of consciousness or presents with unusual symptoms.

History

The patient's history is essential to the evaluation of acute psychosis. The history includes the present illness; past medical and psychiatric illnesses; present and past medications, including the specifics of all medication trials, to the extent possible; family history of medical, neurologic, and psychiatric disorders; a substance abuse history; a thorough review of systems, with particular attention to head trauma; and a thorough mental status examination. The history obtained from the patient should be augmented with information from other informed sources, including family members, significant others, and current and past treaters when possible.

Physical Examination

When performing a physical examination, the physician should pay particular attention to the vital signs, the pupils, and to the presence of any diaphoresis (31).

The neurologic examination should concentrate on any focal signs of cerebral dysfunction and attempt to elicit signs of diffuse cerebral disease.

Laboratory Tests

Laboratory tests for the hospitalized patient include a complete blood count, with hemoglobin and hematocrit; electrolytes; blood glucose; and renal, liver, and thyroid function tests. For those patients who present with unusual signs, symptoms, or abnormal laboratory findings, other tests and consultations may be necessary. These include blood cultures, zinc, magnesium, bromine, ceruloplasmin, ammonia, erythrocyte sedimentation rate, vitamin B_{12} and folic acid levels, arterial blood gases, electrocardiogram, lumbar puncture, human immunodeficiency virus testing, and urine and drug screens for substances.

Electroencephalogram

The electroencephalogram (EEG) is indicated principally when there is a clinical suspicion of epilepsy. Other indications include delirium, significantly altered states of consciousness, head injury, and some cases of first-onset psychosis when the clinical picture is confusing or response to treatment is less than optimal (32).

Imaging

In recent years, neuroimaging techniques have improved dramatically (33). The routine use of computed tomography and magnetic resonance imaging is not standard practice because of the limited translation of findings into actual treatment planning. Imaging techniques can be considered for first psychotic episodes with focal neurologic findings, a history of alcohol abuse, head trauma, seizures, the presence of a movement disorder, an abnormal EEG, cognitive deficits, delirium, and catatonia. The use of magnetic resonance spectroscopy and functional magnetic resonance imaging have made possible the noninvasive, in vivo, study of the biochemistry and cortical activation in schizophrenic patients (34). Although significant differences have been reported for both chronic schizophrenic and first-episode psychotic patients when compared with controls, the role of these techniques in everyday clinical practice has not yet been established.

ASSESSING LEVEL OF CARE

For most of this century, schizophrenic patients were hospitalized for episodes of acute psychosis and, once admitted, many had extended hospital stays. This is no longer the case. Today, hospital level of care is indicated when safety cannot be assured for the patient and others, when medical complications require daily physician and nursing care, or when the patient would be at risk to escape from a less-intensive level of acute care (e.g., residential care). For many schizophrenic patients, particularly those known to a treatment program, brief residential or partial hospital stays will provide the containment, structure, support, and treatment needed for acute care. For those patients who require locked containment at the outset of their psychoses, every effort should be made to transfer them to a residential or ambulatory setting as soon as clinically appropriate. Patients generally prefer less-restrictive environments that permit greater liberty and dignity.

TREATMENT

Psychopharmacologic Management

Antipsychotic Agents

After the discovery of chlorpromazine in the early 1950s (35), the development of antipsychotic agents led to revolutionary changes in the practice of modern psychiatry (36–40). Table 9.2 lists representative available antipsychotic agents. Antipsychotic agents rank third among all drugs prescribed in the United States. The availability of these medications has allowed earlier hospital discharge, encouraged the deinstitutionalization movement of 1960s–1970s, and improved the quality of life and the potential for rehabilitation of patients with schizophrenia and other psychotic disorders (41–43). Antipsychotic medications, including neuroleptics and the newer or atypical antipsychotics, specifically and effectively treat acute psychosis and can limit exacerbations and chronic symptoms of schizophrenia. Antipsychotic drug treatment is a crucial component of the comprehensive clinical management of schizophrenic patients. A careful psychosocial assessment and the development of a therapeutic alliance will enhance medication compliance and thereby enhance the potential for rehabilitation.

NEUROLEPTIC AGENTS

Neuroleptic (literally "neuron seizing") agents have established efficacy in the treatment of the acute psychosis of schizophrenia (44, 45). Improvement of agitation, hostility, and insomnia can be seen within 48 hours. Usually 2 to 3 weeks (or more) are required to see clear beneficial effects on positive symptoms such as hallucinations and acute delusions. Neurolep-

TABLE 9.2.   Representative Clinically Used Antipsychotic Drugs

Agent	Typical dose (mg/day)
Phenothiazines	
Aliphatic side chain	
Chlorpromazine	250–800
Trifluopromazine	100–300
Piperidine side chain	
Mesoridazine	100–300
Thioridazine	250–600
Piperazine side chain	
Acetophenazine	60–120
Fluphenazine[a]	5–25
Perphenazine	4–32
Trifluoperazine	5–25
Thioxanthenes	
Aliphatic side chain	
Chlorprothixene	50–400
Piperazine side chain	
Thiothixene	5–25
Benzepines	
Clozapine	200–600
Loxapine	50–150
Olanzapine[b]	(7.5–20)
Quetiepine[b]	(150–800)
Phenylbutylpiperidines	
Bromperidol	3–6
Droperidol[c]	1–3
Haloperidol[a]	1–20
Pimozide[d]	1–8
Heterocyclic indoles	
Molindone	50–225
Risperidone	1–10
Sertindole[b]	(4–24)
Ziprasidone[b]	(40–160)

Reprinted with permission from Baldessarini RJ, Centorrino F. Results and limits of antipsychotic pharmacotherapy. Rome: Noos-Aggiornamenti in Psichiatria (in press).
[a]Available as depot prodrug fatty ester derivative.
[b]Experimental in mid-1996; typical doses are tentative.
[c]Used in the United States mainly as an anesthetic or preanesthetic sedative and sometimes in psychiatric emergencies.
[d]Oral, relatively long acting.

tics are less effective for negative symptoms, including flat affect, withdrawal, amotivation, and poverty of speech and thoughts (46). Systematic trials of medications at adequate doses and durations are necessary to conclude which agent is most effective for a given patient.

Choice of Agent

Neuroleptic agents are approximately equally effective in groups of psychotic patients when given in adequate dosages. In choosing a medication, the following guidelines apply:

1. The clinician should review medication trials. An antipsychotic that has worked in the past might be considered first. If the patient responded adversely to a drug in the past, this is a relative contraindication to its reuse.

2. When the patient has not been treated previously or there is no information on past trials, the choice of an antipsychotic can be based mainly on the side effect profile. When sedation is preferable, more sedating agents like chlorpromazine or thioridazine may be used. High-potency neuroleptics (e.g., haloperidol, fluphenazine, trifluoperazine, thiothixene) are less sedating, hypotensive, and anticholinergic, but have a greater risk of extrapyramidal side effects. The low-potency neuroleptics (e.g., chlorpromazine and thioridazine) have the opposite side effect profile. Neuroleptics of medium potency—including perphenazine, loxapine, and molindone—have intermediate extrapyramidal and autonomic risks.

3. Psychiatrists should become familiar with the different classes of antipsychotics as well as new medications, drug combinations, and interactions. Psychiatrists should know of the existence of potential new avenues for treatment-refractory patients and, although not all psychiatrists can provide these treatments themselves, they should know how patients may be referred to tertiary care when needed.

Dose

Abundant research evidence accumulated since the early 1980s provides little support for significant gains in clinical improvement or in the speed of recovery with very high doses of neuroleptics (equivalent to several grams of chlorpromazine per 24 hours) (47–49). In current clinical practice, the daily antipsychotic dose in acutely psychotic hospitalized patients averages about 300 mg equivalent of chlorpromazine, despite a sharp fall in duration of hospitalization. The increased use of polypharmacy, particularly the combination of a high-potency benzodiazepine with an antipsychotic agent, provides sedative effects that are useful early in treatment (50).

Route of Administration

Neuroleptics can be given orally or intramuscularly. Oral medications are available in elixirs, tablets, or capsules. Liquid preparations are somewhat more rapidly absorbed than tablets and present less possibility of cheeking. Intramuscular (IM) administration can be used, especially in emergency situations.

Schedule of Administration

Acutely psychotic patients receiving high doses of medication that are rapidly administrated (so-called rapid neuroleptization, in which doses of antipsychotic medication are administered every 30 or 60 minutes until there is evidence of improvement or sedation) do not respond more rapidly or fully, on average, than patients who receive standard doses and routine administration. Furthermore, there is no evidence that patients receiving rapid neuroleptization have shorter hospital stays (51). Higher doses, however, often mean more side effects that require greater amounts of anti-Parkinson agents and an increased risk of toxic effects including extrapyramidal symptoms, hypotension, and delirium. The concurrent use of benzodiazepines provides for rapid sedation, which is different from rapid neuroleptization. The addition of benzodiazepines should be a brief intervention; there is no research available to support that long-term use of these agents is effective.

TABLE 9.3. Adverse Neurologic Effects of Neuroleptic-Antipsychotic Agents

	Reaction features	Maximum risk	Proposed mechanism	Proposed treatment
Acute dystonia	Terrifying spasms of eye, face, tongue, larynx, neck, back; risk high in young men	1–10 days, may recur with IM depots	Compensatory DA excess?	Injected anticholinergic diagnostic + orally preventive if risk high
Parkinsonism	Bradykinesia, rigidity, mask facies, shuffling gait, variable tremor	2–12 weeks, often persists	DA receptor blockade + DA neuron inactivation	Anticholinergics
Malignant syndrome (NMS)	Catatonia, fever, stupor, unstable BP, high CK, can be fatal	Weeks, may recur	DA blockade? Hypothalamic?	Supportive! Bromocriptine? Dantrolene??
Rabbit syndrome	Perioral tremor, reversible, variant of Parkinsonism?	Months	DA blockade?	Anticholinergics
Akathisia (NIA)	Motor restlessness, anxiety, agitation, aggression?	Immediate and persists	Adrenergic?	Lower dose, propranolol, clonidine, anxiolytics?, anticholinergics??
Tardive dyskinesia (TD)	Oral facial lingual dyskinesia, choreoathetosis, dystonia, rarely progressive, often reversible, risk high in elderly and in mood disorders	Months, withdrawal worsens	DA excess?	Prevention best No specific treatment proved Vitamin E? Anti-DA agents if disabling?

Reprinted with permission from Baldessarini RJ, Centorrino F. Results and limits of antipsychotic pharmacotherapy. Rome: Noos-Aggiornamenti in Psichiatria (in press).
BP, blood pressure; CK, serum creatine kinase; DA, dopamine; IM, intramuscular; NIA, neuroleptic-induced akathisia; NMS, neuroleptic malignant syndrome; TD, tardive dyskinesia (and tardive dystonia). Risk of all of these reactions is probably higher with more potent agents. Incidence of TD averages 3–5%/year, but spontaneous remission can occur at 2–3%/year, leaving a prevalence of 20–30%.

Adverse Effects

Central Nervous System Adverse Effects.
Central nervous system adverse effects are summarized in Table 9.3. Typical central nervous system manifestations of antipsychotic agents are extrapyramidal and idiopathic side effects, including dystonia, akathisia (motor restlessness), neuroleptic malignant syndrome (NMS), bradykinesia, rabbit syndrome, tardive dyskinesia, and dystonia (52–55). Akathisia is often difficult to diagnose, may lead to aggressive or self-destructive behaviors, and appears to be a leading cause for drug refusal or noncompliance (36, 39, 55). Neuroleptic medications can lower seizure threshold. Haloperidol, fluphenazine, and molindone may be less likely to induce seizures than other agents (56).

Peripheral Adverse Effects. Hypotension and risk of fall in the elderly (which are greater with the low-potency agents) and hepatic toxicity with jaundice (generally benign allergic, cholestatic type) that responds to stopping medications are common peripheral adverse effects. Less common is bone marrow suppression, which is not consistently dose related. Patients who show fever, sore throat, or signs of infection should have an immediate white blood count to rule out agranulocytosis (36, 39, 57–59).

Anticholinergic Adverse Effects. Anticholinergic (and other adverse autonomic) effects include dry mouth, blurry vision, urinary retention, constipation, confusion, and sedation. Patients with narrow angle glaucoma should not be prescribed neuroleptic agents without ophthalmologic consultation.

Hypothalamic Effects. Hypothalamic adverse effects include increased appetite, decreased libido, breast enlargement, and galactorrhea, which is associated with hyperprolactinemia.

Neuroleptics, Pregnancy, and Lactation

Neuroleptics cross the placenta and can be detected in breast milk. When neuroleptics are required, the risks and benefits must be addressed with the patient and family, and informed consent must be obtained (60).

Long-Acting Depot Antipsychotic Agents

Long-acting injections of esterified antipsychotic drugs (e.g., haloperidol and fluphenazine decanoate) can be administered IM in an oily vehicle every 2 to 4 weeks (61, 62). Treatment with such agents has provided superior average outcome with lower risk of relapse than orally administered neuroleptics (36, 39). These medications are currently underused; they are given principally after noncompliance has led to repeated psychotic relapses. Conservative doses of long-acting agents are not associated with increased risk of adverse effects; for many patients, relapses and readmissions might be prevented or reduced if these agents were used more routinely (61).

Novel Antipsychotic Agents

CLOZAPINE

This atypical antipsychotic agent is effective in greater than 30% of treatment-refractory schizophrenic patients (63–68). Patients with both negative and positive symptoms may continue to improve for up to 10–12 months; there is little evidence for additional gain thereafter (69). Clozapine has been noted to reduce suicide risk by perhaps ninefold in neuroleptic-resistant patients. This decrease in suicide risk was associated with improvement in depression and hopelessness (65, 70).

Patients who are candidates for clozapine therapy are those who have responded inadequately to several trials of standard antipsychotic agents or who have been unable to tolerate neuroleptics because of severe drug-induced Parkinsonism, dystonia, or tardive dyskinesia. Clozapine also may have a beneficial effect in the syndrome of polydipsia and hyponatremia associated with standard neuroleptic treatment (71). The risk of seizures from clozapine is dose related. Anticonvulsant prophylaxis (with valproic acid, not carbamazepine because of its synergistic effect on leukopenia) is recommended when dosages exceed 500–600 mg/day. Other side effects include hypersalivation (responsive to an anticholinergic drug like benztropine or glycopyrrolate), drowsiness (especially in the morning), nocturnal enuresis, hypotension, and hyperthermia (66, 67). Clozapine carries minimal risk of extrapyramidal neurologic side effects (66, 67). Because of the drug's 1–2% risk of agranulocytosis, treatment should not be initiated if the baseline white blood cell (WBC) count is less than 3500/mm^3. Weekly white cell counts are needed after starting treatment because the early detection of granulocytopenia minimizes the risk of agranulocytosis. When a patient has a WBC count between 3000 and 3500/mm^3, twice weekly WBC and differential counts should be performed. If the total WBC count falls below 3000/mm^3, the clozapine should be withheld and the patient closely monitored. Patients with a WBC count below 2000/mm^3 can recover, but should never be re-exposed to the drug (65, 66).

RISPERIDONE

Risperidone is a product of the search for other novel agents that have chemical analogy or pharmacodynamic similarity to clozapine but are safer, more convenient, and less costly than clozapine (72–78). Risperidone can be considered quantitatively atypical in that low doses are associated with limited risks of acute adverse neurologic effects (73, 79–82). Research evidence that risperidone may be superior in efficacy to older agents remains limited (79–83). The narrow dosing range (1–10 mg/day) and lack of an IM form limit its usefulness in acute psychosis or psychiatric emergencies (79, 82, 83). Risperidone strongly elevates prolactin levels and has been associated with several reported cases of NMS (84). Risperidone also has some risk of hypotension and sedation, especially in elderly patients; it should be used cautiously in the elderly population, especially if polypharmacy is involved (85).

Interactions of Antipsychotic Agents With Other Drugs

Neuroleptics, especially low-potency phenothiazines and thioxanthenes, can interact with other drugs (39). Neuroleptics can strongly potentiate sedatives and analgesics as well as alcohol, hypnotics, antihistamines, and cold remedies. Chlorpromazine significantly increases the respiratory depression associated with concurrently administered opioids. Neuroleptic drugs inhibit the actions of direct dopaminergic agonists and of levodopa. Interactions between phenothiazines or risperidone and antihypertensive agents can be unpredictable (due to the potential postural hypotension caused by the low-potency phenothiazines). Clozapine and thioridazine can cause tachycardia and enhance the peripheral and central nervous system effects (confusion, delirium) of other anticholinergic agents. Medications that induce microsomal drug metabolizing enzymes (e.g., carbamazepine, phenobarbital, phenytoin) as well as smoking and caffeine can increase the metabolism of antipsychotic agents, thereby lowering their blood level, sometimes with clinical consequences. Selective serotonin reuptake inhibitors (SSRIs) compete for hepatic oxidases and can elevate blood levels of neuroleptics (39) and clozapine (86).

Experimental Antipsychotic Agents

OLANZAPINE

In double-blind clinical trials, this clozapine-like agent was superior to placebo and comparable to haloperidol in the treatment of positive symptoms; it was also superior to both placebo and haloperidol in the treatment of the negative symptoms of schizophrenia. Olanzapine is a well tolerated drug with little evidence of extrapyramidal side effects; some patients actually show improvement in abnormal movement, akathisia, and dystonia (87–89). The most common side effects of this new agent include sedation, dry mouth, anxiety, nausea, tremor, and orthostatic hypotension. There is no evidence of agranulocytosis, even in patients who had this reaction during treatment with clozapine. Well-tolerated and effective doses range from 7.5–20 mg/day.

QUETIAPINE

Clinical trials comparing this new clozapine-like agent to chlorpromazine (up to 750 mg/day) and haloperidol (12–16 mg/day) showed significant patient improvement in both negative and positive symptoms. Daily dosages range from 150–800 mg/day; 300 mg is a typical dose (90, 91). The major side effects are somnolence, agitation, constipation, dry mouth, weight gain, mildly increased alanine aminotransferase (ALT) and aspartate aminotransferase (AST), postural hypotension, and dizziness. The strengths of quetiapine are low risk of extrapyramidal effects, minimal anticholinergic effects, and no effect on prolactin levels.

SERTINDOLE

Sertindole is another promising new antipsychotic agent with a unique chemical structure. Clinical trials have demonstrated that once-daily dosing between 12 and 24 mg was superior to placebo and comparable with haloperidol (4–16 mg/day) in reducing the positive psychotic symptoms of schizophrenia. Higher doses (20–24 mg) proved effective with negative symptoms (92, 93). Extrapyramidal symptoms were significantly lower when sertindole was compared with haloperidol and statistically indistinguishable from placebo. The most frequent side effects were tachycardia, mild prolongation of the QT interval, decreased ejaculatory volume, mild nasal congestion, and nausea. Sertindole is not sedating, does not have anticholinergic side effects, and does not affect prolactin levels. It has a long half-life (70 hours) that allows for once-daily administration.

ZIPRASIDONE

This novel drug, at daily doses of 120–160 mg, was superior to placebo and comparable to haloperidol (15 mg/day) in reducing positive symptoms; it was also superior to placebo in ameliorating negative symptoms. Extrapyramidal symptoms were infrequent and mild. Its major side effects include somnolence, dizziness, nausea, and orthostatic hypotension. Ziprasidone increases prolactin levels and mildly elevates serum alanine aminotransaminase and alkaline phosphatase levels. No changes in WBC count were noted in clinical trials (94).

Anxiolytic Agents

Anxiolytic agents (e.g., lorazepam, clonazepam) are used commonly as adjunctive agents in the treatment of acute psychosis (50). This practice helps in controlling agitation and limits neuroleptic doses and their untoward side effects.

Mood Stabilizers

Lithium, carbamazepine, and valproic acid are used adjunctively with antipsychotics for treatment-resistant psychotic patients, particularly those with a prominent affective component to their illness (95–97). Anticonvulsants are also helpful for patients who manifest impulsive or violent behavior (96).

Antidepressants

Antidepressants are indicated in schizophrenic patients with a comorbid major depression (98). Major depression in schizophrenia is often underdiagnosed and undertreated because it is mistaken for negative symptoms. SSRIs have also been used to treat negative symptoms, although with limited benefit (99). Antidepressants are also indicated in schizophrenic patients with obsessive-compulsive symptoms or panic attacks; SSRIs may be particularly suitable for such problems.

Beta-Adrenergic Blockers

Propranolol and atenolol are partially effective in managing akathisia (100). Cal-cium channel blockers such as verapamil, nifedipine, and diltiazem have not been demonstrated to be useful for symptoms of schizophrenia, although they may help diminish symptoms of tardive dyskinesia (101, 102).

Electroconvulsive Therapy

Electroconvulsive therapy (ECT) should not be the first-line treatment for the psychosis of schizophrenia, with two possible exceptions. ECT may be useful when the patient presents with a life-threatening catatonia that appears unresponsive to aggressive pharmacotherapeutic efforts, or when the patient cannot tolerate any neuroleptic medication. In general, lack of response to neuroleptic and anxiolytic agents suggests a toxic psychosocial circumstance or a medical condition that has not been recognized.

For patients who warrant ECT because of failed medication trials or persistent or life-threatening illness, informed consent and medical evaluation are required (see Chapter 6). Catatonic and affective symptoms are generally more responsive than those of apathy, autism, and delusions (103).

Alliance and Psychotherapeutic Management

The psychotherapy of schizophrenic patients must be antiregressive (104, 105). Psychosis is an ego regression in response to overwhelming events and the affects they generate. The patient is unable to bear the reality of his or her circumstances and retreats to psychotic denial, distortion, and projection. The clinician working with the psychotic patient, therefore, should support the patient's efforts to use defenses that do not compromise reality and to face the stresses that precipitated decompensation or the feelings and thoughts that seem unbearable. Although psychotic defenses should not be confronted, the clinician can reinforce efforts to bear reality and can deemphasize psychotic productions, which are the ultimate form of withdrawal short of death.

An antiregressive approach eschews primary process (unconscious) productions by the patient. Distortions about reality, including distortions about staff members, are met with reality explanations and an effort to engage the patient in understanding his or her current life difficulties. All the patient's efforts to be adaptive, however rudimentary, should be respected and encouraged. Delusions and hallucinations should not be confronted directly; they are likely to lose their compelling quality as the psychosis resolves and more adaptive defenses are mobilized.

Hope is central to therapeutic work with a schizophrenic patient. Schizophrenia is a disorder that can sap hope and create despair, especially when the illness persists or is highly debilitating. Patients (and families) need to believe that treatment can control symptoms and that longer-term, rehabilitative efforts can achieve functional improvement.

When working with a schizophrenic patient, the clinician must recognize the frightening nature of the psychosis. Psychotic terror can be reduced by effective pharmacotherapy but also requires words to reassure the patient that the terror will subside and that human help is available. As difficult as reality may be for the schizophrenic patient, the retreat into psychosis ushers in a state of dread, sacrifices reality, and erodes self-esteem. The clinician must allow the schizophrenic patient adequate interpersonal distance (these patients are overwhelmed by closeness) but must not avoid the patient or be excessively distant, which can cause feelings of isolation. The patient may respond best to flexible meeting times and sites. For example, brief meetings in open areas may be preferable when the patient is acutely ill, and office settings may be more appropriate when the patient feels safer with staff members and is better able to tolerate discussion of problems, illness, and treatment.

Although major advances have been made in the pharmacotherapy of schizophrenia, the need to establish a trusting, working alliance with these patients should not be minimized. Long-term, effective treatment will always rely on human bonds and a supportive family and living environment.

Family Support, Education, and Intervention

The importance of the family in the life of the schizophrenic patient and in the long-term treatment cannot be overemphasized. Every effort must be made by acute care staff members to meet with and engage the assistance of the family or significant others. This task can be difficult because many families are stigmatized when entering the mental health system; they have often been seen to play a causal role in the illness of the family member. Moreover, many families are burdened, depleted, and ashamed. The clinical team should approach families as partners in what is likely to be a long-term care plan that will depend heavily on their participation.

The current approach to families began in Great Britain in the 1970s. Researchers in social psychiatry discovered that hospitalized patients who returned to their families had higher rates of readmission than those who were discharged to hostels and boarding homes. For those patients who returned to their families, the greatest risk for recurrence was in families who were rated high in expressed emotion (EE), a term defined as actions that were judged as overinvolved, critical, and hostile (106–108). Notably, more than 35 hours of family contact per week was most correlated with a poor outcome. Reducing contact with families lowered relapse rates, which were further reduced by antipsychotic medication (109).

Work by the British was subsequently replicated in the United States (110–112). These studies on English-speaking, Western culture schizophrenics and their families have influenced the clinical approach to families. At first, efforts were made to decrease the direct time that schizophrenic patients spent with their families. Later, psychoeducation of families proved to be an effective means of teaching (especially high EE families) better methods for coping with the symptoms and the demands of the illness, thereby diminishing EE and the negative attitudes of family members (113).

Families and significant others of patients in acute care should be educated about the signs, symptoms, course, and therapeutics of schizophrenia. Every effort must be made to help families feel less guilty and stigmatized than they may already feel. Family work can include training in effective problem-solving, particularly around stressful life events and the demands of psychiatric illness, and helping to transform overinvolvement into concern and criticism into specific behavioral dissatisfactions (114). Families should be urged to get involved with the National Alliance for the Mentally Ill, a peer group that provides education, perspective, and support, as well as national and state efforts to advocate for the mentally ill. Written and video material on schizophrenia is available and should also be recommended to receptive families.

Family intervention cannot cure schizophrenia. However, pharmacotherapy, a working alliance with a psychiatrist (or other mental health professional) who offers reality-oriented problem-solving and active psychotherapy, social skills training, occupational rehabilitation, family psychoeducation and support, and appropriate housing can significantly improve the course and prognosis of this disorder. Families need to be engaged as allies with the treatment team in a potentially life-long endeavor.

Families and patients will often want to receive genetic counseling. Research suggests that both genetic and environmental factors are involved in the transmission of schizophrenia. Most studies indicate that first-degree relatives have a significantly higher risk for the illness (115). The risk for the illness is reported to be 5.6% in the parents of schizophrenics, 12.8% in children with one schizophrenic parent, and 46.3% in children with two affected parents. Kendler (116) estimates the risk for schizophrenia in first-degree relatives to be 5–15 times greater than in the general population. The risk for other psychotic disorders and schizophrenia spectrum disorders is also significantly higher in first-degree relatives. Environmental factors such as seasonality and pregnancy and birth complications account for some of the variance in genetic heritability. Psychosocial stressors play an important role in precipitating the onset and recurrence of illness in vulnerable individuals, although much remains to be learned about the role of stress and the environment in the etiology and pathogenesis of schizophrenia (117, 118).

The Therapeutic Milieu

Milieu treatment traditionally has been based on a belief that interpersonal and group processes can be designed to promote corrective emotional experiences, foster clinical recompensation, and promote psychological growth. By the therapeutic use of staff member involvement, daily structure, and group encounters and activities, patients may change behaviors and enhance ego capabilities. These views derive from and are best illustrated by the therapeutic communities that emerged after World War II (119, 120). The theory and techniques of the early therapeutic communities are now dated; brief lengths of stay, heterogeneous patient populations, and advances in pharmacotherapy have altered dramatically the use of the milieu as a therapeutic agent (121). Acute care settings today must design milieus that are oriented to brief stays, crisis intervention, psychoeducation and medication training, and aftercare planning.

Lessons have been learned from the longer-term milieu care of schizophrenic patients. For example, overstimulating milieus can be unbearable and destabilizing to these patients (122, 123). Overstimulation may occur through frequent meetings or groups, especially those that actively explore or stimulate the expression of feelings, especially anger and aggression. Demanding that schizophrenic patients interact with others can be deleterious because many of these patients require distance, privacy, and relative isolation. Confrontation can also be overstimulating as it both affectively excites and unravels needed defenses.

The difficulties that schizophrenic patients experience in groups parallel those noted above in the milieu. Group therapy for schizophrenic patients began in a format that was sensitive to the limited capacities of these patients for emotional stimulation. In the 1920s, Lazell (124) was treating schizophrenic patients in groups that provided information and education through lectures. His approach avoided uncovering, self-disclosure, and emotional expression, which were subsequently discovered to be unbearable to these patients. Groups for schizophrenic patients (see Chapter 18) in acute treatment settings should be highly structured and offer support, information, and practical advice. In the treatment groups, reality testing must be done when needed, social skills taught and enhanced, and management of illness strategies provided. Patients' self-esteem must be carefully monitored and protected; these patients feel defective and defeated, although they may hide behind a grandiose facade.

Schizophrenic patients may benefit from psychosocial rehabilitation (125). Social skills training and vocational rehabilitation, however, can only be introduced in the acute care setting because rehabilitation requires extended treatment. Integrated systems of care that link ambulatory rehabilitation to acute care can offer patients greater opportunity for optimal aftercare.

CONTROVERSIES IN THE CARE OF SCHIZOPHRENIA

Civil Liberties

Acutely psychotic patients, especially when severely disorganized and frightened, can represent a potential danger to themselves, the community, and those close to them. Commitment and involuntary treatment may be needed. However, because of legal efforts and patient advocacy over many years, the restriction of civil liberties has become highly monitored. Clinicians can find themselves in remarkable binds, such as having the responsibility for a committed patient without any authority to treat the patient (because of the patient's right to refuse treatment except in emergency situations) or bearing potential liability for a patient's dangerousness after discharge when predictive accuracy is very limited.

Despite these litigious times, a clinician's decisions should always be based on clinical judgments. Clinicians should not try to be attorneys or try to forecast a judge's ruling. Clinicians should exercise their best clinical skills, obtain consultation when needed, and always document their thoughts and actions. By following these rules, the patient remains the clinician's foremost priority, which will most likely be beneficial to the patient and will be the best defense in a court of law.

At times, a clinician's difficulties in exercising involuntary commitment or treatment may represent a countertransference problem. This may occur when the clinician anticipates anger and vindictiveness from the patient or family or when a clinician has been the object of a legal or physical attack for previously taking such a stand. Clinicians should be attentive to any countertransference limitations they may experience and seek consultation and supervision at these difficult times.

Pharmacotherapy

Although medications cannot cure schizophrenia, they are vital in controlling acute symptoms, preventing relapse, and creating the conditions for psychosocial interventions and rehabilitation. However, the importance of the traditional neuroleptics and the newer atypical antipsychotic agents only underscores their adverse effects. Especially troubling are NMS and tardive dyskinesia from the older agents and bone marrow suppression from the traditional agents and clozapine.

As newer medications become available, the adverse effects from the pharmacotherapy of schizophrenia continue to diminish. Moreover, newer agents are helping many patients who did not respond to traditional neuroleptics. Until an agent is found that selectively controls psychosis without targeting other central or peripheral organ or neuronal systems (the Holy Grail), the psychiatrist must work closely with patients and families, document informed consent, and choose, by systematic trials, the medication(s) that is most effective with the least adverse effects for the patient.

Psychotherapy

Although the psychotherapy of psychosis has a long history, it has recently come under careful scrutiny. Whereas the evidence for the efficacy of medication and family interventions has met the test of empiric studies, the effectiveness of psychotherapy remains unclear. Moreover, emotionally evocative and confrontational therapies can be overwhelming to the schizophrenic patient, especially during an acute episode.

Yet someone must reach and ally with the schizophrenic patient. Medications may work but the patient must take them, which requires a therapeutic alliance. Like any patient in distress, the schizophrenic patient needs someone to turn to who provides support, places the patient's interests first, provides a reality orientation, explains the illness and its treatments, and offers hope and perspective. This is the critical role for the psychotherapy of schizophrenia.

Substance Use and Schizophrenia

Substance use and abuse is increasingly common in schizophrenic patients, especially in adolescents and young adults (see Chapter 11). Acute care settings should be highly sensitive to this comorbid disorder because of its effects on symptoms, treatment, course, and prognosis. Acute care facilities may want to consider introducing screening instruments in the intake examination to help detect substance use and abuse and using urine tests when suspicion is high and the patient denies any use.

"Just say no" is not an effective approach to the substance-using schizophrenic patient. Patients use substances because they serve them. Drugs can reduce anxiety and thereby enable social contact, provide a means of relating to peers, and provide pleasure in an illness noted for anhedonia. A drug-free life begins with understanding the drug's role in the patient's life. The use of peer supports and 12-step programs are often essential in helping a patient achieve and sustain abstinence.

Managed Care

In the past 10 years, managed care, principally through proprietary utilization review organizations, has irrevocably changed the delivery of psychiatric services. In the past few years, managed care has entered the public sector as state departments of welfare and mental and public health have contracted out Medicaid and public sector mental health and substance abuse services. Many opportunities exist for creating flexible systems of acute care with increased patient access under managed care; however, the danger is that the traditional safety net of so-cial welfare, housing, and rehabilitative services that have been available to chronically ill patients (in many but not all states) and the provision of care beyond acute illness may vanish as states get out of the business of caring for the severely and persistently mentally ill. Although many advocates are voicing this concern, there is great worry that the care of the mentally ill will be subordinated to the cost-cutting goals so prevalent in state government today.

COURSE AND PROGNOSIS

Schizophrenia is a disorder that typically begins in adolescence or early adult life, often with an insidious onset. Most patients will have demonstrated premorbid features of shyness, social withdrawal, awkwardness, and difficulties in establishing close relationships. The onset of schizophrenia is uncommon, although not rare, after age 40 (126).

The perception that all schizophrenic patients have a poor course with significant morbidity may be erroneous and a function of how cohorts were sampled in the past. Longitudinal studies have often followed patients admitted to hospitals, many of whom already had a chronic course. Shepherd et al. and others (124–127) studied first admissions of patients diagnosed with schizophrenia and compared this group with previously admitted patients. In the first admission group, 22% had no relapses in 5 years, 35% had one or more relapses but with limited impairment, and 43% were persistently impaired. The rehospitalized group demonstrated 60% persistent impairment, 29% with one or more relapses and limited impairment, and only 10% with no impairment.

Prognosis in schizophrenia is not as

good as it is for psychotic patients with affective illnesses (128). Variables predicting poorer outcome in schizophrenia include male gender, unmarried status, family history of schizophrenia, insidious onset, significant negative symptoms, relatively few positive symptoms, and lower intelligence (129–132). High levels of EE have been correlated with higher relapse rates, but may also be a function of sampling populations with repeated hospital admissions (131–133). The stress of a chronic illness on a family can possibly evoke dysfunctional responses that, in turn, have an adverse effect on the patient's course and prognosis.

Medication noncompliance also predicts a poorer course (131, 134, 135). In the past, the side effects of neuroleptics (especially sedation, extrapyramidal symptoms, akathisia, and weight gain) were significant factors in patient noncompliance. With the advent of newer antipsychotic agents with more favorable side effect profiles, the longer-term course and prognosis for schizophrenia may be altered in a desirable direction. Patients who are treated with problem-solving, interpersonal, and rehabilitatively orientated psychotherapies (in addition to neuroleptics) also show a better course and prognosis (134, 135).

The risk for suicide in schizophrenia is 15% (136–138). Suicide risk is greatest in those patients who feel hopeless, are aware of the impairment of their illness, have a chronic course, have made previous suicide attempts, and are noncompliant with treatment (139–142). Care must be exercised to identify those patients who are at greater risk and to intervene early when possible (140).

WHO has supported studies on cultural differences in the course and prognosis of schizophrenia. Research evidence suggests that schizophrenic patients in de-veloping countries, as opposed to developed countries, do better over the course of their lifetimes (143). Cultural tolerance may differ across cultures and may account for some of the variance in outcome.

Although schizophrenia is an illness with the potential for great morbidity and mortality, it is most likely that considerable heterogeneity exists for this disorder (144–146). The view that deterioration is the inevitable outcome for schizophrenia is simply not true and may become more inaccurate as pharmacotherapy improves and provides the symptomatic control necessary for psychosocial interventions.

REFERENCES

1. American Psychiatric Press. Diagnostic and statistical manual. 4th ed. Washington, DC: American Psychiatric Press, 1995:273–315.
2. Morel BA. Etudes cliniques: traite theorique et pratique des maladies mentales. Paris: Masson, 1952.
3. Kraepelin E. Dementia praecox. London: Livingston, 1918.
4. Bleuler E. Dementia praecox oder die gruppe der schizophenien: In: Aschoffenburg A, ed. Zinkin J, translator. Handbuch der psychiatrie. New York: Leipzig, 1911.
5. Schneider K. Clinical psychopathology. Hamilton MW, translator. New York: Grune & Stratton, 1959.
6. Silverstein ML, Harron M. First-rank symptoms in the post-acute schizophrenic: a follow-up study. Am J Psychiatry 1978;135:1481–1486.
7. Regier DA, Myers JK, Kramer M, et al. The NIMH epidemiologic catchment area program. Arch Gen Psychiatry 1984;41:934–941.
8. Robbins LN, Helzer JE, Weissman MM, et al. Lifetime prevalence of specific psychiatric disorders in three sites. Arch Gen Psychiatry 1984;41:949–958.
9. Dunham HW. Community and schizophrenia: an epidemiologic analysis. Detroit: Wayne State University Press, 1965.
10. Eaton WW. Update on the epidemiology of schizophrenia. Epidemiol Rev 1991;13:320–328.
11. Dohrenwend BP, Dohrenwend BS. Social status and psychological disorder: a causal inquiry. New York: John Wiley & Sons, 1969.

12. Eaton WW, Day R, Kramer M. The use of epidemiology for risk factor research in schizophrenia: an overview and methodological critique. In: Tsuang MT, Simpson JC, eds. Handbook of schizophrenia. Amsterdam: Elsevier, 1988;3:169–204.

13. Kohn ML. Social class and schizophrenia: a critical review. In: Rosenthal D, Kety SS, eds. The transmission of schizophrenia. Oxford: Pergamon Press, 1968.

14. Faris REL, Dunham HW. Mental disorders in urban areas. Chicago: University of Chicago Press, 1939.

15. Goodman AB, Siegel C. The relationship between socioeconomic class and prevalence of schizophrenia, alcoholism, and affective disorders treated by inpatient care in a suburban area. Am J Psychiatry 1983;140:166–170.

16. Dohrenwend BP, Dohrenwend BS, Gould MS, et al., eds. Mental illness in the United States: epidemiological estimates. New York: Praeger, 1980.

17. Iacono W, Beiser M. Where are the women in first-episode studies of schizophrenia? Schizophr Bull 1992;18:471–480.

18. Riecher A, Maurer K, Loffler W, et al. Gender differences in age at onset and course of schizophrenic disorders. In: Hafner H, Gattz WF eds. Search for causes of schizophrenia. Berlin: Springer-Verlag, 1987:14–33.

19. World Health Organization. Schizophrenia: an international follow-up study. New York: John Wiley & Sons, 1979.

20. Wyatt JW. Neurodevelopmental abnormalities and schizophrenia. Arch Gen Psychiatry 1996;53:11–15.

21. Hartmann H. Ego psychology and the problem of adaptation. New York: International University Press, 1958.

22. Sullivan HS. The interpersonal theory of psychiatry. New York: WW Norton, 1953.

23. Sullivan HS. Schizophrenia as a modern process. New York: WW Norton, 1963.

24. MacKinnon RA, Michels R. The psychiatric interview. In: Clinical practice. Philadelphia: WB Saunders, 1971:230–258.

25. Vaillant G. Adaptation to life. Boston: Little, Brown & Co., 1977:75–90.

26. Vaughn CE, Leff JP. The influence of family and social factors on the course of psychiatric illness. Br J Psychiatry 1976;129:125–137.

27. Kanter J, Lamb HR, Loeper C. Expressed emotion in families: a critical review. Hosp Community Psychiatry 1987;38:374–380.

28. Falloon IRH, Boyd JL, McGill CW. Family management in the prevention of morbidity of schizophrenia. Arch Gen Psychiatry 1985;42:887–896.

29. Leff J. Family factors in schizophrenia. Psychiatr Ann 1989;19:542–547.

30. Sartorius N, Jablensky A, Korten A. Early manifestations and first-contact incidence of schizophrenia in different cultures. Psychol Med 1986;16:909–928.

31. Hoffman RS, Koran LM. Detecting physical illness in patients with mental disorders. Psychosomatics 1984:25:654.

32. Warner MD, Boutros NN, Peabody CA. Usefulness of screening EEGs in psychiatric inpatient population. J Clin Psychiatry 1990;51:363.

33. Andreasen N, Nasrallah HA, Dunn V, et al. Structural abnormalities in the frontal system in schizophrenia. Arch Gen Psychiatry 1986;43:136–144.

34. Yurgelun-Todd DA, Renshaw PF, Gruber SA, et al. Proton magnetic resonance spectroscopy of the temporal lobes in schizophrenics and normal controls. Schizophr Res 1996;19:55–59.

35. Baldessarini RJ, Centorrino F. Results and limits of antipsychotic pharmacotherapy. Rome: Nóos-Aggiornamenti in Psichiatria (In press).

36. Baldessarini RJ. Chemotherapy in psychiatry: principles and practice. Cambridge, MA: Harvard University Press, 1985.

37. Davis JM, Barter JT, Kane J. Antipsychotic drugs. In: Kaplan and Sadock, eds. Comprehensive textbook of psychiatry. 5th ed. Baltimore, MD: Williams & Wilkins, 1989:1591–1626.

38. Carlsson A. Early psychopharmacology and the rise of modern brain research. J Psychopharmacol 1990;4:120–126.

39. Baldessarini RJ. Drugs and treatment of psychiatric disorders: antipsychotic and antianxiety agents. In: Harden W, Rudin W, Molinoff PB, et al., eds. Goodman and Gilman's the pharmacological basis of therapeutics. New York: McGraw-Hill, 1996:399–430.

40. Baldessarini RJ. Fifty years of biomedical psychiatry and psychopharmacology in America. In: Menninger R, Nemiah J, eds. Fifty years of American psychiatry: the 150th anniversary of the founding of the American Psychiatric Association. Washington, DC: APA Press (In press).

41. Anthony WA, Cohen MR, Danley KS. The psychiatric rehabilitation model as applied to vocational rehabilitation. In: Ciardello JA, Bell MD, eds. Vocational rehabilitation of persons with prolonged psychiatric disorders. Baltimore, MD: Johns Hopkins University Press, 1988:59–80.

42. Liberman RP, Van Putten T, Marshall BD Jr, et al. Optimal drug and behavior therapy for treatment-refractory schizophrenic patients. Am J Psychiatry 1994;151:756–759.

43. Bacarach LL. Continuity of care and approaches to case management for long-term

mentally ill patients. Hosp Community Psychiatry 1993;44:465–468.

44. Kane J, Marder SR. Psychopharmacologic treatment of schizophrenia. Schizophr Bull 1993;19:287–302.

45. Hirsch SR, Weinberger DR. Schizophrenia. Cambridge: Cambridge University Press, 1995.

46. Barnes T. Issues in the clinical assessment of the negative symptoms: editorial review. Curr Opin Psychiatry 1994;7:35–38.

47. Baldessarini RJ, Cohen BM, Teicher MH. Significance of neuroleptic dose and plasma level in the pharmacological treatment of psychosis. Arch Gen Psychiatry 1988;45:79–91.

48. Baldessarini RJ, Cohen BM, Teicher MH. Pharmacological treatment. In: Levy ST, Ninan PT, eds. Schizophrenia: treatment of acute psychotic episodes. Washington, DC: American Psychiatric Press, 1990:61–118.

49. Baldessarini RJ, Cohen BM, Teicher MH. Clinical dosing of antipsychotic agents. In: Gram LF, Balant JP, Meltzer HY, et al., eds. Strategies in psychotropic drug development. Heidelberg: Springer-Verlag, 1993:138–148.

50. Baldessarini JR, Kando JC, Centorrino F. Hospital use of antipsychotic agents in 1989 and 1993: stable dosing with decreased length-of-stay. Am J Psychiatry 1995;152:1038–1044.

51. Neborski R, Janowsky D, et al. Rapid treatment of acute psychotic symptoms with high and low dose haloperidol. Arch Gen Psychiatry 1981;38:195–199.

52. Tarsy D, Baldessarini RJ. Clinical and pathophysiologic features of movement disorders induced by psychotherapeutic agents. In: Shah N, Donald A, eds. Movement disorders. New York: Plenum, 1986:365–389.

53. Rosenburg MR, Green M. Neuroleptic malignant syndrome: review of response to therapy. Arch Intern Med 1989;149:1927–1931.

54. Kane JM, Jeste DV, Barnes T, et al. Tardive dyskinesia: a task force report of the American Psychiatric Association. Washington, DC: American Psychiatric Association, 1992.

55. Sachdev P. The identification and management of drug-induced akathisia. CNS Drugs 1995;4:28–46.

56. Markowitz JC, Brown RP. Seizures with neuroleptics and antidepressants. Gen Hosp Psychiatry 1987;9:135–141.

57. Ray WA, Griffin MR, Schaffner W, et al. Psychotropic drug use and the risk of hip fracture. N Engl J Med 1987;316:363–369.

58. Centorrino F, Baldessarini RJ, Flood JG, et al. Relation of leukocyte counts during clozapine treatment to serum concentration of clozapine and metabolites. Am J Psychiatry 1995;152:610–612.

59. Mendelowitz AJ, Gerson SL, Alvir J, et al. Clozapine-induced agranulocytosis: risk factors, monitoring and management. CNS Drugs 1995;8:412–421.

60. Altshuler LL, Cohen L, Szuba MP, et al. Pharmacologic management of psychiatric illness during pregnancy: dilemmas and guidelines. Am J Psychiatry 1996;153:592–606.

61. Kane JM, Honigfeld G, Singer J, et al. Depot neuroleptics: comparative review of standard, intermediate, and low-dose regimens. J Clin Psychiatry 1986;47(Suppl 5):30–33.

62. Davis JM, Metalon L, Watanabe MD, et al. Depot antipsychotic drugs: place in therapy. Drugs 1994;47:741–773.

63. Kane J, Honigfield G, Singer J, et al. Clozapine for the treatment-resistant schizophrenic. Arch Gen Psychiatry 1988;45:789–796.

64. Marder SR, Van Putten T. Who should receive Clozapine? Arch Gen Psychiatry 1988;45:865–867.

65. Wagstaff AJ, Bryson HM. Clozapine: a review of its pharmacological properties and therapeutic use in patients with schizophrenia who are unresponsive to or intolerant of classical antipsychotic agents. CNS Drugs 1995;4:370–400.

66. Baldessarini RJ, Frankenburg FR. Clozapine: a novel antipsychotic agent. N Engl J Med 1991;324:746–754.

67. Centorrino F, Baldessarini RJ, Kando JC, et al. Clozapine and metabolites: concentrations in serum and clinical findings during treatment of chronically psychotic patients. J Clin Psychopharmacol 1994;14:119–125.

68. Lieberman JA, Safferman AZ, Pollack S, et al. Clinical effects of clozapine in chronic schizophrenia: response to treatment and predictors of outcome. Am J Psychiatry 1994;151:1744–1752.

69. Wilson WH. Time required for initial improvement during clozapine treatment of refractory schizophrenia. Am J Psychiatry 1996;153:951–952.

70. Meltzer HY, Okayli G. Reduction of suicidality during clozapine treatment of neuroleptic-resistant schizophrenia: impact on risk-benefit assessment. Am J Psychiatry 1995;152:183–190.

71. Henderson DC, Goff DC. Clozapine for polydipsia and hyponatremia in chronic schizophrenics. Biol Psychiatry 1994;36:768–770.

72. Baldessarini RJ. Dopamine receptors and clinical medicine. In: Neve RL, Neve KA, eds. The dopamine receptors. Totowa, NJ: Humana Press 1996.

73. Meltzer HY, Nash JF. Effects of antipsychotic drugs on serotonin receptors. Pharmacol Rev 1991;43:587–604.

74. Meltzer HY, ed. Novel antipsychotic drugs. New York: Raven Press, 1992.

75. Lieberman JA. Understanding the mechanism of action of atypical antipsychotic drugs: a review of compounds in use and development. Br J Psychiatry 1993;163(Suppl 22):7–18.
76. Meltzer HY. Atypical antipsychotic drugs. In: Bloom FE, Kupfer DJ, eds. Psychopharmacology: the fourth generation of progress. New York: Raven Press, 1995:1277–1286.
77. Kinon BJ, Lieberman JA. Mechanism of action of atypical antipsychotic drugs: a critical analysis. Psychopharmacology 1996;124:2–34.
78. Leysen JE, Janssen PMF, Megens A, et al. Risperidone: a novel antipsychotic with balanced serotonin-dopamine antagonism, receptor occupancy profile, and pharmacologic activity. J Clin Psychiatry 1994;55(Suppl 5):5–12.
79. Claus A, Bollen J, De Cuyper H, et al. Risperidone vs. haloperidol in the treatment of chronic schizophrenic inpatients: a multicenter double-blind comparative study. Acta Psychiatr Scand 1992;85:295–305.
80. Chouinard G, Jones BD, Remington G, et al. A Canadian multicenter placebo-controlled study of fixed doses of risperidone and haloperidol in the treatment of chronic schizophrenic patients. J Clin Psychopharmacol 1993;13:25–40.
81. Marder SR, Meibach RC. Risperidone in the treatment of schizophrenia. Am J Psychiatry 1994;151:825–835.
82. Hoyberg OJ, Fensbo C, Remvig J, et al. Risperidone vs. perphenazine in the treatment of chronic schizophrenic patients with acute exacerbations. Acta Psychiatr Scand 1993;88:395–402.
83. Kleiser E, Lehmann E, Kinzler E, et al. Randomized, double-blind, controlled trial of risperidone vs. clozapine in patients with chronic schizophrenia. J Clin Psychopharmacol 1995;15(Suppl):45–51.
84. Lee H, Ryan J, Mullet G, et al. Neuroleptic malignant syndrome associated with the use of risperidone, an atypical antipsychotic agent. Hum Psychopharmacol 1994;9:303–305.
85. Zarate CA Jr, Siegel A, Nakamura A, et al. Risperidone in the elderly: a pharmacoepidemiological study. J Clin Psychiatry 1996 (In press).
86. Centorrino F, Baldessarini RJ, Frankenburg FR, et al. Serum levels of clozapine and norclozapine in patients treated with selective serotonin reuptake inhibitors. Am J Psychiatry 1996;153:820–822
87. Tollefson GD, Beasley CM, Tran PV, et al. Olanzapine versus haloperidol: results of the multicenter international trial. Schizophr Res. 1996;18:131.
88. Beasley CM, Tollefson GD, Tran P, et al. Olanzapine versus placebo and haloperidol: acute phase results of the North American double-blind olanzapine trial. Neuropsychopharmacology 1996;14:111–123.
89. Robertson GS, Fibiger HC. Effects of olanzapine on regional c-fos expression in rat forebrain. Neuropsychopharmacology 1996;14:105–110
90. Seroquel: a putative atypical antipsychotic drug with serotonin- and dopamine-receptor antagonist properties. J Clin Psychiatry 1995;56:438–445.
91. Borison RL, Arvantis LA, Miller BG. A comparison of five fixed doses of Seroquel (ICI-204, 636) with haloperidol and placebo in patients with schizophrenia. Schizophr Res 1996;18:132. Abstract no. V.D.2.
92. Van Kammen DP, McEvoy JP, Targum SD, et al. Sertindole study group. A randomized controlled, dose-ranging trial of sertindole in patients with schizophrenia. Psychopharmacology (In press).
93. Schulz SC, Mack R, Zborowski J, et al. Efficacy, safety, and dose response of three doses of sertindole and three doses of haldol in schizophrenia patients. Schizophr Res 1996;18:133.
94. Seeger TF, Seymour PA, Schmidt AW, et al. A new antipsychotic with combined dopamine and serotonin receptor antagonist activity. J Pharmacol Exp Ther 1995;275:101–113.
95. Christison GW, Kirch DJ, Wyatt RJ. When symptoms persist: choosing among alternative somatic treatment for schizophrenia. Schizophr Bull 1991;17:217–245.
96. Meltzer HY. Treatment of the neuroleptic-nonresponsive schizophrenic patient. Schizophr Bull 1992;18:515–542.
97. Carpenter WT, Kurz R, Kirckpatrick HB, et al. Carbamazepine maintenance treatment in outpatient schizophrenics. Arch Gen Psychiatry 1991;48:69–72.
98. Siris SG, Bermanzohn PC, Mason SE, et al. Maintenance imipramine therapy for secondary depression in schizophrenia: a controlled trial. Arch Gen Psychiatry 1994;51:109–115.
99. Goff DC, Midha KK, Sarid-Segal O, et al. A placebo-controlled trial of fluoxetine added to neuroleptic in patients with schizophrenia. Psychopharmacology 1995;117:417–423.
100. Lader M. β-Adrenoceptor antagonists in neuropsychiatry. J Clin Psychiatry 1988;49:213–223.
101. Pollack MH, Rosenbaum JF, Hyman JE. Calcium channel blockers in Psychiatry. Psychosomatics 1987;28:356–369.

102. Reiter S, Adler L, Angrist B, et al. Effects of verapamil on tardive dyskinesia and psychosis in schizophrenic patients. J Clin Psychiatry 1989;50:26–27.

103. Salzman C. The use of ECT in the treatment of schizophrenia. Am J Psychiatry 1980;137:1032–1041.

104. Engle RP, Semrad EV. Brief hospitalization, the recompensation process. In: Abroms GM, Greenfield NS, eds. The new hospital psychiatry. New York: Academic Press, 1971.

105. Drake RE, Sederer LI. Inpatient psychotherapy of chronic schizophrenia: avoiding regression. Hosp Community Psychiatry 1986;27:897–901.

106. Brown GW, Monck EM, Carstairs GM. Influence of family life on the course of schizophrenic illness. Br J Prev Soc Med 1962;16:55–68.

107. Brown GW, Rutter ML. The measurement of family activities and relationships. Hum Relations 1966;19:241–263.

108. Brown GW, Birley JLT, Wing JK. Influence of family life on the course of schizophrenic disorders: a replication. Br J Psychiatry 1972;121:241–258.

109. Leff JP, Vaughn CE. The role of maintenance therapy and relative expressed emotion in relapse in schizophrenia: a two-year follow-up. Br J Psychiatry 1981;139:102–104.

110. Vaughn CE, Snyder KS, Freeman W, et al. Family factors in schizophrenia relapse: a replication. Schizophr Bull 1982;8:425–426.

111. Vaughn CE, Snyder KS, et al. Family factors in schizophrenia relapse: replication in California of British research on expressed emotion. Arch Gen Psychiatry 1984;41:1169–1177.

112. Moline RA, Singh S, Morris A, et al. Family expressed emotion and relapse in schizophrenia in 24 urban American patients. Am J Psychiatry 1985;142:1078–1081.

113. Falloon IRH, Boyd JL, McGill CW. Family care of schizophrenia: a problem solving approach to mental illness. New York: Guilford Press, 1984.

114. McFarlane WR. Family therapy in schizophrenia. New York: Guilford Press, 1983.

115. Gottesman I, Shields J. Schizophrenia: the epigenetic puzzle. Cambridge: Cambridge University Press, 1982.

116. Kendler KS. The genetics of schizophrenia. In: Tsuang MT, Simpson JC eds. Handbook of schizophrenia. Amsterdam: Elsevier, 1988;3:437–462.

117. Norman RMG, Malla A. Stressful life events and schizophrenia. Part 2: conceptual and methodological issues. Br J Psychiatry 1993;162:166–174.

118. Stabenau J, Pollin W. Heredity and environment in schizophrenia, revisited: the contribution of twin and high-risk studies. J Nerv Ment Dis 1993;181:290–297.

119. Jones M. The concept of the therapeutic community. Am J Psychiatry 1956;112:647–650.

120. Cummings J, Cummings E. Ego and milieu. New York: Atherton, 1962.

121. Sederer LI. Inpatient psychiatry: what place the milieu? Am J Psychiatry 1984;141:673–674. Editorial.

122. Kahn EM, White EM. Adapting milieu approaches to acute inpatient care for schizophrenic patients. Hosp Community Psychiatry 1989;40:609–614.

123. Gunderson JG. If and when milieu therapy is therapeutic for schizophrenics. In: Gunderson JG, Will O, Mosher EL, eds. Principles and practice of milieu therapy. New York: Jason Aronson, 1983.

124. Lazell EW. The group treatment of dementia praecox. Psychoanal Rev 1921;8:168–179.

125. Liberman RP. Psychiatric rehabilitation of chronic mental patients. Washington, DC: American Psychiatric Press, 1987.

126. Harris MJ, Collum CM, Jeste OV. Clinical prescription of late onset schizophrenia. J Clin Psychiatry 1988;49:356–360.

127. Shepherd M, Watt D, Falloon I, et al. The natural history of schizophrenia: a five-year outcome and prediction in a representative sample of schizophrenics. Cambridge: Cambridge University Press, 1989.

128. Beiser M, Iacono WG, Erickson D. Temporal stability in major mental disorders. In: Robins LN, Barrett JE, eds. The validity of psychiatric diagnosis. New York: Raven Press, 1989:77–98.

129. Kay SR, Maw MS. The positive-negative distraction in drug-free schizophrenic patients. Arch Gen Psychiatry 1989;46:711–718.

130. McGlashan TH. The prediction of outcome in chronic schizophrenia. Arch Gen Psychiatry 1986;43:167–176.

131. Westermeyer JF, Harrow M. Course and outcome in schizophrenia. In: Tsuang MT, Simpson JC, eds. Handbook of schizophrenia. Amsterdam: Elsevier, 1988;3:205–244.

132. Ram R, Bromet E, Eaton W, et al. The natural course of schizophrenia: a review of first-admission studies. Schizophr Bull 1992;18:185–207.

133. Parker G, Johnston P, Hayward L. Parental expressed emotion as a predictor of schizo-

phrenic relapse. Arch Gen Psychiatry 1988;45:806–813.

134. Hogarty GE, Goldberg SC, et al. Drug and sociotherapy in the aftercare of schizophrenic patients, II. Arch Gen Psychiatry 1974;31:609–618.

135. Hogarty GE, Goldberg SC, et al. Drug and sociotherapy in the aftercare of schizophrenic patients, III. Arch Gen Psychiatry 1974;31:618–625.

136. Johns C, Stanley M, Stanley B. Suicide in schizophrenia. Ann NY Acad Sci 1986;487:294–300.

137. Roy A. Suicide in chronic schizophrenia. Br J Psychiatry 1982;141:171–177.

138. Roy A. Suicide in schizophrenia. In: Roy A, ed. Suicide. Baltimore, MD: Williams & Wilkins, 1986.

139. Brent DA, Kupfer DJ, Brometeg EJ, et al. The assessment and treatment of patients at risk for suicide. In: Francis AJ, Hales RE, eds. Psychiatry update, American Psychiatric Association annual review. Washington, DC: American Psychiatric Press, 1988;7.

140. Drake RE, Gates C, Cotton PG. Suicide among schizophrenics: who is at risk? J Nerv Ment Dis 1984;172:613–617.

141. Virkkunen M. Attitude to psychiatric treatment before suicide in schizophrenia and paranoid psychosis. Br J Psychiatry 1976;128:47–49.

142. Amador XA, Friedman JH, Kasapis C, et al. Suicidal behavior in schizophrenia and its relationship to awareness of illness. Am J Psychiatry 1996;153:1185–1188.

143. Leff J, Sartorius N, Jablensky A, et al. The international pilot study of schizophrenia: five year follow-up findings. Psychol Med 1992;22:131–145.

144. Hegarty JD, Baldessarini RJ, Tohen M, et al. One hundred years of schizophrenia: a meta-analysis of the outcome literature. Am J Psychiatry 1994;151:1409–1416.

145. Bleuler M. The course, outcome, and prognosis of schizophrenic psychoses. In: Flach F, ed. The schizophrenias. New York: WW Norton, 1988:1–21.

146. Harding CM, Zubin J, Strauss JJ. Chronicity in schizophrenia: fact, partial fact, or artifact? Hosp Community Psychiatry 1987;38:477–486.

Chapter 10

Trauma and Dissociative Disorders

James A. Chu

DEFINITION

"Psychological trauma is an affliction of the powerless. At the moment of trauma, the victim is rendered helpless by overwhelming force. When the force is that of nature, we speak of disasters. When the force is that of other human beings, we speak of atrocities. Traumatic events overwhelm the ordinary systems of care that give people a sense of control, connection, and meaning . . . Traumatic events are extraordinary, not because they occur rarely, but rather because they overwhelm the ordinary human adaptations to life . . . They confront human beings with the extremities of helplessness and terror, and evoke the responses of catastrophe."
　　　　　　　—Judith Lewis Herman (1)

Traumatization is part of the human experience. Whether by acts of nature or by acts of humans, catastrophic events can overwhelm an individual's ability to cope and can result in a variety of posttraumatic responses. If the traumatization is severe, prolonged, or occurs early in life, posttraumatic stress disorder (PTSD) and dissociative disorders are likely to develop. The traumatic etiologies of these disorders are numerous; generally, they are thought to include combat, physical or sexual assaults, accidents and natural disasters, and other shocking or terrorizing events. Particular traumas are seen more commonly in certain clinical settings. For example, in urban emergency room settings, posttraumatic responses often occur in the aftermath of criminal assaults and rape, whereas in Veterans Administration (VA) facilities, war and combat-related PTSD are more frequent. For the most part, posttraumatic responses to brief or single overwhelming events in an otherwise intact person can be treated in subacute outpatient settings. Acute care delivered in inpatient, partial hospitalization, or intensive outpatient settings generally is necessary if exposure to particularly severe or chronic traumatization has occurred or comorbid psychiatric or substance use disorders are present. Posttraumatic and dissociative disorders most commonly seen in acute care settings appear to result from certain types of prolonged childhood abuse, chronic combat experiences, and long-term battering relationships.

Chronic childhood traumatization poses

a particular problem for our society. Unrecognized or unacknowledged experiences can have profound effects on the psyche. Severe childhood abuse, if untreated, results in sequelae in the form of a variety of posttraumatic responses and alterations in personality development. Furthermore, because the innate capacity to use dissociative defenses is greatest in childhood (2, 3), traumatized and abused children are at most risk for developing severe dissociative disorders, including dissociative identity disorder (DID). Given the prevalence of child maltreatment in the U.S.—a minimum of more than 1 million substantiated cases per year (4)—PTSD and dissociative disorders seen in acute care settings (outside the VA) are due most frequently to severe and persistent childhood traumatization.

DIAGNOSIS

As defined in DSM-IV (5), PTSD has the following four major criteria.

1. A traumatic event that the person experienced or witnessed that involved actual or threatened serious injury or death and evoked a response of intense fear, horror, or helplessness.
2. The traumatic event is persistently reexperienced through recurrent recollections, dreams, or reliving of the experience.
3. Avoidance of stimuli associated with the trauma and general numbing.
4. Persistent arousal symptoms, including sleep difficulties, anger, hypervigilance, startle responses, and difficulty concentrating.

To meet the diagnosis of PTSD, the last three categories of symptoms must be present for more than 1 month, and the disturbance must cause clinically significant distress or impairment in social, occupational, or other functioning. PTSD

is classified as acute if the duration of symptoms is less than 3 months, chronic if the duration of symptoms is 3 months or more, and delayed onset if the onset of symptoms is at least 6 months after the traumatic event(s).

The DSM-IV defines five categories of dissociative disorders: dissociative amnesia, dissociative fugue, depersonalization disorder, DID, and dissociative disorder not otherwise specified (DDNOS) (5). The criteria for each of these disorders requires that the disturbance does not occur exclusively during the course of another dissociative disorder, posttraumatic or acute stress disorder, somatization disorder, substance abuse, or neurologic or medical condition, and that the symptoms cause significant distress or impairment in social, occupational, or other important areas of functioning.

Dissociative Amnesia

"The essential feature of dissociative amnesia is an inability to recall important personal information, usually of a traumatic or stressful nature, that is too extensive to be explained by ordinary forgetfulness."

Dissociative Fugue

"The essential feature is sudden, unexpected travel away from home or one's customary place of daily activities, with inability to recall some or all of one's past . . . accompanied by confusion about personal identity or even the assumption of a new identity."

Depersonalization Disorder

"The essential features of depersonalization disorder are persistent or recurrent episodes of depersonalization characterized by a feeling of detachment or estrangement from one's self . . . The individual may feel like an automaton or as if he or she is living in a dream or a movie. There may be a sensation of being an outside observer of one's mental processes [or] one's body . . . The individual . . . maintains intact reality testing."

DID (Formerly Multiple Personality Disorder)

"The essential feature of dissociative identity disorder (DID) is . . . the presence of two or more distinct identities or personality states (each with its own relatively enduring pattern of perceiving, relating to, and thinking about the environment and self). At least two of these identities or personalities recurrently take control of the person's behavior. [There is also the] inability to recall important personal information that is too extensive to be explained by ordinary forgetfulness."

DDNOS

"The predominant feature is a dissociative symptom that does not meet the criteria for any specific dissociative disorder. Examples include clinical presentations similar to dissociative identity disorder that fail to meet full criteria for this disorder . . . derealization unaccompanied by depersonalization in adults, states of dissociation that occur in individuals who have been subjected to prolonged and intense coercive persuasion . . . dissociative trance disorders . . . loss of consciousness, stupor, or coma not attributable to a general medical condition, [and] Ganser's syndrome."

In acute care settings, dissociative amnesia, dissociative fugue, and depersonalization disorder rarely are seen as single-symptom syndromes. These symptoms are usually part of a more severe posttraumatic or dissociative disorder. Similarly, DDNOS, is seen most commonly as syndromes of severe dissociation—multiple dissociative symptoms and abrupt shifts in of the sense of self—that do not meet the criteria for DID.

EPIDEMIOLOGY

Exposure to traumatic events is extremely common in our society. A sampling of 5877 adults in the U.S. general population (part of the National Comorbidity Study [NCS]) estimated the lifetime exposure to severe traumatic events to be approximately 61% in men and 51% in women (6). Other recent studies have demonstrated similarly high levels of traumatic exposure (7, 8). In research concerning childhood traumatization, one in three adult women (9) and one in six adult men (10) reported some type of childhood sexual abuse. However, it is unclear how this high prevalence of exposure to traumatic events translates into rates of posttraumatic and dissociative disorders. Not every shocking experience, and perhaps not even most traumatic events, results in serious psychopathology. The NCS determined a lifetime prevalence of PTSD at 7.8% (6), much higher than previous general population estimates of approximately 1% (11, 12), probably due to differences in diagnostic criteria and assessment procedures. In the NCS, men were more likely to become symptomatic after such traumas as rape, combat exposure, childhood neglect, or childhood physical abuse; women were more likely to become symptomatic after rape, sexual molestation, physical attack, threats with a weapon, or childhood physical abuse (6). The study found that although men were more likely to be exposed to traumatic conditions than women (61% vs. 51%), women were twice as likely as men to develop PTSD (10% vs. 5%). This result might point to women's increased vulnerability to develop PTSD or to the more severe sequelae of certain forms of traumatization, because women were overwhelmingly more likely than men to be the victims of rape or sexual molestation (odds ratio, 13.33 to 1).

The nature and severity of the events may influence the occurrence of prolonged psychological effects. Moreover, individual variations in response to stressful events are seen; some individuals are better able to cope with trauma and/or show more resiliency to recover from such experiences. Trauma research has not yet explored sufficiently populations that have been exposed to trauma and do not develop posttraumatic or dissociative disorders. Experiences with patients in clinical populations do suggest that some trauma is quite extreme, particularly some reports of malignant childhood abuse. It is likely that such severe experiences would be poorly tolerated by any individual regardless of coping capacity or resilience.

Dissociative symptoms are quite prevalent in clinical populations. As measured by the Dissociative Experience Scale (DES) (2)—a 28-item self-report questionnaire that is the current standard research instrument and an excellent clinical screening tool—approximately 25% of psychiatric inpatients in private and public hospitals, and a similar number of psychiatric outpatients, have dissociative symptoms consistent with posttraumatic or dissociative disorders (13–16). Studies using both the DES and diagnostic interviews show that patients with the highest level of dissociative symptoms, those consistent with DID, are found in approximately 5% of inpatient psychiatric populations (13, 14). The prevalence of dissociative symptoms is considerably higher than generally expected by most clinicians and suggests that even extremely high levels of dissociative symptoms are not rare. However, moderate levels of dissociation associated with PTSD and DDNOS are much more common than higher levels associated with DID.

THE FOUR QUESTIONS

Descriptive and Differential Diagnosis

Dissociation can be defined as the lack of integration of experience, such as a sense of discontinuity of one's experience, or separation of the different parameters of experience. In response to an overwhelming traumatic event, individuals may develop two different groups of dissociative symptoms. The first group serves a defensive function as the psyche attempts to cope with too much stimuli by separating and fragmenting the experience. These symptoms include emotional numbing (dissociated feelings), detachment from one's surroundings (derealization) or from one's body (depersonalization), amnesia (dissociated cognitive awareness), or feeling as though the events are occurring to someone else. Other types of defensive dissociative experiences are less well named, including the ability to remain internally preoccupied for long periods and the ability to ignore pain. In more severe dissociative disorders, dissociated internal thoughts may be perceived as thought insertion ("foreign" thoughts that feel placed in the mind) or even as internal auditory hallucinations. Finally, in response to the most severe childhood traumatization, a person functions as a series of different self-states or "personalities" as an adaptation to intolerable and irreconcilable internal states. The second group of dissociative symptoms relates to the reexperiencing of previously dissociated traumatic experiences. These experiences do not remain dormant but are repeated in a variety of ways. Severe traumatic experiences are reexperienced through so-called "flashbacks" that may include intense reliving of entire events or only waves of feelings and sensations associated with the trauma, as well as repetitive intrusive thoughts, recollections, and nightmares.

Dissociative amnesia is seen occasionally as an isolated response to a severely traumatic experience, whereas pervasive amnesia accompanied by other dissociative symptoms is often a part of a more severe dissociative disorder. Similarly, dissociative fugue (the assuming of another identity and sometimes traveling to another locale) and depersonalization are rarely seen alone but are components of a severe dissociative disorder. DID involves a sense of internal compartmentalization of the sense of self, along with other dissociative symptoms. DDNOS is a catch-all category for dissociative disorders that do not fall into other groups. However, included in DDNOS are patients who do not have the extreme identity separation of DID but have a range of dissociative symptoms and have a fragmented sense of self.

PTSD has been described as a biphasic disorder. Patients alternately experience phases of intrusion and numbing. The intrusive phase is associated with recurrent and distressing recollections in thoughts or dreams and reliving the events in flashbacks. The numbing phase is associated with efforts to avoid thoughts or feelings associated with the trauma, emotional constriction, and social withdrawal. This biphasic pattern is the result of dissociation; traumatic events are distanced and dissociated from usual conscious aware-

ness in the numbing phase, only to return in the intrusive phase. In addition, patients with PTSD have long-standing, heightened autonomic activation that results in chronic anxiety, disturbed sleep, hypervigilance, startle responses, and irritability. This last set of symptoms has led to the classification of PTSD with the anxiety disorders rather than with the dissociative disorders.

Comorbidity of posttraumatic disorders and other DSM Axis I disorders is extremely common, with a number of studies showing comorbidity in the range of 60–99% (6, 8, 11, 17, 18). These findings indicate that features of trauma-related disorders may be similar to symptoms of other syndromes; in fact, posttraumatic and dissociative disorders have been described as "umbrella" disorders. For example, the dysphoria, emotional constriction, and social withdrawal of PTSD may be similar to symptoms of depressive disorders. The illusions of posttraumatic flashbacks, and the hallucinations and thought insertion associated with severe dissociative disorders, are easily confused with psychosis. The NCS found that traumatic events often preceded the development of other Axis I disorders, suggesting that the posttraumatic disorders often are umbrella disorders.

The differential diagnosis of posttraumatic disorders from mood disorders can be subtle. Time-limited assessment of patients may fail to distinguish between traumatized patients and those with more biologically oriented major depression. A comparison of DSM-III criteria between a group of patients with a history of childhood physical or sexual abuse and a group of nonabused patients with a diagnosis of major depression failed to show any significant differences between the two groups—including no differences in neurovegetative signs (19). Subtle distinguishing features included the fact that the traumatized group was more likely to report being afraid to go to sleep (afraid of loss of control) and having more awakenings during the nights, with more anxiety on waking.

The switches in self-states often seen in severe dissociative disorders may mimic the mood changes of bipolar disorder. In general, dissociative switches are much more rapid than the cycling of bipolar disorder. Although sleep disturbance is common in both posttraumatic and dissociative disorders, total sleep time is maintained at a minimum of approximately 4 hours a night. Sleep disturbances that persist at levels less than 2 or 3 hours a night are more consistent with mania or hypomania, particularly in the presence of high energy on waking.

Symptoms of some posttraumatic and dissociative disorders also may mimic psychotic symptomatology. A study of adult psychiatric patients with histories of childhood abuse demonstrated an elevated level of psychotism on the Minnesota Multiphasic Personality Inventory (MMPI) (13). This finding might be explained by the observations of some investigators that symptoms such as hallucinations and even Schneiderian "first rank" symptoms of schizophrenia frequently occur in severe dissociative disorders (20). Recurrent "brief reactive psychoses" should be examined as to whether they may represent posttraumatic flashbacks or dissociative state switches. Intense visual, auditory, somatic, and olfactory illusions or hallucinations are frequent components of flashbacks, and auditory hallucinations are common in severe dissociative disorders as parts of the self "talk" to other dissociated self-states. Differential diagnosis concerning auditory hallucinations may be sharpened by the characteristics of the hallucinations. Dissociative hallucinations almost always are heard as coming from inside the head and generally are a familiar set of voices over time. Psychotic auditory hallucinations tend to be more bizarre (e.g., voices from the radio or TV), are heard from both inside and outside the head, and vary over time.

Certain Axis I disorders may offer ways of coping with the dysphoria of posttraumatic conditions. A history of traumatization, particularly childhood abuse, is substantially higher in patients with substance abuse (6, 21–24), eating disorders (25, 26), and somatization (12, 27–30). The psychological numbing from substance intoxication eases the distress of posttraumatic numbing and isolation and may ease awareness of disturbing symptoms such as amnesia or state switches. Moreover, intoxication may offer an opportunity to release internal tension by acting out intense feelings associated with traumatic events. Eating disorders and somatization can offer avenues of escape from past distressing events and can provide a focus on bodily concerns.

Differential diagnosis is further complicated by the presence of true comorbidity (i.e., two or more disorders, not simply one disorder mimicking another). Very often, the patient will present with pronounced posttraumatic symptoms rather than clear evidence of another disorder. Because PTSD and dissociative disorder are responses to stress, it is hypothesized that the onset of another disorder (e.g., mood disorder or exacerbation of psychosis) results in more stress to the individual and thus increases posttraumatic responses. In virtually all situations in which true comorbidity of Axis I disorders exists, the trauma-related disorder has secondary importance in the hierarchy of treatment. Any acute mood disorder or psychosis should be treated before treating the posttraumatic or dissociative disorder. Similarly, cases of malignant or out-of-control substance use or eating disorders should have first priority.

Ego Defenses and Character Style

Prolonged exposure to trauma produces profound changes in the human psyche. Janoff-Bulman (31) has written about the shattered assumptions of trauma survivors. She notes that most people hold basic assumptions about the world as benevolent and meaningful and about themselves as worthwhile. In contrast, persons who have been severely and chronically abused carry the assumption that their interpersonal world will mirror their abusive past experiences. This is especially true for traumatized children. Chronic experiences of physical, sexual, or emotional abuse, neglect, or terrorization grossly interfere with normal development and change the way a child sees the world and the self.

" . . . The traumatic experience is apt to become fully incorporated into the child's inner world; the basic building blocks of this world are still in the developmental stage, and the victimization is likely to define the world and self-assumptions of the child. These children are apt to have negative assumptions in all domains, for core beliefs are less likely to be disentangled at an early age. The trust and optimism, the sense of safety and security, the feeling of relative invulnerability that are afforded the person with positively based assumptions are absent in the psychological world of these children. Instead, their world is largely one of anxiety, threat, and distrust." (31)

Children who are traumatized extensively experience major disruptions in development that appear to result in characterologic difficulties, most often borderline or narcissistic personality disorders or traits. Recent studies have demonstrated very high rates of traumatic childhood experiences, generally in the range of 60–75%, in adolescent and adult borderline patients, which suggests that childhood trauma often is a critical factor in the development of borderline psychopathology (32–37). In this context, the intrapsychic structures and behaviors of borderline patients can be understood by a model that emphasizes adaptation rather than pathology (38). Major disruptions of normal familial attachments and failure of adequate care and protection result in distortions of normal characterologic development.

Borderline symptomatology often underlies the posttraumatic and dissociative disorders that are seen in acute care settings. However, this symptomatology must be understood in the context of past victimization. The intensity and oscillations of patients' relationships may be understood as recapitulations of early abusive relationships. Patients' behavioral dyscontrol, impulsivity, affective lability, and poor affect tolerance similarly can be traced to failures of care-takers to provide support for the child, resulting in inadequate ego functioning. Patients' fear of abandonment and intense anger may be understood as deriving from actual abandonment, maltreatment, and deprivation. Continually expecting to be victimized and the recapping of abusive and failed relationships leads to a reservoir of bitter disappointment, frustration, self-hate, and rage and results in episodic expressions of intense and poorly controlled anger. Given the borderline patient's disability in using supportive relationships, angry outbursts alternating with impulsive and self-destructive patterns of tension reduction (e.g., suicide gestures and repetitive self-injury) may be the only outlet for the intolerable experience of erupting rage.

The overwhelming consensus is that one of the damaging effects of early abuse is the development of self-hate (1, 6, 9,

39–46). Chronic early victimization frequently creates a set of assumptions in which children view abuse and exploitation as inevitable and even normative. Because young children remain relatively undifferentiated from parental figures on whom they remain physically and emotionally dependent, they cannot see themselves as victims and cannot express rage against their abusers; rather, they view themselves as justly deserving of the abuse and hence as "bad" and defective.

The presence of borderline symptomatology complicates the task of providing adequate treatment to traumatized patients. Interpersonal alienation and poor ego capacities interfere with patient's capacity to cope with stress and to form a therapeutic alliance. A paradigm that takes into account the actual occurrence of major trauma in early life allows clinicians to avoid the prevailing view that patients with borderline symptomatology inherently have abnormal or excessive reactions to current untoward life events. Rather, such patients should be viewed as having adapted to these events by developing protective defenses and patterns of relating and by viewing themselves and others on the basis of unresolved traumatic experiences.

Formulation

Traumatized patients often maintain a tenuous homeostasis between numbing and intrusion, control and dyscontrol, and interpersonal connection and alienation. Often their brittle defenses shatter in the face of stress or changes in the external environment. Current traumatic events or even reminders of a past traumatic event may result in powerful intrusive symptomatology. For example, an attempted rape or a prolonged and painful childbirth may trigger memories of a past sexual assault.

Therapeutic efforts may increase intrusive symptomatology; overly intensive psychotherapy or self-help groups that focus on traumatic experiences may bring on intrusive thoughts, feelings, and recollections as well as autonomic arousal in the form of heightened anxiety, irritability, and nightmares.

Changes in the patient's external environment are frequent precipitants to the decompensations that require acute care. The loss of supportive relationships or important external supports, either temporarily or permanently, often increase symptomatology. The break-up or deterioration of relationships (including dysfunctional relationships); the sudden lack of availability, departure, or death of a friend; the loss of a job or other regular activity; or the vacation of a therapist are frequent etiologies of psychiatric decompensation. These events tend to trigger the dysphoria, anger, panic, helplessness, and despair that are associated with previous traumatic experiences. Unfortunately, as a result of the relational patterns that derive from their early abusive experiences, patients often are unable to turn to others for support. Instead, they expect abandonment and betrayal. Clinicians should understand that these difficulties in relatedness also occur within the therapeutic relationship. Patients view therapists and other mental health professionals with great suspicion, and many severely abused patients are unable to take the emotional risk of trusting the therapeutic relationship. Characteristically, when faced with any major stressor, severely abused patients flee into dysfunctional isolation (the perceived safest alternative) and/or resort to ingrained dysfunctional solutions. Many of these "solutions," including self-destructive or suicidal behaviors, risk-taking or addictive activity, and aggression, result in the need for acute psychiatric care.

Special emphasis should be given to a patient's flight into isolation that results in a profound experience of aloneness. Although patients see this as the safest course, they are alone with their self-hate. A simple formulation is behind many complicated scenarios of decompensation in traumatized patients. Patients who are left alone with their own self-blame and self-loathing often turn to self-destruction or other dysfunctional behaviors as a way of alleviating an intolerable internal experience.

Focal Problems

Psychiatric decompensation with posttraumatic and dissociative symptoms should be evaluated in the context of psychosocial issues and the patient's external environment. Given the common formulation of psychosocial stressors resulting in increased symptomatology and dysfunctional attempts to cope, comprehensive treatment must be focused not only on the symptomatology itself but also on ameliorating the stressors that precipitated decompensation. For example, a patient may present with symptoms such as traumatic nightmares or flashbacks. In addition to attempts to contain and alleviate these symptoms, attention also must be directed toward their precipitants, such as the loss of an important supportive relationship or a current abusive relationship that repetitively threatens the patient.

A dual focus is particularly important when working with patients with severe dissociative disorders. Their intriguing and shifting presentations often may hide the mundane realities that cause their current distress. In many ways, such therapeutic difficulties are not surprising. After all, posttraumatic and dissociative defenses are used to distance and disavow stressful events; there is psychological gain in not attending to them. However, any successful resolution of a crisis situation will necessitate both symptomatic control and restoration of a safe and stable external environment.

As noted previously in the discussions of comorbidity with posttraumatic and dissociative disorders, therapeutic efforts also must be directed at any active biologic processes. Little progress will be made in treating experiences of traumatization in the presence of a major affective or psychotic disorder. Additionally, the biologic expressions of PTSD, including heightened reactivity, chronic severe anxiety, disturbed sleep, and explosiveness, must be addressed. These difficulties are intensely distressing and may interfere with the psychological management of other symptoms. The use of benzodiazepines (e.g., lorazepam, clonazepam, and others) often is only a temporary solution and may lead to tolerance and habituation. Other strategies such as relaxation training and self-soothing techniques, or the use of low-dose neuroleptics, have been used in efforts to reduce autonomic overactivation.

One other area of focal importance is the ongoing outpatient treatment. Acute intensive treatment offers the opportunity for consultations that must be performed with great sensitivity. Because particular characteristics of severely traumatized patients and their therapy appear to result in painful clinical dilemmas (47), ongoing treaters often find themselves beleaguered, emotionally drained, uncertain, and defensive. Issues regarding the pacing of therapy, managing transference-countertransference binds, defining treatment goals, setting limits, and maintaining boundaries are common dilemmas in ongoing treatment (48). Sensitive consultation may be extremely useful in resolving acute difficulties and setting a more productive course for future treatment.

BIOLOGIC EVALUATION

The biology of PTSD has been extensively studied (49–51). However, no current biologic evaluations are available that definitively elucidate the presence of posttraumatic or dissociative disorders. These diagnoses are made on the basis of clinical presentation. Biologic evaluations are useful for eliminating the presence of possible alternative conditions (e.g., electroencephalogram [EEG] evaluations for the differential diagnosis of temporal lobe epilepsy from dissociative disorders).

ASSESSING LEVEL OF CARE

Assessing the level of care for patients with posttraumatic and dissociative disorders follows guidelines that are similar to those used for other psychiatric conditions. Inpatient hospitalization is used to reduce imminent and grave risk to self or others, stabilize out-of-control dysphoric dissociative symptoms, and control agitation. Partial hospitalization and residential treatment are used for less acute situations to help stabilize symptoms and establish a structure for ongoing outpatient care. These step-down treatments offer considerable advantages, not simply in cost-effectiveness, but also in providing team-oriented treatment, an opportunity for patients to have more contact with the community, and a less regressive milieu. However, all intensive treatments should be seen as acute care. The value and fiscal feasibility of providing a long-term asylum for traumatized patients in an acute care setting is questionable. When indicated, such an environment should be designed as a low-intensity, community-based treatment program (e.g., supported and group housing as well as part-time partial hospitalization) to decrease dependency and increase integration into the community.

Intensive office care may be another alternative for the management of crisis in otherwise stable treatment. Because so many decompensations occur in the context of an interpersonal disruption, intensive (3 to 4 times a week) visits may provide opportunities for symptom management and may allow patients frequent contact to reestablish necessary interpersonal connections. However, intensive treatment should be limited to circumscribed crisis periods. Too frequent contacts over a longer period can result in excessive dependency, dysphoric interpersonal intensity, and premature access to overwhelming traumatic memories.

TREATMENT

Complex psychiatric syndromes related to traumatization underscore the need for a sophisticated understanding of the treatment process. The many and varied clinical presentations of trauma-related disorders require clinicians to conceptualize a hierarchy of treatment approaches. In an evolving standard of care, clinician-investigators are advocating a variety of stage or phase-oriented approaches to treatment (1, 48, 52, 53). These models require an initial (sometimes lengthy) period of developing basic skills to maintain supportive relationships, develop self-care strategies, cope with symptomatology, improve functioning, and establish some degree of basic, positive self-identity. This early phase of developing solid skills is essential before embarking on any abreactive work or extensively exploring childhood trauma.

Abreaction, the reexperiencing of the traumatic event in a supportive and therapeutic environment, has been effective in alleviating symptomatology in some traumatized patients. For example, abreaction in combat veterans through deliberately triggering reexperiences of combat has been shown to reduce posttraumatic symptoms (54, 55). No similar studies of abreaction in survivors of chronic traumatization, including childhood trauma, are available. Clinical experience suggests, however, that the eventual reexperiencing of and working through such trauma has a therapeutic effect. Patients who have been able to work through their traumatic experiences successfully often report an ability to tolerate and integrate the experiences. They are able to proceed with their lives with a positive sense of identity and an improved ability to relate to others and are less encumbered by troubling intrusions.

The value of abreaction is questionable in some patients and has led to an erroneous belief that efforts always should be made to immediately explore and abreact abusive experiences. If current difficulties seem even somewhat related to past trauma, some clinicians believe that abreaction is the treatment of choice. Unfortunately, in the treatment of many patients, such a belief is conceptually flawed and inappropriate and can have serious adverse effects, including increased symptoms and decreased functioning. Many patients become overwhelmed by their past experiences; some actually are retraumatized. The key element that is missing in these attempts at abreactive therapy is the ability to use social supports. All models (such as those described in references 54 and 55) of successful use of abreaction are based on patients using a high level of social and interpersonal support. Patients (and their therapists) who aggressively seek to uncover and explore their traumatic pasts long before they are equipped to do so typically find themselves on a psychological roller coaster. These patients overestimate their own capacity for tolerating the torrent of intense experience from premature

abreaction (e.g., periods of intrusive thoughts, feelings, dreams and flashbacks, punctuated by brief periods of numbing).

The Treatment Model

Most accepted models for the treatment of trauma-related disorders divide the course into early, middle, and late stages. The early stage is primarily composed of building basic relational and coping skills. The middle stage involves abreaction and working through traumatic experiences. The late stage consists of consolidation of gains and increased personal growth, particularly in the external world. This discussion focuses only on the early treatment, as all acute care treatment should emphasize stabilization, coping, and crisis management. Further treatment should be based on the ability to avoid crisis and decompensation and should occur in an ambulatory office setting. Crucial areas in early stages of treatment are self-care and symptom control, acknowledgment, functioning, expression, and relationships (SAFER) (48).

Self-Care

Survivors of chronic childhood traumatization are prone to a wide variety of self-destructive and dysfunctional behaviors (44, 56–59). Chronic reexperiencing of the affects related to early abuse, including intense dysphoria, panic, helplessness, and hopelessness, as well as a chronic sense of aloneness and disconnectedness, often leads to suicidal impulses and behavior. Self-mutilation of a nonlethal nature also is extremely common and paradoxically is often used as a self-soothing and coping mechanism. As noted previously, various substance abuse disorders and eating disorders also are seen in these patients. Finally, revictimization is remarkably common, including repetitions of emotional, physical, and sexual abuse (9, 13, 60–63). Clinicians should insist that treatment focus on self-care. Many patients, however, are ambivalent about self-care because self-destructive behaviors have served in coping and self-soothing. For many patients, the most effective strategy for encouraging self-care is the use of an addictions model in which clinicians insist that patients assume the primary impetus and motivation for self-care as a condition of treatment. In the early stage of therapy, many patients will lack the strength to achieve self-care, and lapses will occur in many situations. Lapses should be acceptable when patients demonstrate an ongoing commitment to the principles of self-care. Treatment should require patients to be allied with the goals of preventing self-harm, opposing self-destructive impulses, and understanding the mechanisms of their vulnerability to revictimization. They also must learn to soothe themselves using less self-destructive ways of coping.

Symptom Control

Many of the symptoms associated with severe PTSD and dissociative disorders need to be modulated and controlled to bring some stability into the patient's life. As long as symptoms such as flashbacks, amnesia, or autonomic overactivation are frequently present, the patient is likely to remain in crisis. Limiting the intrusion of traumatic thoughts and feelings often is very difficult and only can be gradually achieved if the patient allies with the therapist in attempting to control the rate and nature of reexperiencing past trauma. Educating the patient as to whether and how this can be done is the most important intervention in properly pacing the therapy, yet it is a difficult proposition, as this

symptomatology is inherently experienced as out of the patient's control. As with issues of self-care, patients must assume the primary responsibility for maintaining control and must wrestle with their internal beliefs that control is impossible to achieve. Early in the treatment process, achieving adequate control may be extremely difficult, and beginning steps to do so may be only minimally successful. However, many of the effective behavioral interventions fall into the category of "grounding" techniques that help to anchor the patient in the present. Patients should be encouraged to develop a crisis plan that grounds them in their environment and current realities when they are beginning to feel consumed by dissociative and posttraumatic symptoms (48, 64). A well-lit environment can be very helpful in grounding patients, particularly in the evening or at night. Too often, patients feel compelled to sit in half-darkened rooms, which only increases their propensity to lose their bearings in current reality. Contact with other persons (particularly eye contact) also is enormously effective. Finally, use of familiar and soothing objects (e.g., mementos, photographs, and stuffed animals) can help reorient patients.

Acknowledgment

Although intensive exploration of past traumatic experiences may be inadvisable in the early stage of treatment, acknowledgment of the central role of the early trauma is crucial. To eschew the role of traumatic experiences is to collude tacitly in the patient's denial of the impact of the abuse and in the erroneous belief of personal defectiveness. Simply acknowledging the possible role of early traumatic experiences helps survivors to understand many of their current difficulties as being adaptive responses to extraordinarily overwhelming events. Patients who are abuse survivors often are remarkably ambivalent about acknowledging the role of trauma in their lives. Although they may be able to understand intellectually the relationship between their early abuse and their current difficulties, emotionally they resist acknowledgment of any such linkage. Many trauma survivors continue to minimize obviously abusive experiences and their effects and insist that they deserve the difficulties in their lives. Virtually all victims of childhood abuse assume inappropriate responsibility for their own abuse. Bright and perceptive patients who can acknowledge that no other children could possibly deserve the abuse they experienced maintain persistently that they were to blame in their personal family situations. This denial appears to be further evidence of the unbearable nature of abuse.

Functioning

In treatment, patients who suffer early abuse often become acutely symptomatic when they are overwhelmed by reexperiencing their trauma. Without persistent efforts on the part of both patients and therapists to maintain some semblance of normal functioning, the reexperiences of trauma can rapidly intrude into every aspect of patients' lives. The syndrome of constant flashbacks, repeatedly occurring crises, desperate efforts to obtain comfort and reassurance, and dysphoric dependence on therapists is seen frequently in out-of-control treatments. In acute care settings, every effort should be made to help patients return to a high level of functioning. Paid employment, a volunteer job, regular activities in the home, school, or training programs are crucial as they both provide a positive sense of self and insist that patients function in the current re-

ality. If patients are unable to meet the challenges of such settings, treatment programs such as therapeutic groups, day programs, or AA-related activities are very useful alternatives. All such activities help patients to reinforce their sense of internal control of their own lives, rather than to feel controlled by past experiences.

Expression

The intense effects associated with posttraumatic symptomatology—including intense depression and hopelessness, panic and terror, and rage—must be expressed in a nondestructive manner. Treatment must help patients find healthier means of expression. Although unspeakable feelings need verbal expression in the early stages of treatment, this verbalization may be quite difficult. Expressive nonverbal therapies may have a special role in permitting and encouraging appropriate expression. Formal expressive therapy is probably best left to trained therapists. However, other clinicians can help patients find nonverbal channels for explosive feelings. Abuse survivors who are unable to speak about their feelings commonly find some relief through art, music, or even a simple program of regular physical activity (movement, dance, exercise, or sports). Even writing may be "nonverbal"—certain patients describe sitting with pen and paper and allowing words to flow out without conscious awareness of the content. In the early stage of therapy, such efforts should be directed primarily at therapeutic expression (e.g., venting tension) rather than exploration of traumatic events.

Relationships

Perhaps the most important task of the early stage of treatment is beginning to establish patterns of mutual and collaborative interpersonal relatedness. Survivors of childhood trauma bring abuse-related interpersonal assumptions of their childhood environments into all their adult relationships, including the therapeutic milieu. Childhood abandonments, betrayals, and abuse often transform treatment settings into an emotional battlefield in which the patient and clinicians take on abuse-related roles—most often victim or abuser, but sometimes rescuer or indifferent bystander (65). Even in acute care settings, the patient and clinicians repeatedly must renegotiate the therapeutic alliance. Because the patient is (unconsciously) compelled repeatedly to precipitate control struggles and other abusive reenactments that disrupt the treatment, clinicians must interpret that process and attempt to reengage patients. The milieu also must support a sense of collaboration and mutuality. Clinicians should be cautioned that being respectful and empathic with patients is not synonymous with excessive care-taking. The patient should be responsible for avoiding the conversion of frequent, acute care regression into passivity and dependency.

The issue of limits and boundaries merits special emphasis. Although authoritarian attitudes and controlling stances are not productive in trauma-related disorders, clear limits and boundaries are essential to minimize regression and maintain a therapeutic milieu. Out-of-control behaviors need not be tolerated in patients with posttraumatic and dissociative disorders, including repetitive self-mutilating or self-destructive behaviors, verbal abuse or violence, and antitherapeutic abreactions. Patients should conform their behavior to unit norms as a condition of their treatment. Florid displays of intense affect in public places, uncontrolled flashbacks or abreactions, or switches into in-

appropriate self-states should be discouraged. Although these tasks can be difficult for many patients, they are essential tenets of treatment. Patients must begin to work on containment of symptoms and impulses, finding appropriate means of expression and learning to maintain healthy relationships.

Psychopharmacologic Management

A variety of psychotropic medications have been proposed as effective treatments for PTSD. Antidepressants have been the most studied agents in the treatment of PTSD. Investigations have shown efficacy of monoamine oxidase inhibitors (MAOIs) (66), tricyclic antidepressants (66–69), and selective serotonin reuptake inhibitors (70–73). Studies also suggest that anticonvulsants (74–76), propranolol (77, 78), and clonidine (78, 79) may be helpful. One open trial suggests that clonazepam is helpful for control of posttraumatic symptoms in DID (80). However, the use of medication in dissociative disorders has been studied less systematically, and investigators agree cautiously that medications are not the primary therapeutic interventions (81, 82). Despite the evidence from the studies cited in this chapter, the usefulness of medications for the treatment of trauma-related disorders remains unclear. A number of these studies were open trials that studied specific traumatized populations (e.g., combat veterans). Further investigations that control for chronicity of traumatization, severity of symptomatology, and premorbid adjustment will clarify the role of medications in posttraumatic and dissociative symptoms.

As previously noted, many patients with posttraumatic and dissociative disorders have significant dysphoria, mood lability, disturbed sleep, and hyperarousal that do not respond readily to standard antidepressant treatment. However, a significant number of traumatized patients with true comorbid major depression and bipolar disorder respond to psychopharmacologic interventions. Similarly, many patients with acute disorders have psychotic disorders in addition to their trauma-related difficulties. The stress imposed by a comorbid Axis I mood or psychotic disorder may heighten dissociative and posttraumatic symptoms. The combination of trauma-related disorder and another Axis I disorder may predispose patients to greater disability with the likelihood of acute, intensive care.

Clinical experience suggests that antidepressants are often useful for PTSD even in the absence of an independent major depression. Although these agents rarely eliminate depressed mood and dysphoria, some clinicians have observed an increase in energy with the use of activating tricyclic antidepressants such as nortriptyline, desipramine, the MAO inhibitors, or the selective serotonin reuptake inhibitors. Similarly, benzodiazepines are commonly used for both panic attacks and chronic anxiety. If possible, benzodiazepines should be used acutely rather than continuously, because they carry the risks of tolerance and habituation and may disinhibit destructive impulses and induce behavioral dyscontrol. Anxiety usually cannot be completely resolved, but medication can help reduce panic so that the patient can work psychologically.

Disturbed sleep is also quite common in an acute care setting. Patients are likely to be fearful of going to sleep and wake up repeatedly with high anxiety and/or nightmares. Benzodiazepines usually are of limited effectiveness over time. A proper sleep routine (getting out of bed and staying awake during the day) and other practical measures such as adequate exercise may be helpful. Trazodone, a sedating antidepressant, has been used in doses of 25–150 mg. Zolpidem, the nonbenzodiazepine hypnotic, has a reduced risk of habituation, but the effects of long-term use remain unclear.

The use of neuroleptic or antipsychotic medications is controversial. However, some patients are so overwhelmed by constant flashbacks, intense dysphoria, and intrusive thoughts that they appear to benefit from the use of low-dose neuroleptic medications (83). The question of whether neuroleptic medication should be continued on a long-term basis should be reviewed carefully with the patient, considering the risk of tardive dyskinesia. The newer generation of antipsychotic medications, particularly risperidone, have some of the advantages of neuroleptics but carry a reduced risk of anticholinergic and Parkinsonian side effects (and perhaps less risk of tardive dyskinesia). Risperidone, given as a bedtime dose of 0.5–3 mg, may have some promise as an effective medication for posttraumatic conditions because it appears to help with sleep and to reduce autonomic overactivation on the following day.

Alliance and Psychotherapeutic Management
Nursing Practice

Patients in acute care with histories of severe traumatization are often very fearful of excessive control and mistreatment. In a hospital setting, members of the nursing staff bear the brunt of this mistrust because of their authority and control over patients' daily lives. Thus, nursing staff have a major responsibility for establishing and maintaining a therapeutic alliance with patients. The staff must have a sophisticated understanding of the effects of early abuse and must be able to empathize with the difficulties experienced by patients. They should be able to project the therapeutic attitudes of acceptance and respect and should be skilled in bridging mistrust during control struggles and in setting limits and establishing boundaries. The negotiation of the therapeutic alliance begins at the time of admission, when issues such as privileges, rooming arrangements, and unit rules provide areas of potential conflict. Patients should be treated respectfully, but patients also must respect the judgments of the staff and the real limitations of the hospital environment. For example, attempts should be made to accommodate the patient in terms of comfort and privacy (e.g., room location or roommate), but nursing staff also must be allowed to consider and weigh the clinical needs of all the patients and to make decisions based on their assessments.

During an episode of acute care, the most traumatized patients are distressed from intrusive reexperiencing of past abuse. Patients suffer from overwhelming effects such as despair, panic, and rage and may have impulses to flee, strike out, or hurt themselves. Effective nursing interventions are critical to patients. Daily structure can be helpful for patients who are experiencing intrusive symptoms such as flashbacks and nightmares. Planned activities, as well as rest and recuperation, are important components of a daily structure. Emotional support and medication also should be provided as necessary. The acute care setting should have flexible rules about sleep and rest. Many patients are afraid of sleeping at night in a darkened room, especially if their abuse occurred at night. The use of night lights should be permitted, and patients should be allowed to get out of bed and sit quietly in an area close to staff for brief periods. Patients may need to sleep during the day if they did not get sufficient sleep during the previous night, but nursing staff should be careful not to allow patients to reverse completely their sleep-wake cycles.

The management of flashbacks and other forms of traumatic reexperiencing involves the use of grounding techniques (48, 64). Patients may find it helpful for a staff member to approach them and maintain contact until the flashback is over. The staff member should let the patient know that he or she is there and should orient the patient to time and place. Staff members may need to speak firmly and give specific instructions to help anchor the patient in the present if the traumatic reexperiencing feels more real than the current environment. However, excessive soothing and care-taking may have the unintended effect of gratifying unmet dependency needs and can prolong reexperiencing episodes.

Educating patients to manage their symptoms may occur through nursing interventions in the milieu. Nursing staff usually are the principal teachers of grounding techniques and other methods to help patients achieve control of dissociative symptoms and to pace the process of abreaction. Nursing staff can help patients overwhelmed by past abusive events by encouraging the containment of painful memories to therapy sessions. Patients can learn to begin to control intrusive thoughts and feelings, rather than to feel completely controlled by them. In addition to grounding techniques, nursing staff can use nonverbal means (e.g., visual imagery such as visualizing "shutting the door" on memories until therapy sessions). When patients become flooded, they can be encouraged to use artwork or journals for brief periods and then to put them away.

Nursing staff are in the unique position of being with patients during periods of crisis, often in the evening or at night. During such times, they have the opportunity to reinforce important messages such as, "It wasn't your fault that you were hurt." Nursing staff can help patients achieve crucial skills in self-care and self-soothing by maintaining adequate food and fluid intake and accessing medical attention as well as encouraging patients to take a warm bath, reading, watch television, or take a brisk walk. Nursing staff also have the critical task of helping patients use other people as resources during periods of crisis, especially by making contact with them and urging patients to trust their support.

Individual Therapy and Case Management

Individual therapy and/or case management is critical in the treatment of complex patients with posttraumatic and dissociative conditions. The individual therapist or case manager is the central professional in formulating a dynamic understanding of the patient's difficulties and implementing a productive treatment plan. Therapists or case managers should be given the autonomy and authority to make important decisions about and with the patient during an acute care episode. Patients often are better able to tolerate hospitalization when decisions affecting them are based on a trusting relationship rather than on inflexible and rigid unit rules. Therapists or case managers also are able to provide specialized services such as specific interventions (e.g., negotiations between alter personalities in a patient with DID), liaison with outpatient professionals, family work, and aftercare planning.

Group Therapy

The use of verbal groups in the acute care treatment of traumatized patients is controversial. Group treatment for posttraumatic disorders has a long tradition (84), whereas the use of groups with dissociative disorders has been discouraged (81, 85, 86). In practice, certain kinds of verbal groups are regressive, whereas others appear to be helpful. Traditional psychotherapy groups that focus on relationships within the group and psychoanalytically based groups that tend to mobilize intense affect are contraindicated. They are considered too overwhelming for patients who have intense relational difficulties and affective instability. Groups that encourage or permit the discussion or details of past abusive experiences are not useful because other patient's stories often trigger patients to reexperience their own trauma.

Verbal groups that are focused on particular tasks appear to be quite useful for many traumatized patients. Some of these groups deal with current symptomatology and the effects of past experiences, but explicitly do not permit detailed discussion of past abuse. These groups have a psychoeducational focus and discuss how to cope with dissociative symptoms and intense feelings, how to remain functional, and how to sustain relationships. Some cognitive behavioral groups (e.g., assertiveness training or relaxation groups) or gender issues groups (e.g., women's issues) also are helpful. Finally, groups that involve activities such as building skills or undertaking tasks are valuable for patients whose self-esteem is shattered and who have little ability to use verbal modalities for relief of intense affect. Recreational activities are a welcome relief from the heavy burdens of psychotherapeutic work and are a good reminder that treatment is intended to improve the quality of patients' lives, not to consume them.

Family Support, Education, and Intervention

Inpatient hospitalization usually brings family issues into the treatment arena. Current families and other persons who are part of the patient's social support system almost always should be involved in the treatment. Spouses or partners simply may need support and education. More often, however, significant relationship problems exist, ranging from a partner who reenacts an abusive relationship to a partner who is overinvolved and overprotective. Children in the home should be assessed for risk as a result of the patient's difficulties. Although many traumatized patients are exemplary parents, others involve their children in the transgenerational cycle or abuse or neglect them through self-absorption in their own difficulties.

In situations involving a history of childhood abuse, contact with families of origin is extremely problematic. Premature disclosure of the abuse "secret" to family members is destabilizing to a family's equilibrium, with potential negative consequences for both the patient and family. Most experts in the treatment of childhood abuse survivors suggest that disclosure and confrontation of a perpetrator should occur only when it is the patient's clear choice and relatively late in treatment, rather than during episodes of decompensation and acute care (41, 87–89).

CONTROVERSY IN THE CARE OF TRAUMA AND DISSOCIATIVE DISORDERS

In recent years, the explosion of reports of childhood abuse has raised questions about the nature of memory for traumatic events. In particular, controversy has arisen concerning amnesia for childhood abuse and the validity and accuracy of recovered memories. Dissociative amnesia is at the core of this controversy. Many clinicians and investigators accept recovered memories of childhood abuse as essentially valid reports of repressed or dissociated early experiences. For some patients, clinical work with recovered memories has been a vehicle for the resolution of psychiatric symptomatology and has led to an enhanced understanding of the traumatic etiologies of their difficulties. Recently, however, a number of investigators have questioned the validity of recovered memory, arguing that such memories can be false and that many clinicians may be colluding in the creation of "pseudo-memories." In particular, a heated debate has emerged in recent years regarding the role of the therapist in the retrieval of dissociated memories of childhood abuse.

Some investigators (90–93) have suggested that traumatic memories are segregated and stored apart from ordinary narrative memory and thus are less subject to ongoing modification in response to new experiences. In contrast to narrative memories, which are integrative, malleable, and part of the individual's personal cognitive schemas, traumatic memories are said to be inflexible, nonnarrative, automatic, triggered, and disconnected from ordinary experience. This nonintegration is considered the basis for remembering through behavioral reenactment, somatic sensation, or intrusive images that are disconnected from conscious verbal memory. Because the memories are unassimilated, they retain their original force—"unremembered and therefore unforgettable" (93). Whereas ordinary narrative memory is dynamic, changing and degrading over time, traumatic memory may be less changeable and has been described as "indelible" (94).

Recent cognitive psychology studies have shown that memories can be remarkably inaccurate. Investigators have studied the nature of memory in stressful experiences, including testing college students under demanding conditions (95–97) and exposing subjects to shocking photographic material (98, 99). Subjects are often remarkably inaccurate in recounting details of their experience (98–101). However, details that are central to the individual are accurately retained.

The role of suggestion in the malleability of memory also has been well established in laboratory studies (102–105). In some protocols, subjects are shown pictures, slides, or videotape of an event and then are asked to recall the event. When subjects are given cues or suggestions, they often make errors concerning peripheral details of the events. Despite evidence that memory content can be influenced by suggestion, emotional arousal, and personal meaning, the bulk of memory research supports the accuracy of remembered events that are known to have occurred. However, there is evidence of memory for events that did not occur. The Swiss psychologist, Piaget (106), a well-known, personal pseudo-memory investigator described such an instance. During his childhood, Piaget had a clear visual memory of someone trying to kidnap him from his pram when he was 2 years old. The memory also involved his nanny chasing away the potential kidnapper and then going home and telling the family. Years later, when Piaget was 15 years old, the nanny returned to the Piaget family and confessed that the incident had never occurred. Her motive had been to enhance her position in the household, but she subsequently suffered guilt about the fabrication and about the watch she had received as a reward.

Piaget's experience suggests that after being told about a past event by a trusted individual, a person may create pseudo-memories of events that never actually occurred. The "memories" may seem valid, and the true source of the information (so-called "source amnesia") may not be recalled. An experiment by Loftus (107) further demonstrated that this phenomenon can readily occur. In the experimental protocol, an older brother attempted to instill in his younger brother a memory of an episode that had never occurred. He told a story about his younger brother being lost in a shopping mall some years previously. Over the next several days, the younger brother began to have fragmentary memories of this "event." By the end of 2 weeks, he had a vivid memory of being lost, complete with essential details and elaborations. Even after being told about the experiment, the younger brother had trouble believing that the incident had not occurred.

The case of Paul Ingram has provided further evidence of the creation of pseudo-memory. As described by Ofshe (108) and Loftus (107), Ingram, the chair of his county's Republican party committee, was accused of sexually abusing his daughter and other children and participating in Satanic cult activities, including ritual sexual abuse and murder. Initially, he denied everything; however, after interrogation and pressure from a psychologist and other advisors, Ingram began to have vivid memories of his involvement in the alleged abuse. Ofshe, an expert witness, attempted to test Ingram's suggestibility. He told Ingram that he had been accused of forcing his son and daughter to have sex together, an event that his children had agreed had not occurred. Ingram initially had no memory of this "event," but after being urged to think about the scene, he began to recall it vividly and eventually confessed to this ersatz abuse. This pseudo-memory does not necessarily invalidate Ingram's other recollections. However, the case does raise issues concerning the effect on memory of legal and clinical questioning, suggestion, and interrogation.

Clinical research generally has supported the concepts of dissociative amnesia and recovered memory. Clinical investigators have found a relatively high rate of self-reported amnesia for childhood sexual abuse (19–62%) in traumatized subjects (109–112). Moreover, these studies suggest that the incidence of amnesia is more highly correlated with early onset of abuse, chronicity of abuse, and severity of abuse (e.g., violence, multiple perpetrators, physical injury, fear of death). Terr's investigations (113–115) with traumatized children also has demonstrated the presence of differential effects depending on the chronicity of abuse. Children who have experienced limited, circumscribed trauma have hyperamnesia—"clear, detailed accounts of their experiences [that] makes one conclude that these memories stay alive in a very special way" (115). In contrast, chronically traumatized children demonstrate extensive amnesia—"they may forget whole segments of childhood—from birth to age 9, for instance" (115). Furthermore, she notes that this kind of chronic traumatization profoundly shifts characterologic development, resulting in "relative indifference to pain, lack of empathy, failure to define or acknowledge feelings, and absolute avoidance of psychological intimacy" (115). Thus, chronically traumatized patients are most likely to suffer amnesia and, given their levels of denial and dissociative defenses, these patients may be most vulnerable to distortions and errors in recall.

Clinicians must use caution in inquiring about histories of childhood abuse. Little evidence suggests that direct questioning about abuse, per se, results in false memories. However, research concerning the use of suggestion and certain types of interrogation has shown that memory content is affected by interactions with others and that pseudo-memory can be induced. Hence, clinicians must be careful not to inquire about possible abuse in a way that is suggestive of any particular responses.

Fantasies, suspicions or partly formed ideas, and dreams about abuse are not the same as the reality of abuse. Especially when memories are fragmentary, clinicians must support the psychological validity of the memories but avoid coming to premature conclusions of its occurrence without sufficient evidence. When recovered memory begins to replace amnesia, clinicians should be open to the possibility of real abuse but should allow patients to reconstruct without suggestion a credible personal history that is consistent with past and current symptomatology.

COURSE AND PROGNOSIS

The course and prognosis of patients with posttraumatic and dissociative disorders varies extensively. The treatment of acute, adult-onset, limited traumatization in persons who are otherwise psychologically intact generally is brief and effective. Such treatment may be accomplished in an office setting. The prognosis for patients with this profile of traumatization is excellent; their symptoms may be mild and intermittent or may resolve spontaneously without substantial psychiatric treatment. Conversely, the treatment of chronic, child-onset, severe traumatization is likely to require extensive use of psychiatric services, including hospitalization and other acute care modalities.

Comprehensive outcome studies on the effectiveness of different treatments for traumatized populations are not available. However, clinical experience suggests that a conservative approach with an initial focus on containment, functioning, and relational issues is most effective. Most exploratory treatment, including attempts at abreaction of traumatic events, should be postponed until acute care services are no longer required.

A subset of traumatized persons who have been persistently victimized since childhood can be described as chronically disempowered (116). The chronic disempowerment of many abuse survivors is not just thoughts or behaviors, but instead constitutes a deeply held belief about the self and the nature of relationships. These survivors cannot act in a way that asserts control or autonomy. They are unable to engage with others in a mutually empowering fashion and repeatedly relate in ways that recapitulate abusive or exploitative past relationships or flee into dysfunctional isolation. Their overwhelming self-hate, isolation, helplessness, and despair becomes a tide of human misery with significant morbidity and mortality.

The treatment of chronically disempowered patients represents a significant challenge for clinicians and the mental health profession. Many patients have been abused so egregiously that they do not believe in their own self-efficacy and are unable to relate to others or engage in treatment. Yet, these patients typically are highly symptomatic and frequently seen in acute care settings. Clinicians must exercise sensitivity and skill to engage them in a way that will minimize regression and promote growth.

In an era of limited health-care resources, the use and type of acute care services for chronically disempowered and traumatized patients must be carefully considered. These patients are frequent users of psychiatric care. Although inpatient hospitalization is indicated when patients are seriously at risk, the hospital should not become an arena for reenactment of abuse or a refuge from living in the real world. Partial hospitalization may be an alternative treatment modality for some patients with persistent symptomatology, but additional knowledge regarding the optimal mix of structure and programming is needed to work with these challenging patients.

Clinicians must be patient and respectful of chronically disempowered survivors of abuse and the psychological prisons that they inhabit. At best, treatment objectives seem formidable to most patients, and the process is long and arduous. Clinicians should insist that these patients begin to share an agenda to help them take control of their lives, even in small increments, and must refuse to collude in reenactments of abuse or revictimization. The ultimate prognosis of many chronically disempowered patients is uncertain. Although many will improve steadily with skillful treatment, others may suffer long-term disability. In either case, clinicians can provide good treatment if they approach therapeutic work with compassion, patience, skill, and a commitment to do no harm.

REFERENCES

1. Herman JL. Trauma and recovery. New York: Basic Books, 1992.
2. Bernstein EM, Putnam FW. Development, reliability, and validity of a dissociation scale. J Nerv Ment Dis 1986;174:727–734.
3. Saunders B, Giolas MH. Dissociation and childhood trauma in psychologically disturbed adolescents. Am J Psychiatry 1991;148:50–54.
4. National Research Council, Commission on Behavioral and Social Sciences and Education, Panel on Research on Child Abuse and Neglect. Understanding child abuse and ne-

glect. Washington, DC: US Government Printing Office, 1993.

5. American Psychiatric Association. Diagnostic and statistical manual of mental disorders. 4th ed. Washington, DC: American Psychiatric Press, 1994.

6. Kessler RC, Sonnega A, Bromet E, et al. Posttraumatic stress disorder in the National Comorbidity Study. Arch Gen Psychiatry 1995;52:1048–1060.

7. Resnick HS, Kilpatrick DG, Dansky BS, et al. Prevalence of civilian trauma and posttraumatic stress disorder in a representative national sample of women. J Consult Clin Psychol 1993;61:984–991.

8. Breslau N, Davis GC, Andreski P, et al. Traumatic events and posttraumatic stress disorder in an urban population of young adults. Arch Gen Psychiatry 1991;48:216–222.

9. Russell DEH. The secret trauma: incest in the lives of girls and women. New York: Basic Books, 1986.

10. Finkelhor D, Hotaling G, Lewis IA, et al. Sexual abuse in a national survey of adult men and women: prevalence, characteristics and risk factors. Child Abuse Neglect 1990;14:19–28.

11. Helzer JE, Robins LN, McEvoy L. Posttraumatic distress in the general population. N Engl J Med 1987;317:1630–1634.

12. Davidson JRT, Hughes D, Blazer D, et al. Posttraumatic stress disorder in the community: an epidemiological study. Psychol Med 1991;21:1–19.

13. Chu JA, Dill DL. Dissociative symptoms in relation to childhood physical and sexual abuse. Am J Psychiatry 1990;147:887–892.

14. Ross CA, Anderson G, Fleisher WP, et al. The frequency of multiple personality disorder among psychiatric inpatients. Am J Psychiatry 1991;148:1717–1720.

15. Saxe GN, van der Kolk A, Berkowitz R, et al. Dissociative disorders in psychiatric inpatients. Am J Psychiatry 1993;150:1037–1042.

16. Surrey J, Michaels A, Levin S, et al. Reported history of physical and sexual abuse and severity of symptomatology in women psychiatric outpatients. Am J Orthopsychiatry 1990;60:412–417.

17. Kulka RA, Schlenger WE, Fairbank JA, et al. Trauma and the Vietnam war generation. New York: Brunner/Mazel, 1990.

18. Shore JH, Vollmer WM, Tatum EI. Community patterns of posttraumatic stress disorder. J Nerv Ment Dis 1989;177:681–685.

19. Chu JA, Dill DL, Murphy DE. Depressive and post-traumatic symptomatology in adults with histories of childhood abuse. Unpublished manuscript available through Dr.

Chu, McLean Hospital, Belmont, MA 02178.

20. Kluft RP. First-rank symptoms as a diagnostic clue to multiple personality disorder. Am J Psychiatry 1987:144:293–298.

21. Davidson JRT, Fairbank JA. The epidemiology of posttraumatic stress disorder. In: Davidson JRT, Foa EB, eds. Posttraumatic stress disorder: DSM-IV and beyond. Washington, DC: American Psychiatric Press, 1993:145–169.

22. Kilpatrick DG, Resnick HS. Posttraumatic stress disorder associated with criminal victimization in clinical and community populations. In: Davidson JRT, Foa EB, eds. Posttraumatic stress disorder: DSM-IV and beyond. Washington, DC: American Psychiatric Press, 1993:111–143.

23. Loftus EF, Polonsky S, Fullilove MT. Memories of childhood sexual abuse. Psychol Women Q 1994;18:64–84.

24. National Victim Center and Crime Victims Research and Treatment Center. Rape in America: a report to the nation. Arlington, VA: National Victim Center, 1992.

25. Hall RCW, Tice L, Beresford TP, et al. Sexual abuse in patients with anorexia and bulimia. Psychosomatics 1986;30:73–79.

26. Welch SL, Fairburn CG. Histories of childhood trauma in bulimia nervosa: three integrated case controls. Am J Psychiatry 1994;151:402–401.

27. Barksy AJ, Wool C, Barnett MC, et al. Histories of childhood trauma in adult hypochondriacal patients. Am J Psychiatry 1994;151:397–401.

28. Morrison J. Childhood sexual histories of women with somatization disorder. Am J Psychiatry 1989;146:239–241.

29. Pribor EF, Dinwiddie SH. Psychiatric correlates of incest in childhood. Am J Psychiatry 1992;149:53–56.

30. Pribor EF, Yutzy SH, Dean T, et al. Briquet's syndrome, dissociation, and abuse. Am J Psychiatry 1993;150:1507–1511.

31. Janoff-Bulman R. Shattered assumptions: towards a new psychology of trauma. New York: Free Press, 1992.

32. Herman JL, van der Kolk BA. Traumatic antecedents of borderline personality disorder. In: van der Kolk BA, ed. Psychological trauma. Washington, DC: American Psychiatric Press, 1987:111–127.

33. Herman JL, Perry JC, van der Kolk BA. Childhood trauma in borderline personality disorder. Am J Psychiatry 1989;146:490–495.

34. Ludolph PS, Westen D, Misle B, et al. The borderline diagnosis in adolescents: symptoms and developmental history. Am J Psychiatry 1990;147:470–476.

35. Ogata SN, Silk KR, Goodrich S, et al. Childhood sexual and physical abuse in adult patients with borderline personality disorder. Am J Psychiatry 1990;147:1008–1013.

36. Westen D, Ludolph P, Misle B, et al. Physical and sexual abuse in adolescent girls with borderline personality disorder. Am J Orthopsychiatry 1990;60:55–66.

37. Zanarini MC, Gunderson JG, Marino MF. Childhood experiences of borderline patients. Compr Psychiatry 1987;30:18–25.

38. Saunders EA, Arnold FA. A critique of conceptual and treatment approaches to borderline psychopathology in light of findings about childhood abuse. Psychiatry 1993;56:188–203.

39. Brown A, Finkehor D. The traumatic impact of child sexual abuse: a conceptualization. Am J Orthopsychiatry 1985;55:530–541.

40. Carmen EH, Rieker PP, Mills T. Victims of violence and psychiatric illness. Am J Psychiatry 1984;141:378–383.

41. Courtois C. The incest experience and its aftermath. Victimology 1979;4:337–347.

42. Gelinas DJ. The persisting negative effects of incest. Psychiatry 1983;46:312–332.

43. Herman J, Russell D, Trocki K. Long-term effects of incestuous abuse in childhood. Am J Psychiatry 1986;143:1293–1296.

44. Shapiro S. Self-mutilation and self-blame in incest victims. Am J Psychother 1987;41:46–54.

45. Shengold L. Soul murder. New Haven: Yale University Press, 1989.

46. Summit RC. The child sexual abuse accommodation syndrome. Child Abuse Neglect 1983;7:177–193.

47. Chu JA. Ten traps for therapists in the treatment of trauma survivors. Dissociation 1988;1:24–32.

48. Chu JA. The therapeutic roller coaster: dilemmas in the treatment of childhood abuse survivors. J Psychother Prac Res 1992;1:351–370.

49. Charney DS, Deutch AY, Krystal JH, et al. Psychobiologic mechanisms of posttraumatic stress disorder. Arch Gen Psychiatry 1993;50:294–305.

50. Krystal JH, Kosten TR, Southwick S, et al. Neurobiological aspects of PTSD: review of clinical and preclinical studies. Behav Ther 1989;20:177–198.

51. van der Kolk BA. The body keeps the score: memory and the evolving psychobiology of posttraumatic stress. Harvard Rev Psychiatry 1994;1:253–265.

52. Brown DP, Fromm E. Hypnotherapy and hypnoanalysis. Hillsdale, NJ: Lawrence Erlbaum Associates, 1986.

53. Lebowitz L, Harvey MR, Herman JL. A stage-by-dimension model of recovery from sexual trauma. J Interpersonal Violence 1993;8:378–391.

54. Foa EB, Steketee G, Rothbaum BO. Behavioral/cognitive conceptualizations of posttraumatic stress disorder. Behav Ther 1989;20:155–176.

55. Keane TM, Fairbank JA, Caddell JM, et al. Implosive (flooding) therapy reduces symptoms of PTSD in Vietnam combat veterans. Behav Ther 1989;20:245–260.

56. Briere J, Runtz M. Symtomatology associated with childhood sexual victimization in a non-clinical adult sample. Child Abuse Neglect 1988;12:331–341.

57. de Yong M. Self-injurious behavior in incest victims: a research note. Child Welfare 1982;61:577–584.

58. Himber J. Blood rituals: self-cutting in female psychiatric patients. Psychotherapy 1994;31:620–631.

59. van der Kolk BA, Perry JC, Herman JL. Childhood origins of self-destructive behavior. Am J Psychiatry 1991;148:1665–1671.

60. Briere J, Runtz M. Post sexual abuse trauma: data and implications for clinical practice. J Interpersonal Violence 1987;2:367–379.

61. Chu JA. The revictimization of adult women with histories of childhood abuse. J Psychother Prac Res 1992;1:259–269.

62. Dutton MA, Burghardt KJ, Perrin SG, et al. Battered women's cognitive schemata. J Traumatic Stress 1994;7:237–255.

63. Follette VM, Polusny MA, Bechtle AE, et al. Cumulative trauma: the impact of child sexual abuse, adult sexual abuse, and spouse abuse. J Traumatic Stress 1996;9:25–35.

64. Benham E. Coping strategies: a psychoeducational approach to post-traumatic symptomatology. Am J Psychosoc Nurs 1995;33:30–35.

65. Davies JM, Frawley MG. Treating the adult survivors of childhood sexual abuse. New York: Basic Books, 1994.

66. Kosten TR. Alexithymia as a predictor of treatment response in PTSD. J Traumatic Stress 1992;5:563–573.

67. Davidson JRT, Kudler HS, Saunders WB, et al. Predicting response to amitriptyline in posttraumatic stress disorder. Am J Psychiatry 1993;150:1024–1029.

68. Davidson JRT, Kudler HS, Smith R, et al. Treatment of posttraumatic stress disorder with amitriptyline and placebo. Arch Gen Psychiatry 1990;47:259–266.

69. Reist C, Kaufmann CD, Haier RJ, et al. A controlled trial of desipramine in 18 men with posttraumatic stress disorder. Am J Psychiatry 1989;149:513–516.

70. Davidson JRT, Roth S, Newman E. Fluoxetine in post-traumatic stress disorder. J Traumatic Stress 1991;4:418–423.

71. Klein NA. Sertraline efficacy in depressed combat veterans with posttraumatic stress disorder. Am J Psychiatry 1994;151:621.

72. Nagy LM, Morgan CA, Southwick SM, et al. Open prospective trial of fluoxetine for posttraumatic stress disorder. J Clin Psychopharmacol 1993;13:107–114.

73. van der Kolk BA, Dreyfuss D, Michaels M, et al. Fluoxetine in posttraumatic stress disorder. J Clin Psychiatry 1994;55:517–522.

74. Lipper S, Davidson JRT, Grady TA, et al. Preliminary study of carbamazepine in posttraumatic stress disorder. Psychosomatics 1986;27:849–854.

75. Wolf ME, Alavi A, Mosnaim AD. Posttraumatic stress disorder in Vietnam veterans: clinical and EEG findings. Biol Psychiatry 1988;23:642–644.

76. Fesler FA. Valproate in combat-related posttraumatic stress disorder. J Clin Psychiatry 1991;52:361–364.

77. Famularo R, Kinscherff R, Fenton T. Propranolol treatment for childhood posttraumatic stress disorder. Am J Dis Child 1988;142:1244–1247.

78. Kolb LC, Burris B, Griffiths S. Propranolol and clonidine in the treatment of chronic posttraumatic stress of war. In: van der Kolk BA, ed. Posttraumatic stress disorder: psychological and biological sequelae. Washington, DC: American Psychiatric Press, 1984:97–107.

79. Kinzie JD, Leung P. Clonidine in Cambodian patients with posttraumatic stress disorder. J Nerv Ment Dis 1989;177:546–550.

80. Loewenstein RJ, Hornstein N, Farber B. Open trial of clonazepam in the treatment of post-traumatic stress symptoms in multiple personality disorder. Dissociation 1988;1:3–12.

81. Putnam FW. Diagnosis and treatment of multiple personality disorder. New York: Guilford Press, 1989.

82. Ross CA. Multiple personality disorder: diagnosis, clinical features and treatment. New York: John Wiley & Sons, 1989.

83. Saporta JA, Case J. The role of medication in treating adult survivors of incest. In: Paddison P, ed. Treating adult survivors of incest. Washington, DC: American Psychiatric Press, 1984:101–134.

84. van der Kolk BA. Group psychotherapy with posttraumatic stress disorders. In: Kaplan HI, Sadock BJ, eds. Comprehensive textbook of group psychotherapy. Baltimore: Williams & Wilkins, 1993:550–560.

85. Kluft RP. Aspects of treatment of multiple personality disorder. Psychiatr Ann 1984;14:51–55.

86. Kluft RP. The hospital treatment of multiple personality disorder. Psychiatr Clin North Am 1991;14:695–719.

87. Herman J. Father-daughter incest. Cambridge: Harvard University Press, 1981.

88. MacFarlane K, Korbin J. Confronting the incest secret long after the fact: a family study of multiple victimization with strategies for intervention. Child Abuse Neglect 1983;7:225–240.

89. Schatzhow E, Herman JL. Breaking secrecy: adult survivors disclose to their families. Psychiatr Clin North Am 1989;12:337–350.

90. Crabtree A. Dissociation and memory: a two hundred year perspective. Dissociation 1992;5:150–154.

91. Kolb LC. A neuropsychological hypothesis explaining posttraumatic stress disorders. Am J Psychiatry 1987;144:989–995.

92. van der Kolk BA, Ducey CP. The psychological processing of traumatic experience: Rorschach patterns in PTSD. J Traumatic Stress 1989;2:259–274.

93. van der Kolk BA, van der Hart O. The intrusive past: the flexibility of memory and the engraving of trauma. Am Imago 1991;48:425–454.

94. LeDoux JE. Emotion as memory: anatomical systems underlying indelible neural traces. In: Christianson S-A, ed. The handbook of emotion and memory. Hillsdale, NJ: Lawrence Erlbaum Associates, 1992:289–297.

95. Eriksen C. Defense against ego threat in memory and perception. J Abnormal Soc Psychol 1952;3:253–256.

96. Eriksen C. Individual differences in defensive forgetting. J Exp Psychol 1953;44:442–443.

97. Tudor TG, Holmes DS. Differential recall of successes and failures. J Res Personality 1973;7:208–224.

98. Christianson S-Å, Loftus E. Memory for traumatic events. Appl Cogn Psychol 1987;1:225–239.

99. Kramer TH, Buckhout R, Fox P, et al. Effects of stress on recall. Appl Cogn Psychol 1991;5:483–488.

100. Christanson S-Å, Loftus E. Remembering emotional events: the fate of detailed information. Mem Cogn 1991;5:81–108.

101. Holmes DS. Evidence for repression: an examination of 60 years of research. In: Singer J, ed. Repression and dissociation: implication for personality theory, psychopathology, and health. Chicago: University of Chicago Press, 1990:85–102.

102. Loftus EF, Korf NL, Schooler JW. Mis-

guided memories: sincere distortions of reality. In: Yuille JC, ed. Credibility assessment. Norwell, MA: Kluwer Academic Publishers, 1989:155–173.

103. Loftus E. Reacting to blatantly contradictory information. Mem Cogn 1979;7:368–374.

104. Schooler J, Gerhard E, Loftus E. Qualities of the unreal. J Exp Psychol: Learning Memory and Cognition 1986;12:171–181.

105. Schumaker JF, ed. Human suggestibility: advances in theory, research, and application. New York: Routledge, 1991.

106. Piaget J. Plays, dreams and imitation in childhood. New York: Norton, 1962.

107. Loftus EF. The reality of repressed memories. Am Psychol 1993;48:518–537.

108. Ofshe RJ. Inadvertent hypnosis during interrogation: false confession due to dissociative state, misidentified multiple personality and the satanic cult hypothesis. Int J Clin Exp Hypnosis 1992;40:125–126.

109. Briere J, Conte J. Self-reported amnesia in adults molested as children. J Traumatic Stress 1993;6:21–31.

110. Herman JL, Schatzow E. Recovery and verification of memories of childhood sexual trauma. Psychoanal Psychol 1987;4:1–4.

111. Loftus EF, Polonsky S, Fullilove MT. Memories of childhood sexual abuse. Psychol Women Q 1994;18:64–84.

112. Williams LM. Recall of childhood trauma: a prospective study of women's memories of child sexual abuse. J Consult Clin Psychol 1994;62:1167–1176.

113. Terr L. Remembered images of psychic trauma. Psychoanal Study Child 1985;40:493–533.

114. Terr L. What happens to memories of early childhood trauma? J Am Acad Child Adolesc Psychiatry 1988;27:96–104.

115. Terr LC. Childhood traumas: an outline and overview. Am J Psychiatry 1991;148:10–20.

116. Chu JA. Treating chronically disempowered survivors of childhood abuse. Unpublished manuscript available through Dr. Chu, Belmont, MA 02178.

Chapter 11

Substance-Related Disorders

Gwen Zornberg and Roger Weiss

DEFINITION

Although prevailing social attitudes toward the use of alcohol and other brain-altering drugs vary considerably, most societies view as problematic substance use that deviates from socially accepted norms or endangers physical or mental health in general. However, the continual shift in the professional lexicon produced by reconvening committees of experts reflects the complex effects of these chemical substances on mood, cognition, perception, and behavior.

DSM-IV (1) divides substance-related disorders into substance dependence or substance abuse. DSM-IV has dropped the term "psychoactive substance-induced organic mental disorders" along with the concept of organic mental disorders. Because it is beyond the scope of this chapter to cover all substances in exhaustive detail, the discussion focuses on three main substances of abuse covered in the American Psychiatric Association Practice Guidelines (2)—alcohol and other sedative-hypnotics, cocaine and other stimulants, and opioids. These substances also are the predominant chemical classes seen in clinical acute care settings.

DIAGNOSIS

Substance dependence is defined in DSM-IV as a maladaptive pattern of substance use. The behavioral and physiologic criteria imply a preoccupation with the substance, loss of control, and continued use despite adverse consequences. DSM-IV (1) has operationalized the diagnosis of dependence as meeting at least three of seven of the following criteria during a 12-month period:

1. Tolerance, as represented by a need for increased amounts to achieve intoxication or desired effect, or significantly diminished effect with continued use of the same amount of the substance.
2. Withdrawal, as manifested by either the withdrawal syndrome characteristic of the substance or if the same or a closely related substance is taken to avoid withdrawal.

3. Consumption of a substance in larger amounts or over a longer period than intended.

4. The persistent desire or attempts to cut down or control substance use.

5. Much time is spent in obtaining or using the substance.

6. Interference of substance use with important social, occupational, or recreational activities.

7. Recurrent use despite persistent physical or psychological problems.

The diagnostic criteria for substance dependence are the same regardless of the particular substance(s) an individual uses. However, certain criteria are likely to be more prominent with some drugs than others. For example, although all substances listed in the DSM-IV substance-related disorders produce intoxication, certain drugs do not produce the physiologic responses of tolerance or physical dependence. For instance, although cocaine is extremely addicting, sustained cocaine use induces tolerance to its euphoriant effects but does not produce severe physiologic withdrawal symptoms. Similarly, withdrawal symptoms are not characteristic of hallucinogen or phencyclidine (PCP) use. If the patient meets criteria for substance dependence and the first two physiologic criteria as well, a diagnosis of substance dependence with physiologic dependence should be specified. If tolerance and withdrawal are not present, a diagnosis of substance dependence without physiologic dependence should be specified.

The DSM-IV criteria for substance abuse emphasize that the criteria for substance dependence never have been met, but that behavioral and cognitive problems associated with substance use have led to clinically significant impairment or distress. DSM-IV has operationalized the definition for substance abuse as meeting at least one of the following criteria during a 12-month period: failure to fulfill major role obligations at work, school, or home; recurrent substance use despite physically hazardous situations; recurrent legal problems associated with substance use; and continued use despite social or interpersonal problems caused or amplified by the effects of the substance. When substance abuse is present, episodes of substance use may be relatively brief and interspersed. Some individuals who abuse substances may be able to preserve generally adequate social and occupational functioning.

The course of substance-related disorders provides important insight into the severity of illness. Remission is defined as not meeting criteria for either substance dependence or abuse for at least 1 month. If none of the criteria has been met during 12 months or longer, the disorder is in sustained remission. Early remission is defined as no evidence of substance dependence or abuse for less than 1 year. In DSM-IV, full remission indicates that no criteria for substance dependence or abuse have been met during the specified period. In contrast, partial remission denotes that one or more criteria—but not full criteria—for either substance dependence or abuse have been met during the early or sustained period. Thus, a patient who has met only one criterion of substance dependence for 3 months would be in early partial remission. Remission is also characterized in DSM-IV by the presence or absence of agonist (e.g., methadone maintenance) and/or antagonist (e.g., maintenance naltrexone) therapy or containment "in a controlled environment" with restricted access to alcohol and other substances.

Patients with substance-related disorders comprise one of the most varied populations seen in psychiatric practice. For example, these patients differ according to the number and classes of drugs used; the type and number of comorbid Axis I and Axis II psychiatric disorders; individual strengths and vulnerabilities; social, familial, cultural, and environmental context; and course of illness.

In medical and psychiatric settings, polysubstance dependence frequently is seen, which may pose greater challenges to assessment and treatment than a single substance use disorder (3). There are three major reasons for polysubstance dependence: to counteract or buffer intolerable symptoms of intoxication or withdrawal from another substance (e.g., the use of alcohol to palliate the symptoms of cocaine-induced stimulation); to enhance the effects of another psychoactive substance (e.g., the use of benzodiazepines to intensify opioid effects); and to take advantage of the availability of mind-altering substances (particularly important in adolescents).

EPIDEMIOLOGY

In the general population, the lifetime risk of having a substance-related disorder is greater than for any other psychiatric illness (4). Men account for the particularly high risk; the 26.6% lifetime risk for men and women combined derives largely from the high lifetime prevalence for men of 35.4%. In contrast, the lifetime prevalence of substance-related disorders for women is only 16.1% (4). Although most individuals who have been introduced to alcohol or have experimented with drugs do not progress to problematic use, patients with substance-related disorders seen in treatment settings often suffer a chronic illness of dependence with recurrent episodes.

Alcohol

It is estimated that roughly 15–20% of persons who drink alcohol become de-

pendent (5). Overall, the risk for alcohol use disorders ranges from approximately two to three times that of other substance use disorders (5). It is most likely that the greater risk from alcohol derives from greater exposure and availability of alcohol, as drinking is legal and socially condoned.

Estimates of problematic alcohol use may be lower than the true risk. Surveys comparing alcohol production with admitted use only account for approximately half of estimated alcohol consumption (6, 7). The 1-year prevalence for alcohol dependence is estimated to be 7.2%, with a lifetime risk of 14.1% (4).

Gender, age, socioeconomic status, and family history are robust risk factors for alcohol use disorders. However, the data regarding race as a risk factor are conflicting and inconclusive, no doubt because most studies have not succeeded in disentangling the effects of socioeconomic status from race. Generally, drinking behavior begins in youth. The median age of onset of alcohol use disorders is 21 years, with 90% of these individuals experiencing their first symptom by age 38 (8). The incidence rates of alcohol use disorders then drop steeply after the third decade of life until they rise sharply after age 65 (9, 10). Although the prevalence of drinking rises with income level for both men and women, the rate of weekly drunkenness increases as income drops (11). Moreover, divorced or separated persons are at higher risk than married or unmarried persons (12). Family studies reveal a seven-fold risk in first-degree relatives of alcoholics (13). Both heredity and shared family culture characteristics likely play a role (14). Recent data suggest that reduced response to alcohol in early adulthood may predispose one to later alcohol use disorders (15).

Nonalcohol Substance Use Disorders

The current national burden of drug dependence is reflected in the 1-year prevalence of 1.8% in Americans ages 15–54 who are actively drug dependent (4). This 1-year prevalence is nearly double the cumulative annual incidence of 0.6% (16), suggesting that drug dependence tends to be a chronic disorder (5).

There are four major risk factors for nonalcoholic substance-related disorders: gender, age, family history, and nationality. Despite prior anecdotal reports, no credible evidence suggests that race is a causal factor apart from social disadvantage (5). The 12-month prevalence ranges from 1.7% to 3.8% for men and from 0.7% to 1.9% for women (4, 9). This lower rate in women appears to be the result of shorter periods of drug use (16, 17). However, differences between the sexes in predisposing factors remain unknown. Data from the Epidemiology Catchment Area study showed the peak incidence of drug use disorders during ages 18–29 (9). The National Comorbidity Survey study found the peak prevalence for any substance use disorder (including alcohol) occurred from ages 25 to 34 years and that prevalence trails off with rising age (4). Although some children of drug dependent parents do not use drugs, a number of those who experiment with substances become dependent (18). Finally, the prevalence of active cases of substance-related disorders for all controlled substances other than opium (19) is more consistently elevated in the United States than in other nations. The reasons for these international differences remain unclear.

Sedative-Hypnotic Drugs

The benzodiazepine sedatives, hypnotics, and anxiolytics are among the most widely prescribed medications. They are frequently prescribed to treat anxiety, insomnia, akathisia, and medication side effects. Approximately 5–10% of individuals with psychiatric illness who are treated with these medications develop a pattern of problem use (3). Although one recent study found no significant difference in the pattern of benzodiazepine use in patients with anxiety disorders, with or without a history of alcoholism (20), most clinicians hesitate to prescribe these drugs to patients with a history of substance use disorder. They fear abuse either of the benzodiazepine itself or the patient's drug of choice (e.g., alcohol). Although the data remain inconclusive on the risk of misuse of medically prescribed benzodiazepines, regulatory limitations on their prescription have been accompanied by frequent street use with resulting medical hazards (21).

Cocaine and Other Stimulants

The lifetime prevalence estimate for cocaine dependence is 2.7% of adults; for other stimulants the risk is 1.7% (16, 22). Roughly 15% of all cocaine users become dependent (5). Crack, a smokeable form of cocaine, tends to be most likely associated with pathologic use (23).

Opioids

The lifetime prevalence for heroin dependence ranges from approximately 0.4% to 0.7% of the general population (22). Among heroin users, approximately 30% become dependent (16). Whereas the development of opioid dependence in a medical setting tends to consist of middle class women who suffer chronic pain (24), addicted health professionals with their high level of access are an important subgroup requiring intervention (25).

THE FOUR QUESTIONS

Descriptive and Differential Diagnosis

Substance-related disorders are the great masqueraders of psychiatry. The primary goal of the acute assessment is accurate diagnosis so that the appropriate level of care and treatment plan can be selected. Any psychiatric or medical evaluation should include a physical examination, thorough psychiatric interview, and laboratory tests to gather critical diagnostic information.

The comprehensive substance-use evaluation in the acute care setting should include an assessment of four major variables: specific substance(s), dosage, duration and frequency of use, and time elapsed since last use.

Two primary factors pose the major obstacles to accurate descriptive diagnosis in the acute evaluation—masking of symptoms and discriminating substance-related from non–substance-related syndromes.

The masking of substance-related disorder symptoms is one of the major impediments to accurate diagnosis in the acute setting. Patients may either purposely or unintentionally conceal symptoms. Typically, this occurs because patients fear the negative consequences of disclosure or because they are using the defense mechanism of denial. Moreover, in the acute setting, a variety of factors may explain why a timely diagnosis is not reached. The clinician may hesitate to stigmatize the patient, fear provoking an angry patient, wish to avoid a lengthy assessment and complex treatment process in an agitated patient, lack adequate education about management of substance abuse, or have strong countertransference reactions to patients with substance-related disorders (26–28).

Researchers have found that certain features of the assessment situation can impede the ability to obtain an accurate substance use history. The most common obstacles consist of patient expectation of negative consequences, disturbed cognitive processes, poor motivation, and personality traits (e.g., defensiveness or need for approval) (29). The clinician's nonjudgmental attitude will facilitate the collection of accurate clinical information on sensitive topics. Experts have described better results when exploratory questions are framed with, "How did you feel?" rather than, "Why did you pick up this time?" (30).

The linchpin of accurate diagnosis lies in the clinician's ability to obtain a thorough clinical history, which can be a challenging task in an acute care setting. Therefore, the major goal after the initial evaluation, beyond medical stabilization, is to collect adequate and reliable clinical information. Key informants, such as family members and significant others (when they are available), can provide crucial information. Toxicology testing also adds valuable data to inform the clinical picture. Urine and serum toxicology and alcohol Breathalyzer tests are the mainstay of rapid biochemical screening.

The choice of serum versus urine toxicology screening depends on the immediate clinical goal. Blood screens should be used when a clinician suspects overdose and needs to know the present level of the substance in the patient. Urine screens should be used for evaluating recent drug use over the past few days to weeks.

When the patient is admitted to an acute care setting, the clinician almost always should obtain a urine toxicology screen. Patients may not be aware of what substances they have ingested. For example, they may have used an illicit drug that was sold as another psychoactive substance or they may not be able to remember the substances that they self-administered. Furthermore, some individuals may not wish to reveal substance use. Studies have found that a substantial proportion of persons admitted to psychiatric units demonstrates positive results on urine toxicology screens. Indeed, one study found that 50% of patients seen in an emergency department who had positive urine toxicology tests for cocaine denied any recent cocaine use (31).

Substance use syndromes can pose great diagnostic challenges when clinicians attempt to disentangle substance-related from non–substance-related psychiatric syndromes. Substance use can induce virtually any symptom seen in psychiatric practice. Both intoxication and withdrawal induce changes in mood, perception, cognition, and behavior, as shown in Table 11.1. Even personality disorders, such as antisocial personality disorder, can be mimicked by chronic substance use (32).

Substance-related disorders not only masquerade as other psychiatric disorders, they also frequently coexist. Although depressive disorders generally have been considered the most common comorbid psychiatric diagnosis in clinical populations of patients dependent on drugs and alcohol (33), bipolar disorder is the Axis I illness most likely to coexist with alcohol and drug disorders, with a lifetime prevalence ranging from 4.6% to 7.4% (34). Other common comorbid diagnoses include generalized anxiety disorder, panic disorder, depression, and antisocial personality disorder (34). The evaluating clinician needs to be aware that substance-related disorders are more likely to be underdiagnosed in psychotic patients than in any other patient population (35).

Common screening measures to detect substance-related disorders include the CAGE interview (see below), the Michigan Alcohol Screening Test (MAST), and the alcohol Breathalyzer test. Screening with self-report scales and structured interviews offer another approach to gathering important diagnostic information necessary for designing treatment plans and reducing the chance of overlooking critical diagnostic information.

The CAGE questionnaire, a prime example of a self-report screening instrument for alcoholism, has become a valuable and commonly used adjunct for evaluation (36). The strength of this questionnaire derives from its brevity and ease of application, combined with high accuracy for detecting problem drinking. The wording of the questions represented by the acronym is easy to remember during an acute evaluation.

- C—"Have you ever felt the need to Cut down on your drinking?"
- A—"Have you ever felt Annoyed by others criticizing your drinking?"
- G—"Have you ever felt Guilty about your drinking?"
- E—"Have you ever felt the need for a morning Eye-opener?"

Validation studies show a sensitivity of 80% to the presence of a substance use disorder when investigators define the threshold of positivity at two or more positive responses (37). Screening with the CAGE questionnaire in pregnant women may be improved by modifying the item exploring feelings of guilt; with pregnant women, experts recommend replacing this question with one evaluating for tolerance to alcohol (38).

The brief pencil-and-paper MAST is also a simple and widely used screening tool. One study showed that four of the questions used on the MAST allowed the evaluator to classify correctly 83% of patients with an alcohol use disorder. These four questions are, "Do relatives complain about your drinking?" "Do you feel guilty about your drinking?" "Has drinking created family problems?" and "Have

Table 11.1. Diagnoses Associated With Class of Substances

Substance	Dependence	Abuse	Intoxication	Withdrawal	Intoxication delirium	Withdrawal delirium	Dementia	Amnestic disorder	Psychotic disorder	Mood disorders	Anxiety disorders	Sexual dysfunctions	Sleep disorders
Alcohol	X	X	X	X	I	W	P	P	I/W	I/W	I/W	I	I/W
Amphetamines	X	X	X	X	I				I	I/W	I	I	I/W
Caffeine			X								I		I
Cannabis	X	X	X		I				I		I		
Cocaine	X	X	X	X	I				I	I/W	I/W	I	I/W
Hallucinogens	X	X	X		I				I[a]	I	I		
Inhalants	X	X	X		I		P		I	I	I		
Nicotine	X			X									
Opioids	X	X	X	X	I				I	I		I	I/W
Phencyclidine	X	X	X		I				I	I	I		
Sedatives, hypnotics or anxiolytics	X	X	X	X	I	W	P	P	I/W	I/W	W	I	I/W
Polysubstance	X												
Other	X	X	X	X	I	W	P	P	I/W	I/W	I/W	I	I/W

Reprinted with permission from the American Psychiatric Association (DSM-IV), 1994.

[a]Also hallucinogen persisting perception disorder (flashbacks).

X, I, W, I/W, or P indicates that the category is recognized in DSM-IV. In addition, I indicates that the specifier "with onset during intoxication" may be noted for the category (except for intoxication delirium); W indicates that the specifier "with onset during withdrawal" may be noted for the category (except for withdrawal delirium); and I/W indicates that either "with onset during intoxication" or "with onset during withdrawal" may be noted for the category. P indicates that the disorder is persisting.

there been any alcohol-related inpatient psychiatric admissions?" (39).

In addition to screening measures, other standardized interviews can enhance assessment during the course of treatment. Once a patient has been diagnosed with a substance-related disorder, some clinicians administer the Addiction Severity Index (ASI) to measure severity of addiction-related problems (40). The ASI evaluates the nature of problems associated with substance abuse at the start of treatment and after discharge (41). This instrument is used to measure severity of illness by identifying personal and family problems in seven areas: medical condition, alcohol use, drug use, family and social status, employment, legal involvement, and psychiatric status.

The ASI, however, is a structured interview that requires a trained and experienced clinician. It takes 45–60 minutes to complete and 10–15 minutes to score, thus limiting its use in the general acute care setting. Another disadvantage stems from the failure of the ASI to address health issues specific to women, such as pregnancy (42).

After a substance use disorder has been diagnosed, the evaluating clinician must identify any coexisting psychiatric and medical disorders while simultaneously defining the immediate and longer-term goals of treatment. Neglect of comorbid illness seriously interferes with diagnosis, treatment, and recovery.

Ego Defenses and Character Style

Traditionally, clinicians have described denial as the hallmark defense mechanism in substance-related disorders. Denial has been used to explain inaccurate clinical information obtained at evaluation and failure to abstain after ending treatment (29).

In addition to a defense mechanism, this concept has been described as an antisocial personality trait, a reaction to confrontational therapeutic approaches, lack of awareness, and impaired perception of internal and external stimuli (29, 43, 44).

Clinical experience indicates that denial is overused. Many patients who appear to be in denial because of their behavior (e.g., repeated substance use despite negative consequences) are instead hopeless about recovery despite their recognition of the seriousness of their condition. The greatest potential pitfalls to recovery may result from an oxymoronic blend of pathologic optimism (denial) combined with fatalistic pessimism (demoralization). Focusing only on the denial (i.e., trying to instill fear) rather than the demoralization (trying to instill hope) is likely doomed to failure.

In addition to assessing the severity of a patient's problems, the clinician and the treatment team should evaluate motivation for recovery, which is an important factor in predicting outcome. Prochaska et al. (45) have characterized motivation according to a gradient of readiness to give up substance use: precontemplation (denial), contemplation (ambivalence), preparation, action, and maintenance.

In this context, the term precontemplation denotes denial of the need for abstinence; in the contemplation stage, the patient admits the need for abstinence but does not feel ready to undertake the necessary steps. Preparation implies the attempt to achieve sobriety without help. Action implies that the patient has reached the point to begin active work on abstinence. Maintenance of sobriety (i.e., "cruise control") is achieved after the consolidation of at least 3 months of sobriety (45). Understanding the patient's level of motivation is critical to the alliance and treatment (46). Indeed, one aim of the acute evaluation is to facilitate the patient's progress to the next stage of motivation for change.

Formulation

In examining the circumstances that have led a patient to seek treatment in an acute care setting, the meaning of the event(s) to the individual should be explored. Marlatt and Gordon (47) emphasize that in addition to interpersonal conflicts and environmental shifts, the intolerance of affective states such as depression and anger frequently provoke relapse.

The reasons for decompensation of individuals with substance-related disorders are frequently associated with changes in the external environment. This is in contrast to many other Axis I psychiatric disorders (e.g., bipolar disorder or schizophrenia) in which a biologic cycling of mood or eruption of psychosis can precipitate a deterioration of a condition even in a relatively stable environment. The individual with an alcohol or drug dependence problem usually persists in chronic use within a particular social homeostasis. When this equilibrium is disrupted, the resulting adverse consequences can result in the patient seeking emergency treatment. Common examples of events that trigger acute destabilization include loss of a spouse, loss of enabling by a spouse, legal problems, and employment difficulties.

☐ **C A S E E X A M P L E**

Sara R. was a 42-year-old married mother of two who had been treated for bipolar I disorder for 10 years. Her alcohol dependence had been in remission for 2 years. Before her previous hospitalization, although she could recall no apparent stressors, she became severely depressed after a brief hypomanic period. As she grew increasingly apathetic, she returned to out-of-control drinking. She felt that her hopelessness was the driving force behind her ignoring the consequences that her drinking had on her children and her marriage.

☐ **C A S E E X A M P L E**

Bill D. was a 30-year-old married salesman with three children who was so preoccupied with drinking that he had been oversleeping and arriving at work late on most days and intoxicated on some. Bill's wife had been covering for him, calling his employer and explaining that he was arriving late because he had to care for one child who had fallen ill. Bill remained in denial about the impending collapse of his marriage and the possible harm he might cause his family by driving them around while intoxicated. After attending her first Al-Anon meeting, Bill's wife stopped making excuses for Bill at work and he was soon fired. Bill then sought emergency treatment for depression.

Research on substance dependence, comparing individuals in treatment with those who are not, offers some insight regarding the motivation of persons with substance-related disorders to seek treatment. One study found that depressive disorders and other psychiatric syndromes were key features distinguishing persons dependent on opiates who sought treatment from those who eschewed treatment (48). This report, in addition to the high association between depression and substance use disorders reported in clinical settings, suggests that depression is frequently a major motivating factor for seeking treatment. Thus, it is important to assess newly admitted substance patients for depression and hopelessness complicating depression (33). As part of the acute intervention, the clinician should explore where the patient lies on the dimensional spectrum from hopeful to hopeless. Apathy stemming from hopelessness may pave the way for relapse, as patients who feel no hope of successful recovery may not appear to be "trying." A similar evaluation along the spectrum of fear of adverse consequences and unwarranted fearlessness is also important. A reawakening of a patient's concern for the damage inflicted on his or her life, along with a fear of the consequences of backsliding, can buttress motivation when combined with hope for a better quality of life.

Focal problems

During an evaluation of the patient's clinical status, the clinician must decide the best management approach. In the acute care setting, the clinician may need to minimize stimulation and avoid "talking down" to a patient intoxicated on PCP, whereas a patient intoxicated on marijuana tends to respond well to this calming approach in a supportive environment. Once the patient has been deemed medically stable, discerning the level of care required for the acute treatment of a patient with substance use disorder may begin, including a check for signs and symptoms of intoxication and withdrawal, depending on the substances used. Moreover, in this patient population, the major focal problem areas that typically require intervention to restore a safe equilibrium, which allows these patients to progress out of an acute care setting, include risk of violence to self or others, medical issues, and disruptions in the social environment.

Risk of Violence

Patients with substance-related disorders are three to four times more likely to complete a suicide attempt than the general population (49) and are more likely to commit homicide than the general population (50). As a result, experts in this area recommend that an evaluation for alcohol and drug use be performed for any individual presenting in the acute care setting with risk of violence to self or others (2). Conversely, any patient presenting for evaluation of a substance-related disorder should be assessed thoroughly for any risk of violence to self or others. The evaluating clinician should be familiar with substances that predict relatively high risks of violence and should be able to recognize when in the phases of use the patient is most at risk. Generally, intoxication states due to cocaine, phencyclidine (PCP), and alcohol tend to be associated with violence. Alcohol is also associated with violence during withdrawal, as is the use of opioids and sedative-hypnotic medications.

Medical Problems

Medical care is not well rendered or coordinated in this population; consequently, these patients often are medically ill when they present for alcohol or drug abuse treatment. Because of the high prevalence and toxicity of chronic alcohol use, alcohol disorders are responsible for most general medical problems seen in substance use programs (2). Acute medical problems such as hepatitis or delirium thus require medical stabilization during the acute treatment of these patients.

Medical problems related to chronic alcohol use can be divided into three major categories (51)—illnesses caused by alcohol toxicity (e.g., cardiomyopathy, cirrhosis, pancreatitis, hepatitis, dementia, gastritis), nutritional diseases caused by insufficient dietary intake (e.g., Wernicke-Korsakoff's syndrome and peripheral neuropathy related to deficient thiamine intake), and medical complications due to the problematic use of alcohol (e.g., withdrawal seizures, delirium tremens, automobile and other accidents, head injuries).

In the acute setting, medical issues must be addressed that are specific to particular groups. For example, fertile women should be evaluated for pregnancy with a beta human chorionic gonadotropin test. Accumulating evidence suggests that substance use during pregnancy poses a risk of damage to both the mother and the fetus (52).

Increasingly, infectious diseases are appearing as secondary complications of substance-related disorders. The most common infectious diseases that greatly compound the morbidity and mortality of substance-related disorders include human immunodeficiency virus (HIV) infection, hepatitis, tuberculosis, syphilis, and infective endocarditis. Injection drug use is not the sole means of HIV transmission among substance abusers. Patients are at high risk to contract HIV through sharing needles and through unprotected sex with multiple partners while intoxicated with crack cocaine or even alcohol (53). One study revealed that among individuals who used substances administered intravenously, needle sharing correlated highly with depression and other psychopathology and not with a lack of education about HIV risk factors (54). For these reasons, clinical suspicion of the presence of these infections should be high whenever signs and symptoms of substance-related disorders are present. Virtually every patient in the acute care setting should have (or have had) a PPD (tuberculosis) test, a serologic

screen for syphilis, and liver function tests to screen for alcoholic and/or viral hepatitis.

Legal Issues

A number of individuals with substance use disorders do not seek treatment until they are forced to interface with the judicial system. Some patients may not demonstrate motivation in treatment until obliged to undergo treatment under a court-mandated order. Nonetheless, many patients who are legally compelled to enter treatment show similar outcomes to those who enter voluntarily (55).

In addition to the role of the legal system in facilitating treatment entry, the clinician should know that federal law and regulations demand that strict confidentiality be maintained in regard to substance use treatment to protect the individual's right to privacy. Exceptions to these regulations mandating strict confidentiality include the following (2).

1. Written consent from the patient.
2. A medical emergency.
3. A court order.
4. Disclosure in response to a crime committed at the treatment facility.
5. The report of child abuse.
6. Compliance with the duty to warn.

Social Environment

To move to a less intensive level of care, patients may require psychosocial intervention to deal with the consequences of a lifestyle centered on their addiction. For example, many patients have housing difficulties or live with an addicted partner, which may require immediate attention before a feasible treatment plan can be implemented.

BIOLOGIC EVALUATION

In the acute care setting, the physical examination and laboratory work-up may contribute valuable diagnostic information. The physical examination may reveal evidence of recent and past substance use such as intravenous or intranasal drug use, overdose, sepsis, nutritional deficiency, or signs of intoxication, withdrawal, and delirium. Physical signs and symptoms to look for include "tracks" (scars from multiple injections) and abscesses on the skin; perforated septum and/or ulcerated nasal mucosa from intranasal cocaine use; cigarette burns between the index and middle fingers or on the chest that suggest periods of alcoholic stupor; painless enlargement of the liver; severe, constant upper abdominal pain and tenderness radiating to the back that indicates pancreatic inflammation possibly due to alcohol; and reduced sensation and weakness of hands and feet perhaps due to neuropathy secondary to chronic alcohol use (56). It is also important to evaluate for signs of acute alcohol-related complications, including gastrointestinal bleeding, and acute mental status changes perhaps due to head injury or amnestic (Wernicke's) syndrome.

Systematic evaluation of the degree of intoxication or withdrawal is imperative in the acute evaluation of individuals with substance-related disorders. In addition to serum and/or urine toxicology screen, primary indications for toxicologic analysis of blood or urine samples to confirm drug ingestion include acute change in mental status and suspicious behavior. Analysis also should be done on a random basis as part of a deterrent to further substances use.

As noted earlier, it is imperative to obtain serum levels of substances when an overdose is suspected, as serum levels reasonably reflect current levels of drugs. In contrast, urine toxicology, which measures the end-products of earlier serum levels of substances, is useful in gauging recent use. For alcohol, the Breathalyzer test (which is convenient, reliable, and inexpensive) is preferable to urine testing and provides an immediate result.

The clinical use of toxicology screening is enhanced by a thorough understanding of the test methodologies and the elimination half-lives of the various drugs of abuse (28). To interpret negative results on toxicology screens, it is essential to know the maximum amount of time that a drug or its metabolite may still be detected (28). Cocaine or heroin use may be detectable for only 24–48 hours after last use, whereas marijuana or benzodiazepine metabolites may appear in the urine for several weeks after last use. Correlation of clinical status to toxicology data also is critical. For example, for the same amount of ingested alcohol, women tend to have higher blood alcohol concentrations than men due to reduced gastric oxidation of alcohol (57). Moreover, when the blood alcohol level is roughly 250–300 mg/100 mL, and the patient is alert without dysarthria, the clinician should be alert for moderate to severe withdrawal symptoms as the blood alcohol level decreases (28). Treatment of the patient should be within the context of the clinical situation and not simply based on laboratory data.

During the initial phases of treatment of substance use disorders, toxicology screens are important in monitoring for relapse. The toxicology screen bolsters the patient's motivation to engage in frank discussion and report lapses and relapses to the clinician. Over the course of time, as the patient's self-motivation becomes established while consolidating sobriety,

Table 11.2. Criteria for Level of Care in Substance-related Disorders (American Society of Addiction Medicine)

Level of care	I (Outpatient)	II (Partial hospital)	III (Inpatient)
Acute intoxication and withdrawal	Stable	Minimum risk	Unstable
Biomedical conditions and complications	Stable	Does not interfere with treatment	Unstable
Emotional/behavioral conditions and complications	Substance-use related	Mildy unstable or diagnosed comorbid psychiatric illness	Unstable
Degree of treatment acceptance	Cooperative with treatment plan	Requires structure	Does not accept severity of problems
Relapse potential	Able to maintain abstinence	High likelihood of relapse	Unstable in less intensive level of care
Recovery environment available	Stable	Moderate hindrance to recovery	Strong hindrance to recovery

Reprinted with permission from the American Society of Addiction Medicine, 1991.
Based on information from reference 63.

the need for toxicology screens may decrease.

In addition to toxicology screens, laboratory evaluation also should be used to detect adverse sequelae of alcohol and drug use (28). The biologic evaluation should include urinalysis, complete blood count, blood chemistry, and liver enzymes. Gamma-glutamyl transpeptidase (GGTP) remains the best serum indicator of chronic alcohol use with reasonable sensitivity and specificity (58).

A neurologic examination is indicated when the history and physical examination suggest the presence of neurologic deficits over a sustained period of abstinence. Alcoholism causes both acute and chronic disturbances of cognitive, perceptual, and perceptual-motor functions (59). During the first few weeks of abstinence, great recovery of function typically is seen, although even after 1 year of alcohol use, abnormalities of psychomotor speed, visuospatial competence, abstracting ability, and perceptual motor function can be evident (60).

ASSESSING LEVEL OF CARE

Outpatient detoxification can be accomplished safely in certain, but not all, outpatient settings (61, 62). The American Society of Addiction Medicine (ASAM) has concluded that adequate evaluation to determine the appropriate level of care requires a multidimensional assessment (63). A discussion of Level IV of ASAM criteria, which pertains to medically intensive treatment rather than management directly overseen by clinicians, is excluded in this chapter. Table 11.2 outlines the six major problems areas to be evaluated.

Although widely used, empiric data validating these guidelines (or variations on them) are still lacking. Indeed, research on "patient-treatment matching" remains sparse throughout the field (64). However, the importance of multidimensional evaluation to determine the appropriate treatment setting generally is accepted.

TREATMENT

Psychopharmacologic Management

After medical stability has been assured in the acute care patient, the pharmacologic treatment of substance-related complications may consist of two stages—detoxification and consolidation of sobriety through maintenance treatment and rehabilitation.

For treatment of withdrawal (Table 11.3), regardless of the specific substance(s), three groups of clinical signs are most informative and require careful monitoring.

1. Vital signs (to evaluate for impending delirium tremens or surreptitious drug use).
2. Eye signs (to evaluate for pupillary dilatation seen in opioid withdrawal, nystagmus as seen in sedative-hypnotic intoxication, vertical and horizontal nystagmus and lateral rectus palsy seen in Wernicke's disease).
3. Mental status changes (to evaluate for somnolence or disorientation as seen in delirium).

Alcohol

INTOXICATION

Simple alcohol intoxication is characterized by slurred speech, ataxia, coordination, nystagmus, and flushed face. In addition, behavioral disinhibition, poor judgment, impaired attention, poor recent memory, emotional lability, irritability, and depression may be seen. Fluctuating alterations of consciousness or a rapid change in cognition in excess of those warrants additional medical evaluation.

WITHDRAWAL

When an alcohol-dependent patient is admitted to an acute care setting, the patient should be evaluated for signs and symptoms of withdrawal. Of all psychoactive substances listed in DSM-IV, alcohol presents the greatest risk of morbidity and mortality from withdrawal. Common manifestations of alcohol withdrawal include elevated pulse and blood pressure, sweating, tremulousness of the upper extremities, insomnia, anxiety, and agitation. The severity of the syndrome is further influenced by the presence or absence of other complicating medical conditions such as head injury. Infrequently, hallucinations or delusions may be seen. In a small percentage of patients suffering alcohol dependence, grand mal seizures may occur between 12 and 48 hours after drinking. Delirium tremens (alcohol withdrawal delirium) is present when the alcohol withdrawal syndrome progresses in severity to encompass disorientation, agitation, and hallucinations associated with autonomic hyperactivity. Delirium tremens is a medical emergency requiring stabilization on an acute care medical unit. Delirium sometimes occurs after an alcohol withdrawal seizure. However, if the seizure follows a period of delirium, another cause of the seizure (e.g., subdural hematoma) should be assumed and a vigorous work-up should be pursued.

In patients with chronic alcohol dependence complicated by malnutrition, Wernicke's encephalopathy (i.e., acute alcohol-induced persisting amnestic disorder) may occur; this is characterized by confusion, ataxia of gait, and oculomotor disturbances. Korsakoff's psychosis (i.e., chronic alcohol-induced persisting amnestic disorder) results in some patients with Wernicke's encephalopathy. Unlike Wernicke's disease, Korsakoff's psychosis generally is not reversible. Due to poor gastrointestinal absorption caused by a severe degree of long-term alcohol use, treatment of both diseases consists of an initial administration of parenteral thi-

Table 11.3.   Clinical Features of Psychoactive Substance Withdrawal Syndromes

Withdrawal syndromes vary in duration and intensity and may consist of any or all of the following signs and symptoms

Uncomplicated alcohol withdrawal
  Coarse tremor, particularly in the upper extremities
  Gastrointestinal distress
  Feeling weak or ill
  Elevated vital signs
  Depressed, irritable, or anxious mood
  Transient perceptual disturbances
  Headache
  Inability to sleep
  Hyperreflexia
  Generalized seizures

CNS depressant withdrawal (at least three of the following must be present)
  Gastrointestinal distress
  Feeling weak or ill
  Elevated vital signs
  Irritable or anxious mood
  Postural hypotension
  Coarse tremor
  Generalized seizures
  Marked inability to sleep

Withdrawal delirium (alcohol and CNS depressants)
  Frank delirium in conjunction with elevated vital signs
  Stimulated withdrawal (including cocaine)
  Dysphoric mood and at least one of the following lasting at least 24 hours after last substance use
    Sleep disturbance
    Fatigue
    Agitation
    Drug craving

Opiod withdrawal (at least three of the following must be present)
  Drug craving
  Gastrointestinal distress
  Myalgias
  Lacrimation
  Rhinorrhea
  Dilated pupils
  Yawning
  Elevated temperature
  Sleep disturbance
  Piloerection
  Sweating

Reprinted with permission from Adelman SA, Weiss RD. In: Sederer LI, ed. Inpatient psychiatry: diagnosis and treatment. Baltimore: Williams & Wilkins, 1991.

amine, 50–100 mg, intramuscularly or intravenously (in less severe cases, oral thiamine) followed by thiamine, 50 mg; folate, 1 mg; and 1 multivitamin tablet daily for at least 3 days. Because intravenous glucose solution may precipitate Wernicke's encephalopathy in predisposed patients, these patients must be given thiamine before glucose infusion (that does not contain thiamine and magnesium sulfate).

DETOXIFICATION

The mainstay of alcohol detoxification has long been based on tapering dosages of medium- to long-acting benzodiazepines. Chlordiazepoxide is used frequently due to an onset of action within 2 hours, a peak effect within 4 hours, and a half-life of active metabolites up to 30 hours. One typical protocol is to administer immediately 50 mg orally and then repeat this dose as needed every 2 hours for withdrawal symptoms (e.g., elevated blood pressure, tremulousness) over the next 24 hours. Within the first 24 hours, 400–600 mg may be given. Throughout this time, the patient is monitored frequently for objective signs of withdrawal such as hypertension, tremor, and tachycardia. The total dose given on day 1 may then be tapered by 25% per day over 4 days. Other benzodiazepines such as diazepam, oxazepam, and lorazepam are also used frequently. Oxazepam is particularly popular for treating patients with liver disease. Studies have found that carbamazepine and valproate may be used successfully for the treatment of alcohol withdrawal (65). In general, monitoring the patient closely during detoxification is critical to avoid oversedation and severe withdrawal symptoms. The dosage may need to be adjusted (either upward or downward) throughout the course of the detoxification period, depending on the patient's current clinical status.

MAINTENANCE TREATMENT

Disulfiram (Antabuse) provides negative reinforcement that can discourage drinking behavior by interfering with the metabolism of acetaldehyde, an intermediate in the metabolism of alcohol. Disulfiram, in dosages ranging from 125 to 250 mg/day, may reduce the rate of relapse if used appropriately within a comprehensive treatment program. It is particularly effective for older, socially stable, highly motivated patients.

A prerequisite for disulfiram use is informed consent. The patient must clearly understand the toxic and potentially lethal effects of this medication. When a patient drinks alcohol while taking a stable regimen of disulfiram, symptoms may include flushing and feelings of warmth in the face and neck, throbbing headache, profound anxiety, chest pain, coughing, respiratory depression, constriction in the throat, cardiac arrhythmias, and death. This medication is virtually contraindicated in patients with heart disease, cirrhosis, diabetes, or other extremely debilitating medical conditions. The patient and clinician need to factor into the decision-making process the risk of reversible (and rarely, irreversible) liver toxicity when considering the advantages and disadvantages of this treatment. Hepatotoxicity should be monitored through levels of alanine aminotransferase, the most sensitive laboratory indicator of hepatic damage due to disulfiram (66).

Two recent placebo-controlled, double-blind studies have found that naltrexone, at a dose of 50 mg/day, can reduce alcohol use in dependent individuals (67, 68). The mechanism of action is not understood completely but may involve blocking the primary subjective effects of a drink. Adverse effects of naltrexone include gastrointestinal irritation, small increases in blood pressure, light-headedness, and drowsiness. The most dangerous side effects derive from elevated liver function tests. Thus, liver enzymes should be monitored at baseline and then each month for the first 6 months of treatment. Once therapy has begun, treatment should be discontinued if the liver enzymes elevate to three times baseline.

Sedative-Hypnotic Medications

INTOXICATION

The signs of intoxication with sedative-hypnotic drugs resemble alcoholic inebriation but without alcoholic breath. Common manifestations include slurred speech, sedation, poor motor coordination, impaired memory, confused thinking, irritability, disorientation, and severe rage reactions as seen in extreme cases. Physical examination may reveal horizontal and vertical nystagmus and signs of cerebellar dysfunction.

OVERDOSE

Usually, severe overdose can be assumed if greater than 10 times the full hypnotic dose has been taken. Severe overdose on central nervous system depressants is associated with cerebrocortical and medullary signs of central nervous system depression. Coma or stupor may be seen, accompanied by absent gag, corneal, and deep tendon reflexes. On recovery, the patient's potential for suicide should be assessed. The terminal overdose condition is characterized by the development of shock, hypothermia, pulmonary involvement, and renal failure.

WITHDRAWAL

Signs of sedative-hypnotic withdrawal resemble alcohol withdrawal syndromes consisting of anxiety, tremulousness of the upper extremities, irritability, disinhibition, anxiety, tachycardia, hyperreflexia, insomnia, tachycardia, and postural hypotension.

Treatment of benzodiazepine withdrawal proceeds generally by gradually reducing the substance of dependence or substituting a longer-acting benzodiazepine in dosages to achieve equivalent potency (e.g., 1 mg of clonazepam for 2 mg of alprazolam). The method chosen and speed of reduction will depend on the substance of dependence, the patient's clinical status, and the clinical setting. As with alcohol withdrawal, the physician attempts to reduce the dose as quickly as possible without exposing the patient to medical danger, namely, a high seizure risk. For long-term, high-dose benzodiazepine users, detoxification may take weeks and often must be completed in an aftercare program.

Opioids

INTOXICATION

Opioid intoxication is accompanied by a sense of tranquillity and euphoria for several hours depending on the dosage and type of drug used. Signs include miosis and decreased pulse, blood pressure, and respiratory rate. Tolerance to euphoria, analgesia, sedation, and respiratory depression begins after roughly 1 week of regular use. Opioid overdose is a common concomitant of opioid use disorders due to shifting levels of tolerance and uncertainty about the true dose of illegally obtained drugs.

WITHDRAWAL

Withdrawal from a short-acting opioid such as heroin begins 6 to 12 hours after the last dose. The most prominent symptoms of withdrawal include drug craving, pupillary dilatation, myalgias, nausea, insomnia, elevated blood pressure, pulse, and body temperature. Among patients with long histories of dependence, insomnia and malaise may last for months after detoxification.

A variety of pharmacologic regimens have been devised to hasten the usual duration of opioid detoxification. Detoxification from opioids tends to be less medically hazardous than from alcohol and sedative-hypnotic agents. Because the opioid withdrawal syndrome presents less medical risk, the main objectives of medical detoxification are improving the patient's level of comfort and engaging the patient in rehabilitation. The method selected depends on the support system available and the patient's ability and willingness to tolerate the physical discomfort of withdrawal.

DETOXIFICATION

Detoxification using methadone hydrochloride is aided by its long half-life (from 24 to 36 hours) and its similarity to commonly abused drugs such as heroin. Dosages of methadone ranging from 10 to 40 mg/day generally will prevent abstinence symptoms in patients physically dependent on heroin and other short-acting opioid drugs such as oxycodone. Due to its long half-life, methadone may be administered once or twice a day. One common protocol in the acute care setting is to administer 10 mg of methadone on the manifestation of objective signs of withdrawal (i.e., elevated pulse or blood pressure, dilated pupils, sweating, gooseflesh, rhinorrhea, or lacrimation), followed by 10 mg as needed up to every 4 hours, based on objective signs of withdrawal during the next 24 hours. The patient then is tapered off the total methadone dose given in the first day by 5 mg each subsequent day.

Alternatively, in settings in which the use of methadone is either impossible or undesirable, clonidine frequently is used to reduce the signs and symptoms of withdrawal (including elevated pulse and blood pressure, mydriasis, nausea, vomiting, intestinal cramps, and diaphoresis and diarrhea). Clonidine is less successful in relieving myalgias and insomnia. Patients first should be given a test dose of 0.05 mg of clonidine to monitor for stability of blood pressure. Then clonidine is administered at a dosage of 0.1—0.3 mg every 6 hours, up to 1.2 mg/day for outpatients and 2.0 mg/day for inpatients. The medication is withheld if the patient's blood pressure drops below 90/60 mm Hg. Because clonidine is not a controlled substance, the medication can be used in a wider range of settings than can methadone. A second advantage of clonidine stems from the physician's ability to begin treatment with opioid antagonists more quickly after detoxification. The most common side effects of clonidine are hypotension and/or sedation.

Other protocols for opioid detoxification, still in the experimental stages, are beyond the scope of this chapter. Some examples include detoxification using the mixed opioid agonist-antagonist buprenorphine and rapid detoxification using a combination of clonidine and naltrexone, sometimes preceded by buprenorphine.

MAINTENANCE TREATMENT

The mainstays of maintenance therapy of opioid dependence are replacement or antagonist medications. Replacement treatment is based on observation bolstered by empiric research that certain patients are unable to abstain completely from opioids for months or years after withdrawal. Methadone maintenance treatment, in which an inexpensive, legal, quality controlled, oral drug replaces heroin, has been shown to be effective in improving the medical condition and quality of life of a number of patients. No optimal dose of methadone has been found for maintenance; 40–60 mg/day constitutes a low dose, whereas more than 60 mg/day is considered high. The dosage schedule and concomitant rehabilitation program need to be tailored to each patient. In the adolescent population, clinicians tend to avoid prescribing methadone maintenance as a first-line approach to treatment because the long-term nature of this treatment could inhibit development (2). Similar to methadone, L-alpha acetylmethadol is an oral agent that is longer-acting than heroin and palliates urges to turn to intravenous administration of heroin.

Naltrexone, a pure opioid antagonist, binds to endogenous receptors to block the effect of opioid drugs. It is important to wait for 7 to 10 days after last opiate use before beginning naltrexone. If used after detoxification from methadone, naltrexone may produce better treatment outcome (69). However, the success of this drug in patients dependent on opioids has been limited because of very low compliance.

Cocaine

The use of cocaine and other stimulants produces hypertension and other signs of sympathetic hyperactivity including tachycardia, increased body temperature, tremor, and in high doses paranoia. Overdose may lead to dangerous elevations of blood pressure, tachycardia, ventricular arrhythmias, hyperthermia, seizures, myocardial infarction, or stroke.

Pharmacologic management generally is not recommended as part of the initial treatment of the cocaine-dependent patient without a coexisting psychiatric illness. Despite positive studies initially with certain drugs, especially desipramine, replication of these results has been spotty. However, the potential efficacy of disulfiram for cocaine dependence has been considered because of many relapses to cocaine occur after an individual has ingested alcohol.

Medications for Treatment of Other Psychiatric Syndromes

The prescription of psychotropic medications for substance use disorder patients after detoxification is a complicated issue. Diagnosing psychiatric disorders in substance abusers can be difficult; as stated previously, intoxication and withdrawal syndromes can profoundly affect mood, perception, and cognition. Some clinicians have tried to deal with this problem by creating rules such as "a patient has to have stopped all drugs and alcohol for 1 month (or longer) before any psychiatric disorder can be diagnosed." Unfortunately, these rules are overly simplistic, because withdrawal syndromes from different agents (e.g., alcohol and cocaine) are very different from each other and mimic some disorders but not others. Therefore, in trying to make a specific psychiatric diagnosis and instituting the proper treatment, the clinician should be cognizant of the expected withdrawal symptoms, the specific characteristics of the disorder being considered, and the time period at which these two symptom pictures would overlap. Thus, certain psychiatric disorders (e.g., eating disorders) can be diagnosed even during periods of active substance use, whereas other disorders (e.g., an anxiety disorder in a patient withdrawing from long-term benzodiazepine use) may not be diagnosed for weeks.

When the diagnosis is clear (e.g., a patient has had a psychiatric disorder either before the onset of the substance-related disorder or during periods of sustained abstinence), then treatment of the coexisting psychiatric disorder generally is not greatly affected by the patient's coexisting substance use disorder. For example, the choice of an antidepressant in a substance abuser is not ordinarily different because the patient has a coexisting substance use disorder. Rather, the usual considerations (e.g., previous medication history, side effect profile, cost, family history) apply in choosing an antidepressant.

Several exceptions to the general guidelines listed above should be considered. First, most experts generally discourage the use of benzodiazepines, whenever possible, because of their reinforcing characteristics, potential for abuse, and potential for stimulating the desire to return to the original substance of abuse (70). Second, monoamine oxidase inhibitors may be risky in this population given the risk of precipitating a hypertensive crisis by relapsing on substances such as Chianti wine, beer (particularly draft beer, which has higher levels of tyramine), and sympathomimetic drugs such as cocaine. Third, anecdotal reports suggest that some patients with psychotic disorders who have been switched from standard neuroleptics to clozapine have reduced their substance use. In some cases, this may be related to a reduction in symptoms of akathisia, for which some patients have been reported to self-medicate with substances of abuse.

Alliance and Psychotherapeutic Management

Once medically stabilized, the patient's ability to benefit from psychotherapy emerges. A solid alliance encourages the patient's adherence to treatment goals, improves quality of life, and reduces morbidity by preventing relapse. In fact, the strength of the alliance between the patient and clinician is a direct predictor of outcome (71).

Early in recovery, the clinician helps patients to sort out their emotions, perceptions, and behaviors while assessing the damage inflicted on their lives. During the early phase of recovery, psychotherapeutic approaches mainly consist of supportive, cognitive behavioral, and social skill oriented approaches. Exploratory psychotherapy focused on understanding the root causes of addiction is ineffective, especially to the exclusion of efforts to stop current use while the patient is actively abusing substances. Patients use this approach to bolster their rationalization for continued substance use.

The therapist should help the patient to develop a set of individualized cognitive and behavioral strategies to prevent relapse (72–74). These skills include setting goals, self-monitoring, analyzing drinking, identifying high-risk situations and conditional cues, refusing substances, and learning alternative ways of coping. Brief motivational interventions, which may be effective for less severely ill individuals with substance-related disorders, attempt to bolster the patients' inner resources and relationships by cultivating their confidence in their ability to change alcohol and drug use behavior. Over one to three sessions, patients learn to deal with sobriety and distinguish where they are from where they want to be. These interventions can enhance the efficacy of treatment at a later date.

Group therapy provides the mainstay of treatment for substance use disorders in the acute care setting. Groups focus on early recovery skills, motivation for abstinence, illness education, introduction to self-help groups, and skills to manage craving.

Self-help groups such as Alcoholics Anonymous (AA), Cocaine Anonymous (CA), and Narcotics Anonymous (NA) can be highly effective in the treatment of alcoholism and other substance-related disorders. These groups provide valuable role models, clear guidelines, and hope relevant to all phases of recovery. Unlike treatment offered by clinicians, AA groups and sponsors are available almost continuously. AA offers all four components required for successful rehabilitation as studied by Vaillant (75)—effective substitute behaviors for drinking, awareness of immediate negative consequences of continued drinking, repair of some social and medical damage caused by drinking, and restoration of self-esteem and hope. The confrontation of denial combined with reinforcement of techniques to maintain abstinence practiced in AA has been extremely effective in consolidating long-term abstinence. However, only a small minority of substance abusers enter self-help groups and continue with them. Moreover, many patients need additional professional treatment. Therefore, it is important to engage patients in alternate or complementary psychotherapeutic and/or pharmacologic treatment instead of simply referring all patients to self-help groups.

Family Support, Education, and Intervention

The social environment and the individual's ability to cope under particular social circumstances play a major role in the stability of persons with substance-related disorders. As emphasized above, perceived losses are frequent cues for relapse. Marital and family conflict or job loss can tip the fragile balance and overwhelm the individual's ability to cope substance free. Family therapy can be an important factor in successful treatment (76), but only when the treatment is designed to encourage and support continued abstinence. Education should include an understanding of the experiences of both the patient and the family to avoid conflict during early recovery, thus reducing the likelihood of relapse. Al-Anon, a separate organization of significant others, spouses, and family members, offers support and valuable information on coping with a substance dependent individual.

Therapeutic Milieu

Specialized clinical settings provide strong peer support and confrontation as well as knowledgeable clinical staff to treat illnesses with high levels of disability and morbidity (77). Studies on the factors correlated with the most effective inpatient care have found that the most effective units provide group orientation with peer support and confrontation (78). In addition, a philosophy that centers on patient involvement in the planning and implementing of treatment has been considered more effective (79). Finally, the medical orientation of the inpatient unit to treat substance-related disorder predicts greater likelihood that patients will complete treatment (80), as does the presence of good interpersonal skills among inpatient staff (81, 82).

Partial Hospitalization

Similar to the inpatient milieu, the partial hospital provides programs with an intensive, multidimensional therapeutic approach. The intensity of the partial hospital centers on group therapy, psychopharmacologic supervision, individual and family counseling, vocational rehabilitation, random urine screening, treatment of coexisting psychiatric illness, and patient and family education about substance use disorders. Patients live at home rather that at the hospital. One randomized, controlled study compared the effectiveness and cost of inpatient versus day hospital treatment in the rehabilitation of cocaine dependence. Although a significantly greater number of inpatients actually completed treatment, major improvement was found in substance use disorders in day hospital treatment with respect to psychosocial functioning and general health condition (83). Of those patients who completed treatment, the inpatient and day hospital groups did not differ based on relapse rates or involvement in postrehabilitation aftercare. However, the treatment costs of the day hospital were 40–60% less than the inpatient treatment costs.

Residential Treatment

In general, residential treatment benefits individuals who find themselves preoccupied exclusively with substance use. This treatment setting may be indicated when the patient does not require an inpatient level of care, but lacks the support and skills needed to remain abstinent and has a living situation that is not conducive to recovery.

Therapeutic communities provide an alternative long-term residential environment that centers specifically on cultivating a drug-free lifestyle through peer pressure and behavior modeling. Generally, these environments tend to be highly confrontational; often, therapeutic communities are staffed by recovering addicts. Usually, they are not recommended as

first-line treatment for patients with substance-related disorders, but tend to be appropriate for patients with high relapse histories and difficulties with honesty and work skills.

DECISION TO TRANSFER TO THE NEXT LEVEL OF CARE

The decision to shift to the next level of care requires decision-making involving not only the most apparent problems with substance use, but the equally important problems regarding the law, unemployment, family conflict, and coexisting medical and psychiatric disorders. The decision to choose among outpatient, inpatient, or partial hospital level of care is based on a number of criteria such as the individual's severity of illness and degree of motivation, availability of drug-free social supports in the community, low-risk employment, and a living situation conducive to abstinence. The guiding principle is to realize the least restrictive, but most effective, level of care at that point in the patient's clinical course. Inpatient treatment typically is indicated in the following medically hazardous situations.

- Complicated detoxification by more than two drugs used (because of the need for frequent medical reevaluation and medication adjustment).
- Risk of imminent harm from a dangerous mixture of a high degree of denial and current risk of danger to self or others that requires external limits.
- A pattern of poor response to bona fide outpatient treatment modalities.
- Concomitant psychiatric and medical disorders that greatly hinder outpatient treatment.

Controlled outcome research has shown that patients who respond best to inpatient treatment are those who demonstrate greater severity of their illness, less social stability, increased psychiatric comorbidity, and employment problems (84, 85). In contrast, empiric evidence has shown that the worst response to inpatient treatment occurs in those individuals who inject substances intravenously or who have antisocial personality disorder (86).

CONTROVERSIES IN THE CARE OF SUBSTANCE USE DISORDERS

Inpatient Versus Outpatient Care

The indications for inpatient treatment of substance use disorders remains one of the greatest controversies in the clinical realm. This is due, in large part, to its expense. Wide variation in per diem costs and treatment exists across hospitals, yet the direct and indirect costs of untreated substance-related disorders are extremely high. For example, in one study, 70% of persons with substance-related disorders in a community sample supported their habits, at least in part, through illegal means (48). The primary challenge lies in maximizing both cost-saving and treatment effectiveness.

Prior trends in criteria for inpatient care have been based largely on political concerns, not clinical research data. The choice always should be determined on the basis of the patient's needs.

In the available studies of treatment outcome, the majority are not randomized, controlled trials. Two frequently cited studies suggest that patients fare equally well in residential and nonresidential treatment settings (87, 88). In the first study, although the authors concluded that inpatient and outpatient treatment approaches produce similar results, the data suggest

that patients with the most severe illnesses (and complicated by lack of social supports) benefited the most from impatient care (87). The results of the second study are marred by selection effects because the authors excluded the more unstable patients who would be expected to have greater need for inpatient care (88).

A review of the literature indicates that there are only three randomized, controlled trials in which the results are less likely to be highly skewed by methodologic problems (83, 89, 90). In cocaine addicts, two studies found inpatient care equivalent to partial hospital care (83, 89). In these studies, the patients were randomly assigned to either 28 days of inpatient care or partial hospital treatment (83, 89). After 4 months of follow-up in the first study (89) and 7 months in the second study (83), both groups showed equal levels of improvement. However, treatment costs in the day hospital treatment were 40–60% less than inpatient treatment costs (83). In a third trial (90), the patients were randomly assigned to one of three treatment regimens—compulsory inpatient treatment (abstinence-based with subsequent referral to AA), compulsory attendance at AA meetings, and a choice of options. After a 2-year follow-up, the group assigned to mandatory inpatient treatment before attending AA relapsed significantly less than those attending mandatory AA meetings alone; the group with a choice of options showed intermediate outcomes. In this study, the cost of total inpatient care was only approximately 10% more than an initial referral to AA or choice of treatment because of the higher rates of additional inpatient treatment for relapse. The authors concluded that although the cost of inpatient care was somewhat greater initially, inpatient programs provided greater sustained protection from relapse (90). However, no intermediate options were offered (e.g., intensive outpatient or partial hospital treatment).

In summary, the present controversy about the role of inpatient care will remain unresolved until direct analyses of treatment matching of homogenous subgroups of patients can be conducted.

Psychopharmacologic Treatment of Coexisting Psychiatric Disorders

One of the most difficult issues that clinicians face in treating substance abuse patients on an acute care service concerns the prescription of a benzodiazepine after detoxification has been completed. A patient entering an acute care setting for treatment of alcohol or opioid dependence may be taking a prescribed benzodiazepine (most commonly clonazepam or alprazolam) daily. Typically, the benzodiazepine is prescribed for treatment of an anxiety disorder. What should the clinician do? Some take a very hard line on this subject and maintain that patients with a substance use disorder should not be prescribed benzodiazepines under any circumstances. Others contend that benzodiazepines are an effective treatment for panic disorder and therefore should be used liberally. Anecdotal case reports have shown that, in some patients, benzodiazepines can be administered safely to patients with other substance use disorders.

Because prescription of benzodiazepines to substance abusers is a complicated issue, it should be approached as such; simple rules, although appealing, generally do patients a disservice. Rather, the clinician should consider the risks and benefits of using a benzodiazepine for each patient. If a patient has panic disorder, there are other pharmacologic and nonpharmaco-

logic treatments that are available and should be tried. If alternatives have been tried without success, a benzodiazepine appears to be working well, and the patient's physician agrees that the patient has not been abusing the medication, then the patient probably should continue taking the benzodiazepine. In summary, these drugs clearly should not be a first-line (or even second-line) treatment for patients with substance use disorders.

COURSE AND PROGNOSIS

The course of substance-related disorders in the general population is highly variable. Whereas certain individuals progress on a relentless downhill course, some may remit permanently and others may relapse sporadically. Individuals who use substances at an earlier age will be more likely to become dependent. Regardless of the chemical substance used (alcohol, cocaine, or opioids) or the treatment setting, outcomes for dependence on different substances are based similarly on the severity of illness on admission (91). A worsening prognosis can be expected in those who demonstrate a recent shift to more risk-taking behavior. Examples include a change from a medical to an illicit source of substance, a shift to a more potent or dangerous form of the substance or mode of administration, and the onset of criminal activity to support the habit.

Alcohol and drug dependence are illnesses that respond to treatment, especially in socially stable and employed individuals. The majority of patients treated for substance dependence are able to improve and lessen, if not stop, compulsive use. More than 90% of those who are abstinent for 10 years will remain substance free at least 20 years (92). The best prognosis tends to be seen in older patients who are in a stable marriage, are dependent on alcohol rather than illicit drugs, and have families who participate in treatment (93). Because sustained abstinence often leads to substantial medical and psychosocial recovery—and may prevent infections that are devastating to both the individual and society—early intervention is imperative in the course of substance-related illnesses.

REFERENCES

1. American Psychiatric Association. Diagnostic and statistical manual of mental disorders. 4th ed. Washington, DC: APA, 1994.
2. Mirin SM, Batki SL, Bukstein O, et al. Practice guidelines for the treatment of patients with substance use disorders: alcohol, cocaine, opioids. Am J Psychiatry 1995;152(Suppl):5–59.
3. Schuckit MA. Drug and alcohol abuse: a clinical guide to diagnosis and treatment. 3rd ed. New York: Plenum Press, 1989.
4. Kessler RC, McGonagle KA, Zhao S, et al. Lifetime and 12-month prevalence of DSM-III-R psychiatric disorders in the United States. Arch Gen Psychiatry 1994;51:8–19.
5. Anthony JC, Helzer JE. Epidemiology of drug dependence. In: Tsuang MT, Tohen M, Zahner GEP, eds. Textbook in psychiatric epidemiology. New York: Wiley-Liss, 1995:361–406.
6. Embree BG, Whitehead PC. Validity and reliability of self-reported drinking behavior: dealing with the problem of response bias. J Stud Alcohol 1993;54:334–344.
7. DeLint J. Words and deeds: responses to Popham and Schmidt. J Stud Alcohol 1981;42:359–361.
8. Helzer JE, Burnam A, McEvoy LT. Alcohol abuse and dependence. In: Robins LN, Regier DA, eds. Psychiatric disorders in America. The Epidemiologic Catchment Area Study. New York: The Free Press, 1991:53–81.
9. Eaton WW, Kramer M, Anthony JC, et al. The incidence of specific DIS/DSM-III mental disorders. Data from the NIMH Epidemiologic Catchment Area Program. Acta Psychiatr Scand 1989;79:163–178.
10. Ojesjo L, Nagnell O, Lanke J. Incidence of alcoholism among men in the Lundby community cohort, Sweden, 1957–1972. J Stud Alcohol 1982;43:1190–1198.
11. Hilton ME. The demographic distribution of drinking patterns in 1984. In: Clark WB, Hilton ME, eds. Alcohol in America. Albany, NY: State University of New York Press, 1991:73–86.
12. Regier DA, Farmer ME, Rae DS, et al. One-month prevalence of mental disorders in the United States and sociodemographic characteristics. The Epidemiologic Catchment Area Study. Acta Psychiatr Scand 1993;88:35–47.
13. Merikangas KR. The genetic epidemiology of alcoholism. Psychol Med 1990;20:11–22.
14. Pickens RW, Svikis DS, McGue M, et al. Heterogeneity in the inheritance of alcoholism. Arch Gen Psychiatry 1991;48:19–28.
15. Schuckit MA, Smith TL. An 8-year follow-up of 450 sons of alcoholic and control subjects. Arch Gen Psychiatry 1996;53:202–210.
16. Anthony JC, Helzer JE. Syndromes of drug abuse and dependence. In: Robins LN, Regier DA, eds. Psychiatric disorders in America. New York: The Free Press, 1991:116–54.
17. Kandel DB, Raveis VH. Cessation of illicit drug use in young adulthood. Arch Gen Psychiatry 1989;46:109–116.
18. Merikangas KR, Rounsaville BJ, Prusoff BA. Familial factors in vulnerability to substance abuse. In: Glantz M, Pickens R, eds. Vulnerability to drug abuse. Washington, DC: American Psychological Association, 1992:75–97.
19. Hughes PH, Canavan KP, Jarvis G, et al. Extent of drug abuse: an international review with implications for health planners. World Health Stat Q 1983;36:394–497.
20. Mueller TI, Goldenberg IM, Gordon AL, et al. Benzodiazepine use in anxiety disordered patients with and without a history of alcoholism. J Clin Psychiatry 1996;57:83–89.
21. Robertson JR, Treasure W. Benzodiazepine abuse. Nature and extent of the problem. CNS Drugs 1996;5:137–146.
22. Anthony JC, Warner LA, Kessler RC. Comparative epidemiology of dependence on tobacco, alcohol, controlled substances, and inhalants: basic findings from the National Comorbidity Survey. Exp Clin Psychopharmacol 1994;2:1–24.
23. Gorelick DA. Progression of dependence in male cocaine addicts. Am J Drug Alcohol Abuse 1992;18:13–19.
24. Lass H. Most chronic pain patients misuse drugs, study shows. Hosp Trib World Serv 1976;6:2.
25. McAuliffe WE, Rohman M, Santangelo S, et al. Psychoactive drug use among practicing physicians and medical students. N Engl J Med 1986;315:805–810.
26. Lisansky ET. Why physicians avoid early diagnosis of alcoholism. N Y State J Med 1975;75:1788–1792.

27. Clark WD. Alcoholism: blocks to diagnosis and treatment. Am J Med 1981;71:275–285.
28. Schottenfeld RS. Assessment of the patient. In: Galanter M, Kleber HD, eds. The American Psychiatric Press textbook of substance abuse treatment. Washington, DC: American Psychiatric Press, 1994:25–33.
29. Babor TF, Brown J, DelBoca FK. Validity of self-reports in applied research on addictive behaviors: fact or fiction? Behav Assess 1990;12:5–31.
30. Kaufman E, Reoux J. Guidelines for the successful psychotherapy of substance abusers. Am J Drug Alcohol Abuse 1988;14:199–209.
31. Shaner A, Khalsa E, Roberts L, et al. Unrecognized cocaine use among schizophrenic patients. Am J Psychiatry 1993;150:758–762.
32. Vaillant GE. Natural history of alcoholism, Part V. Is alcoholism the cart or the horse to sociopathy. Br J Addict 1983;78:317–326.
33. Woody GE, Blaine J. Depression in narcotic addicts: quite possibly more than a chance association. In: Dupont RI, Goldstein A, O'Donnell J, eds. Handbook on drug abuse. Rockville, MD: NIDA, 1979:277–285.
34. Kessler, RC. Epidemiology of psychiatric comorbidity. In: Tsuang MT, Tohen M, Zahner GEP, eds. Textbook in psychiatric epidemiology. New York: Wiley-Liss, 1995:179–198.
35. Woodward B, Fortgang J, Sullivan-Trainor M, et al. Underdiagnosis of alcohol dependence in psychiatric inpatients. Am J Drug Alcohol Abuse 1991;17:373–388.
36. Ewing J. Detecting alcoholism. The CAGE questionnaire. JAMA 1984;252:1905–1907.
37. Buchsbaum DG, Buchanan RG, Welsh J, et al. Screening for drinking disorders in the elderly using the CAGE questionnaire. J Am Geriatr Soc 1992;40:662–665.
38. Sokol RJ, Martier SS, Ager JW, et al. The T-ACE questions: practical prenatal detection of risk-drinking. Am J Obstet Gynecol 1989;160:863–870.
39. Searles JS, Alterman AI, Purtill JJ. The detection of alcoholism in hospitalized schizophrenics: a comparison of the MAST and the MAC. Alcohol Clin Exp Res 1990;14:557–560.
40. McLellan AT, Kushner H, Metzger D, et al. The fifth edition of the Addiction Severity Index. J Subst Abuse Treat 1992;9:199–214.
41. McLellan AT, Cacciola JS, Fureman I. The Addiction Severity Index (ASI) and the Treatment Services Review (TSR). In: Sederer LI, Dickey B, eds. Outcomes assessment in clinical practice. Baltimore, MD: Williams & Wilkins, 1996:70–75.
42. Friedman AS, Granick S, eds. Assessing drug abuse among adolescents and adults: standardized instruments. Rockville, MD: NIDA Clinical Reports Series, 1994.
43. Miller WR. Motivational interviewing with problem drinkers. Behav Psychother 1983;11:147–172.
44. Tarter RE, Alterman AI, Edwards KL. Alcoholic denial: a biological interpretation. J Stud Alcohol 1979;45:214–218.
45. Prochaska JO, DiClemente CC, Norcross JC. In search of how people change: applications to addictive disorders. Am Psychol 1992;47:1102–1114.
46. Miller WR, Rollnick S. Motivational interviewing: preparing people to change addictive behavior. New York: Guilford Press, 1991.
47. Marlatt GA, Gordon JR. Determinants of relapse: implications for the maintenance of behavior change. In: Davidson PO, Davidson SM, eds. Behavioral medicine: changing health lifestyles. New York: Brunner/Mazel, 1980:410–452.
48. Rounsaville BJ, Kleber HD. Untreated opiate addicts. how do they differ from those seeking treatment? Arch Gen Psychiatry 1985;42:1072–1077.
49. Murphy GE. Suicide and substance abuse. Arch Gen Psychiatry 1988;45:593–594.
50. Langevin R, Paitich D, Orchard B, et al. The role of alcohol, drugs, suicide attempts and situational strains in homicide committed by offenders seen for psychiatric assessment: a controlled study. Acta Psychiatr Scand 1982;66:229–242.
51. Weiss RD, Mirin SM. Alcoholism. In: Hyman SE, Jenike MA, eds. Manual of clinical problems in psychiatry. Boston: Little, Brown & Co., 1990:163–169.
52. Mishra A, Landzberg BR, Parente JT. Uterine rupture in association with alkaloidal (crack) cocaine abuse. Am J Obstet Gynecol 1995;173:243–244.
53. Avins AL, Woods WJ, Lindan CP, et al. HIV infection and risk behaviors among heterosexuals in alcohol treatment programs. JAMA 1994;271:515–518.
54. Metzger D, Woody G, DePhilippis D, et al. Risk factors for needle sharing among methadone-treated patients. Am J Psychiatry 1991;148:636–640.
55. Leukefeld CG, Tims FM. Compulsory treatment for drug abuse. Int J Addict 1990;25:621–640.
56. Beeder AB, Millman RB. Treatment of patients with psychopathology and substance abuse. In: Lowinson JH, Ruiz P, Millman RB, et al., eds. Substance abuse: a comprehensive textbook. 2nd ed. Baltimore: Williams & Wilkins, 1992:675–690.

57. Frezza M, DiPadova C, Pozzato G, et al. High blood alcohol levels in women. N Engl J Med 1990;322:95–99.
58. National Institute on Alcohol and Alcoholism. Alcohol alert: screening for alcoholism. 8:PH285. Rockville, MD: National Institute on Alcohol and Alcoholism, April 1990.
59. Parsons OA, Butters N, Nathan PE, eds. Neuropsychology of alcoholism: implications for diagnosis and treatment. New York: Guilford Press, 1987.
60. Lishman WA. Organic psychiatry. 2nd ed. Oxford, UK: Blackwell Scientific, 1987.
61. Hayashida M, Alterman AI, McLellan AT, et al. Comparative effectiveness and costs of inpatient and outpatient detoxification of patients with mild-to-moderate alcohol withdrawal syndrome. N Engl J Med 1989;320:358–365.
62. Collins MN, Burns T, Van Den Berk PAH, et al. A structured programme for out-patient alcohol detoxification. Br J Psychiatry 1990;156:871–874.
63. Hoffman NG, Halikas JA, Mee-Lee D, Weedman RD, eds. Patient placement criteria for the treatment of psychoactive substance use disorders. Washington, DC: American Society of Addiction Medicine, 1991.
64. McLellan AT, Luborsky L, Woody GE, et al. Predicting response to alcohol and drug abuse treatments: role of psychiatric severity. Arch Gen Psychiatry 1983;40:620–625.
65. Kosten TR, McCance E. A review of pharmacotherapies for substance abuse. Am J Addict 1996;5:58–65.
66. Wright C, Moore RD, Grodin DM, et al. Screening for disulfiram-induced liver test dysfunction in an inpatient alcoholism program. Alcohol Clin Exp Res 1993;17:184–186.
67. O'Malley SS, Jaffe AJ, Chang G, et al. Naltrexone and coping skills therapy for alcohol dependence. a controlled study. Arch Gen Psychiatry 1992;49:881–887.
68. Volpicelli JR, Alterman AI, Hayashida M, et al. Naltrexone in the treatment of alcohol dependence. Arch Gen Psychiatry 1992;49:876–880.
69. Rawson RA, Washton AM, Resnick RB, et al. Clonidine hydrochloride detoxification from methadone treatment: the value of naltrexone aftercare. In: Harris LS, ed. Problems of drug dependence. Washington, DC: NIDA Research Monograph 34. U.S. Government Printing Office, 1980:101–108.
70. Roth M. Anxiety disorders and the use and abuse of drugs. J Clin Psychiatry 1989;50(Suppl):30–42.
71. Luborsky L, McLellan AT, Woody GE, et al. Therapist success and its determinants. Arch Gen Psychiatry 1985;42:602–611.
72. Marlatt GA, Gordon JR. Determinants of relapse: implications for the maintenance of behavior change. In: Davidson PO, Davidson SM, eds. Behavioral medicine: changing health lifestyles. New York: Brunner/Mazel, 1980:410–452.
73. Eriksen L, Bjornstad S, Gotestam KG. Social skills training in groups for alcoholics: one year treatment outcome for groups and individuals. Addict Behav 1986;11:309–329.
74. Brandsma JM, Pattison EM. The outcome of group psychotherapy with alcoholics: an empirical review. Am J Drug Alcohol Abuse 1985;11;151–162.
75. Vaillant GE. The natural history of alcoholism: causes, patterns, and paths of recovery. Cambridge: Harvard University Press, 1985.
76. Steinglass P, Bennett L, Wolin SJ, et al. The alcoholic family. New York: Basic Books, 1987.
77. Substance abuse: the nation's number one health problem. Key indicators for policy. Waltham, MA: Institute for Health Policy, Heller Graduate School, Brandeis University, 1995:7–65.
78. Stinson DS, Smith WG, Amidjaya I, et al. Systems of care and treatment outcomes for alcoholic patients. Arch Gen Psychiatry 1979;36:535–539.
79. Vannicelli M. Treatment contracts in an inpatient alcoholism treatment setting. J Stud Alcohol 1979;40:457–471.
80. Smart RG, Gray G. Multiple predictors of dropout from alcoholism treatment. Arch Gen Psychiatry 1978;35:363–367.
81. Valle SK. Interpersonal functioning of alcoholism counselors and treatment outcome. J Stud Alcohol 1981;42:783–790.
82. McLellan AT, Woody GE, Luborsky L, et al. Is the counselor an active ingredient in substance abuse rehabilitation? J Nerv Ment Dis 1988;176:423–430.
83. Alterman AI, O'Brien CP, McLellan AT, et al. Effectiveness and costs of inpatient versus day hospital cocaine rehabilitation. J Nerv Ment Dis 1994;182:157–163.
84. McKay JR, Murphy RT, Longabaugh R. The effectiveness of alcoholism treatment: evidence from outcome studies. In: Mirin SM, Gossett JT, Grob MC, eds. Psychiatric treatment: advances in outcome research. Washington, DC: American Psychiatric Press, 1991:143–158.
85. McLellan AT, Luborsky L, Woody GE, et al. An improved diagnostic evaluation instru-

ment for substance abuse patients: the Addiction Severity Index. J Nerv Ment Dis 1980;168:26–33.

86. Harrison PA, Hoffman NG, Streed SG. Drug and alcohol addiction treatment outcome. In: Miller NS, ed. Comprehensive handbook of drug and alcohol addiction. New York: Marcel Dekker, 1991:1163–1197.

87. Miller WR, Hester RK. Inpatient alcoholism treatment: who benefits? Am Psychol 1986;41:794–805.

88. McCrady B, Longabaugh R, Fink E, et al. Cost effectiveness of alcoholism treatment in partial hospital versus inpatient settings after brief inpatient treatment: 12-month outcome. J Consult Clin Psychol 1986;54:708–713.

89. O'Brien CP, Alterman A, Walter D, et al. Evaluation of treatment for cocaine dependence. In: Harris LS, ed. Problems of drug

dependence 1989. Washington, DC: NIDA Research Monograph 95. U.S. Government Printing Office, 1990:78–84.

90. Walsh DC, Hingson RW, Merrigan DM, et al. A randomized trial of treatment options for alcohol-abusing workers. N Engl J Med 1991;325:775–782.

91. McLellan AT, Alterman AI, Metzger DS, et al. Similarity of outcome predictors across opiate, cocaine, and alcohol treatments: role of treatment services. J Consult Clin Psychol 1994;62:1141–1158.

92. Vaillant GE. What can long-term follow-up teach us about relapse and prevention of relapse in addiction? Br J Addict 1988;83:1147–1157.

93. Brecht ML, Anglin MD, Woodward JA, et al. Conditional factors of maturing out: personal resources and preaddiction sociopathy. Int J Addict 1987;22:55–69.

Chapter 12

Disorders of the Geriatric Population

Stephen L. Pinals and Andrew Satlin

ASSESSMENT OF THE GERIATRIC PATIENT

A comprehensive evaluation of the geriatric patient combines the examination of medical, neurologic, and psychiatric disorders with a critical assessment of functional capacity. A broad and detailed initial evaluation is required to determine the most appropriate treatment setting and level of care. As the average length of hospital stay and allotted clinical time in all treatment settings decreases, the necessity of a thorough and concise assessment becomes more crucial. This endeavor is often challenging; shrinking clinical resources make it difficult to collect pertinent history from an increasingly ill, geriatric medical and psychiatric population. Thus, a complete assessment of the geriatric patient must involve an efficient multidisciplinary team approach and whenever possible the use of collateral sources of information, such as families or other caregivers.

PSYCHIATRIC INTERVIEW

The evaluation of a geriatric patient begins with the referral, which is generally initiated by family members, caretakers, or involved agencies. Immediate family and referring professionals such as social workers, visiting nurses, case managers, or primary care providers typically comprise an integral part of the assessment process. Developing a strong therapeutic alliance with the family is often essential in the assessment, diagnosis, and treatment of the elderly. Clinical staff members should be open, responsive, trustworthy, and respectful of the patient's confidentiality. Thus, an interview should be conducted privately with the patient first, before family or caretakers are invited to join in with the patient's permission. In this manner, patients have an opportunity to divulge confidential information, and family members then may verify historical data and recent changes in functioning. In see-

TABLE 12.1. Medical Causes of Depression in the Elderly

Endocrine disorders
  Addison's disease
  Cushing's disease
  Diabetes mellitus
  Hyperparathyroidism and hypoparathyroidism
  Hyperthyroidism and hypothyroidism
  Pituitary disorders
Infections
  Central nervous system infections
  Upper respiratory infections
  Urinary tract infections
Malignant disease
  Brain tumors
  Leukemia
  Metastatic disease
Medications and drugs
  Alcohol
  Anticonvulsants
  Antihypertensives
  Anti-Parkinsonian
  Antipsychotics
  Cimetidine
  Digitalis
  Sedative/hypnotics
  Steroids/hormones
Metabolic disorders
  Anemia
  Hepatic encephalopathy
  Hyperglycemia and hypoglycemia
  Hyperkalemia and hypokalemia
  Hypernatremia and hyponatremia
  Hypoxemia secondary to
    Chronic bronchitis
    Congestive heart failure
    Emphysema
    Myocardial infarction
    Pneumonia
  Malnutrition
  Uremia
  Vitamin B_{12} deficiency
Neurologic disorders
  Alzheimer's disease
  Huntington's disease
  Normal pressure hydrocephalus
  Parkinson's disease
  Pick's disease
  Seizure disorders
  Stroke
  Subdural hematoma
  Wilson's disease

ing the family, understanding their dynamics and available resources will also allow for more appropriate recommendations regarding placement, ancillary services, rehabilitation, and treatment.

The psychiatric interview generally opens with an inquiry into the patient's understanding of the evaluation. This may be followed by the clinician providing a brief description of the goals and objectives of the examination. Careful consideration should be given to any possible sensory impairments, such as loss of vision or hearing, that may require special attention or alterations in interview style. As the patient begins to describe elements of the presenting illness, particular attention must be given to recent environmental and physical changes that may have precipitated his or her decompensation. The elderly are very susceptible to mental status disturbances induced by acute stressors such as separations, deaths, changes in residence, caretakers, or supports. Many physical illnesses, infections, medicines, or disabilities predispose geriatric patients to delirium or decrements in functioning.

The mental status examination in geriatric psychiatry is distinguished by the significantly greater prevalence of dementia, delirium, and cognitive deficits in older patients. The mental status examination begins with an inspection of the patient's general appearance, posture, and behavior. Initial impressions are frequently suggestive of the underlying diagnosis and may help to guide the interview process. For example, a malodorous and disheveled elderly patient with blank facies, limited speech, and psychomotor retardation may have advancing dementia or untreated depression. Confused or disorganized responses to opening questions may lead the examiner to initiate cognitive testing and to turn the interview toward the primary caretaker.

Speech and language disturbances must be evaluated carefully because they may indicate either psychiatric illness or organic disorders (e.g., stroke). The rate, quantity, prosody, articulation, fluency, and spontaneity of speech should be observed, and language comprehension, naming, and repetition should be assessed. Patients with dementia may demonstrate fluent or nonfluent aphasia depending on the nature and location of the brain lesion(s). The presence of paraphasias such as the incorrect substitution of a word (verbal paraphasia) or a syllable (literal paraphasia) may also be evidence for a dementing process.

Standardized cognitive examinations such as the Mini-Mental Status Examination (1) are widely used to assess orientation, attention, concentration, memory, language, and constructional ability. This brief (10 minutes) standardized instrument is a valuable screening tool and substitutes nicely for more elaborate screening tests.

BIOLOGIC EVALUATION

Geriatric patients presenting with changes in mental status require thorough medical and neurologic evaluation. Numerous physical disorders present with psychiatric symptoms such as anxiety, depression, and psychosis. Collaboration with a specialist in geriatric medicine can help to focus the evaluation. Common medical disorders in the elderly that exacerbate or mimic psychiatric conditions are listed in Table 12.1. Chronic medical conditions most commonly found among the elderly are arthritis, hypertension, and diabetes (2). Laboratory tests are routinely ordered for screening purposes on admission to a psychiatric hospital. A useful and cost-efficient screening battery includes a chest radiograph, electrocardiogram (ECG), urinalysis, blood urea nitrogen, and vitamin B_{12}

assay (3). Beyond ordering these tests, the astute physician should order only those laboratory tests that are clearly indicated by the clinical presentation.

Although electroencephalography (EEG) is the oldest, safest, and most affordable type of functional brain imaging, its clinical usefulness is limited. EEG is generally nonspecific in the diagnosis of most illnesses of the elderly, although it may provide information consistent with dementia, delirium, or seizure disorders. Whereas the majority of patients with dementia demonstrate brain wave slowing and abnormal EEGs (4), it is difficult to distinguish the type of dementia responsible. Increased brain wave slowing is also found in cases of delirium (5), and the degree of slowing may reflect the severity of encephalopathy (6). Consequently, despite recent advances with quantitative EEG, this test remains clinically limited due to its lack of specificity in differentiating between delirium and dementia.

Computed tomography (CT) is most beneficial in the identification of brain tumors, abscesses, subdural hematomas, and hydrocephalus. Magnetic resonance imaging (MRI) offers much improved resolution of brain anatomy and is more useful in diagnosing vascular and white matter disease. Both CT and MRI detect cerebral atrophy, but this finding is nonspecific because it may occur in the healthy elderly and those with degenerative dementia. Both methods of neuroimaging have a central role in the differential diagnosis of dementia. Due to its relatively lower cost, CT may be considered to be a useful screening test for elderly patients presenting with mental status changes that are not attributable to other known medical conditions. Other imaging techniques, such as single photon emission computer tomography (SPECT), have demonstrated hypoperfusion in the temporoparietal area of

patients with Alzheimer's dementia (7). This finding is consistent with the temporoparietal and hippocampal hypometabolism found in research studies using positron emission tomography (PET) in Alzheimer's patients (8). Advances in functional neuroimaging techniques (SPECT and PET) show great promise for improving clinical diagnosis in geriatric psychiatry.

LEVELS OF CARE

Assessing the functional capacity of the geriatric inpatient begins with an evaluation of physical health and rehabilitative needs. One goal of this assessment is to refer patients to the least restrictive environment, which allows for an optimal amount of self-reliance while providing an appropriate level of structure and care. Throughout this evaluation process, recognizing and addressing issues of safety must be of paramount concern. A full assessment of functional capacity ideally involves professionals from multiple disciplines. In the acute care setting, nurses and physical and occupational therapists may consult in the assessment of mobility, ambulation, communication skills, personal hygiene, and activities of daily living to determine the most appropriate level of care. Physicians must assess the degree of treatment and medication compliance before recommending a suitable level of care. Social workers or case managers must evaluate family and personal resources and determine the validity of requests of referring parties and outside agencies.

Patients requiring the least structure or assistance will generally adapt best to home care with visiting nurses and home health aides. Local outreach teams may provide maintenance treatment or crisis intervention. Elderly patients needing more supervision and structure may require referrals to appropriate levels of residential care ranging from assisted living to nursing home facilities. Day programs and partial hospitalization programs often complement these supported living arrangements by providing daily structured activities, regular monitoring, and evaluation by a treatment team (9). Patients who are unable to be cared for in any of these environments or who are at risk of harming themselves or others require acute psychiatric hospitalization. In addition, patients who receive treatments that are unsafe to render outside a hospital (e.g., electroconvulsive therapy [ECT] or tricyclic medications for unstable cardiac patients) require inpatient admission, at least for the initiation of treatment.

To leave the acute care setting, geriatric patients must demonstrate an adequate capacity to care for themselves and remain safe in the home environment. Elderly patients who are unable to care for themselves must be able to accept care from health-care providers. Primary caretakers and follow-up referral appointments should be clearly established before discharge from acute hospitalization.

DSM-IV DIAGNOSES

The most common illnesses in geriatric psychiatry requiring acute levels of care include mood, dementing, and psychotic disorders. Within each of these broad Axis I categories fall numerous diagnoses described by the *Diagnostic and Statistical Manual of Mental Disorders*, 4th edition (DSM-IV) (10). This section briefly reviews those disorders that most commonly require acute care, with particular attention to late-onset disorders and to the epidemiology, differential diagnoses, treatment, course, and prognosis of disorders more specific to the elderly population. Possible underlying character issues, vulnerabilities,

and focal problems whose understanding will optimize treatment and allow the patient to leave acute care are described.

Mood Disorders

Epidemiology

Affective disorders are among the most common illnesses that geriatric psychiatrists encounter. Epidemiologic catchment area studies estimate the 1-year prevalence of DSM-III major depression to be approximately 1.0% and bipolar I and II both to be 0.1% in patients older than 65 years of age (11, 12). There is evidence that the incidence of major depression does not increase with age, as was once suspected; rather, it may actually decrease (13), especially when risk factors such as physical illness, disability, and cognitive impairment are controlled (14). Major depression tends to occur more commonly in institutional settings than in the community (15). Among nursing home residents, the prevalence of major depression has been estimated to be from 6–25%, and significant depressive symptoms may occur in an additional 30% of the cases (16). In one large community survey, Blazer et al. (17) found that elderly people experienced depressive subtypes ranging from mild dysphoria (19%) to symptomatic depression (4%), to dysthymia (2%), to mixed depression and anxiety (1.2%), to major depression (0.8%). In this and other studies (13), no cases of manic episodes were found, leading some authors to conclude that bipolar disorder in the elderly is rare (18). However, because the first manic attack may not occur for many years after a depressive episode, many people believed to have unipolar depression actually may suffer from bipolar disorder (19). Other investigators have found the prevalence of acute mania in the elderly to be less than 1% (20). However, because manic episodes in the geriatric population tend to be longer, have more frequent cycles, and require more intensive care, approximately 5% of acutely hospitalized elderly patients have mania (21). As a consequence, these patients use more clinical services than would be expected based on the epidemiologic data.

Descriptive and Differential Diagnosis

The DSM-IV diagnostic criteria defining depression, dysthymia, and bipolar disorders are the same in both elderly and younger adults. However, geriatric patients with affective disorders may present with different profiles of symptoms and complaints. For example, older patients may display more psychomotor agitation or retardation (22). Small et al. (23) found that depressed geriatric patients tended to have a greater number of somatic complaints and fewer expressions of guilt compared with a middle-aged control group. Depression in the elderly is also associated with much higher rates of completed suicide than in other age groups (24).

Major depression that occurs for the first time in people older than 60 has been termed late-onset depression. This syndrome may have a presentation, course, and outcome that are distinct from the depressive disorder of earlier life (25). Late-onset depression appears to have a greater occurrence of delusions (26, 27), although this has not been uniformly validated (28–30). In a study by Brown et al. (31), late-onset depressed patients had more somatization and hypochondriasis than an earlier-onset group. It is not clear whether consistent clinical differences between older and younger patients and between early and late-onset depression are empirically demonstrable (32).

The differential diagnosis of mood disorders in the geriatric population must first include medical illnesses, with particular attention to infections and metabolic, endocrine, neurologic, and degenerative disorders (Table 12.1). Cardiovascular disease, stroke, and Alzheimer's and Parkinson's diseases are all associated with depression in the elderly (33–36) and may present with a range of mood disturbances (37). A close examination of patients with dementia reveals that 20% or more may have coexistent major depression (38), although the rates may vary depending on criteria and method of evaluation (39). Geriatric patients are predisposed to toxic reactions from medications as the result of polypharmacy and drug interactions that may present as a depressive disorder (40). A differential diagnosis for depression must also include dysthymia and anxiety disorders because considerable overlap among these disorders can be seen in the elderly.

Ego Defenses and Character Style

The prevalence of personality disorders in the elderly ranges from 10–70% (41). In at least three studies, the personality disorders most likely to occur in those patients with major depression were dependent, compulsive, and avoidant types (42–44). Evidence also suggests that long-standing depressive personality traits may be a vulnerability or risk factor for major depressive episodes in the elderly (45). The high comorbidity of these personality traits with major depression may contribute to the recurrent nature of depressive disorders (46).

Formulation

The elderly are more likely to suffer from the loss of family, friends, health, home, and financial and social stability. Thus, they are especially susceptible to sadness and grief. A mood, sleep, or appetite disturbance with lethargy, fatigue, and social withdrawal resulting from physical illness, interpersonal loss, or change in environment is often difficult to distinguish from the signs and symptoms of major depression. Because the geriatric population is particularly prone to suffer from chronic illnesses, acute losses, or changes in lifestyle, they are more likely to experience bereavement and adjustment mood disorders, which may evolve into prolonged grief reactions or precipitate episodes of major depression.

Focal Problems

Geriatric patients require special consideration in treatment planning before transition to less-restrictive care. Caretakers may be exhausted from providing 24-hour supervision and managing the household. An overwhelmed spouse, son, or daughter may not freely admit to being angry or resentful for devoting their lives to caring for a chronically depressed relative. For this reason, acute management of the elderly patient must include a thorough evaluation of the home environment and primary care providers. Family meetings in the acute setting often allow the treatment team to observe underlying family dynamics and make recommendations for long-term care. This may include support groups for family members, psychoeducational sessions, or home services such as visiting nurses and home health aides.

Elderly patients and their families also benefit from a gradual transition back home with referrals to less-restrictive environments such as day programs or partial hospitalization. Group therapies and structured activities provide an extended supportive network for depressed elderly patients and allow clinicians to continue their

clinical and safety assessment over time. In this manner, recently acutely ill patients can continue to be closely monitored in a therapeutic milieu, can more readily obtain medical or laboratory testing and medication adjustments, and can receive ECT. A gradual transfer from the acute care setting also allows for greater continuity of treatment and collaboration with outpatient providers. For example, if a primary care physician prescribed a sedative-hypnotic to an elderly patient that resulted in ataxia or confusion, there would be ample opportunity to address this problem or seek an alternative referral for follow-up care.

Treatment

Psychopharmacologic management of depression in the geriatric population uses principles similar to those in treatment strategies used in younger adults. However, psychiatrists treating depression in the elderly must carefully consider the following issues:

1. Medical evaluation.

   a. Thorough physical examination.

   b. Laboratory testing (liver and thyroid function tests, electrolytes, complete blood count, vitamin B_{12}, folic acid, urinalysis).

   c. ECG.

2. Pharmacokinetics of psychotropic drugs (47).

   a. Hepatic and renal drug clearance decreases with age, leading to increased drug half-life and possible accumulation.

   b. Volume of distribution changes as total body fat increases relative to decreasing muscle mass and total body water.

   c. Fat-soluble psychotropics are dis-

TABLE 12.2. Antidepressants in the Elderly

Antidepressants	Example agents	Starting doses	Side effects
Heterocyclics	Nortriptyline	10 mg	Anticholinergic, hypotension,
	Desipramine	10mg	sedation, and cardiovascular
SSRIs	Fluoxetine	5–10 mg	Restlessness, insomnia, and
	Paroxetine	10 mg	gastrointestinal
	Sertraline	25 mg	
SNRIs	Nefazodone	50 mg	Sedation, gastrointestinal,
	Venlafaxine	25–37.5 mg	anticholinergic
Atypicals	Trazodone	25 mg	
	Bupropion	75 mg	Sedation, hypotension, anxiety,
			and tremor
MAOIs	Phenelzine	7.5 mg	Hypotension, sedation, and
	Selegiline	5 mg	hypertensive crisis

SSRIs, selective serotonin reuptake inhibitors; SNRIs, serotonergic-norepinephrine reuptake inhibitors; MAOIs, monoamine oxidase inhibitors.

tributed more widely in body fat and remain in the body longer.

3. Pharmacodynamics and neurotransmission (48).

 a. Normal aging leads to reduced concentrations of neurotransmitters.

 b. Decreased numbers and altered sensitivity of certain presynaptic and postsynaptic receptors occur with aging.

 c. Postsynaptic receptors may have decreased compensatory functioning.

4. Medication regimen.

 a. Numerous prescriptions increase risks for drug interactions.

 b. Simplicity in dosing may reduce inappropriate dosing and poor medication compliance.

 c. Written instructions and pill dispensers may improve compliance.

As a result of their greater sensitivity to medications, side effects, and risk for drug toxicity, older patients are typically initially given medication doses one third to one half of those used in younger adults (Table 12.2). Furthermore, adequate drug trials may need to be extended for as long as 9 weeks in geriatric patients to achieve a maximal therapeutic response rate (49).

Research in geriatric psychopharmacology has predominantly focused on the use of heterocyclic antidepressants (HCAs) and, more specifically, nortriptyline in the treatment of major depression. The literature suggests that nortriptyline is an effective antidepressant with a therapeutic window that is similar in older and younger patients. However, as with other HCAs, low initial dosages should be used to assess for the tolerability of side effects such as orthostatic hypotension, oversedation, tachycardia, and anticholinergic toxicity (Table 12.2). Elderly patients may be at significant risk for anticholinergic side effects such as dry mouth, constipation, urinary retention, blurred vision, and confusion. In general, the secondary amines (such as nortriptyline and desipramine) have relatively milder anticholinergic and sedative properties compared with the tertiary amines (imipramine, amitriptyline, doxepin, etc.); therefore, the secondary amines are typically better tolerated. Cardiotoxicity is the most potentially dangerous side effect of heterocyclics in the elderly, particularly for those with pre-existing conduction defects or ischemic heart disease. In patients who have recently suffered from myocardial infarction, class I antiarrhythmics chemically similar to the HCAs have demonstrated a trend toward increased mortality (50). Thus, for patients with serious conduction alterations, ischemic heart disease, or recent myocardial infarction, heterocyclic antidepressants should be avoided entirely or monitored closely with frequent ECGs.

More recently, selective serotonin reuptake inhibitors (SSRIs) have become first-line agents and mainstays in the treatment of depression. This is especially true among elderly patients who are likely to benefit from the improved side effect profile, easier absorption, and decreased interactions with other medications compared with standard antidepressant medications (51). Although the SSRIs offer no advantage over heterocyclics in terms of efficacy (52, 53), they may prove more beneficial as a result of their increased tolerability and compliance over time. As with heterocyclic medications, SSRIs are generally initiated at lower doses in the elderly to reduce common side effects such as insomnia, restlessness, or nausea.

Similar dosages are recommended for other classes of antidepressants. For example, low doses of trazodone (25–50 mg) are frequently used as an adjunct medication when insomnia is the presenting complaint. The advantage of this drug is its highly sedative quality and lack of anticholinergic side effects, although elderly patients must be monitored for episodes of orthostatic hypotension or oversedation. Venlafaxine is a novel antidepressant that combines activity on two receptor systems and is the first of a new line of agents known as serotonergic-norepinephrine reuptake inhibitors (SNRIs). Elderly patients must be monitored carefully for hypertension at higher doses of this medication as well as for side effects observed

with both standard HCAs and SSRIs. Nefazodone has a similar multiple-receptor effect, at least at high doses, and may be of particular benefit in patients with anxiety or insomnia. Bupropion is a highly effective antidepressant and frequently used medication in the geriatric population due to its relatively safe and tolerable side effect profile (53). Monoamine oxidase inhibitors (MAOIs) are also as effective as HCAs in treating elderly patients with depression, without the cardiac toxicities associated with HCAs (54). However, orthostatic hypotension, anticholinergic-like symptoms, and the risk of hypertensive crisis tend to limit their use with geriatric patients. One study comparing nortriptyline and phenelzine over 7 weeks in elderly depressed outpatients found equivalent efficacy rates of approximately 60% versus 13% for placebo (55). A 1-year maintenance treatment study revealed that the patients receiving phenelzine did significantly better than those receiving either nortriptyline or placebo (56).

The use of mood stabilizers in elderly patients for stabilization of bipolar disorder and substance-induced mania as well as augmentation of antidepressant therapy is very similar to their use in younger adults. Differences in lithium treatment occur in the distribution and excretion of the drug, which leads to higher plasma levels for equivalent dosages used in younger patients. Thus, older patients may often begin treatment with and be maintained on relatively lower doses of lithium (Table 12.3). The pretreatment evaluation for geriatric patients being considered for mood stabilizers is similar to that performed in younger adult patients. Blood levels of mood stabilizers should be monitored approximately every 3 months or more frequently if indicated.

Elderly patients taking lithium require ECGs, thyroid function tests, and creati-

TABLE 12.3. Mood Stabilizers in the Elderly

Mood stabilizers	Starting dose	Blood levels
Lithium	150–300 mg bid	0.2–0.6 mEq/l
Carbamazepine	100–200 mg bid	4–8 µg/ml
Valproic acid	125–250 mg bid	50–100 mg/ml

nine clearance every 6–12 months. In medically compromised or frail elderly patients, side effects such as confusion, polyuria, polydipsia, nausea, diarrhea, tremor, and ataxia may be more severe. Elderly patients are also at greater risk for cardiotoxicity and extrapyramidal effects from lithium (57). Concomitant neurologic illness is one of the predisposing factors that increase the risk of lithium toxicity (58). Alternatives to lithium include carbamazepine and valproic acid, which bring comparable risks for neurotoxicity and peripheral side effects in the elderly. However, these alternatives may be useful in older bipolar patients with diminished renal function or cardiovascular disease such as congestive heart failure or conduction abnormalities. Patients taking carbamazepine and valproic acid also require pretreatment physical examinations, laboratory testing (liver function tests, complete blood count, platelet count), and regular monitoring as would occur with younger adult patients.

Stimulants such as methylphenidate and dextroamphetamine are useful in treating depressed elderly patients who are apathetic, withdrawn, and unmotivated (59, 60). These medications are particularly useful in medically ill patients who have become demoralized and discouraged by their decline. Low doses (2.5–5 mg) each morning, with increases every 2–3 days up to 20 mg/day, may produce immediate results such as improved energy, attention, and interest level (61). Methylphenidate is particularly beneficial with very old patients because it has fewer toxic side effects than standard antidepressants (62). Side effects of amphetamines are dose related and include insomnia, tachycardia, and transient increases in blood pressure. Amphetamines may also produce agitation, restlessness, or confusion, and for this reason should be avoided in patients with dementia. Responses may diminish over time as tolerance to these medications develops after several weeks (61).

Geriatric patients with delusional depression or major depression with psychotic features generally respond poorly to HCAs alone (63, 64). Although combining antidepressants with neuroleptics may improve response rates, ECT is often the safest and most effective treatment available for elderly patients with delusional depression (65). Some evidence indicates that geriatric patients with delusional depression may have a particularly good response to ECT when compared with patients without symptoms of psychosis (66, 67). Several studies suggest that older patients, in general, may have a higher response rate to ECT than younger patients (68–70). ECT is also indicated for those depressed elderly patients who are at risk for suicide, are medically ill, or refuse to eat and drink (71–73). Predictors of a good response to ECT include symptoms of psychosis, guilt, agitation, anhedonia, and neurovegetative signs (74–76).

Depressed elderly patients with concomitant cognitive deficits or underlying dementing illness may also be good candidates for ECT, despite concerns that ECT may exacerbate their cognitive impairment. Although ECT may transiently produce posttreatment confusion or memory loss, it does not exacerbate dementia or preexisting cognitive impairment (61, 77); for some patients, ECT may actually improve cognitive dysfunction (40). Careful evaluation of baseline functioning, accompanying medications, electrode placement, and frequency of ECT treatments will help to minimize cognitive side effects. In general, unilateral electrode placement in patients with dementing illness minimizes the risk of post-ECT confusion. Other specific complications of ECT in the elderly include cardiac problems such as cardiac ischemia, arrhythmias, or worsening of congestive heart failure (78, 79). Although geriatric patients tend to have a greater incidence of preexisting cardiac disease, they will usually tolerate ECT better than tricyclic antidepressants (71, 80).

Following a series of ECT treatments, patients are customarily given an antidepressant drug or lithium to reduce the risk of recurring depression. Patients who consistently relapse despite adequate medication coverage may be candidates for maintenance ECT. Because elderly patients often require longer recovery periods after each ECT treatment, the ECT series can be provided while patients are making the transition from acute hospitalization to partial programs and on to an outpatient clinic. Maintenance ECT may begin 1–2 weeks after the initial series and gradually be reduced to treatments every 2–4 weeks (81). Retrospective reports suggest that maintenance ECT is both safe and efficacious (82, 83), particularly for patients who no longer meet criteria for hospital level of care but who suffer from chronic, relapsing disorders.

Individual, group, and family psychotherapy in elderly depressed patients is a critical component of comprehensive treatment. Numerous studies document that the geriatric population is highly responsive to psychotherapy (84–86). Research reveals that cognitive behavior therapy is as effective in older adults as in younger patients with depression (87). Brief psychodynamic or insight-oriented approaches are as beneficial as cognitive behavior therapy in reducing symptoms of depression in geriatric patients; however, some evidence shows that the benefits from cognitive behavior therapy are better maintained on follow-up of 1 year (84, 88).

In considering treatment plans for elderly patients, reminiscence and life review therapy has proven to be particularly useful (89). Although findings are inconsistent, empiric self-report studies suggest that this psychodynamic therapy may reduce depression and anxiety in some elderly patients while increasing feelings of self-esteem and life satisfaction (90). Therapy for caregivers and family members are also important components of the treatment plan for the elderly. Ongoing family therapy or regular psychoeducational meetings may help to foster cooperation, support, and understanding of primary caretakers, which may improve long-term compliance and treatment outcome.

Course and Prognosis

Anecdotal evidence suggests that older depressed patients are more likely than younger patients to suffer a relapsing course with poorer outcome. However, few large-scale, long-term, standardized studies have been conducted and none offers empiric evidence that major depression is significantly more chronic in later life (91, 92).

Numerous factors have been found to

TABLE 12.4.   Causes of Dementia

Degenerative
  Alzheimer's disease
  Parkinson's disease
  Pick's disease
  Huntington's chorea
  Frontal lobe dementia
  Diffuse Lewy body disease
  Progressive supranuclear palsy
Vascular
  Multi-infarct dementia
  Subarachnoid hemorrhage
  Vasculitis
Infectious disorders
  AIDS encephalopathy
  Syphilis
  Meningitis
  Brain abscess
  Creutzfeldt-Jakob disease
Toxic
  Alcohol/drugs
  Heavy metals
  Carbon monoxide
Metabolic disorders
  Hypothyroidism
  Hypoglycemia
  Vitamin B_{12} deficiency
  Wilson's disease
Neoplastic
  Meningioma
  Metastatic tumor
Mechanical
  Normal pressure hydrocephalus
  Subdural hematoma
  Dementia pugilistica
Genetic disorders
  Adrenoleukodystrophy
  Gaucher's disease
  Porphyrias

be predictors of poor outcome at 1-year follow-up in the elderly: psychosis, medical illness, cognitive impairment, severity of initial symptoms, major life events, and lack of social support (92–94). Patients with delusional depression tend to have higher relapse rates than patients with nondelusional depression (95). High relapse rates in both major depression and delusional depression are often the result of inadequate treatment (96). Outcome studies of late-life depression should standardize symptom assessment and focus on a broader view of overall functioning by including measures of cognition, health, social supports, bereavement/grief, and quality of life (97). Studies should examine the effects of decreasing length of hospital stay, expanding utilization of partial hospitalization, and overall effectiveness of outpatient treatment in determining the course and prognosis of depression in the elderly.

Dementing Disorders

Epidemiology

A recent community-based survey estimated the prevalence of Alzheimer's disease (AD) in the United States to be approximately 4 million (98). After all forms of heart disease, cancer, and stroke, AD is considered to be the fourth leading cause of death in the United States (99). Several studies confirm that the prevalence of AD rises dramatically with each decade of life (100–102). One review of 20 studies estimated that AD affects 1% of persons between 65 and 75 years of age and 10% of those older than 75 years of age. (103). Another study found that the prevalence jumped to 45% for persons older than age 95 (104). However, estimates vary considerably due to variations in the clinical and pathologic criteria for diagnosis. The occurrence of vascular dementia is believed to be in the 10–25% range, but similar variables hamper these estimates (105, 106).

Descriptive and Differential Diagnosis

Dementia is a syndrome of acquired impairment of intellectual and memory functioning associated with one or more of the following cognitive deficits: aphasia, apraxia, agnosia, and disturbances in executive functioning such as planning, organizing, sequencing, or abstracting. Dementia is usually characterized by a gradual onset and persistent decline of cognition that is sufficiently severe to interfere with social or occupational functioning (10). At least 65 known disorders cause primary or secondary symptoms of cognitive impairment consistent with dementia (Table 12.4).

The most common form of dementia—AD—is a progressive, degenerative illness characterized by a gradual decline in memory, language, visuospatial skills, personality, and cognition (107). Initial presentations may include patients who are increasingly forgetful, repetitive, and unable to learn new information. In patients with AD, storage and retrieval of learned information are progressively impaired, and cues are typically not helpful; this is distinct from patients with subcortical or frontal lobe injury (108). Language deficits most commonly begin as a relative paucity of speech and eventually develop into word-finding problems, anomia, and fluent aphasia with impaired comprehension (109). Patients with AD may also exhibit apraxia or impaired ability to execute motor activities despite intact motor functioning and comprehension of the task. Examples include the inability to cook, dress, bathe, or toilet. Agnosia describes the inability of demented patients to recognize or identify objects despite adequate sensory function. In advanced stages of AD, patients are unable to name friends or family members. Impairments of executive functioning are manifested by difficulties following multistep commands, generating word lists, or describing similarities and differences between related words.

Personality changes in AD may occur in the form of increased irritability, impulsivity, egocentricity, indifference, or social withdrawal (110, 111). Symptoms of anxiety and agitation may progress to displays of verbal outbursts or nonverbal anger, perhaps as a result of increasing awareness of the progressive cognitive decline (112). Behavioral disturbances in AD are more common than symptoms of psychosis (113), although increased agitation frequently occurs as a reaction to disturbing hallucinations or delusions. AD patients may experience paranoid delusions such as, "Someone is stealing my things," as a psychological compensation for memory deficits (114). Hallucinations are less common than delusions in AD; when present, visual and auditory hallucinations appear to be equally as common, in contrast to patients with schizophrenia (115). Psychotic symptoms tend to be more prominent in the later stages of the illness and are associated with greater functional and intellectual deterioration (116).

Vascular dementia is distinguished from AD by its abrupt onset, stepwise deterioration, and history of stroke and/or hypertension. These patients may also have gait disturbances, emotional lability, and focal neurologic signs and symptoms (107). Subtypes of vascular dementia are defined by the number and type (large vs. small) of vessels involved in a cerebrovascular accident. Each subtype describes variable combinations of motor, sensory, and neuropsychological deficits based on the disrupted anatomic region (117).

Dementia, which may occur in approximately 30% of patients with Parkinson's disease (118), is considered subcortical; this is distinct from the cortical dementia of AD. However, these conditions often have similar clinical presentations and at times have overlapping pathologic findings. Subcortical dementias may be distinguished by a relative preservation of insight, language, calculation, and memory (e.g., priming, encoding, and recognizing information with cues). However, patients with subcortical dementia tend to have more depression, apathy, and earlier impairment of motor functioning (e.g., dysarthria, gait disturbance, and incoordination) (119). Other examples of subcortical dementia include Huntington's disease and progressive supranuclear palsy.

Delirium is distinguished from dementia primarily by the fluctuating level of consciousness and the relatively transient nature of the cognitive dysfunction. Patients with delirium also tend to have a rapid onset, diurnal fluctuation of symptoms, mood shifts, and acute behavioral changes (120). The geriatric population is particularly susceptible to delirium due to a greater risk for medical and vascular diseases, infections, hypoxia, toxic effects from medications, trauma, poor nutrition, and a reduced capacity for homeostatic regulation. Patients with delirium typically have difficulty in their ability to focus, maintain, and shift attention. Alterations in sleep-wake cycles and more frequent illusions or visual hallucinations are associated findings of delirium. Treatment is guided by the identification and correction of the underlying etiology.

The term pseudodementia (121), or the preferable term "dementia syndrome of depression," describes the reversible cognitive impairment often found in depressed geriatric patients. Patients with pseudodementia generally have a more rapid onset, a fluctuating course with prominent depressed mood, and a shorter duration of symptoms than those patients with dementia from known organic causes. As a result of their depression, these patients may refuse to participate in activities or attend to activities of daily living. Pseudodementia patients frequently may reply, "I don't know," to simple questions. In contrast, dementia patients usually try to conceal their deficits and genuinely attempt to answer mental status questions despite numerous "near misses" (122). Although many differences have been found between dementia and depression, considerable overlap still exists between these two diagnoses. Recent research suggests that cognitive dysfunction secondary to depression may represent an early marker for progressively developing dementia (123).

Ego Defenses and Character Style

A patient's gradual awareness of cognitive decline may serve to mobilize specific ego defenses determined in part by premorbid character structure. Elderly patients with aggressive, compulsive, or rigid personality styles may experience more difficulties with cognitive impairment than patients with premorbid versatility in adaptation (124). Ego defenses such as suppression, denial, and rationalization can allow the mildly demented patient to defend against overwhelming fear and anxiety. Similarly, regression and withdrawal defenses in older patients may provide coping mechanisms in the face of an uncertain future. Clinical experience suggests that premorbid aggressive or impulsive character traits are amplified in states of dementia, although no known research can substantiate this impression.

Formulation

As the pathogenesis of dementia is gradually elucidated, various clinical characteristics can be related primarily to the underlying brain disease. However, environmental factors and major life events also aggravate symptoms of dementia. For example, a change in routine, caregiver, room, or nursing home may precipitate behavioral disturbances or affective and psychotic symptoms. Patients with limited cognitive capacities are generally less adaptable to life changes and more likely to respond with fear, frustration, and anger. At times, disruptive behaviors can be understood as a confused attempt to communicate or adapt to changing circumstances (125). When comprehension and sensory input are impaired, patients may perceive the environment to be threatening and react accordingly. For this reason, demented patients who require acute care initially may experience a worsening of symptoms as a consequence of their change in environment. The potential benefit of acute treatment must be weighed carefully against its disruptive effects. With each change, cognitively impaired individuals are more vulnerable to further deterioration. Thus, physicians must be alert to the psychosocial and environmental context of acute behavioral disturbances and exacerbations of symptomatology. Psychiatric hospitalization may often be avoided by thorough clinical assessment and intervention with elderly patients in their homes or nursing facilities.

Focal Problems

The safety assessment of demented patients presents a great challenge because their level of functioning may change precipitously and, as noted above, acute stressors may lead to impulsive behaviors. One of the more difficult problems in AD is coping with wandering behavior. Other behavioral disturbances found in dementia include yelling, hoarding, sexualizing, and assaulting. Many behavioral problems result in some form of restrictive management such as isolation and physical or chemical restraints. These techniques often lead to further decrements in functioning or escalations of behavior.

Inpatient evaluation of behavior problems involves multidisciplinary treatment approaches to maximize patient safety and preserve optimum independence. For example, wandering patients may require occupational therapy evaluation for intensive group activity programs in accordance with the level of cognitive impairment. Physicians and nurses should assess patients for underlying medical illnesses or drug interactions that may precipitate changes in behavior. Psychopharmacologic evaluation may identify ways to lower the risk of unwanted behavior by initiating medication trials or reducing side effects such as akathisia, dystonia, and anticholinergic symptoms. Psychiatrists, psychologists, and social workers will often be involved in educating caregivers, either at home or in nursing facilities, to provide emotional support and possible recommendations for cognitive behavioral techniques to deescalate or redirect patients. Other strategies to address the problem of wandering among demented patients include "wander guards" or alarm devices that may reduce the incidence of unmonitored departures.

Treatment

The main neuropathologic findings in AD are amyloid plaques, neurofibrillary tangles, and neuronal loss in the cerebral cortex and hippocampus. The most prominent neurotransmitter abnormality is the reduced level of acetylcholine resulting from the loss of the synthesizing enzyme choline acetyltransferase. Although several drugs that focus on cholinergic neurotransmission are currently being investigated, at this writing, only one medication has been approved for use in patients with AD. Tetrahydroaminoacridine (THA) or tacrine (Cognex; Parke-Davis, Morris Plains, NJ) is a reversible cholinesterase inhibitor that has been shown to produce small improvements in

cognition in some studies (126), although these benefits may be clinically insignificant (127) and transient (128). The use of this medication is also limited by its hepatotoxicity and gastrointestinal side effects.

Consequently, the psychopharmacologic treatment of AD is oriented toward managing the secondary features of the illness, including psychosis and mood and behavioral disturbances. Affective and psychotic symptoms in AD are treated in a manner similar to their treatment in other psychiatric disorders in the elderly. The psychopharmacologic management of behavioral disturbances begins with neuroleptics, despite their variable efficacy. Behavioral disorders may be less responsive than psychotic symptoms to neuroleptic treatment (129). The clinical efficacy of neuroleptics in treating behavior problems remains unclear due to a lack of placebo-controlled, double-blind studies with adequate diagnostic homogeneity (130). Nevertheless, neuroleptics are widely used for behavior problems and may function in part by alleviating underlying symptoms of psychosis. The antipsychotics appear to be therapeutically similar. They differ primarily in their potency and side effect profile. The elderly are particularly sensitive to extrapyramidal symptoms, cardiovascular effects, sedation, and tardive dyskinesia (114, 115, 130, 131). Lower-potency neuroleptics should generally be avoided due to the higher incidence of anticholinergic side effects, including urinary retention, constipation, and confusion. These medications also produce greater sedation and orthostatic hypotension, thereby increasing the risk for falls in the elderly. Higher-potency agents must be used with caution due to their greater risk for causing dystonia and Parkinsonian side effects. Selecting a low initial dose of a midrange-potency neuroleptic, such as perphenazine (1–2 mg), may help to avoid the potential side effects of high-potency and low-potency agents.

Clozapine is also an acceptable alternative for demented patients with paranoid or socially disturbing behavior who cannot tolerate standard neuroleptics. However, its use is limited by the high risk for sedation and orthostatic hypotension (132). The additional burden of weekly blood draws to monitor for leukopenia often makes this medication intolerable for demented patients. Risperidone is another novel antipsychotic agent with a lower propensity for extrapyramidal symptoms and may have clinical usefulness in reducing agitation and behavioral disturbances in demented patients (130). These two atypical antipsychotics will be discussed below in the section dealing with psychotic disorders.

Several other medications, including anticonvulsants, anxiolytics, and antidepressants, have been used in the management of behavioral disorders. In particular, lithium (133), valproic acid (134), carbamazepine (135, 136), trazodone (137), buspirone (138), SSRIs (139, 140), and beta blockers (141) have all been reported to have some efficacy. Unfortunately, data suggesting improvement in behavioral disturbances are rarely from double-blind, placebo-controlled studies.

Benzodiazepines may also reduce agitation in some demented patients; patients suffering from insomnia, anxiety, and tension may be more likely to respond (142). However, because geriatric patients appear to be at greater risk for side effects such as sedation, ataxia, dizziness, falls, confusion, and paradoxical disinhibition, low doses of shorter-acting agents metabolized by conjugation only (e.g., lorazepam, 0.5–1.0 mg, or oxazepam, 10–30 mg/day) are generally preferred (142).

An organized approach to the assessment of behavior disturbances may reduce the need for pharmacologic management. An initial period of observation coupled with information from multiple sources will help to document problematic behaviors and identify target symptoms for intervention. A thorough medical evaluation may uncover an underlying infection, metabolic disorder, medication side effect, or painful lesion. An assessment of the environment may reveal etiologic factors such as alterations in daily routines, roommates, staff members, or family supports.

Behavioral interventions must be specifically designed for the individual's level of cognition and physical ability. Some simple tactics include decreasing overall sensory stimulation, redirecting patients, restructuring or clarifying daily routines, and designating one trusted caretaker to interact directly with the patient. Increasing physical activity, exercise, or pacing often allows for a safe release of motor restlessness. Frequent, brief, and supportive social contacts with a calm, reassuring voice and an occasional gentle touch may substantially reduce episodes of agitated behavior. Education of patients and caregivers may reduce confusion and disruptive behavior while providing an environment to express ongoing fears and uncertainty. Supporting the efforts of overburdened caretakers—whether they are relatives, aides, nurses, or other professionals—and explaining the potential origins and management of behavioral disturbances will enhance their efforts and provide an essential alliance for clinical staff in an ongoing and irreversible set of problems.

Course and Prognosis

The course of dementia may be variable depending on the etiology and stage of the illness. The Global Deterioration Scale is one means of assessing the progressive decline in cognition, behavior, emotions, and functioning among patients with AD (143). The rate of deterioration is highly variable and may range from periods of slow advancement over decades to rapid deterioration within 1 year. Most AD patients experience a steady decline, with survival lasting 5–12 years after onset (107). Initial deficits appear in areas of language, concentration, and short-term memory. During the middle stages, cognitive impairments progress and patients may develop behavior and motor problems. Behavioral disturbances are a fairly common complication in the advanced stages of AD and may be associated with a worse prognosis (144). In the final stages of AD, the patient is completely bedridden with rigidity or spasticity, is aphasic, incontinent, unable to swallow, and has minimal or no cognitive capacity. Patients often die of infection, sepsis, aspiration pneumonia, or dehydration.

Psychotic Disorders

Epidemiology

Elderly patients with psychosis comprise a broad and diverse group, including patients with early onset and late-onset schizophrenia, delusional disorder, delirium, dementia, mania, schizophreniform, and schizoaffective disorders. One recent literature review found that 13% of all schizophrenic inpatients have an onset of psychosis in their 50s, 7% in their 60s, and 3% after age 70 (145). Other studies estimate that 10% of elderly patients admitted to psychiatric hospitals have late-onset schizophrenia (146, 147). Late-onset schizophrenia occurs 6–20 times more frequently among females than males (146, 148). Prior epidemiologic studies may be compromised by varying diagnos-

tic criteria and sampling difficulties in elderly patients with psychosis because they tend to be socially isolated and avoid treatment.

Delusional disorder may occur in younger adults but generally begins in mid-adulthood or later, with onset at an earlier average age for men (40–49 years) than for women (60–69 years) (149). Although difficult to determine, the DSM-IV estimates the prevalence of delusional disorder to be approximately 0.03%, with a lifetime risk between 0.05% and 0.1% (10).

Descriptive and Differential Diagnosis

DSM-IV uses the term late-onset schizophrenia for patients who meet criteria for schizophrenia with the prodrome and symptoms occurring after 45 years of age (10). This disorder was originally termed paraphrenia by Kraepelin (150) in 1919 and is distinguished from early-onset disease by the age of onset and its clinical phenomenology. Late-onset schizophrenia is commonly characterized by systematized, persecutory delusions and auditory hallucinations (145). Schneiderian first-rank symptoms may also occur, but formal thought disorder, negative symptoms, and inappropriate affect are rare (151, 152). The differential diagnosis for late-onset schizophrenia includes medical and neurologic disorders such as stroke, tumors, demyelinating diseases, metabolic abnormalities, central nervous system infections, endocrinopathies, vitamin deficiencies, and drug/medication toxicity. Careful neurologic, medical, and laboratory examination guided by the clinical presentation is critical to the identification of reversible causes of psychosis.

Delusional disorder describes patients with at least 1 month of nonbizarre delusions. Delusions are either unspecified in type or subgrouped by their predominant theme (e.g., erotomanic, grandiose, jealous, persecutory, or somatic delusions). Delusional patients do not typically have prominent hallucinations, thought disorder, affective symptoms, or a deteriorating course. Elderly patients with delusional disorder are distinguished from those with dementia or delirium by their relatively intact cognition and sensorium.

Ego Defenses and Character Style

Premorbid personality characteristics such as paranoid and schizoid traits appear to contribute to social isolation and precede psychosis in a sizable number of patients with late-onset schizophrenia (146, 148, 152). Although many never marry, late-onset patients are more likely than early-onset schizophrenics to marry, hold a job, and raise children (151). Later-onset psychosis allows for extended premorbid opportunities to socialize appropriately, develop more mature ego defenses, and maintain long-term relationships.

Formulation

Numerous potential stressors may affect the elder schizophrenic patient and precipitate an initial episode or recurrence of psychosis. Social isolation, psychosocial loss, illness, or environmental change may increase the vulnerability of an elderly patient with underlying psychosis. Common risk factors in this population are the sensory deficits from auditory and visual impairments (152–154) such as cataracts and conductive deafness. Either impairment may lead to reduced social contact, thus contributing to increased isolation, suspiciousness, and misinterpretation of environmental cues (155). Treatment of these problems may improve social interactions

and lessen the intensity of psychotic symptoms. Other medical illnesses and disabilities, changes in functioning or lifestyle, and alterations in environment, caregivers, or daily routine may contribute to exacerbations of psychosis in the elderly.

Focal Problems

The elderly patient with psychosis is at high risk for medication or treatment noncompliance and resulting relapse. One common explanation for noncompliance in this population is the absence of the primary caregiver. Family members may become overwhelmed, angry, or physically ill, resulting in their withdrawal from caretaking. Acute hospitalization may serve both to stabilize the patient and to give caretakers temporary relief from their responsibilities. An aftercare plan may include the use of depot neuroleptics and a community psychiatric nurse, which may improve compliance and treatment response (156). Aftercare appointments with transportation arrangements and adequate emergency services must be clearly established before discharge from the acute setting. Interpersonal supports and social services should also be evaluated, with appropriate recommendations for day programs, senior centers, groups, or activities that may improve the older patient's daily structure and decrease reliance on a primary caretaker.

Treatment

Elderly patients with late-onset schizophrenia typically experience symptom relief with relatively low doses of neuroleptics, although the extent of treatment response varies. Similar to patients with early onset schizophrenia, late-onset patients with no auditory hallucinations or affective symptoms tend to have a more limited response to treatment (157). In one study, patients with premorbid schizoid traits had a poor medication response, whereas first-rank symptoms, gender, or a positive schizophrenia family history did not effect treatment response (152). In general, neuroleptics will control relapses and ameliorate the positive symptoms of psychosis (e.g., hallucinations, delusions, thought disorder, and bizarre behavior) (158). Neuroleptics may also be effective for delusional disorder but are more likely to decrease the intensity of delusions than to eliminate them entirely.

As previously noted, neuroleptic use is limited by the side effects of sedation, anticholinergic and Parkinsonian effects, postural hypotension, and tardive dyskinesia. Because of their increased propensity for side effects, geriatric patients need to be maintained with significantly lower neuroleptic doses than younger adults. Clozapine is an effective atypical antipsychotic agent that can be used in some refractory elder schizophrenics (159). Although clozapine has few extrapyramidal side effects or risks for tardive dyskinesia, other side effects such as sedation and postural hypotension may leave elderly patients at much greater risk for falls or injury (160). For this reason, clinicians should begin clozapine at doses of 12.5 mg, gradually titrate to minimize side effects, and closely monitor patients for agranulocytosis and drug interactions (161). Risperidone is another useful therapeutic alternative to standard neuroleptics because of its preferable side effect profile and, according to one study, similar efficacy to clozapine (162). Geriatric patients may require starting doses as low as 0.25–0.5 mg with slow titration to avoid problems with stiffness, sedation, and postural hypotension.

Developing an alliance and therapeutic rapport is often the first task in building trust and creating an environment for good treatment compliance. Family support and periodic educational sessions may also contribute to a greater understanding of the course and treatment of the illness. Medication and psychotherapy groups may be appropriate for some less paranoid patients. Day programs or partial hospitalization can provide a supportive setting to monitor therapeutic progress and treatment compliance and can assist isolated elderly patients with socialization skills.

Course and Prognosis

The course of late-onset schizophrenia is often chronic and unremitting. Spontaneous remissions are uncommon, and most patients require maintenance medication. Noncompliance in late-onset schizophrenia tends to occur frequently and is highly correlated with increased risk for relapse. There is some evidence that a subgroup of late-onset schizophrenics will eventually develop dementia (146, 157, 163). The reported incidence of dementia in patients with late-onset psychosis varies considerably; however, it appears to be significantly higher in these patients than in a comparable group of nonpsychotic older patients (164). Cerebrovascular disease or structural brain injury may also be associated with late-onset psychosis (164, 165), and evidence suggests that stroke patients with psychosis are less likely to respond to treatment (166). The course of late-onset delusional disorder may fluctuate with remissions and relapses or remain more chronic with residual symptoms (167). There is little evidence, however, that delusional disorder leads to a higher incidence of dementia among geriatric patients.

CONTROVERSIES IN GERIATRIC PSYCHIATRY

Informed Consent in the Elderly

Several studies in recent years have suggested that elderly patients generally have less capacity than younger patients to give competent consent for medical or psychiatric treatment (168–170). Because competence is strictly a legal term, the concept of decision-making capacity has gained considerable attention in clinical practice. A clinician's assessment of a patient's decision-making capacity before initiating treatment (171) is crucial, particularly in elderly patients who are at greater risk for debilitating illness, long-term care, and potentially poorer outcomes as a result of their treatment decisions (172).

Identifying patient groups that are at particular risk for having difficulties with decision-making may assist clinicians in protecting elderly patients from poorly informed consent while preserving the rights of more competent elderly patients. Grisso and Appelbaum (173) identified four standards commonly found in the law that describe distinct aspects of decision-making capacity. These are the ability to express a choice; understand information regarding treatment; appreciate the significance of one's own illness, treatment, and situation; and manipulate information rationally to make reasonable decisions.

Specific instruments have been designed to assess these different components of the decision-making process. Using these criteria and instruments, one recent large-scale study found that schizophrenic patients demonstrated significant impairment in decision-making capacity compared with depressed or medically ill patients or healthy controls

(173). Other studies have found that older populations, particularly those with medical illness and lower verbal abilities and/or educational levels, had more impairment in decision-making capacity than had younger populations (170, 174–176). However, depression and other psychiatric illnesses do not necessarily predispose geriatric patients toward diminished decision-making capacity (172).

Geriatric psychiatrists who are considering the prescription of new medications or ECT should document their patient's educational level, cognitive capacity, verbal skills, and current sensorium. The physician must then assess the patient's understanding of the illness, treatment, alternative treatments, and potential risks and benefits of having or not having the prescribed treatment. Health-care providers must be responsible for adequately assessing a geriatric patient's ability to make these decisions and identifying more vulnerable patients who are at risk for making inadequate decisions. Patients suffering from late-stage dementia, acute psychosis, or severe affective disorders may require protection from improper consent with the appointment of a health-care proxy or medical guardian.

Suicide in the Elderly

The rates of suicide among the elderly are the highest of any age group and have steadily increased since 1980. According to the Centers for Disease Control and Prevention, almost one in five of every suicides committed between 1980 and 1992 occurred among persons 65 years and older. White men 85 years and older are at the greatest risk for suicide, and the rate has risen most dramatically among all persons 80 years and older during this period. Although women may attempt suicide more often, men are far more successful in their attempts (177). The most common method of suicide for elderly men and women is by firearm. However, unlike the active, impulsive suicide attempt often seen in younger populations, late-life suicide is more likely to be passive, premeditated, and lethal (178). Rates of suicide in the elderly may be even higher than those reported due to numerous unrecognized or unreported cases. Older patients who passively commit suicide by refusing medications, nutrition, or treatment may suffer deaths attributed to secondary complications.

Numerous factors contribute to the escalating rates of suicide among the elderly. As noted previously, late life is often marked by social isolation, stressful events, and profound losses (e.g., spouse, family member, friends, home, or health). Many studies have found that both physical and psychiatric illness are correlated with increased rates of suicide among the elderly (178). In fact, elderly patients with affective disorders are at significantly greater risk for suicide, and this risk is considerably higher than that associated with younger depressed patients. Suicidal elderly persons are also less likely to suffer from comorbid substance abuse or psychotic illness, which are more commonly found in younger populations (24, 178). Unfortunately, the identification of neurobiologic correlates or personality types specific to suicide have not been clearly defined.

The challenge for geriatric health providers is to identify and treat those elderly persons at risk for suicide. This process is complicated by the fact that few elderly persons seek mental health assessment when at risk for suicide. However, an older person is likely to visit his or her primary care physician in the month before a suicide attempt (24, 178). Thus, one important responsibility for geriatric

mental health providers is to increase their efforts to educate primary care clinicians in the recognition and treatment of affective disorders. Particular emphasis must be placed on the difficult decision to refer elderly patients for acute psychiatric assessment. Current demographics suggest that the number of suicides in the elderly will tend to increase in the decades ahead. The timely identification of major depression and treatment with appropriate medications, ECT, psychotherapy, and increased social supports may serve to stem the rising tide of suicide in the elderly.

REFERENCES

1. Folstein MF, Folstein SE, McHugh PR. Mini-mental state: a practical method for grading the cognitive state of patients for the clinician. J Psychiatr Res 1975;12:189–198.
2. Soldo BJ, Manton KG. Health status and service needs of the oldest old: current patterns and future trends. Milbank Q 1985;63:286–319.
3. Kolman PBR. The value of laboratory investigation of elderly psychiatric patients. J Clin Psychiatry 1984;45:112–116.
4. Leuchter AF, Daly K, Rosenberg-Thompson S, et al. The prevalence of electroencephalographic abnormalities among patients with possible organic mental syndromes. J Am Geriatr Soc 1993;41:605–611.
5. Engel G, Romano J. Delirium, a syndrome of cerebral insufficiency. J Chronic Dis 1959;9:260–277.
6. Brenner RP. Utility of electroencephalography in delirium: past views and current practice. Int Psychogeriatr 1991;3:211–229.
7. Jagust WJ, Budinger TF, Reed BR. The diagnosis of dementia with single photon emission computed tomography. Arch Neurol 1987;44:258–262.
8. Benson DF, Kuhl DE, Hawkins DR, et al. The fluorodeoxygluose 18F scan in Alzheimer's disease and multi-infarct dementia. Arch Neurol 1983;40:711–714.
9. Howard R. Day hospitals: the case in favour. Int J Geriatr Psychiatry 1994;9(7):525–529.
10. American Psychiatric Association. Diagnostic and statistical manual of mental disorders. 4th ed. Washington, DC: American Psychiatric Association, 1994.

11. Weissman MM, Bruce M. Affective disorders. In: Robins LN, Berger DA, eds. Psychiatric disorders in America. New York: Free Press, 1991:53–80.
12. Blazer DG. Epidemiology of late-life depression. In: Schneider L, Reynolds CF, Lebowitz BD, et al., eds. Diagnosis and treatment of depression in late life: results of the NIH consensus development conference. Washington, DC: APA Press, 1994;9–19.
13. Myers DK, Weissman MM, Tischler GL, et al. Six-month prevalence of psychiatric disorders in three communities. Arch Gen Psychiatry 1984;41:959–967.
14. Berkman WF, Berkman CS. Depression symptoms in relation to physical health and functioning in the elderly. Am J Epidemiol 1986;124:372–388.
15. Parmalee PA, Katz IR, Lawton MD. Depression among institutionalized aged: assessment and prevalence estimate. J Gerontol 1989;44:22–29.
16. Katz IR, Parmalee PA. Depression in elderly patients in residential care settings. In: Schneider L, Reynolds CF, Lebowitz BD, et al., eds. Diagnosis and treatment of depression in late life. Washington, DC: APA Press, 1994:437–462.
17. Blazer D, Hughes DC, George LK. The epidemiology of depression in an elderly community population. Gerontologist 1987;27:281–287.
18. Allen A, Blazer DG. Mood disorders. In: Sadavoy J, Lazarus LW, Jarvik LF, eds. Comprehensive review of geriatric psychiatry. Washington DC: APA Press, 1991:337–351.
19. Shulman K, Post F. Bipolar affective disorder in old age. Br J Psychiatry 1980;136:26–32.
20. Young R, Klerman GL. Mania in late life: focus on age at onset. Am J Psychiatry 1992;149:867–876.
21. Stone K. Mania in the elderly. Br J Psychiatry 1989;155:220–224.
22. Brodaty H, Peters K, Boyce P. Age and depression. J Affect Disord 1991;23:137–149.
23. Small GW, Komanduri R, Gitlin M, et al. The influence of age on guilt expression in major depression. Int J Geriatr Psychiatry 1986;1:121–126.
24. Conwell Y. Suicide in elderly patients. In: Schneider LS, Reynolds CS, Liebowitz BD, et al., eds. Diagnosis and treatment of depression in late life. Washington, DC: APA Press, 1994:397–418.
25. Kalayam B, Shamoian CA. Treatment of depression: diagnostic considerations. In: Salzman C, ed. Clinical geriatric psychopharmacology. 2nd ed. Baltimore: Williams & Wilkins, 1992;115–135.
26. Meyers BS, Kalayam B, Mei-tal V. Late-onset delusional depression: a distinct clinical entity? J Clin Psychiatry 1984;45:347–349.
27. Meyers BS, Greenberg R. Late-life delusional depression. J Affect Disord 1986;11:133–137.
28. Charney DS, Nelson JC. Delusional and nondelusional unipolar depression: further evidence for distinct subtypes. Am J Psychiatry 1981;138:328–333.
29. Glassman AB, Roose SP. Delusional depression: a distinct clinical entity? Arch Gen Psychiatry 1981;38:424–427.
30. Nelson JC, Conwell Y, Kim K, et al. Age at onset in late-life delusional depression. Am J Psychiatry 1989;146:785–786.
31. Brown RP, Sweeney J, Loutsch E, et al. Involutional melancholia revisited. Am J Psychiatry 1984;141:24–28.
32. Caine ED, Lyness JM, King DA, et al. Clinical and etiological heterogeneity of mood disorders in elderly patients. In: Schneider L, et al., eds. Diagnosis and treatment of depression in late life. Washington, DC: APA Press, 1994:21–53.
33. Wesner RB, Winokur G. American archival study of depression before and after age 55. J Geriatr Psychiatry Neurol 1988;1:220–225.
34. Robinson RG, Starr LB, Price TR. A two-year longitudinal study of mood disorders following stroke: prevalence and duration at six month follow-up. Br J Psychiatry 1984;144:256–262.
35. Burns A. Affective symptoms in Alzheimer's disease. Int J Geriatr Psychiatry 1991;6:371–376.
36. Cummings JL. Depression and Parkinson's disease: a review. Am J Psychiatry 1992;149:443–454.
37. Robinson RG, Boston JD, Starkstein SE, et al. Comparison of mania with depression after brain injury: causal factors. Am J Psychiatry 1988;145:172–178.
38. Price TRP, McAllister TW. Safety and efficacy of ECT in depressed patients with dementia: a review of clinical experience. Convuls Ther 1989;5:61–74.
39. Weiner MF, Edland SD, Luszczynska H. Prevalence and incidence of major depression in Alzheimer's disease. Am J Psychiatry 1994;151:1006–1009.
40. Sargenti CJ, Ringos AL, Jeste DV. Psychotropic drug interactions in the patient with late-onset psychosis and mood disorders (part 1). Psychiatr Clin North Am 1988;11:235–252.
41. Agronin M. Personality disorders in the elderly: an overview. J Geriatr Psychiatry 1994;27:151–191.
42. Abrams RC, Alexopoulos GS, Young RC. Geriatric depression and DSM-III-R personality disorder criteria. J Am Geriatr Soc 1987;35:383–386.

43. Thompson LW, Gallagher D, Czirr R. Personality disorder and outcome in the treatment of late-life depression. J Geriatr Psychiatry 1988;21:133–153.

44. Fogel BS, Westlake R. Personality disorder diagnoses and age in inpatients with major depression. J Clin Psychiatry 1990;51:232–235.

45. Hirschfield RMA, Klerman GL, Lavori P, et al. Premorbid personality assessments of first onset of major depression. Arch Gen Psychiatry 1989;46:345–350.

46. Costa PT, McCrae RR. Depression as an enduring disposition. In: Schneider LS, Reynolds CS, Liebowitz BD, et al., eds. Diagnosis and treatment of depression in late life. Washington, DC: APA Press, 1994:155–167.

47. Abernathy DR. Psychotropic drugs and the aging process: pharmacokinetics and pharmacodynamics. In: Salzman C, ed. Clinical geriatric psychopharmacology. 2nd ed. Baltimore: Williams & Wilkins, 1992:61–76.

48. Sunderland T. Neurotransmission in the aging central nervous system. In: Salzman C, ed. Clinical geriatric psychopharmacology. 2nd ed. Baltimore: Williams & Wilkins, 1992:41–59.

49. Georgotas A, McCue RE, Cooper TB, et al. How effective and safe is continuation therapy in elderly depressed patients. Arch Gen Psychiatry 1988;45:929–932.

50. Glassman AH, Roose SP, Bigger JT. The safety of tricyclic antidepressants in cardiac patients. JAMA 1993;269:2673–2675.

51. Jenike M. Serotonin selective reuptake inhibitors in the elderly. J Geriatr Psychiatry Neurol 1994;7:133–134.

52. Katona C. Optimizing treatment for the elderly depressive: new antidepressants in the elderly. J Psychopharm 1993;7(Suppl 1):131–134.

53. Roose SP, Dalack GW, Glassman AH, et al. Cardiovascular effects of bupropion in depressed patients with heart disease. Am J Psychiatry 1991;148:512–516.

54. Georgotas A, McCue RE, Hapworth W, et al. Comparative efficacy and safety of MAOI's versus TCA's in treating depression in the elderly. Biol Psychiatry 1986;21:1155–1166.

55. Georgotas A, McCue RE, Friedman E, et al. Response of depressive symptoms to nortriptyline, phenelzine and placebo. Br J Psychiatry 1987;151:102–106.

56. Georgotas A, McCue RE, Cooper TB. A placebo-controlled comparison of nortriptyline and phenelzine in maintenance therapy of elderly depressed patients. Arch Gen Psychiatry 1989;46:783–786.

57. Jefferson JW. Lithium and affective disorder in the elderly. Compr Psychiatry 1983;26:166–178.

58. Himmelhoch JM, Neil JF, May SJ, et al. Age, dementia, dyskinesias, and lithium response. Am J Psychiatry 1980;137:941–945.

59. Chiarello RJ, Cole JO. The use of psychostimulants in general psychiatry: a reconsideration. Arch Gen Psychiatry 1987;44:286–295.

60. Roccaforte WH, Burke WJ. Use of psychostimulants for the elderly. Hosp Community Psychiatry 1990;41:1330–1333.

61. Alexopoulos GS. Treatment of depression. In: Salzman C, ed. Clinical geriatric psychopharmacology. 2nd ed. Baltimore: Williams & Wilkins, 1992:137–174.

62. Gurian B, Rosowsky E. Low-dose methylphenidate in the very old. J Gen Psychiatry Neurol 1990;3:152–154.

63. Spiker DG, Perel JM, Hanim I, et al. The pharmacological treatment of delusional depression. part II. J Clin Psychopharmacol 1986;6:339–342.

64. Georgotas A, McCue RE, Cooper T, et al. Clinical predictors of response to antidepressants in elderly patients. Biol Psychiatry 1987;22:733–740.

65. Fogel BS. Electroconvulsive therapy in the elderly, a clinical research agenda. Int J Geriatr Psychiatry 1988;3:181–190.

66. Pande AC, Grunhaus LJ, Haskett RF, et al. Electroconvulsive therapy in delusional and non-delusional depressive disorder. J Affect Disord 1990;19:215–219.

67. Wilkinson AM, Anderson DN, Peters S. Age and the effects of ECT. Int J Geriatr Psychiatry 1993;8:401–406.

68. Weiner RD. The role of electroconvulsive therapy in the treatment of depression in the elderly. J Am Geriatr Soc 1982;30:710–712.

69. Coryell W, Zimmerman M. Outcome following ECT for primary unipolar depression: a test of newly proposed predictors. Am J Psychiatry 1984;141:862–867.

70. Black DW, Winokur G, Nasarallah A. A multivariate analysis of the experience of 423 depressed inpatients treated with electroconvulsive therapy. Convuls Ther 1993;9:112–120.

71. Benbow S. The use of electroconvulsive therapy in old age psychiatry. Int J Geriatr Psychiatry 1987;2:25–30.

72. Alexopoulos G, Young R, Abrahms RC. ECT in the high-risk geriatric patient. Convuls Ther 1989;5:75–87.

73. Hay DP. Electroconvulsive therapy in the medically ill elderly. Convuls Ther 1989;5:8–16.

74. Salzman C. Electroconvulsive therapy in the elderly patient. Psychiatr Clin North Am 1982;5:191–197.

75. Sackheim HA. The efficacy of electroconvulsive therapy. Ann N Y Acad Sci 1986;462;70–75.
76. Greenberg L, Fink M. The use of electroconvulsive therapy in geriatric patients. Clin Geriatr Med 1992;8:349–354.
77. Pritchett JT, Kellner CH, Coffey CE. Electroconvulsive therapy in geriatric neuropsychiatry. In: Coffey CE, Cummings JL, eds. Textbook of geriatric neuropsychiatry. Washington, DC: APA Press, 1994:634–659.
78. Alexopoulos GS, Shamoian CA, Lucas J, et al. Medical problems of geriatric psychiatric patients and younger controls during electroconvulsive therapy. J Am Geriatr Soc 1984;32:651–654.
79. Burke WJ, Rubin EH, Zorumski CE, et al. The safety of ECT in geriatric psychiatry. J Am Geriatr Soc 1987;35:516–521.
80. Zielinski RJ, Roose SP, Devanand DP, et al. Cardiovascular complications of ECT in depressed patients with cardiac disease. Am J Psychiatry 1993;150:904–909.
81. Hay DP. Electroconvulsive therapy. In: Hay DP, ed. Comprehensive review of geriatric psychiatry. Washington DC: APA Press, 1991:469–485.
82. Decina P, Guthrie EB, Sackheim HA, et al. Continuation ECT in the management of relapses of major affective episodes. Acta Psychiatr Scand 1987;75:559–562.
83. Jaffe R, Dubin W, Shoyen B, et al. Outpatient electroconvulsive therapy: efficacy and safety. Convuls Ther 1990;6:231–238.
84. Gallagher DE, Thompson LW. Treatment of major depressive disorder in older adult outpatients with brief psychotherapies. Psychother Theory Res Pract 1982;19:482–490.
85. Gallagher DE, Thompson LW. Effectiveness of psychotherapy for both endogenous and non-endogenous depression in older adult outpatients. J Gerontol 1983;38:707–712.
86. Lazarus LW, Sadavoy J, Langsley PR. Individual psychotherapy. In: Sadavoy J, Lazarus LW, Jarvik LF, eds. Comprehensive review of geriatric psychiatry. Washington, DC: APA Press, 1991;487–512.
87. Teri L, Curtis J, Gallagher-Thompson D, et al. Cognitive-behavioral therapy with depressed older adults. In: Schneider LS, Reynolds CS, Liebowitz BD, et al., eds. Diagnosis and treatment of depression in late life. Washington, DC: APA Press, 1994;279–291.
88. Thompson LW, Gallagher DE. Depression and its treatment in the elderly. Aging 1985;348:14–18.
89. Lewis MI, Butler RN. Life review therapy: putting memories to work in individual and group psychotherapy. Geriatrics 1974;29:165–173.
90. Teri L, McCurry SM. Psychosocial therapies. In: Coffey CE, Cummings JL, eds. Textbook of geriatric neuropsychiatry. Washington, DC: APA Press, 1994:661–682.
91. Keller MB, Shapiro RW. Major depressive disorder: initial results from a one-year prospective naturalistic follow-up study. J Nerv Ment Dis 1981;169:761–767.
92. Murphy E. The prognosis of depression in old age. Br J Psychiatry 1983;142:111–119.
93. Balldwin RC, Jolley DJ. The prognosis of depression in old age. Br J Psychiatry 1986;149:574–583.
94. George LK, Blazer DG, Hughes DC, et al. Social support and the outcome of major depression. Br J Psychiatry 1989;154:478–485.
95. Robinson DG, Spiker DG. Delusional depression: a one-year follow-up. J Affect Disord 1985;9:79–83.
96. Meyers BS. Effects of somatic treatment in longitudinal studies of geriatric depression. Int J Geriatr Psychiatry 1991;6:687–690.
97. Pearson JL, Reynolds CF, Kupfer DJ, et al. Outcome measures in late-life depression. Am J Geriatr Psychiatry 1995;3:191–195.
98. Evans DA, Funkenstein H, Albert MS, et al. Prevalence of Alzheimer's disease in a community population of older persons: higher than previously noted. JAMA 1989;262:2551–2556.
99. Weiler PD. The public health impact of Alzheimer's disease. Am J Public Health 1987;77:1157–1158.
100. Bachman DC, Wolf PA, Linn R, et al. Prevalence of dementia and probable senile dementia of the Alzheimer's type in the Framingham study. Neurology 1992;42:115–119.
101. Kokmen E, Beard CM, O'Brian PC, et al. Is the incidence of dementing illness changing? A 25-year time trend study in Rochester, MN. Neurology 1993;43:1887–1892.
102. Ebly EM, Parhad IM, Hogan DB, et al. Prevalence and types of dementia in the very old: results from the Canadian study of health and aging. Neurology 1994;9:1593–1600.
103. Ineichen B. Measuring the rising tide: how many dementia cases will there be by 2001? Br J Psychiatry 1987;150:193–200.
104. Gottfries CG. Neurochemical disorders of dementia disorders. Dementia 1990;1:56–64.
105. Kase CS. Epidemiology of multi-infarct dementia. Alzheimer Dis Assoc Disord 1991;5:71–76.

106. Chui HC, Victoroff JI, Margolin D, et al. Criteria for the diagnosis of ischemic vascular dementia proposed by the state of California Alzheimer's disease diagnostic and treatment centers. Neurology 1992;42:473–480.

107. Friedland RP. Alzheimer's dementia: clinical features and differential diagnosis. Neurology 1993;43(Suppl 4):545–551.

108. Miller BL, Chang L, Oropilla G, et al. Alzheimer's disease and frontal lobe dementias. In: Coffey CE, Cummings JL, eds. Textbook of geriatric neuropsychiatry. Washington, DC: APA Press, 1994:389–404.

109. Cummings JL, Benson F, Hill MA, et al. Aphasia in dementia of the Alzheimer's type. Neurology 1985;35:394–397.

110. Rubin EH, Morris JC, Berg L. The progression of personality changes in senile dementia of the Alzheimer's type. J Am Geriatr Soc 1987;37:721–725.

111. Petry S, Cummings JL, Hill MA, et al. Personality alterations in dementia of the Alzheimer's type: a 3 year follow-up study. J Geriatr Psychiatry Neurol 1989;2:203–207.

112. Reisberg B, Franssen E, Schon SG, et al. Stage specific incidence of potentially remediable behavioral symptoms in aging and Alzheimer's disease: a study of 120 patients using the BEHAVE-AD. Bull Clin Neurosci 1989;54:95–112.

113. Devanand DP, Brockington CD, Moody BJ, et al. Behavioral symptoms in Alzheimer's disease. Int Psychogeriatrics 1992;4:161–184.

114. Devanand DP, Sackheim HA, Mayeux R. Psychosis behavioral disturbance and the use of neuroleptics in dementia. Compr Psychiatry 1988;29:387–401.

115. Wragg RE, Jeste DV. Overview of depression and psychosis in Alzheimer's disease. Am J Psychiatry 1989;146:577–587.

116. Jeste DV, Wragg RE, Salmon DP, et al. Cognitive deficits of patients with Alzheimer's disease with and without delusions. Am J Psychiatry 1992;149:184–189.

117. Reichman WE. Nondegenerative dementing disorders. In: Coffey CE, Cummings JL, eds. Textbook of geriatric neuropsychiatry. Washington, DC: APA Press, 1994:389–404.

118. Huber ST, Friedenberg DL, Shuttleworth EC, et al. Neuropsychological impairments associated with the severity of Parkinson's disease. J Neuropsychiatry Clin Neurosci 1989;1:154–158.

119. Koller WC, Megaffin BB. Parkinson's disease and Parkinsonism. In: Coffey CE, Cummings JL, eds. Textbook of geriatric

120. Conn DK. Delirium and other organic mental disorders. In: Sadavoy J, Lazarus LW, Jarvik LF, eds. Comprehensive review of geriatric psychiatry. Washington, DC: APA Press, 1991:311–336.

121. Kiloh LG. Pseudo-dementia. Acta Psychiatr Scand 1961;37:336–351.

122. Allen A, Blazer DG. Mood disorders. In: Sadavoy J, Lazarus LW, Jarvik LF, eds. Comprehensive review of geriatric psychiatry. Washington, DC: APA Press, 1991:337–352.

123. Kral VA, Emery OB. Long-term follow-up of depressive pseudo- dementia of the aged. Can J Psychiatry 1989;34:445–446.

124. Verwoedt A. Individual psychotherapy in senile dementia. In: Miller N, Cohen G, eds. Clinical aspects of Alzheimer's dementia and senile dementia (aging). New York: Raven Press, 1981;15:187–208.

125. Cohen-Mansfield J, Marx MS, Werner P. Agitation in elderly persons: an integrative report of findings in a nursing home. Int Psychogeriatr 1992;4(Suppl 2):221–240.

126. Eagger S, Morant N, Levy R, et al. Tacrine in Alzheimer's disease: time course of changes in cognitive function and practice effects. Br J Psychiatry 1992;160:36–40.

127. Growdon JH. Treatment for Alzheimer's disease? N Engl J Med 1992;327:1306–1308.

128. Small GW. Tacrine for treating Alzheimer's disease. JAMA 1992;268:2564–2565.

129. Petrie WM, Lawson EC, Hollander MH. Violence in geriatric patients. JAMA 1982;248:443–444.

130. Devanand DP, Levy SR. Neuroleptic treatment of agitation and psychosis in dementia. J Geriatr Psychiatry Neurol 1995;8(Suppl 1):18–27.

131. Harris MJ, Panton D, Calgiuri MP, et al. High incidence of TD in older outpatients on low doses of neuroleptics. Psychopharmacol Bull 1992;28:87–92.

132. Oberholzer AF, Hendriksen C, Monsch AU, et al. Safety and efficacy of low-dose clozapine in psychogeriatric patients: a preliminary study. Int Psychogeriatr 1992;4:187–195.

133. Holton A, George K. The use of lithium carbonate in severely demented patients with behavioral disturbances. Br J Psychiatry 1985;146:99–100.

134. Sival RC, Haffmans PMH, Van Gert PP, et al. The effects of sodium valproate on disturbed behavior in dementia. J Am Geriatr Soc 1994;42:906–907.

135. Liebovici A, Tariot PN. Carbamazepine treatment of agitation associated with de-

mentia. J Geriatr Psychiatry Neurol 1988;1:110–112.

136. Patterson JF. A preliminary study of carbamazepine in the treatment of assaultive patients with dementia. J Geriatr Psychiatry Neurol 1988;1:21–23.

137. Lawlor BA, Radcliff J, Mochan SE, et al. A pilot placebo-controlled study of trazodone and buspirone in Alzheimer's disease. Int J Geriatr Psychiatry 1994;9:55–59.

138. Hermann N, Eryavec G. Buspirone in the management of agitation and aggression associated with dementia. Am J Geriatr Psychiatry 1993;1:249–253.

139. Nyth AL, Gottfries CG. The clinical efficacy of citralopram in treatment of emotional disturbances in dementia disorders. A Nordic multicentre study. Br J Psychiatry 1990;157:894–901.

140. Burke WJ, Folks DG, Roccaforte WH, et al. Serotonin reuptake inhibitors for the treatment of coexisting depression and psychosis in dementia of the Alzheimer's type. J Am Geriatr Psychiatry 1994;2:352–354.

141. Weiler PG, Mungas D, Bernick C. Propranolol for its control of disruptive behavior in senile dementia. J Geriatr Psychiatry Neurol 1988;1:226–230.

142. Tariot PN, Schneider LS, Katz IR. Anticonvulsant and other non-neuroleptic treatment of agitation in dementia. J Geriatr Psychiatry Neurol 1995;8(Suppl 1):28–39.

143. Reisberg B, Ferris SH, de Leon MJ, et al. The global deterioration scale for assessment of primary degenerative dementia. Am J Psychiatry 1982;139:1136–1139.

144. Rosen J, Zubenko GS. Emergence of psychosis and depression in the longitudinal evaluation of Alzheimer's disease. Biol Psychiatry 1991;29:224–232.

145. Harris MJ, Jeste DV. Late-onset schizophrenia: an overview. Schizophr Bull 1988;14:39–55.

146. Kay DWK, Roth M. Environmental and hereditary factors in the schizophrenias of old age (late paraphrenia) and their bearing on the general problem of causation in schizophrenia. J Ment Sci 1961;107:649–686.

147. Blessed G, Wilson D. The contemporary natural history of mental disorder in old age. Br J Psychiatry 1982;141:59–67.

148. Herbert ME, Jacobson S. Late paraphrenia. Br J Psychiatry 1967;113:461–469.

149. Jeste DV, Manley M, Harris MJ. Psychoses. In: Sadavoy J, Lazarus LW, Jarvik LF, eds. Comprehensive review of geriatric psychiatry. Washington, DC: APA Press, 1991:353–368.

150. Kraepelin E. Dementia praecox and para-

phrenia. 8th German ed. Edinburgh: Livingstone, 1919.

151. Jeste DV, Harris MJ, Pearlson GD, et al. Late-onset schizophrenia: studying clinical validity. Psychiatr Clin North Am 1988;11:1–14.

152. Pearlson GD, Kreger L, Rabins PV, et al. A chart review study of late-onset and early onset schizophrenia. Am J Psychiatry 1989;146:1568–1574.

153. Naguib M, Levy R. Late paraphrenia: neuropsychological impairment and structural brain abnormalities on computed tomography. Int J Geriatr Psychiatry 1987;2:83–90.

154. Prager S, Jeste D. Sensory impairment in late-life schizophrenia. Schizophr Bull 1993;19:755–772.

155. Pearlson GD, Rabins PV. The late onset psychoses: possible risk factors. Psychiatr Clin North Am 1988;11:15–33.

156. Howard R, Levy R. Which factors affect treatment response in late paraphrenia? Int J Geriatr Psychiatry 1992;7:667–672.

157. Holden NL. Late paraphrenia or the paraphrenias? A descriptive study with a 10 year follow-up. Br J Psychiatry 1987;150:635–639.

158. Lacro JP, Harris MJ, Jeste DV. Late life psychosis. Int J Geriatr Psychiatry 1993;8:49–57.

159. Frankenberg FR, Kalunian D. Clozapine in the elderly. J Geriatr Psychiatry Neurol 1994;7:129–132.

160. Pitner JK, Mintzer JE, Pennypacker LC, et al. Efficacy and adverse side effects of clozapine in four elderly psychotic patients. J Clin Psychiatry 1995;56:180–185.

161. Chengappa KN, Baker RW, Kreinbrook SB, Adair D. Clozapine use in female geriatric patients with psychoses. J Geriatr Psychiatry Neurol 1995;8:12–15.

162. Heinrich K, Klieser E, Lehmann E, et al. Risperidone versus clozapine in the treatment of schizophrenic patients with acute symptoms: a double blind, randomized trial. Prog Neuropsychopharmacol Biol Psychiatry 1994;18:129–137.

163. Lesser IM, Miller BL, Boone KB, et al. Psychosis as the first manifestation of degenerative dementia. Bull Clin Neurosci 1989;54:59–63.

164. Pearlson GD, Petty RG. Late-life-onset psychoses. In: Coffey CE, Cummings JL, eds. Textbook of geriatric neuropsychiatry. Washington, DC: APA Press, 1994:261–278.

165. Miller BL, Lesser IM, Boone KB, et al. Brain lesions and cognitive function in late-life psychosis. Br J Psychiatry 1991;158:76–82.

166. Flint A, Rifat S, Eastwood R. Brain lesions and cognitive function in late-life psychosis. Br J Psychiatry 1991;158:866.

167. Almeida OP, Howard R, Forstl H, et al. Late-life paraphrenia: a review. Int J Geriatr Psychiatry 1992;7:543–548.

168. Stanley B, Guido J, Stanley M, et al. The elderly patient and informed consent: empirical findings. JAMA 1984;252:1302–1306.

169. Taub HA, Baker MT, Sturr JF. Informed consent for research: effects of readability, patient age, and education. J Am Geriatr Soc 1986;34:601–606.

170. Taub HA. Informed consent, memory, and age. Gerontologist 1980;20:686–690.

171. Appelbaum PS, Lidz CW, Meisel A. Informed consent, legal theory and clinical practice. New York: Oxford University Press, 1987.

172. Christensen K, Haroun A, Jeste D, et al. Decision-making capacity for informed consent in the older population. Bull Am Acad Psychiatry Law 1995;23:353–365.

173. Grisso T, Appelbaum PS. Comparison of standards for assessing patients' capacities to make treatment decisions. Am J Psychiatry 1995;152:1033–1037.

174. Fitten LJ, Lusky R, Hamann C. Assessing treatment decision-making capacity in nursing home residents. J Am Geriatr Soc 1990;38:1097–1104.

175. Taub HA, Kline GE, Baker MT. The elderly and informed consent: effects of vocabulary level and corrected feedback. Exp Aging Res 1981;7:137–146.

176. Cassileth BR, Zupkis RV, Sutton-Smith K, et al. Informed consent-why are its goals imperfectly realized? N Engl J Med 1980;302:896–900.

177. Centers for Disease Control and Prevention. Suicide among older persons— United States, 1980–1992. MMWR 1996;45:3–6.

178. Kennedy GJ, Metz H, Lowinger R. Epidemiology and inferences regarding the etiology of late-life suicide. In: Kennedy GJ, ed. Suicide and depression in late life. New York: John Wiley & Sons, 1996.

Chapter 13

Disorders of Childhood and Adolescence

Gordon Harper

INTRODUCTION

Among the many acute psychiatric problems seen in children and adolescents, this chapter focuses on two: suicidal behavior and disruptive behavior. These two problems have been selected for discussion for several reasons, including the frequency of occurrence as seen by general psychiatrists and general physicians; differences from adult disorders in their etiology, presentation, and management; and importance of prompt and effective clinical management.

Other acute problems in child and adolescent psychiatry that are likely to be encountered by the nonchild psychiatrist (e.g., acute psychosis) can be managed according to principles defined in the chapters on depression, mania, and psychosis (with appropriate modification of dosages for the child or younger adolescent) (Table 13.1). Other acute problems, less familiar to adult psychiatrists, include crises in children with eating disorders, pervasive developmental disorders, obsessive-compulsive disorders, and issues of child pro-

tection (children at risk of abuse, neglect, or molestation). Such problems should be referred to a child and adolescent psychiatrist.

SUICIDAL BEHAVIOR

Definition

Suicidal behavior refers to any behavior or statement by a child or adolescent deemed to represent a suicidal risk. The term "parasuicide" (especially in the British literature) refers to any self-injurious behavior that is without suicidal intent.

Diagnosis

The recognition of a patient at risk of suicide represents a serious challenge. Up to 80% of suicide attempters were not recognized to be at risk by their primary care physicians (1). In general, children and adolescents at suicidal risk verbalize and behave similarly to suicidal adults. Similar risk factors apply, such as the presence of mood disorders, substance abuse, isola-

TABLE 13.1.   Medications Frequently Administered to Children and Adolescents

	Starting dose	Therapeutic range
Stimulants		
Methylphenidate (Ritalin; Ciba-Geigy, Woodbridge, NJ)	5–10 mg every morning or twice a day	10–50 mg/day, divided doses
Dextroamphetamine (Dexedrine; Smith-Kline Beecham, Pittsburgh, PA)	2.5–5 mg every morning or twice a day	5–30 mg/day, divided doses
Alpha-2 adrenergic agonist		
Clonidine (Catapres; Boehringer Ingelheim, Ridgefield, CT)	0.05 mg by mouth twice a day	3–12 μg/kg/day
Antidepressants		
Serotonin reuptake inhibitors		
Fluoxetine (Prozac; Eli Lilly, Indianapolis, IN)	10 mg by mouth four times a day	20–40 mg/day
Sertraline (Zoloft; Pfizer, New York, NY)	25 mg by mouth four times a day	50–200 mg/day
Paroxetine (Paxil; Smith-Kline Beecham, Pittsburgh, PA)	10 mg by mouth four times a day	20–40 mg/day
Tricyclics		
Nortriptyline (Pamelor; Sandoz Pharmaceuticals, East Hanover, NJ)	10–25 mg by mouth four times a day	To a serum level of 50–150 ng/mL
Imipramine (Tofranil; Ciba-Geigy, Woodbridge, NJ)	10–25 mg by mouth four times a day	3–5 mg/kg/day

tion, and interruption of important relationships. More than with adults, impulsive suicidal behavior in children and adolescents—especially in adolescents—may occur in the absence of a diagnosable mood disorder.

Epidemiology

After accidents, homicide and suicide rank as the second leading cause of death among adolescents (2). In the past three decades, adolescent suicide rates have increased by 200%, and 2000 adolescents take their own lives in the United States each year. In the same period, suicide rates among children have increased fivefold. The most common methods of suicide are guns and hanging among males and ingestions among females. Males more often complete suicide, and females more often attempt suicide (3). Two thirds of adolescents who kill themselves appear, in retrospect, to have had major depression.

Hispanic females are at especially high risk of potentially lethal ingestions, without clear suicidal intent, at times of interpersonal crisis. Risk for suicide among gay and lesbian youth, both "out" and "closeted," appears to be several times greater than for the general population, particularly when significant others are unsympathetic or outwardly homophobic and hostile. Both suicide and attempted suicide are increased among childhood victims of molestation and incest, before and after disclosure and protective intervention.

The Four Questions

Descriptive and Differential Diagnosis

Suicidal risk exists independently of other diagnoses, although specific disorders (especially mood disorders and substance abuse) may contribute. In an acute crisis, the first key goal is to assess suicidal risk, independent of disorder. For example, apart from whether a mood disorder is present, a teen-ager may be at significant suicidal risk due to an unexpected personal loss, isolation, limited support, substance use, impulsivity, and access to lethal means of self-harm. The same may be true of other categoric diagnoses, such as personality or psychotic disorders, parent-child problems, or child-at-risk status.

A child is at high suicidal risk when abiding hopelessness exists along with a preformed plan, especially when the child is isolated from others. Substantial risk may also exist without a plan if depression, lability, and limited coping strategies are present. An unsympathetic or blaming family atmosphere compounds the risk.

Ego Defenses and Character Style

Limited personal resilience, inflexible perfectionist standards, and brittle defenses with consequent breakthrough impulsivity, rage, or despair increase risk of self-harm.

□ C A S E   E X A M P L E

A high-achieving, ambitious, 14-year-old boy enjoyed consistent success in distance running and academics. His parents noted that he "took setbacks less easily" than his brother and sister did, but he encountered no major defeats until he was not chosen for a regional track team he had counted on making. Self-reproaches like, "I am nobody, I can do nothing," were quite at odds with his other accomplishments and characterized the depression that developed in the next 6 months and his suicide attempt. Treatment provided an opportunity for him (and his parents) to appreciate the fragility of his premorbid self-esteem and to renegotiate his perfectionistic expectations of himself.

Formulation

In the formulation, the clinician considers factors contributing to suicidal risk, some of which are chosen for intervention. For example, in an adolescent at risk, contributing factors might include the following:

◆ Biologic factors, such as untreated major depression.
◆ Psychological-developmental factors, such as a rigid, self-critical personality style with overreliance for self-esteem and self-cohesion on particular activities or relationships.
◆ Family factors, such as parental limitations in finding ways to talk with a teen-ager, parent-child relationships that feel either smothering or abandoning, or the death of another child, with unresolved family feelings and expectations of the living teen-ager that are felt but are not undiscussed.
◆ Treatment factors (such as no treatment) or a clinician's underestimating a patient's despair, perhaps after being misled by the teen-ager's superficially upbeat manner.
◆ School and peer factors, such as a current setback in academics or in relation-

ships, or a mismatch at school between poorly recognized learning needs and a conventional academic program.

□ CASE EXAMPLE

A 15-year-old girl with anorexia nervosa and major depression was regarded by others and herself as academically gifted. She took accelerated classes, but her exceptionally diligent study habits resulted only in average grades. She had been overachieving relative to her abilities at a heavy personal cost, and was not able to keep up the pace of increasingly difficult academic demands. Her feeling that she had to be an academic star prevented her from backing off from this program. Her illness and near-lethal overdose provided her and her parents with an opportunity to recognize her average abilities and to adjust their academic expectations. They were able to give up the dream that she would be an exceptional student in favor of appreciating her as a good student.

Focal Problem

Suicidal risk is a problem that requires acute intervention. The corresponding goal to reduce that risk, not just to decrease current symptoms, is a vital distinction in the acutely ill child or adolescent. These patients often feel less suicidal after an attempt due to hospitalization or acknowledgment by others of their despair or removal from an overwhelmingly stressful personal environment. The clinical problem and the corresponding goal must not be defined too narrowly if an effective risk-reducing intervention is to occur. A criterion such as, "Hospitalized for acute suicidal ideation," with the implica-

tion that the patient should be discharged once acute suicidal ideation no longer exists, underestimates the risk and inappropriately defines the clinical task because the contextual element in the child's disorder is missed. The goal of intervention must be to decrease the suicidal risk in the patient while outside the hospital, not within it.

□ CASE EXAMPLE

A 16-year-old girl had major depression that had been slow to respond to outpatient treatment, including individual therapy and a course of a serotonin reuptake inhibitors. She was hospitalized after inconsolably sobbing, with suicidal intent, in her psychiatrist's office. As happens with many patients, her acute distress decreased once she was hospitalized. Although still depressed, she was not suicidal. Acute care directed only to current symptoms would have led to discharge at this point. However, the problem being treated was suicidal intent outside the hospital, not suicidal intent while hospitalized. Attention was directed to the circumstances causing the patient to become acutely distressed. Repeated review of the events preceding admission finally revealed that a heated argument, previously undisclosed despite repeated inquiries, had occurred the morning of admission. The patient's older sister had yelled at her, expressing the family's resentment at her illness and reviling her for "not trying." With the identification of this immediate precipitant—and the family's lack of knowledge about depression—discussion, ventilation, psychoeducation, and reconciliation were possible, allowing the patient to return home safely.

Biologic Evaluation

Toxicologic screens of serum or urine play a crucial part in the assessment of suicidal patients, especially for an undisclosed ingestion. Physical examination noting autonomic and neurologic signs of ingested licit or illicit drugs may be the first indication of an ingestion. All psychiatric patients with unexplained physical symptoms or with histories suggestive of possible ingestions, as well as medical patients without clearly explainable symptoms, should receive toxicologic screens. The general medical examination may provide the first clue in the assessment of other patients (e.g., those with general cognitive or language impairment) who might not complain verbally of undetected infections or other diseases.

Transfer to Next Level of Care

When the patient and his or her caretaker are unable to contain a suicidal risk, a higher level of care is required. With children and adolescents, even more than with adults, the risk is a function of both the status of the patient and the caretakers. A depressed child or adolescent at significant risk can be maintained in the community if adults recognize the risk, are sympathetic to the child or adolescent, and are able to provide supervision and reduce availability of dangers (including access to medicines and firearms). Patients at higher risk, even with caretakers available, require a more secure level of care.

A patient is ready for transfer to a less-restrictive level of care when the acute risk has subsided, when risk continues but the patient is able to behave in a safe manner, or when the environment has become more protective. The emphasis must al-ways be on the reduction of risk where the child will reside, not simply in the hospital or residential center.

Treatment

Although depression is the psychiatric disorder most often seen in suicidal risk and most suicidal adolescents may be diagnosed with major depression (even postmortem), antidepressant medication is not part of the first-line intervention for adolescents and children in suicidal crisis. Beginning an antidepressant trial may be important in the acute phase, but most patients will move out of acute care before an antidepressant medication effect has been achieved. This is due to length of time necessary for the onset of clinical effect, pressure from family and payers for expeditious treatment, and efficacy of psychosocial interventions (below) in acutely lowering risk.

Electroconvulsive therapy (ECT) is used only rarely in children and adolescents. The use of ECT is restricted to the older adolescent (older than 16 years of age) with a life-threatening melancholic depression or severe mania that is refractory to pharmacologic and psychosocial interventions (4).

Alliance and Psychotherapeutic Management

For all suicidal children and adolescents, the family attitude toward the child and the illness is a critical dimension of assessment and intervention. The family must be located along a continuum from nonvalidating, challenging responses ("... Depressed? How can he be depressed? Why, just yesterday, I saw him ... " or, "It's just manipulation; when he wants to, he can ... "), to pseudo-accepting interrogation ("Just tell us why you feel that way, we just want to understand . . . "), to sympathetic acknowledgment and acceptance of the child's pain ("It hurts to hear that you're feeling that way, but I'm glad you told us. If you want to talk about any part of what's going on, we'll be glad to listen, we'll stick with you, no matter how it goes . . . ").

For the child, expression by the family that his or her distress and hopelessness are understood and accepted is the first intervention, followed by inquiry about isolation and communication ("How much has anybody understood what it's been like for you? Who? Do they get it? Do you think they could?"). Emphasis belongs on acknowledgment and acceptance, not on inquiry (usually experienced as challenging) as to putative causes. The idea that a depressed person, child, or adult could cite "causes" for major depression fits more with popular notions (and with the wish of family members to "talk away" a painful and perplexing condition) than with modern biopsychosocial concepts of mood disorders.

After acknowledgment and acceptance, it is possible to be open to current stressors or dilemmas the child or adolescent faces, but without suggesting that talking about these will "make it go away."

Education of both child and family members about risk factors and mood disorders as illnesses is a critical intervention. Conversations and printed material, particularly self-help literature and information from the American Psychiatric Association and the American Academy of Child and Adolescent Psychiatry, are useful.

Negotiating a "plan for safety" ("If you were to feel like hurting yourself, what would you do? Could you let someone know? Who? How would you reach them?") helps the child or adolescent learn about affect recognition, communication, and management and provides a concrete measure of readiness for a less-

restrictive level of care. While in a more restrictive environment, such as a hospital or acute residential program, the patient has an opportunity to explore new ways of managing in relation to others. In addition to providing protection from self-harm behavior, staff members of the therapeutic milieu are trained and motivated to talk about the patient's feelings (which may be new discourse for the patient), to offer empathy and support, to mediate crises arising among peers and with family members, and to provide the patient the experience of a culture of acknowledgment and open communication.

Controversies in the Care of Disorders of Childhood and Adolescence

Samariteens

The role of Samaritans or Samariteens, a volunteer, nonprofessional group who offer telephone conversation to self-identified suicidal individuals, is under debate. Some suicidologists believe that the Samaritans offer a valuable service, whereas others view their efforts as futile at best or, at the very least, as interference with the effective professional intervention given to patients with serious clinical disorders.

Public Education

The risks and benefits of public education regarding suicide are also controversial. One school of thought argues for increasing public awareness, whereas another side points out the risks that can arise from a journalistic or cinematic portrayal of suicides and of copy-cat suicide. This is the so-called Werther phenomenon, which was named after the protagonist in Goethe's novel of the 1780s that inspired a wave of imitative suicides throughout Europe. Still another view is that that the models used in suicide-prevention education programs, which identify suicidal behavior as the product of accumulating stress impinging on an undifferentiated population, are at odds with increasing scientific evidence pointing to those with diagnosable mood disorders as the at-risk group (5).

Preventive Interventions

This treatment is also controversial. Early data show efficacy of preventive intervention in promoting adaptation, which may reduce the risk of subsequent depression or mood disorder in children of parents with major mood disorder (6). Further demonstration of the efficacy of this concept is needed but is difficult to obtain when the interval between intervention and later symptomatic behavior is very lengthy.

Involuntary Treatment

Ethical concerns relating to involuntary treatment of children and adolescents is less controversial than with adults. The hospitalization of teen-agers with adjustment problems (including those with mood disorders) is highly controversial, particularly treatment given in proprietary facilities. In the recent past, such practices led to civil investigations and stiff penalties.

Several other aspects of clinical practice are also controversial, including maintaining a balance between confidentiality and disclosure of clinical information regarding at-risk behaviors to parents, other clinicians, or schools; using nonhospital residential facilities instead of hospitals, either to divert patients from the hospital setting prematurely or to use the facility as a less-restrictive level of care if clinical care is inadequate to meet the needs of the patient; the necessary discontinuing of relationships as patients move from one facility to another; and, in all facilities, using restraint or seclusion to protect the self-endangering patient. The frequency with which a patient is restrained or secluded reflects not only the severity of the condition but the philosophy and skill development of the particular program. Typically, success in implementing psychological "holding"—through the daily program, the attitudes and skills of the clinical and direct care staff, and the attention to countertransference to patients—is accompanied by decreased use of physical holding, restraint, and seclusion.

Course and Prognosis

Suicidal ideation occurs at a rate of 12% in children and 53% in adolescents and carries a significant risk. Throughout adolescence, thoughts of suicide and suicidal behavior increase. Among depressed preadolescent outpatients, 18% will attempt suicide within the next 7 years. Identification of individuals at risk is difficult: 50% of those completing suicide had no previous attempt, and 50% had no prior mental health contact. However, two thirds of adolescents who succeeded in committing suicide had expressed suicidal thoughts, and many are more likely than controls to have consulted a physician in the recent past.

DISRUPTIVE BEHAVIOR

Definition

Assaultive, disruptive, or unmanageable behavior is one of the most important and most frequently referred problems in child and adolescent psychiatry. Rather than depending on the judicial system to manage such children, modern psychiatry emphasizes the subjective experience of the child. Clinicians must identify any *Diagnostic and Statistical Manual* (DSM) diagnosable disorder and treat it like other DSM disorders.

The disruptive behavior of a child or adolescent is defined contextually; the definition is relative to and dependent on the perspective of adults. The fourth edition of the DSM (DSM-IV) (7) groups familiar diagnoses like attention-deficit/hyperactivity disorders (ADHD) (inattentive, impulsive, or combined types) and conduct disorders (CD) (beginning in childhood or adolescence) with oppositional defiant disorder (ODD), which is marked by negative and uncooperative behavior. These disorders and the mood disorders, especially major depression and bipolar disorder, overlap considerably.

Diagnosis

Diagnostic possibilities among disruptive children include ADHD, CD, and ODD mentioned above, as well as major depression, bipolar disorder, and Tourette's disorder. The clinician must ascertain whether undiagnosed or underappreciated learning disabilities, mental retardation, obsessive-compulsive disorder, psychosis, substance use, posttraumatic symptoms or undetected abuse, neglect, or molestation are part of the problem. Undiagnosed sensory handicaps (auditory or visual) or language impairment may be the first points of intervention for disruptive behavior. Intermittent explosive disorder and panic disorder, more frequently seen in older adolescents and young adults, should also be considered.

Epidemiology

Disruptive behaviors and the disorders contributing to them are common in chil-

dren and adolescents. ADHD occurs in 3–5% of the population; CD occurs in 6–16% of boys and 2–9% of girls; and ODD occurs in 2–16% of children.

Four Questions

Descriptive Diagnosis

Diagnosis begins with an historical characterization of the pattern and sequence of the disruptive behavior(s). Long-standing, stable patterns point to constitutional factors (e.g., ADHD, ODD, mental retardation, learning disability), whereas recent onset disruptive behavior signifies other possibilities (e.g., reactive disorders, mood disorders). Few disruptive behaviors in children and adolescents are contextually independent; the pattern of context variability (home versus school, one class versus another, early versus late in the day, one parent versus another, quiet versus stimulating environment) aids the diagnostician in distinguishing what are the environmental and psychological triggers for disruptive behavior. The clinician must seek data from informants with first-hand knowledge to determine the antecedent of the behavior.

A comprehensive developmental assessment provides an impression of the child's general competence; resilience; long-term success or difficulty in state, mood, and impulse regulation; and degree of identification with responsible self-management. The developmental history usually provided by parents is filtered through their hopes, dreams, and disappointments with the child, their relationships to therapists, and their feelings about the present crisis. The clinician must recognize such a filter and use it to help define the attitudes and behaviors of those caring for the child. If a child is no longer in family custody (i.e., through social services, mental health, or juvenile justice), data from the earlier years may be lacking. However, an attempt should be made to obtain these data and data from current caretakers to give those currently responsible for the child the most complete account of past and current strengths and vulnerabilities.

Ego Defenses and Character Style

Regardless of the categoric disorder (e.g., ADD, ODD, mood disorders), assessment of children with disruptive behavior must be based on ego defenses. Flexibility of defenses, capacity to use aggression adaptively, and ego structure that can withstand frustration characterize children best able to manage themselves and their behavior.

□ CASE EXAMPLE

An 11-year-old boy was hospitalized in crisis after threatening his mother with a knife during an argument and then threatening suicide. He had been out of school for more than 1 year, complaining of academic frustration and teasing by his peers. His mother, a single parent and an immigrant with little facility in English, encouraged her daughter's school attendance but endorsed her son's avoidance of school. She viewed him as vulnerable and potentially explosive. The boy's developmental assessment indicated borderline mental retardation, academic delay, and a limited set of skills that resulted in withdrawal and explosive intimidation. Although possible categoric diagnoses of retardation, mood disorder, and anxiety disorder were considered, equal importance was given to the boy's immature defenses and adaptive rigidity.

□ CASE EXAMPLE

An 11-year-old boy who was a survivor of repeated physical and sexual abuse by his biologic parents and by foster care family members was repeatedly hospitalized from group homes, where his explosive temper and violent responses to confrontation led to injuries of several staff members. Although he was not considered psychotic or even paranoid, he was extremely sensitive to physical challenges and responded violently to "hands-on" management. Although the sequelae of earlier trauma played a part in his sensitivity, no single diagnosis—not a mood, anxiety, or intermittent explosive disorder—captured the brittle defenses against vulnerability and the concurrent susceptibility to overwhelming rage with which he had to contend.

Formulation

The formulation consists of the following factors that contribute to the disruptive behavior requiring intervention:

◆ Biologic factors such as undiagnosed learning or sensory impairments, constitutional high activity and impulsivity (ADHD), untreated mood disorder (unipolar or bipolar), or temporolimbic dysfunction.

◆ Individual developmental factors such as the residue of trauma, poorly integrated anger or aggression, and affective-cognitive factors such as an "easily giving-up" learning and interpersonal style.

◆ Family factors such as inconsistent child management, ambivalent socialization, or outright endorsement of disruptive or criminal behavior; enabling behavior regarding substance use; undetected physical and sexual abuse or neglect; exhaustion as a result of repeated behavioral and emotional turmoil.

♦ School and peer factors such as hazing or an educational mismatch between the child's needs and a school program.

♦ Treatment factors such as the need for external help in impulse control (for example, through juvenile probation through the Child-in-Need-of-Services [CHINS] mechanism) or lack of consensus among treaters.

□ CASE EXAMPLE:
BIOLOGIC AND
INDIVIDUAL FACTORS

A 14-year-old boy with a history of obsessive-compulsive disorder and Tourette's syndrome had tyrannized his family for years. He demanded that they comply with rules related to his contamination fears. He screamed when frustrated and threatened to injure his sisters or mother if thwarted. In addition to the diagnosable disorders listed above, his cognitive style indicated a feeling of helplessness. He was unable to manage his behavior, viewing his "disorders" and current behavior as beyond his control. Individual factors included both the diagnosable disorders and his immaturity in accepting responsibility for his behavior and its effect on his life.

□ CASE EXAMPLE:
FAMILY FACTOR

A 17-year-old girl presented in crisis after being suspended from a private school for repeated erratic and disrespectful conduct. Her parents requested an emergency evaluation, "Because the school requires it." In inappropri-ately high spirits with the girl present, they recounted a history of "troubling incidents" and offered many spontaneous excuses. Later, with their daughter absent, they voiced their serious concern with the girl's long-term labile temper and alcohol abuse. Their ambivalence regarding responsible conduct and their enabling behavior regarding substance use were important factors in helping staff members to treat their daughter effectively.

□ CASE EXAMPLE:
TREATMENT FACTOR

A 12-year-old boy with bipolar disorder was hospitalized after increasingly violent confrontations at home. He had demanding tirades and whining regressions, and his tantrums and their management dominated his family's life. Treatment had been limited to pharmacologic efforts to stabilize the boy's mood and temper, without individual therapy for the boy or concerted efforts to help the parents manage their son or deal with their disappointment with the boy's illness. The treatment approach was considered too limited.

Focal Problem

The definition of the focal problem depends on the referrer. For example, whose distress has brought the child to this level of care? Who is hurting? Once the referrer's perception and agenda are identified, the clinician can define the problem requiring intervention in contextual terms. The effective delineation of a focal problem will describe the level of change required in the disruptive behavior to return the child to school and to family. Clinical staff members, together with those most affected by the behavior, must make the assessment.

□ CASE EXAMPLE

A 16-year-old girl was diagnosed with an organic personality disorder after sustaining a cerebral injury associated with childhood leukemia and its treatment. She was hospitalized after impulsively attempting to jump out a window at a rehabilitation school after a confrontation over school rules. Many treatment approaches were available to the inpatient team—pharmacologic and psychological approaches for the child as well as psychological and educational approaches for the family. In the treatment system at school, a staff consultation enabled a focus on the girl's (and family's) lack of understanding of the rules and the school staff's difficulty recognizing her processing problems. A focused intervention and early return to the school resulted.

Biologic Evaluation

Some disorders that result in disruptive behavior, although presumably neuropsychiatric disorders, are not accessible as yet to quantifiable biologic assessment; consequently, these disorders are defined clinically. This is true of ADHD (for which clinical assessment is the gold standard, despite the use of instruments like the Child Behavior Check List and despite parents' frequent assumption that the physician can test for ADD).

Mood disorders, including bipolar disorder, are also assessed clinically even when a biologic foundation is posited. In temporolimbic dysfunction (sometimes called temporal lobe epilepsy), electroencephalography (EEG)—preferably with depth (sphenoidal) electrodes—supplements the clinical assessment. However, temporolimbic dysfunction may exist despite an apparently "normal" EEG. In suspected substance abuse, toxicologic urine screens and random periodic urine screens are essential. When unacknowledged substance abuse is suspected, the clinician should readily screen for substances with urine testing.

Level of Care

Some children's disruptive crises respond to environmental manipulation without containment in a hospital or residential facility. Temporarily withdrawing the child from school or moving the child to a less-stimulating or less-challenging program within the school may effect a beneficial change. At other times, temporarily allowing an adolescent to live with another family (e.g., with a relative or friend) will achieve the same goal. In protective cases, removing a molesting parent from the home or limiting contact with a molesting parent may be effective. A more restrictive level of care should be used only when necessary, according to the principle of using the least restrictive alternative.

As in the earlier discussion of suicidal behavior, the clinical goal is to stabilize the child for the receiving level of care, not only for the current level.

Transfer to Next Level of Care

The decision to transfer either to a higher or lower level of care depends on the ability of the child and the child's caretakers to change the factors that contribute to the disruptive behavior. At each level of care, the challenge is to anticipate how the child will function at the next level of care and thus be proactively guided in intervention. In this approach, picturing the patient in a less-restrictive level of care shapes the interventions needed to sustain the child in the future.

☐ CASE EXAMPLE

A 10-year-old boy had stabilized his tantrums and aggressive behavior during a brief admission. He became attached to the inpatient staff members and to his peers there. As he prepared for discharge to a therapeutic group home, he presented several requests for privileges, changes of roommates, and new ways to talk about temper management. His disruptive behavior recurred when these requests were taken at face value. A shift in focus was required: discussion focused on the management of events at the group home to which he must go and on the strategies for coping while he "learned the ropes" there. He was able to refocus his energies on where he was going, not on where he was currently. He began working on a "good-bye book" and soon effected a successful transition.

Treatment

Increasing evidence indicates that pharmacologic agents, particularly the stimulants (methylphenidate and dextroamphetamine) in the treatment of ADHD, provide prompt and effective intervention in disruptive behaviors. Nonstimulants such as clonidine and guanfacine are serving an increasing role in the treatment of ADHD disorders and in posttraumatic and Tourette's disorders. These agents are useful as first-line treatment because they act promptly, are easily prescribed, and are well tolerated. Although effective, mood stabilizers (e.g., lithium carbonate, divalproex sodium, and carbamazepine) and the tricyclic antidepressants are more

difficult to prescribe and are less likely to provide immediate relief. In refractory cases, neuroleptics may play a role in managing severely disruptive behavior. ECT has no role in these disorders.

☐ CASE EXAMPLE

A 13-year-old girl with irritability and depressed mood met the criteria for depression. During a 5-day admission to a day hospital, antidepressant therapy was begun and was well tolerated, but did not ameliorate her dysphoria for at least 2 weeks. In the short term, clonidine (0.1 mg by mouth three times a day) produced immediate relief from irritability. The patient, her family, and peers were grateful.

☐ CASE EXAMPLE

A 7-year-old boy was admitted to an acute residential facility after disruptive behavior in school that frightened the other students and teacher. The acute admission resulted in a respite for all parties and for a calm assessment of a rapidly building massive frustration. Several factors were recognized as precipitants to the event; however, acute intervention brought about the recognition of a previously undiagnosed attention-deficit disorder (nonhyperactive type). A trial of methylphenidate (5 mg by mouth twice a day, then 10 mg by mouth twice a day) enabled the boy to return to school with improved functioning.

Alliance and Psychotherapeutic Management

With disruptive children the first intervention includes redefining the child not as "being the problem" (a bad child or just like his jailed father), but as "having a problem." The clinician assesses the family's capacity to develop a more sympathetic view of the child and to ally with treatment.

For some children, a useful acute intervention involves mobilizing adults outside the immediate family who can provide a role model for responsible self-management. Such a role may be played by another family member, a member of the clergy, or a probation officer mobilized through the CHINS system.

Family support takes the form of defining opportunities to help. Criticism or finding fault is not useful. Developing consistent child management approaches at home that combine sympathetic understanding with consensus-developed consequences for behavior can be presented as an opportunity to help a child in need and to control disruptive behavior.

The therapeutic milieu, in hospitals or residential centers, is used according to principles developed by Cotton (8) and Trieschman et al. (9). The milieu first contains behaviors, then helps the child develop alternatives.

Treatment begins with containment, both to give the child a feeling of safety and to interrupt established habits and interactions. Treatment continues with the freely expressed acceptance of the child, combining nurturance with the expression of confidence that the child is worth more than his or her symptoms or reputation. Teaching new ways to cope through modeling and direct skills instruction provides alternatives to the child's familiar behavior patterns. Treatment must be coordinated between office and hospital as well as between individual therapy with the child and work with the family.

◻ **C**ASE **E**XAMPLE

An 11-year-old boy with a background of severe abuse and neglect had been living in a foster home. He was admitted to acute care after becoming combative and making verbal suicide threats. Review of his recent experience in care indicated that major depression had not been recognized and that his interactions with his foster parents had become increasingly oppositional and tense. Although the diagnosis of major depression was appreciated by the foster parents and antidepressant medication was ultimately useful, prompt return to better functioning—with return to the community—was achieved by interventions in the therapeutic milieu. These interventions gave the boy an opportunity to interact with new adults; to "take time" and "back off" from struggles; to have his inner pain (and recently evoked memories of past abuse) acknowledged by the direct care staff, with time provided for crying and for constructing a "life book"; and to develop his own incentives for better behavior control.

Controversies in the Care of Disruptive Behaviors

Scientific debate continues as to the extent that specific disorders, especially bipolar disorder, contribute to disruptive behavior disorders in childhood. Evidence for the efficacy of antidepressant therapy has been less convincing for children than for adults; nonetheless, good practice now includes offering a therapeutic trial to children meeting criteria for major depression. Early treatment of mood disorders may prevent the neurophysiologic changes (kindling) that result in a worsening of the mood disorder, with repeated and more severe episodes over the course of a lifetime (10).

Disagreement exists as to who should take responsibility for the services needed by children with disruptive behavior. Historically, acute health services, special education services, the juvenile justice system, social services, and mental health services have all participated (11). An integration of efforts has been difficult to achieve, particularly as different departments within state government, state government as a whole, private insurance carriers, and managed care organizations—all operating under the slogans of efficiency, privatization, and market competition—take advantage of the historical diffusion of responsibility for children's services to "cost-shift" to someone else's budget. Such opportunistic and short-sighted maneuvers do not reflect the value that society must place on delivering care to the next generation.

Recent developments to counter these tendencies include the "system of care" model implemented in Ventura County, California, the nationwide Child and Adolescent Service System Program (CASSP) funded by the National Institute of Mental Health (NIMH), and the service innovation promoted by the Robert Wood Johnson Foundation and the Center for Mental Health Services of the NIMH (11).

"Carving out" mental health services from other health services, particularly when cost reduction is the main goal, has made service coordination and integration more difficult.

The use of stimulants in ADHD has been controversial. The use of these agents is frequent and highly variable, both internationally and within every country. Ideologic criticisms from such groups as the scientologists has affected the public attitude; however, increasing evidence attesting to the efficacy of the drugs, and the benefits of years of success as opposed to years of failure, have been more important. In general, because the stimulants (when useful) are so dramatically effective, they should not be prescribed for "soft" efficacy. The medication should be discontinued unless significant benefit is achieved.

Course and Prognosis

For many children, disruptive behavior disorders carry a lifetime burden of mood and affect lability and unstable personal relationships at home and at work. Prognosis depends on early identification of contributing factors and their remediation.

REFERENCES

1. Slap GB, Vorters DF, Khalid N, Margulies SR. Adolescent suicide attempters: do physicians recognize them? J Adolesc Health 1992;12:286–292.
2. Clark DC. Suicidal behavior in childhood and adolescence: recent studies and clinical implications. Psychiatr Ann 1993;23:271–283.
3. Brent DA, Perper JA, Allman CJ. Alcohol, firearms, and suicide among youth: temporal trends in Allegheny County, Pennsylvania, 1960 to 1983. JAMA 1987;257:3369–3372.
4. Bertagnoli MW, Borchardt CM. Case Study: A review of ECT for children and adolescents. J Am Acad Child Adolesc Psychiatry 1990;29:302–307.
5. Garland A, Shaffer D, Whittle B. A national survey of school-based, adolescent suicide prevention programs. J Am Acad Child Adolesc Psychiatry 1898;28:931–934.
6. Beardslee WR, Wright E, Rothberg PC, et al. Response of families to two preventive intervention strategies: long-term differences in behavior and attitude change. J Am Acad Child Adolesc Psychiatry 1996;35:774–782.
7. American Psychiatric Association. Diagnostic and statistical manual of mental disorders. 4th ed. Washington, DC: American Psychiatric Association, 1994.
8. Cotton N. Lessons from the lion's den: thera-

peutic management of children in psychiatric hospitals and treatment centers. San Francisco: Jossey-Bass, 1993.

9. Trieschman AE, Whittaker JK, Brendtro LK. The other 23 hours. Chicago: Aldine, 1969.

10. Post AM. Transduction of psychosocial stress into the neurobiology of recurrent affective disorder. Am J Psychiatry 1992;149:999–1010.

11. England MJ, Cole RF. Building systems of care for youth with serious mental illness. Hosp Community Psychiatry 1992;43:630–633.

Chapter 14

Borderline and Antisocial Personality Disorders

Joseph Triebwasser and Lloyd I. Sederer

BORDERLINE PERSONALITY DISORDER: DEFINITION

Borderline personality disorder (BPD) is a persistent disturbance in the ability to manage affects, tolerate aloneness, sustain stable and trusting relationships, and control self-destructive impulses (1, 2). The intermittent inability of BPD patients to maintain physical safety periodically forces others to see to their safety. Although the term "borderline" was used as early as the 1930s to denote patients who oscillated between neurotic and psychotic levels of functioning, the contemporary BPD concept—as clarified in the 1970s by Gunderson, Kernberg, and others—refers instead to a consistent set of dysfunctional traits and symptoms (3–5). Although BPD patients have unstable affects, behaviors, and object relations, these vulnerabilities show stability over time. For this reason, BPD patients have sometimes been called "stably unstable" (6).

Patients with BPD can present a chal-lenge, given their impulsivity, rage, and externalization of responsibility for their circumstances and behaviors. The primitive defense mechanisms seen in BPD can elicit feelings of guilt, anger, and self-doubt even in the most experienced treaters (2, 7). In cases involving multiple clinicians, BPD patients have a remarkable ability to evoke strong, intense conflicts within a treatment team (8, 9). These challenges are heightened by the ever-present risk of suicide and the manipulative and provocative behavior that BPD patients exhibit regarding this risk.

DIAGNOSIS

According to the *Diagnostic and Statistical Manual*, 4th edition (DSM-IV) (1), the diagnostic criteria for BPD involve a pervasive pattern of instability of interpersonal relationships, self-image, and affects as well as significant impulsivity (beginning by early adulthood and present in a variety of contexts) as indicated by five (or more) of the following:

1. Frantic efforts to avoid real or imagined abandonment (note: this criterion is distinct from suicidal or self-mutilating behaviors, which are included in Criterion 5).
2. A pattern of unstable and intense interpersonal relationships characterized by alternating extremes of idealization and devaluation.
3. Identity disturbance, defined as a significantly and persistently unstable self-image or sense of self.
4. Impulsivity in at least two areas that are potentially self-damaging (e.g., spending, sex, substance abuse, reckless driving, binge eating) (note: this criterion also does not include suicidal or self-mutilating behaviors covered in Criterion 5).
5. Recurrent suicidal behavior, gestures, or threats or self-mutilating behavior.
6. Affective instability due to a significant reactivity of mood (e.g., intense episodic dysphoria, irritability, or anxiety usually lasting a few hours and only rarely more than a few days).
7. Chronic feelings of emptiness.
8. Inappropriate, intense anger or difficulty controlling anger (e.g., frequent displays of temper, constant anger, or recurrent physical fights).
9. Transient, stress-related paranoid ideation or severe dissociative symptoms.

EPIDEMIOLOGY

The prevalence of BPD in the United States is considered to be 3–5%; the rate of diagnosis (2:1 to 4:1) is much higher in women than in men (1, 10, 11). BPD patients tend to be high utilizers of mental health resources, so that the disorder is highly prevalent among clinical populations, especially in psychiatric acute care settings (10, 12).

THE FOUR QUESTIONS

Descriptive Diagnosis

BPD affects a large and heterogeneous population, ranging from mildly symptomatic patients perplexed about identity issues to profoundly disturbed individuals unable to function independently. Many clinicians have developed mental images of the subgroup of BPD patients most likely to present for acute psychiatric care. These images often are accurate, but they may also be drawn from the powerful and often unpleasant emotional responses that some BPD patients evoke (13).

Although recognizing and assessing a clinician's emotional reactions to a patient can be a useful tool in evaluation and treatment, the DSM-IV criteria should be the basis for arriving at diagnoses.

Differential Diagnosis

Substance-Related Disorders

Acute intoxication or chronic dependence on psychoactive substances can mimic almost any psychiatric condition, including BPD. In particular, the volatility, manipulativeness, and chaotic life circumstances of many substance-dependent patients can resemble the clinical picture seen in BPD patients (14). Certain substance-dependent patients who function on a borderline level while actively "using" demonstrate a more mature personality structure after prolonged abstinence. For this reason, clinicians should avoid assigning a definitive diagnosis of BPD in the absence of information about the patient's clinical presentation during a sustained drug- and alcohol-free period (15).

Psychotic Disorders

BPD patients' episodes of "micropsychotic" or "quasipsychotic" thinking can resemble symptoms of schizophrenia and related psychotic syndromes. However, the thought disturbance in BPD is generally transient and rarely involves highly complex, bizarre, or elaborate delusions. BPD patients' hallucinations frequently involve visual percepts and often have a recognizable basis in the patient's emotional life (e.g., seeing a beloved, deceased grandmother waving and beckoning). Also, although object relations in BPD are stormy, BPD patients are usually markedly more interpersonally related than schizophrenic patients.

Mood Disorders

The dysphoria and suicidal ideation in BPD can resemble the core symptoms of major depressive disorder, and BPD patients' reactivity to situational and interpersonal stressors can parallel the rejection sensitivity seen in atypical depression (see Chapter 6). The anger and affective instability of BPD patients can be mistaken for the irritability and lability of bipolar disorder (see Chapter 8). Furthermore, when the mood shifts in BPD occur quickly, they can resemble the mood swings of patients with rapid cycling bipolar disorder. These areas of similarity and overlap between BPD and mood disorders have prompted some researchers to suggest that BPD is, in fact, an atypical or attenuated presentation of a chronic affective disturbance (16–22).

However, certain clinical features are more typical of BPD than of a mood disorder, and their presence suggests the need to consider BPD, even in patients with a known affective illness. These features include a history of persistent functional disturbance since adolescence; a chronic history of active or, more usually, passive suicidal ideation (patients with BPD, but not an uncomplicated mood disorder, are likely to report having felt suicidal "all the time" or "for as long as I can remember"); a history of repetitive hospitalizations for suicide risk or attempts; and a history of self-mutilation in the absence of suicidal intent.

Conversely, the coexistence of a mood disorder in a BPD patient should be suspected if prominent neurovegetative symptoms or persistent, elaborate psychotic symptoms are present. Uncomplicated BPD does not cause a prolonged, decreased need for sleep, which should suggest mania or an organic condition such as substance intoxication.

Dissociative Disorders

Because many BPD patients use dissociation as a defense, a number suffer from dissociative disorders (including dissociative identity disorder, which was formerly called multiple personality disorder).

BPD by itself does not cause patients to experience significant periods of "lost" time or to undergo sudden, dramatic changes in name or appearance. Uncomplicated dissociative disorders do not involve self-mutilation and manipulative suicide attempts. If one of a dissociative identity disorder patient's "alters" meets the criteria for BPD, then the diagnosis of BPD should be assigned.

BPD and Comorbidity

DSM-IV's multi-axial system encourages clinicians to avoid an "either-or" approach to psychiatric diagnoses. Instead, it urges clinicians to be as inclusive as necessary. This is especially relevant to patients with BPD, who have a high frequency of co-morbid Axis I and II mental disorders (23–27).

Ego Defenses and Character Style

BPD patients have an immature character structure marked by deficits and conflicts suggestive of a failure to achieve the developmental goals of the first 3 years of life (28). Early writings about BPD sought a pathogenic explanation in insufficiently stable or nurturing parents (28–31). More recent literature has emphasized biologic and constitutional factors, as well as a putative relationship between BPD and a history of childhood physical or sexual abuse (32, 33).

Symptomatic BPD patients demonstrate primitive defense mechanisms and a paucity of adaptive ones. Certain defenses are especially associated with, although not limited to, BPD patients. These include splitting, projective identification, devaluation, and primitive idealization (5). Other less-specific, maladaptive defenses that BPD patients use extensively include denial of unpleasant realities, dissociation, and projection. Projective defenses can lead to a mistrustful and even paranoid stance toward others (including treaters).

Formulation

Although BPD patients' decompensations may seem to happen "on their own" or "out of the blue," they more commonly occur in the context of specific life stressors. An acute care treatment team can identify these stressors and respond to them with focused interventions.

The lives of BPD patients tend to be chaotic and crisis-ridden, which stems in part from the instability of their affects and object relations. Moreover, their difficulty managing anger can lead to failures and rageful outbursts at work and home. Impulsivity and deficits in mature defenses lead to poor decision-making and contingency planning. Difficulties forming attachments and understanding others' efforts at autonomy interfere with parenting skills.

Comorbid psychopathology contributes to BPD patients' situational difficulties. For example, substance abuse impairs functioning in all spheres and causes medical and legal problems. Eating disorders cause physical fragility, and shame associated with this behavior fosters social isolation. Likewise, dissociative symptoms can lessen a patient's ability to function occupationally or interpersonally.

Focal Problems

When caring for a BPD patient, a treatment team must rapidly define and reach a consensus on the goals for the current episode of care. At least five key parties should participate in the consensus: the patient, the acute care clinical team, the referring clinician (or clinical team), the patient's family or significant other, and the payer. Unanimity is especially important with BPD patients because of their tendency to split and project.

The team must distinguish between goals that seem attractive or desirable and those that are necessary prerequisites for discharge. The latter category, goals that must be accomplished before the patient leaves acute care, should share at least three characteristics: they should be realistic, clinical (not situational or environmental), and almost always relate clearly and directly to the reduction of suicide risk.

The acute care team should encourage the patient, family, and referring clinician to focus on realistic goals and should discourage preoccupation with or pursuit of elusive or unattainable goals. To accomplish this focus, the acute care team may need (1) to emphasize repeatedly that expectations should be limited during the current care episode and (2) to urge patients and families not to pin their hopes on one outcome alone. The patient and family should be reminded to operate exclusively within the realm of available options (even if those options are imperfect) and not to expect ideal solutions.

The clinical team may need to emphasize its own limitations. A BPD patient's transference to a clinician or clinical team may include attributing to them exaggerated, almost magical power. In such a situation, the patient may not understand, for example, that an inpatient social worker cannot force a partial hospital program to accept the patient or force a family to take the patient back into their home.

Treatment goals should focus on clinical issues rather than on the relief of situational or environmental stressors. Although treaters may appropriately try to ameliorate problematic external circumstances (e.g., family discord, housing difficulties) during an acute episode of care, discharge should never be contingent on resolving these problems. The constraints inherent in trying to control others, as well as the potential to reinforce BPD patients' tendencies to externalize responsibility for their predicaments, make the clinical focus more attainable.

Reduction of suicide risk means that the patient is either no longer intent on dying or has sufficient control over his or her suicidal intentions to take responsibility for personal safety. This is an internal psychological event; the treatment team must remember (and remind the patient and family when necessary) that the decision to live or die belongs to the patient.

To this end, it is useful to avoid identifying an external stressor as the cause of a BPD patient's suicidal ideation or behavior; rather, it is preferable to say that the stressor "precipitated," "was involved in," or "led up to" the suicidal intent. Similarly, the sentence, "The patient became suicidal because his therapist went on vacation," is less accurate than, "The patient became suicidal after his therapist went on vacation."

Just as suicide risk is not caused directly by external events, it is also not made inevitable by a dysphoric mood state. Subjective improvement in mood should not be the chief criterion for discharging a BPD patient from acute care; the patient may remain dysphoric longer than the acute episode of care. BPD patients must be made aware of the possibility of being dysphoric without becoming actively suicidal. BPD patients who fail to understand this concept often enter a pattern of frequent and lengthy hospitalizations, which contribute to regression and render the patient less able to maintain safety without institutional support. Specific situations (which involve the patients' own actions) that frequently serve as precipitants for BPD patients' decompensations include:

♦ Noncompliance with medications.
♦ Use of alcohol or illicit drugs.
♦ Ejection from a living situation (e.g., home, halfway house) because of acting out.
♦ Legal difficulties.

Relapse prevention in such cases may be furthered by:

♦ Changing the nature or mode of administration of the patient's medications to make compliance easier.

- Clarifying ground rules or expectations necessary for a patient to return to his or her prior living situation through a family or treatment plan.
- Teaching the patient behavioral techniques to avoid destructive or self-destructive behavior.
- Referring the patient to community resources (e.g., a visiting nurse to increase medication compliance, a drug or alcohol rehabilitation center, local volunteer opportunities to help mobilize the patient and reduce regression).

Other precipitants, less clearly related to the patient's own behavior, include:

- Medical problems.
- Illness or death of a family member or friend.
- The need to change a living situation for financial or logistical reasons.
- A change in a medication that may have made the patient worse (e.g., severe side effects, antidepressant-induced hypomanic symptoms, or a disinhibiting benzodiazepine).
- A therapist's (or other treater's) vacation, illness, or termination.

Situations are often corrected with the passage of time (e.g., when a therapist's vacation ends or a harmful medication is metabolized). When required, intervention by the treatment team may involve referral to community resources (e.g., an aftercare mental health provider or internist, a support group for relatives of the terminally ill, or services for the homeless).

If the focal problem involves outpatient treatment, a consultation by the acute care team can be useful. For example, a therapist whose vacation triggered a decompensation may benefit from advice about planning for the next vacation or, more importantly, focusing more effectively on the patient's dependency and abandonment issues.

BIOLOGIC EVALUATION

No known physical or laboratory abnormality is specific to BPD.

Physical examinations should include inspecting the skin for possible complications of self-mutilation (e.g., infections or excessively wide or deep cuts) and checking for tetanus. Presence of visible cuts or scars should be recorded, because even the referring treatment team may be unaware of the extent of the problem.

Laboratory and other specific studies should be obtained when clinically indicated. Examples include a suspected overdose, suspected recent substance abuse, active bulimia or anorexia nervosa, and behavioral or mental status findings that are a significant departure from the patient's norm or that cannot be explained by psychopathology alone. Certain clinical circumstances (e.g., a wish to rule out porphyria or complex-partial seizures) may warrant a more elaborate workup. In most cases, however, nonemergency tests can be performed on an ambulatory basis.

ASSESSING LEVEL OF CARE

Assessing Suicide Risk

The decision regarding the level of care for a BPD patient is based primarily on the level of suicide risk (34). Clinicians should distinguish between a passive wish to die ("passive suicidality") and an active intention to kill oneself ("active suicidality"). In the acute care setting treaters should focus on active suicidality, which is a psychiatric emergency, rather than on passive suicidality, which is rarely (if ever) an indication for acute containment. Active suicidality should not be confused with the presence of a suicide plan. Although the latter may be an ominous harbinger of risk, it may represent nothing more than a patient's fantasized way of dying. Many BPD patients have suicide plans for years but never act on them. The determinant of suicide risk is active intent, not passive wishes or fantasies.

There is also a distinction between "suicidal" and "parasuicidal" behavior. Parasuicidal behavior refers to physically self-destructive acts (e.g., cutting or burning one's skin) that are not intended to be lethal and that patients do not view as suicide attempts. Parasuicidal behavior, in the absence of suicidal intent, is generally not an indication for acute care; exceptions include self-mutilation that is medically dangerous or a new onset or alarming increase in parasuicidal behavior.

When relating his or her history, a BPD patient consciously or unconsciously may omit information vital to the assessment of suicide risk. The evaluating clinician should seek other sources of information, including the obvious informants (family, friends, referring treaters), witnesses to the patient's behavior, or statements that prompted the referral to acute care. The evaluating clinician should also check all recent case documents (e.g., police reports and emergency department notes) for worrisome information that otherwise might remain unnoticed.

Safety contracts with BPD patients must be evaluated carefully before being accepted as valid, and trust should be based on at least two judgments: whether the patient is able to accurately gauge and communicate his or her level of risk, and whether the alliance is sufficiently reliable to prevent the patient from knowingly misleading the treater.

A BPD patient's assurances of safety should be disbelieved or at least questioned when clinicians also observe:

♦ Worrisome or provocative hints about suicide.

♦ Statements by the patient to family, friends, or fellow patients that contradict those the patient has made to staff members.

♦ A markedly hostile or fearful attitude toward treaters, which casts doubt on the patient's ability to communicate accurately or openly.

♦ Prominent expressions of hopelessness, especially when combined with an inability to speak about the future.

A BPD patient can be treated in a nonsecure setting only with consistent and convincing assurances of safety. Any residual suicidal ideation must be passive, not active, and the patient must be confident that if the suicidal ideation were to become active again, he or she would seek appropriate help before acting. Generally, clinicians should not accept as convincing a patient's statement about "trying" to access help before attempting suicide; instead, the question should be whether the patient predicts that he or she would definitely seek help before attempting suicide.

Because evidence indicates that concurrent substance abuse or depression increases the risk of suicide in BPD patients, clinicians should look for and treat these comorbid conditions (35–37). It is unclear how this concept can be incorporated in assessing long-term individual risk. For example, little evidence demonstrates that treating a comorbid depression reduces a BPD patient's lifetime suicide risk.

Although clinicians should be aware that comorbidity represents an increased risk, an overemphasis on this risk may lead to unnecessary hospitalizations and ensuing iatrogenic problems. Treaters cannot and should not hospitalize all or even most BPD patients with concurrent substance abuse or depression. Nor is it feasible or advisable to delay the discharge of already hospitalized BPD patients until their depression resolves. Extra weeks (or months) in the hospital may increase the long-term risk of suicide if the patient's level of adaptive functioning diminishes during hospitalization.

Levels of Care

Clinicians should try to triage a BPD patient to the least-restrictive setting available, that is, a setting that is the least intensively staffed and that gives the patient the most responsibility for his or her safety and self-care (see Chapter 4).

Locked Inpatient Units

A locked holding unit may be the best initial disposition for a BPD patient requiring acute containment. The patient's active suicidal intent may be transient, and suicide risk may diminish to an acceptable level within hours or 1–2 days.

If a patient's suicide risk persists despite clinical interventions and the passage of time, the patient may need referral for continued locked-door care. Locked inpatient units are indicated for patients who are at acute risk for serious self-harm or escape from the treatment setting or whose level of agitation requires secure containment. A locked unit is needed when the following symptoms are present:

◆ Inability to give consistent or convincing assurances of safety.
◆ A history of recent suicide attempts with high degrees of intent or of suicide attempts in treatment settings.
◆ A history of escape or behavioral dyscontrol while in treatment settings.
◆ A high degree of physical agitation.

Unlocked Inpatient Units

Unlocked inpatient units are indicated for patients who do not require a locked unit but who would be at substantial risk for rapid decompensation if triaged directly to the community. Although many such patients can be referred to an acute residential program (see below), others may be ineligible for immediate residential treatment for reasons that might include:

◆ A history before admission of significant medication noncompliance—most acute residential programs will not treat patients who do not take their medications reliably.
◆ A history before admission of refusal to attend groups or other prescribed treatment—for clinical and financial reasons, many residential programs will not treat patients who will not participate readily in assigned activities.
◆ Acute medical problems that require 24-hour nursing care—many acute residential programs are understaffed and will not accept patients who may require urgent medical attention.
◆ A judgment that the patient's condition is so fragile that greater staff support is necessary than that offered by a residential program.

Acute Residential Programs

Acute residential programs are used for patients in crisis who do not appear actively unsafe and who meet the residential program's requirements for admission (see above). A patient is referred to an acute residential program rather than to outpatient treatment alone for the following reasons: recent multiple presentations to acute care despite an intensive outpatient program, and an unsupportive or actively destructive home environment (e.g., an abusive relationship, drug or alcohol use in the household, or a marked absence of social supports) that puts the patient at high risk for immediate relapse.

Shelters or Other Community Domiciles

For the patient whose primary difficulties are situational, referral to a shelter or other community domicile rather than to a treatment setting may be indicated. Reasons for this level of care include the following: the inadequacies of the home environment seem likely to be chronic; if the patient recently has had multiple, unfruitful residential placements for the same problems; and dysfunction in the home environment appears to be the only active treatment issue or the only reason the patient is in acute care. Payers typically do not reimburse for inpatient or residential treatment if the only problem is the lack of an adequate domicile.

Outpatient Treatment

Direct referral to outpatient treatment can occur if living outside a treatment setting will not place the patient at active risk for suicide or immediate relapse.

An ongoing outpatient treatment may benefit from a consultation by the acute care team. Should the need arise to intensify the outpatient program, potential interventions include:

◆ Increased frequency of clinical contacts.
◆ Referral to a partial hospital program.
◆ Referral to a rehabilitation program.
◆ Referral to a "drop-in center" or "social club."
◆ Participation in self-help groups.

When the patient's social isolation appears to have contributed to the decompensation, enhancement of social supports may also help to prevent future relapse.

TREATMENT

General Principles

BPD is a chronic condition in which patients have deficits in their ability to maintain responsibility for their physical safety. The goal of treatment is to help BPD patients resume this responsibility and retain it over the long term. Interventions that are "responsibility enhancing" contribute to this goal, whereas "responsibility depriving" interventions militate against it (38).

A BPD patient enters into acute psychiatric care because clinicians consider this step necessary to save the patient's life. Because a treater or institution assumes the patient's self-preservatory functions, acute psychiatric care carries with it the risk of iatrogenic toxicity. Responsibility-depriving interventions can reduce the patient's wish or ability to maintain responsibility for his or her safety.

Although the risk of fostering a BPD patient's regression and dependency can never be eliminated, it can be reduced. Means of doing so are to keep acute care stays as brief and as focused as clinically possible and to hold the patient responsible for his or her actions as much as is clinically reasonable. The clinical focus for the patient should aim for symptom and problem management and impulse control. Open-ended psychological exploration should be avoided in favor of a practical approach to improving the patient's safety status. Treatment should focus more on controlling behavior than on understanding it and more on improving behavior than on improving the patient's mood.

Treaters should not judge an acute episode of care to be a success simply because a BPD patient addresses "important" issues, memories, or affects, because this action can be destabilizing for these patients and thereby impairs clinical recompensation. The effectiveness of an acute episode of care should be judged by the speed with which it enables the patient to be discharged safely from acute care, to engage in aftercare, and most important to remain out of acute care in the future.

Psychopharmacology

No single, generally accepted pharmacologic algorithm exists for treating the symptoms of BPD, and no Food and Drug Administration (FDA)-approved medication is available specifically for this disorder (39). Overall, BPD tends to be less responsive to somatic interventions than mood and anxiety disorders; in BPD patients with comorbid Axis I disorders, the BPD will adversely affect the medication responsiveness of the Axis I symptoms (40–42). However, because many BPD patients do respond (at least partially) to medications and because of the high morbidity and mortality of the disorder, many clinicians consider the potential benefits of judicious medication trials in BPD to outweigh the risks.

In the acute care treatment of BPD, the primary role of medications is to help calm agitated patients and enable them to regain control of their behavior. Other medication interventions, such as trials of antidepressants or mood stabilizers, can be started during acute care, but their delayed onset of action precludes their helpfulness as emergency interventions.

Many BPD patients in outpatient treatment are already in the midst of medication trials when they present to acute care. The acute care psychiatrist should collaborate and consult with the ambulatory care psychiatrist, resisting the temptation to discontinue an outpatient regimen and start over. This temptation may stem from the desperation (and impatience) with which the patient asks for a medication change, which can create a split between the acute care and ambulatory teams. A reasonable outpatient medication algorithm should not be interrupted unless there is a compelling clinical reason to do so.

Antipsychotic Agents

Antipsychotics are among the best studied and most useful medications for BPD patients (43). Among the symptoms shown to be reduced by these agents are "micropsychotic" symptoms, impulsivity, self-destructiveness, and, significantly, dysphoric mood (44–49).

Antipsychotic agents administered either orally or intramuscularly can be used in the acute management of BPD patients to help reduce agitation or panic. Their benefits (i.e., effectiveness, nonaddictiveness, low risk of disinhibition) should be weighed against their disadvantages (which include a long half-life, the risk of dystonic reactions, akathisia, neuroleptic malignant syndrome, and tardive dyskinesia). As a rule, it is best to use benzodiazepines and antihistamines as acute anxiolytics, sedatives, or chemical restraints before turning to neuroleptics.

Evidence shows that clozapine, like the traditional antipsychotic agents, can be useful in the treatment of BPD (50). Clinical experience suggests that clozapine can help even those patients who have been refractory to other medication interventions, although BPD patients who show a dramatic response to clozapine tend to be those who also meet criteria for schizoaffective disorder.

Antidepressant Agents

Many if not most BPD patients presenting for acute care meet the criteria for major depression. However, the presence of concurrent major depression does not necessarily predict the patient's response to antidepressant medications (48, 49). There is evidence that tricyclic antidepressants (TCAs) are not as effective as antipsychotics in relieving BPD symptoms, including dysphoria, and may cause clinical worsening in some cases (48, 49, 51).

Fluoxetine has become a popular agent in this patient population because of ease of administration, relative paucity of side effects, and low lethality if taken in overdose. There is some promising research on fluoxetine in BPD (52–54). Fluoxetine's relatively high cost can be a deterrent to its use; however, the overall cost of a course of fluoxetine (or other recently introduced serotonin reuptake inhibitors) may be lower than that of an older antidepressant because administering a medication with greater side effects and medical risks may require extra blood tests, electrocardiograms (ECGs), or referral to an internist.

Patients and family members may be aware of the controversy triggered by a 1990 report that associated fluoxetine with increased suicide risk (55). However, subsequent studies have shown, to the satisfaction of most clinicians, that fluoxetine is no more likely than other antidepressants to make patients more suicidal, and that some apparent cases of fluoxetine-induced suicide risk were due to untreated side effects (56–63). Nonetheless, because BPD patients have a tendency to look for external causes to explain their difficulties, clinicians should mention the claim that fluoxetine can worsen suicide risk and should explain the rationale for prescribing it for these patients.

Because BPD may exhibit a phenotypic similarity with atypical depression, which has been shown to respond preferentially well to monoamine oxidase inhibitors (MAOIs) (64), these agents can be useful in BPD. However, few BPD patients who present regularly for acute care have sufficient impulse control for the safe prescription of MAOIs, and clinicians should generally be wary of using MAOIs in this population.

Mood Stabilizers

Lithium, which is prescribed to many BPD patients, has received surprisingly little study in this population. There is evidence that lithium can help decrease irritability and lability in some patients (65). The anticonvulsants, carbamazepine and valproic acid, have shown some efficacy in reducing impulsivity and behavioral dyscontrol (66, 67).

Benzodiazepines

Anxious BPD patients who are given benzodiazepines usually report subjective improvement, although one study using alprazolam found an increase in impulsivity (68). Because of this possible disinhibiting effect and BPD patients' high risk of substance abuse or dependence, the prescription of maintenance benzodiazepines to BPD patients should be undertaken cautiously. This is especially true in view of the benzodiazepines' potential lethality if discontinued abruptly or taken in overdose, particularly in combination with alcohol.

Benzodiazepines administered either orally or intramuscularly play an important role in the management of acutely anxious or agitated BPD patients. If a patient is dangerously agitated, benzodiazepines can be used even if the patient has a history of abuse or dependence, although a clinician might first test whether antihistamines alone are effective. The benzodiazepine should be discontinued or tapered once the emergency has resolved.

The Therapeutic Milieu

A well-regulated treatment milieu can further a BPD patient's recompensation, just as a poorly functioning milieu can impede it. A treater's firm but fair insistence that the patient meet basic behavioral expectations can be the most effective avenue toward enhanced control over impulsive behavior and a chaotic inner world (69, 70).

To meet the needs of BPD patients, milieu rules and regulations should be:

- Achievable.
- Clearly stated to the patient and family as early in the treatment encounter as clinically sensible.
- Consistently articulated and implemented by members of the treatment team, without significant discrepancies from one treater to another.
- Internally consistent.
- Geared toward promoting adaptive behaviors and discouraging regression.

While in the treatment milieu, patients should be asked to conform to the behavioral standards of normal adult society. This creates a safe and reassuring environment for patients and staff and indicates to the patient that the role of acute care treatment is to prepare for a return to the outside world, not for further acute care treatment.

In arriving at specific milieu rules and policies, treatment teams should observe a hierarchy of priorities:

- Patients must not compromise their safety or that of staff members or other patients—in addition to not behaving assaultively or suicidally, patients must not sequester contraband (such as medications, alcohol, or sharp objects) on the unit (in eating disordered patients, failure to maintain adequate food and fluid intake can also be considered a safety issue).
- Patients must demonstrate decency—when in public areas, they should show respect for themselves by not dressing revealingly or seductively, sobbing for prolonged periods, or engaging in regressed behavior (e.g., walking around with a blanket or stuffed animal); they should also show respect for others by avoiding rude, demeaning, or inconsiderate actions; they should not engage in sustained verbal abuse toward treaters, visitors, or fellow patients and should behave maturely and appropriately during clinical interviews (e.g., not eat, lie on the bed, or sit on the floor).
- Patients must pay attention to basic self-care, including taking responsibility for maintaining personal hygiene and knowing their medication regimen and schedule.
- Patients must care for the environment (e.g., follow trash disposal rules or clean the area after using the bathroom or eating).

Treaters should respond promptly, firmly, and consistently to infractions of important milieu policies. Limit-setting, especially when accompanied by clear explanation and discussion, discourages future acting out and helps the patient accept responsibility for deviant behavior. Limit-setting should always be understood as a negative consequence of acting out, rather than as a punishment, and should always be performed in the interests of furthering the patient's treatment or protecting the community, rather than out of countertransference anger. If the patient's acting out has occurred in the context of a psychotic transference, clinicians should provide reality testing to elicit and correct distorted images of the treatment team.

A common form of limit-setting is the adjustment of "privileges" or "levels of restriction" (i.e., the patient's freedom to leave the unit or hospital grounds). Granting or denying privileges should be based on a thorough assessment of the patient's safety status, clinical condition, and progress toward discharge. Acting out as an indicator of the patient's clinical condition should be included in this assessment; this behavior may be a means of communicating anxiety about discharge. An effective clinical response would not be a restriction of privileges but a clarification of the patient's concerns and continued movement toward discharge.

Limit-setting often angers BPD patients, and they and their families may object strongly to treatment they consider punitive or unfair. In these situations, the treatment team should stand firm regarding reasonable limit-setting, explaining that failure to respond to the acting out would be enabling and countertherapeutic. Acting out often represents the patient's unspoken wish to ascertain that the treatment team cares and is in control, especially when the patient feels out of control. Experience indicates that some BPD patients, including those who bristle and struggle with staff members during an acute episode of care, subsequently are grateful for appropriate limit-setting.

Psychotherapy

Acute care teams can help in the psychotherapeutic treatment of BPD patients in several ways, including assessment and consultation to an ongoing therapy (71, 72), therapeutic referral of patients new to treatment, and psychotherapy in the acute care setting.

Acute care consultations to ongoing therapies are necessarily brief and incomplete. At the very least, the acute care team should screen for fundamental problems such as a regressive transference, a disruptive countertransference, a therapeutic approach that is more stimulating or provocative than the patient can tolerate, and insufficient attention to a key symptom or issue (e.g., substance abuse or unsafe sexual behavior).

If the acute care treaters uncover a significant problem in the psychotherapy, they may recommend consultation or at least a serious rethinking of the psychotherapy around this issue. At other times, supervision may be an important suggestion. Because acute care encounters generally are too brief for this process to reach completion, the psychotherapist can be urged to pursue the team's recommendations after discharge.

In assessing ambulatory psychotherapies of BPD patients, the clinician should bear in mind that the lack of clinical progress may be a reflection of the severity of the disorder rather than any shortcoming in the psychotherapy. Therapists should not be blamed (implicitly or explicitly) for the patient's suicide attempt or acting out. Often, the acute care team's most appropriate contribution to an ongoing therapy is to offer the therapist encouragement and support, including emphasizing areas of clinical progress that may have been overlooked.

A BPD patient who is new to treatment or "between therapists" should be assessed for suitability for psychotherapy and which type of therapy or therapist would be the best match. If the patient is referred to psychotherapy, the follow-up appointment should occur promptly after the discharge from acute care to take advantage of what may be a short-lived period of motivation and cooperativeness. Acute care teams often offer some form of psychotherapy, especially if the treatment episode lasts more than 1 or 2 days (73, 74). For clinical, logistic, and financial reasons, acute care therapy often occurs in a group setting (see Chapter 18).

Acute care psychotherapy in BPD

should focus on practical, concrete issues such as discharge planning, coping skills, relapse prevention, and psychoeducation. The primary questions to be addressed are how can the patient work toward being discharged safely from acute care, and how can the patient work toward remaining out of acute care once discharged. Acute care therapy groups should focus on building adaptive coping skills (e.g., relaxation training, grounding techniques, and anger management). Certain groups may have fairly specific foci (e.g., psychoeducation groups that focus on specific disorders or medications or dual diagnosis groups). Recently, dialectical behavior therapy—a treatment approach incorporating group and individual sessions and emphasizing skill building and avoiding reinforcement of self-destructive behavior—has shown promising results in controlled clinical trials (75–77).

With obvious exceptions, such as gender-oriented groups (i.e., men's group, women's group) or groups designed to orient new patients, all groups should be mandatory for all BPD patients. Because of a tendency to resist a treatment and a propensity for splitting, BPD patients may try to schedule an individual therapy session or meet with a psychiatrist during group time. The team should, with rare exceptions, see this behavior as resistance and actively intervene.

The Treatment Team

Treating BPD patients effectively is one of the most difficult tasks undertaken by a psychiatric acute care team (78, 79). In addition to presenting the usual diagnostic and therapeutic challenges, BPD patients are prone to psychological defenses that can undermine a team's efforts to work together productively (80). Effective multidisciplinary treatment requires not only professional training and expertise on the part of team members, but also psychological insight into and successful management of disruptive individual and group countertransferences.

Certain strategies can be helpful in decreasing the emotional toll that the care of BPD patients can exact on a treatment team. Treatment team members should be familiar with the existence and nature of countertransference and should be able to identify it when it occurs. An emotional response is normal with any clinical population, especially BPD patients. It is considered countertransference, however, if the emotion is out of awareness, out of proportion to the patient's actual behavior or personality, or if it interferes with the quality of care.

The team's treatment philosophy should be clear, coherent, and consistent and should be acceptable to the team members. Inevitably, team members will disagree about specific situations; however, there should be consensus regarding fundamental and frequently recurring issues (e.g., criteria for admission and discharge from acute care, indications for the use of seclusion or isolation, policies regarding privileges or levels of restriction, and when and how to set limits on acting out).

Team members should have well-defined clinical roles, which should be exceeded only in special circumstances; role violations and ambiguous or changing role definitions are common causes of conflicts among clinicians. For example, role violations might include a nonphysician expressing doubt to a patient that a newly added medication will work, or several clinicians independently arranging aftercare for the patient.

Even within the best organized treatment teams, BPD patients occasionally produce sharply divergent emotional responses or clinical opinions. This may be a sign that the team has taken on the patient's problems or conflicts. When frictions arise, the team should identify areas of consensus and agreement as well as decrease the focus on areas of conflict. The team should also designate certain individuals to make final treatment decisions. Information gathering and opinion sharing are the work of the entire team. A clinical decision is ultimately the responsibility of one specific person—the attending psychiatrist who bears medicolegal responsibility for the patient in acute care.

FAMILY SUPPORT, EDUCATION, AND INTERVENTION

Working effectively with a BPD patient's family (or close friends) can be a key factor in the success or failure of a clinical encounter. Often, these patients' relationships with family members are strained, and a family crisis is a common stressor that leads a BPD patient to acute care.

A BPD patient's family difficulties can stem from anger toward family members for allegedly not understanding or helping, difficulty separating from parents and establishing an adult self, family members' anger toward the patient because of a suicide attempt, and the family's frustration with the patient's limitations in functioning.

Treatment teams can help families of BPD patients in three important ways: education, support, and crisis intervention. Education about the patient's symptoms, behaviors, and treatment can help a family respond more effectively and decrease the likelihood of enabling or counterproductive responses. Family education about BPD may touch on several key areas:

- Suicidality—the magnitude of the suicide risk in BPD, the difference between active and passive suicidality, the difference between suicidal and parasuicidal behavior, how to recognize suicidality, and what to do in an emergency.

- The patient's responsibility in suicide prevention—the limitations of a family's (or treatment team's) ability, even on a locked inpatient unit, to prevent the suicide of a patient determined to die; and the eventual unfeasibility of trying to make the patient's everyday world "suicide-proof" (e.g., by locking the medicine cabinet or taking away the patient's car keys).

- Splitting and secrecy—BPD patients' propensity for splitting, the danger inherent in the family's knowledge of clinical information that is not known to the treatment team, the need for the family to convey information about active suicidality to the treatment team even if the patient objects, and the fact that in the long run the patient will be reassured by the family's sharing of potentially life-saving clinical information with treaters.

- Enabling versus health-promoting behaviors—the difference between the patient's request and what is best for the patient, the need for the family to say "no" if the patient's request is detrimental to health or treatment, and the importance of reasonable behavioral expectations to prevent regression.

- Medications—the need for alliance with the prescribing clinician (complying with medications; communication with the prescriber if not complying); the expected delay before newly prescribed medications start working; the need for systematic, adequate medication trials (i.e., dosage, duration); the chance that any given medication will not be effective or the chance that medications in general will be ineffective or only partially effective in alleviating the patient's problems.

♦ The role of acute care and inpatient treatment—the potential for toxicity of acute care or inpatient treatment, given the risks of regression and dependency; and the major focus on short-term suicide prevention (although clinicians should emphasize that the determined patient can succeed anywhere, including on a locked hospital ward).

♦ The role of limit-setting—the need for family (and clinicians) to set limits on acting out, and the need to explain that limit-setting is a behavioral technique (i.e., a consequence for unhealthy behavior) and not a punishment.

Because of the toll that BPD symptoms can take on a patient's family, particularly during a decompensation, families may need significant support from the acute care team.

A team member should be selected to work with the family and to elicit an account of their experiences with the patient, especially the events leading up to the crisis. In addition to providing support and education, meetings with the family may yield potentially vital clinical information. Treaters should listen for signs of a family's guilt in not being able to cure or help the patient. Many families need to be reassured and educated about the extent and limits of their role and responsibility. Families should also be informed about community resources for continued ongoing support.

If a family crisis has precipitated the patient's presentation to acute care, a focused family intervention may be clinically useful. The intervention may consist of arranging a family meeting to lessen tensions and reopen lines of communication. Such a meeting will often result in changing household ground rules or establishing consequences for acting out. These family meetings should focus on resolving immediate conflicts, negotiating compromises, and arriving at guidelines for getting along and continuing the dialogue after discharge. Generally, the meetings should not attempt to probe family dynamics or members' grievances toward one another.

THE DECISION TO TRANSFER TO THE NEXT LEVEL OF CARE

Given the risk for clinical regression and dependency, BPD patients should be transferred to a lower level of care as soon as it is safe and feasible to do so. The most important and, for the clinician, the most anxiety-provoking transfer of a BPD patient is that from a "secure" setting to a "nonsecure setting." This transfer should occur when the patient's risk for suicide or serious self-harm is low enough for the patient to assume primary responsibility for safety. Such a transfer should preferably occur only after the patient, family, acute care treaters, and outside treaters have agreed to the plan. If the decision to move ahead is not unanimous, it should be justified carefully in the clinical record.

When the decision is made to transfer a BPD patient home or to another unsupervised setting, at least one aftercare appointment scheduled by the time of discharge, and at least one clinical contact should occur shortly after discharge. All patients, even those who seem to be at relatively low risk for relapse, should have a "crisis management plan" that the patient and family can understand and accept.

MEDICOLEGAL ISSUES

Perhaps more than any other patient group, BPD patients prompt clinicians to worry about litigation (81, 82). Factors that increase a clinician's anxiety may include:

◆ Concern that a BPD patient's splitting, devaluation, or hostile transference will lead to an unrealistically negative view of the clinician.
◆ Perception that family members do not understand the nature or severity of the patient's disorder or that they themselves engage in borderline defenses.
◆ Fear that a jury would view the clinician's limit-setting as harsh or punitive.
◆ Unconscious guilt and fear of punishment because of hatred in the countertransference (83–85).
◆ Patients' or family members' overt threats of filing a lawsuit.
◆ Recognition that the patient may in fact have a poor outcome.

When malpractice cases involving BPD patients go to court, experience reveals that the term "borderline personality disorder" is rarely used and that the patient's Axis I disorders are typically cited (86). This adds to a clinician's potential liability difficulties because many treatment interventions or techniques appropriate for BPD patients may seem unusual or puzzling in other contexts, such as a court of law.

To safeguard against incurring liability with BPD patients, as with all patients, the clinician should provide good care, seek consultation at times of difficulty, and document care thoroughly and in a timely manner. Clinicians documenting the treatment of a BPD patient can demonstrate their professionalism by using neutral, objective language. Overly euphemistic language can minimize the patient's difficulties, which may make a poor outcome more difficult to explain. Hostile or judgmental language can suggest that the clinician dislikes the patient. Clinicians should emphasize that treatment decisions were based on carefully considered clinical assessments and never solely on patients' reports (including safety contracts) or families' recommendations or requests.

In the medical record, the documentation of important treatment decisions in the care of BPD patients should include:

◆ A detailed (but concise) description of the reasoning process that led to the decision.
◆ A list of the reasons for not choosing an opposite or alternative approach.
◆ When indicated, a corroboration from colleagues who are not directly involved in the case—either through formal (written) consultations or through documenting verbal, curbside consultations (with the consultant's permission).
◆ An acknowledgement that in the subset of BPD patients with chronic active suicidality, there is no risk-free treatment plan; in such cases, the documentation should emphasize the clinician's reasons for believing the treatment plan to be the one with the lowest (although still present) risk.

CONTROVERSIES IN THE CARE OF PATIENTS WITH BPD

Perhaps more than any other area of clinical psychiatry, BPD is fraught with disagreement and controversy. Conflicts among clinicians treating these patients can be heated and emotional and can impede or even reduce the effectiveness of care.

Diagnostic Issues

Clinicians frequently disagree about whether the diagnosis of BPD is warranted in a given patient. Experience indicates that a treater's likelihood of diagnosing BPD often reflects underlying biases or preconceptions. Some clinicians, for example, overdiagnose BPD (finding symptoms in every help-rejecting or otherwise difficult patient), which leads to significant clinical inaccuracies. Emotional responses to a patient should never replace DSM-IV criteria as guides for diagnosis.

Alternatively, a clinician might underdiagnose BPD for the following reasons: belief that the label is judgmental or pejorative; fear that the diagnosis will promote undue pessimism among patients, families, and fellow treaters; fear that the diagnosis will discourage other clinicians from attempting aggressive pharmacotherapy; or belief that Axis II assessments must await resolution of all Axis I symptoms. In the authors' opinion, all the above lines of reasoning can lead to serious error.

Clinicians should not avoid the diagnosis of BPD (which is not a criticism or an insult) for fear of stigmatizing a patient. Treaters should also not feel constrained by a fear of demoralizing the family or fellow clinicians. The former deserve accurate and realistic clinical information, and the latter need to know the full diagnostic profile to provide effective treatment. Furthermore, an accurate diagnosis of BPD should help, not hinder, pharmacologic treatment because the presence or absence of BPD may have profound implications for pharmacologic decision-making.

Clinicians who believe that Axis II assessments must await the full disappearance of Axis I symptoms are probably overinterpreting data about the confounding effects of Axis I symptoms on Axis II diagnoses. In fact, Axis II disorders can often be diagnosed in the presence of significant Axis I symptoms, especially if the evaluator possesses reliable information about the patient's long-term history (87).

Treatment Dilemmas

The Role of Hospitalization

Some clinicians view the hospitalization of BPD patients as an important and helpful treatment modality that provides a safe environment for grappling with painful memories, affects, or psychotherapy issues. Other treaters view hospitalization as a necessary evil, which can cause BPD patients more harm than good over time.

In the authors' opinion, evidence demonstrates that the "necessary evil" model is closer to the truth. The treatment goal for suicidal BPD patients is to help them resume responsibility for their physical safety. Hospitalization, especially if repetitive, inevitably deprives patients of at least some of this responsibility; thus, it is inherently regressive. Although the tendency of a hospitalization to promote regression can be reduced, the risk of regression (and demoralization) is ever present.

The regressiveness of the hospital setting can be one of its principal attractions for BPD patients. The patient may confuse this issue by seeming to struggle against being hospitalized. However, because hospitalization results from a patient's own statements or behaviors, the underlying wish to be contained and cared for is likely present. Unfortunately, the patient's struggle or ambivalence about hospitalization may represent a wish to experience the admission as cruel and coercive rather than a genuine wish to avoid a hospital stay. BPD patients "vote with their feet": repeated hospitalizations most likely indicate that the patient wished to be hospitalized, even if this wish was unstated or unconscious.

Given the inevitable risk that hospital level of care poses for the BPD patient, hospitalization should be kept to a minimum. Once the patient is in the hospital, treatment should be directed toward achieving a safe discharge and reducing the need for a repeat hospitalization.

The Treatment Milieu: Limit-Setting Versus Permissiveness

Treatment milieus aim to promote healthy, mature behaviors and discourage regressive, maladaptive ones. The milieu should not mirror the chaos and dyscontrol of the BPD patient's inner world. Rules and expectations should be clear and understandable. Patients should be asked to conform to the behavioral norms of adult society. Bizarre or childish behavior should be discouraged.

Although some clinicians argue that BPD patients must be allowed to regress during an acute episode of care, excessive tolerance of symptomatic behavior may make it harder, not easier, for a BPD patient to resume mature functioning. In addition, an overly tolerant milieu appeals to a BPD patient's wish to regress; therefore, such a setting may stimulate any desire to be rehospitalized.

Psychoeducation and BPD: To Tell or Not To Tell?

Clinicians may encounter families who have never been told the true nature of the BPD patient's problem. Often, these families have been led to believe that the patient suffers solely from an Axis I disorder, especially an affective disorder.

An overreliance on evasions and euphemisms when educating BPD patients' families is not recommended. For example, they should not be told that the problem is solely depression, posttraumatic stress disorder, or rapid cycling bipolar disorder (to cite three frequently given diagnoses). The patient may in fact suffer from one or more of these disorders, but the family should be informed about a comorbid BPD, which has a distinct phenomenology, treatment strategy, and prognosis.

Role of Medications in Treating BPD

Clinicians should avoid doctrinaire or absolute positions on the use of medications (88). Except for patients who repeatedly fail to comply with prescribers' instructions or use medications to act out, most BPD patients are appropriate candidates for psychopharmacology, especially in the presence of a comorbid Axis I disorder. Furthermore, because certain core symptoms of BPD have been reported to respond to medications, it is reasonable to attempt pharmacologic interventions even in patients without prominent Axis I symptoms. Medications may be especially useful when BPD symptoms are "state-dependent" (i.e., flare up only when the patient enters an Axis I illness episode like a major depression).

Conversely, BPD patients respond to medications less often and less fully than patients with uncomplicated Axis I disorders. Therefore, BPD patients must be dissuaded from adopting a passive, purely pharmacologic attitude toward their illness and expecting that sooner or later the right medication regimen will solve all their difficulties. Instead, clinicians should urge, to the extent clinically feasible, that BPD patients maintain their safety as well as their occupational and social functioning despite ongoing symptoms and limited medication responses. The patient's need to remain functional and safe must be uncoupled from the success or failure of pharmacologic interventions.

Role of Psychotherapy in Treating BPD

Traditionally, a modified version of analytically oriented psychotherapy was considered the treatment of choice for BPD (89). More recently, cognitive behavioral, supportive, and "relational" models have come to the fore. A specialized form of cognitive behavioral therapy, dialectical behavioral therapy, has attracted attention as the only psychosocial intervention for parasuicidal patients to be subjected to a controlled clinical trial (76).

The volatility and disorganization of BPD patients in acute care render them unsuitable for any form of therapy that is overly challenging or provocative. Therefore, certain psychotherapy interventions and techniques are relatively contraindicated:

- ◆ Substantially exploring the patient's early history and experiences, which may distract the patient from focusing on the present.
- ◆ Encouraging the patient to uncover memories of past traumas, which can induce overwhelmingly powerful affects of sorrow and rage.
- ◆ Conducting unstructured, affectively evocative psychotherapy sessions, which can be disorganizing for a BPD patient. Such sessions can also allow avoidance of dealing with the paramount issues that prompted the need for acute care and of focusing on a plan to effect a safe and appropriate return to the community.

- ◆ Being too neutral or inactive during therapy sessions, which can promote distorted and potentially psychotic transference reactions.

COURSE AND PROGNOSIS

Although BPD patients treated in acute care settings tend to show persistence and even worsening of symptoms when reassessed after 2–5 years, the long-term course and prognosis of the disorder is heterogeneous (90, 91). The course of BPD follows a common pattern in which symptoms reach their highest frequency and greatest severity in the young adult years, with a gradual attenuation of symptoms (including a decrease in life-threatening behaviors) as surviving patients move toward middle age. BPD patients followed over the course of decades may eventually no longer meet diagnostic criteria for the disorder (36, 37, 92, 93). This pattern is by no means universal, however, and BPD patients with comparatively mild symptoms in young adulthood may become significantly more impaired in middle age.

According to available research, the lifetime rate for suicide in BPD patients is 3–9.5% (93). No long-term outcome data have demonstrated convincingly whether psychiatric treatment has enduring benefit or harm for these patients or whether treatment—including medications, psychotherapy, and hospitalization—increases or decreases the long-term suicide risk (93).

ANTISOCIAL PERSONALITY DISORDER: DEFINITION

Antisocial personality disorder (APD) is marked by the pervasive disregard for the rights, property, and physical safety of others, which results in criminal, violent, or other destructive behavior (1). Individuals with APD characteristically show little if any genuine remorse for their antisocial behaviors; if anything, these persons seem bewildered by any negative consequences from their actions. Although APD is considered a mental disorder in that its manifestations cause significant impairment in life functioning, it differs from most mental disorders in its intractability to psychiatric treatment. Not infrequently, interactions with the mental health system are an avenue by which APD patients avoid punishment for crimes they have committed. Moreover, as a rule, mental health settings are poorly equipped to address the needs of individuals with APD because clinicians are not trained to work with criminal problems that more properly belong within the correctional system.

DIAGNOSIS

The DSM-IV defines APD by the following criteria (1):

A. A pervasive pattern of disregard for and violation of the rights of others occurring since age 15 years, as indicated by three (or more) of the following:

1. Failure to conform to social norms with respect to lawful behaviors, as indicated by repeatedly performing acts that are grounds for arrest.

2. Deceitfulness, as indicated by repeated lying, use of aliases, or conning others for personal profit or pleasure.

3. Impulsivity or failure to plan ahead.

4. Irritability and aggressiveness, as indicated by repeated physical fights or assaults.

5. Reckless disregard for safety of self or others.

6. Consistent irresponsibility, as indicated by repeated failure to sustain consistent work behavior or honor financial obligations.

7. Lack of remorse, as indicated by being indifferent to or rationalizing having hurt, mistreated, or stolen from another.

B. The individual is at least age 18 years.

C. Evidence of conduct disorder with onset before age 15 years.

D. The occurrence of antisocial behavior is not exclusively during the context of schizophrenia or a manic episode.

EPIDEMIOLOGY

APD is thought to have a prevalence of 1–3% in males and 1% in females (1, 11). Some authors have questioned whether the APD tends to be underdiagnosed in women, who may be given the diagnosis of BPD or mood or dissociative disorder. Another concern is the potential tendency of clinicians to overdiagnose APD in an economically disadvantaged population. Some drug and alcohol treatment centers, like prisons, report extremely high rates of APD (1).

THE FOUR QUESTIONS

Descriptive and Differential Diagnosis

Although some APD patients present with "typical" histories that include recent and frequent interactions with the penal system, the lack of such a history should not be taken as proof that a patient does not have APD. Older APD patients, in particular, may no longer engage in the violent or prominently destructive behavior characteristic of their younger counterparts, although they may still be prone to exploitativeness. In addition, a diagnosis of APD should not be assumed simply because a patient has a history of arrests or imprisonment. Many other mental disorders—such as substance abuse, mania, and psychosis—can lead to illegal behavior.

To maintain diagnostic rigor, clinicians should adhere to two often overlooked provisos of the DSM-IV criteria. First, the patient must be at least 18 years of age; younger patients with significant antisocial behavior should be assigned a diagnosis from the DSM-IV section entitled, "Disorders Usually First Diagnosed During Infancy, Childhood and Adolescence" (1). Second, APD should be diagnosed only when the patient has met criteria for conduct disorder before the age of 15 years. If no reliable information is available about the patient's early years, then only a provisional diagnosis of APD should be made. In addition, because the well-known triad of childhood warning signs of APD (enuresis, cruelty to animals, fire-setting) are not included in the DSM-IV criteria, they should not be relied on for diagnosis.

Many psychiatric disorders place patients at risk for illegal behavior secondary to impulsivity, poor judgment, irritability, or a response to delusions or hallucinations.

Substance abuse can lead a patient to behave sociopathically, especially if the substance is illegal or expensive. A diagnosis of APD in a substance abuser without a childhood history of conduct disorder should be deferred until there is a sustained period of abstinence. Comorbid substance abuse is common in APD patients and significantly worsens the prognosis and the risk of violence (94–96).

Psychotic patients may behave illegally if their actions are compelled by delusions or commanded by hallucinations. In particular, paranoid patients may become violent to defend themselves against individuals they consider threatening or dangerous. The irritability of manic conditions can lead to assaultiveness, and grandiosity can cause manic patients to disregard both laws and the instructions of police or judges. In all these cases, however, illegal behavior is accompanied by signs and symptoms suggestive of a mood or thought disorder that can explain the legal infractions. The criminality in APD occurs independently of other psychiatric causes (1).

Ego Defenses and Character Style

Patients with APD tend to use the immature defenses characteristic of primitive personalities. They are prone to projection, in which they attribute their anger and aggressiveness to others, and denial, especially of their antisocial behavior and its consequences. Many APD patients also make extensive use of dissociation, a tendency that both leads to and is exacerbated by psychoactive substance abuse.

Formulation

APD patients often present to acute psychiatric care when faced with the consequences of their antisocial behavior (e.g., arrests, restraining orders, or court hearings). Legal difficulties may be compounded by comorbid substance abuse through arrests for drug use or possession or crimes committed to fund the addiction.

APD patients are also prone to work-related problems; trouble maintaining steady employment is one criterion of the disorder. Financial difficulties typically ensue, and homelessness is not uncommon; these factors are due to financial problems and the tendency of APD patients to be ejected from domiciles as a result of violence, stealing, or substance abuse. Hence, the interpersonal lives of APD patients are often tumultuous and impoverished.

An APD patient's entry into acute psychiatric care sometimes seems prompted, in whole or in part, by the hope of secondary gain. For example, for legal purposes, a patient with APD may try to demonstrate evidence for a major Axis I mental disorder or show motivation for or compliance with psychiatric treatment. Alternatively, a "crisis" may have been designed to elicit sympathy from a spouse or family member. Clinicians suspecting a hidden motive should be careful not to assume that the presentation to acute care was caused solely by a desire to trick or manipulate; there may be a genuine clinical reason for the presentation in addition to the patient's covert agenda.

Focal Problems

The goal of acute care for the APD patient should almost always aim to diminish or eliminate an acute safety risk, usually of suicide or homicide. Lengths of stay should be kept as short as clinically possible to avoid encouraging the patient to view the hospital as a refuge from the real world.

If the patient has behaved violently before or during the acute episode of care or has made a verbal threat against others, the treatment team should assess early on whether they are bound by a "duty to warn" the potential victims (see Chapter 21) and whether a second opinion, especially one from a forensically trained psychiatrist or psychologist, is indicated.

In developing a treatment plan for an APD patient, the acute care team should seek as much detailed information as possible concerning the events that led to the presentation. This knowledge often proves crucial for effective management of the patient's treatment, especially discharge planning. For example, if the presentation to acute care involved the police, the team should ask the following questions:

- Was the patient merely transported by the police or was he or she arrested?
- Was the patient charged with a crime?
- Is a court hearing scheduled?
- Is the patient out on bail?
- Is hospitalization required for purposes of a court-ordered evaluation?
- Is the patient on parole or probation for a previous crime?
- Is an active restraining order in effect against the patient?

Similarly, if the precipitant to the hospitalization occurred in the patient's home, the acute care team should determine whether the patient can return there and if there are any preconditions to the return.

ASSESSING LEVEL OF CARE AND TRANSFERRING TO THE NEXT LEVEL OF CARE

APD patients should be treated in the least-restrictive, least-regressive level of care that is consistent with the patient's and community's safety. A potential complication in the placement or discharge planning process occurs when receiving programs are reluctant to accept certain APD patients because of concerns about noncompliance or disruptiveness.

Aftercare plans for all APD patients should be documented in the clinical record, and relevant appointments should have been made by the time of transfer or discharge.

TREATMENT

Psychopharmacologic Management

Medication regimens for APD patients should aim to treat comorbid conditions and to control specific behaviors and symptoms (especially violence and impulsivity). This is in contrast to treating the personality disorder itself, which is generally regarded to be resistant to pharmacologic interventions.

Psychiatrists should exercise care when prescribing abusable medications to an APD patient, given the risks that the patient will become addicted or that the supply will be sold to persons who are. Because of claims in the courts and the media that fluoxetine can cause or increase the likelihood of violent crimes, clinicians prescribing this medication or other selective serotonin reuptake inhibitors (SSRIs) to an APD patient should discuss this issue with the patient. The exchange should be documented in the chart, although a linkage between SSRIs and violence is not supported by the research literature (97).

Reducing the risk of violence is often a central goal of medication intervention in this population. The first-line agents for effecting a nonspecific reduction in violent behavior are the beta-blockers, which are effective, nonaddictive, and generally well tolerated (98). Propranolol has been the best studied (99–102), but other beta-blockers including metoprolol (103), nadolol (104, 105), and pindolol (106) have demonstrated comparable efficacy. Other studies have reported some benefit from prescribing lithium (107) or anticonvulsants (101, 108–110). There is some evidence that SSRIs can help reduce impulsivity (111) and aggression (112).

At times, the patient, family, or refer-ring treaters will press for an "emergency" medication intervention to control an APD patient's violent behavior. The acute care team should clarify the potential delay (weeks or months) in the effectiveness of any such intervention and that the patient's risk of violence should not be expected to diminish acutely through a medication change.

APD patients who also carry a diagnosis of attention-deficit/hyperactivity disorder (ADHD), residual type, may be candidates for psychostimulant treatment (113). Not infrequently, patients and families ask for these agents to be prescribed. Clinicians should exercise extreme caution when prescribing stimulants to APD patients because of (1) the high risk of dependence and illicit use of these drugs and (2) the risk that a stimulant will increase agitation and potentially the risk of violence. A nonsedating TCA (e.g., desipramine), rather than an amphetamine, should be considered as the first-line agent when a clear diagnosis of ADHD is made (114). Buspirone also has been reported to be effective in adult ADHD (115).

Alliance and Psychotherapeutic Management

Forming an alliance with APD patients is extremely difficult due to their dishonesty, distrust of others, and difficulty sustaining relationships with others, including treaters. Clinicians should be cautious in assuming that a reliable, dependable alliance has been formed with an APD patient. That said, it is possible (especially in the acute care setting) to form a temporary alliance with these patients around a well-defined, short-term goal, especially if the patient believes the goal coincides with his or her best interests (116).

Clinicians should expect APD patients to be deceitful and manipulative and should not blame themselves if they are "fooled." Many APD patients spend a lifetime conning people; a clinician should not expect to beat them at their own game. APD patients can develop strong transference reactions, especially when the treater represents an authority figure. The transference often consists of perceiving treaters as being either uncaring or overly harsh and punitive. Sometimes APD patients, fearing the former, will struggle around limits to verify that treaters care enough to stand up to them. A treatment team's emotional response to an APD patient may be extremely powerful and difficult to manage (117, 118). Clinicians may fear that the patient will become assaultive or they may harbor anger at the patient for criminal (especially violent) behavior. The patient's manipulative, deceitful, or exploitative behavior in the treatment setting—especially if directed toward other patients—may increase the staff's animosity. Fear or anger toward an APD patient should be considered countertransference if the emotions are out of proportion to the patient's actual behavior or if they interfere with the clinician's wish or ability to provide good care. Society does not authorize delivering or withholding care based on personal opinions about a patient; even convicted murderers on death row are afforded appropriate medical and psychiatric care.

APD is not amenable to psychodynamic psychotherapy, especially in an acute care setting. Acute care therapy with APD patients should be structured and goal directed. It should also emphasize anger management and impulse control. Therapy should include appropriate assertiveness training (to offer alternatives to the patient's customary use of aggression or manipulation to make his or her wants known) and nonviolent conflict resolution (119). APD patients with comorbid substance abuse or dependence should be required to attend either treater-led or self-help recovery groups.

FAMILY SUPPORT, EDUCATION, AND INTERVENTION

Families of APD patients are often in crisis by the time the patient presents to acute care, either because of their physical, emotional, and financial damage or their anxiety about the patient. Spouses or other partners may be unwilling to resume living with APD patients after discharge, a situation that may result in patients having nowhere to live.

When interacting with APD patients' families, acute care clinicians should obtain as complete a history as possible of the patient's behaviors (especially recent acts), including violence toward family members. In addition to providing useful information for the treatment team, this inquiry shows the family that the treatment team cares about the family's problems and wishes to help. Staff members should determine whether the patient can return to the family or other prior living arrangements after discharge.

Treaters should give the family information about support groups and other community resources. Families of APD patients may benefit from individual counseling or from attending Al-Anon meetings if the patient has comorbid substance abuse. If the family seems especially overwhelmed or uneducated about the patient's symptoms and behaviors, a referral for supportive, psychoeducational, outpatient family therapy may be indicated. In cases in which family members appear to have significant psychiatric pathology, treaters should discern tactfully whether these problems are being treated. If not, a referral of a family member to outpatient psychiatric services may be helpful.

The clinical team may also illustrate to the family their enabling or counterproductive behaviors, such as repeatedly paying the patient's debts or allowing the patient to live with the family despite continued aggressiveness.

Every acute care center should develop a treatment approach to address the patient's violent behavior toward family members or significant others. A balance between protecting the victim and the clinician's responsibility to the patient should be sought. In most cases, helping to protect the family from the patient is in the best interests of both family and patient and can be justified as such to the patient and in the clinical record.

THE THERAPEUTIC MILIEU

Patients with APD do best in a highly structured milieu with clear behavioral expectations and predictable consequences for infractions. Although some flexibility in response to minor rule-breaking can be useful, APD patients usually work better with clinicians whom they perceive to be firm and consistent. An absence of consequences for destructive or countertherapeutic behavior may lead the patient to believe that the treatment team is either indifferent or afraid. Any behavior that harms another person (including undermining the treatment of other patients) should elicit an immediate limit-setting response. Serious rule infractions may represent cause for terminating treatment.

COURSE AND PROGNOSIS

Like all personality disorders, APD has a chronic course with continued symptomatic behavior through young adulthood. The mortality associated with the condition is significant, with a high incidence of death through suicide, accident, and homicide.

Evidence suggests that the more dramatic antisocial behaviors exhibited by these patients, especially homicide and other violent crimes, decrease over time. The high death rate in this population and the decreasingly florid clinical picture as patients age have given rise to the saying, "You never meet an old sociopath." However, the underlying character deficits in APD (selfishness, dishonesty, lack of remorse) seem to persist through the life cycle, and middle-aged and elderly APD patients may continue to show significant deficits in functioning (120).

REFERENCES

1. American Psychiatric Association. Diagnostic and statistical manual of mental disorders. 4th ed. Washington, DC: American Psychiatric Association, 1994.
2. Gunderson JG. Borderline personality disorder. Washington, DC: American Psychiatric Press, 1984.
3. Gunderson JG, Kolb JE. Discriminating features of borderline patients. Am J Psychiatry 1978;135:792–796.
4. Gunderson JG, Singer M. Defining borderline patients: an overview. Am J Psychiatry 1978;132:1.
5. Kernberg O. Borderline conditions and pathological narcissism. Northvale: Jason Aronson, 1975.
6. Schmideberg M. The borderline patient. In: Arieti S, ed. American handbook of psychiatry. New York: Basic Books, 1959;1:398–416.
7. Fine M, Sansone R. Dilemmas in the management of suicidal behavior in individuals with borderline personality disorder. Am J Psychother 1990;44:160.
8. Friedman H. Some problems of inpatient

management with borderline patients. Am J Psychiatry 1969;126:299–304.

9. Stanton A, Schwartz M. The mental hospital: a study of institutional participation in psychiatric illness and treatment. New York: Basic Books, 1954.

10. Swartz M, Blazer D, George L, et al. Estimating the prevalence of borderline personality disorder in the community. J Pers Disord 1990;4:257–272.

11. Weissman M. The epidemiology of personality disorders: an update. J Pers Disord 1993;7(Suppl):44–62 .

12. Zanarini M, Frankenburg F, Chauncey D, et al. The diagnostic interview for personality disorders: interrator and test-retest reliability. Compr Psychiatry 1987;28:467–480.

13. Cornfield RB, Share IA. Countertransference in the treatment of the borderline personality. Psychiatr Clin North Am 1994;17:851–856.

14. Vaillant G. The natural history of alcoholism. Cambridge: Harvard University Press, 1983.

15. Sederer LI. Multiproblem patients: psychiatric disorder and substance abuse. In: Milkman HB, Sederer LI, eds. Treatment choices in alcohol and drug abuse. Lexington, MA: Lexington Books, 1990:163–181.

16. Akiskal HS, Yerevanian BI, Davis GC. The nosological status of borderline personality: clinical and polysomnographic study. Am J Psychiatry 1985;142:192–198.

17. Lahmeyer HW, Val E, Gaviria FM, et al. EEG sleep, lithium transport, dexamethasone suppression, and monoamine oxidase activity in borderline personality disorder. Psychiatry Res 1988;25:19–30.

18. Gunderson JG, Elliot GR. The interface between borderline personality disorder and affective disorder. Am J Psychiatry 1985;142:277–288.

19. Gunderson JG, Phillips KA. The current view of the interface between borderline personality disorder and depression. Am J Psychiatry 1991;148:967–975.

20. McGlashan TH. The borderline syndrome. Part 2: is it a variant of schizophrenia or affective disorder? Arch Gen Psychiatry 1983;40:1319–1323.

21. McNamara E, Reynolds CF, Soloff PH, et al. EEG sleep evaluation of depression in borderline patients. Am J Psychiatry 1984;141:182–186.

22. Stone MH. Contemporary shift of the borderline concept from a subschizophrenic disorder to a subaffective disorder. Psychiatr Clin North Am 1979;2:577–594.

23. Dulit RA, Fyer MR, Haas GL, et al. Substance use in borderline personality disorder. Am J Psychiatry 1990;147:1002–1007.

24. Miller FT, Abrams T, Dulit R, et al. Substance abuse in borderline personality disorder. Am J Drug Alcohol Abuse 1993;19:491–497.

25. Oldham J, Skodol A, Kellman H, et al. Comorbidity of axis I and axis II disorders. Am J Psychiatry 1995;152:571–578.

26. Perry CJ. Depression in borderline personality disorder. Am J Psychiatry 1985;142:15–21.

27. Pope H, Jonas J, Hudson J, et al. The validity of DSM-III borderline personality disorder. Arch Gen Psychiatry 1983;40:23–30.

28. Adler G. Borderline psychopathology and its treatment. Northvale: Jason Aronson, 1985.

29. Mack JE. Borderline states: an historical perspective. In: Mack JE, ed. Borderline states in psychiatry. New York: Grune & Stratton, 1975:1–28.

30. Mahler MS. On human symbiosis and the vicissitudes of individuation. New York: International Universities Press, 1968.

31. Winnicott DW. The theory of the parent-infant relationship. Int J Psychoanal 1960;41:585–595.

32. Herman J, Perry CJ, van der Kolk B. Childhood trauma in the borderline personality disorder. Am J Psychiatry 1989;146:490–495.

33. van der Kolk BA, Hostetler A, Herron N, et al. Trauma and the development of borderline personality disorder. Psychiatr Clin North Am 1994;17:715–730.

34. Maltsberger JT. Suicide risk. New York: New York University Press, 1986.

35. Kullgren G. Factors associated with completed suicide in borderline personality disorder. J Nerv Ment Dis 1988;176:40–44.

36. McGlashan T. The Chestnut Lodge follow-up study. Part 3: long-term outcome of borderline personalities. Arch Gen Psychiatry 1986;43:20–30.

37. Stone M, Stone D, Hurt S. The natural history of borderline patients. Part 1: global outcome. Psychiatr Clin North Am 1987;10:185–206.

38. Schwartz D, Flinn D, Slawson P. Treatment of the suicidal character. Am J Psychother 1974;28:194–207.

39. Soloff P. Is there any drug treatment of choice for the borderline patient? Acta Psychiatr Scand Suppl 1994;379:50–55.

40. Baer L, Jenike M, Black D, et al. Effect of axis II diagnoses on treatment outcome with clomipramine in 55 patients with obsessive-compulsive disorder. Arch Gen Psychiatry 1992;49:862–866.

41. Reich J, Green A. Effect of personality disorders on outcome of treatment. J Nerv Ment Dis 1991;179:74–82.

42. Shea MT, Glass DR, Pilkonis PA. Frequency and implications of personality disorders in a

sample of depressed outpatients. J Pers Disord 1987;1:27–42.

43. Cowdry R. Do borderline patients benefit from treatment? Symposium at the APA Annual Meeting, 1994.

44. Cowdry R, Gardner D. Pharmacotherapy of borderline personality disorder. Arch Gen Psychiatry 1988;45:111–118.

45. Frances A, Soloff P. Treating the borderline patient with low-dose neuroleptics. Hosp Community Psychiatry 1988;39:246–248.

46. Gunderson J. Pharmacotherapy for patients with borderline personality disorder. Arch Gen Psychiatry 1986;698–700.

47. Teicher M, Glod C, Aaronson S, et al. Open assessment of the safety and efficacy of thioridazine in the treatment of patients with borderline personality disorder. Psychopharmacol Bull 1989;25:535–549.

48. Soloff P, George A, Nathan R, et al. Progress in pharmacotherapy of borderline disorders. Arch Gen Psychiatry 1986;45:691–697.

49. Soloff P, George A, Nathan R, et al. Amytriptyline vs. haloperidol in borderlines: final outcomes and predictors of response. J Clin Psychopharmacol 1989;9:238–246.

50. Frankenburg FR, Zanarini MC. Clozapine treatment of borderline patients: a preliminary study. Compr Psychiatry 1993;34:402–405.

51. Soloff P, George A, Nathan R. Paradoxical effects of amytriptyline in borderline patients. Am J Psychiatry 1986;143:1603–1605.

52. Cornelius JR, Soloff P, Perel JM, et al. A preliminary trial of fluoxetine in refractory borderline patients. J Clin Psychopharmacol 1991;11:116–120.

53. Markovitz PJ, Calabrese JR, Schulz SC, et al. Fluoxetine in the treatment of borderline and schizotypal personality disorders. Am J Psychiatry 1991;148:1064–1067.

54. Salzman C, Wolfson AN, Schatzberg A, et al. Effect of fluoxetine on anger in symptomatic volunteers with borderline personality disorder. J Clin Psychopharmacol 1995;15:23–29.

55. Teicher MH, Glod C, Cole JO. Emergence of intense suicidal preoccupation during fluoxetine treatment. Am J Psychiatry 1990;147:207–210.

56. Beasley CM Jr, Dornseif BE, Bosomworth JC, et al. Fluoxetine and suicide: a meta-analysis of controlled trials of treatment for depression. Br Med J 1991;303:685–692.

57. Beasley CM Jr, Potvin JH, Masica DN, et al. Fluoxetine: no association with suicidality in obsessive-compulsive disorder. J Affect Dis 1992;24:1–10.

58. Fava M, Rosenbaum JF. Suicidality and fluoxetine: is there a relationship? J Clin Psychiatry 1991;52:108–111.

59. Goldstein DJ, Rampey AH Jr, Potvin JH, et al. Analyses of suicidality in double-blind, placebo-controlled trials of pharmacotherapy for weight reduction. J Clin Psychiatry 1993;54:309–316.

60. Hamilton MS, Opler LA. Akathisia, suicidality and fluoxetine. J Clin Psychiatry 1992;53:401–406.

61. Jick H, Ulcickas M, Dean A. Comparison of frequencies of suicidal tendencies among patients receiving fluoxetine, lofepramine, mianserin or trazodone. Pharmacotherapy 1992;12:451–454.

62. Rothschild AJ, Locke CA. Reexposure to fluoxetine after serious suicide attempts by three patients: the role of akathisia. J Clin Psychiatry 1991;52:491–493.

63. Wheadon DE, Rampey AH Jr, Thompson VL, et al. Lack of association between fluoxetine and suicidality in bulimia nervosa. J Clin Psychiatry 1992;53:235–241.

64. Liebowitz MR, Klein DF. Hysteroid dysphoria. Psychiatr Clin North Am 1979;2:555–575.

65. van der Kolk BA. Uses of lithium in patients without major affective illness. Hosp Community Psychiatry 1986;37:1986.

66. Gardner DL, Cowdry RW. Positive effects of carbamazepine on behavioral dyscontrol in borderline personality disorder. Am J Psychiatry 1986;143:519–522.

67. Wilcox JA. Divalproex sodium as a treatment for borderline personality disorder. Ann Clin Psychiatry 1995;7:33–37.

68. Gardner DL, Cowdry RW. Alprazolam-induced dyscontrol in borderline personality disorder. Am J Psychiatry 1985;142:98–100.

69. Abroms GM. Setting limits. Arch Gen Psychiatry 1968;19:113–119.

70. MacDonald DM. Acting out. Arch Gen Psychiatry 1965;13:439–443.

71. Bernstein SB. Psychotherapy consultation in an inpatient setting. Hosp Community Psychiatry 1980;31:829–834.

72. Jacobs DH, Rogoff J, Donnelly K, et al. The neglected alliance: the inpatient unit as a consultant to referring therapists. Hosp Community Psychiatry 1982;5:377–381.

73. Numberg HG, Suh R. Time-limited psychotherapy of the hospitalized borderline patient. Am J Psychother 1982;36:82–90.

74. Sederer LI, Thorbeck J. First do no harm: short-term inpatient psychotherapy of the borderline patient. Hosp Community Psychiatry 1986;37:692–697.

75. Linehan MM. Dialectical behavior therapy for borderline personality disorder: theory and method. Bull Menninger Clin 1987;51:261–276.

76. Linehan MM. Cognitive-behavioral treat-

ment of borderline personality disorder. New York: Guilford Press, 1993.

77. Linehan MM, Tutek DA, Heard HL, et al. Interpersonal outcome of cognitive behavioral treatment for chronically suicidal borderline patients. Am J Psychiatry 1994;151:1771–1776.

78. Brown LJ. Staff countertransference reactions in the hospital treatment of borderline patients. Psychiatry 1980;43:333–345.

79. Kaplan CA. The challenge of working with patients diagnosed as having a borderline personality disorder. Nurs Clin North Am 1986;21:429–438.

80. Gabbard GO. Splitting in hospital treatment. Am J Psychiatry 1989;146:444–451.

81. Gutheil TG. Medicolegal pitfalls in the treatment of borderline patients. Am J Psychiatry 1985;142:9–14.

82. Gutheil TG. Borderline personality disorder, boundary violations and patient-therapist sex: medicolegal pitfalls. Am J Psychiatry 1989;146:597–602.

83. Groves JE. Taking care of the hateful patient. N Engl J Med 1978;298:883–887.

84. Maltsberger JT, Buie DH. Countertransference hate in the treatment of suicidal patients. Arch Gen Psychiatry 1974;30:625–633.

85. Winnicott DW. Hate in the countertransference. Int J Psychoanal 1949;30:69–74.

86. Wike P. Risk management in the contemporary treatment of BPD. Symposium at the American Psychiatric Association Annual Meeting, 1996.

87. Loranger A, Lenzenweger M, Gartner A, et al. Trait-state artifacts and the diagnosis of personality disorders. Arch Gen Psychiatry 1991;48:720–728.

88. Swenson CR, Wood MJ. Issues involved in combining drugs with psychotherapy for the borderline inpatient. Psychiatr Clin North Am 1990;13:297–306.

89. Kernberg O. Technical considerations in the treatment of borderline personality organization. J Am Psychoanal Assoc 1976;24:795–829.

90. Links PS, Mitton MJ, Steiner M. Stability of borderline personality disorder. Can J Psychiatry 1993;38:255–259.

91. Carpenter W, Gunderson J, Strauss J. Considerations of the borderline syndrome: a longitudinal comparative study of borderline and schizophrenic patients. In: Hartocollis P, ed. Borderline personality disorders. Baltimore: Williams & Wilkins, 1986:303–326.

92. Paris J, Brown R, Nowlis D. Long-term follow-up of borderline patients in a general hospital. Compr Psychiatry 1987;28:530–535.

93. Paris J. Follow-up studies of borderline personality disorder: a critical review. J Pers Disord 1988;2:189–197.

94. Arndt IO, McLellan AT, Dorozynsky L, et al. Desipramine treatment for cocaine dependence. Role of antisocial personality disorder. J Nerv Ment Dis 1994;82:151–156.

95. Draine J, Solomon P, Meyerson A. Predictors of reincarceration among patients who received psychiatric services in jail. Hosp Community Psychiatry 1994;45:163–167.

96. Westermeyer J, Walzer V. Sociopathy and drug use in a young psychiatric population. Dis Nerv Syst 1975;36:673–677.

97. Heiligenstein JH, Beasley CM Jr, Potvin JH. Fluoxetine not associated with increased aggression in controlled clinical trials. Int Clin Psychopharmacol 1993;3:277–280.

98. Sorgi P, Ratey J, Knoedler D, et al. Depression during treatment with beta-blockers: results from a double-blind placebo-controlled study. J Neuropsychiatry Clin Neurosci 1992;2:187–189.

99. Elliott FA. Propranolol for the control of belligerent behavior following acute brain damage. Ann Neurol 1977;5:489–491.

100. Jenkins SC, Maruta T. Therapeutic use of propranolol for intermittent explosive disorder. Mayo Clin Proc 1987;62:204–214.

101. Mattes JA. Comparative effectiveness of carbamazepine and propranolol for rage outbursts. J Neuropsychiatry Clin Neurosci 1990;2:159–164.

102. Yudofsky S, Williams D, Gorman J. Propranolol in the treatment of rage and violent behavior in patients with chronic brain syndromes. Am J Psychiatry 1981;138:218–220.

103. Kastner T, Burlingham K, Friedman DL. Metoprolol for aggressive behavior in persons with mental retardation. Am Fam Physician 1990;42:1585–1588.

104. Alpert M, Allan ER, Citrome L, et al. A double-blind, placebo-controlled study of adjunctive nadolol in the management of violent psychiatric patients. Psychopharmacol Bull 1990;26:367–371.

105. Ratey JJ, Sorgi P, O'Driscoll GA, et al. Nadolol to treat aggression and psychiatric symptomatology in chronic psychiatric inpatients: a double-blind, placebo-controlled study. J Clin Psychiatry 1992;53:41–46.

106. Greendyke RM, Kanter DR. Therapeutic effects of pindolol on behavioral disturbances associated with organic brain disease: a double-blind study. J Clin Psychiatry 1986;47:423–426.

107. Luchins DJ, Dojka D. Lithium and propranolol in aggression and self-injurious behavior in the mentally retarded. Psychopharmacol Bull 1989;25:372–375.

108. Barratt ES. The use of anticonvulsants in

aggression and violence. Psychopharmacol Bull 1993;29:75–81.

109. Giakas WJ, Seibyl JP, Mazure CM. Valproate in the treatment of temper outbursts. J Clin Psychiatry 1990;51:525.

110. Mattes JA. Carbamazepine vs. propranolol for rage outbursts. Psychopharmacol Bull 1988;24:179–182.

111. Kafka MP, Prentky R. Fluoxetine treatment of nonparaphilic sexual addictions and paraphilias in men. J Clin Psychiatry 1992;53:351–358.

112. Kafka MP. Successful treatment of paraphilic coercive disorder (a rapist) with fluoxetine hydrochloride. Br J Psychiatry 1991;158:844–847.

113. Simeon JG, Wiggins DM. Pharmacotherapy of attention-deficit hyperactivity disorder. Can J Psychiatry 1993;38:443–448.

114. Wilens TE, Biederman J, Mick E, et al. A systematic assessment of tricyclic antidepressants in the treatment of adult attention-deficit hyperactivity disorder. J Nerv Ment Dis 1995;183:48–50.

115. Wender PH, Reimherr FW. Buproprion treatment of attention-deficit hyperactivity disorder in adults. Am J Psychiatry 1990;147:1018–1020.

116. Gerstley L, McLellan AT, Alterman AI, et al. Ability to form an alliance with the therapist: a possible marker of prognosis for patients with antisocial personality disorder. Am J Psychiatry 1989;146:508–512.

117. Durst R, Oren Wolman N, Vass A, et al. Predicaments of the closed ward staff. Isr J Psychiatry Relat Sci 1991;28:1–7.

118. Gabbard GO, Coyne L. Predictors of response of antisocial patients to hospital treatment. Hosp Community Psychiatry 1987;38:1181–1185.

119. Vaillant PM, Antonowicz DH. Cognitive behavior therapy and social skills training improves personality and cognition in incarcerated offenders. Psychol Rep 1991;68:27–33.

120. Black DW, Baumgard CH, Bell SE. The long-term outcome of antisocial personality disorder compared with depression, schizophrenia and surgical conditions. Bull Am Acad Psychiatry Law 1995;23:43–52.

SPECIFIC INTERVENTIONS AND TREATMENTS

Chapter 15

—————

Case Management

Lisa Dixon and Jack Scott

INTRODUCTION

Case management in the care of persons with serious mental illness has assumed a critically important role over the past decade. We can be as certain of the expanding importance of case management as we can of the future scarcity of health-care resources. Evaluation of case management programs is likely to focus on the acute care of persons with serious mental illness because they are at greatest risk for consuming the most expensive resource, namely hospitalization. Also, they are the most in need of help and care and perhaps are the most unable to obtain what they require from the treatment system without assistance.

In a recent national survey, respondents from 323 case management programs most frequently ranked prevention of hospitalization as the top program priority (1). Crisis intervention, a function clearly related to reducing hospital risk, was rated the second most important activity performed by case managers. More than 95% of case management programs surveyed provide crisis intervention services (which accounts for approximately 18% of case manager time). This survey emphasizes the importance of reducing hospitalization and its related service, crisis intervention.

Historically, two primary functions of case management have emerged. In the public sector, case management has evolved from the desire to ensure access to care and delivery of services to under-served or needy persons (2). Conversely, in the private sector, case management is frequently perceived as a mechanism of utilization review, aimed at limiting service to reduce costs (2). As the distinction between the private and public sectors vanishes, case managers unquestionably must integrate both of these functions. The following examples illustrate this point.

☐ **CASE EXAMPLES**

Mr. W was diagnosed with schizophrenia. His caretaking mother recently died, and he became acutely psychotic after 3 years of stability. He was withdrawn, heard voices of his dead mother, and forgot to go to his medication appointments. He spent all his money on fast food, which left him penniless 2 weeks before his next disability check.

Ms. K was a woman whose sub-threshold manic symptoms worsened because of recent cocaine use as she awaited the results of a human immunodeficiency virus (HIV) test. She was ashamed, hostile, and agitated and was finally evicted from her housing program.

A case management program provided Mr. W with his medication, assisted him with food until his next check, and provided social and emotional support while he grieved his mother's loss. His rent was paid, and instead of entering the hospital, Mr. W began the process of deciding whether he wanted to live alone or make alternative group living arrangements. A case management program identified a short-term crisis bed for Ms. K, arranged for an increase of her medication, and provided an environment that facilitated sobriety while she discussed her fears about HIV. A scenario was averted in which Ms. K presented to an emergency department psychiatrist who, knowing little of her resources and difficulties, resorted to hospitalization. With case management, Ms. K felt safe enough to stabilize psychiatrically and made alternative housing plans.

In both the public and private sectors, case management will be essential in providing care to those in need who have limited resources. This chapter discusses the defining characteristics of case management for acutely ill patients as well as the clinical tasks of acute care and their relationship to case management. The effectiveness research on the different case management models and their respective uses in clinical practice are reviewed.

DEFINING CASE MANAGEMENT

There are probably as many definitions of case management as there are case managers. Bachrach (3) asserts that there is not yet a consensus in the definition of case management for persons with long-term mental illness. Case management programs have been classified according to models, staffing dimensions, focus, and "people-program-system" dimensions (1). Sledge et al. (2) provide an analysis of case management characteristics and tasks in psychiatry. This perspective lends itself well to analysis of the acute care work of case managers. It also allows differentiation of clinical tasks important for acutely ill persons from tasks more relevant to persons in a more stable phase of illness. The framework of tasks outlined by Sledge et al. has been adapted to summarize the defining features of case management and underline those elements that are most important for the acutely ill. Sledge et al. divide case management into activity, accountability, and authority (2).

ROLE OF THE CASE MANAGER

Table 15.1 shows the various activities of case managers that are relevant in the care of persons in an acute phase of illness.

Patient Identification

Patient identification refers to the boundary management function—who is in-

TABLE 15.1.   Case Management Activities

Patient identification
Needs assessment
Linkage
Brokering
Advocacy
Coordination
Planning
Direct service

cluded and who is excluded—of case managers, particularly at the initiation of services. The case manager is responsible for ensuring that persons who are appropriate for a service receive it and, similarly, that persons who are not appropriate for a service do not receive it. An important example of this function occurs in the work of case management teams that have adopted the Assertive Community Treatment (ACT) model (described later in this chapter). For ACT (an expensive program) to achieve cost-effectiveness relative to less-intensive case management models, patients must be selected on the basis of high levels of previous service utilization. Mr. W, the patient discussed above who had 3 years of stability before the death of his mother, would not be appropriate for referral to an ACT program. Had Mr. W experienced multiple hospitalizations in the year preceding his mother's death, ACT might have been appropriate. This is an example of boundary management through proper case identification.

Outreach for persons who are underserved can be an important aspect of the patient identification process. Numerous treatment programs have emerged recently to engage homeless persons with serious mental illness. These programs inevitably require case management to attend to the multiple needs of homeless persons (4). The following case example illustrates outreach and patient identification.

☐ **C A S E   E X A M P L E**

Ms. J was a 43-year-old woman with a long history of paranoid schizophrenia. She was significantly disorganized, with elaborate delusions regarding the imagined conspiracies of child protection authorities and her own grandmother to take her children from her. She shunned the mental health system, believing that all her difficulties were due to the aches and pains she experienced and that all she needed was the "right medicine for [her] back." Despite her psychosis, she managed to maintain herself as a homeless person, receiving daily food from soup kitchens and sometimes shelter from charitable organizations. A local case management program visited the soup kitchen regularly to evaluate clients for eligibility for case management services. The case management program established that Ms. J met their eligibility criteria because she was both homeless and suffered from a serious mental illness. She also had been a frequent user of emergency department services, although she had mostly avoided hospitalization. After outreach and identification, the next task for the case management program was to engage Ms. J in services.

Needs Assessment

Related to patient identification, the assessment of patient needs is crucial in the care of acutely ill persons. An important question is whether hospitalization is necessary or whether a less-intensive intervention is appropriate. Other needs such as psychiatric treatment, housing, rehabilitation, income, and entitlements are also evaluated. With the possible exception of rehabilitation, each need has the potential to be important in the acute phase of illness.

Linkage

This activity refers to the process in which a case manager facilitates the patient's access to existing services. The following case serves as an example.

□ CASE EXAMPLE

Ms. A was a 71-year-old woman with a long history of fragile bipolar disorder. Her medications included valproate and clonazepam. Ms. A lived with a board and care provider from whom she received meals but had marginal supervision and support. Although Ms. A tried hard to take medication as prescribed, she sometimes "forgot." One day in the late spring, Ms. A presented to her case manager wearing bright pink sunglasses and a new flowered dress. She was singing loudly in the waiting room. Her case manager recognized this behavior as a sign of mania for Ms. A. The case manager also knew that the patient's friendly and cheerful affect indicated that she was in an early phase. In conjunction with the psychiatrist, the case manager made the assessment that a local crisis bed would be sufficient to stabilize Ms. A. She called the crisis center, ensured that the appropriate paper work was completed, and transported the patient for a brief 3-day stay, averting hospitalization.

In this case, the case manager had to be aware of the existing services and needed to execute the necessary steps to obtain

the crisis bed. Although this task may seem trivial, without an appropriate linkage, Ms. A very easily may have escalated to the point of requiring hospitalization.

Brokering

Service brokering is an extension of linkage. The case manager might have to work diligently with an agency to obtain a priority position on a waiting list or to bend the rules where some ambiguity exists. In the case of Ms. A, she recently had taken a drink of alcohol. The crisis bed service had guidelines that prohibited persons with a recent drug/alcohol history from admission, but the case manager negotiated with the crisis bed service to establish that the alcohol was not the primary problem and that there was no medical risk.

Advocacy

Advocacy extends even further along the continuum of linkage and brokering. As an advocate, the case manager attempts to change the rules of the system to enhance appropriate access to services. Although the case manager does not advocate during the acute phase of his or her client's problem, advocacy is an important task in the case manager's overall job. Needed services are often not developed or sustained without advocacy.

For example, case managers of an urban community program for homeless mentally ill adults frequently worked with a transitional shelter program serving persons with severe mental illness. This shelter required that all clients with a history of a substance use disorder attend a detoxification program before admission and then attend daily Alcoholics Anonymous (AA) or Narcotics Anonymous (NA) meetings. The case management program did not believe that a medical detoxification was appropriate for all patients with a substance use history. The case management program also believed that daily AA or NA meetings were not always helpful for all clients. Thus, the case management program advocated for a change in the rules. To effect this change, the management of both organizations were required to meet and consider the other's perspectives and beliefs. Ultimately, advocacy produced a change in shelter rules. As a result, more housing options were available for persons with acute (or subacute) illness.

Coordination

Coordination involves ensuring that each multiple service—whether a crisis center, substance abuse treatment, or a housing program—is provided in an effective manner consistent with the other services offered. In the example of Ms. A who was in an early phase of hypomania, the case manager would need to ensure that appropriate psychiatric services and medication were available in addition to linking her with a crisis center.

Planning

Planning most frequently requires working with a team representing different areas of expertise to determine patients' needs and how best to meet them. Planning implies anticipating difficulties or problems and having responses to different contingencies worked out in advance, as seen in the following example.

☐ **C A S E E X A M P L E**
Ms. B, a 40-year-old woman, had a long history of institutionalization as a teen with impulsive, child-like behaviors and intermittent alcohol abuse. After 10 years of homelessness, Ms. B was living in an independent apartment subsidized through a federal housing support program. She was managing adequately but required ongoing support and frequent interaction with the superintendent of her building when her behavior was loud or disruptive. The most problematic incidents occurred every 4–6 months when Ms. B would abuse alcohol. During these episodes she frequently became aggressive and depressed and expressed suicidal ideation. The team developed a protocol (as part of a planning process) for responding to these infrequent but predictable acute circumstances. The team would make a home visit and give the patient several nonhospital choices for maintaining her safety during the acute period. They also developed a plan with the patient to deal with any consequences of her disruptive behaviors. Finally, the team established a relationship with the building superintendent who was concerned enough about the patient to communicate with the team at the earliest possible point in the patient's episodes.

Multidisciplinary team planning must include a psychiatrist because of the frequent necessity to have access to a medical opinion in assessing the need for or provision of services such as medication or hospitalization.

Direct Service

Most case managers for persons in the acute phase of illness provide some direct service to the client. The role may be that of a "therapist" or a substance abuse counselor, a rehabilitation aide, or a housing specialist. Clinical skills are essential to respond appropriately to acutely ill patients. Case managers vary considerably in their background, orientation, and training and thus in their comfort with and capacity to provide services directly. However, patients in the acute phase of illness frequently require rapid response. Those case managers without extensive clinical background will need to learn rapidly on the job. Supervision and ongoing training are particularly important for case management systems that employ less extensively trained staff.

ACCOUNTABILITY AND AUTHORITY OF THE CASE MANAGER

The capacity of case managers to meet the needs of patients in the acute phase of illness and to perform the identification, assessment, and linkage functions outlined above is to some extent a function of the organizational structure within which they work. Key structural elements of an organization include accountability and authority. Accountability addresses the following questions: "Who is the case manager's direct boss?" "Who evaluates the case manager's performance?" "Who is ultimately responsible for the case manager's work?" The case manager may report to a clinician, a program chief, or an administrator. In the case of a clinician (in which case the clinical role of the case manager is emphasized), conflicts may occur when senior clinical supervisors are oriented to traditional office practice or are unfamiliar (hence, uncomfortable) with assertive case management strategies (2). The case manager may report to a program chief or administrator if he or she functions at the systems level (e.g.,

private sector utilization review). The case manager may conflict with a clinician who perceives the case manager as attempting to either deprive the patient of needed services or the clinician of his or her own authority and expertise.

The case manager may have very limited authority, negotiated authority, or extensive authority (2). Case managers with limited authority may have limited credentials (e.g., a bachelor's degree without a license as opposed to a master's degree with a clinical license) and/or work for agencies with limited clinical authority. Negotiated authority emerges from a team process in which the case manager assumes the authority of the team after he or she and the team collaborate on a plan of necessary action. Extensive authority may be the province of senior staff members within any system. Authority, however, is never complete (2).

Several critical issues emerge in the care of acute psychiatric patients. First, accountability and authority must be paired. If the case manager or the case management team is charged with reducing hospitalization, then the team must have authority over decisions relevant to the use of hospital care. An example to the contrary occurs when an emergency department psychiatrist who is not accountable to the same authority as the case management team has the final decision about admission. This emergency department physician may not understand the services that the case management team has to offer to support the patient in the community. This physician may also be under pressure to fill hospital beds. Once the patient is hospitalized, the inpatient physician may then have the authority to discharge the patient and may be accountable to yet a different organizational entity. These limitations on case management authority are addressed in the ACT model; psychiatrists

TABLE 15.2. Task Areas of Psychiatric Practice

Task area	Focus
Medical	Disease; cure, stabilize or arrest the course of illness
Rehabilitation	Functional deficit; efforts to habilitate or rehabilitate the individual
Social control	Deviance and control of social behavior
Growth and development	Personal growth, capacity to experience self-sufficiency and well-being
Social welfare	Provision of food, shelter and other services crucial for survival

serve as members of the team and provide inpatient/outpatient continuity of care teams.

The organizational structure must align supervisors and frontline case managers with accountability for a common set of outcomes. A clinical supervisor who understands how to diagnose and prescribe medications but who does not endorse a community-based treatment approach aimed at avoiding hospitalization would not align physician leadership with line staff and would generate interpersonal conflict. This arrangement would likely result in quality and cost problems. Convergent goals exist, for example, between a case manager working for an insurance company who has to approve or disapprove services, and a "public" sector case manager who is more traditionally concerned with increasing access to care but also needs to reduce the use of medically unnecessary resources.

Accountability and authority in case management are most critical with acutely ill persons who, in the absence of adequate care, are likely to experience adverse outcomes such as suicide, violence, and homelessness. A medical marketplace emphasizing the minimal use of intensive and costly services must ensure through the authority invested in clinical staff that undertreatment will not be delivered. All programs, public and private, must be accountable for evaluating and preventing this occurrence.

TASK AREAS OF PSYCHIATRIC PRACTICE

An outline of the five domains of psychiatric practice as described by Astrachan et al. (5) and Sledge et al. (2) is shown in Table 15.2.

The medical and social control tasks are the most germane in the case management of the acutely ill patient. Attention to rehabilitation and growth and development issues may serve as prevention for stabilized patients, but these domains are not relevant in the acute phase. Lack of attention to social welfare needs can precipitate acute episodes, and resolution of social needs may help to resolve acute episodes. Thus, social welfare—although not strictly a part of traditionally defined primary, secondary, or tertiary medical care—requires case management attention for persons with serious mental illness.

Medical

The case manager has a vitally important role in the provision of medical services for acutely ill patients. In both the public and private sector, only "medically necessary" services are typically approved. Clinical case management models in which the case manager has clinical training and background are ideal for acute care services. Crisis services, evaluation, assessment, and linkage to medical care are the staples of this task area. The following case illustrates a typical medical intervention conducted by a skillful case manager.

□ C A S E E X A M P L E

Ms. F was a 43-year-old, divorced woman with a long history of bipolar disorder. She had a history of multiple psychiatric hospitalizations and reluctantly acknowledged that she had a mental illness. After a particularly damaging episode of mania, she found herself penniless. She then began to work with a community-based clinical case management team. She was persuaded to take low-dose lithium, and case managers provided Ms. F with a 7-day supply of medication packed in unit dosages to facilitate medication compliance and monitoring. One day, Ms. F's daughter, with whom she had a close but emotionally charged relationship, called the team after visiting her mother. The daughter was concerned that Ms. F had left the oven on, had allowed the bathtub to overflow, and was irritable. The case manager was unable to reach Ms. F by telephone because it was left off the hook. The case manager then went to Ms. F's apartment. Ms. F initially refused to allow the case manager to come in, but opened the door a few inches. After a brief conversation through this crack in the door, the case manager persuaded Ms. F to allow her to enter. It was obvious to the case manager that Ms. F was hypomanic and had been noncompliant with her medication. With the support of Ms. F's daughter and in consultation with the psychiatrist, the case manager persuaded Ms. F to resume medication at a slightly increased dose. The case

manager presented a choice between admission to the emergency department and/or hospitalization (which Ms. F abhorred) or management of her illness appropriately in the community with medication. The case manager clinician skillfully addressed the medical problem raised by the patient's manic syndrome by using her knowledge of psychopathology and treatments, using her alliance with the patient, and coordinating her efforts with family and psychiatric care.

Social Control

This task area principally involves situations in which the state deems the patient unable to make decisions or to be responsible for his or her own behavior, resulting in a threat to the safety of the patient or the public. In the care of the acutely ill, judgments to involve the police or legal system are frequently required. Involuntary treatment or its specter may be necessary to exert social control, as is illustrated in the following example.

□ C A S E E X A M P L E

Mr. S was a 50-year-old, single man with a history of bipolar disorder and stroke. He was frequently noncompliant with the medication that controlled his illness because he did "not like the side effects" of mood stabilizers. Mr. S had a history of threatening and violent behavior when ill. He was a very tall man who could be intimidating. One spring, Mr. S began working very long hours cutting lawns. The team became concerned that Mr. S was hyperenergetic. He was not being responsible with his income and had missed his rent payment. During a home visit, the case manager followed an electrical cord from an outlet above the patient's bed to a large hedge trimmer with very sharp blades lying on the patient's bed. The case manager also observed several electrical fire hazards. When the case manager questioned Mr. S about the condition of his apartment, he became agitated. The case manager was aware of Mr. S's history of violence and rapidly backed off, attempting to reassure the patient. However, within a few hours, it became necessary for the case manager and psychiatrist to have the police take Mr. S to the hospital.

Social Welfare

Deprivation of basic needs such as food and shelter can precipitate or be a consequence of an acute episode of psychiatric illness. Case managers help to ensure the provision of basic needs in a clinically relevant manner. For example, a case manager may recognize that a patient prefers to eat in soup kitchens with an occasional restaurant meal rather than to purchase food and cook. Case managers are in the optimal position to determine housing arrangements that are most acceptable to the patient and to try to arrange for that housing. Case management programs also frequently work to obtain income entitlements for patients; case managers may serve as representative payees if patients are unable to manage their funds.

CASE MANAGEMENT MODELS IN MENTAL HEALTH CARE

To this point, a conceptual framework (activities, accountability, and authority) has been described for comparing the ba-

sic features of different case management programs. A discussion of four case management models follows, focusing on the case manager's activities, the task areas within each model, and their authority structures. The four models considered are the generalist, personal strengths, intensive case management, and ACT. Following this discussion, the empiric evidence on the effects of these models on reduction of psychiatric hospitalization and the costs of treatment are examined.

In practice, the distinctions among various case management models (particularly between the intensive case management and ACT models) may be difficult to discern. Thus, the descriptions below provide broad outlines of "pure" types; models in actual practice typically blend features from different types.

Generalist Model

Also known as the broker model, the generalist model is essentially social casework in which a nonclinician case manager advocates on behalf of the patient. Typically a person with a bachelor's level (or less formal) education in human services, the generalist case manager does not provide formal treatment or rehabilitation services. He or she works with the patient to identify unmet needs, assists the patient directly or indirectly to access services, and coordinates on behalf of the patient the service activities of multiple agencies and providers. The generalist case management model has four basic objectives: continuity of care, accessibility of services, accountability, and efficiency (6).

In many ways, generalist case managers are only as effective as their mental health service delivery system. Where services are comprehensive and accessible, they can be an effective advocate on behalf of the patient (7). In more poorly serviced or restricted environments (or for patients with needs for highly specialized or difficult-to-access services), generalist case managers are less effective. The reduced scope of authority of generalist case managers is particularly evident in decisions to hospitalize or discharge, which typically lie outside their purview.

Personal Strengths Model

This case management model (also known as the Kansas model) focuses on clients' strengths and resources, rather than psychopathology, and seeks to empower the client to achieve goals through active case manager support (8). In this model, the case manager assists the client in achieving his or her goals rather than imposing externally derived treatment goals on the client. Advocacy and a strong emphasis on an active and dynamic one-to-one relationship between the case manager and the client are central features of the personal strengths model. This model is intended to be adjunctive to and independent of the delivery of mental health services (9).

The personal strengths case management model bears certain similarities to the generalist model. Like the generalist model, case managers following the personal strengths model are typically not mental health professionals with credentials. In a survey of 12 personal strengths case management programs, all case management staff were undergraduate and graduate social work students supervised by an experienced social worker (8). This model also does not provide direct clinical treatment services; rather, the focus is on meeting basic daily social, financial, and interpersonal needs. The model also emphasizes a one-to-one relationship between a client and a case man-

ager. Case managers operating within this model would not have control over decisions to hospitalize or discharge, although it is likely that they would be involved with the patient during the hospital stay.

The personal strengths model also has some similarity to the intensive case management and ACT models described below. Like these models, the personal strengths case management model emphasizes the delivery of services in vivo, that is, outside the case manager's office. Services are delivered as often as necessary and are available 7 days per week, 24 hours per day.

Intensive Case Management

Intensive case management incorporates a stronger clinical emphasis (often including the delivery of mental health treatment services), assertive outreach and in vitro office and hospital service delivery, and smaller caseload sizes (i.e., ratios of 1:10–1:20). Intensive case managers tend to work with clients on a one-to-one basis to facilitate access and appropriate use of mental health and other needed services. Examples of intensive case management approaches include social network and clinical case management models (9). Many of these programs incorporate some (but not all) of the critical features of the ACT model (see below).

Intensive case management involves the provision of case management services and mental health/substance abuse treatment by clinically trained staff members who all serve as members of a treatment team. For that reason, it is likely that intensive case managers will have more influence (if not control) over the hospital admission and discharge processes.

ACT

ACT provides a comprehensive range of mental health/substance abuse treatment and rehabilitation and supportive services through a multidisciplinary community-based team. The basic characteristics of ACT programs are assertive engagement, in vivo delivery of services, a multidisciplinary team approach, staff responsibility and continuity over time, caseloads with high staff-to-client ratios, and brief but frequent contacts (high service intensity). ACT teams also provide close liaisons with the client's support system and a treatment focus on alternatives to hospital care (10). ACT programs control the decisions to admit and discharge from inpatient care. The ACT approach strives to reduce the incidence of inpatient psychiatric care and to reduce length of stay when hospital care must be used.

The ACT model, developed and evaluated in Madison, Wisconsin, was called the Training in Community Living Program (or TCL) (11). The TCL model was subsequently replicated and evaluated in controlled studies in Australia, Michigan, and London. The TCL model has been modified and adapted for different settings. One specific adaptation of this model, known as assertive outreach, was developed and evaluated at Thresholds, a large psychosocial rehabilitation agency in Chicago. This model has subsequently been adapted and evaluated at sites in Indiana, Illinois, and Pennsylvania. Despite some differences in their structure and operation, both the TCL and the assertive outreach models embody the key elements of the ACT approach. Moreover, a broad consensus exists among experts concerning these critical elements, which has led to recent efforts to assess the fidelity of implementation of the ACT model (12–15).

EFFECTS OF CASE MANAGEMENT ON PSYCHIATRIC HOSPITALIZATION

There is clear and consistent evidence from literature reviews and empiric studies to support the claim that ACT reduces the rate and duration of psychiatric hospitalization (16). In a meta-analysis of nine studies involving the assertive outreach approach, Bond et al. (17) concluded that, "As a rule of thumb, providing assertive outreach programs for frequent users of hospitals can be expected to reduce inpatient days by about 50%." Four points should be noted, however. First, the reduction in the use of psychiatric hospitalization may be offset partially by an increased use of other community-based alternative services, such as 24-hour crisis intervention and residential services. Therefore, reductions in the use of inpatient services may not be as pronounced where these other services are unavailable.

Second, the effectiveness of ACT models in reducing rehospitalization may be a function of their capacity to control hospital admissions, length of stay, and discharge. As an illustration, in the evaluation of the Daily Living Programme (DLP) (18), the DLP team initially had control over the length of hospital stays. DLP patients were hospitalized at approximately the same rate as control patients, but length of stay was approximately 80% shorter. At a later time, control over discharge decisions was assumed by non-DLP staff members, at which point the average lengths of stay increased significantly.

Third, reductions in hospital use have tended to cease after ACT treatment is discontinued (11, 19–20).

Fourth, the degree of fidelity to the original ACT program model appears to be an important determinant of the magnitude of the reduction in psychiatric inpatient utilization. McGrew et al. (13) assessed the effect of program fidelity for assertive outreach on reductions in psychiatric hospital days in a sample of 18 programs using this model. They found a significant association between the total fidelity index score and two fidelity index subscale scores (staffing and organization) and overall reductions in psychiatric hospital days.

Evidence also shows that intensive case management programs can reduce use of inpatient care, although not to the same extent as ACT (16). One problem complicating the interpretation of this literature is the wide variability in program characteristics defined as "intensive case management." A review of this literature did not indicate the extent to which the case management intervention explicitly targeted reductions in hospital utilization, nor did it determine the degree of control exercised by the program over hospital admission and discharge decisions. Caseload size and composition also varied. Thus, it could not be determined whether the intensive case management programs that focused on reducing hospital use and were effective achieved these results because of the intensity and character of alternate services provided or the ability to control the hospitalization process. Conversely, studies did not indicate whether programs that did not significantly reduce hospital use failed because they lacked one or more of these elements.

The evidence was unclear for the effectiveness of other case management models. In two evaluations of the personal strengths model, Modrcin et al. (21) found no effect on rehospitalization rates, whereas Macias et al. (22) reported no reduction in subsequent inpatient utilization. In an evaluation of the generalist model, Franklin et al. (7) reported a significant increase in hospital use among individuals who received case management. In short, existing studies did not demonstrate that the other models reduced psychiatric inpatient utilization. These results suggest that individuals with schizophrenia or other chronic mental illnesses with high levels of service utilization require an intensity of case management services that may not be present in the personal strengths and generalist models.

EFFECTS OF CASE MANAGEMENT ON COSTS OF CARE

Previous studies have examined the effects of ACT and intensive case management services on the economic costs of care and have shown that TCL programs are either less costly than comparison programs or, when more costly, that the higher costs may be offset by an increased earning capacity on the part of service recipients (16). In addition, several studies have shown that the sources of treatment costs change as a result of TCL programming, with a reduction in costs attributable to inpatient care and an increase in structured residential and/or outpatient costs. These shifts are compatible with the program theory underlying the TCL model. The evidence for cost-savings from the TCL programs appears stronger and more consistent than from the assertive outreach adaptation.

Some evidence indicates that intensive case management approaches may be less costly than their comparison approaches, but that shifts in costs from inpatient care to outpatient and residential services occur (23–26). However, Wright et al. (27) found that total costs (based on billings for services across the service delivery system) decreased significantly for each of 4 years of intensive case management.

The lack of extensive economic analyses of other case management program models (e.g., personal strengths and generalist models) preclude forming any conclusions about their costs.

CONCLUSION

Case management and case managers have the dual goals of enhancing access to care and limiting expenditures. Case managers can enhance patient outcomes and save costs in the care of the acutely ill psychiatric patient. A full range of case management activities (from patient identification to direct service) is important for acutely ill persons. Case managers must focus explicitly on reducing the consumption of resources (e.g., reduction of hospitalization), must have authority commensurate with this responsibility, and must work within an organizational structure that is committed unambiguously to this goal. A number of well-defined and well-researched case management models, including ACT, have documented effectiveness for patients who are high users of services.

REFERENCES

1. Ellison ML, Rogers ES, Sciarappa K, et al. Characteristics of mental health case management: results of a national survey. J Ment Health Admin 1995;22:101–112.
2. Sledge SH, Astrachan B, Thompson K, et al. Case management in psychiatry: an analysis of tasks. Am J Psychiatry 1995;152:1259–1265.
3. Bachrach LL. Continuity of care and approaches to case management for long term mentally ill patients. Hosp Community Psychiatry 1993;44:465–468.
4. Center for Mental Health Services. Making a difference. DHHS publication no

SMA94–3014. Rockville, MD: DHHS, 1994:94–3014.
5. Astrachan B, Levinson DJ, Adler DA. The impact of national health insurance on the tasks and practice of psychiatry. Arch Gen Psychiatry 1976;33:785–794.
6. Intagliata J. Improving the quality of community care for the chronically mentally disabled: the role of case management. Schizophr Bull 1982;8:655–674.
7. Franklin J, Solovitz B, Mason M, et al. An evaluation of case management. Am J Public Health 1987;77:674–678.
8. Rapp CA, Wintersteen R. The Strengths model of case management: results from twelve demonstrations. Psychosoc Rehab J 1989;13:23–32.
9. Meisler N, Santos AB. Case management of persons with schizophrenia and other severe mental illnesses in the USA. In: Moscarelli M, Rupp A, Sartorius N, eds. Handbook of mental health economics and health policy, schizophrenia. Chichester: John Wiley & Sons, 1996;1:179–194.
10. Taube CA, Morlock L, Burns BJ, et al. New directions in research on assertive community treatment. Hosp Community Psychiatry 1990;41:642–646.
11. Stein LI, Test MA. Alternative mental hospital treatment. Part 1: conceptual model, treatment program, and clinical evaluation. Arch Gen Psychiatry 1980;37:392–397.
12. Brekke JS, Test MA. A model for measuring the implementation of community support programs: results from three sites. Community Ment Health J 1992;28:227–247.
13. McGrew JH, Bond GR, Dietzen L, et al. Measuring the fidelity of implementation of a mental health program model. J Consult Clin Psychol 1994;62:670–678.
14. McGrew JH, Bond GR. Critical ingredients of assertive community treatment: judgements of the experts. J Ment Health Admin 1995;22:113–125.
15. Teague GB, Drake RE, Ackerson TH. Evaluating use of continuous treatment teams for persons with mental illness and substance abuse. Psychiatric Services 1995;46:689–695.
16. Scott JE, Dixon LB. Assertive community treatment and case management for schizophrenia. Schizophr Bull 1995;21:657–668.
17. Bond GR, McGrew JH, Fekete DM. Assertive outreach for frequent users of psychiatric hospitals: a meta-analysis. J Ment Health Admin 1995;22:4–16.
18. Marks IM, Connolly J, Muijen M, et al. Home-based versus hospital-based care for people with serious mental illness. Br J Psychiatry 1994;165:179–194.

19. Test MA. Training in community living. In: Liberman RP, ed. Handbook of psychiatric rehabilitation. New York, Macmillan, 1992:153–170.

20. Audini B, Marks IM, Lawrence RE, et al. Home-based versus out-patient/in-patient care for people with serious mental illness—phase II of a controlled study. Br J Psychiatry 1994;165:204–210.

21. Modrcin M, Rapp CA, Poertner J. The evaluation of case management services with the chronically mentally ill. Eval Prog Planning 1988;11:307–314.

22. Macias C, Kinney R, Farley OW, et al. The role of case management within a community support system: partnership with psychosocial rehabilitation. Community Ment Health J 1994;30:323–339.

23. Borland A, McRae J, Lycan C. Outcome of five years of continuous intensive case management. Hosp Community Psychiatry 1989;40:369–376.

24. Jerrell JM, Hu TW. Cost-effectiveness of intensive clinical and case management compared with an existing system of care. Inquiry 1989;26:224–234.

25. Burns T, Raftery J, Beardsmore A, et al. A controlled trial of home-based acute psychiatric services. Part II: treatment patterns and costs. Br J Psychiatry 1993;163:55–61.

26. Quinlaven R, Hough R, Crowell A, et al. Service utilization and costs of care for severely mentally ill clients in an intensive case management program. Psychiatric Services 1995;46:365–371.

27. Wright RG, Heiman JR, Shupe J, et al. Defining and measuring stabilization of patients during four yearns of intensive community support. Am J Psychiatry 1989;146:1293–1298.

Chapter 16

Family Support and Intervention

Ira D. Glick and John F. Clarkin

FAMILY MODEL OF INTERVENTION

The nature and quality of work with the family has varied enormously throughout the history of the treatment of acute psychiatric illness. The regard and help given families has tended to reflect prevailing theories of individual patient psychopathology and a tendency for clinicians to temporarily "adopt" patients from their families. Shorter lengths of hospital stay and a now-developed literature on family theory and practice have combined to inform us of the limits of hospital practice and the importance of including, allying, and relying on families for the effective short- and long-term care of the acute psychiatric patient (1, 2).

This chapter focuses on a new model (or orientation) for the evaluation and treatment of families. The model is empiric rather than theoretical (where data exist). General guidelines for family work are provided, and specific approaches for specific diagnostic disorders elaborated.

Table 16.1 contrasts the individually oriented model with the family oriented model that is advocated for the acute care of psychiatric patients (3).

Background

In the 1970s, a family with a member presenting for care in a psychiatric hospital was regarded, at best, as a source of information for the social worker and as payer of the bill. At worst, the family was perceived as a malignant force, composed of pathogenic people who played a major role in causing the patient's symptoms and who tended to interfere with the patient's treatment. Staff members acted in loco parentis and often inappropriately blamed the family for the patient's symptoms. Remarkably, the family frequently was not allowed to visit during the early part of hospitalization. In many cases, families were only too happy to stay away because the psychiatric hospital was associated with fear and stigma. Already fragile family ties were consequently broken. Hospital

TABLE 16.1. Family Therapy in Individually and Family Oriented Treatment: A Comparison

Issue	Individually oriented	Family oriented
Locus of pathology	In the neurobiologic system or psychodynamics of the individual	Dysfunctional individual behavior related to dysfunction in family interactions as well as individual neurobiologic and psychodynamic factors—a biopsychosocial model
Locus of change and healing	In the biosystem or the intrapsychic system of the individual	In the individual within the family as a significant piece of the individual's ecology
Diagnosis	DSM-IV, Axes I, II, III	DSM-IV, Axes IV and V, and characterization in relation to the symptoms or complaints
Role of the staff	To care for and provide therapy for the patient	To facilitate changes in education through family interaction or planned interactions with patient
Role of family therapy	A modality to work on those aspects of the patient's problem that seem to be related to family functioning	The orienting therapy of the overall treatment program
Discharge planning	Related to the condition of the individual and his or her ability to function	Related to the condition of the family and its ability to provide safety and continued growth for members

staff members tended to want to remove the patient from the family setting. When this did not occur, patients were sent back to families without the problems addressed or the ties rebuilt.

In other cultures, families typically are considered a vital part of the psychiatric care of their members (4). Because of the scarcity of trained professionals in other cultures, families are required to care for the needs of the identified patient. In fact, family members often stay with the patient in or near the hospital. In other cultures, the patient is assumed to be an integral part of his or her family, and it is unthinkable that the patient would return anywhere but to the family (5).

Although family intervention has increased in acute care settings during the past 20 years, this has not been without problems (6). In a prescient article published in 1977, Anderson (7) outlined some of the difficulties:

"Regrettably, however, the family therapy literature is not particularly helpful to those working on inpatient units; such concepts as 'defining the family as the patient' tend to alienate both the medical staff of an institution and the already overwhelmingly guilt-ridden families. The polarized approaches of family therapists, who generally operate on a 'system' model, which overemphasizes interactional variables, and of psychiatrists, who generally operate on a 'medical' model, which overemphasizes individual variables, disregard the complex and complementary interplay of biological, psychodynamic, and interactional factors."

This quote highlights the problem of integrating theories of etiology and pathogenesis, a problem shared by patient, family, and hospital staff. To be sure, advances have been made since 1977. For example, the research on expressed emotion (EE) in the family environments of schizophrenics has demonstrated the interplay between biology and environment, thereby focusing treatment (8). In addition, research designs that include pharmacotherapy in various doses combined with family intervention (9, 10) recognize (and provide data on) the importance of simultaneously attacking biologic and social factors in illness.

In the 1990s the family has become a "colleague" on the treatment team. Accordingly, the prescription for acute care for families has undergone major changes. Because patients are typically more ill and more disabled, both mentally and physically, the families of these patients tend to be more burdened, compromised, and financially depleted. They need more support than ever.

Function of the Acute Team for the Family

Brief acute psychiatric intervention (through hospitalization and other acute residential services), which is the norm in the United States, provides a safe and controlled environment in which to treat acute symptoms of depression, mania, suicidal ideation, alcoholism, severe personality disorder, schizophrenia, and psychotic thought and behavior. In addition, acute care with residential support serves major functions for the family of the patient. The (identified) patient is temporarily removed from an overwhelmed family environment. In an acute family crisis, removal from home can decrease behavioral eruptions and offer substantial relief to a desperate family. During this separation, a critical goal is to evaluate and change the family's maladaptive patterns of interaction (11).

Acute residential care can also dramatically symbolize the problems of patient and family and thus can allow for their resolution. Psychiatric intervention can disrupt a rigidly pathologic pattern of family interaction, throw the family temporarily into turmoil, and create an opportunity to change that can be more rapid and substantial than without separation. Moreover, 24-hour care permits observation, evaluation, and discussion of family interaction patterns that can instill motivation for marital and family treatment after discharge. Acute care may also set the stage for overt (as opposed to previously covert) consideration of separation in deadlocked marital or parent-child interactions.

Staff members in an acute care setting should consider four family-relevant functions when a patient with a serious mental illness presents for treatment (12):

1. Treat the patient.
2. Evaluate the family, identifying those members with special difficulties who need immediate or intense support.
3. Develop an alliance with the family, which can later be shifted to community-based care.
4. Begin psychoeducation of the families (therapy and consultation are regarded as distinct interventions).

In performing the above functions, especially the second, it is important that the clinician identify family patterns of coping with the patient's mental illness and intrafamilial differences in coping that evoke conflict (e.g., when one parent sees the patient as "bad" and another as "sick"). The family response must always be understood in its cultural context. Finally, a good clinician should recognize that the family's ability to cope can change over time.

Some families with a seriously mentally ill member are able to cope successfully. Clinicians should not presume that something must be wrong with the family because a patient has a serious mental illness. The National Alliance for the Mentally Ill does not accept the assertion of many family therapists that the whole family "is the patient." Alliance family members prefer to serve as "members of the treatment team" (D. Richardson, personal communication, 1996).

Later in this chapter, these functions will be translated into goals.

Functions of Acute Treatment for Families

Although most family interactions are not a major or sole cause of serious individual symptoms, it seems clear that acute intervention with a family member can serve important functions (adaptive and maladaptive) for a family system:

1. The family is in crisis and uses acute care to adaptively resolve the crisis (13–15). For example, some dysfunctional couples have described the process of coping with a psychotic episode in one member as a strongly positive experience for both (16).

2. The family extrudes an identified patient from the family in a misguided and maladaptive attempt to solve a crisis.

3. The family uses the health-care system to obtain treatment for a member other than the identified patient. The identified patient is not necessarily the only "sick" one (nor even the "sickest" one) in the family (17). A family approach allows for observing and evaluating all family members and advocating for appropriate treatment (including medication) for those members who may require it. Clinicians concentrating on one individual may overlook or not have access to psychological disturbances in a close relative.

4. The family uses the health-care system as a means to regain a "lost" member. For example, an alcoholic father who is never home is finally convinced to enter treatment. The family's motivation to regain a functioning father and spouse has overcome the need to keep him "sick."

5. The family turns to an acute care system as a necessary respite from family burdens caused by an identified patient with a chronic or deteriorating condition (e.g., childhood or adult schizophrenia).

☐ CASE EXAMPLE OF EXTRUSION

The M family consisted of mother, boyfriend, and two teen-age daughters; the older daughter had anorexia nervosa, and the younger was functioning well in school. The mother had long-standing paranoid schizophrenia and was extremely dependent on her own mother. The mother had been divorced about 10 years previously but had recently become involved with a boyfriend.

After the mother became very involved in this relationship and was considering marriage, she began to argue frequently with the elder daughter. When the anorectic daughter began eating less and became paranoid, the mother contacted a pediatrician, stating that her daughter was seriously ill and needed hospitalization. The mother confided to the family therapist that she was unable to take care of her daughter because caring for her daughter would prevent her from spending time with her boyfriend, threatening the relationship. The pediatrician hospitalized the daughter.

This case illustrates how one family member can extrude another in the service of individual needs. To prevent the loss of her boyfriend, the mother restructured the family by having her daughter (the identified patient) hospitalized.

As these clinical situations illustrate, the treatment program is inadequate unless the family is included. Acute care psychiatry will not be able to provide effective and efficient care without a focus on the family.

Process of Family Treatment in Acute Care

The process of family intervention involves (*a*) alliance with the family, (*b*) assessment, (*c*) definition of the problem, (*d*) goal setting, (*e*) the start of treatment (in some cases), and (*f*) referral for continued care after discharge. Intensive psychoeducation about a specific illness and a specific treatment for that illness is an essential service. Particular attention should be paid to single-parent families and remarried families who have to cope with serious long-term mental illness. The Alliance for the Mentally Ill has found that approximately 60% of its members are single parents who often express the opinion that mental illness in a child caused the marital breakup.

Allying with the Family

Contact with the family should start as early as possible. If hospitalized, contact should preferably start before hospitalization, when the family is trying to arrange admission, or certainly by the time of admission. A principal focus with the family should be discharge planning. Moreover, the family must be helped to understand that hospital treatment of the identified patient involves (or requires) education, support, and involvement of all family members. This should be made a condition of all acute care. A family representative should be appointed as the accountable communicating link with the primary clinician (outside formal treatment sessions).

A more relevant question should be whether to use a psychoeducational or a consultative approach and in which order. Grunebaum and Friedman (18) suggested that the first encounter be psychoeducational rather than consultative. Therapists need the family "in order to learn about the history of the patient's illness and the family's story. Families need us to teach them about what they are facing, often for the first time" (18). Consultation is more appropriate later in treatment.

Evaluating the Family

Evaluating the family should involve the presence of the identified patient unless he or she is too psychotic or cognitively impaired. The evaluation should follow the customary outline for acute work and begin with the construction of a family genogram. In addition, an examination of immediate events, especially notable family events and changes, that led to the contact should be performed. The evaluation should help to answer whether family intervention is needed and, if so, with what focus.

Most importantly, a necessary goal of the family evaluation should be to move the family from a frightened defensive stance (in which they presume they will draw blame) to a position of early trust and collaboration with the treatment team. The clinician also seeks to enable the family to find the best possible coping mechanisms for the patient's symptoms. Coping mechanisms must be understood by clinicians and family members as the best of difficult alternatives. Adaptation to illness is a process of building adaptive responses.

Negotiating Goals of Family Intervention

Keeping in mind that acute treatment is brief, the therapist should immediately focus on the general goals of family intervention and on the goals specific to the individual family. Negotiating these goals with the family should be accomplished by the end of one or two evaluation sessions. Negotiation must be done with confidence, delicacy, firmness, and empathy. Families are upset about the condition of the patient, may see no need for their participation in therapy, or may be hostile to the treatment team for not quickly "curing" their family member. In the worst scenario, the family consciously or unconsciously seeks to extrude the patient. These varied responses often occur because of the burden of dealing with illness.

Educating the family about the illness helps to reduce guilt. Information about the type and length of treatment, as well as realistic expectations of change, will reduce anxiety and allow for focus. Realistic expectations can diminish subsequent disappointment and devaluation of the treatment and staff. Education about needed family assistance will help in discharge planning and treatment compliance. Family sessions can vary in length from 30–60 minutes and may be scheduled on a daily, biweekly, or weekly basis, depending on need, goals, and/or anticipated discharge date.

It has been found that psychoeducation rarely proceeds as smoothly as its description might imply. Families frequently resist participating in treatment, deny the patient's illness, or magnify its severity and intractability. These are the complexities and challenges of family intervention. The family intervention must then switch from educational to interpretative to overcome or circumvent family resistance to treatment.

Common Goals of Acute Family Intervention

Six goals dictate the focus and course of acute family intervention. Although one inpatient family intervention research study (19) focused on two major diagnostic groups (schizophrenic spectrum and major affective disorders patients), these goals can be generalized to major mental illnesses.

Whatever the patient's diagnosis, the family faces multiple tasks, including (1) understanding the patient's illness, (2) appreciating their influence on the illness, (3) allying with treatment staff, (4) acknowledging the future course of the illness, (5) adjusting their expectations of the ill member, and (6) deciding on a discharge treatment plan, including the optimal living arrangement for the family member. These tasks are enormous, especially for the first episode of illness, and consequently require considerable, focused attention from therapeutic staff members.

The following six goals and corresponding treatment strategies of acute family intervention are designed to meet systematically the needs of families. When this is accomplished, the family becomes a major asset in the patient's recovery. When family needs are not met, the family will respond with aversion, hostility, and chaos, which add to a patient's risk of destabilization.

Goal 1: Accepting the Reality of the Illness and Understanding the Current Episode

This goal is the cornerstone of all other goals. Unless some acceptance and understanding of the illness and the seriousness of the episodes are achieved, the family cannot aid in future treatment.

Clinicians can choose from a number of techniques to accomplish this goal. All techniques require a working alliance that is accomplished by appreciating and expressing the family's burden. Clinical staff members should inquire as to each family member's perception and understanding of the illness. Although clinical staff members may not agree with a family member's view, they can empathize with the family's attempts to cope. To reduce inordinate feelings of responsibility for the illness, therapists can provide the family with facts about the illness and (especially in the case of schizophrenia and major mood disorders) articulate the biologic and genetic causes. When the family realizes that staff members are not blaming them, trust can begin. The therapist may then explore the emergence of the current episode to identify family stresses and environmental problems. Finally, the family can be educated about the course of the disorder, including early warning signs, progression, relapse, and recurrence.

Goal 2: Identifying Current Episode Stressors

Once the family has tentatively accepted the reality of the illness, the next step should be to identify precipitating current episode stressors while they are still fresh in the family's mind. The abstract notion that stress can influence a psychiatric illness can become a reality when the link between theory and reality is forged.

The strategies and techniques for achieving this second goal are mainly educative, cognitive, and problem solving. The clinician should encourage the family to think about recent stresses, inside and outside the family, that may have contributed to the patient's regression. In addition, the family can rank the stresses and assign priorities for brief interventions.

Goal 3: Identifying Potential Future Stressors Within and Outside the Family

The first two goals are principally concerned with the immediate and remote

past and offer a didactic approach to illness. If these goals can be accomplished (even partly), there may be a natural pull to consider the future. In fact, in some cases, a future orientation (e.g., discharge) can come too early. This can generally signal defensive denial that must be met with a refocus on Goals 1 and 2.

The family's attitudes toward the patient and treatment have an impact on outcome. For example, positive parental attitudes about hospital treatment have correlated with patient improvement, whereas resistance to treatment has correlated with discharge against medical advice (20–22). In addition, Greenman et al. (23) found that certain parental concerns on admission to the hospital have an impact on patient behavior. Interestingly, these concerns were linked to gender: mothers were concerned with limit-setting (i.e., preventing impulsive and self-destructive behavior), whereas fathers "had difficulty supporting treatment because they were afraid that taking such a position would anger the patient, leading to a loss of their relationship with the patient" (23).

Goal 4: Elucidating Stressful Family Interactions

Informing a family that they can be the cause of stress is both intellectual and vague. However, demonstrating how a family's behavior can destabilize the patient (e.g., becoming paranoid or disorganized or smashing an object), can lead to real learning.

In the past decade, an impressive body of evidence has suggested that families high in EE run an increased risk of patient relapse. Originally, high EE was thought to be specific to schizophrenia, but recent research demonstrates this difficulty in families with chronic affective and other disorders (24). Increased family

EE can be found in almost all chronic psychiatric illnesses. Because techniques that lower EE can result in better patient outcome, there is a great deal to offer families with dysfunctional coping mechanisms.

Although the first three goals are mediated by cognitive and educative strategies, techniques that demonstrate how family interactions stress the patient more closely approximate traditional (or system-oriented) family therapy. A systems-clarifying technique is illustrated by the following statement: "Every time you criticize him, as you did just now, he puts his head down and murmurs something under his breath that sounds like nonsense." This technique can help the clinician show the family that an interaction does not cause the disorder (thereby reducing guilt) but is likely to trigger current symptoms (thereby focusing controllable and adaptive behavior). The family's frustration and anger toward the patient's behavior, which led them to criticize, can be successfully redirected.

Goal 5: Planning Strategies for Managing and/or Minimizing Future Stressors

By the middle or toward the end of an acute episode of illness, family members can believe that their troubles are over. The next goal of family intervention should be to help families recognize the need for planning to ensure that history does not repeat itself.

The therapist can initiate discussion of the possible return of symptoms and ways in which the family can cope with this eventuality. Family members also need to be encouraged to discuss their expectations of the patient's future level of functioning. For some families, expectations must be realistically lowered; for others, hope needs to be stimulated. Families need

help anticipating potential stressors related to the patient's reentering the community, including occupational, educational, and social functioning.

Goal 6: Accepting the Need for Continued Treatment

This goal, central to preventing relapse, brings the family full circle with the first goal, reducing denial of the illness. Families who have experienced repeated episodes of illness have little problem anticipating the possibility of relapse. However, because these families are often discouraged and burdened, they need support and encouragement. For families going through a first hospitalization, the danger of denying future illness and the need for aftercare should be recognized.

The therapist can use the family technique of visualizing in the future to replay the causes of the current illness. How would the patient tell the family (or vice versa) that something is the matter? What are the early signs of illness? Who would the family contact? Additional education about the course of the condition further emphasizes the need for aftercare.

Not every family will need work on all goals. Some families will be so traumatized or limited that only the initial basic goals can be approached.

The ultimate goal of family intervention is to include the family in the gains of acute care. If the family can understand precipitating stressors, modulate high EE, and ensure continued treatment, the transition from acute to ambulatory care will be facilitated greatly. This is especially important in the current environment, which promotes reduced hospitalization to limit regression and especially to reduce health-care costs through brief stays.

Particular Decisions in Hospital Family Intervention

Timing

When to make contact and when to start therapy are the two key elements of timing. Contact with the family should start during the decision-making process leading to acute care (e.g., in the emergency department). Family therapists typically disagree about when the patient should be present. Some believe that family intervention with the patient should begin only when the active symptoms have begun to diminish (25). This position seems to rationalize the delay in family intervention and treatment. Many patients, even in a psychotic state, become more coherent during well-planned and focused family sessions.

Staffing

Who should provide the family intervention? The primary clinician or therapist would be in the best position to work with the family because he or she has an overall grasp of the case. Moreover, both the individual and family treatment should be performed by the same clinician. However, time constraints or the need for supervision may make this impossible. Primary clinicians may be from any discipline (psychology, social work, nursing), but experience with families and training in the theory and practice of family therapy are critical. Also, experience with the disorders that are prevalent in acute care psychiatry is important.

The partial hospital or inpatient milieu is especially advantageous for identifying patterns of family interaction. Accurate, on-the-spot observation of a family may reveal how a patient's symptoms may be aggravated. For example, an adolescent who repeatedly recreates problem family interactions with female staff members on the psychiatric unit can be shown that this behavior is similar to the way he reacts to his mother.

Family Techniques

A variety of family therapy techniques needed in the acute setting include:

1. Individual family intervention.
2. Multiple family group and conjoint couples group (26).
3. Family psychoeducational workshops (also known as family survival skills workshops or family support groups) (27).

Today, family therapy is rarely used for hospitalized or acute care patients. For psychotic patients, family intervention complements medication and rehabilitative therapies. For nonpsychotic patients, family intervention is part of a treatment plan consisting of pharmacotherapy and individual therapy.

☐ CASE EXAMPLE

A 17-year-old boy was admitted to the hospital after having been extremely agitated and disoriented at home, where he refused to eat or sleep. A schizophrenic disorder was the working diagnosis. In the hospital, he continued to be very paranoid, eating only with a parent and avoiding other patients. Staff members met with the boy, and his mother and explained their observations and concerns as well as how a medication could help. They also discussed side effects and how to evaluate the effectiveness of the drug (e.g., thinking more clearly and understanding activities around him). He was told he could help the staff members decide the best dose.

The boy hesitated and the mother

had questions, but she convinced him that he should begin a neuroleptic. Two days later, he reported that he felt better and wanted to stop the medication. Staff members spoke with the patient and his mother again and indicated that more time was needed to keep the patient well. Again, the mother persuaded the boy to continue taking the drug. Some days later, he said he felt better but wondered if an increased dose would help him sleep better. In another meeting with the boy and his mother, a new dosage was arranged.

Discussions regarding the medication provided the boy and his mother with a cooperative, respectful relationship with each other and with staff members. Decisions were not made for him; instead, he was included in them. As the hospitalization progressed, he more readily questioned his family and the staff, and the answers he received helped to clarify and quiet his psychotic confusion. The neuroleptic and the contextual experiences described had worked synergistically.

The acute treatment team must make a "choice" of a family treatment model: psychoeducational or psychodynamic or a systems-structural approach. All three are useful, but at different times in the course of a disorder or with different disorders. Because of the brief duration of acute care and the cognitive impairment of an acutely ill patient, a psychoeducational approach is recommended, reserving psychodynamic and structural approaches for continued care.

A good description of the need for psychoeducation is found in the following communication from a parent of a patient with schizoaffective disorder:

"When my daughter and son-in-law entered the clinic with their newborn son, diagnosed with spina bifida and hydrocephalus, the chief nurse said, 'You will be with this child every hour of the day. We will teach you what to look for, and then you will be able to tell us what is wrong with the baby.' When my other daughter accompanied her son to the allergist about the boy's asthma, the doctor gave specific instructions about the dosage of medicine and the desired response. The doctor told her when to go up and come down with the medication dosage and what to do in an emergency. As a pathologist who has worked closely with my son who has schizoaffective disorder, I believe it is important that a parent or family member be involved equally in the treatment of mental disorders. The principle is that a patient and his family should be given medical education and training to enable them to carry out the treatment program."

The care of a mental disorder, like many persistent or unstable illnesses, requires daily attention to symptomatology, stresses, and treatment. Professional care is simply not possible at this level of intensity. The patient and family need to be educated and supported to implement the treatment plan.

A WORKING MODEL OF ACUTE FAMILY INTERVENTION

The Group for the Advancement of Psychiatry Committee on the Family has summarized the new family model as follows:

"Hospitalization should be viewed in most cases as an event in the history of the family, an event that can be devastating or valuable depending upon the skills and orientation of the therapeutic team. Hospitalization viewed in this way becomes central in understanding the role of the patient in the family system and in supporting the family as well as the patient. The hospital becomes an important therapeutic adjunct not only for severely dysfunctional individuals and their families, but also for families stuck in modes of relating that appear to interfere with the development and movement of individual members. For these families, hospitalization aims to disrupt the family set; this disruption can be used to help the family system to change in more functional ways" (28).

Family-oriented programs can be implemented within existing hospital resources. Moreover, acute care environments may be readily revised to include family members in patient care. (This trend is also noted in other specialties, such as "rooming in" in obstetric and pediatric units.) Effective programs involve the entire staff, from admission clerks on, in building an alliance with the family. On acute teams, families should be advised that the changes they make in relating will always increase anxiety because the status quo has been changed. Stewart (29) described this as "the engagement of the family with the institution in a relationship that achieves mutual understanding and support and establishes clarity, acceptance, and commitment to mutually agreed upon goals for the treatment of the hospitalized patient." Active reaching out can be done at all levels of acute care (not just at the hospital level of care) and can be considered different from a commitment to change-oriented family treatment. The family model proposed in this chapter avoids staff overidentification with the patient, which can pit staff members against the family. It also reduces the stigma of psychiatric treatment and increases aftercare compliance.

Different staff-family interactions are possible and helpful; alliance building, staff and family interaction around medications, visits, and formal family therapy sessions geared to change may all have a therapeutic function (29).

Table 16.2 is a summary of acute family intervention.

GUIDELINES FOR RECOMMENDING FAMILY INTERVENTION IN AN ACUTE CARE SETTING

The guidelines for recommending family intervention in acute care are similar to those for outpatient settings. If the family is present and available, family intervention should not be withheld (30).

A careful distinction should be made between evaluation and psychoeducation and family treatment. As a rule, every family should be evaluated and educated about illness and family treatment. When indicated, family treatment should be started in the acute care setting, although most goals will be accomplished in a continued care setting.

Examples of acute situations that called for family intervention included:

◆ A suicidal and depressed adolescent living in the parental home was hospitalized after a car accident. There was some suspicion that the father was an alcoholic and that the parents were not aware of the adolescent's depression or of his day-to-day functioning.

◆ A 22-year-old college student presented with an acute psychotic episode in the fall of his first year away from home. Family sessions were needed to educate about the unexpected illness, help the parents and the patient evaluate their mutual expectations for his performance, and encourage follow-up psychiatric care.

◆ A 39-year-old divorced woman living with her 11-year-old and 13-year-old children was hospitalized after a paranoid psychotic break in which she stabbed herself in the abdomen in the presence of the children. Family ses-

TABLE 16.2.   Acute Family Intervention (31)

Definition: Acute family intervention (AFI) is work with patients and their families together in one or more family sessions. It aims at favorably affecting the patient's course of illness and course of treatment through increased understanding of the illness and decreased stress on the patient.

Description:

I.   Assumptions

   1.   AFI does not assume that the etiology of the major psychotic disorders lies in family functioning or communication.

   2.   It does assume that present-day functioning of a family (with which the patient is living or is in frequent contact) can be a major source of stress or support.

II.   Aims

   1.   AFI aims to help families understand, live with, and deal with patients and their illness; to develop the most appropriate possible ways of addressing the problems the illness presents and its effects on the patient; and to understand and support the necessary acute and long-range treatment.

   2.   AFI aims to help patients understand family actions and reactions and to help patients develop the most appropriate intrafamily behavior to decrease their vulnerability to family stress and decrease the likelihood that their behavior will provoke family maladaptive behaviors.

III.   Strategy and techniques

   A.   Evaluation

      1.   Evaluation is accomplished in one or more initial family sessions, with the patient present when conditions permit. Information gained from other sources is also used.

      2.   The patient's illness and its potential course are evaluated.

      3.   The present effect and the possible future effect on the family are determined.

      4.   The family's effect on the patient is evaluated, with particular reference to the stress caused by expressed emotion and criticism.

      5.   Family structure and interaction and the present point in the family life cycle are evaluated to determine whether particular aspects of the patient's role in the family are exacerbating or maintaining the illness or otherwise impairing the patient.

   B.   Techniques

      1.   The family and patient are usually seen together.

      2.   Early in treatment an attempt is made to form an alliance with the family that gives them a sense of support and understanding.

      3.   Psychoeducation:

         a.   The family is provided with information about the illness, its likely course, and its treatment; questions are answered.

         b.   The idea that stress from and in the family can exacerbate the illness is discussed.

         c.   The ways in which conflicts and stress arise within each family are discussed, and a problem-solving approach is taken in planning ways to decrease stress in the future.

         d.   The ways in which the illness and the patient's impaired functioning have burdened the family are discussed, and plans are made to decrease such a burden.

      4.   In some cases, the initial evaluation or subsequent sessions suggest that particular resistances due to aspects of family structure or family dynamics interfere with accomplishing (2) and (3) above. If it is judged necessary and possible, one or a series of family sessions may attempt to explore resistances and effect changes in family dynamics. Such attempts may use some traditional family therapy techniques. Families may be encouraged to seek family therapy after the patient's discharge.

sions with the children were needed to assist the mother who was in a denial phase, to explain her illness, and to talk about the future. An urgent need also existed for the children to discuss their feelings about witnessing their mother stab herself.

   ◆   A 23-year-old woman who lived with

her parents was hospitalized following an exacerbation of schizophrenia occasioned by her younger sister leaving for college. The patient also had stopped taking her medication. The parents were suspected of high EE (they were critical of their daughter, and one parent was with her constantly). Family treatment was started to increase the likelihood of aftercare, including medication, family therapy, and a partial hospital program.

Indications for family intervention come from the patient, the family, and the observable interactions between the family and the patient's illness. Patient-related criteria include current living conditions (e.g., living with spouse or family of origin) and life cycle issues (e.g., patient is a young adult trying to separate or an older adult living with or dependent on the family). Family criteria include conflict that contributes to the patient's difficulties or psychiatric illness in another family member. Criteria related to the interaction of the family with the patient's illness are family denial and/or inadequate support of illness, family resistance to treatment, and danger of harm to the family.

Contraindications include the patient who is striving (with a good chance for success) for independence from the parents and parents in severe conflict for whom marital therapy may be indicated.

Empiric Studies

Glick et al. (31) have reported the only controlled study of family intervention in an inpatient setting. Inpatient family intervention (IFI) (emphasizing family psychoeducation) was compared with hospitalization without family intervention for patients with schizophrenic and affective disorders. The sample included 169 pa-

tients and their families for whom family intervention was indicated. The families were randomly selected for inclusion in one of the two treatment conditions (mentioned above). Assessments were made at admission, discharge, and 6 and 18 months after admission using patient and family measures from the vantage points of patient, family, and independent assessors.

Overall, family intervention in the hospital setting was found to be effective but not for everyone (31–34). For some patients and families, IFI appeared not to add anything to standard hospital treatment. The positive effect of IFI was seen primarily in female patients with affective disorder and their families, to a lesser extent in good prehospital functioning schizophrenics, and in patients with other diagnoses.

At follow-up, the statistical interactions indicated that any therapeutic effect was generally restricted to female patients with schizophrenia or major affective disorder. The effect of family treatment on male patients with these diagnoses was minimal or slightly negative. It was noted that the effect of IFI on schizophrenia did not appear until 18 months after admission, with the most striking effect in the poor prehospital functioning group. Similarly (and in contrast to the discharge results), for patients with affective disorder, the follow-up results revealed positive findings favoring the IFI. However, these positive findings were only seen in the bipolar subgroup. Composite means showed that family treatment was somewhat better for the families of patients (primarily females) with major psychoses, whereas families of patients with other diagnoses did better without family intervention.

Clinical research on hospital treatment(s) has typically focused on outcomes for patients; outcomes for families are unknown. One three-country study of family outcome after an episode of major affective disorder found that families were less well off financially (because of hospitalization costs), were frequently less functional, and without psychoeducation were unprepared for the next episode (35).

Clinical experience suggests that the specific interventions of psychoeducational groups can help the often demoralized family of a patient with chronic mental illness to reestablish itself as a viable unit and lessen the burden of shame, guilt, despair, and isolation (36).

A study on effectiveness in outpatient settings in three countries (8) has shown that family intervention coupled with medication significantly lowers the risk of relapse for outpatients with schizophrenia. Therefore, it might be extrapolated from this study that family intervention may be needed as part of the multimodal prescription for most Axis I disorders.

Treatment of Nonpsychotic Psychiatric Illness

Families who have a member with a severe personality disorder and/or substance abuse are frequent users of acute care services. The following section briefly reviews family approaches to nonpsychotic patients.

Personality Disorders

The most common personality disorders presenting for acute care are schizotypal, obsessive-compulsive, and borderline personality disorder.

SCHIZOTYPAL PERSONALITY DISORDER

This disorder is thought to be a less severe variant of schizophrenia. Although treatment principles are essentially the same, the lack of psychotic features makes it diffi-

cult for the family to accept an underlying organic illness (rather than a moral failing). Psychoeducation and family intervention are generally needed to help these families.

OBSESSIVE-COMPULSIVE DISORDER

It is now generally well accepted that obsessive-compulsive disorder is related to an underlying selective basal ganglia dysfunction. Families, however, often believe the symptoms, (obsessions and compulsions) can be controlled voluntarily. Controlled studies demonstrate the effectiveness of medication and behavioral therapy for managing this disorder. Family therapy serves an important adjunctive role of decreasing patient anxiety, increasing coping skills, and improving family functioning through education and support.

BORDERLINE PERSONALITY DISORDER

Research during the past decade suggests strong evidence of disturbed biologic underpinnings in this disorder. Lacking adequate perceptual and cognitive capabilities, these patients suffer from "oscillations of attachment" and difficulty regulating interpersonal distance (37). In addition, many borderline patients are self-destructive and/or have major problems relating to their families. Family evaluation and often family treatment are indicated for most cases of borderline personality disorder (37).

Addictive Disorders

The following facts regarding addictive disorders are now well accepted (38) (see Chapter 11 for more details on this subject).

1. The problems of alcohol and substance disorders affect and are affected by the patient's family situation.

2. Marital and family interventions are a necessary component for any patient hospitalized or receiving acute care for an addictive disorder.

3. Family work aims to reduce or end the substance abuse and enhance communication within the family.

4. The few controlled studies performed on alcohol or substance abuse indicate that the family approach seems more effective than individual psychotherapy for both alcohol and substance abuse.

5. Increasingly, family members are recognized as primary patients deserving treatment in their own right.

6. Family treatment techniques include psychoeducational and structural and psychodynamic techniques. Participation in spouse and family groups such as Al-Anon and Nar-Anon are essential to long-term care.

Community-Based Support Groups

An accepted practice among mental health professionals is to encourage family members to use community-based support groups and to form such groups if none are available (39).

During the past decade, a number of excellent books have been written for families with mentally ill members. The National Alliance for the Mentally Ill has the most current list of readings for families.

Hospitals and clinics have also developed manuals for patients and families that describe management and treatment of mental illness. These can serve as important homework reading for families requiring acute care.

Controversies in Treatment

1. Is the family considered in treatment, a part of treatment, or a member of the treatment team? Good treatment should involve all three aspects. First, most families have problems coping with the illness of the identified patient, and many have problems separate from the identified patient. Second, the family's presence in the treatment process (compared with individual or drug treatment) makes them a de facto part of the treatment (in fact, consent to treatment should be obtained). Third, Wynne et al. (40) argue that the long-term nature and seriousness of recurrent or chronic mental illness, as well as the family's experience dealing with a particular member, require the family's expertise to be harnessed.

Initially, most families feel most comfortable as partners with the treatment team. Later, families may feel ready to become part of treatment or enter into treatment. This step often occurs after the patient has stabilized. Over time, clinicians should blend all three positions to achieve the best outcome for patients and families.

2. Should the initial goals of family therapy be oriented around family change or family consultation? This long-standing controversy emanates from the traditional family as etiologic model. The best way to engage family members is to make contact with them "where they are," provide psychoeducation, and respond to requests for information and support. The initial consultation serves as a means to form an alliance with the family. Change cannot occur without this first step.

3. Many family therapists believe that schizophrenic and other major functional psychoses are purely family systems, psychological and social but not biologic problems. Are they? In part, this belief is based on the inference that improvement (or recovery) is not possible without medication. Stein (41) found that mental illnesses, "like virtually every disease, are in-

fluenced by biological, psychological, and social factors." Treating schizophrenic or any other major mental disorder requires biologic, psychological, and social approaches and anything else that will help.

4. Many families believe that major mental illnesses are solely "brain" illnesses. This belief creates confusion in the minds of some families when they are offered a psychosocial treatment such as family therapy. Why would a biochemical problem be treated with a psychosocial treatment? The answer is that any family living with a member who has sustained cognitive and other brain function defects will have major problems in the management of the disorder and with the feelings attached to chronic illness.

5. How much does family intervention add to medication in the treatment of patients with acute mental illness? Most studies indicate concern that modalities are additive (42). Medication is effective for positive (and probably negative) symptoms, and family intervention helps with the complicating interpersonal problems of illness.

An interesting question addressed by The Treatment Strategies in Schizophrenia Collaborative Study is whether family intervention can result in lowered doses of medication and thereby reduction in the risk of tardive dyskinesia. Using a three-by-two design, the study involved the use of standard-dose versus low-dose neuroleptic versus an early intervention strategy (i.e., use medication once the patient starts to relapse), coupled with two kinds of family strategies (a weekly, applied, behaviorally oriented family treatment compared with a monthly supportive group). The greater the family involvement in either applied or supportive treatment, the fewer the patient's symptoms and the less need for medication. However, the addition of family intervention did not interact

with the drug conditions. Neither family strategy lowered the amount of medication needed. In fact, the targeted strategy was not found efficacious for the population of patients with chronic schizophrenia. Conversely, long-term drug maintenance often helped the patient participate more meaningfully in family therapy. Importantly, patients taking lower doses of medication were found to be more socially responsive and involved in therapy (43).

6. Family treatment in the acute setting lacks evidence of effectiveness. Therefore, the enormous resources in time, staff, and money should not be allocated to this modality. Although the accusation (until recently) was mostly true, clinical experience and recent studies (31–35) suggest that the controversy surrounding the effectiveness of family treatment should be reformulated. The central questions are, "Who requires intervention and what is an effective intervention?" Experience indicates that intervention works best for females with affective disorder (especially bipolar disorder) and females with chronic schizophrenia. The families of all patients with schizophrenia and bipolar disorder seem to derive some benefit from family intervention, as opposed to family therapy (31). Consequently, until further studies are conducted, family intervention should be considered for all patients. This approach should be prescribed on the basis of available knowledge and requires a case-by-case evaluation of the patient and the family. Other studies show consistent patterns of effectiveness (44–46).

REFERENCES

1. Glick ID, Hargreaves WA. Psychiatric hospital treatment for the 1980s: a controlled study of short versus long hospitalization. Lexington, MA: Lexington Books, 1979.
2. Glick ID, Klar HM, Braff D. Guidelines for hospitalization of chronic psychiatry patients.

Hosp Community Psychiatry 1984;35:934–936.

3. Group for the Advancement of Psychiatry. The family, the patient, and the psychiatric hospital: toward a new model. New York: Brunner/Mazel, 1985:24.

4. Bell J, Bell E. Family participation in hospital care for children. Children 1970;17:154–157.

5. Bhatti RS, Janikramaiah N, Channabassavanna SM. Family psychiatric ward treatment in India. Fam Process 1980;19:193–200.

6. Harbin HT. Families and hospitals: collusion or cooperation? J Psychiatry 1978;135:1496–1499.

7. Anderson CM. Family intervention with severely disturbed inpatients. Arch Gen Psychiatry 1977;34:697–702.

8. Schooler NR, Keith SJ, Severe JB, et al. Maintenance treatment of schizophrenia: a review of dose reduction and family management strategies. Psychiatry Q 1995;66:279–292.

9. Glick ID, Clarkin JF, Goldsmith SJ. Combining medication with family psychotherapy. In: Beitman B, ed. Combined treatments, the American Psychiatric Press review of psychiatry. Washington, DC: American Psychiatric Press, 1993:585–610.

10. Goldstein MJ, Rodnick EH, Evans JR, et al. Drug and family therapy in the aftercare of acute schizophrenics. Arch Gen Psychiatry 1978;35:1169–1177.

11. Rabiner E, Malminski H, Gralnick A. Conjoint family therapy in the inpatient setting. In: Gralnick A. ed. The psychiatric hospital as a therapeutic instrument. New York: Brunner/Mazel, 1969:160–177.

12. Kahn EM, White EM. Adapting milieu approaches to acute inpatient care for schizophrenic patients. Hosp Community Psychiatry 1989;40:609–614.

13. Sampson H, Messinger S, Towne RD. Family processes and becoming a mental patient. Am J Sociol 1962;68:88–96.

14. Sampson H, Messinger S, Towne RD. The mental hospital and family adaptation. Psychiatry Q 1962;36:704–719.

15. Langlsey D, Kaplan D. The treatment of families in crisis. Orlando: Grune & Stratton, 1968.

16. Dupont R, Ryder R, Grunebaum H. Unexpected results of psychosis in marriage. Am J Psychiatry 1971;128:735–739.

17. Bursten B. Family dynamics, the sick role, and medical hospital admissions. Fam Process 1965;4:206–216.

18. Grunebaum H, Friedman H. Hosp Community Psychiatry 1989;4:20. Letter.

19. Glick ID, Clarkin JF, Spencer JH, et al. Inpatient family intervention. a controlled evaluation of practice: preliminary results of the six-months follow-up. Arch Gen Psychiatry 1985;42:882–886.

20. Goldstein E. The influence of parental attitudes on psychiatric treatment outcome. Social Casework 1979;60:350–359.

21. Daniels RS, Margolis PM, Carson RC. Hospital discharges against medical advice. Arch Gen Psychiatry 1963;8:120–130.

22. Akhtar S, Helfrich J, Mestayer RF. AMA discharge from a psychiatric inpatient unit. Int J Soc Psychiatry 1981;27:143–150.

23. Greenman DA, Gunderson JG, Canning D. Parents' attitudes and patients' behavior; a prospective study. Am J Psychiatry 1989;146:226–230.

24. Miklowitz DJ, Goldstein JM, Neuchterlein KH, et al. Family of bipolar affective disorder. Arch Gen Psychiatry 1988;45:225–231.

25. Guttman HA. A contraindication for family therapy: the prepsychotic or postpsychotic young adult and his parents. Arch Gen Psychiatry 1973;29:352–355.

26. Davenport YB. Treatment of the married bipolar patient in conjoint couples psychotherapy groups. In: Lansky MR, ed. Family therapy and major psychopathology. New York: Grune & Stratton, 1981.

27. Anderson CM, Hogarty GE, Reiss DJ. Family treatment of adult schizophrenic patients: a psychoeducational approach. Schizophr Bull 1980;6:490–505.

28. Group for the Advancement of Psychiatry. The family, the patient and the psychiatric hospital: toward a new model, New York: Brunner/Mazel, 1985:27–29.

29. Stewart R. Building an alliance between the families of patients and the hospital: model and process. Natl Assoc Private Psychiatr Hosp J 1982;12:63–68.

30. Gould E, Glick ID. The effects of family presence and family therapy on outcome of hospitalized schizophrenic patients. Fam Process 1977;16:503–510.

31. Glick ID, Clarkin JF, Hass GL, et al. Clinical significance of inpatient family intervention. Part VII: conclusions from the clinical trial. Hosp Community Psychiatry 1993;44:869–873.

32. Spencer JH, Glick ID, Haas GL. A randomized clinical trial of inpatient family intervention. Part III: overall effects at follow-up for the entire sample. Am J Psychiatry 1988;145:1115–1121.

33. Glick ID, Spencer JH, Clarkin JF, et al. A randomized clinical trial of inpatient family intervention. Part IV: follow-up results for subjects with schizophrenia. Schizophr Res 1990;3:187–200.

34. Clarkin JF, Glick ID, Haas GL, et al. A ran-

domized clinical trial of inpatient family intervention. Part V: results for affective disorders. J Affect Disord 1990;18:17–28.

35. Glick ID, Burti L, Minakawa K, et al. Effectiveness of psychiatric care. Part II: outcome for the family after hospital treatment for major affective disorder. Ann Clin Psychiatry 1991;3:187–198.

36. Greenberg L, Fine SB, Cohen C, et al. An interdisciplinary psychoeducation program for schizophrenic patients and their families in an acute care setting. Hosp Community Psychiatry 1988;39:277–282.

37. Glick ID, Dulit RA, Wachter E, et al. The family, family therapy & borderline personality disorder. J Psychother Prac Res 1995;4:237–246.

38. U.S. Department of Health and Human Services. Sixth special report to the U.S. Congress on alcohol and health. DHHS publication no. 87–1519. Washington, DC: Superintendent of Documents, U.S. Government Printing Office, 1987;129.

39. Solomon P, Draine J. Adaptive coping among family members of persons with serious mental illness. Psychiatric Services 1995;46:1156–1160.

40. Wynne L, McDaniel SH, Weber TT. Professional politics and the concepts of family therapy, family consultation and systems consultation. Fam Process 1987;26:153–166.

41. Stein L. The effect of long-outcome studies on the therapy of schizophrenia critique. J Marital Fam Ther 1989;15:133–138.

42. Glick ID, Clarkin J, Hass G, et al. A randomized clinical trial of inpatient family intervention. Part VI: mediating variables and outcome. Fam Process 1991;30:85–99.

43. Schooler N, Keith SJ, Severe JB, et al. Relapse and rehospitalization during maintenance treatment of schizophrenia: the effects of dose reduction and family treatment. Arch Gen Psychiatry (In press).

44. Faloon IRH, Boyd J, McGill C, et al. Family management in the prevention of morbidity of schizophrenia: clinical outcome of a two-year longitudinal study. Arch Gen Psychiatry 1985;42:887–896.

45. Walling DP, Dott SG. Quality of life: a pilot study—comparison of crises, stabilization and hospitalization. Psychol Bull 1994;30:725. Abstract.

46. Postrado L, Lehman AF. Quality of life and clinical predictors of rehospitalization of persons with severe mental illness. Psychiatric Services 1995;46:1161–1165.

Chapter 17

Focal Psychotherapy

Michael J. Bennett

INTRODUCTION

With the proliferation of managed systems of care, clinicians are increasingly pressed to provide a clear rationale for their interventions. Although the care of acute psychiatric disorders has changed dramatically over recent decades, the vast majority of such care has occurred without oversight; consequently, variations in practice are likely to result from idiosyncratic differences rather than differences in knowledge. Changes in the financing and delivery of health care have forced practitioners to account for their differences. Psychotherapy, assumed by its critics to be unmeasurable and by its adherents to be immeasurable, is proving to be neither. As one of a number of useful treatment strategies, psychotherapy must justify its place among treatment alternatives by addressing the question, "When is it medically necessary?"

MEDICALLY NECESSARY PSYCHOTHERAPY

The concept of medical necessity may be a response to the fear of moral hazard, namely that mental health services (if made too readily available) will be overly and inappropriately used (1). Sabin and Daniels have described the following three frames of reference for medical necessity: an intervention is required to restore normalcy to a medically defined deviation and/or to reduce disability; personal capability to manage successfully in life is limited and must be enhanced; and welfare is compromised in that potential for happiness is constrained, and intervention is required to restore or promote a sense of well-being (2). The restoration of normalcy is most commonly used in managed systems in determining both the need for and the appropriateness of (i.e., is the treatment appropriate to the disorder) services. If intervention is required to restore normal function to a medically defined deviation, then interventions will be judged as medically necessary to the extent that they can be proven effective in achieving that purpose. When used with this level of specificity and precision, psychotherapy is medically necessary. Targeted or focal psychotherapy is a medically necessary treatment used to mitigate or reverse specified impairments caused by mental disorders.

DEFINING FOCAL PSYCHOTHERAPY

Before attempting a definition, it is important to note that focal psychotherapy is not necessarily brief. The common assumption that brevity and focality are equivalent stems from the fact that all brief psychotherapy is focused. When the concept of focality is applied as a guiding principle to meet the acute care needs of a population, it must be applicable to the full range of reasons for which patients seek treatment. If focality is applied simply as a feature of a particular school or model of psychotherapy (3–6), the criteria for exclusion or inclusion common to such schools are inconsistent with this aim. The remainder of this chapter presents a proposal for using the concept of focality to meet the needs of patients.

The definition of focal psychotherapy stems from the common element in all acute help-seeking behavior: the patient or someone close to the patient is in pain, likely due to the patient's being "stuck" or immobilized. Help-seeking behavior can be understood as a result of both the impasse and the pain that it produces. Only some form of change will alter the impasse and alleviate the pain. The common objective of all forms of focused treatment is to facilitate that change. Focal psychotherapy may be defined as a treatment intervention, usually brief, that is designed to

achieve a specific outcome; that outcome is derived from the patient's immediate motive for seeking help, fashioned (reframed) into necessary and achievable change. Focal treatment is problem driven (although not necessarily problem centered) because the necessary change can be identified only by thoroughly assessing and understanding the timing of the patient's presentation. To be successful, focal psychotherapy must answer three questions: "Why now?" "What now?" and "What next?"

Why Now?

When patients seek to alleviate pain, the first question must be, "Why now?" Frequently called the "operative" or "operational diagnosis," the proximate cause for the patient's presentation should be distinguished from the familiar concept of precipitant (7). The precipitant is the event that initiated the patient's distress and putatively led to a sequence of responses—attempts to adapt, compensate, mobilize resources, or reestablish balance. These responses are analogous to the body's efforts to restore homeostasis when stressed. Such adaptive efforts provide important clues to an individual's strengths, both real and imagined. Although it may fail, the "why now" often can be found in the adaptive effort. The following case demonstrates this point.

☐ C A S E   E X A M P L E

Ms. R was a 36-year-old, single attorney whose latest in a series of unsuccessful romances failed when her boyfriend announced that he had decided not to leave his wife. She attempted to contact her best friend but reached only her voice mail. She then called her mother, who criticized her for "being stupid enough to be involved with a married man," and went on to berate her for being "a highly educated tramp who sleeps with anything in pants." The patient hung up the telephone and proceeded to overdose. She was discovered by her roommate and brought to the emergency department, where the admitting note indicated, "Broke up with boyfriend."

In this case, the precipitant was the breakup, but the patient's attempt to adapt failed. Her aloneness and her appeal to her critical and rejecting mother amplified the pain of the breakup. The "why now" was the second rejection, which compounded the first and proved to be the last straw. Theoretically, the "why now" contains Ms. R's acute need for help and provides important clues as to her expectations (or fears) of any therapeutic encounter. If this theory is correct, a therapist's ability to effectively engage this patient would be aided by a full understanding of the complete sequence of events rather than an oversimplified and empathically inadequate "Broke up with boyfriend."

In the following case, accurate attunement to the patient's motive and expectations might have been life saving.

□ **CASE EXAMPLE**

Mr. J was a 58 year-old-hospital administrator who was laid off when his hospital downsized. Although he attempted to find work, his age and symptoms of an evolving depression were substantive impediments. Three months into unemployment, he stopped sending out resumes and spent most of his time in bed. He refused to seek psychiatric help and began to abuse alcohol. On the morning of his presentation to the emergency department, his wife had placed the want ads in front of him at the breakfast table and announced

that she would leave him if he failed to find work within the next month. That afternoon he spoke with his primary care physician, saying that his depression was intolerable and he was considering suicide. His physician sent him to the emergency department by ambulance, and he was admitted with the diagnosis of major depression. He began taking antidepressants and by the third hospital day was noted to be in better spirits. That night, following a visit from his wife who reiterated her deadline, he left the hospital, bought a gun, and shot himself.

In this case, the patient's depression—not the patient—was treated. A failure to understand the "why now" led the staff to a false sense of security. The patient's wish for hospitalization may have represented an adaptive response to his wife's threat, until her reiteration of the deadline undermined his hope. Although the admitting diagnosis was correct, the patient's motive was not identified and therefore was insufficient to establish a focused treatment plan, which would have included his wife. The fact that diagnosis is a necessary but not sufficient basis for treatment is explicated more fully in considering the elements in a biopsychosocial assessment of "What now?"

What Now?

An intervention that is problem driven must expand beyond the specific problem (or life dilemma) to a picture of the person with the problem. If the operational diagnosis answers the question, "What brings the patient (at this particular time)?" this step asks, "What does the patient bring?" The answer lies only partly in a formal diagnosis (e.g., the patient may bring a mental disorder) because the diagnostic system tends to be unidimensional. It lacks a longitudinal perspective (the patient in his or her life cycle), emphasizes psychopathology but overlooks other impediments (i.e., impoverishment, homelessness, limited intelligence, or cognitive capacity), and ignores health measures.

A three-dimensional picture of the person with the problem can be obtained only by a thorough assessment of the patient's biologic, psychological, and social matrix. The context surrounding the presenting problem and its solution must be found. This understanding involves the reason(s) for the patient's presenting pain and an inventory of the resources and limiting factors that are unique to the individual and that will facilitate or impede efforts to mitigate that pain through some form of corrective action or necessary change.

Figure 17.1 summarizes the elements of a biopsychosocial assessment. Emphasizing the presenting pain, the evaluator must start with the patient's request for help (the explicit agenda) to generate a hypothesis about the change that is required and the steps that must be taken to facilitate that change. This sequence takes place only when the evaluator understands the context of the presenting problem. As the following case illustrates, the patient's presenting pain is best understood by knowing both its factual history and its resonance with the patient's world view, which has been termed mythology.

□ CASE EXAMPLE

Ms. L was an 18-year-old college freshman referred for help because of episodes of panic following a mugging in which her wallet was stolen but she was not physically injured. Although her symptoms improved rapidly while she was taking alprazolam, she found it increasingly difficult to go to class and was considering withdrawing from school. When her psychiatrist raised the dose of medication, the patient abruptly dropped out of treatment and 1 month later left school. Sometime later, she wrote to him to indicate that she was doing well in treatment with a cognitive therapist. She explained that her mother was an alcoholic and she had been afraid for many years of becoming an addict. She apologized for not having informed him that she had discontinued her alprazolam after finding herself "liking it too much."

In addition to recognizing mythology, the biopsychosocial assessment identifies the impairments to be reversed as well as the resources and limiting factors that will, respectively, support or undermine treatment.

Identification of the resources that the patient brings to the acute treatment encounter is important because these resources are often not apparent or are eclipsed by the patient's acute pathology. Resources, both internal (adaptive capacities) and external (interpersonal, financial), should be considered in general and with specific reference to the corrective action (necessary change) sought. As Figure 17.1 indicates, an inventory of resources complements the therapeutic agenda, "What is the patient ready, willing, and able to change?"

A second task—one that is usually more complex—is to identify the limiting factors that will impede necessary change. When treating the acutely ill patient, the therapist will frequently confront a panoply of confounding clinical information that can undermine the focus, trivialize the presenting life dilemma or problem, or frighten the therapist into abandoning the emphasis on the present. The most important question with regard to a given limiting factor is, "What is its relevance to the necessary

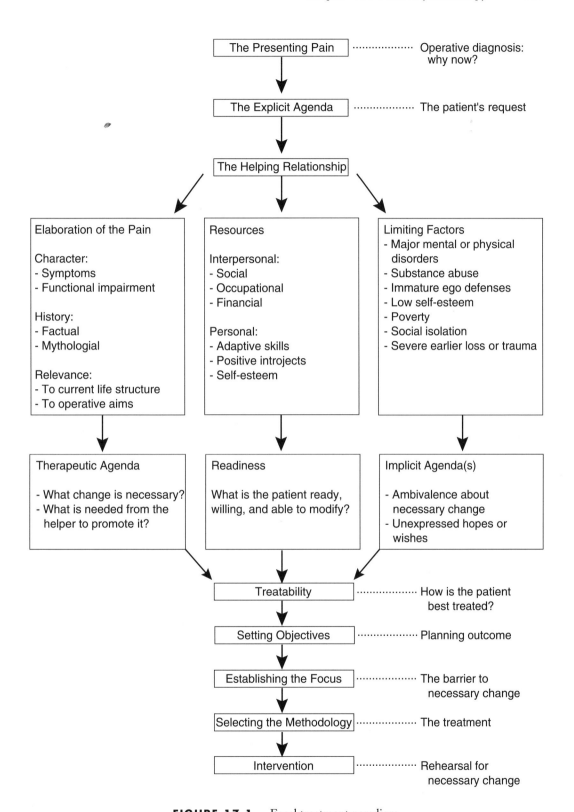

FIGURE 17.1.   Focal treatment paradigm.

change?" Depending on the response, a second question may need to be asked, "What must be done to mitigate or minimize the obstacles to necessary change?" As with the evaluation of resources, the evaluation of limiting factors should center on the patient's reason for being there at the time, "What limitation(s) must be addressed (either first or concurrently) to allow the patient to succeed in resolving the presenting life dilemma?" The following case example illustrates a therapist's approach to this question.

□ C A S E   E X A M P L E

R.B. was a 36-year-old engineer with bipolar disorder who presented in an acutely manic state after stopping his maintenance lithium 1 month earlier. According to his wife, his present difficulties began after he received a poor performance evaluation 6 weeks earlier. Attributing his problems with performance to "not being able to think straight since they put me on that damned drug," he had stopped his medication. He became progressively manic and was brought in by the police after he had punched his supervisor during an argument.

Mr. B's problems were characterized as follows: his operational diagnosis ("why now") was his loss of control and angry outburst; this behavior was, in turn, related to his active bipolar disorder and to his anger at his supervisor for having given him an unfavorable performance review. The necessary change was Mr. B's resumption of maintenance mood stabilizing medication. Factors that supported this change included his previously good work history, his supportive wife, and the leverage from his current legal and work difficulties. Factors that limited the

change were his acute manic state and the likelihood that he had experienced cognitive impairment from lithium. His psychiatrist chose to address these issues by first stabilizing his affective disorder with antipsychotic medication during a brief hospitalization, and then working with Mr. B after his discharge to accept maintenance treatment with valproic acid. The focus of psychotherapy was on Mr. B's concern about cognitive function, which proved to be central to his poor performance and his lowered sense of self-worth.

As the case of Mr. B indicates, focused treatment requires more than patient compliance; a clear appreciation of the patient's presenting pain opens the door to an alliance. An unmotivated patient does not exist; the question is, "What is the patient's motive for being here at this time?" For Mr. B, the presenting pain (his motive) involved intermediaries and the leverage they were able to exert on him. This is often the case with adolescent patients, chemically dependent patients, patients who are undergoing court-ordered or school-ordered evaluations, and many others who present with behavioral rather than symptomatic problems. For these patients, an initial strategy may involve generating motive by turning up the heat, that is, building the leverage into the structure of the intervention. In the case of Mr. J (discussed previously), appropriate involvement of his wife in the treatment might have countered his regression while averting the tragic outcome.

As Figure 17.1 illustrates, the evaluator's ability to identify the necessary change to mitigate the presenting pain is the most essential part of the treatment planning process. However, to complete the evaluation process, the patient's readiness for that change must be assessed. Readiness, which is only partly volitional, can be viewed as a resource and an indicator of health. In contrast, any limiting factors create obstacles to the necessary change and must either be mitigated (if possible) or recognized as limitations. Where does the *Diagnostic and Statistical Manual* (DSM) diagnosis fit within this framework?

The DSM-IV diagnosis, which is a condition of establishing medical necessity in most managed systems of care, is a compendium of symptoms and functional impairments (some acute, some not acute) associated with the patient's presenting state. Although necessary, a DSM-IV diagnosis is not sufficient as a basis for planning treatment. This is because the diagnosis bears only an indirect relationship to the patient's motive for being there. Diagnosis must be made relevant through personalization. The formal diagnosis (the patient's disorder) should be linked with the operational diagnosis ("why now") through development of a formulation. A clinical hypothesis can then be shared with the patient in the form of a reframe or a starting point in the negotiation that eventuates in an agreed-on therapeutic focus. The process of reframing will be addressed later in this chapter.

Although the therapist may understand the patient's life impasse as a diagnosable disorder, it is not a formulation and offers little basis for a reframe. To avoid the common pitfall of treating the disorder rather than the patient, the therapist must concentrate on the patient's subjective experience of pain and the discrepancy between life's demands and the patient's ability to meet them. This discrepancy constitutes the barrier to necessary change and the putative focus of treatment. The therapist's ability to understand the patient's dilemma in human terms and convey a personalized appraisal linking formal and operational diagnoses is illustrated by the following case.

□ CASE EXAMPLE

K.M. was a 64-year-old, unemployed roofer who was brought to his primary care physician by his daughter because he had resumed drinking (after many years of sobriety) after the death of his wife. He had repeatedly refused treatment but agreed to seek help after vomiting bright red blood. The patient's father died of gastric cancer and he was worried that he had symptoms of the disease. When seen by his physician, the patient was disheveled, sad, and worried. He acknowledged poor sleep (waking frequently during the night), recent weight loss, poor appetite, crying spells, and a loss of interest in family and friends. Usually an avid reader, he had not been able to concentrate on books or newspapers for several months. He had become socially isolated and had vague thoughts of suicide without intent or plan. After exploring his lethality with him in some depth, his doctor told him the following:

"You know yourself to be an alcoholic and have managed that disease very well for a long time. Right now, you are using alcohol again to try to make yourself feel better because you have been very depressed since [your wife] died. But alcohol made you bleed last night, and since you really don't want to die and you want to please your daughter, you are here today. While I doubt that you have cancer, you are poisoning yourself and must stop or you may die. Are you worried enough to consider an alternative to alcohol?"

In this case, the necessary change is the patient's gaining control over his drinking. His resources that support such change are his daughter, good insurance, previous record of sobriety, primary care physician, and fear of dying. Limiting factors include dual DSM disorders (alcohol abuse and major depressive disorder), unemployment and social isolation, a medical disorder (not yet diagnosed), and his age. The operational diagnosis ("why now") is the bleeding episode and his fear of cancer. This fear may be also construed as a resource in that it indicates a probable wish to live and counterbalances his suicidal ideation. In presenting a reframe to this patient, the physician has chosen to share his formulation in terms the patient understands and can probably accept. His manner of reframing, which is to issue a challenge, may reflect his understanding of how this patient may best be engaged. Note that the challenge includes reinforcement (you have done it before) and an implicit promise of help, both in the service of the necessary change. Because the negotiation is at an early stage, the physician has not yet addressed what the psychiatric treatment will be (which would be premature) and has not made any suggestions about what the patient should do (i.e., return to AA). The ball, however, has been placed in the patient's court. The focus of care will be determined by the barrier (or barriers) to the necessary change.

What Next?

Before considering focused interventions any further, recent changes in the treatment environment and the effects on the evolving paradigms of treatment should be considered.

Table 17.1 compares traditional psychiatric values with those emerging in a changing practice environment. The most important determinant of that change is the shift in funding, which emphasizes the care of populations and thereby redefines the relationship between clinicians and the patients. A fixed budget may be allocated across an identified population in four ways: (1) much care to many (which is unaffordable), (2) much care to few (unconscionable), (3) limited care to few (inadequate), or (4) limited care to many. A shift from option 2 to option 4 is underway, and this shift is profoundly shaping the treatment individual patients will receive.

Traditional psychiatric care has been based on a two-person model, insulated from the context in which the patient lives and works. Therapy is often considered to be curative (it goes on until the patient is healed), and the therapist is viewed as an artisan-healer who personally provides the healing milieu. In contrast, evolving systems of care seek to serve the needs of populations. Consonant with the highly subspecialized nature of contemporary mental health care, treatment is collaborative rather than insular. It is based on context (the work site, home, community) and more on rehabilitation and recovery models than on cure. It is also multimodal (often involving more than one helper at a time or in sequence), rather than centered on a single healing relationship. More of a guide than a healer, the therapist organizes and oversees care, is available intermit-

TABLE 17.1. Changing Values, Changing Paradigms

Parameter	Traditional	Emerging
Priority	Individual patients	Populations
Milieu	Insular (dyadic)	Collaborative
Site	Out of context	In context
Role of therapist	Artisan-healer	Catalyst
Objective	Cure	Recovery

tently rather than continuously, and exercises a facilitating or catalytic role.

These value changes in our health-care system shape individual interventions. Plans of treatment are likely to involve multiple helpers who are acting in concert. In addition, collaborative care implies active liaisons with nonmedical resources such as family, friends, employment services and supports, self-help programs, and various community resources. Over time, contact with the formal health-care system takes place at points of need, whereas ongoing rehabilitation programs occur primarily outside the formal health-care system. This pattern occurs in both acute and chronic care, because acute episodes of mental illness are frequently recurrent events that exceed the threshold of nonmedical or self-care. The function of the caregiver is to appraise correctly the medical necessity, develop a plan of treatment, and either perform or orchestrate a focal intervention. The purpose is to facilitate a necessary change that will allow the patient to return to his or her developmental trajectory and/or program of recovery. The key to understanding the therapist's role in these evolving systems is to appreciate how people change.

STAGES OF CHANGE

Prochaska and DiClemente (8) have identified five stages of change. As indicated in Figure 17.2, the wheel implies that change involves time and that the patient may need to go through the sequence more than once. Relapse, in fact, is conceptualized as a step in the process. Moving from precontemplation (not yet considering the change), to contemplation (considering it but not yet ready to act on it), to determination (preparation for change), to action, and then to maintenance, the patient brings motives and resistance that will ei-

ther facilitate or impede progress around the wheel. As elaborated by Miller and Rollnick (9) in their work on motivational interviewing, the treater should recognize where the patient is in the sequence and then shape the intervention to move the patient from one phase to the next. Considered longitudinally—with an eye toward the natural history of illness and recovery—this framework suggests that the therapist perform focused interventions, at times separated by intervals of treatment-free progress (momentum), set in motion by the prior episode of care. The therapist is challenged to think strategically—not in terms of treating a disorder, but treating a patient who may have a disorder which he or she is learning to manage. Depending on the nature of the disorder, "management" may correspond to "cure" (i.e., with successful management of the situational stressor associated with an adjustment disorder) or to the concept of recovery (which involves illness management).

Three alternative frames of reference may be useful in developing a strategic approach to psychotherapy. The first is based on the primacy of pathogenesis and advocates reversing the lasting or increasing impact of causative historical events through abreaction. This involves the recovery of memories and their associated affects, usually in the context of a healing two-person relationship, to integrate and master one's history. This approach encourages continuous, often lengthy courses of psychotherapy; it is costly and can be risky. The second strategy, commonly associated with cognitive and behavioral methods, places primary emphasis on changing those factors in the present that reinforce pathogenic processes. These factors, which might be termed pathostatic, can often be mitigated through strategic interventions, freeing the individual to use intact strengths and capacities to overcome

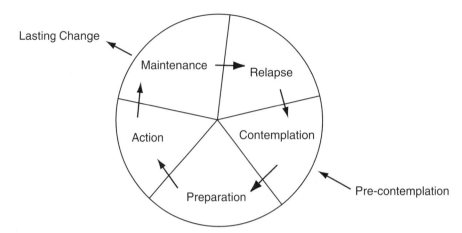

FIGURE 17.2.   Miller and Rollnick's wheel of change derived from Prochaska and DiClemente's six stages of change.

pathology. An example would be treatment that attempts to mitigate the pathostatic influence of a codependent spouse on a chemically dependent patient's continuing drug use.

A third alternative, which might be considered homeopathic and may be useful alone or as an adjunct to either of the other two, is to evoke or reinforce the individual's thrust toward health by drawing on resources that exist (and can be found) outside the health-care system. For example, Viederman (10) has pointed out the health-inducing potential of people found within the patient's ordinary life, such as mentors. Therapy focused on solution emphasizes the patient's power to mobilize internal problem-solving skills toward the same ends (11). The therapeutic value of contextual healing resources, which might be called patholytic, can be illustrated though the following case example.

□ CASE EXAMPLE

Ms. L came to treatment because she episodically had begun to experience somatic symptoms similar to those that had caused the recent death of her emphysemic mother. Ms. L's res-

piratory symptoms were treated unsuccessfully with a series of anxiolytic and antidepressant medications, and she sought psychotherapy on the recommendation of her internist. Initial sessions, which established the patient's failure to grieve as causative, focused on her relationship with her mother and a presumed pathogenic identification. She made good progress in her grieving, but her symptoms persisted. Two months into her therapy, she announced to her therapist that she had begun to work with a respiratory therapist who had identified problems in her posture and breathing habits. She began to practice prescribed exercises and found herself feeling progressively better. Never previously interested in sports or physical activity, she took up swimming. She proudly shared her symptomatic improvement and terminated psychotherapy.

FOCAL INTERVENTION

The phase grid illustrated in Table 17.2 was developed to help supervisees work with the "stuck case" (12, 13). Based on an

TABLE 17.2. Phases of Focal Psychotherapy: Catalyzing Change

Phase	Location	Motive	Resistance	Agent(s)	Mode	Timeframe
1: Establishing the helping relationship	Telephone or office	1. Pain 2. Failure of alternatives	Unwillingness or inability to accept help	Patient and helper	Courtship (precollaborative)	Early in first session
2: Reframing	Telephone or office	Perception of impasse	Commitment to mythology	Helper	Consultant to consultee	Late in first session
3: Selecting a focus	Office	1. Readiness to collaborate with helper 2. Readiness for change	1. Presence of covert agendas 2. Lack of readiness for change	Patient and helper	Collaborative	First or second session
4: Rehearsing for change	Office and patient's life setting; homework	1. Hope for normalcy or health restoration 2. Vision of better self	1. Felt need for the maladaptation 2. Secondary gain 3. Lack of hope	Patient and helper	Collaborative	Through the intervention
5: Trial and error	1. Outside the health setting 2. Occasional office or telephone	1. Momentum from therapy (optimism) 2. Early success 3. Reinforcement from significant others	1. Pain of change (loss) 2. Fear of failure 3. Early failure 4. Counterpressure by significant others	Patient and significant others	Internalization of gains; active and independent	After the intervention; months to years

Modified from Bennett M. The catalytic function in psychotherapy. Psychiatry 1989;52:351–365. Reprinted with permission.

assumption similar to the wheel shown in Figure 17.2, the phase grid characterizes a focal intervention as consisting of five overlapping phases: (1) establishing the helping relationship, (2) reframing the presenting problem in the form of an hypothesis that accounts for the presenting pain and implies the necessary change(s), (3) establishing the focus, (4) rehearsing for change, and (5) implementing change through trial and error.

Each phase may be characterized by its place in the sequence, its primary locus, the agents involved, and the likely timeframe. Central to this schema is the relationship between those forces that drive the process forward, termed "motive," and those that tend to retard it or drive it backward, termed "resistance." The balance between these two factors, which changes and evolves through an episode of treatment, is the crucial variable in determining success or failure. Therefore, the therapist should monitor and influence that balance in a favorable way so that motive will predominate. Although oversimplified, the graphic depiction offers an infrastructure that illustrates many of the points made in this chapter.

Phase 1: Establishing the Helping Relationship

The foundation of all effective psychotherapy is the establishment of a relationship suitable for the work. In the evolving health-care environment, most psychotherapists can no longer see only patients of their choosing. Therapists must examine ways to initiate and maintain relationships with a wide variety of patients, including those who may resist treatment. Success lies in the ability to appreciate the patient's presenting agenda(s). A patient may present with an explicit agenda (the request that the patient makes of the therapist) and an implicit agenda (wishes and hopes that the patient brings and unconscious predispositions toward helping figures). Failure to understand and address implicit expectations risks an unwitting endorsement of wishes or fears, potentially undermining the objectives of therapy. The following case illustrates this point.

☐ CASE EXAMPLE

B.W. was an 18-year-old high school senior who was brought to a clinic by her mother, who was worried about her daughter's peculiar eating habits. The mother, who was slightly overweight, seemed particularly concerned about how the patient looked to others. B.W.'s pattern was to avoid eating solid food, sometimes for weeks at a time. At 105 pounds and 5 feet, 4 inches, she was visibly underweight. The mother also felt that the patient was depressed, which B.W. readily acknowledged. The evaluator took a careful history of eating behavior and questioned mother and daughter about depressive symptoms. Axis I diagnoses of anorexia and major depression, recurrent, were made. The patient was not suicidal, and her physiologic state did not call for hospitalization. A decision was made to treat her on an outpatient basis. B.W. agreed to a course of fluoxetine and left with a prescription and a return appointment in 2 weeks.

The patient came alone to the second session and appeared more depressed. She indicated that she had stopped the fluoxetine 1 week earlier, although she had experienced some decrease in depressive symptoms and had begun to eat more normally. She was unable to account for stopping her medication but told the therapist that she had been fighting with her mother about her decision to do so. The therapist put down her prescription pad and took a new history. In the course of asking the patient why she was in a struggle with her mother, B.W. shared important new information. She had been sexually abused by an uncle (her mother's brother) while in her early teens; her mother, when informed of this, had not believed her. During the past year, as she had become sexually active for the first time, she had found herself conflicted, angry, and unable to respond. Her depressive symptoms began in that context. As the therapist listened, she became aware that her patient's implicit agenda was to reach her mother and have her pain and anger acknowledged. When this was pointed out to her, she smiled for the first time. A series of joint meetings were arranged, with a plan to include her father.

This case illustrates important principles. As Table 17.2 indicates, the motive for establishing a helping relationship in any patient is pain and the failure of (adaptive, sometimes maladaptive) efforts to relieve that pain. Obstacles to engagement include inability (e.g., the intoxicated patient), unwillingness (e.g., the sociopathic patient), or both (e.g., the abuse victim or the severely character-disordered patient who may be untrusting, ambivalent about seeking help, or too angry or frightened to engage). In the case of B.W., the patient was willing and able to engage, but her agenda was missed. Rather than characterizing B.W. as resistant to treatment or noncompliant, the therapist first considered that she had not listened properly to

her patient; fortunately, she was willing to try again.

Phase 2: Reframing

In the earlier discussion of assessment and diagnosis, formulation was characterized as the evaluator's understanding of the linkage between the operational and formal diagnoses or, in an overall sense, the unifying hypothesis that puts the current pain into historical perspective and proposes the change(s) necessary to resolve it. The step that immediately precedes the patient's commitment to take necessary action is reframing. The therapist offers to help the patient in a way that is specific and limited to his or her treatment needs at the time. The reframe is the answer to the question, "Where am I stuck, and what do I need from you to become unstuck?" The therapist is the consultant, and the patient is the consultee who is invited to suspend belief in his or her explanation of the impasse.

Because these explanations are likely to be associated with basic convictions about self and others (a personal mythology), the ability and/or willingness of the patient to consider the hypothesis proffered may involve a fundamental openness to reorienting. Some patients find it extremely difficult to tolerate the temporary state of receptivity involved because it may threaten the need to remain in control of the process. Others cling tenaciously to their idiosyncratic explanations of pain, as seen with paranoid, compulsive, or somatizing patients. When accomplished, the reframe not only develops a focus but also accomplishes four other goals: normalizing the painful impasse, serving as informed consent, empowering the patient, and providing a critical opportunity to consolidate the helping relationship. Success in achieving a reframe depends on the therapist's skill in presenting the hypothesis respectfully, as the following case illustrates.

□ C ASE E XAMPLE

O.S. was a 72-year-old retired engineer who suffered a stroke 2 years earlier. He presented with paranoid ideation after quarrelling with his daughter over her insistence that she begin to manage his financial affairs. Always independent, he had distrusted bankers, accountants, and lawyers all his life and had managed his finances without calling on advice or assistance. When seen for evaluation, he was convinced that "experts" were manipulating his daughter with the aim of stealing his money; he was suspicious of the doctor, questioned each step of the evaluation, and refused to divulge any historical information concerning his finances. He was oriented but showed pronounced gaps in recent memory, poor judgment, and difficulty performing tests of cognition. Underneath his irritability, there was evidence of diminished self-esteem and mild depression. The evaluating psychiatrist was informed by his daughter that he had refused all medication offered by his primary care physician.

After taking a careful history, insofar as was possible under the circumstances, Dr. L asked the daughter to wait outside while he spoke with the patient. The reframe was offered as follows: "You are clearly having difficulty knowing who is trustworthy and, as a result, find yourself at odds with the person you love the most. Can we agree that your mental machinery, which has served you so well for so long, is wearing out?" Seeing no reason to indicate that he had gone too far, Dr. L continued, "I don't know you well enough to be sure this is the case, but may I venture a guess about why you are being so ornery?" Accepting the lack of response as permission, Dr. L concluded, "I wonder if you are not worried about leaving your daughter and, as a result, are pretending that the final phase of your life is not an issue." At this point, O.S. softened considerably and looked sad. He and Dr. L were able to agree on moving toward empowering his daughter to act on his behalf while he was still around and could help her assume that mantle.

Follow-up visits were characterized by a reduction in paranoid thinking but an increase in depression. Able to acknowledge his concerns and underlying depression, O.S. accepted a course of medication.

Phase 3: Developing the Focus

The concept of focus is central to all time-efficient therapy and therefore can be found in any literature on brief psychotherapy (14, 15). Whereas all brief therapy is focused, most but not necessarily all focused psychotherapy turns out to be brief. Duration must be kept distinct from focus. The organizing precept of focus states that psychotherapy involves a commitment to change through some form of action. The focus is the obstacle or barrier to that action. In the model discussed in this chapter, the action of greatest interest is the necessary change. Commitment to a focus, therefore, is tantamount to a commitment to take action. The patient's recognition and acceptance of the need for corrective action (acceptance of the reframe) will evoke an opposite reaction (inaction, persistence) as well, because there is always ambivalence about change. Commitment to a focus includes surrender of previously unexpressed or covert agendas and the losses associated with change. In the next case, the therapist's formulation had to be revised as a result of a covert agenda manifesting itself only after treatment based on an erroneous premise had begun.

□ CASE EXAMPLE

Mr. M was a 49-year-old auto worker referred for psychotherapy by his employee assistance counselor. He had been placed on probation by his employer for repeated absences from work and declining job performance. A recovering alcoholic, he indicated that he had stopped attending AA meetings 3 months earlier and had been drinking daily since that time. He related his slip to his discovery that his wife was considering divorce. When asked what he wanted from therapy, Mr. M stated that he wished to save his marriage. As the evaluation proceeded, Dr. L uncovered depressive symptoms and proposed to Mr. M that he was self-medicating and was perhaps trying to relieve the pain about his marriage. She proposed that he consider alternative forms of treatment that did not produce the same side effects as his present choice of antidepressant. A plan was developed in which Mr. M would ask his wife to join him for an evaluative session, would contact his sponsor, and would return to AA. If his depressive symptoms continued or should worsen, Dr. L would provide medication after Mr. M was no longer abusing alcohol.

The next two sessions took place without Mrs. M, who, according to her husband, was refusing to come to "counseling" and was planning to leave him. Despite this, Mr. M looked better. His depressive symptoms had diminished. He claimed to be sober and attending AA, and he appeared to be accepting the likelihood of life without his wife. When Dr. L asked him why he had been so upset by his wife's behavior earlier and was so accepting now, he confessed that he had been having an affair for the past year and had moved out of his house the day before their first meeting. In retrospect, he attributed his past depression to his own conflict, now resolved, about ending his marriage.

As the focus directs attention to the barrier(s) to taking necessary action, the operational and DSM-IV diagnoses may be placed in longitudinal perspective. The patient is at a nodal point involving a choice between successful maturation and persistent or worsening impasse. Such nodal points are likely to be repetitive "windows of opportunity" to address, through resolution of the present impasse, propensities that have contributed to it. Although treatment-free intervals may occur, repeated episodes of care (the usual pattern of service use in any population) may build on each other.

This "macro" and longitudinal view of focused treatment episodes is analogous to the "micro" level in which the identification of necessary change is the prerequisite to ending an episode of treatment. The focus, which is a barrier to necessary change and to discharge, is relevant to contemporary forms of treatment involving varying sites and intensities. As the following case demonstrates, focus may be defined from a systems perspective as that barrier to necessary change that accounts for the patient's need to be treated at a given level of care rather than at a lower level.

□ CASE EXAMPLE

V.R. was a 14-year-old high school student with a long history of behavioral problems and probable attention deficit hyperactive disorder. He was brought to the emergency department by his mother, a single parent, after a particularly violent quarrel in which he had threatened her with a knife. Ms. R was requesting hospital admission for her son and an out-of-home placement because she "no longer could manage him." The patient's history included polydrug abuse, sexual promiscuity, and fights with peers. Although he occasionally missed classes, V.R. managed to do reasonably well in school. He also befriended the minister of the local church and had developed some rapport with the social worker at the Department of Social Services. When seen in evaluation, V.R. presented as sullen, uncommunicative, and angry with his mother. He attributed his threats against her to her efforts to keep him from seeing his friends.

At the point of entry, V.R. constituted some danger and was clinically unstable. He initially required intense services to restore stability and reevaluate the existing treatment plan. Although V.R. had many problems (and some conspicuous assets as well), the focus was on the factors leading to his current potential for harming his mother. Less-intense treatment could be provided only when his dangerousness diminished. Depending on the resources available, the focal objective (diminishing acute danger of violence) could be pursued in various alternative sites capable of providing containment, evaluation, and crisis intervention. Any question of residential placement could not be made until the focal objective had been attained.

Phase 4: Rehearsing for Change

If the focus is the barrier to necessary change, the treatment plan must address the patient's preparation for that change. This process, which takes place partly within an office but increasingly draws on healing elements within the patient's own life, must be tailored to the patient's preferred method of learning and to the specific change involved. The choice of treater, method, and strategy should not reflect the clinician's preference, but the patient's need.

Phase 4 in a focal intervention may involve other treaters in addition to the evaluator and may involve concurrent or sequential specialized interventions (e.g., concurrent use of family and individual methodology as well as pharmacotherapy for some patients with depressive disorders). This fourth treatment phase underscores the importance of an array of treatment options tailored to the needs of the patient identified in the earlier phases of treatment.

To achieve necessary change, the patient must be committed to the focus, agree to surrender any secondary gains that are attached to the present (mal)adaptations, and believe strongly in a positive outcome. If hope for a better self or a better life are lacking, the patient will bog down in this phase. Covert depression or demoralization may occur at this point in treatment, and the therapist must be able to recognize and address them. Such affective shifts often result from personal mythology as yet unexpressed (e.g., convictions about fundamental lack of worth or the impossibility of change). Covert depression should be treated not as an alternative to the focus, but in support of it. The following case illustrates this point.

□ **C A S E   E X A M P L E**

Ms. G was a 22-year-old woman treated for a posttraumatic stress disorder that emerged in the context of an abusive interpersonal relationship. Treatment focused on helping her disengage from her destructive partner after she had been helped symptomatically and had learned basic elements of self-soothing. In the eighth therapy session, as she spoke of a recent contact with her mother, she became overwhelmed with sadness and a sense of despair that her life could ever improve. For the first time in her therapy, she recalled how her mother had "fallen apart" after her father's death (which had occurred when Ms. G was 12) and how she had been told repeatedly at that time that "a woman without a man is a worthless nothing."

Over the next two sessions, Ms. G proceeded to work on separating from her boyfriend, but she remained demoralized and frequently spoke of how powerless she felt. Although this could be understood at this point as related to her mythology (a woman without a man is a worthless nothing), further abreaction did not appear helpful. She did not present a picture of major depression, and medications did not appear indicated. Instead, Ms. G was referred to a brief cognitive group for young women entitled, "Finding Our Power in Femininity," offered through a local adult education program. She responded well to the positive message and the support of peers, enabling her to use her psychotherapist more effectively. Her spirits lifted and she could then terminate her relationship with her abusive boyfriend. She retained several relationships begun through her support group.

Rehearsal involves office work, homework, and practice. Corresponding to the action phase of Prochaska and DiClemente (8), rehearsal may draw heavily on collaterals (e.g., family, friends, and other helpers) and on existing and newly developed non–health-care resources (e.g., church or synagogue and community organizations). When seen as a significant impedance to the process, the lack of hope should be explored to mitigate its influence. Even in the course of a psychodynamic or interpersonal form of psychotherapy, a strategic cognitive or behavioral intervention that directly addresses demoralization may be useful (16).

It is important to emphasize that resistance is not a character fault in the patient but an indicator of the demands of change. Blaming the patient for the failure of treatment is both inappropriate and wrong. Resistance is a universal feature of all patients and all therapies and can help the therapist understand why and where the patient is stuck. Moreover, like any other form of energy or purpose emanating from the patient, resistance to change may be capitalized on and used in the service of achieving treatment goals. Cummings and Sayama have named this approach "psychojudo" (17).

Phase 5: Trial and Error

The median psychotherapy episode involves 10 or fewer visits (18). A significant number of patients come once. Given these facts, therapists are advised to make the most of their time with the patient and, from the outset, address the issue of the work continuing outside and after the office visits. The fifth phase of treatment is not as much a discrete phase as it is a consistent message of, "Try out what you learn here." Leaving treatment (and to some extent leaving each treatment session) provides most patients with a "honeymoon" period of increased energy and optimism, often characterized by risk-taking and momentum. However, success is not guaranteed. When failure occurs or when significant others in the patient's life undermine (or are threatened by) the gains of therapy, benefits will be diminished or even reversed. Conversely, early success and reinforcement by significant others reinforces treatment gains.

Patients may return and should be encouraged to do so if they feel the need, although perhaps be encouraged to wait a few months to get beyond immediate feelings about the termination. Patients will often bring a spouse or significant other to address issues that have surfaced by changes produced by treatment. The gains of treatment are typically internalized after the episode has ended.

Focal treatment is never terminated absolutely, just as one's ongoing relationship with an internist, an accountant, or an attorney is not terminated. If focused care is directed toward current impasses and impairments and future needs are not predictable, return is to be expected and accepted by patients, families, and therapists.

For those patients with persistent and recurrent self-compromising behavioral patterns (Axis II disorders and their variants), a pattern of intermittent focal episodes of treatment may be an effective and affordable alternative to an extended, continuous psychotherapy. Good focal work must address adaptive responses, cognitive predispositions, and other aspects of characteristic function. For those patients who suffer from chronic and recurrent disorders, focal treatment may represent a realistic and limited use of the resources of the health-care system. This is especially true if needs for maintenance care, rehabilitation (or habilitation), and recovery are also met, either within or outside the boundary of formal health care.

FUTURE OF FOCAL PSYCHOTHERAPY

As the private mental health-care system changes from a dyadic, office-based specialty to organized systems of care, lessons can be learned from the following services: military psychiatry, with its emphasis on focality, treatment in context, and triage with rapid return to function; the community health center movement, with its values of treating the patient in his or her milieu, practicing prevention, and addressing the public health issues that often manifest themselves as individual pain and pathology; liaison psychiatry, with its interdisciplinary ambience, short time-frame, and reliance on indirect service; and HMO psychiatry, with its rediscovery of the full range of brief methodologies and integration of medical and mental health care. These systems of care contribute to the evolving culture and ethos of contemporary organized health care, featuring an array of treatment options linked by adequate assessment, treatment planning, and care management. The principles involved in the formulation of targeted interventions will be central to meeting the needs of patients in an affordable way (19).

Ultimately, the principles of time-effective psychiatric treatment cannot be separated from those of health care in general. The goal is to provide humane care with appropriate and optimal understanding to the person in pain, according to need. Future systems of care will benefit from the growing science of outcome assessment, further informing and standardizing the processes by which we evaluate and meet the needs of our patients (20). Beyond science, however, the core of mental health care will always require a combination of skill and compassion brought by succeeding generations of practitioners to succeeding generations of patients.

REFERENCES

1. Taube CA, Goldman H, Burns B, et al. High users of outpatient mental health services. I: definitions and characteristics. Am J Psychiatry 1988;145:19–24.
2. Sabin J, Daniels N. Determining "medical necessity" in mental health practice. Hastings Center Report 1994;24:5–13.
3. Mann J. Time-limited psychotherapy. Cambridge: Harvard University Press, 1973.
4. Malan D. The frontiers of brief psychotherapy: an example of the convergence of research and clinical practice. New York: Plenum, 1976.
5. Sifneos P. Techniques of short-term anxiety provoking therapy. In: Davanloo H, ed. Basic principles and techniques in short-term dynamic psychotherapy. New York: Spectrum, 1978:433–453.
6. Davanloo H. Basic principles and techniques in short-term dynamic psychotherapy. New York: Spectrum, 1978.
7. Cummings N, Sayama M. Focused psychotherapy: a casebook of brief, intermittent psychotherapy throughout the life cycle. New York: Bruner/Mazel, 1995:90–93.
8. Prochaska JO, DiClemente CC. Transtheoretical therapy: toward a more integrative model of change. Psychother Theory Res Pract 1982:19:276–288.
9. Miller WR, Rollnick S. Motivational interviewing: preparing people to change addictive behavior. New York: Guilford Press, 1991:15.
10. Viederman M. Personality change through life experience I: a model. Psychiatry 1986;49:204–217.
11. De Shazer S. Keys to solution in brief therapy. New York: WW Norton, 1985.
12. Bennett M. The catalytic function in psychotherapy. Psychiatry 1989;52:351–365.
13. Bennett M. Treatment planning for adult outpatients. In: Feldman J, Fitzpatrick R, eds. Managed mental health care. Washington: APA Press, 1992:203–217.
14. Budman S. Theory and practice of brief therapy. New York: Guilford Press, 1988;62.
15. Friedman S, Fanger M. Expanding therapeutic possibilities: getting results in brief psychotherapy. Lexington, MA: Lexington Books, 1991:105–106.
16. Bennett M. Focal behavioral psychotherapy for acute narcissistic injury: "de mopes"—report of a case. Am J Psychotherapy 1985;39:126–133.
17. Cummings N, Sayama M. Focused psychotherapy: a casebook of brief intermittent psychotherapy throughout the life cycle. New York, Bruner/Mazel, 1995:41–85.
18. Budman S. Theory and practice of brief therapy. New York: Guilford Press, 1988:5–6.
19. Bennett M. View from the bridge: reflections of a recovering staff model HMO psychiatrist. Psychiatr Q 1993;64:45–75.
20. Sederer L, Dickey B. Outcomes assessment in psychiatric practice. Baltimore: Williams & Wilkins, 1996.

Chapter 18

Group Psychotherapy

Susan Kemker and Howard D. Kibel

INTRODUCTION

Acute psychiatric treatment has two tasks: to bring under control those symptoms that threaten the daily living of the patient and to engage the patient in a treatment process that extends beyond the hospital. Accomplishing one task without the other is of temporary benefit at best and wasteful at worst. Groups are a powerful modality for engaging patients in treatment. They provide patients with an arena for working through tensions they may feel in the milieu, facilitate the development of more constructive relationships with peers and staff members, and set the stage for learning a range of skills necessary for functioning in the community. Groups can also educate patients about their illness and its treatment.

In the past 20 years, the parameters of acute care have changed dramatically. However, groups continue to play a crucial role in forming the alliance between patients and the therapeutic milieu. New treatment approaches are evolving to meet the demands of acute care settings.

This chapter describes the history of groups and the development of three basic models of treatment. The challenges of making group therapy effective in the acute care setting are also discussed.

HISTORY OF MILIEU-BASED GROUP PSYCHOTHERAPY

Until recently, all milieu-based treatment was provided in hospitals. Clinicians first wrote about the value of inpatient groups in the early 1920s. After presenting a series of lectures to hospitalized veterans, Lazell [1] noticed that they became more socialized and less fearful of the psychiatrist. An innovative theory at that time was that patients could be supportive of each other, and Marsh [2] built on this idea that today might be termed "milieu therapy." He described the mental hospital as an "educational-social-industrial community."

As a result of the influx of psychoanalytically trained refugees from Europe in the late 1930s, therapists began applying

Freudian principles to inpatient groups. Wender, who worked analytically with nonpsychotic patients in a small private hospital, saw the small group as symbolic of the family of origin, with relationships influenced by transference (3).

During World War II, the military hospital was frequently the center of major advances. Indeed, Menninger (4) remarked that one of military psychiatry's contributions to the field was the use of group psychotherapy. Wartime clinicians were often forced to use group methods to address the large number of psychiatric casualties. At the Northfield Military Hospital in England, three analytically oriented approaches were developed that ultimately became cornerstones in the theory of group dynamics (5–7). Foulkes (5) described the nurturing, healing power of the group as a whole, which later came to be called the "mother group" (8). He also delineated the complex interrelationship between the small therapeutic group and the psychiatric ward. Main (6) believed that patients should be given an active, adult role in shaping the unit culture and that the problems of the milieu were matters to be dealt with by the community as a whole. He coined the term "therapeutic community," which was further expanded by Jones (9), another British military psychiatrist. Bion (7) was the first to introduce community meetings in the hospital.

During the immediate postwar period, inpatient group psychotherapy received increasing attention as a treatment modality. Setting the stage for later interpersonal group models, Semrad (10) evolved a group technique that strongly emphasized the value of group interaction. The therapist's role was primarily that of a facilitator, who, "Makes comments, listens, smiles and does whatever seems appropriate to keep up a free and easy conversation" (10). The therapist promoted an atmosphere of tolerance, accepting patients' psychotic productions and their underlying emotions. Catharsis and group unity were seen as key therapeutic elements. Contrary to most programs today, in which group attendance is prescribed by treatment plan, Semrad (10) was adamant that patients come entirely of their own free will. Standish and Semrad were among the first authors to point out the value of group cohesion for psychotic patients (11).

Frank coined the term "group cohesiveness" as a major therapeutic factor (12, 13). Emphasizing the importance of patient interaction, he described the group as a place for interpersonal learning, helping each patient to obtain a more accurate picture of himself or herself in the eyes of others (14). Role models within the group would further serve as powerful agents for change. Frank served as an early influence for Yalom, who observed his work during his psychiatric residency at Johns Hopkins University.

By introducing the concept of interpersonal feedback in the here-and-now context of the group, the human potential movement of the 1960s and 1970s profoundly affected the way groups were run both inside and outside the hospital. In 1946, the social psychologist Kurt Lewin discovered the value of interpersonal feedback in a leadership training workshop he ran for the Connecticut State Inter-Racial Commission (15). He founded the National Training Laboratories, which subsequently influenced clinicians and researchers to consider a broader treatment model—one that involved here-and-now, social, and interpersonal forces. Adapting this model to psychiatry, Lieberman et al. (16) completed the Stanford University encounter group study, which corroborated the importance of feedback as a curative factor. In a study of encounter group casualties, Yalom and Lieberman (17) cautioned that feedback was too powerful an intervention to be used indiscriminately by untrained leaders. Yalom (18) was the first to develop and present a comprehensive approach to interpersonally oriented group psychotherapy. He later modified his approach for inpatients (19).

The optimism of the postwar period was tempered by reports of negative experiences with inpatient groups, especially those modeled after analytically oriented outpatient groups. At Brooklyn State Hospital, Lawton (20) and Pinney (21) reported on a program of weekly, 90-minute groups in which patients were encouraged to help one another with deep-seated conflicts. The therapists were generally passive, at times making transference interpretations. The authors maintained that these groups were generally useful but acknowledged that some members became dangerously hostile toward one another. In addition, paranoid patients sometimes incorporated the leaders' comments into their delusional system and had to be removed from group.

Frank also found that the traditional psychoanalytic group, particularly one with a nondirective approach with a focus on feelings, heightened inpatients' anxiety (13). He emphasized the need for inpatient groups to keep tension "within bounds" and turned his efforts to task-oriented groups and social skills training.

Summing up the growing discomfort of the time, Slavson (22) maintained that psychotic patients were too fragile in their defenses and ego strength to tolerate insight-oriented group therapy, due to the associated uncovering of unconscious drives and painful affects. Instead, he advocated supportive, reality-oriented discussions that would foster "growing relatedness as a result of the comfort, intimacy, and sharing that occur in a small group" (22). Other studies have concluded that inpatient groups that uncritically transpose outpatient expressive techniques or encourage the expression of affect may be of little value or even detrimental (23, 24).

CURRENT MODELS OF GROUPS IN THE ACUTE CARE SETTING

Over time, many—although far from all—authors have supported Slavson's contention that an uncovering, insight-oriented group approach may specifically be harmful for schizophrenic patients (25).

Major changes in the conditions of hospitalization have added to the difficulties of inpatient groups. In the past 20 years, hospital stays have shortened dramatically. By the mid 1980s, the average length of stay was reduced to less than 1 month, with an increasingly acute and heterogeneous patient population (26). Since that time inpatient stays have decreased even further, with current average lengths of stay ranging from 3–10 days. New treatment facilities have evolved, including partial hospitals with dormitory living and intensive outpatient transitional programs. Regardless of their theoretical orientation, inpatient group therapists have had to tailor their approach to fit these new settings.

The following section describes three different models of groups and their main subtypes. All groups discussed are designed to fit appropriately into acute care settings. They tend to be more structured than outpatient groups, and leaders are much more active and "real" in their behavior with the patients. Some are more specifically directed toward regressed or psychotic patients; others are designed to engage a heterogeneous membership.

These models characterize the predominant theoretical orientation of the therapist in terms of goals, values, and role definitions. However, an outsider looking in on a group may be unable to identify the particular model being used for two reasons: the models have overlapping goals and the proponents of one model invariably borrow from the other. The "free and easy conversation" described by Semrad (10) appears to be the hallmark of a well-run group, regardless of its theoretical backdrop. The leader's notion of how this is accomplished is the distinguishing feature of each model.

Skills Development Model

Most of the very early writers subscribed to a skills development model that uses groups to set the stage for learning. These groups tend to be highly structured, and the leader teaches patients and demonstrates what they are expected to learn to stay out of the hospital. Patient interactions take the form of problem-oriented discussions or exercises and role-playing. The structure and task orientation of these groups attempt to keep anxiety and tension well within bounds. It is sometimes difficult, however, to include patient agendas in these sessions (e.g., concerns related to life on the unit). Patients should not be placed in the role of passive, reluctant students. Instilling energy and spontaneity while staying faithful to the task is a major challenge. Included in the skills development model are the following group classifications (27): educational skills, problem-solving skills, social skills, and cognitive behavioral skills.

Educational Groups

In these groups, patients are given information about their mental illness and trained to deal with symptoms more effectively (28, 29). Patients discuss their symptoms and prevention, treatment, and precipitants of illness. They are encouraged to share experiences and offer advice regarding various coping strategies. The presumption is that the increased knowledge and perspective gained in the group will help patients manage their lives better after discharge.

Although not specifically labeled as such, most of the specialty groups in acute care programs would be considered educational. Groups organized around topics such as medication, orientation, discharge planning, and relapse prevention generally involve some instruction from the leader, followed by patient discussion. The interactions that occur often take the form of sharing experience and advice, rather than exchanging feedback, being confrontational, or providing interpretation.

In his work with groups of schizophrenic patients, Kanas (25) has developed an integrative treatment model that uses elements of educational, psychodynamic, and interpersonal groups. In the acute setting, the groups are educationally oriented. Patients discuss ways of managing their psychotic experiences, and the leader takes an active role in structuring the group and imparting information. Cohesion is established through the sharing of a common problem. As opposed to more purely educational groups, however, Kanas' integrative groups assign patients a more active role in determining the meeting agenda, so that interpersonal aspects of the group process can be stimulated.

Problem-Solving Groups

These groups take patients through a series of steps in dealing with problems, especially those in the interpersonal realm (30). With the group's help, a member is encouraged to first clarify a problem, then devise and evaluate a set of alternative solutions. Role-playing is part of the group's activity. Patients are urged to work on problems outside the group and report back on their efforts. For example, a patient admitted to a partial hospital program for self-mutilating behavior may reveal to the group her urge to cut herself when severely stressed. The group would help her to articulate fully the nature of her stress—feeling very numb, "dead," and worthless after a fight with her boyfriend. The patient would then examine the needs giving rise to the impulse to cut herself, including the wish to feel pain to be released from the "dead" feeling. With help from the group, she would explore coping measures such as communicating her needs more effectively before such fights occur, notifying the staff or a friend if she becomes distressed, or redirecting the impulse by placing her hands in icy water. She would practice these measures outside, keeping the group informed of her progress. This work assumes that the development of problem-solving skills will improve self-esteem, help in the performance of day-to-day living, and empower the patient to manage a variety of affects and tasks that were previously avoided. Problem-solving groups have been used with a wide range of ages and diagnostic categories. To participate in this approach, patients must have some ability to think abstractly, translate problems to and from a role-playing scenario, and be motivated to do homework outside the group.

Social Skills Groups

These groups help patients acquire better interpersonal skills through work on the basic components of social behavior. Their usefulness has been particularly well documented with chronically psychotic patients whose mannerisms may exacerbate their already severe social isolation (31). Social skills groups are considered to be an integral part of any psychosocial rehabilitation approach. Sessions often focus on the different verbal and nonverbal components of conversation. For example, the group might discuss the role of gestures and facial expressions, then rehearse smiling and nodding to indicate interest and agreement in conversations with others.

Cognitive Behavioral Groups

These groups are designed to alter the cognitions that appear to evoke painful affects (32). With the aid of didactic instruction, homework assignments, and group sharing, members are taught how to identify and then modify maladaptive cognitions. Patients with anxiety and depression appear to respond particularly well to cognitive behavioral groups. For example, many severely depressed patients interpret losses and setbacks as absolute evidence of global personal worthlessness.

The group works as follows. A depressed member shares his feelings of ineffectiveness as a father and provider, especially since being laid off from work. The group might respond by first asking him to explore how often and persistently he has these thoughts and how severely they affect his mood. He might then be challenged regarding his logic: is he totally ineffective and forever unemployed? His cognitive connections would be broken down further (e.g., the thought that employment totally determines the capacity for fatherhood). Once acknowledgment of the toxicity and failed logic in this thinking is made, the group can explore coping measures. These often include alternative mental imagery or a more reasonable version of the original cognition such as, "I hate not having my job today, but I am still a caring father and provider." As homework, the unemployed father would monitor the intensity and frequency of his self-defeating thoughts and practice restructuring them.

When administered in groups, cognitive behavioral treatment can be very effective, offering a sense of universality and playing a powerful, supportive role. As members share their pain, they experience a "welcome to the human race" feeling (19), which begins to mitigate their shame. In an atmosphere of trust, members tend to be more willing to relinquish cognitive distortions. Homogeneous groups tend to amplify this effect because members share a common problem.

Cognitive behavioral techniques may be applied to various patient groups. Many patients suffer from cognitive distortions that induce and sustain negative affective states, and these must be addressed if the patient is to improve. Therefore, cognitive behavioral techniques are frequently used in groups for the treatment of substance abuse (33), eating disorders, and affective disorders.

Interpersonal Models

In formulating his interpersonal model of group psychotherapy, Yalom (18) integrated the work of three disparate sources: analysts from the postwar period, the social psychologist Kurt Lewin, and the encounter movement. This input led him to conclude that a group was the therapeutic arena par excellence for interpersonal learning. The most powerful curative element was feedback that occurred in the here-and-now context of the group. In a later adaptation of his model for inpatients, Yalom (19) continued to stress the importance of feedback but, for more highly structured groups, advocated titration of the impact on fragile patients.

Interpersonal groups focus on relationships as the key determinants of patients' responses to treatment. In the acute care setting, the formation of peer attachments often determines whether patients feel supported and nurtured or whether they are pushed further into isolation and paranoia. Therefore, a crucial role of group therapy is to promote healthy interactions in the milieu. As Yalom (19) insisted, "Inpatient therapy groups, if properly led, decrease conflict between patients, facilitate the inclusion of isolated and withdrawn patients, promote a sense of cohesiveness and mutual respect, and break down interpersonal barriers of fear and stereotype." Furthermore, a patient's initial experience of treatment, regardless of the health-care setting, plays an important role in the acceptance of treatment after discharge.

Yalom proposed the use of a structured "focus group" for psychotic patients and an "interactional group" for more highly functioning patients. In both groups, effective communication was stressed. The interactional group began with a patient agenda, in which each member identified a problem with relating to others that he or she would like to explore. The group then worked on providing feedback as to how these problems could be acted out in the group. The leader's job was to provide structure by defining the task, encouraging members to actively participate, and helping to translate an "outside" problem into a here-and-now event. For example, one patient might share that she feels alone most of the time. Beyond watching for moments in which this member alienates herself from the rest of the group, the leader could respond by asking her to select someone in the group she would like to know better. If she answered that there was no one in the group she would like to know, feedback would be available immediately in the reactions of the other members.

Patients are rarely confronted so directly in the focus group. Their interactions are structured by exercises, both verbal and nonverbal, that are designed to relieve tension in the room and still facilitate a here-and-now discussion. For example, the group might work on the task of completing various sentences and then discussing the answers. Particularly evocative statements are: "Two things I want to change about myself are . . . ; two things I like about myself and do not want to change are . . . "

Controversy exists regarding the ability of psychotic patients to tolerate interpersonal feedback. Some authors contend that feedback can only be introduced gingerly, if at all (34). Others argue that interpersonal learning and group cohesion go hand in hand, even for the most fragile patients (35). Experience indicates that feedback, when judiciously used, can help patients feel more (rather than less) cared about and secure.

Psychodynamic Models

A number of authors have promoted a psychodynamic approach, with attention to such elements as group transferences, resistances, and historical and developmental factors (36). In general, however, these authors are describing concepts to understand the group experience rather than a method of care. One exception is Kibel (37, 38), who developed a group model based on an integration of object relations and general systems theory. This model was first developed on a short-term care unit with patients who had a variety of disorders, mostly psychotic. It can be applied to both chronically and acutely ill patients who are unable to manage negative affects, especially anger, and has been used in short-term and intermediate-stay settings.

According to systems theory, the small therapy group is a subgroup of the larger psychiatric program (39), whose dynamics directly or symbolically reflect those of the milieu in which it resides (40). Thus, hostility toward one staff member may constitute a dramatization of conflicts between patients and the staff at large, including the group therapist.

The group's goal is to help patients understand their experiences in the milieu, which may reduce pathologic defenses. If this goal is achieved, patients may benefit in other ways such as relating more effectively, becoming allied with the program more easily, and managing aggressive impulses more effectively.

The focus of an object relations/systems group is generally on events in the treatment milieu, most particularly those triggering noxious affects and paranoid sensitivities among the patients. The therapists, who symbolize authority in the group, help the patients as follows. First, they respond to patients in an accepting manner, diffusing projections and setting the tone of the group as a safe place. Then, they clarify events in the milieu, validating the reality testing of the patients and helping them to see their reactions as human and understandable. Once patients realize that even their chaotic reactions can be understood, they tend to feel less paranoid and aggressive. Thus, they can move past their distortions and relate to the therapist and each other in a more authentic, less suspicious manner.

For example, groups in acute care programs repeatedly react to the high patient turnover, and staff absences further intensify a patient's sense of loss. In the following case, a partial hospital group met after an extended holiday, during which many staff members were absent. The therapist arrived to find an empty room. The patients were loitering in the hall instead of arranging the chairs in the room, as was their custom. The therapist rounded up the group and began the session by discussing all the absences, including his own, the previous week. He also announced that one of the absent members would not be returning, due to job pressures. During the silences that followed, the therapist empathized with the group's difficulty engaging, given the long weekend and the missing staff members. The group launched into a discussion of funerals, hunting, and dead animals, but ultimately shifted to speaking more directly about their sense of loss. One of the individuals who was being discharged announced he was having a party, to which the group was invited. The members became quite animated and chose to stay together after the end of the session to plan the party. The therapist viewed this "acting out" as healing for the group and supported the plan.

In the above example, the group could not form and the therapist had to "round them up." The therapist was tolerant, keeping in mind the context, and actively pursued engagement of the group. He explained the silences as the group's reaction to absences and losses, which helped members to voice their losses—at first metaphorically through talk of funerals and death and then more directly.

Events in the milieu affect not only patients but staff members as well. Therapists must constantly monitor their own reactions that, if unprocessed, can adversely affect a group. In one example, a pair of seasoned, generally quite effective coleaders allowed a hostile patient to escalate and dominate the session with loud, disruptive behavior. In reflecting on the process, the leaders realized that they were displaying onto the patient their reactions to her referring physician, a powerful figure in the academic hierarchy. With this awareness, they were effective in managing the next session of the group.

GROUP THERAPY AND THE CHALLENGE OF THE ACUTE CARE SETTING

A group of acutely ill patients is always regarded as part of the larger therapeutic setting, whether in a hospital, a transitional residence, or an intensive outpatient program (39). Therapists may differ with respect to their theoretical orientation, but most agree that an effective relationship with the larger program is crucial to the success of any group. The previous section addressed the distinguishing features of three different models of group psychotherapy. The next section focuses on those elements of the acute care setting that have a bearing on all psychotherapy groups.

Patient Population

Hospital stays for acute psychiatric patients are now very limited, perhaps only a few days. Stays in transitional programs—such as the partial hospital, short-term residence, or intensive outpatient setting—are also limited to a few weeks or less. For this reason, groups almost never have the same membership from one session to the next. In addition, patients are highly diverse in their level of functioning, motivation, diagnosis, age, and cultural and socioeconomic background. Their admission to the hospital and assignment to groups are often involuntary. Once in the group, they do not know what is expected of them and are primarily preoccupied with the leaders as need-fulfilling objects (35). They may be unable to participate, due to uncontrollable destructive impulses, or tolerate the stimulation of the group.

Therapists hoping to give these patients a safe and beneficial group experience must carefully control the frequency, length, group assignment, and criteria for inclusion/exclusion. Goals for the group must also be realistic. Goals must be limited and narrow enough to be attainable, but ambitious enough to be worth the effort. Finally, the therapists must be active as both group leaders and model participants, providing structure and supporting members' efforts to communicate with each other.

Frequency of Stays

Although frequency varies from program to program, the general consensus is that the shorter the length of stay, the more frequent the sessions should be. At the very least, patients should be introduced to the experience of group therapy because this modality is common to most aftercare programs. As they attend further sessions, members are more likely to deepen their attachment to the group and its leaders, becoming less anxious and more available for the learning experience provided. A meeting time of 45–60 minutes is considered optimal because this is long enough to provide for closure but short enough to be tolerated by disorganized or psychotic patients.

Group Assignment

In general, groups are assigned according to treatment team or level of patient functioning. Commonly, one group "level" is for actively psychotic patients, and another "level" is for patients with severe character pathology or affective illness, including

those with bipolar illness who readily recompensate (41). Yalom (19) advocates the use of a "lower" level group, which is structured and supportive, for psychotic and regressed patients. The "higher" level group, for more highly functioning patients, is less structured, encourages greater self-disclosure and sharing of interpersonal feedback, and identifies problems to be worked on after discharge from the program. Kanas (42) similarly favors a separate group for patients with schizophrenia and other primary psychotic disorders, especially in short-term settings in which they are clinically more impaired. He maintains that cohesiveness can be established quickly because the patients share common problems. Discussions in these groups are often centered around ways of coping with psychotic thoughts and perceptions. The behaviorally oriented social skills groups also tend to be homogeneous (31).

Perhaps the greatest disadvantages of group levels are the demands placed on staff members. It is difficult to communicate with the treatment providers about the progress of all patients in the groups. Leaders are forced either to attend all team meetings in a given program or to keep a group log (much easier said than done), which cannot convey all relevant clinical information. The prospect of treatment teams being uninformed of group dynamics, regardless of their therapeutic value, looms quite large. Thus, although levels of groups are well tailored for patients, they are poorly suited to staff members.

When compared with their "levels" counterparts, groups assigned to a given treatment team have the opposite advantages and disadvantages. Team groups share the same treatment providers, and the leaders of the group are members of the team. In previous years, when acute treatment occurred almost exclusively in hospitals, team group assignments were relatively simple. Currently, however, acute treatment is not exclusively an "inpatient" phenomenon. Patients may proceed stepwise through various stages of care (i.e., hospitalization, followed by partial hospitalization with overnight stays in a dormitory setting, followed by intensive outpatient treatment). One or more of these stages may occur in the same physical setting, such as a floor or ward of the hospital. Frequently, a case manager or primary therapist will provide follow-up for a few patients through all the different acute settings until they are discharged to a more permanent aftercare arrangement. In these circumstances, groups are assigned according to primary therapists, who are able to provide continuity through each treatment stage. Those who believe in team or case manager assignments argue that these groups are more easily integrated into the structure of the milieu (38). In addition, patients are given the message that the group is an essential part of their treatment.

One frequently cited disadvantage of team groups is the mixing of psychotic and nonpsychotic patients. Leaders face the very difficult task of establishing cohesion within this very diverse patient population. Disruptions and bizarre behavior are common, and the more highly functioning patients may complain bitterly about the "sicker" ones. The leaders must avoid a situation in which only the more articulate and vocal members speak, leaving the others silent and uninvolved. Conversely, they must not structure the group so much around the psychotic patients that the others are bored and alienated. When the treatment setting allows, Yalom (19) advocates two daily group sessions—a levels group and a team group.

Patient Preparation

Patients who are new to a program may be excluded from the first group session until they are more acclimated to the milieu or they may be "briefed" in a very small intake group (43). In most programs, patients enter groups almost immediately after admission. Their orientation often consists of a short opening statement at the beginning of each session, which usually includes the time, place, and length of the meetings; a summary of the group's purpose; and boundaries of confidentiality.

The introduction is really a statement of the leaders' expectations. Acutely ill patients are invariably quite confused regarding their expected behavior and contribution to a group. In the opening statement, the leaders must address goals and flow of information in the group. For example, an interpersonally oriented therapist may stress the value of understanding more about one's relationships with others, and patients may be encouraged to talk about their reactions to each other in the group. The skills development groups may emphasize learning new ways of coping or solving problems. The psychodynamic group may encourage patients to discuss and clarify their experience with their treatment program, especially those events on the unit that upset or confuse them.

A structured format and predictable flow create a sense of safety in the group. The time and length of meetings, generally announced in the introduction, are important parts of the structure. The leaders should adhere to the time boundaries whenever possible and guide the patients in their role as group members.

Confidentiality is another aspect of safety in groups. Addressing this issue at the beginning of the meeting can diffuse patient paranoia. Patients need to know that the leaders will discuss information revealed in groups with the treatment team, but not with other patients. In some programs, patients are cautioned not to discuss the contents of the group meeting with nonmembers. This norm is impossible to enforce in an acute setting, but when violations occur, they become an important issue for discussion. Yalom (19) suggests that material revealed in group be considered confidential, in that its dissemination is confined to the treatment program rather than the small group alone.

Patient Selection

Criteria for group inclusion tend to be very broad. Bizarre, psychotic behavior alone is not considered a basis for automatic exclusion. The goal of most groups is to promote an atmosphere of tolerance, and patients are faced with psychotic behavior on a daily basis in the milieu. It is generally agreed that patients should be excluded when they threaten their safety or that of the group by either dangerous or violently disruptive behavior. Patients may also be excluded if they are so impaired by organicity or psychotic regression that they are unable to communicate even simple needs or tolerate even modest external stimulation.

Before brief hospital stays, patients might have been allowed to exclude themselves from a group simply on the basis of not wanting to come. As previously noted, some pioneers of inpatient group treatment insisted that groups be totally voluntary (10). Currently, however, with sharply limited time for treatment, most clinicians require acutely ill patients to attend groups. Some even advocate an active "rounding up" process to increase attendance and convey to patients that their presence in group is an important element in their treatment (35).

Realistic Goals: Starting with the Treatment Alliance

Realistic goals are crucial to the morale and sense of direction of the group. Overly ambitious leaders risk creating an environment that promotes unnecessary feelings of defeat. The therapist cannot take on the goals of overall treatment, which would include the amelioration of psychotic behavior. A more attainable and universal goal of groups is to foster an effective treatment alliance (19, 39). Regardless of their theoretical orientation, all group therapists seek to provide an experience "so relevant, comfortable, and effective that patients will elect to continue it" (19).

Patients are often ambivalent about entering a hospital and forming a treatment alliance with staff. On the one hand, they desire a safe haven where they can be nurtured and protected (at times from their own impulses). Conversely, they are demoralized, sensing that they have failed to function adequately (41). They may fear even further loss of control and resent having to submit to the rules and structure of the milieu. Thus, they vacillate between feeling drawn to staff members and being pitted against them. This ambivalence is inherent in the relationship between the patients and the treatment team. It is played out in all areas where compliance is an issue, including medications and disposition planning (39).

The small group offers patients an opportunity to deal with their ambivalence more directly in their relationship with the leaders, who represent the staff at large. Patients are encouraged to articulate feelings that might otherwise be acted out and validate their reactions to the loss of autonomy and the tensions that are part of life in the acute setting. This approach helps to demystify their experience of the milieu and alleviate anxiety (38). Peers provide further support through a sense of shared experience.

Because of their social nature, groups demonstrate that talking helps and promote an atmosphere of open communication and mutual support (19, 38). Once patients are more comfortable and engaged in the treatment program, more specific goals are possible. For those groups focusing on skills development, learning will take place more quickly. In the interpersonal groups, patients will feel safe enough to give and receive feedback. In the psychodynamically oriented groups, patients will begin to correct negative transference reactions to the therapists, their peers, and the staff.

Methods

A passive, reflective leader may be appropriate in the outpatient setting but can be deleterious to a group of acutely ill patients (23). In the acute setting, group members do not know what they are supposed to do and are often highly anxious around others. The leaders must serve as both facilitators and models of group involvement. Their behavior and degree of commitment to the group tend to set the tone of the meetings (35). Animated, involved leaders are more likely to have animated, involved groups.

Leaders demonstrate their commitment to the group by rounding up the members and starting each session on time (35). They show interest in the members by responding to their contributions, no matter how psychotic or bizarre, and by checking in with members who are silent or preoccupied (38). By dealing with their own behavior, including lateness or mistakes in empathy, they encourage candor and openness.

Leaders orchestrate the session's flow by preventing lengthy silences and by

managing disruptions from inside or outside the group. Patients who become agitated or threatening need to be controlled quickly and supportively and may be escorted from the group by one of the leaders. In addition, the leaders must consider recent events on the unit in terms of their overall effect on the group (38). Frequently, patients have difficulty discussing their reactions to such events as violent behavior or a suicide attempt in the milieu. Instead, they might act out by refusing to talk or becoming disorganized or overly hostile. The inexperienced clinician frequently asks how to deal with such a group. The more relevant question is, "What is happening on the unit to make the patients anxious" (38). Discussion of the event is often more useful than exploration of the affect, as paranoid patients often have difficulty "owning" their responses.

Treatment Team

"If one is to build an effective inpatient group therapy program, one's starting place, then, must be the belief system of the staff" (19). Therapy groups require substantial human resources, time, space, and communication; these resources are in ever shorter supply on most treatment units. For this and other reasons, therapists wishing to create a viable group program must go beyond identifying their own treatment philosophy vis-a-vis patients. In fact, their first priority must be their relationship with other staff members. Without the active support of the treatment team, a therapeutic group will not survive. The staff's view of the group will also strongly influence patients' attitudes and, in turn, the group's success.

To fully appreciate the staff's effect on the survival of the small group, a group can be envisioned that is neither supported by the staff nor integrated into the overall treatment plan. This "negative model" might include the following:

1. Human resources. This group has a single leader due to staff shortage or lack of interest. When this leader is away, no group session takes place. The leader is overwhelmed by other responsibilities and receives no coverage during the sessions. At any point in the meeting, the leader may be summoned to address some crisis on the unit. Cancellations due to audits or other unit mandates are frequent. The leader assembles the group alone, without help from other staff members.
2. Time. The sessions are held less than twice per week, despite the shrinking length of stay. In fact, the frequency is decreasing because of the demands of high patient turnover. Meetings often begin late. Patients may not be able to stay the entire length of the meeting, as they are being called out for individual therapy, medications, or medical appointments.
3. Space. The designated meeting room is often being used for other purposes at the time the group is supposed to assemble.
4. Communication. The leaders do not participate in the team meetings and do not communicate the content of the group, even when patients are revealing crucial information about themselves. Conversely, leaders are not apprised of clinical changes in the patients. Group meetings are frequently disrupted by patients who are dangerously out of control.

If therapists want to avoid the above pitfalls and gain needed structural supports, they must build on the group process of the staff. An effective small group requires an active dialogue between group leaders and the treatment team. This free exchange of information allows the team to work through conflicts and reach a consensus regarding treatment goals and the role of the group. Perhaps the most powerful way to accomplish this goal is to involve team members in the group leadership. In programs that follow a model of case management, the case managers can serve as the group leaders; this helps to ensure integration of the group into the overall treatment. Coleadership that provides shared responsibilities and cross-coverage of staff further protects the continuity and therapeutic power of the group.

Staff group cohesion is perhaps the only buttress against the tensions and external pressures inherent to acute treatment. Persuasive evidence indicates that the ward's effectiveness is seriously undermined by covert, unexpressed staff conflicts (44). The therapeutic group, which is considered by many to be a microcosm of the unit (38), is equally crippled by the lack of staff cohesion.

CONCLUSIONS

In times of dwindling resources and shrinking staffs, the phrase "less time to do more" perhaps has never had such power in the field of psychiatry. Patients enter and leave hospitals more rapidly, often sicker and more disaffiliated than ever before. Stabilizing the acutely ill is an arduous task, but patients must be engaged in the treatment process if enduring success is to be achieved. Since the 1920s, group therapy has been a powerful instrument for assimilating patients into treatment cultures in hospitals, mental health centers, clinics, and private offices. Although the conditions of care have changed, the task of groups remains the same. The models and techniques have evolved continuously to accommodate new treatment settings. A team of staff members who can maintain their sense of cohesion and communication under the external pressures of patient high acuity and rapid turnover is crucial to acute care.

REFERENCES

1. Lazell EW. The group treatment of dementia praecox. Psychoanal Rev 1921;8:168–179.
2. Marsh LC. An experiment in the group treatment of patients at the Worcester State Hospital. Ment Hyg 1933;17:397–416.
3. Wender L. The dynamics of group psychotherapy and its application. J Nerv Ment Dis 1936;84:54–60.
4. Menninger WV. Lessons from military psychiatry for civilian psychiatry. Ment Hyg 1946;30:571.
5. Foulkes SH. Therapeutic group analysis. New York: International Universities Press, 1965.
6. Main T. The hospital as a therapeutic institution. Bull Menninger Clin 1946;10:66.
7. Bion WR. Experiences in groups. London: Tavistock, 1961.
8. Scheidlinger S. On the concept of the mother-group. In: MacKenzie KR, ed. Classics in group psychotherapy. New York: The Guilford Press, 1992:284–294.
9. Jones M. Group treatment with particular reference to group projection methods. Am J Psychiatry 1944;101:292.
10. Semrad EV. Psychotherapy of the psychosis in a state hospital. Dis Nerv Sys 1948;9:105–111.
11. Standish CT, Semrad EV. Group psychotherapy with psychotics. J Psychiatr Soc Work 1951;20:143–150.
12. Frank JD. Group therapy in the mental hospital. Washington, DC: American Psychiatric Association Mental Hospital Service, 1955.
13. Frank JD. Group therapy in the mental hospital. In: Rosenbaum M, Berger M, eds. Group psychotherapy and group function. New York: Basic Books, 1963:453–468.
14. Powdermaker FB, Frank JD. Group psychotherapy: studies in methodology of research and therapy. Cambridge, MA: Harvard University Press, 1953.
15. Marrow AJ. The practical theorist; the life and work of Kurt Lewin. New York: Basic Books, 1969.
16. Lieberman M, Yalom ID, Miles M. Encounter groups: first facts. New York: Basic Books, 1973.
17. Yalom ID, Lieberman MA. A study of encounter group casualties. In: MacKenzie KR, ed. Classics in group psychotherapy. New York: The Guilford Press, 1992:270–283.
18. Yalom ID. The theory and practice of group psychotherapy. 3rd ed. New York: Basic Books, 1985.
19. Yalom ID. Inpatient group psychotherapy. New York: Basic Books, 1983.
20. Lawton JJ. The expanding horizon of group psychotherapy in schizophrenic convalescence. Int J Group Psychother 1951;1:218–224.
21. Pinney EL. Reactions of schizophrenics to group psychotherapy. Int J Group Psychother 1956;6:147–151.
22. Slavson SR. Group psychotherapy and the nature of schizophrenia. Int J Group Psychother 1961;11:3–32.
23. Beutler LE, Frank M, Schieber SC, et al. Comparative effects of group psychotherapies in a short-term inpatient setting: an experience with deteriorating effects. Psychiatry 1984;47:66–76.
24. Pattison EM, Brissenden E, Wohl T. Assessing special effects of inpatient group psychotherapy. Int J Group Psychother 1967;17:283–297.
25. Kanas N. Group therapy for schizophrenic patients. Washington, DC: American Psychiatric Press, 1996.
26. Marcovitz RJ, Smith JE. Short-term group therapy: a review of the literature. Int J Short-Term Psychother 1986;1:49–57.
27. Brabender V. Inpatient group psychotherapy. In: Kaplan HI, Sadock BJ, eds. Comprehensive group psychotherapy. 3rd ed. Baltimore: Williams & Wilkins, 1993:607–619.
28. Maxmen JS. An educative model for inpatient group therapy. Int J Group Psychother 1978;28:321–338.
29. Maxmen JS. Helping patients survive theories: the practice of an educative model. Int J Group Psychother 1984;34:355–368.
30. Coche E. Problem-solving training: a cognitive group therapy modality. In: Freeman A, Greenwood V, eds. Cognitive therapy: applications in psychiatric and medical settings. New York: Human Sciences Press, 1987:83.
31. Liberman RP, Mueser KT, Wallace CJ. Social skills training for schizophrenics at risk for relapse. Am J Psychiatry 1986;143:523.
32. Freeman A. Cognitive therapy: an overview. In: Freeman A, Greenwood V, eds. Cognitive therapy: applications in psychiatric and medical settings. New York: Human Sciences Press, 1987:19.
33. Kemker SS, Kibel HD, Mahler JC. On becoming oriented to inpatient addiction treatment: inducting new patients and professionals to the recovery movement. Int J Group Psychother 1993;43:285–301.
34. Feilbert-Willis R, Kibel HD, Wikstrom T. Techniques for handling resistances in group

psychotherapy with severely disturbed patients. Group 1986;10:228–238.

35. Pam A, Kemker S. The captive group: guidelines for group therapists in the inpatient setting. Int J Group Psychother 1993;43:419–438.

36. Rice CA, Rutan JS. Inpatient group psychotherapy: a psychodynamic perspective. New York: Macmillan, 1987.

37. Kibel HD. Inpatient group psychotherapy. In: Alonso A, Swiller H, eds. Group therapy in clinical practice. Washington, DC: American Psychiatric Press, 1992:93–111.

38. Kibel HD. Group psychotherapy. In: Leibenluft E, Tasman A, Green SA, eds. Less time to do more: psychotherapy on the short-term inpatient unit. Washington, DC: American Psychiatric Press, 1993:89–109.

39. Kibel HD. Inpatient group psychotherapy: where treatment philosophies converge. In:

Langs R, ed. The yearbook of psychoanalysis and psychotherapy. New York: Gardner Press, 1987:94–116.

40. Klein RH, Kugel B. Inpatient group psychotherapy: reflections through a glass darkly. Int J Group Psychother 1981;31:311–328.

41. Rutchick IE. Group psychotherapy. In: Sederer LI, ed. Inpatient psychiatry. 2nd ed. Baltimore: Williams & Wilkins, 1986:263–279.

42. Kanas N. Group therapy with schizophrenic patients: a short-term, homogeneous approach. Int J Group Psychother 1991;41:33.

43. Leopold HS. Selective group approaches with psychotic patients in hospital settings. Am J Psychother 1976;30:95–102.

44. Stanton AH, Schwartz MS. The mental hospital; a study of institutional participation in psychiatric illness and treatment. New York: Basic Books, 1954.

Chapter 19

Home-Based Care

David Fassler, Gail Hanson-Mayer, and Elizabeth G. Brenner

INTRODUCTION

Historically, families facing life or death behavioral crises were obliged by both health insurance reimbursement structures and the dearth of appropriate community treatment services to send their children away from home to inpatient psychiatric treatment (1, 2). Although inpatient treatment efforts to protect and treat children could be effective in the short term, the capacity of psychiatric institutions to provide enduring solutions to chronic crisis situations was typically compromised by a lack of care continuity and an inattentiveness to the site of many precipitating events—the home and community environment (2–4). With insurance companies and other payers demanding increasingly shorter lengths of stay and families often reacting negatively to treatment decisions beyond their control, hospitals frequently have been faced with unresolved safety issues. The effort to manage acute costs while providing effective treatment during times of crisis can create additional pressures for care

providers, families, and children. Professionals have struggled to assess danger, families have fought to get consistent help, and payers have searched for answers to life and death questions about care delivery.

In the current behavioral health-care environment, major developments centered on clinical and financial resource issues have accelerated the refinement of innovative approaches to providing effective treatment when a serious crisis occurs with a child and his or her family. Although hospitalization can be an absolute necessity when safety is directly and imminently threatened, acute care cases that do not present an immediate threat to safety can be treated optimally in community-based settings (5). Many hospitalizations can be avoided completely, and lengths of stay for hospitalized patients can be reduced significantly when both inpatient treatment and intensive community-based treatment are readily available.

This chapter reviews the ways in which home-based family treatment is uniquely

TABLE 19.1. Age Distribution of Family and Home Consultation Service Clients—1995

Age group (yr)	Percentage of total clients
0–4	1%
5–12	16%
13–17	50%
Older than 17	33%

suited to the diversion of children from out-of-home treatment settings and the facilitation of rapid and safe discharges. Home-based family treatment can create a context in which safety can be restored and lasting change promoted in even some of the most complex and critical circumstances. This chapter specifically examines the Family and Home Consultation Service (also known as the family team) of Choate Health Management, Inc., Woburn, Massachusetts. The service is an intensive outpatient program designed to provide brief, crisis intervention treatment to children and families in crisis in an effort to prevent out-of-home placement, such as psychiatric hospitalization. Although the model was originally designed for child welfare and then child and adolescent psychiatric populations, it has become apparent that adults in psychiatric crisis can frequently benefit from these services (Table 19.1).

FAMILY TEAM APPROACH

New cases are referred to the Family and Home Consultation Service for either stepdown or diversion from hospital, residential placement, or other higher levels of care. The intensive home-based services provided by the family team incorporate a theoretical model that combines historical public sector in-home family services with cutting edge family therapy. The scope of our service includes the provision of services for clients in both the public and private sectors. Among the challenges encountered by the team in the present health-care environment are the tasks of decreasing lengths of stay, keeping with a crisis intervention model, and shifting to accommodate managed care systems.

PROGRAM DESCRIPTION

An approach that begins at the point of crisis, often in the emergency department or psychiatric hospital, and then literally carries the effort to change into the family's home and/or community is uniquely suited to create a climate of lasting change. Home-based family treatment is able to dramatically reduce hospital lengths of stay because it delivers immediately available, time- and skill-intensive services that address both the crisis of safety and the crisis of treatment failure (6–9). Interventions occur wherever they are most appropriate for each family. The critical meaning of "home-based" work for the family team is that ultimately change takes place in the home environment. Pragmatic issues of safety and other considerations determine whether actual sessions are held in the home or at other community sites.

Interventions under the program model are designed to interrupt not only the presenting crisis, but the entire pattern of crisis that has led up to the referral, and to engage all relevant nuclear and extended family members and treating professionals at the point of crisis. By meeting with families and treating professionals in home or community settings, a team of family therapists creates a series of powerful interventions meant to interrupt the failure pattern within these groups at the same time. It is, in fact, a short-term intervention capable of creating long-term change.

In the initial stages of the program's development, the family team struggled to choose the best family treatment model to create better therapeutic interventions. Ultimately, as the team evolved and borrowed from the work of many significant systems theorists, the team formed its specific approach. The creation of a systems meeting that took the traditional case conference and added families to the process was a significant team development.

During its developmental stages, the team tested a broad range of theoretical models and techniques. From the beginning, the team attempted to share power. Issues of power and hierarchy among and between team members and clients were primary areas of concern as the model developed. Particular emphasis was placed on finding ways to empower clients to create their own change. The family team works within a cotherapy model, and the sharing of leadership inevitably presents challenges that generally parallel the hurdles that families in treatment face.

The team has always consisted of clinicians who are highly dedicated to working with families in crisis, embracing the Chinese definition of the word crisis that translates to mean both danger and opportunity. In the context of moving in to stabilize a crisis situation, the team works to facilitate change while managing safety issues.

A primary goal of treatment is to diminish the crisis that precipitated the referral. Services are delivered at a variety of locations, including the team's offices, hospital emergency departments, families' homes, outpatient clinics, schools, churches, and other community settings. The locations of the interventions are determined by clinical and other pragmatic concerns. Once the worrisome symptoms and behaviors are stabilized, a plan for continued success is developed with the family and collateral providers. In most cases, clients return to the care of collateral providers or begin traditional outpatient treatment.

Intensive family therapy and case management are provided by two master's level clinicians working together to manage cases of high acuity on an outpatient basis. Cotherapists consult with one another, as well as with the entire team and team supervisors, to ensure that safety issues are addressed objectively and progress is being achieved. A child psychiatrist is consulted on every case to assess issues of danger, development, and diagnosis. Individual family members are evaluated by the treating team and referred for a psychiatric evaluation when clinically indicated. Psychological and neuropsychological testing are accessed as needed. The team uses consultation when a specific expertise is needed.

Within the program, significant progress can be made toward the goals of family reunification or out-of-home placement prevention with families who generally have a history of being in chronic crisis. With the development of a short-term treatment model based on crisis intervention and family therapy theories, long-term change that ensures a combination of clinical success and reduced mental health costs can be attained.

Role of the Psychiatrist

The psychiatrist within the home-based team model assumes multiple roles. A psychiatrist acts as a team member in the role of consultant and attends weekly meetings with the entire staff to review cases in depth. All cases are reviewed at least once in this forum. The cotherapists on the case present the reason for referral and information gathered about family history, family functioning, and the identified client. The working treatment plan and formulation are also presented. Particular questions, problems, and worries about the case, as well as any differences between team members, are brought to the team discussion. All team members offer suggestions or questions about how to move the case safely and effectively through crisis intervention treatment. The consulting psychiatrist's role is to pay particular attention to issues related to safety, diagnostic questions, and psychopharmacology. The psychiatrist also assists in the coordination of treatment and provides input with respect to clinical/administrative and/or medicolegal issues.

When family members are in need of psychiatric/psychopharmacologic evaluation or treatment, a referral is made by the team. If possible (given clinical, geographic, and other pragmatic considerations), the referral can be made to the team's consulting psychiatrist for outpatient services. Because of the relatively short length of treatment within the program, there is a preference for facilitating a lasting connection for clients with providers in their community. Within the context of the larger Choate system of services, the team can quickly access a psychiatric evaluation in a number of geographic areas. Families can also use providers with whom they have had previous relationships. In such cases, clinicians on the case communicate with these providers to help ensure well-coordinated treatment.

PROGRAM RESULTS

The program has provided hospital stepdown and diversion services to children and families in crisis for the past 4 years. When the service began as a public sector program, there was uncertainty about methods of addressing safety issues successfully in the absence of an out-of-home placement. There was even greater uncertainty concerning the ability to provide successful treatment within the 13 weeks allowed under the public sector contract. Without the respite from the initial problem that out-of-home placement typically provides, the family team discovered that the level of worry motivated family supports to rally and move more quickly to change in positive ways. As experience grew, lengths of treatment decreased (in some cases to just 1 week). Also under the program, the home-based treatment process can better diffuse and redirect the challenges encountered when issues of safety and length of treatment collide within a context of treatment failure. In effect, the family team facilitates a process that places responsibility for change in the hands of family and community supports rather than with substitute care takers who will not own the problem permanently.

Subsequently, the public sector model has been adapted to the private sector. Experience reveals that this treatment approach is well suited to handling the multiple difficulties and dangers that can be faced in providing crisis treatment in managed care situations.

For children in crisis, family system issues are usually present. Although the majority of the program's clients are children and adolescents, services are also ef-

TABLE 19.2. Diagnostic Case Mix—1995

Diagnosis	Percentage of total
Major depression/depression	29%
Adjustment disorder	13%
Bipolar	9%
ADHD	9%
PTSD	8%
Eating disorder	8%
Oppositional defiant disorder	7%
Anxiety	4%
Dysthymia	3%
Substance abuse	3%
Conduct disorder	2%
Psychotic	2%
Other	3%

ADHD, attention deficient hyperactivity disorder; PTSD, posttraumatic stress disorder.

fective with adult clients and their families when there are family systems issues.

From January 1995 to October 1995, 109 families were seen by the family team, with 84 families having completed treatment and 25 still with the program at that time. The daily census ranged from a low of 22 families to a high of 36 families during the peak period. The caseload was primarily handled by six licensed or license-eligible clinicians, one bachelor's level clinician, and one social work intern.

The program's client base featured a wide range of psychiatric disorders. Experience in 1995 yielded the case mix shown in Table 19.2.

Because the program treats individuals and families having a wide spectrum of difficulties, the cases range in complexity. This variance was reflected in lengths of treatment, ranging from a single day for crisis evaluation to months for families chronically in crisis with identified patients who remained highly acutely ill over time. The length of treatment for clients during the period averaged 71 days.

The completed 1995 cases were evenly divided between the two types of referrals as follows: stepdown (41 cases; 49%) and diversion (43 cases; 51%).

The presenting problem for referrals remained consistent with previous periods, with the vast majority of clients referred in life-threatening situations. The following is a breakdown of presenting problems for which initial referrals were made:

- Suicidal attempt/danger—32 cases (38%).
- Aggression/assaultiveness—29 cases (35%).
- Eating disorders—4 cases (5%).
- Substance abuse—6 cases (7%).
- Anxiety—3 cases (4%).
- Psychosis—1 case (1%).
- Parenting/child protective issues—9 cases (10%).

Despite the severity of problems in the families referred to the family team, the majority were able to be diverted from hospitalization or residential placement. Only 16 clients required hospitalization (5 cases; 6%), placement (7 cases; 8%), or respite (4 cases; 5%) during treatment with the family team.

PROVISION OF SERVICES

Services are used with the following frequency and time frames:

- Telephone response to referral—within 15 minutes of referral.
- Face-to-face crisis evaluation—within 24–48 hours of referral.
- Family therapy sessions—1–3 times per week.
- Parent guidance—1–2 times per week.
- Systems meetings—1–3 per course of treatment.
- Pharmacotherapy—as needed.
- Telephone contact with family—1–7 times per week.
- Telephone contact with collaterals—as needed.
- Telephone response to family in crisis—within 15 minutes, 24 hours per day, 7 days per week.

CRITICAL COMPONENTS OF THE PROGRAM MODEL

Referral

Before face-to-face contact with the family or client, referrals are made to the program director or clinical director. The source of the referral is often an insurance company or state agency asking for involvement with a family or client. Referrals may also come from outside professionals such as therapists, psychiatric hospitals, or medical personnel.

The program is grounded in the belief that, in times of crisis, services should be immediately available to those in need. Consequently, the home-based treatment program is accessible to families, treating professionals, and payers on a continuous basis, 7 days per week. Clients who are already in the service may telephone at any time for support and crisis intervention. New referrals can be taken at any time. When a crisis evaluation cannot be accessed immediately from the team, an affiliated 24-hour emergency service can be consulted. The client's mental status and safety risk are evaluated to help both family members and treating professionals make any immediate changes needed to establish safety.

A number of questions need to be posed at the point of the referral. These questions can help to assess the appropriateness of the case and level of risk involved and can begin to develop some understanding of what treatment is needed.

Receiving the Referral

Included in the questions pertaining to the referral are the following: "Who made the referral?" "Who is asking for help in the case?" "Are there specific consequences if the family does not follow through with the family team or meet certain treatment goals?" In some situations, questions related to mandated reporting and protective issues must be addressed before the family can make an informed decision about its future. Subsequent to the referral, the team contacts every treating professional to fully understand the successes and failures of treatment over time. This active, collaborative case management helps everyone involved make the decisions necessary to change the course of treatment.

Contacting the Family

Is the family expecting a telephone call from the team and, if so, what do they think and feel about this? Do they feel pressured into accepting the team's help? Some contact with the family before the initial face-to-face meeting affords the opportunity to explain the program and its services. If the family is coming in to participate in a family evaluation, fundamental issues will include assessment of the level of risk or dangerousness within the family; questions about what precipitated the request for outside intervention, what conditions eventuated in the crisis, and which individuals were involved; and a determination of who the family members are and whether extended family or friends are aware of the "problem" and are involved in it.

□ CASE EXAMPLE

The clinical director of the Family and Home Consultation Service was called by Dr. W, the crisis coordinator of a managed care company, who asked that the family team see Daniel M and his family as soon as possible. Dr. W indicated that Daniel's mother, Elaine, was concerned that her son seemed depressed and that a local substance abuse counseling agency felt that he was suicidal and may be abusing drugs. Dr. W also indicated that Daniel's parents had divorced when he was 4 years old and that Daniel, 14 years old at the time of referral, had been physically abused by his biologic father. Dr. W felt that the precipitant of the crisis was the stepfather's move out of the house. Elaine was called within 1 hour of the referral by the clinical director.

Elaine was upset by Daniel's behavior and she indicated that he refused to obey her rules at home. Daniel would typically threaten to kill himself and then leave the home and not return for a number of hours. Further questioning revealed that Elaine had an older son, Marco (18 years old), and a daughter, Sheila (10 years old). Elaine was remarried and said that her husband, Manuel, was a help to her but that he spoke no English. Elaine's son, Marco, also tried to help her with Daniel.

Further discussion indicated that there was then no current violence within the family, and that Elaine was willing to try to bring in all family members from the home.

Case Summary

The case of Daniel M has many of the typical aspects of referrals to the program. There was the suicide threat by Daniel, which was associated with parental conflicts, as well as a question of possible substance abuse by Daniel. The existence of past domestic violence is often a factor in this kind of family crisis.

The program encounters many other types of initial referral contact in its work. For example, when the identified patient already has been psychiatrically hospitalized, the case usually begins while the patient is still in the hospital and involves an initial meeting with the family and treating professionals to assess how the family team can best help. Cases may also be presented to the family team when a family member has made a suicide attempt and is being stabilized on a medical unit. The family team assesses the patient and family to help decide if psychiatric hospitalization is necessary.

Family Evaluation

The family evaluation is the centerpiece of our service's work. A cotherapy team from the program meets with the identified client and family in crisis within 24–48 hours of a referral. The evaluation includes the client's mental status and present threat to safety as well as the family's and professionals' capacity to establish safety for the identified client in his or her present situation. The team makes every effort to help the client, family, and treating professionals make the changes required to keep the client at home. A major objective is to understand and change the context that has allowed the situation to become dangerous. The team determines the appropriate level of care with the family at the time of evaluation. Options include outpatient services, respite care, day treatment, inpatient care, or continued care with our service.

Critical issues

Critical issues to be covered during the family evaluation include:

1. What are family members hoping for in connection with their situation? Do they desire a better understanding as to why the problems are occurring? Do they have a particular goal in mind? Exploration of family members' hopes, worries, and goals has two purposes. First, exploration obliges the family to be active in the evaluation. Second, thoughts within the family are carefully explored in a manner that encourages members to discuss their different perspectives, and how these differences affect them, and to begin to explore solutions to the problems that bring them into the family evaluation.

2. What are the safety concerns within the family? What has happened in the past regarding issues of dangerous behavior? Have there been previous suicide attempts or threats by the identified member or by anyone else in the family? Have there been any instances of domestic violence within the family? Are there any threats or instances of violence from out-

side the family? Individual concerns are explored thoroughly.

3. What is the family history? It is often important that a family genogram be completed during the family evaluation. The genogram should cover at least three generations and provide information concerning mental illness, substance abuse, suicidal ideation, medical problems, relationships between members, and other noteworthy family events or issues. Particular attention should be paid to any pattern of events that could be connected to the presenting crisis.

4. What are the mental status and safety issues of the identified client? During the family evaluation process, it is necessary to interview separately the family member who is in significant crisis to assess mental status and risk to self and others.

5. What is the treatment history? A thorough discussion of the treatment history is undertaken.

6. Are there significant medical concerns within the family?

7. When and why should the team take a break during the family evaluation? Members of the clinical team may be so affected by the family that their clinical perspective may be influenced. The effects on team members can provide additional information toward the team's understanding of the family. Continuing treatment with a family in crisis in the absence of such self-awareness on the part of team members significantly reduces the team's ability to be helpful. A break is taken to allow team members to confer and plan a treatment strategy in the light of both the facts and the feelings elicited by the family.

8. How should the treatment plan be developed? The treatment plan is a collaborative effort between the team and family. There are instances when the team needs to take charge of the process in the short run. These situations typically involve the

presence of significant risks to a member(s) of a family. When a family member needs to be hospitalized due to a risk to self or others, it is desirable to obtain family agreement and assistance in the process of hospitalization. In lower-risk situations allowing for more clinical options, the family needs to be a significant part of developing the treatment plan.

9. What are the family therapy techniques used to interview a family during the evaluation? Circular questions are particularly effective for helping a family have a series of experiences that enable an understanding of family problems and past attempted solutions. These questions frequently ask the family to reflect on how they are affected by other family members and to listen to how they affect members of their family. Other treatment techniques will be discussed in later sections of the chapter.

Phases of the First Family Session

The structure of the first family session is a developmental model that implies and applies to the later phases of family treatment. Although the successful completion of early phases of the session is needed to move forward to the subsequent phases, it is also true that—if an impasse is reached—returning to earlier phases may be critical at later points of treatment. A team of two clinicians meets with the family. The symbolic power of bringing two clinicians into the room helps to provide sufficient containment in high-risk situations and allows for the introduction of more ideas and perspectives. During a life-threatening crisis, conducting the evaluation session in a community setting is often preferable to the home to assess safety issues with the least amount of risk. Rediscovering a sense of progress is critical to the family's effort to regain their competence in the wake of a life-threatening crisis. Creating a context for this shift of competence from professionals to the family is fundamental to extinguishing the crisis and creating the capacity for long-term change. The team should be expert at facilitating the family's rediscovery of change, but the family itself should become expert at change.

During the course of the first week, significant efforts are made to consult with other professionals involved to determine the most appropriate treatment plan. Each session is custom designed to build on the one before it, in a manner that helps the family get as close as possible to the changes they had initially outlined. It is important that this shift of who is in charge of change is made when there are no outstanding safety issues present. The team always takes a clear stand on safety issues. Initially, however, they support the family's efforts to establish safety itself. Once the immediate threat to safety has receded, those clinical issues that have had the family stuck in the pattern of crisis can be addressed.

In the beginning of the first family session, the team reflects on the reasons the case has been referred. Who is worried about the child and/or family? What was the family's involvement in the referral process? Is the family interested in an intensive therapy intervention? What has the family been told by others about the program? What are the expectations or worries that other providers or payers have about the family and their use of the program? The team should enter the case in as open and neutral a way as possible to establish itself as a service to help the family accomplish its own identified goals. The specific phases of family therapy are discussed below.

Joining

The joining phase sets the stage for the process of the treatment in several ways. By acknowledging that the process of family therapy can be unsettling for the clients, team, and collaterals, it is honored as hard work. A social connection is made with each person in the room. The cotherapists make the initial move by introducing themselves and describing the work of the program. References to all members of the family are included in the description of the process to help reduce the anxiety of the identified patient. When beginning the process of speaking systemically, the family team is also careful to avoid increasing the anxiety of family members who may be susceptible to feeling blamed and may attempt to get away from a process of joining.

Problem Definition

In performing this phase of family therapy, some basic premises that inform the work of family therapists should be recalled. The manner in which the team asks about the problem can affect the way the family sees the problem, thereby implying or creating alternate solutions. Each family member is asked at this stage about how he or she sees the problem. Frequently, answers that imply that a particular person in the family is the problem can be expected. In the beginning phases of treatment, such responses are taken at face value to validate individual ideas and feelings. To keep the therapy focused and accomplish crisis stabilization in as brief a period as possible, it is helpful to connect family members' definition of the problem to the reason for referral or the crisis at hand.

Enactment or Observation

The goal of this phase of the first session is for the cotherapy team to understand how the presenting problem is connected to the system. Therefore, what occurs at this point is a systems observation during which the cotherapists watch the family's process to discover patterns. To promote discussion, it may help to ask the family to talk about an aspect of the problem definition, while the cotherapists both interact with and observe the process. Another method is to ask the family to engage in an activity together (e.g., act out a play with puppets or play a board game). A more direct way to get the desired information is to ask tracking questions to elicit information about who does what with regard to the problem. At this stage of treatment, the goal is to understand the problem in context so that questions about what happens before, during, and after the problem starts are relevant.

Assessing the Safety of Family Members/Identified Patient

By this point, the cotherapy team has a significant amount of information about the family and the presenting problem. Safety issues should be assessed thoroughly to enable the family to leave the office with a plan that adequately protects the safety of all its members. To intervene appropriately, it is crucial to understand family members' behaviors, coping strategies, and symptoms regarding relevant psychiatric problems. These elements should be assessed in the context of all family members' positions and the family pattern regarding safety issues. If one person is deemed to be in danger of inflicting harm to self or others, that family member should be assessed individually by the team. The team must feel certain that there are individual and family plans to create/support safety until the next scheduled meeting.

Taking a Break/Redefining the Problem in Systems Terms

This next phase allows the cotherapy team to give the family time to relax and affords the team an opportunity to consult. One goal of a cotherapy meeting outside the presence of the family is to ensure that the cotherapists believe safety issues have been addressed adequately. If safety issues are unresolved, consultation is necessary. Assuming that safety issues are adequately addressed, the cotherapists' task is to redefine the problem systemically. Redefinition is the culmination of the previous stages of the first family session. The therapists may agree on a statement of the problem definition that is similar enough to the family's concept to be seen as helpful, but different enough to enlarge, refocus, and/or reframe the course of thinking. They may then choose to discuss this redefinition with the family or create another intervention to end the session.

Contracting

Contracting is another fundamental phase of the first family session. It is important to suggest that the therapy will have an endpoint. Knowing that there is a limited timeframe can work to mobilize the family.

Systems Consultation

The systems consultation entails intervention with the family and collateral providers during the course of the program. The creation of a new view or perspective about the family is a primary goal. With systems consultation meetings, the effect of the work moves beyond the family alone; the relationships between the other professionals and the family are altered, introducing empowering ideas into the entire system. Critical issues that need to be addressed to conduct a successful systems consultation include:

1. How do you invite the professionals to a meeting during which they will be asked to talk about their work while their clients are present?

   a. The initial telephone call with the other professionals to invite them to the systems meeting needs to focus on establishing a connection with the professionals. Professionals working with the family need to have a clear idea about the family team's role and how the team has come to be involved with the family.

   b. The historical or diagnostic information collected from the collateral providers creates a context for the experience of treatment. In addition, professionals often want their data and ideas to be heard and attended to before they further discuss their work experiences with the family.

   c. "What has it been like to work with the client and/or family?" is a question that opens the door to the experience of the work. The team can then hear about what has been frustrating, worrisome, delightful, moving, puzzling, frightening, and (most importantly) real.

2. What are the goals of a system meeting? At the simplest level, the goal is to affect the other professionals working with the family. The beliefs of collateral providers about the family can powerfully restrain or help the family in their efforts

to change. If the family is able to make progress in changing through their work with the family team, such change needs to be brought to the professional system to challenge any contrary beliefs about the family. A face-to-face meeting in which the changes are revealed and the professionals are asked to respond to them can be effective. It is most helpful to elicit the effect of these changes on the professionals' previous views about the family.

3. The systems consultation should be conducted by a senior clinician on the family team who may or may not have had much involvement with the family. This clinician must be experienced in conducting difficult meetings with professionals and families and must be able to respond to the ideas, beliefs, and experiences of the participants in the meeting without being prejudiced about what should happen in the meeting.

4. How do you start a systems consultation? The question of, "Who do we start with?" is answered before the meeting through discussion of the cotherapy team's clinical position, the work they have done with the family, and an understanding of the professionals' experience with the family. For instance, the cotherapy team may have seen something in their work with the family that opens up new possibilities for change. In such a case, it may be advantageous to begin the consultation with one of the therapists on the family team.

5. What are the important issues to focus on and questions to ask during the course of the systems consultation? After the family highlights their work with the family team, a comparison between what the professionals are hearing and their previous experiences with the family or client should be the focus of the family team's questions. For example, "How does what you heard fit with your own experiences with the family?" or "How might what you

are hearing about the family influence your work with the family?" These questions ask the other professionals to reflect on how the family's current efforts compare with their own previously held views about the family.

6. How do you end a systems consultation? Ending a systems consultation involves operationalizing the changes that the family and professionals have discussed in their views about the family and the problem. "What will be different now?" is a question that needs to be answered by each participant. The professionals may talk about working on different problems or a different kind of partnership as a result of a new understanding of the family's capabilities. The consultation leader also asks the family to respond to the new ideas and the new directions in its work with the professionals. The family team is asked about its future work with the family and is encouraged to propose a short-term plan that fits with the professionals' and family's ideas.

□ **C A S E E X A M P L E**

The systems consultation again involved the M family—consisting of Elaine, Manuel, Marco, and Daniel, the identified patient. The professionals at the consultation were Mr. F, Daniel's classroom teacher; Mrs. M, the resource room teacher; Ms. A, the guidance counselor; and Mr. D, a community outreach worker. The family team of cotherapists, Ken and Betty, were present. The clinical director of the family team, Matt, was invited to facilitate the meeting.

Matt began the 90-minute systems consultation by asking each person to introduce themselves. During the family meeting before the systems consultation, the family had decided to discuss the past abuse and the idea that the abuse was a factor in Daniel's behavior problems. Daniel wanted to introduce the work of the family. Matt began by asking Daniel, "What do you think is important to talk about here at this meeting?" Daniel told the group that his family was talking about some bad things that happened in the past. This was as much as Daniel could say, but he felt comfortable with his mother filling in more of the details. Elaine talked about the family's history of abuse at the hands of her first husband and her feeling that this was part of Daniel's difficulties. She wanted the school personnel to know that the family was working on the problem with Ken and Betty. Matt then turned to Betty and asked, "What do you think is important to add to what Daniel and his mother have said?" Betty indicated that family therapy was an important beginning for the family and that it was vital that they receive support. In addition, Betty felt that Elaine was working to lead her family in the process of recovery and her leadership needed to be strongly recognized.

It was then time to ask for active involvement by the school personnel in the systems consultation. Matt asked the guidance counselor, Ms. A, "How does what you are hearing fit with your own work with Daniel and his family?" This question asked the guidance counselor to acknowledge the family's beginning work. Ms. A had not known about Daniel's and his family's past. She indicated that she thought their present work was very important and could be difficult, but she hoped she could find a way to support them. Ms. A indicated that she was still worried about Daniel's safety and that she wished he could

be in a hospital while the work was being done. Matt mentioned that the team did not think Daniel required that level of care and he wanted to know more about the guidance counselor's worry. He asked, "What do you think Daniel and the family may need from the professionals to help them be safe during this process?" This question served to circle the process of looking for solutions within the family and professionals system present in the room and sought a level of conversation that could bring the group together in a shared effort to establish a higher degree of safety and a shared sense of responsibility. Mrs. M, the resource room teacher, joined the conversation at that point to talk about issues of safety at school. She felt that Daniel might need a smaller classroom setting with more attention to help him be calmer at school. The community outreach worker, Mr. D, said that he could provide a regular place for Daniel to go for support, cooling off, or simply "hanging out." Matt noticed that the school personnel were rushing to provide what they thought the family needed without directly addressing the family members.

Matt asked Elaine, "What do you think the impact of the solution offered by the school staff would be, and are there additional ideas that you have that would help to increase safety?" Elaine indicated that she thought the ideas mentioned by the school staff would be helpful in conjunction with continuing work with the family team.

With only 10 minutes left in the meeting, Matt was aware of the need to begin to close. Matt turned to Elaine and asked her, "What thought do you have about what may need to happen next?" Elaine responded, "His stepfather and I need to work on rules and the consequences for not following them." Matt then confirmed with Ken and Betty that this was a topic they could work on with the family. Matt next turned to the resource room teacher and said, "Sounds like the school is wanting to reevaluate what Daniel's school needs are. We are talking about a formal evaluation, aren't we?" The resource room teacher agreed and left to get the formal paperwork for Elaine to sign. Matt saw that some new work would be developing over the next 2–3 weeks and that it would probably be helpful for another systems consultation to be held in 3 weeks to discuss any progress. The group agreed, and the next meeting was scheduled.

Case Summary

The opinions of professionals about family safety cannot be disregarded without jeopardizing the value of the systems consultation. In the case example, Matt attempted to prompt the professionals in the room to discuss with the family how the level of safety could be enhanced. He tried to establish that the people at the meeting could influence the level of safety. What resulted was a clarification of what was actually unsafe. A smaller, more structured classroom setting seemed to be needed for more safety at school. Elaine may have needed some help regarding rules and consequences and how to communicate with Daniel to create a safer structure at home. The school needed to reevaluate Daniel's school placement, and the family team was available to help Elaine with issues at home. These two efforts could probably increase the

level of safety, and the systems consultation engaged the system of professionals and family to take action.

PARAMETERS OF SHORT-TERM WORK

In family-based, short-term crisis intervention work, the brief work should be framed properly at the outset, particularly when the dynamics of dealing with families in acute distress may lead in a less-efficient direction. The primary questions to be asked in the context of crisis intervention work with families include, "What can happen so that the identified patient and other family members can be safe?" "What needs to happen so that the symptom or problem can be resolved?" "When will traditional outpatient treatment be a sufficient level of psychiatric care for the family?"

Families who come to our service are in crisis because they are at an impasse. Often, the solutions being applied to the problem were part of that problem. A shift in the way a problem is understood can allow people to create a new solution, rather than to apply the same solution that has not been working. A change in understanding a problem can create different feelings and different behavioral responses. Generally, a change that affects belief systems about a problem and is connected directly to the issue of safety or crisis is effective.

As advocates of crisis abatement, it is essential that the therapy team stays neutral to the various descriptions of the problem presented by family members and collateral providers. Rather, the team tries to broaden the possibilities for the situation by testing out new ideas with the family. Attempts are made to move individuals from linear thinking (blame, narrow view of problems) to systemic thinking (responsibility, broader view of problem). A team that remains unattached to the correctness of its own ideas is free to allow many new ideas into the system.

To keep the work short term, any shift in the family's functioning that positively affects the presenting problem is amplified. Discreet and manageable goals are created with the family, and the focus is on how each family wants to define itself.

The shift to a more systemic understanding of the problem often takes the family on a path from blame to individual responsibility. It is not necessary for all family members to change for goals to be accomplished. Sometimes only one of the individuals sees the problem in a different way and changes his or her behavior. Often, this shift is sufficient to allow the waves of change to affect other parts of the system. It is important for the team to continually assess its own ideas about change. If the team is taking too much responsibility for the problem (i.e., working too hard), the family may be prevented from solving their own problem. Is the team acting as a positive force? If the team reaches an impasse with the family, it is important to step back and try something different (e.g., get consultation, involve other providers, involve new family members, or see a new combination of family members).

Are there some families and problems that are not amenable to the family team model of treatment? On occasion, treatment simply serves to clarify patterns of interaction and behavior that indicate that brief intensive family therapy is not the solution. A case in which safety issues preclude the family from remaining intact to solve the problem is an example. In such cases, intensive family therapy can assist in treatment planning for longer-term family or other treatment. Cases in which no family members are willing to participate

in treatment are also contraindicated for this service.

How can outcomes of brief, intensive, home-based treatment be assessed? Ideally, cases end with these measures of success: the family's hopes have been realized, out-of-home placement has been avoided, the family experiences a sense of being in charge of the change and using it, and relationships in the system are available to be seen, experienced, and changed as future challenges arise.

□ **CASE EXAMPLE**

The program director was called by a social worker at an inpatient child psychiatric unit to invite the family team to attend the discharge conference for Joe B. Joe, a 12-year-old boy, lived with his mother; his parents were divorced 5 years earlier. Joe was admitted to the hospital after he had attempted to strangle his mother, Mary, on three occasions. Precipitants to these episodes were two incidents during which Mary had encouraged Joe to do his homework and one time when she refused to go out in a snowstorm to buy him a Nintendo tape. The hospital social worker reported that Mary carried a diagnosis of schizophrenia, paranoid type. The social worker also reported that several collateral providers were recently involved in the case, including the child protective agency.

Attendees at the conference were the child protective agency, the hospital treatment team (including a child psychiatrist, nurse, and social worker), the family team, Joe's school guidance counselor, a representative from the town-funded youth services agency, and a representative from a local mental health agency (where Mary received medication and had recently begun individual psychotherapy) that would be able to provide long-term, home-based services to assist Mary with budgeting and other aspects of community living. In addition to these providers, the hospital staff had made a referral to their affiliated outpatient clinic for Joe to receive outpatient psychotherapy and medication management. While in the hospital, Joe was diagnosed with oppositional defiant disorder and rule out bipolar disorder and was participating in a trial of Depakote (Abbott Laboratories, Chicago, IL).

The program director clarified the referrent's goals for the family team's involvement as follows: facilitate Joe's transition home by coordinating services of various providers, clarify the context in which violence at home occurs, and help Joe and Mary resolve conflicts at home without an escalation to violence, and assess Mary's ability to parent Joe effectively.

During the first in-home session 2 days after Joe's discharge, the team found Joe very worried about discussing the events that led to his hospitalization. Joe indicated that he was embarrassed about the incidents of violence toward his mother. However, Joe appeared to minimize the past incidents and evade responsibility for them. Mary appeared worried about Joe's anger. When the team asked her about this, Mary stated that, if the session angered Joe, she feared repercussions from Joe after the team left the home. The team took this opportunity to create some rules and parameters regarding safety with Joe and his mother. Ultimately, the family team left Joe in charge of the discussion, allowing him to stop a particular subject at any time. Additionally, the team took a nonblam-

ing stance by identifying the discussions about the past as necessary to plan for a better future. Joe agreed with the team that he did not want to continue to physically hurt Mary in any way.

The team interviewed Joe about his family history. As the interview progressed, the team asked Mary to share her view of the family story, while making it clear that different family perspectives were not a "right or wrong" situation. Joe was able to share significant events that he believed had shaped his life. In particular, he described the memory of his father pushing his mother down the stairs when Joe was 5 years old. Mary corroborated the incident and described it as the defining moment that led to her divorce.

Case Summary

Despite the compelling information about Joe's relationship with his father, it was determined that working more intensively with Joe and Mary, rather than involving the father, would be more effective for immediate crisis stabilization. This decision was based on the knowledge that the crises that had precipitated the hospitalization occurred between Mary and Joe. The primary intervention that occurred during the first family session was to redefine the problems of violence between Joe and Mary as sequelae to the history of domestic violence shared by them both, rather than an artifact to be blamed on one or the other.

After the first in-home session, the team began a series of telephone calls with collateral providers to gather more information and to inform them of the problems as perceived by the team. It became clear that the ongoing family treatment needed to occur either at the hospital-affiliated clinic where Joe would be receiving his treatment (to facilitate communication and limit the number of providers) or through the child protective agency that offered a more intensive in-home service that would afford the ability to coordinate services through intensive case management. Given the significant needs and limited resources of the family, the team advocated for the more intensive service with a plan to access traditional outpatient family therapy, if needed.

THERAPEUTIC POSITIONING

The Family and Home Consultation Service practices family therapy that takes a narrative approach to the systemically oriented work. The approach incorporates the historical underpinnings of the family therapy field as it evolved toward the postmodern era. Therefore, many influences of structural, strategic, and systemic thinking are present in the model. Therapeutic positions that prioritize empowerment and self-determination are integral to the model because such approaches fit with the goals of short-term work.

As to structural issues, the team may form a hypothesis that family functioning problems are related to the way the family is organized with regard to power and authority. This information forms a basis for discussion with family members about how they see themselves and their power in connection with differences, conflicts, and concerns.

A systemic approach is to determine whether the organization of the cotherapy team or provider system reflects the problematic family functioning. Because systems often organize isomorphically to reenact or reflect the patterned problem in the family, team processes can give solutions for systems issues.

The team as a whole and the cotherapists try to avoid the replication of family problem patterns during intervention. Systems theory dictates that family dynamics tend toward homeostasis, thereby making the team vulnerable to becoming engaged in the continuity of the pattern. Systems theory also leads to examination of problems in the functioning of relationships. Situations are generally seen as more problematic because of difficulties in relationships, rather than problems within the identified patient.

To create a long-lasting solution to the crisis, it must be understood in the context of the patterns of crisis in each family. These patterns include not only the threats to safety that have worried everyone involved in treatment, but all attempts to solve these safety issues over time. From a strategic standpoint, failed solutions become entangled with safety issues in a way that creates a crisis in treatment. A lasting solution to the presenting crisis must include a change in the method of attempting to change so as to avoid a continuation of the unproductive pattern.

The team is organized to prevent unproductive conflict. The constructivist perspective—that there are multiple correct perspectives, answers, and ideas—allows the team to view clients' struggles with a broader attitude of acceptance and permits varying ideas among team members to be applied in each case.

Reflecting teams inform the intervention team in numerous ways. Within cotherapy teams, there is always the opportunity for one therapist to have more distance on the problem by using a second-order or reflective position. The second-order position allows the team member to see issues that may be difficult to address or discern from an actively engaged position. The cotherapy team can reflect with one another in the presence of the family, or one person can reflect (thus allowing the family the opportunity to sit back and listen to therapists offer ideas about them).

The importance of language, as recognized in the narrative model, is a critical aspect of treatment. A family's world is brought to life by the language it uses. Using the family's language in a way that is similar enough to engage them but different enough to create the possibility for change is a key aspect of the work.

Gathering family history through the use of a genogram is integral to the model. Intergenerational work is adapted to the short-term approach. A theme-focused model that uses the genogram as a tool to broaden the family's understanding is applied. After collecting information on the presenting problem from the perspective of all family members and providers, and depending on the timing of the use of the genogram, the team develops ideas that are explored in the context of the genogram. Themes that appear to move the family toward change are developed until their usefulness is exhausted. Thematic material is used to paint a larger context explaining family and relational problems without blaming individuals, past or present.

☐ CASE EXAMPLE

The team continued its work with Mary and Joe, focusing on the theme of preventing violence in the family. Mary seemed surprised when Joe raised the episodes of past violence as being so integral to his current life. She apologized to Joe for not having been able to protect him from suffer-

ing in these ways. Mary revealed that it was during this early violent period that she first began to experience episodes of hearing voices and sought psychiatric help. The team asked if Mary and Joe had ever discussed the ramifications of her illness on their mother-son relationship. They had not.

The team reframed Joe's violence with his mother as an effect of having been exposed to the violence of his father. Joe's dislike of his father's behavior was discussed in terms of whether he wanted to follow in those footsteps or make a different choice for his life.

Detailed attention was then paid to the patterns of behavior at home that precipitated violent episodes. It became clear that Mary's schizophrenia caused her to be overly worried about Joe in ways Joe felt were intrusive. It was also evident that Joe had taken on the role of a parent with his mother. The combination of these two patterns culminated in Joe taking charge of his mother through violence to retain control and "get her off his back." The role confusion was discussed in light of both Mary's problems with mental illness and normative developmental hurdles of adolescence. Mary decided to try to leave the issues of homework to be resolved between Joe and the school, with the exception of reminding him in a limited way. The school was consulted in this plan and agreed to help Mary to worry less about Joe's schooling by taking on the issue more fully in the school.

Mary and Joe also spoke in depth of ways to help Joe manage his anger safely. Joe was able to describe some anger management skills he had begun to learn in the hospital. He was able to make plans to implement these strategies at home. Mary was able to support Joe's plans.

Case Summary

Creating a therapeutic space for Joe and Mary to tell the story of how they had been affected by violence and by Mary's mental illness allowed for the development of a workable problem definition that was nonblaming and therefore nonthreatening. In this atmosphere, both Mary and Joe were able to look at alternate solutions to their dilemmas. Mary could begin to see herself as a good enough mother without having to protect Joe from having the responsibility of doing his homework. She was able to engage in discussions about the normative process of letting go with teen-agers in an atmosphere of feeling understood. Joe started taking responsibility for his homework and dealing appropriately with his own anger. The team had positioned itself with the family to find a definition of the problem that permitted change.

COTHERAPY RELATIONSHIP

The use of cotherapists as the primary treating system places a high value on the use of a team approach. A team of therapists is more effective than a single therapist because of the added resources in the form of ideas, areas of expertise, and values that are brought to the case. The collaborative process involved in treating a case with a cotherapy team requires preparation and discussion of the case outside the session. In many ways, the value of a cotherapy team boils down to the old adage "two heads are better than one." In addition, two clinicians are better able to tolerate high levels of stress and acuity, which facilitates the ability to perform hospital diversion work.

Successful cotherapy depends on the ability of the cotherapy team to work together effectively. The act of cotherapy requires that a therapist observe and be observed. It is important to develop an atmosphere of openness and trust in the cotherapy and larger team relationships so that effective communication can occur. Each member of the team has a responsibility to the development of open communication, respect, and trust.

The struggles of cotherapists can be likened to those of a married couple in that there is intimacy in a dyad that can have a positive or negative effect on the ability to work together under stress. The cohesiveness of even an experienced cotherapy team can be tested by strong feelings elicited from working with families, and cotherapy teams need to develop strategies to communicate and solve problems.

When the cotherapists cannot agree on how to best proceed with a case, they should consult with either a clinical supervisor or the whole family team. Unresolved conflict within the cotherapy team is often reflective of conflicts within the family, isomorphic to the family system. Supervisor and team consultation are part of the process of resolving systems problems. The systemic model guides the team in finding useful, nonlinear, nonblaming ways to look at the struggles that are inherent to team work. Tolerating differences, another fundamental aspect of the cotherapists' relationship, avoids rigidity and promotes creativity in the team's work.

This egalitarian model of cotherapy does not require both therapists to be equally active in all sessions. Cotherapists' positions can shift back and forth depending on the particular family, the clinicians' feelings at the time, and particular strategies that are devised before and during the session.

TRAINING COTHERAPISTS

Training clinicians and interns who are new to cotherapy mirrors the treatment process itself. New team members are empowered to the point of being in an equal cotherapy relationship. Cotherapy relationships that remain unequal over time are not effective in modeling collaboration, mutual respect, and conflict resolution. In addition, such relationships do not allow for the benefits of multiple perspectives being entered into the family system. The pace of the process and the amount of time it takes to participate equally in the cotherapy process depends on the new member's level of experience and personal style. Interns begin by observing videotapes and live work and by discussing the model in supervision.

When beginning cotherapy, the new team member is expected to seek guidance from the cotherapist, taking a less-active position in the sessions as the two clinicians develop a working relationship. The more seasoned team member is responsible for the modeling of the work and the cotherapy process. Actively engaging the new team member in the cotherapy process can happen in the presence of families by asking the new clinician for input or questions for the family. The senior clinician has more responsibility for forming the cotherapy team and directing the work in the beginning stages of the training process.

As the new team member becomes comfortable, he or she is encouraged to interview the family and to try out ideas and hypotheses. It is important for the new therapist to be able to signal the senior therapist if he or she requires help or support. The more seasoned therapist can assist the new team member by reflecting on the process, asking questions of the team member, asking questions of the family, and bringing in other concerns and worries.

CULTURAL ISSUES

The crises encountered by our service vary in context across a wide range of racial, ethnic, linguistic, cultural, and socioeconomic components. The program attempts to resolve problems that affect and, conversely, are influenced by many aspects of a family's life; therefore, the family team must acknowledge, study, value, and incorporate into the team's work the culturally distinct beliefs, customs, and habits of the family that may have a bearing on the outcome of the case.

Although cultural sensitivity can be important in any course of treatment, it is particularly consequential when the site of treatment is focused on the heart of culture—the home. Further, a program such as ours, which seeks to correct misdirected systemic interactions, must maintain flexibility in avoiding too narrow a vision of systemic variants and possibilities. The implications of certain interactive patterns vary, depending on the social and cultural milieu. By definition, a program in which the family helps to set its own goals and solutions entails the need for a heightened cultural awareness.

CONCLUSIONS

Home-based family treatment and its capacity to intervene quickly and safely in the community will continue to have significant effects on concepts of acute care provision for families with psychiatric problems. Successfully shifting intensive treatment into community-based settings helps in reevaluating ideas about acute treatment and in redefining the role of psychiatric hospitals in providing this care for children, adults, and families. The opportunity created by the clinical strategy, in conjunction with the financial pressures of managed care, will speed the revolution in acute treatment. Psychiatric hospitals and other out-of-home placement settings will no longer be the treatment of choice for children and families in crisis. Instead, these treatment settings will provide care primarily in situations that present an immediate threat to safety. Psychiatric hospitals will play this specific role in relationship to an entire spectrum of community-based programs. Day treatment, respite, and intensive clinically based and school/vocational based services are already part of this spectrum of care for children and adults. Home-based family treatment is a link that makes the transition from hospital to community-based services successful by bringing to light safety issues in relation to broader treatment questions.

Despite recent progress in the home-based treatment field, much work lies ahead for improving current approaches. Available research on the outcomes of intensive family-centered systems of care has been sparse (10). Measures of family functioning need to be refined and advanced so that the effectiveness of programs in resolving crises can be more accurately assessed. As home-based programs gain further experience, more sophisticated and systematic methods of collecting data on family characteristics and dynamics, the nature of presenting problems, and specific approaches deployed in treatment will serve to better identify some of the as

yet unrealized potential of already successful intensive treatment models.

By moving intensive treatment into the community and the home and by reinforcing the central roles of the family and community in the treatment process, home-based family treatment expands the options available to hospitals, families, treating professionals, and payers. In this manner, home-based family treatment programs can help ensure that needed clinical services continue to be provided within the broader sphere of change—the health-care system.

ACKNOWLEDGMENTS

The authors thank Thomas Denton, MSW, Michael Longo, MA, and Stuart Koman, PhD, for significant contributions toward the evolution and development of the Family and Home Consultation Service. Their contributions to training materials and protocols currently used are also appreciated. The authors also thank Caroline Marvin, PhD, Charles Verge, PhD, and the Family Institute of Cambridge for contributions to the development of the theoretical framework on which the program was based.

REFERENCES

1. Friedman RM. Mental health and substance abuse services for adolescents: clinical and service system issues. Admin Policy Ment Health 1992;19:159–178.
2. Saxe L, Cross T, Silverman N. Children's mental health: the gap between what we know and what we do. Am Psychol 1988;43:800–807.
3. Pfeiffer SI, Strzelecki SC. Inpatient psychiatric treatment of children and adolescents: a review of outcome studies. J Am Acad Child Adolesc Psychiatry 1990;29:847–853.
4. Dougherty D. Children's mental health problems and services. Am Psychol 1988;43:808–812.
5. Friedman RM, Kutash K. Challenges for child and adolescent mental health. Health Aff 1992;11:125–136.
6. Grant Bishop EE, McNally G. An in-home crisis intervention program for children and

their families. Hosp Community Psychiatry 1993;44:182–184.

7. AuClaire P, Schwartz IM. Are home-based services effective? Child Today 1987;16:6–9.

8. McCleave Kinney J, Madsen B, Fleming T, et al. Homebuilders: keeping families together. J Consult Clin Psychol 1977;45:667–673.

9. Hinckley EC, Ellis WF. An effective alternative to residential placement: home-based services. J Clin Child Psychol 1985;14:209–213.

10. Evans ME, Armstrong MI, Thompson F, et al. Assessing the outcomes of parent and provider designed systems of care for children with emotional and behavioral disorders. Psychiatr Q 1994;65:257–272.

SUGGESTED READINGS

Anderson CM, Stewart S. Mastering resistance: a practical guide to family therapy. New York: The Guilford Press, 1983.

Gilligan S, Price R, eds. Therapeutic conversations. New York: WW Norton, 1993.

Hoffman L. Foundations of family therapy: a conceptual framework for systems change. New York: Basic Books, 1981.

Hoyt MF, ed. Constructive therapies. New York: The Guilford Press, 1994.

Imber-Black E, ed. Secrets in families and family therapy. New York: WW Norton, 1993.

McGoldrick M, Pearce JK, Giordano J. Ethnicity and family therapy. New York: The Guilford Press, 1982.

Trepper TS, Barrett MJ. Systemic treatment of incest: a therapeutic handbook. New York: Brunner/Mazel, 1989.

Walters M, Carter B, Papp P, et al. The invisible web: gender patterns in family relationships. New York: The Guilford Press, 1988.

Section III

ADMINISTRATIVE ASPECTS OF ACUTE CARE PSYCHIATRY

Chapter 20 The Medical Record in the Acute Care Setting

Chapter 21 Legal Issues in Acute Care Psychiatry

Chapter 22 Treatment Guidelines and Algorithms in Acute Care Psychiatry

Chapter 23 The Salience of Neuroscience in the Education of Psychiatrists

Chapter 24 Training Residents in Psychodynamic Psychiatry

Chapter 25 Ethical Issues in Acute Care

Chapter 26 Assessing Quality of Care in Clinical Practice

Chapter 27 Professional Satisfaction and Compensation

Chapter 20

The Medical Record in the Acute Care Setting

Thomas G. Gutheil

INTRODUCTION

Special Considerations for Case Records

Acute care psychiatry presents several considerations that impinge on medical record-keeping. The first consideration is that acute care psychiatry is viewed by many clinicians as a veritable subspecialty by itself. In effect, this book is an expression of this viewpoint.

The second consideration is that the acute care setting may be compared with an intensive care unit in general medicine. Although not always obvious or manifest, issues of life and death usually engross most patients sick enough to arrive at the emergency department or to require admission, given the high admission threshold most contemporary facilities maintain. These ultimate issues coupled with the manifestations of florid mental illness give to the acute care patient's experience a drama, an intensity, and an urgency rarely seen in more leisurely outpatient circumstances. Such factors have been repeatedly associated with an increase in potential liability for clinicians, an issue highly relevant to record-keeping.

A third important consideration, intensified by the short-term stays characteristic of much modern care, is the difficulty in assessing data in the old leisurely way. Today, a large amount of information with a justifying thrust must be gathered promptly and as promptly recorded for use in utilization review operations.

A fourth consideration, frequently lacking in legal assessments of a given case, is that acute care clinicians must weigh the effects of interventions on other ward patients and on their "own" patients. The hospitalized patient is inevitably a member of a social milieu, an arrangement that contrasts with the unitary model of outpatient practice. The implications for record-keeping of a milieu orientation are reviewed in this chapter.

The final consideration is that acute care psychiatric treatment customarily involves multidisciplinary care delivered by different personnel. These separate contributions must be orchestrated in constructive collaboration in a relatively short time, which poses unique problems for the record-keeping process.

This chapter is divided into clinical and legal aspects of the record-keeping process. Because confidentiality is a topic intimately related to record-keeping, the third section addresses that subject. Finally, the specific organization of the material in the record is outlined in Appendix 20A.

CLINICAL ASPECTS

Although the case record is an instrument that is fraught with medicolegal implications, its primary purpose is the care of the patient. The following specific functions of the record in serving the clinical aims of treatment are reviewed.

Archival Function

A major function of the record is the durable storage of information about patients and the care delivered to them by the institution. This storage may be short term (chart entries may be consulted immediately) or long term (charts may be reviewed decades after a first admission).

One implication of these time courses is the importance of writing the record in language whose meaning will endure. Topical allusions, excessively idiosyncratic abbreviations, crypticisms, and simple illegibility may result in the record's failure to achieve its archival value. The following case demonstrates this point.

☐ **C A S E   E X A M P L E**

A resident wrote, "LOL in betzopenia with possible 'Big S' admitted from BNH for a Charlie's special." This might be translated as, "Little old lady with dementia (facetiously characterized as deficiency of Betz cells) who may have schizophrenia admitted from a bad nursing home (i.e., a nursing home whose administration is characterized by a tendency to refuse readmission of the patient after psychiatric intervention, in contrast to a good nursing home) for that extensive workup of reversible causes of dementia especially favored by the chief resident that year, one Dr. Charles."

The original chart entry is shorter, terser, more richly evocative and, no doubt, almost telepathically connotative to those staff members on the ward during that particular year. However, the coherency of this entry will predictably become more obscure with the passage of time. Moreover, the disrespectful tone of the case example poses other difficulties that will be discussed later.

Planning Function

The chart is most useful if it generates plans of operation for treatment. The database is valuable in identifying problems in biologic, psychiatric, and social areas and in suggesting directions for further exploration or intervention. The treatment plan—the operational heart of the record—consists of the current available data, the necessary further investigations and tests, and the appropriate responses to the patient's needs.

Like a musical score, the treatment plan orchestrates the contributions from the members of the treatment team into a collaborative, harmonious effort. In addition, the plan is goal oriented (preferably measurable ones), which avoids the twin treatment pitfalls of amorphousness. i.e, treatment grinds along directionless or, like Leacock's (1) protagonist, "rides madly off in all directions." Both amorphous and all-encompassing treatment goals are impossible to fulfill in this life.

□ **C A S E   E X A M P L E**

A treatment plan read, "All members of the team should get this guy by the lapels, shake some sense into him, and turn his life around."

A preferable plan for the case in question might have been, "Psychotherapy for hysterical seizures and medical control of diabetes by psychiatrist; vocational assessment and training in marketable skills by occupational therapist; family therapy by social worker aimed at family's acceptance of severity of his illness; and increased socialization by nursing staff."

The improved version, while still brief, details specific tasks that allow for measurable goals. Although the goals are not explicitly stated in the example, they may be inferred because of the precision of the task definitions. Measurable goals also serve the purpose of justifying admission, length of stay, and reimbursement.

Documentary Function

The documentary function of the record is linked to its archival and planning functions. Documentation serves to validate the delivery of care, an issue of great clinical and forensic power that is discussed further under legal aspects. The power of this function can best be captured in the axiom familiar from the legal system: "If it isn't written down, it didn't happen" (2). Good work deserves credit by careful recording. Complex and difficult decisions made in an emergency situation gain protection from liability through scrupulous documentation.

□ **C A S E   E X A M P L E**

A suicide malpractice case was won because the clinician recorded, "No suicidal ideation, plan, or intent; reasonable future plans."

It must be stressed that, as often as not, the data to be documented are significant by their absence. Significant negatives such as "denies suicidal intent," the absence of change, the absence of concurrent medical conditions, or signs of tardive dyskinesia can only be conveyed through documentation.

Justificatory Function

In these times of heightened accountability, data must serve not only to record, guide, and document, but also to justify. The need for certain interventions and their clinical, legal, or fiscal (reimbursement) validity rests firmly on a foundation of documented information. Among the items requiring justification are examinations, interventions, and most importantly admission to the acute care setting.

Many patients who are ranting, raving, and out of control in the emergency setting rapidly calm down on the ward. To the inexperienced viewer, they may appear ready for discharge the instant they reach the acute care unit. This familiar clinical phenomenon might cast retrospective doubt on the need for the admission unless the record states that no less a step than admission would provide appropriate clinical care. Many apparently tranquil inpatients cannot be returned responsibly to the very outside situation that fostered their decompensation without significant changes either in their clinical condition or their extrahospital environment. Furthermore, third-party payers may not allow reimbursement for inadequately justified admissions, resulting in crushing economic burdens on patients and their families.

Utilization Function

Closely related to the justificatory function, the utilization function addresses aspects of quality control and utilization review (an amalgam of documentation and justification with planning) affecting litigation, reimbursement, and other important variables. Utilization review is an intrahospital checks-and-balances mechanism by which patients are evaluated after admission about the appropriateness of the decisions to admit and/or treat. The question might be phrased, "Is this patient receiving a level of acute care appropriate to his or her condition or might lower-level (less-intense) care serve equally well?" This determination frequently affects third-party reimbursement. At times, utilization review requires the completion of a particular form that addresses the above question.

The principle is that certain services or procedures must be accounted for in terms of indications, needs, and justification. Admissions, use of special diagnostic tools such as imaging and neuropsychological testing, or special interventions such as electroconvulsive therapy and clozapine administration must be justified in terms of clinical appropriateness and expense. Professional review organizations (PROs) require similar recording.

Education Function

A good case record in an acute care setting with a teaching component should instruct the trainee about etiology, precipitant, interventions, and response. That is, the record should be able to serve as a

profitable focus in supervisory and training meetings.

More importantly, the act of thinking through the conceptualization of the case before recording is a vital method of instruction, both for supervision and self-instruction, in systematic clinical evaluation and treatment planning. When asked to reread an unclear chart entry, many a clinically confused trainee will recognize the muddy clinical thinking at the core of the problem.

□ **C ASE E XAMPLE**

A trainee noted that her chart order that significantly increased a psychotic patient's privileges closely followed an entry that stressed the patient's profound suicidal ideation. The trainee realized that her countertransference anger at this abusive patient had led her to minimize the patient's lethality. The order was then corrected.

Research Function

Recorded data are the essential raw material for research. Research data may be gathered from project-specific research instruments or directly from the actual case record, as often occurs in longitudinal studies. For research purposes, a premium is placed on recording observations that initially may seem incidental or uninterpretable. Explanatory hypotheses may emerge long after the data are gathered, assuming the data are available for retrospective review.

LEGAL ASPECTS

As in almost every sphere of modern life, the mental health system has increasingly become involved with the legal and judicial systems. The implications of this involvement are especially relevant to record-keeping in the acute care setting. This section overlaps with its clinical predecessor, largely because the legal system assigns such an importance to formal aspects of care and records in particular. Attorneys often have difficulty grasping the intuitive elements of psychiatric care and the more elusive aspects such as the art of therapy, the role of the unconscious in human functioning, the therapeutic alliance, and ambivalence. From a legal perspective, they expect concrete matters such as contracts, documents, and explicit testimony to be detailed by the psychiatric case record. This difference in conceptual models may lead to misunderstanding (3).

□ C A S E   E X A M P L E

An attorney agreed to refrain from serving a writ of habeas corpus (for the immediate release of a patient) because the doctor predicted that the patient's condition would probably improve enough over the weekend to permit a Monday discharge. However, the patient's condition worsened unexpectedly over the weekend, and discharge required postponement on clinical grounds. At a later commitment hearing, the attorney presented these events as though the physician had promised (i.e., contracted) to discharge the patient that Monday. In conceptualizing the matter as a breach of contract, the attorney failed to grasp the significance of the change in the patient's clinical state as determining the psychiatric decision.

From this general view, the following sections discuss particular legal issues relevant to inpatient record-keeping.

Malpractice Prevention Versus Fostering Good Practice

The clinician's central concern with good patient care is certainly fostered by good record-keeping. In these litigious times, the important role of records in preventing suits for negligence and other wrongs as well as in protecting patients' rights should not be overlooked. Because the "fostering" and "preventing" aspects of the record are so intertwined, they are presented together under the legal rubric.

"Process-Progress" Distinction

Court subpoenas, insurance companies, and other sociopolitical forces conspire to make the record less private than is desirable. The entire record should be written in an objective, descriptive manner. The patient's verbal expression and behavior should be recorded in diplomatic language. Unconscious fantasy content, psychodynamic formulations, dream material, and technical descriptive terms or jargon that are likely to be misunderstood should be scrupulously avoided; this is material not for progress notes, but for process notes. In fact, the record should consist of progress notes only. Process notes, verbatim accounts, and the dynamic issues just listed (if any) should be maintained separately in the clinician's private file. A question is sometimes raised about this point when the SOAP (subjective, objective, assessment, plan) record schema is endorsed; "subjective" is often interpreted as verbatim (i.e., a quotation in the patient's own words). Even in this model, compromising words and quotes should be avoided.

□ CASE EXAMPLE

Digressing from the main course of examination in a malpractice trial, an attorney seized on a note mentioning the patient's "homosexually eroticized relationship" to the therapist. The attorney then attempted to discredit the therapist by introducing testimony to the effect that the patient had never been gay. Although the attorney had misconstrued the meaning of the phrase, this apparent "contradiction" was damaging to the therapist's credibility and potentially stigmatizing to the patient.

In keeping with the guideline of carefully selecting terminology, "homosexuality" might be replaced with "positive feeling" or "identity confusion." In another example, the term "developmental" might be substituted for "infantile" or "primitive" when the recording of these terms is unavoidable in communicating about the patient to subsequent caretakers. In all other cases, such material should not appear in the "public" record at all.

Professional Tone

The professionalism rightly expected of inpatient caretakers should extend to the tone of the written record. In practice, the following terms should be excluded from the record: judgmental or moralistic comments ("the patient is being really evil to the nurses"); inappropriate preciousness ("patient is back to being her sweet widdle self"); facetiousness or sarcasm ("if this patient gets any more grandiose, we'll have to crown him Messiah and be done with it"); casual and pejorative slang ("the patient is being a real brat"); gratuitous interpolations ("patient plans to work in therapy at being less entitled [hah!] in the future"); and any other lapses of professional demeanor conveyed in written form. No matter how satisfying such entries may be to write or how cute and funny to read to one's colleagues, it should be noted (2) first, that the entries are rarely quite so comic when they are read aloud in open court and, second, such material invariably conveys disrespect for the patient. This attitude is destructive to one's actual attitude toward and work with the patient and to the caring posture one would wish conveyed toward that same patient at, for instance, a trial for negligence (3). All the clinical descriptions from the mock examples above can be expressed quite adequately and appropriately in neutral and objective terms.

Reference to Other Patients and Staff Members

A patient's interaction with specific other patients may be highly significant and relevant to his or her acute care; thus, it may be important to refer to patient B on patient A's chart. For example, two patients who provoke each other to fight or sexualize will have to be kept apart on clinical grounds. This information should be recorded to guide and inform staff members on subsequent shifts to prevent harm.

However, if patient A later releases his record to an appropriate reader, that reader is not entitled to gratuitous information about patient B. Therefore, to protect patient B's identity from future readers, only the first name and last initial of the "other" patient(s) should be used. However, current staff members will still be able to identify the patient.

Staff members should be mentioned by name and discipline. For example, "patient threatened Ms. Smith, RN," instead of "patient threatened Betty."

Judgment Calls and Thinking Aloud for the Record

Clinical work repeatedly requires exercising clinical intuition, making judgment calls, and taking calculated risks. For patients in acute care settings, these critical decisions often but not always focus around the question of when the patient is clinically ready to leave the hospital or to experience some liberalization of constraints.

The secret of sound documentation without spending too much time writing lies in the notion, "Don't write more, write smarter." Efficiency is achieved by focusing on three pivotal issues of documentation, which coincidentally represent three critical points of clinical decision-making:

1. Conducting risk-benefit analysis for each alternative. That is, both alternatives in a given situation—hospitalizing and not hospitalizing, treating and not treating with medications—have both risks and benefits.
2. Exercising clinical judgment at decision points. Clinical judgment should be structured in two parts: "What did you assess or determine?" and "What was your response?"
3. Recording patients' observed capacity to participate in their own treatment. This helps clarify patient responsibility for following-up on a regimen and justifies delegation of monitoring to the patient.

The resulting conciseness is highly desirable for the busy clinician. More importantly, a record of such key decision-making issues makes clear to a jury that, even if your conclusions are wrong, your care is not negligent.

One exception to the above rule of brevity is the high-risk, complex, or highly ambiguous clinical situation requiring a judgment call. In such cases, the usual austerity and restraint that should characterize writing for the record must be compromised, and the clinician should "think out loud for the record" (2, 3). This phrase means that the clinician should go to great lengths to detail the factual underpinnings and incremental steps of reasoning that led to the decision in question. Equal care should be given to the explicit weighing of benefits and risks and advantages and costs that enter into the clinical reasoning.

The essence of judgment calls and thinking aloud relates to the critical distinction between a legitimate error in judgment and negligence. Careful decision-making based on careful assessment that leads to a regrettable result is not negligence. Failure to make such assessment and decision (or failure to record) is negligent and, given a bad result, could provide grounds for malpractice.

□ **C ASE E XAMPLE**

A resident was considering releasing a patient in an against-medical-advice discharge rather than filing for commitment. The patient was a persistently suicidal borderline male intermittently self-lethal and highly resistant to taking responsibility for himself. In writing the discharge note, the resident included observations of the patient's state, notations about the goals of treatment in fostering responsibility in the patient, the justifications for this approach, reports of the views of supervisors and consultants, candid acknowledgment of the risk of suicide, review of the disadvantages of hospitalization (regression, absence of an end point, failure of even the hospital to ensure safety), iteration of the various supports and safeguards outside the hospital (e.g., "patient was given the hospital telephone number and instructed to call if the situation worsens"), and an outline of contingency plans (2).

Although the amount of detail described above may seem excessive or unnecessary, the record is made in preparation of a calculated risk that may or may not turn out favorably, no matter how necessary the plan may be for managing the patient. If the judgment call is correct, a slight amount of time is lost. If not, details documenting careful assessment and exercise of judgment become enormously important.

Recording comments by professional colleagues is also an important step. As an informal peer review, this documentation demonstrates that the decision on the judgment call has the support of at least one or more colleagues in the field, a situation similar to the second opinion obtained in general medicine. Professional support for an opinion powerfully refutes the accusation of negligence, because the clinician demonstrated care by obtaining consultation and assessed the community standard of another average reasonable practitioner. Consultation thus conforms with the standard of care.

Forensically Significant Events

In the practice of acute care psychiatry, certain events are more likely to be the focus of medicolegal attention. Such events might include admissions and discharges; assaults, falls, accidents, and injuries; ill effects from treatments, especially sensitive treatment (e.g., electroconvulsive therapy); special procedures (seclusion, restraint); escapes or failures to return from pass; threats or other evidence of dangerousness; and concurrent medical conditions (illnesses, allergies). These clinical events and their attendant decisions require record-keeping commensurate with their potential forensic significance. At times the documentation requires signifi-

cant negatives (i.e., the absence of a particular finding such as no homicidal or suicidal ideation), as shown in the following case.

☐ **C ASE E XAMPLE**

A patient was inappropriately and without clinical basis sent by a court to a hospital because of alleged dangerousness. Realizing that this issue would adumbrate the eventual discharge, the clinician, in anticipation of discharge, regularly recorded in the progress notes the absence of dangerous behavior, threats, and so on.

The documentation of forensically significant events should address any potential questions such as, "Was normal neurologic function present after a fall with head injury?" "Are radiographs indicated?" "Were vital signs checked?" and "Were pupils checked?"

In a complementary manner, noting evidence for dangerousness is useful when a possible future commitment petition is envisioned.

Special Medicolegal Issues

Certain documents with specific medicolegal significance must be included in the record. These include the legal status paper (voluntary or involuntary admission by court or civil commitment) and consent forms for special procedures. The consent form should always be matched by a progress note in the body of the chart outlining the conversation with the patient in which the information about the procedure in question was conveyed. The note should also comment on answers given to the patient's questions, if any. These data should document the fact that consent is truly informed and that certificates of guardianship and similar papers bear on matters of competence (3). For court-committed patients, the relevant court documents should also be included.

Specificity about the sources of data often has medicolegal significance. Direct observation of behavior and speech must be distinguished from secondary sources.

□ **C ASE E XAMPLE**

A record entry read, in part: "4/19/96 5 p.m. I saw Mr. Jones in the day room become agitated and strike Rhonda W. across the face (note that the alleged crime for which Mr. Jones is being evaluated, as reported by the arresting officer on admission, is assault and battery on an older woman)."

Note the distinctions between primary observations ("I saw"), secondary observations ("as reported"), and the careful use of "alleged" to refer to any actual or potential criminal charges. Note also the use of time and date for recording specific incidents in which time course may be essential (e.g., does Rhonda W. develop neurologic symptoms 2 or 10 hours after the injury?).

A more extensive discussion of record-keeping may be found elsewhere (3, 4). A critical point concerning the alteration of records is made in the following section.

Altering the Record

In a recent article on malpractice by an experienced attorney (5), this subject matter was introduced by the sidebar, "Altering Medical Records is the Dumbest Thing a Doctor Can Do."

The point is relatively simple. Not only is it unwise to attempt to fudge records after a bad outcome, it is nearly impossible. An entire forensic specialty exists called "questioned documents"; the modern technology available to this field is truly astonishing, ranging from chemical tests that specify the age of ink on a page to ultraviolet light that examines the relative compression of paper fibers.

To alter a record appropriately—that is, to enter a correction or emendation—the critical notion to consider is "transparency," or care in documentation that makes clear (i.e., transparent) when the original was written, when the correction was entered, and what both said. For example, to change yesterday's note, write today's date and time and describe the change (e.g., review of yesterday's note reveals omission of father's visit).

CONFIDENTIALITY

Confidentiality is the term for a person's right not to have revealed to third parties information shared "in confidence" with a second party, such as a mental health professional. As mentioned earlier, this issue is closely related to record-keeping.

Practical Aspects of Confidentiality

Originally an ethical principle, confidentiality now rests on a number of explicit and implicit legal bases. The underlying principle is that identifiable information about a patient cannot be shared with third parties without that patient's explicit (usually written) consent. There are exceptions to this rule, and implied in the act of consenting to the release of information are several considerations.

1. Consent should be given for particular data or particular kinds of data, with the amount or degree of detail specified.

2. A single consent is good for a single release of information. A second request, even from the same source, requires a second consent.

3. Even with consent, the clinician is expected to use discretion in how much or what kind of information to release. The standard is set by the needs of the situation, narrowly construed.

4. Although acceptable during emergencies and other conditions, oral consent is generally far less desirable than written consent for obvious documentary reasons.

Pitfalls in Confidentiality

The most common breach of confidentiality in acute care settings occurs when staff members carelessly discuss patients by name in public places like elevators, corridors, or cafeterias. This harmful practice must be eschewed, not only because confidentiality is compromised but also because it is a blow to the morale of other patients, next of kin, and visitors. The casual insensitivity thus demonstrated conveys a lack of respect or seriousness of purpose regarding patients in general.

To the surprise of some clinicians, confidentiality extends (i.e., bars sharing information) to even the patient's family, the patient's attorney, the patient's former therapist, and the clinician's professional colleagues who are not directly involved in the patient's care.

On the other hand, supervisors are usually considered part of the treatment team and are thus viewed as within the "circle" of direct information. The same is true for ward personnel directly involved with the patient's care. Thus, ward staff members who keep a patient's secrets from each other are not observing confidentiality but acting in a manner destructive to good patient care (3, 6).

Clinicians often wonder how much in-formation to share with a consultant when the latter gives advice on a case. It is customary to obtain the patient's permission for the consultation and, hence, for the implicit sharing of information. If some difficulty arises—the patient is paranoid, hesitant, reluctant, and ambivalent—the patient should be presented anonymously (e.g., the patient is a 50-year-old man) to obtain at least some consultative benefit from a second opinion without compromising confidentiality. This approach also spares consultants who are wary of litigation. Because their duty is to the clinician/consultee, not the patient, the latter cannot sue the consultant for malpractice.

An important point is that patients bear no burden of confidentiality, which may serve a valuable purpose when the clinician's communications are complicated by conflicts of interests or uncertainty about whose interests one is actually serving. In sticky situations, the patient may legitimately pass on information to family, other caretakers, or even potential victims of his or her own aggression (7).

Record Keeping and AIDS Patients

In regard to acquired immunodeficiency syndrome (AIDS), issues of record-keeping and confidentiality are in a constant state of flux. Individual jurisdictions vary widely in their regulations and laws on this matter, and clinicians must familiarize themselves with local rules (8–11).

In particularly murky situations in which laws and regulations provide no illumination, two rules may help. First, an ethical analysis of competing advantages and disadvantages may provide some guidance for an appropriate intervention and a refutation of the charge of negligence. Second, AIDS can be treated provisionally like syphilis, using public health reporting measures and sanctions via appropriate public health agencies.

Exceptions to the Principle of Confidentiality

Under certain circumstances, information from a patient's record may be released without the patient's consent. These cases include the following:

1. To meet emergency needs of the acute care patient. Clinicians should follow the "best interests" doctrine narrowly construed. For example, a limited revelation might apply to the family of a floridly psychotic teen-ager needing to be queried regarding his possible phencyclidine (PCP) use. In this and similar cases, an attempt should be made to obtain consent, and that effort should be documented.

2. To treat incompetent patients. Consent of the guardian or next of kin in emergencies is required.

3. To protect against harm from a patient. In some jurisdictions—but, inconsistently, not in others—the clinician is obligated to breach confidentiality if necessary to protect third parties from harm from a patient, e.g., warning the putative victim of death threats without the patient's consent (3) or calling the police. However, a patient's allegation of having committed past crimes does not trigger a reporting requirement.

4. To comply with special reporting requirements. In some jurisdictions reporting requirements govern venereal disease, child abuse, and other issues. Local statutes should be checked.

In the interests of the alliance, all breaches of confidentiality for one of these emergency reasons should be reviewed with the patient, addressing the necessity of the breach and its impact and consequences. The patient's feelings and the clinical state that necessitated the breach should be reviewed, explored, and worked through.

The aim of this review of the structure and function of the psychiatric record is to clarify the complex medicolegal nimbus surrounding charting and also to offer an insight into the manner in which good clinical care may be fostered by attention to careful recording of clinical data. See Appendix 20A for details of the chart itself.

REFERENCES

1. Leacock S. Laugh with Leacock. New York: Pocket Books, 1980.
2. Gutheil TG. Paranoia and progress notes; a guide to forensically informed psychiatric record keeping. Hosp Community Psychiatry 1980;31:479–482.
3. Appelbaum PS, Gutheil TG. Clinical handbook of psychiatry and the law. Baltimore: Williams & Wilkins, 1991.
4. Slovenko R. On the need for record keeping in the practice of psychiatry. J Psychiatry Law 1979;7:399–440.
5. Toberoff M. A surefire way to destroy your malpractice defense. Med Econ 1995;72:166–172.
6. Gutheil TG. Legal defense as ego defense: a special form of resistance to the therapeutic process. Psychiatr Q 1979;51:251–256.
7. Wulsin LR, Bursztajn H, Gutheil TG. Unexpected clinical features of the Tarasoff decision: the therapeutic alliance and the duty to warn. Am J Psychiatry 1983;140:601–603.
8. McGuire J, Nieri D, Abbott D, et al. Do Tarasoff principles apply in AIDS-related psychotherapy? Ethical decision making and the role of therapist homophobia and perceived client dangerousness. Prof Psychol Res Pract 1995;26:608–611.
9. Morrison CF. AIDS: ethical implications for psychological intervention. Prof Psychol Res Pract 1989;20:166–171.
10. Stanard R. Legal and ethical implications of HIV and duty to warn for counselors: when does Tarasoff apply? J Counseling Dev 1995;73:397–400.
11. Hughes RB. AIDS-related ethical and legal issues for mental health professionals. J Ment Health Counseling 1994;16:445–458.

Appendix 20A

Contents of the
Psychiatric Record in
Acute Care Settings

Because the majority of acute care facilities tend to develop their own systems of record-keeping in idiosyncratic fashion, discussion in this appendix must be limited to those general principles defining the purpose and hence the content of the sections of the record.

ADMISSION NOTE

This section heralds the transformation of an individual into an acute care patient. This is a shift of enormous sociolegal impact, rife with implications of changed status, altered rights, liabilities, duty of care, potential stigma, and the like. In keeping with the seriousness of the patient's passage over this administrative cliff, this section should emphasize the justificatory aspect of the record. Why was admission the best (or the only, or the only feasible, or the most appropriate) approach? Why would no less a step suffice? What was the "last straw" for this patient that "broke the back" of ambulatory nonacute care? The answer to these questions must be clear in the note.

Ideally, entry into acute care, especially hospital admission, is a carefully planned and weighed prescription. In reality, it is often a precipitous event, partaking of the urgency of a life-or-death emergency department intervention. Like the emergency department workup, the admission note should focus on critical, decisive elements. Deeper, more discursive elaboration may follow in the definitive record. After identifying data, chief complaints, and a cogent present illness have been recorded, a brief history relating social circumstances and family history should be obtained. Particular attention should be paid to medical history, noting past and current medical conditions and their pharmacotherapy, if any; current medications, drugs, and alcohol, including over-the-counter preparations; allergies or previous adverse drug reactions; and dietary considerations. The clinician should ask about the presence of weapons in the home.

The tentative formulation and working diagnosis should guide the early interventions, expressed in a goal-directed fashion (e.g., thorazine 50 mg by mouth, test dose, then 100 mg three times a day for hallucinations). The working diagnosis and acute interventions should be recorded together with planned investigations and laboratory tests.

The informants or others who accompany the patient are often extremely important to the patient, although this may not always be obvious. The admission note should record their names and telephone numbers as well as similar data for previous mental health or medical and social contacts, if available. If this information is not obtained on admission, it is often far more difficult to track down later.

A physical examination, including careful neurologic assessment, is a central part of each hospital admission workup and may be indicated for acutely disturbed patients whose differential diagnosis is not clear and who are being considered for less than hospital level of care.

STATUS PAPER

This vitally important document is, quite literally, the only indication that medical hospitalization is occurring and not kidnapping or false imprisonment. Clinical experience reveals the surprising finding that the most dangerously vague status indicators accompany patients sent by the courts. For this reason, the clinician should carefully scrutinize the documentation sent with court-ordered patients. Ambiguities should be clarified as rapidly as possible with the clerk of the court.

INITIAL INTAKE

Whether termed "intake," "presenting problem list," "staffing report," "conference plan," or a similar title, this section of the record should reflect a current, detailed portrait of the patient in the acute state, drawn from the available data gathered in the early workup from all involved disciplines. The best working diagnosis or clinical formulation belongs in this section, as well as the various planned modalities of treatment, with attention to the utilization perspective noted earlier in this chapter.

TEAM TREATMENT PLAN

As the operational core of the chart and the veritable compass of the course of acute care, this section should focus on data gathering, task assignment, and goal definition. A problem-oriented format often helps to organize this section. Regular updating should include the evolution of the illness, the treatment, the acute course, newly emerging data, and the pooled wisdom of staff members, supervisors, consultants, and others.

PROGRESS NOTES

These regular recordings of the developments of the patient's progress should follow the principles outlined in this chapter. Most of the considerations described apply particularly to progress notes.

Progress notes must always be dated. For significant events, the time should also be indicated. Progress notes should always be signed by name and discipline; additional titles should be added when pertinent (e.g., S. Wilson, RN, night supervisor). The frequency of entry should be governed by the acuteness of the illness and the course of treatment. Of course, ad hoc entries can be made whenever significant events occur.

DISCHARGE SUMMARY

In addition to marking the termination of one phase of total treatment (e.g., hospitalization) and the onset of another (e.g., aftercare), this section also heralds passage over another administrative cliff to outpatient status. Ambulatory care often lacks many of the implicit supports and opportunities for monitoring care that would be present in the acute care setting. This fact places a burden on the treatment planners to address this deficit, which must be done in the discharge summary.

Many institutions send only the discharge summary to other caretakers when information is requested (with patient's release, of course). Thus, the discharge summary is an important part of the record. This fact places two potentially contradictory burdens on its author: completeness (because all critical data must be included) and circumspection (because this document is the most "public" piece of the chart by virtue of its transmissibility).

The discharge summary should contain identifying data, chief complaint, brief statement of the admission picture enriched by subsequent information and understanding, a summary of the hospital course specifically including forensically important events and their outcomes or remedies, a comparison of admission and discharge diagnoses, statements of condition (e.g., improved) and prognosis (e.g., guarded), and a very detailed outline of planned aftercare, preferably including specifics of the first planned outpatient or aftercare appointment.

An example of an aftercare plan is as follows: "Perphenazine (32 mg, h.s., daily), 10 pills were given to pt.; a prescription for 2 weeks' supply given, to be filled by patient's mother. Needs to be monitored by Dr. Smith; pt. has 1st appt. with him on 5/17/96 at 2:30 PM; given appt. slip. Therapy per Jonesville CMHC clinic; case reviewed with Ms. Adams, MSW, who will follow pt. 1st appt. 5/14/96 at 10 AM pt. given map to clinic."

If some aspect of dangerousness characterized the admission (suicide attempt, homicide threats), current dangerousness should be assessed at discharge. If discharge is occurring (as not uncommonly happens) in the context of a calculated risk, this decision must be meticulously spelled out, with determinants, risks, and benefits of discharge and benefits of alternative courses of action made explicit. The care with which this is done may prove decisive (in the event of even an adventitious postdischarge bad outcome) in differentiating a justified judgment call from negligence.

GENERAL ELEMENTS OF THE RECORD

Other important parts of the record include consent forms (witnessed) for special procedures, laboratory and consultation reports, and special forms (e.g., seclusion reports and other statutorily required documents). The responsible clinician's initials or countersignature indicates that these documents have been reviewed.

Some jurisdictions have mandated special considerations for AIDS and human immunodeficiency virus-related data, such as keeping this information in a separate part of the chart or in an entirely separate chart and/or requiring separate, specific consent for release of this information (8–11). Because of regional inconsistencies in this area, local regulations must be consulted.

Chapter 21

Legal Issues in Acute Care Psychiatry

Stuart A. Anfang and James T. Hilliard

INTRODUCTION

Over the past three decades, psychiatry has witnessed an explosion of statutory and case law on the care and treatment of mentally ill patients. Particularly for acutely ill patients, the evolution of legal doctrine around such issues as informed consent, civil commitment, right to refuse treatment, and duty to protect third parties has affected the daily clinical practice of psychiatrists (1, 2). A similar expansion has occurred in malpractice liability. Once, psychiatrists were sued infrequently; now, clinicians are facing increasing claims of negligence around questions of psychiatric treatment and diagnosis. Finally, the dramatic changes in mental health care, including the advent of managed care and the restricted availability of resources, have forced clinicians to become increasingly aware of the legal aspects of the treatment they are striving to deliver.

Previous books on acute care psychiatry have focused on inpatient settings. As care is increasingly delivered in other acute care settings, such as partial hospitalization and residential programs, the legal context must be understood in broader terms. Many of the same basic principles apply across all levels of care. This chapter examines psychiatric malpractice, considering areas of risk and prevention. A special section discusses emerging issues of liability in the managed care marketplace, and the fundamental concepts central to risk management—including confidentiality, informed consent, and patient rights—are examined. Finally, the role of the clinician interacting within the legal system is covered, bringing a therapeutic perspective to an inherently adversarial process. Documentation in the medical record, a critical area of both risk management and good clinical care, is discussed in more detail in Chapter 20.

MALPRACTICE

Elements

A medical malpractice lawsuit is based on a theory of negligence committed by the

431

physician (3–5). The plaintiff in a medical malpractice suit must prove by a preponderance of the evidence (more likely than not) that the physician was negligent. Four conditions frequently referred to as "the four Ds" must be established: the physician had a *duty* to care for the patient, the physician *derelictly* breached that duty, the injuries caused were the *direct* and proximate result of the physician's breach, and the injuries suffered by the plaintiff are compensable *damages* resulting from the physician's malpractice.

Duty of Provider

The duty owed by physicians to their patients stems from the existence of a physician-patient relationship; if no relationship exists, no medical malpractice can be claimed. Once the physician-patient relationship has been established, the duty owed to the patient is that of reasonable, nonnegligent care. Physicians are expected to practice with the reasonable degree of skill and knowledge ordinarily possessed by equally qualified members of the profession practicing in similar circumstances. Thus, a psychiatrist is held to the standard of practice of other reasonable psychiatrists. Historically, the standard was based on the specific community in which the individual doctor practiced. However, with advances in science, communication, and continuing education, the medical standard is now usually defined as the national standard of practice, as reflected for example, in major textbooks or practice guidelines issued by national specialty organizations.

The issue of duty of care in a particular specialty usually arises when a physician, aware that he or she lacks specialized knowledge or training, continues to treat the patient despite that lack of expertise. Physicians have a duty to recommend and refer patients to specialists or more knowledgeable providers when they recognize their own limitations in treating particular ailments. When physicians do treat patients who clearly should have been referred to specialists, they will be held to the standard of care required of the specialist.

The standard of care can be proved in various ways. When acceptable and appropriate alternative medical procedures are available, the physician is not subject to liability for malpractice merely by choosing one of these procedures despite a resulting injury to the patient. It must be established that the choice or implementation of treatment was below the standard of reasonable practice. Standards may be established by expert testimony, often referring to published literature or generally accepted rules and guidelines, to define the minimum standard against which the physician will be judged.

Breach of the Standard (Negligence)

The lawyer's adage that "bad results do not make a malpractice case" clearly illustrates negligence as a key element in a malpractice action. Proof of an unfavorable medical result without more evidence showing that negligent behavior caused the bad result will not establish the physician's liability. Proof of negligence ordinarily requires expert medical testimony to establish breach of the standard of care. If the allegation of negligence is obvious for a simple and widely known treatment (e.g., the psychiatrist has sex with a patient during therapy sessions), negligence can be inferred from the common knowledge of lay jurors. To prove negligence, a particular event, conversation, or action might need to be recreated. When the doctor and the patient are recounting their different recollections of an event, the jury must decide which version is the most credible. Therefore, in a malpractice case, the proof of what occurred may be more important than what actually occurred. Timely records are often crucial when recreating proof of events that may have occurred years before the trial or deposition.

Damages

Negligence without damages precludes an action for malpractice. In law, damages fall into several categories including general (such as pain and suffering), special (such as economic losses due to medical or funeral expenses and loss of earnings or earning capacity) and punitive (such as proof of willful, wanton, or malicious conduct).

Direct Causation

Causation is the final key element of proof for a malpractice claim. As a general rule to prove causation, an act or omission by a physician is considered the proximate cause of the patient's injury if it produced a foreseeable harm that would not have otherwise occurred. Intervening events out of the physician's control may alter the liability. For example, if the patient awakened after surgery to discover that the wrong leg had been amputated, the plaintiff can rely on the theory of res ipsa loquitur (the thing speaks for itself). In contrast, if it can be demonstrated that the patient was partially responsible for the adverse result (e.g., not heeding care recommendations or reporting early side effects), the physician's liability may be reduced or dismissed.

Data

Although data regarding the frequency and success of malpractice claims would interest both insurers and insured physicians, the relevant numbers are difficult to estimate accurately. There are several explanations for this problem. Only a small number of malpractice claims actually reach public trial, and only a smaller percentage of these lead to an appeal with a published opinion. Malpractice insurers have traditionally been reluctant to reveal a detailed breakdown of the type and frequency of filed claims and have provided only aggregate or summary data. Also, cases often continue over several years in different legal stages, making it hard to estimate the true incidence of malpractice claims. Finally, the same act of negligence could be described differently in different suits and could be expressed as multiple counts. For example, a borderline patient who develops tardive dyskinesia after being erroneously treated for schizoaffective disorder could claim misdiagnosis, negligent prescription of medication, failure to monitor for side effects, failure to obtain proper informed consent, or a combination of charges.

Despite the questionable reliability of the data available, some general observations can be made based on reported trends. According to the most recent data maintained by the American Medical Association, psychiatrists represent approximately 6% of all physicians (6). In 1993, psychiatrists accounted for approximately 3% of all malpractice claims incurred that year. Although psychiatrists continue to be sued less frequently than other specialists, the incidence of malpractice claims for psychiatrists has been rising dramatically over the past 10 years, with increasing average awards. Simultaneously, insurance premiums have been rising dramatically, particularly in high-risk urban areas and for high-risk practitioners (7). Recently, the insurance group offering coverage for members of the American Psychiatric Association (APA) estimated that the chance of a psychiatrist being sued in any given year is approximately 8%, up from 5% 3 years ago (8). High-risk practices have been identified as those involved in treating large numbers of psychopharmacology patients at multiple sites; supervising several other therapists in high-volume clinics; increasing use of limited, episodic care and emergency crisis intervention; and using hypnosis or "recovered memory techniques" for patients with reportedly repressed memories. The malpractice carrier sponsored by the APA has begun to shift from a practice of allowing the clinician to make the final decision about settling a claim to a policy of allowing an impartial tribunal to hold the ultimate vote on settling a claim that appears likely to lose at trial. This trend will likely be followed by other insurers.

Not surprisingly, topping the list of claims against psychiatrists (9–11) are suicide, medication-related negligence, misdiagnosis, and negligent treatment. Breach of confidentiality, lack of informed consent, and failure to protect a third party are less common grounds. Recently, claims for sexual misconduct and other boundary violations have increased dramatically; these suits often result in very high cash awards by settlement or trial. These areas are discussed in more detail below.

Finally, sobering if not reassuring "rules of thumb" offered by malpractice attorneys can place these issues in an appropriate context (12–14). Approximately 33% of 100 general claims filed with an insurer will be dropped before a formal claim has been entered with the court. Another 30% will be closed due to lack of prosecution by the plaintiffs, dismissal by an impartial screening tribunal, or summary judgment in favor of the defendant. Approximately 20–30% of cases will proceed to negotiation or arbitration, often resulting in some

reasonable settlement award. Finally, 5–10% of all malpractice cases will go to trial; of these, 80–90% result in verdicts for the defendant. Therefore, of the original 100 claims filed, only one or two cases will conclude in a jury verdict against the defending doctor. These verdicts, with their multimillion dollar awards, are the cases that inspire headlines and frighten physicians. The 20–30 cases that result in a settlement reflect the fact that negligence is recognized in a significant number of cases for which patients receive (presumably) appropriate compensation.

Areas of Malpractice Claims

Suicide

Suicide represents one of the more common malpractice claims against psychiatrists and frequently results in high financial awards. The allegations generally fall into two categories: failure to detect or assess suicidal intent and failure to respond with appropriate interventions. If the patient's condition is the direct cause of the suicidal action, then the question is, "How responsible is the clinician?" Recognizing that mental illness often reduces the judgment or impulse control of patients, the courts usually assume implicitly that a patient may not be competent to control his or her own behavior. This implication leaves others, including the physician, to bear much if not all the responsibility. A guiding focus of management of the suicidal patient, therefore, attempts to engage the patient (and when appropriate friends and family) in the process of assessment and treatment. Good clinical practice can translate into good risk management (15, 16).

The assessment of suicidal intent, including the difficulties of accurate prediction, is discussed in detail in Chapter 2.

Clinicians are not considered negligent for failing to predict accurately suicidal acts, provided that they acted within the professional standard of care. Ultimately, the jury in a malpractice trial will decide on the standard of care for that particular case based on the (often conflicting) testimony of expert witnesses. However, the prudent clinician can look to the literature for useful parameters and practice guidelines created by professional organizations and malpractice insurers (17, 18). Although these guidelines do not necessarily set the standard of care, they can be identified as a reasonable professional consensus that reflects the minimum expectations of the psychiatric community. Clinicians should recognize that such guidelines can help or hinder a malpractice defense, particularly if the standard of care described is far different from the treatment delivered (19). Ultimately, of course, judgments regarding a particular patient must be based on all the clinical data available for that patient.

Typically, the clinician will evaluate for suicidal ideation and history at the time of initial assessment or acute care admission. Further data to assess seriousness and degree of urgency should be obtained. With any significant change in the clinical situation, including any new self-destructive behavior or ideation, suicidal ideation should be reevaluated. For inpatients, the evaluation should be repeated when the patient is to be given greater freedom of privileges or reductions in precautions, especially at the time of discharge. If the patient falsely denies suicidal ideation but then becomes self-destructive, the clinician will be expected to have made a reasonable assessment of the patient's credibility based on the clinical context. Most clinicians recognize that a patient who is intent on suicide will eventually succeed despite all reasonable precautions. The psychiatrist's task is to reduce the likelihood of suicide for treatable patients while recognizing realistic limitations of his or her capabilities.

Chronically suicidal patients pose special clinical challenges, but the risk management process remains the same. In these cases, engaging the patient and other supports in the treatment planning process is important. Informed consent requires that the patient be made aware of the risks and benefits of a proposed discharge or transition to a less-restrictive level of care. In developing the therapeutic alliance, the psychiatrist should maximally promote the patient's efforts to take more responsibility for his or her actions. Acknowledging the risks of continued hospitalization, such as regression or the consumption of limited lifetime hospitalization benefits, the treatment team and the patient may choose to tolerate short-term risk to gain longer-term functioning.

Documentation is essential for all assessments of suicidal ideation. As discussed below, "If it's not written down, it didn't happen." Documentation should include an analysis of the relevant data, the possible choices with their associated risks and benefits, and the rationale for the decided course of treatment. If possible, the patient's (and family's) participation and understanding of the decision process should be included. Documentation should always be completed as close as possible to the time of decision for discharge or increased privileges. Finally, for high-risk or challenging cases, consultation with colleagues is extremely useful for clinical guidance and for demonstrating what a reasonable practitioner would do under similar circumstances. Although frequently underused, consultations should always be noted in the record.

In the event of a tragic outcome, the clinician's feelings of sadness, failure, self-reproach, and anger are mirrored by the surviving family and friends of the patient (20). The treatment team should reach out to the survivors, offering support and if necessary treatment referrals. Although a debated suggestion, attending the wake or funeral service can be an appropriate and often appreciated show of support on the clinician's part. Such efforts represent both good clinical care and effective risk management.

Medications/Somatic Treatments

For psychiatrists, these malpractice cases are similar to those faced by other physicians within medicine and surgery. Such cases include use of an inappropriate medication or an inappropriate dosage, failure to monitor side effects and blood levels, and prescription of a drug despite known contraindications. Psychiatrists should be up to date with the basic clinical psychopharmacology literature, particularly as newer psychotropic agents are continually being introduced. Caution should be used when prescribing unfamiliar agents for the first time, and consultation should be considered when necessary. Commonly accepted guidelines regarding premedication workup, regular blood levels when appropriate, and scheduled monitoring of other laboratory values (e.g., liver functions, white blood cell counts) should be followed, and the results should be documented in the record.

Informed consent is central to the correct prescription of medications, as in all nonemergent treatments in medicine (21). Informed consent is an ongoing process that evolves as the relationship with the patient and the patient's clinical status change. Informed consent should not be seen merely as a legal requirement or a risk prevention tool; rather, it is an opportunity to engage the patient in a therapeutic partnership that respects the patient's autonomy and encourages an acceptance of treatment responsibility (22).

Neuroleptics pose a special difficulty for psychiatrists for two reasons: the severity of possible side effects, such as tardive dyskinesia, and the impaired judgment and potential incompetence of acutely psychotic patients for whom the medications are typically prescribed (23). Tardive dyskinesia is a recognized side effect that can occur with the appropriate, nonnegligent prescription of antipsychotics. The courts require clinicians to warn their patients of the risk of tardive dyskinesia and other major side effects and to continue monitoring for its occurrence (24). Several notable court cases have resulted in large financial judgments and settlements against psychiatrists for failure to obtain adequate informed consent or to monitor appropriately (25, 26). Unfortunately, judges and juries often have misconceived notions of the severity and probability of neuroleptic side effects. Clinicians must explain the accurate risk-benefit analysis of neuroleptic use to the legal profession in general and to the court hearing a particular case.

Although often a challenging task, except in emergency situations such as danger to self or others, the physician should always obtain proper consent before beginning a neuroleptic (or any medication) (27, 28). Information should be provided at a level of detail appropriate to the patient's clinical situation; it can be counterproductive to provide the acutely psychotic patient with detailed statistics on the incidence of tardive dyskinesia over 10 years of use. Basic information regarding risks and benefits, however, should be provided and documented. As the patient improves, and if continued use of neuroleptic is indicated, a more thorough discussion will be necessary. The argument that the patient will not accept the medication if the risks are known or the contention that such knowledge will be a detriment is unlikely to hold up in court. If incompetency is an issue, substituted consent from the court or a legal guardian must be obtained.

Finally, once a patient has consented to a neuroleptic, the psychiatrist is responsible for monitoring side effects and the patient's continued consent. Clinicians should be aware of any standard of care, such as the APA guidelines on tardive dyskinesia (29). A regular examination for early abnormal movements (AIMS [Abnormal Involuntary Movement Scale]) is important, along with periodic discussions with the patient about the ongoing risks and benefits. The patient's continued informed consent should be documented in the record, typically at the time of the AIMS or at the emergence of signs suggestive of tardive dyskinesia. As appropriate, psychiatrists should try to wean patients to the lowest necessary dose. Newer antipsychotic agents, such as clozapine (lower tardive dyskinesia, higher neutropenia), offer the possibility of different risk-benefit profiles and should be considered with the patient as they become available. For chronic patients, it is helpful to involve family members and the treatment team in the ongoing informed consent dialogue.

Misdiagnosis

Misdiagnosis typically refers to negligence in recognizing the true nature of a patient's condition. To claim malpractice, some harm caused by the faulty diagnosis must be demonstrated, usually by failure to provide appropriate care and treatment. Clinicians are well aware that ambiguities, diagnostic errors, and genuine disagreements are unavoidable in the practice of

psychiatry. Negligence does not mean simply arriving at a mistaken diagnosis, but implies that the clinician failed to use the appropriate procedures and information that a reasonable, competent colleague would use to make an accurate diagnosis. For example, a clinician might fail to seek neurologic evaluation for an atypical psychotic patient, although an organic disorder should have been suspected, and proceed to treat the patient as having a schizophrenic illness. If the patient is improperly treated with neuroleptics and develops tardive dyskinesia, liability may be found. If the patient ultimately presents with a progressive brain tumor that should have been suspected and identified earlier, liability may be found if it can be demonstrated that harm occurred from the delay in diagnosis (30). Again, clinicians are held to the standard of a reasonable, prudent practitioner practicing with the same information and resources. In the absence of suggestive signs or symptoms, not every patient requires a full neurologic workup simply for risk management reasons; good clinical practice standards should always be the guide.

An area of growing controversy regarding misdiagnosis involves "false memory" cases of repressed memories of alleged past abuse. Recently, a number of celebrated cases involve a patient or a third party who brings a malpractice suit against a clinician for negligent diagnosis and treatment (31). These cases often involve outpatient treaters, but inpatient hospitals and psychiatrists have also been named. Typically, the damages result not merely from a diagnostic error, but because the therapist actively encouraged an action leading to harm (e.g., having a public confrontation or bringing civil or criminal charges against the alleged abuser). As case law and scientific evidence emerge in this area, clinicians are advised to be cautious when dealing with such cases (32). Treaters are advised to take a neutral stance, to be circumspect about suggesting the patient take actions outside therapy, and to define carefully their role as clinicians rather than as forensic evaluators or legal advocates. As always, proper documentation and consultation with other (especially expert) clinicians are important risk management strategies.

Dangerousness

In the past, psychiatrists have been liable for negligently allowing a dangerous patient to be discharged or to escape from an inpatient facility if the patient later causes harm to a third party. In 1976, the California Supreme Court, in the well-known case of Tarasoff v. Regents of the University of California, imposed on clinicians a "duty to protect" third parties from dangerous patients—inpatient or outpatient (33). The court stated that when clinicians know or should know that their patients represent a danger to others, they have a duty to take whatever steps are reasonably necessary to protect those identifiable third parties. Clinicians opposed to such a duty have raised arguments that accurate predictions of future dangerousness are difficult and that the risk of cautious "false-positive" predictions could lead to unnecessary breaches of confidentiality and unnecessary hospitalization. In addition, such actions could discourage some patients from seeking therapy at all. Generally the courts have not been impressed with these arguments, and most states now have adopted some version of the duty to protect by case law or statute (34, 35).

Although some court decisions suggest that clinicians would have a duty to protect potential victims who are not specifically threatened, the duty usually is limited to situations in which a patient makes an overt threat against a clearly identifiable victim (36). The statutes defining this duty vary by state, but usually specify one or more possible options for discharging the duty, including warning the victim, notifying the police, and/or hospitalizing the patient, voluntarily or involuntarily. If the psychiatrist discharges the duty in good faith and with reasonable clinical judgment, the statutes typically hold the doctor immune from liability for breach of confidentiality and for negligence. It is essential for all clinicians to be familiar with the specific duty to protect obligation in their jurisdiction as defined by statute or case law.

Clinical approaches that deal with a duty to protect situation (37, 38) are covered extensively in the literature. One recommendation is to conduct a thorough clinical assessment of the threat, involve the patient in the decision whenever possible, document reasoning and obtain consultation with a colleague if necessary, and do what is clinically appropriate for the situation, including hospitalization if necessary. When clinically appropriate, either voluntarily or involuntarily hospitalization can provide a less public means of managing a dangerous patient without breaching confidentiality. For some patients, particularly those who pose a chronic threat of danger to others, management outside the inpatient setting may be necessary. Whenever possible, the patient should be engaged in the problem as part of the therapeutic alliance, allowing for an exploration of violent impulses and an acceptance of responsibility for controlling these actions. Some clinicians have advocated including potential victims who are relatives or acquaintances of the patient in a joint meeting that allows for the expression of anger and hostility in a more productive, less dangerous way. For patients who are managed outside the inpatient setting, psychiatrists should monitor closely for any acute change in clinical status that may increase the risk of danger.

Sexual Misconduct

Over the past several years, awareness and concern about sexual contact between clinicians and patients has been growing (39, 40). In the past, this may have been quietly "deplored, but tolerated." A therapist who fell in love with his patient could refer the patient to another treater and then continue the romantic relationship. Remarkably, some therapists argued that sexual contact was a beneficial, therapeutic aspect of treatment. As the public and the profession have become more aware of the frequency of sexual misconduct (anonymous surveys have indicated that between 5% and 15% of therapists admit to sexual activity with patients, the majority being male therapists) and its harmful effects on patients, a clear standard has emerged. Therapists (including psychotherapists and psychopharmacologists) can never have sex with their current patients. This position is articulated in the ethical code of the APA and other professional organizations (41, 42). The APA has taken the position that this ethical prohibition against sexual conduct extends to former patients, although some have argued that romantic relationships might be acceptable under certain circumstances following a specific period after the treatment relationship has ended (43). Clinicians should note that malpractice insurers have tried to argue that sexual misconduct does not represent negligence (which is covered) but is an intentional act (which would not be cov-

ered under most policies). Some insurers include language in the malpractice contract explicitly excluding coverage for liability due to sexual misconduct. Clinicians facing a claim for sexual misconduct must be aware of their insurers' positions on this matter. In addition, several states have enacted legislation criminalizing patient-therapist sex, making it easier for patients to sue and requiring registration boards to suspend professional licenses (44). The message is clear that sex with patients will not be tolerated.

On inpatient units and in residential programs, the risk of sexualized acting out with a vulnerable patient is often increased, especially with nonprofessional staff members such as mental health workers (45–48). Psychiatrists may be held liable for such acting out by staff members under their supervision via the doctrine of respondeat superior (let the master respond), which essentially holds supervisors responsible for their agents' actions. A malpractice plaintiff searches for the potential defendant with the "deepest pockets," which will almost always be the physician, the administrator, and/or the hospital rather than the nonprofessional staff member. Inpatient and residential program staff members should receive supervision and education that address the powerful transference and countertransference feelings that sexually provocative patients can inspire. When an apparent incident of sexual misconduct occurs, appropriate documentation and consultation is recommended. When a charge of sexual misconduct is made, the defending clinician or administrator must determine whether this is a real incident or an imagined fantasy from an angry patient (49, 50). Legal consultation is often valuable in these complicated scenarios.

Termination Versus Abandonment

Although this issue most frequently occurs in the context of outpatient treatment, the principles are relevant for inpatient and other acute care settings such as residential and day programs. The law recognizes abandonment as the sudden termination of the patient's care, and the clinician is responsible for insuring that a termination is appropriately handled. Typically, if a clinician unilaterally ends the treatment, a proper referral should have been arranged or at least identified, and the patient should be engaged in the termination process to the appropriate extent. Frequent reasons for termination include threats to the therapist, nonpayment of professional fees, therapeutic impasse, and uncooperative or oppositional patients. Clinicians should first explore the meaning of the difficulties with the patient, when possible. Supervision or consultation can be very helpful, particularly for a therapeutic impasse or for a "hated" patient (51).

If anticipated, termination should be planned in advance to avoid later charges of abandonment. The patient should be notified, the process discussed, and a termination date scheduled. An appropriate referral should be identified and, ideally, the patient will agree to professional contact to facilitate an orderly transfer of care. The clinician should always document the reasons for termination, the efforts to avoid termination, and the processes of notification, planning, and referral. Termination for financial reasons should indicate a careful documentation of the discussions over time, including referral to a public clinic or other source of free or reduced care. Clinicians may wish to specify that the patient is welcome to return to treatment if the bill is paid or the financial situation changes.

Malpractice Prevention

Clinical Consultation

Along with an initial evaluation and examination before diagnosis, clinical consultation may be necessary and appropriate before or during treatment (52, 53). Consultations can protect the treater from a claim of malpractice by demonstrating reasonable and prudent care as validated by another practitioner. When seeking a clinical consultation, certain steps should be followed. First, whenever possible, the patient's permission should be requested to avoid any possible claim of breach of confidentiality. The patient's name or specific identifying information to be used in a "curbside" clinical consultation may not necessarily be used. Under certain circumstances, it may not be possible to obtain the patient's prior permission; in those cases, identifying information should be limited and the consultant should clearly understand the confidential nature of the discussion. (See further discussion under confidentiality below.) For more serious cases, a formal consultation—including a personal evaluation by the consultant—would be necessary.

The provider seeking the consultation should document the discussion, particularly if the consultant is unlikely to keep notes. The consultant should be asked for permission to record his or her name. If a formal consultation is requested, and especially if the consultant has seen the patient or is being reimbursed, the consultant should make a note in the treatment record (54). Such notes should include a brief outline of the problems discussed and the consultant's recommendations. In those cases in which patients have claimed a violation in the standard of care by substandard treatment or other allegations, the recorded presence of one or more clinical consultations have proven extremely beneficial as a defense. Clinicians must be aware of the converse tenet as well: if a consultant's documented recommendations are not followed and an adverse incident occurs, the clinician must be able to justify why the consultant's suggestions were not followed. Such justification should be written in the record at the time of disagreement and not after an adverse event.

Legal consultation can be helpful during the course of treatment, especially for interpretation of a statutory duty (e.g., to protect a third party or report child abuse). If clinically relevant to the management of treatment, information should be documented in a manner similar to a clinical consultation. If the information is limited to a discussion of possible risk management strategies in the event of an adverse outcome, it may not be appropriate for inclusion in the record. Discussion with a legal consultant can clarify correct documentation in these circumstances.

Records/Documentation

"If it's not written down, it didn't happen," is a commonly held precept for trial lawyers and the courts. Contradictory memories and recollections are not the best means of proving facts in a courtroom; therefore, records become extremely important to prove or disprove certain allegations. At a minimum, most states require records of evaluation, diagnosis, and treatment to be made; additional requirements govern records in inpatient facilities. Records are maintained for three major reasons: continuity of care, insurance reimbursement, and potential claims or litigation that may arise. The timeliness of records is crucial in the event a complaint is made against the treater. Records that are made when no controversy exists may be the best evidence to resolve an allegation of negligent treatment. Conversely, records made after a controversy develops or allegations are filed are suspect in terms of their objective honesty (55).

Many treaters are reluctant to place certain information into the records for fear of harming the patient at a later time. A clinician should adhere to the following legal rule: if the material is clinically important, it should be included in the record despite any personal opinion that the information, if disclosed, may be harmful to the patient. Usually the patient controls access to the confidential record and bears responsibility for allowing that release. At times, careful documentation of statements made or allegations brought into therapy by the patient is essential for the protection of both the patient and the treater. A patient's statements expressing sexualized transference issues or threatening the treater should be carefully recorded as protection in the event a future claim is made. A simple entry, such as "Patient wanted to hug; I responded with a handshake," timely entered could be critical evidence in favor of an innocent treater against a claim for boundary violations in therapy.

Occasionally, a patient will ask that the medical record be changed to reflect his or her view of an occurrence or disagreement with the treater's opinion (56). Also, the treater may fail to include an item in the record or, on review, may realize that there was an incorrect statement or change in opinion. If the record needs to be changed, any correction should be made so that the original entry is recognizable and the correction is obvious, dated, and explained. Patients wishing to change or to explain what is in their record should have the opportunity to spell out their disagreement; their written version can be identified as their response and should be added to the permanent record. The treater should almost never change a record based on the request of the patient unless, in rare cases, a clear inaccuracy of the record exists, such as through a transcription error or a misunderstanding of information. Again, such changes should always be explained, and the date of the entry, not an earlier date, should be recorded.

Patient-Doctor Relationship/Alliance

Although the maxim that "patients do not sue the doctors they like" is frequently inaccurate, it is true that doctors who are perceived as brusque, distant, and uncaring are more likely to face a malpractice claim in the event of an adverse outcome. Like most tenets of good risk management, fostering a strong patient-doctor alliance is also critical for good clinical care (57). Malpractice suits do result from patient and family anger and frustration with a caregiver in the context of adverse outcomes, rather than from simple negligence. Patients and families are surprisingly interested in hearing about the inherent uncertainties and ambiguities in psychiatric treatment. Through a candid discussion, those uncertainties become part of the informed clinical dialogue and are accepted by both patient and doctor as a reasonable risk given clinical realities (22). Such dialogue should be a continuous part of the treatment process and can extend even after an unfortunate outcome. "The secret to the care of the patient is caring for the patient" may be the most useful guiding maxim in malpractice prevention.

MANAGED CARE AND LIABILITY

The dramatic changes in the health-care delivery system created by managed care have created new legal dilemmas for providers and institutions (58–59). Managed care organizations (MCOs) are increasingly named as defendants in malpractice suits. Case law continues to evolve in this area, and legislatures are starting to write additional regulations and obligations clarifying the responsibilities of MCOs. As the liability aspects of managed care become better defined, clinicians must be mindful of their own liability and obligations, which may become even greater. Even if a managed care company is found liable for negligent care, the physician may not escape some responsibility.

Malpractice claims against MCOs have focused on three general areas: negligent selection of unqualified panel clinicians, negligent provision of care (usually for staff model health maintenance organizations in which the physicians are "supervised" employees), or inappropriate utilization review (such as falling below the standard of medical care) (60). This last area is the most common cause of concern to psychiatrists, particularly in inpatient settings. Every inpatient psychiatrist has had patients whose "days have been cut off " and who were "discharged sicker than some of the patients who used to be admitted." Early cases, such as Wickline v. California suggested that physicians have a "duty to appeal" adverse decisions; the doctor who "complies without protest" despite his or her better medical judgment "cannot avoid his [or her] ultimate responsibility for the patient's care (61)." Later decisions clarified that if the conduct of the utilization review program was "a substantial factor" in causing a bad outcome, the MCO may share liability with the physician (62). Increasingly, courts are joining state legislatures to make it clear that MCOs are held to reasonable standards of behavior, although the clinician who makes the ultimate medical decision is also to be held to a reasonable standard of good practice. How is that reasonable standard determined?

For the clinician treating the acutely ill patient, the first question is whether the patient needs treatment and, if so, what treatment is necessary. Some have advocated providing the patient with "informed consent" at the outset, explaining the patient's rights under the managed care plan and the possibility that benefits may be withheld. Such disclosure may be needed throughout the treatment process. If the MCO agrees, payment for treatment proceeds. When the MCO limits benefits, the clinician must reassess the patient's current treatment needs. If the patient can terminate treatment without harm, then an appropriate discharge or termination should be planned. If further treatment is necessary to avoid harm, then the MCO's decision should be appealed initially. Appeals can be time-consuming as clinicians argue through several levels of bureaucracy. How far should an appeal go? In general, the degree of the appeal depends on the degree of harm expected if treatment stops. As the appeal proceeds, the patient should be notified and brought into the process, taking into account whether treatment should be continued and whether alternative payments options are available. Ultimately, if the MCO refuses further payment, the clinician and the patient have several choices: continue with free care, obtain alternative payment, transfer to another setting if feasible (such as a public hospital), or terminate treatment if appropriate. In risk management, both the physician and the patient should make the choice; an opportunity exists to emphasize shared risk and responsibility and to promote alliance.

In this regard, early managed care contracts had gag or nondisparagement clauses, suggesting that clinicians could not fully inform patients about a disagreement over benefits or that alternative treatment was available beyond what the MCO would authorize. With the public's growing dissatisfaction with managed care, increasingly chronicled by the media, legislators in several states have moved to prohibit such restrictions. An important legal point must be made, however, relevant to all state legislation, which typically includes claims of malpractice that would be filed in state courts. Health insurance provided as a self-insured corporate employee benefit is regulated under the federal Employee Retirement Income Security Act (ERISA) statute (63, 64). ERISA "preempts" much of state regulation of such self-insured plans and also appears to immunize or protect many health plans from significant negligence liability. It is estimated that perhaps half of all U.S. managed care patients are covered under ERISA plans. In recent court cases, however, this ERISA protection has been challenged in certain ways, removing some of the obstacles to holding MCOs liable for their decisions. It has been suggested that federal legislation may be necessary to hold ERISA plans liable in malpractice claims. Psychiatrists who individually sign agreements with MCOs must be aware of "hold harmless" clauses commonly inserted into these contracts. These clauses require the clinician to indemnify the managed care company for any potential liability in the event of an adverse outcome; malpractice insurance may not cover the costs of such indemnification. Although these clauses are being challenged in courts and legislatures, clinicians are advised not to agree to indemnify MCOs. Psychiatrists must be aware of these developments while keeping a watchful eye on their evolving relationship with the managed care companies and the patients they insure (65).

CONFIDENTIALITY

Confidentiality is the right of an individual not to have communications made in confidence divulged to third parties without permission. For medicine, this right is grounded in an ethical tradition dating back to the times of Hippocrates and is based primarily on the concept that patients would not reveal important, personal information to their physician for fear of disclosure. More recently, the law has recognized this right through judicial decisions and legislative statutes, with some variation across jurisdictions. Generally, with exceptions discussed below, identifiable data about a patient can be disclosed to third parties only with the patient's specific consent (1, 66, 67).

Exceptions

The principal exception to the right of confidentiality occurs in an emergency situation in which the patient's physical health or safety is at risk. A common example would be to provide information to the emergency department clinician evaluating the psychiatrist's psychotic, noncompliant patient. When the clinician believes the patient is incompetent to give consent, a substitute consent should be obtained from a guardian or close relative, if available. When acting to hospitalize a patient voluntarily or involuntarily, most states allow the clinician to disclose relevant information such as suicidal or homicidal threats. Many states also require clinicians to disclose relevant information while protecting third parties from their patient's potentially violent acts (see below).

Information can be shared without the patient's explicit consent under other circumstances. The "circle of confidentiality" is defined as the extended treatment team within an institution, usually the inpatient facility, although now the circle may include staff members across the acute continuum of care. Physicians, therapists, supervisors, nurses and allied personnel, and consultants who actually examine the patient are all considered within the circle for treatment purposes, and information should be shared freely for optimal clinical care. The shared information should be limited to data relevant for appropriate clinical treatment. The patient's consent is required if information is to be shared with individuals outside the circle, including the patient's family, friends, attorney, employer, outside therapist, past treaters, and police. The patient's lawyer, as legal representative, is entitled to information only with the patient's consent. In contrast, the guardian (or parent of a minor)—as the legally responsible individual—is considered to be inside the circle of confidentiality. For clinical purposes, it is often useful to share information with outside parties, particularly outside treaters, and the patient should be encouraged to give appropriate releases as necessary. Although a clinician cannot disclose information without the patient's consent, there is no restriction on the clinician receiving information provided by concerned outsiders. For example, if a suicidal patient refuses to give consent for the psychiatrist to provide information to family members, the clinician can still listen to important information provided by the parents. As a general rule, if the psychiatrist does receive such outside information, the therapeutic alliance can be enhanced by informing the patient about the unilateral contact.

Disclosure of information to third-party payers can be a vexing problem for both clinicians and patients. Patients are often asked to sign general consents releasing all information as a prerequisite of insurance coverage for treatment. Managed care reviewers are scrutinizing cases more thoroughly and are requiring an increasing amount of data, which often include copies of the actual records. Patients may be forced to refuse consent and bear the cost of treatment themselves. Clinicians must use careful judgment to record only essential information and to avoid recording embarrassing or compromising nonessential information, particularly in the case of those employers who process claims internally. Increasingly, to preserve the patient's right to confidentiality, professional organizations are working with insurer groups and legislators to try to limit the information required for the documentation of care.

Disclosure of human immunodeficiency virus (HIV) status requires special consideration. Many states have passed restrictive laws with significant penalties for release of information without the patient's permission. Some statutes do allow physicians to reveal HIV information to certain third parties at risk for exposure. Similarly, substance abuse treatment programs receiving federal funding may require very specific written consent language to release information. Clinicians should be aware of the relevant case and statutory law in their jurisdiction. Legal consultation is helpful in complicated situations.

A lawyer's request or subpoena for records can provoke anxiety for a clinician. Any litigant in a dispute can receive a subpoena to require the appearance of a witness or the production of records in court or at deposition. Under a subpoena, a therapist is not required to testify or release records to the court; it only requires that the therapist appear with the records. Records should not be altered or destroyed in response to the subpoena. The judge must decide whether the material in question is protected by confidentiality. Under no circumstances should the clinician release information without the patient's consent or the court's order. On receiving a subpoena, it is good practice to consult with an attorney to clarify the therapist's rights and responsibilities. If circumstances allow a patient to claim privilege, it is useful to notify the patient's attorney.

Those outside the legal profession are often confused about the distinction between confidentiality and privilege and may inaccurately use the terms interchangeably. Privilege is actually a subsection of confidentiality and refers primarily to testimony in judicial settings. Privilege is held when an individual has the right to prohibit testimony by another person based on information imparted in confidence. Only the patient can invoke privilege, and only the patient (or the court) can waive privilege. The extent of privilege and its exceptions are strictly defined by case law or statute in each jurisdiction. Among the common exceptions are the patient-litigant exception (the patient's mental status is relevant to the litigation), the patient represents a danger to self or others, the patient has brought a malpractice suit against the clinician, a court-ordered examination is required to evaluate competency to stand trial or criminal responsibility, some child custody cases, the patient fails to pay his or her bill and the therapist brings suit, and the patient testifies about some aspect of the confidential relationship. Clinicians should consult with their attorneys about the specific situation before offering testimony.

Mandatory Reporting

In every state, the legislature has determined as a matter of public policy in specified situations that disclosure is more important than maintaining confidentiality. These "mandatory reporter" requirements range from sexually transmitted diseases and gunshot wounds to abuse of children, the elderly, and the disabled. Recently, some states have required reporting of impaired physicians, patient-therapist sexual relations, and in some instances patients suffering from certain disorders that can impair driving. All clinicians should be aware of the reporter requirements in their jurisdiction, which vary in regard to detail, obligation, and practitioners covered (e.g., only physicians, all mental health practitioners, and other caregivers). The legislation provides specific information regarding the reportable circumstances, the information to be released, and the mechanism for notification within a certain timeframe. The obligation to report generally covers information gathered in the professional context. If a therapist witnesses a child being abused while on vacation, most jurisdictions would not mandate a report; however, the therapist may feel a moral obligation to contact an authority. Furthermore, there is no expectation of any confidentiality without a therapist-patient relationship.

The statutes typically provide civil immunity to the clinician who fulfills his or her obligation in good faith (the obvious exception is when the reporter is also the perpetrator). Failure to comply with the reporting mandates may subject the clinician to civil or criminal penalties. If harm occurs that would have been avoided had the clinician reported the situation earlier, civil liability for negligent practice is possible. If the clinician believes that the situation is potentially reportable, it is best to notify the appropriate authorities. Some institutions have internal review boards to provide prescreening and information to potential reporters. Allegations are then screened by the state agency, based on the available evidence and information. The clinician may be contacted at a later date for further data. Depending on the statutory requirements in that jurisdiction, disclosure of further information may be barred without the patient's consent. Clinicians should document in the treatment record, if there is one, that a mandated report has been made. Legal consultation is helpful for clarification in complicated cases.

Therapists commonly ask whether a patient's confession of past crimes during a treatment session is reportable. In general, there is no such obligation (68, 69). The traditional common law principle of misprision (requiring citizens to report felonies) has been rejected by contemporary U.S. courts; an exception would involve a clinician who actively helped a patient to conceal a crime (e.g., provide an alibi or hospitalize the patient to avoid criminal investigation). When possible and appropriate, some experts have advocated that the patient reveal the information to the authorities as a means of satisfying legal, ethical, and therapeutic goals. If the patient with a criminal history is at risk for committing similar acts in the future, such as a serial rapist or pedophile, the clinician will likely have a duty to take appropriate action to protect potential victims.

PATIENTS' RIGHTS

Informed Consent

Over the past 30 years, the doctrine of informed consent has evolved into a central tenet of the ethical practice of modern psychiatry and medicine (21, 70). Physicians, especially surgeons, were required to obtain consent before proceeding with a physical treatment or operation; however, it was common for physicians to provide a simple explanation of the nature and purpose of the proposed treatment to get the patient's simple assent. Beginning in the late 1950s, courts and clinicians began to reconsider this issue. With the increased recognition of patient autonomy and the variety of medical treatment options available, it was important to consider the patient's need for information before an informed decision could be made.

Generally, informed consent can be separated into three components: information, voluntariness, and competence (71). Adequate information is necessary to make an adequate consent; accepting a consent based on insufficient information can constitute malpractice. The question for the clinician is how much and what information is necessary for a patient to make an informed choice. Courts have split on this issue, but the most common answer is what a "reasonable person" would want to know to accept or reject treatment, such as what are the potential risks and benefits of the proposed treatment, are there any alternative treatments, and what are the consequences of no treatment at all. The patient should be encouraged to express any specific concerns. It is usually not practical, or even possible, to present the patient with an exhaustive recitation of facts and statistics because this information can be overwhelming. The clinician should engage the patient in the process as an active participant, tailoring the discussion to the particular situation. In general, the clinician should provide more detailed information when the desired outcome is less likely or the significance of the potential risk or benefit associated with that outcome is greater. As always, the record should reflect the information that has been discussed, especially if proposing somatic treatments such as electroconvulsive therapy (ECT), antipsychotic medications, and other psychotropic drugs.

Voluntary Consent

Voluntariness requires the patient to give consent freely, without coercion. Questions have been raised whether institutionalized patients can ever be free of a subtle coercion inherent in a dependent situation. Psychiatric patients, like all individuals, are subject to transference reactions toward caretakers that can render them easily influenced or particularly stubborn. Given that such subtle forms of coercion are inherent in all interpersonal relationships, the courts generally have prohibited coercion that is clearly considered to be illegitimate or undue influence. For example, withholding cigarettes or promising to help a patient get extra privileges would be considered coercive influences. However, a clinician or family member may strongly urge the patient toward consenting to the proposed treatment. Clinicians should be sensitive to the dynamics of the treatment relationship, taking the opportunity to make the patient's voluntary choice an enfranchising, therapeutic experience.

Competency

Competency is a legal concept not yet defined in a consistent or clinically instructive way. Competence generally refers to the ability to understand and manipulate relevant information in a rational manner germane to the informed consent process. Four components in considering competency are: understanding the information, appreciating its relevance for the person's particular situation, expressing a consistent choice, and rationally manipulating the relevant information in coming to that choice (72, 73). Patients may be strong in one area and weak in another; clinicians must probe the patient's decision process to weigh the degree of competency. A patient with psychotic depression who refuses ECT because of concern about electrocution may be less competent to refuse than the patient who is concerned about side effects of confusion and memory loss. Competency is dependent on both time and context and varies with the patient's changing condition. The degree of competency necessary to make an informed choice often depends on the nature of the decision. Choosing to participate in experimental psychosurgery requires a higher degree of competency than accepting an aspirin for a headache. Competency should be assessed specific to the decision required; patients may be competent to refuse medications but may not be able to manage their own financial affairs.

In general, an involuntarily committed patient is presumed competent unless legally adjudicated otherwise. When discussing proposed treatment, the clinician assumes that the patient is competent but must be sensitive to those conditions that might challenge that assumption. Active psychosis, delirium, organic impairment, intoxication, dementia, severe depression, and mental retardation are clinical presentations that should lead the clinician to assess more thoroughly the patient's ability to make an informed choice. Although clinicians are usually most concerned about patients who refuse recommended treatment, it is important to recognize that some patients are "incompetent acceptors," consenting to recommended treatment despite significant deficits in competency. Particularly for treatments that carry a greater potential risk, the clinician should make a more formal assessment of competency and seek judicial intervention if necessary.

Exceptions

Clinicians should not view informed consent as an inflexible process when applied to clinical psychiatric practice. The courts recognize four exceptional situations in which the usual requirements of informed consent do not apply (1). First, in medical emergencies, if stopping to obtain informed consent from the patient or substitute decision maker would pose a life-threatening delay of treatment, clinicians may treat without a formal consent. The law assumes as "implied consent" that any rational patient facing an acute life-threatening situation would agree to the recommended treatment. In psychiatry, such emergencies are typically limited to violent, self-destructive, or delirious patients who require immediate restraint to prevent physical harm to themselves or others. Although clinicians may recognize as emergent more ambiguous situations, such as the psychotically depressed patient who refuses food and treatment, the courts have been more rigid, requiring informed consent by the patient or substitute decision maker in those circumstances.

Historically, physicians have maintained in certain circumstances that to disclose all potential information to the patient would be antitherapeutic and emotionally damaging. Giving the patient a diagnosis of terminal cancer was a common example. Arguing the Hippocratic maxim of primum non nocere (first do no harm), clinicians have persuaded the courts to make a second exception for therapeutic privilege in such circumstances. In psychiatric practice, however, this exception can rarely be invoked. For example, information about tardive dyskinesia cannot be withheld simply because the patient might refuse treatment with neuroleptics. If diagnostic information might damage a fragile patient, it can be withheld until the patient is more able to hear the information. In general, for treatment decisions in psychiatry, seeking a determination of incompetency and substituted judgment if appropriate is preferable to relying on therapeutic privilege.

A third exception is the patient's right to waive informed consent; the clinician is not required to force information on an unwilling patient. A patient who waives consent must be informed that he or she has the right to the information being waived. In addition, the clinician should consider the reason why a patient chooses not to know and the meaning of the potential denial. After appropriate clarification, the competent waiver of informed consent should be noted in the record.

The fourth exception is the incompetent patient. By definition, once a patient has been adjudicated by a court to be incompetent, he or she cannot then give informed consent. Consent must be obtained from a substitute decision maker as determined by the court. The court usually considers two forms of competence, general and specific. General competency is the ability to handle all of one's personal affairs in a reasonable manner, and specific competency refers to the task in question (e.g., competency to make treatment decisions, to execute a will, or to stand trial).

General competency is questioned when advancing dementia renders an elderly patient unable to tend to basic daily needs. The family may request a guardianship evaluation, usually in probate court, where a psychiatrist may be asked to offer a determination of mental competency. Unfortunately, the law offers clinicians only vague guidance as to the court's standard for incompetence. Evaluating clinicians should be familiar with the standards in their jurisdiction and may want to seek clarification from the court or the representing attorneys. The presence of mental illness alone or the status of involuntary commitment is not sufficient to establish incompetence. In assessing a patient's capacity, the clinician should examine the four basic aspects of capacity described above, taking into consideration the environmental demands that will be placed on the patient.

Decisions regarding specific competency to consent to general medical treatment tend to be made outside the courtroom. In the hospital, psychiatrists are frequently asked to make clinical assessments of "incompetence," which are not legally authoritative but do strip the patient of decision-making capacity in practical terms. A substitute decision maker, usually a family member, is informally allowed to consent for the patient. This nonjudicial process has fostered considerable debate, balancing the potential for abuse by colluding physicians and family with the need to make urgent decisions without the expensive and cumbersome delay of a judicial proceeding. As a standard practice endorsed by leading legal, medical, and ethical groups, hospitals continue to rely on these informal psychiatric determinations of decision-making capacity. However, the courts do make exceptions for extraordinary treatments, which include a variety of procedures that require judicial approval for substituted consent, even if a general guardian has been appointed by the court. Beginning with forced sterilization, the list of exceptional treatment in many states now routinely includes psychosurgery and ECT (74). Several states, such as Massachusetts, include treatment with neuroleptics in that category. Therefore, when seeking such treatment for a presumably incompetent patient, psychiatrists must be aware of the regulations in their jurisdiction and typically must seek a more formal, often judicial assessment.

Finally, clinicians should be sensitive to the therapeutic implications of the incompetence assessment process. As treatment progresses, patients will ideally be restored toward competency and come to understand the full ramifications of the process of being deemed incompetent. Physicians should engage the patient, when possible, in a dialogue about the experience in an effort to enhance the therapeutic alliance and promote future compliance. As the patient regains decision-making capacity, the physician should seek to initiate the judicial review process and prepare data for the judicial restoration of competency. Because the court adjudicates formal incompetency, the court typically restores legal competency. Sometimes a court finding of incompetency is valid only for a specified hospital admission or for a fixed period before automatic expiration or review. Once the court has become involved, the psychiatrist never restores competency. Therefore, the treating clinician must keep aware of the patient's legal status regarding competency and must alert the court of any changes in the patient's clinical status regarding decision-making capacity.

Admission

Voluntary admission to a psychiatric hospital is typically defined by state statute. The majority of hospital admissions, including state hospitals, are voluntary admissions. Most states allow for a conditional voluntary admission—a hospital can detain a patient, usually for several days after notice is given of a desire to leave. Thus, the hospital can assess the patient's ability to meet criteria for involuntary commitment or can arrange appropriate discharge plans. Patients should be informed of these regulations before consenting to a voluntary admission. Voluntary admissions usually indicate to the clinician the patient's willingness to engage in treatment (75). Despite that therapeutic advantage, with declining inpatient resources in an era of managed care, some hospitals (particularly state hospitals) no longer accept voluntary patients. In an effort to control utilization, these institutions maintain that a patient who is "healthy enough" to consent to hospitalization does not require inpatient treatment.

Clinicians frequently ask whether a patient has to be competent to consent to hospitalization. Given the discussion about informed consent for treatment, it might seem reasonable to set a high standard of competency; however, this standard might deprive many patients in need of potential treatment and further clog a crowded court system with extra involuntary commitment petitions. Most states do not explicitly require legal competence for a voluntary admission, but for states that do, a 1990 U.S. Supreme Court decision (Zinermon v. Burch) held that the state was required to screen out potentially incompetent patients (76). This decision did not include states whose statutes failed to comment on the issue of competency for voluntary hospitalization. In practice, the decision appeared to have a less dramatic effect than originally expected (77). Clinicians should be aware of the rules in their state, but in general should make an informal assessment of the patient's competency to consent to hospitalization in the same manner as competency to consent to treatment is assessed.

Involuntary Hospitalization

Traditionally, the state's authority to commit a mentally ill person has derived from two important precepts—parens patriae (parental authority) and police power (78). In the former, the state assumes a parental authority to care for citizens unable to care properly for themselves; with police power, the state intervenes in cases involving individuals who pose a danger to others. Before the 1970s, the presence of mental illness and the need for treatment were the usual standards for commitment. However, with increased concern for the civil rights of the underprivileged, the courts began to reject these standards as unconstitutionally overbroad. In Lessard v. Schmidt, a 1972 U.S. District Court decision, the court held that commitment required evidence of dangerousness to self or others (79). State statutes were redrawn until every state required dangerousness (and mental illness) to be a requisite for involuntary commitment. Judicial hearings were required along with the panoply of rights and protections usually associated with criminal proceedings. Researchers raised concerns that dangerousness was notoriously difficult for clinicians to predict; clinicians worried that nondangerous patients in need of treatment would be "dying with their rights on" (80). Despite these objections, studies have demonstrated that most patients in need of treatment are committed, often under a "grave inability to care for self" criterion common in most states (81). Beyond the requirements of the statute, the legal system appeared to accommodate with "common sense" to make appropriate decisions for seriously mentally ill persons. In recent years, several states have moved to expand their commitment statutes to allow for formal outpatient commitments and to broaden the definition of dangerousness to include deterioration into potential harmfulness (82, 83).

Procedures and standards outlined in involuntary commitment statutes vary across jurisdictions. Clinicians should keep current on the regulations in their state. Most states allow for a brief involuntary hospitalization based on a physician's commitment certification. In some states, the police, court, or other clinician can order an emergency commitment. At the end of the emergency commitment period, a judicial hearing is usually required to extend the involuntary hospitalization. The patient is represented by an attorney who can challenge the petition for further commitment. The psychiatrist provides the court with factual data and expert opinion, but the judge or jury ultimately decide the question of further commitment. After the initial commitment, judicial or administrative review is usually required at fixed time intervals to extend the hospitalization if necessary.

Given the inherently adversarial nature of the commitment process, it may be difficult for a clinician to maintain a working therapeutic relationship with the patient who may refuse treatment and voluntary hospitalization. Patient education, family involvement, and a process that is more advocacy than adversarial can help to marshal the patient's insight into the need for continued treatment.

Treatment

As discussed above, both voluntary and involuntary patients have the right to accept or reject proposed treatment with medications (84) and the right to the information necessary to make an informed consent. A patient's refusal to take medications can be overridden only if the patient has been adjudicated incompetent or the failure to treat in an imminent emergency would result in a serious risk of physical harm to the patient or others. Once a potentially incompetent patient refuses medications, a legal proceeding is required to order treatment (85). Jurisdictions vary in terms of procedure, ranging from administrative review to full judicial hearing. Once a patient is found incompetent, a substitute decision maker is appointed to make the treatment choice (86); such a decision maker can be the physician, a guardian, a neutral third party, or the judge. Depending on the state, the standard can range from the best interests of the patient (determining how a typical reasonable patient would choose) to a "substituted judgment" standard (requiring the decision maker to determine how this specific patient, with his or her specific interests, would choose if competent). For example, in a Massachusetts case (Rogers v. Commissioner), a mental patient may refuse treatment unless adjudicated incompetent by a judge, who then must make a substituted judgment treatment decision (87). Other jurisdictions allow more for clinical judgment once incompetence has been determined, a model that has been upheld by federal court decisions. For more extraordinary treatments such as ECT and psychosurgery, states commonly regulate their use even with a patient's informed consent. As before, clinicians should be familiar with the relevant cases and regulations in their jurisdiction.

After an adjudication of incompetence, a judge will likely appoint a guardian to monitor a patient's ongoing treatment and, in some cases, to make ongoing treatment decisions. If a patient is known to have a guardian, any proposed changes in the treatment plan should be reviewed first with that person. State statutes, through such mechanisms as durable powers of attorney and living wills, permit a competent person to designate a friend or family member to make decisions on his or her behalf in the event competency becomes an issue at a later time. These documents vary in scope and authority depending on the language of the authorizing legislation. They are invoked most frequently in medical cases dealing with the withholding of life support for unconscious patients. If mentally ill patients, when competent, could indicate their preference for hospitalization, medication, or ECT, it might obviate the need for a court hearing later if the patient, then incompetent, refuses treatment. Without specific legislative or court guidance on the validity of this practice, a judicial hearing still would be required in the face of an actively refusing, incompetent patient.

INTERACTING WITH THE LEGAL SYSTEM

Understanding the Adversarial Process

Psychiatrists must remember that their roles in the legal system are as clinicians, not lawyers (88). Whereas the medical system strives to take a supportive, advocacy stance toward the patient, the legal system is by nature an adversarial process (89). In this process, a clinician's motives and opinions may be maligned by an attorney zealously representing a client. Non-lawyers are often amazed to see opposing attorneys, after an afternoon of blistering, bitter infighting before the jury, go out for a drink as old friends. A clinician whose reputation is nastily impugned under cross-examination may find that the lawyer offers "no hard feelings" following the judge's verdict. To assuage the potential effect of these assaults on their ego and self-esteem, psychiatrists new to the legal process should recognize that this is "the way of doing business" (90, 91).

Psychiatrist as Witness

As a witness in a commitment or guardianship hearing, the psychiatrist may be asked to provide factual data, expert opinion, or both. Ideally, the attorney working with the psychiatrist should discuss what questions might be asked and what the witness might anticipate under cross-examination. The lawyer should review the relevant rules of evidence, including when hypothetical questions might be asked and when testimony might be disallowed as hearsay (based on facts not directly perceived by the witness and usually inadmissible). As discussed above, privilege belongs to the patient and normally prevents the introduction of confidential clinical material other than for the exceptions described above. In commitment and guardianship hearings, such material is required by the court, and most jurisdictions require that the patient be forewarned by the clinician that the usual rules of confidentiality will not apply. For cases involving civil commitment, guardianship, or other legal proceedings, the psychiatrist (and other mental health professionals on the team) should inform the patient from the outset of clinical contact that the material discussed can and will be used in court if necessary. This warning of the limits of confidentiality should be documented appropriately in the chart, and the patient should be reminded of the warning as necessary. An alert patient's attorney can use the lack of a properly documented warning to invoke the patient's privilege, drastically limiting a clinician's testimony. Giving sworn testimony in an imposing courtroom under the scrutiny of judge and jury can be an intimidating experience. Rigorous cross-examination can be frustrating, if not frightening (92). The clinician/witness should resist the temptation to argue back or to lose professional composure. The argument should be left to the lawyers.

Transference/Countertransference Issues

The clinician should maintain a clinical perspective regarding the patient and avoid overidentifying with the aggressor. Particularly in cases of patient refusal of hospitalization or medication, the psychiatrist may feel more like a tormentor than a treater. Conversely, in cases of alleged malpractice, the psychiatrist may feel like the victim. When a patient's care appears to revolve more around the legal rather than the clinical aspects of the case, the psychiatrist must pause and reflect. Fear of legal reprisals may interfere with quality of care. The legal conflict inevitably engenders powerful transference and countertransference reactions, which the clinician must monitor carefully. Consultation or supervision with colleagues can be invaluable in gaining both supportive and objective perspective (2, 52, 53). Legal consultation with an attorney who is familiar with mental health issues is important for education and counsel about the relevant issues of the case.

CONCLUSION

The legal aspects of psychiatric practice, like clinical and economic aspects, continue to evolve dramatically with the changes in the health-care system. It has been observed, however, that the legal system has a certain equilibrium with regard to mental health law; seemingly revolutionary changes are often followed by gradual shifts toward a more reasonable and rational position (93). For the clinician practicing in today's rapidly changing environment, the best risk management advice remains the same: take good care of the patient and act as a clinician, not as a lawyer. Psychiatrists should respect the patient's clinical needs and legal rights and follow good practices of appropriate documentation and consultation to be successful in promoting and protecting a patient's interests, as well as their own.

REFERENCES

1. Appelbaum PS, Gutheil TG. Clinical handbook of psychiatry and the law. 2d ed. Baltimore: Williams & Wilkins, 1991.
2. Simon RI. Clinical psychiatry and the law. 2d ed. Washington, DC: American Psychiatric Press, 1992.
3. Simon RI, Sadoff RL. Psychiatric malpractice: causes and comments for clinicians. Washington, DC: American Psychiatric Press, 1992.
4. Bonnie R. Professional liability and the quality of mental health care. Law Med Health Care 1988;16:229–240.
5. Klein JI, Glover SI. Psychiatric malpractice. Int J Law Psychiatry 1983;6:131–157.
6. American Medical Association. Physician masterfile and socioeconomic monitoring system. Chicago: AMA, 1994.
7. MacBeth JE, Wheeler AM, Sither JW, et al. Legal and risk management issues in the practice of psychiatry. Washington, DC: Psychiatrists' Purchasing Group, 1994.
8. Levenson AI. 1996–1997 professional liability policy renewal. Washington, DC: Psychiatrists' Purchasing Group, 1996.
9. Volk LA, ed. Forum: claims data overview. Cambridge: Risk Management Foundation, 1995.
10. Data on file, Physician Insurers Association of America. Rockville, MD: 1996.
11. Data on file, Psychiatrists' Purchasing Group. Washington, DC: 1996.
12. Slawson PF. Psychiatric malpractice: the low frequency risks. Med Law 1993;12:673–680.
13. Slawson PF. Psychiatric malpractice: recent clinical loss experience in the United States. Med Law 1991;10:129–138.
14. Slawson PF. Psychiatric malpractice: ten years' loss experience. Med Law 1989;8:415–427.
15. Jacobs DG, ed. Suicide and clinical practice. Washington, DC: American Psychiatric Press, 1992.
16. Maris RW, Berman AL, Maltsberger JT, eds. Assessment and prediction of suicide. New York: The Guilford Press, 1992.
17. American Psychiatric Association. Practice guidelines for major depressive disorder in adults. Am J Psychiatry 1993:150(Suppl):1–26.
18. Jacobs DJ, Gutheil TG, Harburger J, et al. Guidelines for identification, assessment, and treatment planning for suicidality. Cambridge: Risk Management Foundation, 1995.
19. Appelbaum PS. Practice guidelines in psychiatry and their implications for malpractice. Hosp Community Psychiatry 1992;43:341–342.
20. Ness DE, Pfeffer CR. Sequela of bereavement resulting from suicide. Am J Psychiatry 1990;147:279–284.
21. Appelbaum PS, Lidz CW, Meisel A. Informed consent: legal theory and clinical practice. New York: Oxford University Press, 1987.
22. Gutheil TG, Bursztajn H, Brodsky A. Malpractice prevention through the sharing of uncertainty: informed consent and the therapeutic alliance. N Engl J Med 1984;311:49–51.
23. Appelbaum PS, Schaffner K, Meisel A. Responsibility and compensation for tardive dyskinesia. Am J Psychiatry 1985;142:806–810.
24. Mills MJ, Eth S. Legal liability with psychotropic drug use: extrapyramidal syndromes and tardive dyskinesia. J Clin Psychiatry 1987;48(Suppl):28–33.
25. Clites v. Iowa, 332 NW2d 917 (Iowa 1982).
26. Faigenbaum v. Oakland Medical Center, 373 NW2d 161 (Mich 1985).
27. Wettstein RM. Informed consent and tardive dyskinesia. J Clin Psychopharmacol 1988;8:65–70.
28. Munetz MR, Roth LH. Informing patients about tardive dyskinesia. Arch Gen Psychiatry 1985;42:866–871.
29. American Psychiatric Association. Task force report: tardive dyskinesia. Washington, DC: American Psychiatric Association, 1992.
30. Kokensponger v. Athens Mental Health Center, 578 NE2d 916 (Ohio 1989).
31. Appelbaum PS, Zoltek-Jick R. Psychotherapists duties to third parties: Ramona and beyond. Am J Psychiatry 1996;153:457–465.
32. Beahrs JO, Connell JJ, Gutheil TG. Delayed traumatic recall in adults: a synthesis with legal, clinical, and forensic recommendations. Bull Am Acad Psychiatry Law 1996;24:45–55.
33. Tarasoff v. Regents of the University of California, 551 P. 2d 334 (Cal 1976).
34. Beck JC, ed. The potentially violent patient and the Tarasoff decision in psychiatric practice. Washington, DC: American Psychiatric Press, 1985.
35. Beck JC, ed. Confidentiality versus the duty to protect: foreseeable harm in the practice of

psychiatry. Washington, DC: American Psychiatric Press, 1990.

36. Anfang SA, Appelbaum PS. Twenty years after Tarasoff: reviewing the duty to protect. Harvard Rev Psychiatry 1996;4:67–76.

37. Appelbaum PS. Tarasoff and the clinician: problems in fulfilling the duty to protect. Am J Psychiatry 1985;142:425–429.

38. Monahan J. Limiting therapist exposure to Tarasoff liability: guidelines for risk containment. Am Psychol 1993;48:242–250.

39. Lazarus JA. Ethical issues in doctor-patient sexual relationship. Psychiatr Clin North Am 1995;18:55–70.

40. Gabbard G, Nadelson C. Professional boundaries in the physician-patient relationship. JAMA 1995;273:1445–1449.

41. American Psychiatric Association. The principles of medical ethics, with annotations especially applicable to psychiatry. Washington, DC: American Psychiatric Association, 1995.

42. American Psychological Association. Ethical principles of psychologists and code of conduct. Am Psychol 1992:47:1597–1611.

43. Appelbaum PS, Jorgenson L. Psychotherapist-patient sexual contact after termination of treatment: an analysis and a proposal. Am J Psychiatry 1991:148:1466–1473.

44. Appelbaum PS. Statutes regulating patient-therapist sex. Hosp Community Psychiatry 1990;41:15–16.

45. Gutheil TG, Gabbard GO. The concept of boundaries in clinical practice: theoretical and risk management dimensions. Am J Psychiatry 1993;150:188–196.

46. Gutheil TG. Borderline personality disorder, boundary violations, and patient-therapist sex: medicolegal pitfalls. Am J Psychiatry 1989;146:597–602.

47. Simon RI. Treatment boundary violations: clinical, ethical, and legal considerations. Bull Am Acad Psychiatr Law 1992;20:269–288.

48. Strasburger LH, Jorgenseon LM, Sutherland P. The prevention of psychotherapist sexual misconduct: avoiding the slippery slope. Am J Psychother 1992;46:544–555.

49. Sederer LI, Libby M. False allegations of sexual misconduct: clinical and institutional considerations. Psychiatric Services 1995;46:160–163.

50. Gutheil TG. Approaches to forensic assessment of false claims of sexual misconduct by therapists. Bull Am Acad Psychiatr Law 1992;20:289–296.

51. Groves JE. Taking care of the hateful patient. N Engl J Med 1978;298:883–887.

52. Gutheil TG, Bursztajn HJ, Brodksy A, et al. Decision making in psychiatry and the law. Baltimore: Williams & Wilkins, 1991.

53. Reiser SJ, Bursztajn HJ, Appelbaum PS, et al.

Divided staff, divided selves: a case approach to mental health ethics. Cambridge: Cambridge University Press, 1987.

54. Garrick TR, Weinstock R. Liability of psychiatric consultants. Psychosomatics 1994;35:474–484.

55. Gutheil TG. Paranoia and progress notes: a guide to forensically informed psychiatric record keeping. Hosp Community Psychiatry 1980;31:479–482.

56. Roth LH, Wolford J, Meisel A. Patient access to records: tonic or toxin? Am J Psychiatry 1980;137:592–596.

57. Gutheil TG, Havens LL. The therapeutic alliance: contemporary meanings and confusions. Int Rev Psychoanal 1979;6:467–481.

58. Inglehart JK. Managed care and mental health. N Engl J Med 1996;334:131–135.

59. Stone AA. Paradigms, pre-emptions, and stages: understanding the transformation of American psychiatry. Int J Law Psychiatry 1995;18:353–387.

60. Appelbaum PS. Legal liability and managed care. Am Psychol 1993;48:251–257.

61. Wickline v. California, 228 Cal. Rptr. 661 (Cal. App. Ct. 1986).

62. Wilson v. Blue Cross of Southern California, 271 Cal. Rptr. 876 (Cal. App. Ct. 1990).

63. Hoge SK. ERISA. Part I: barriers to reforming health care. J Practical Psychiatry Behav Health 1996;2:188–190.

64. Hoge SK. ERISA. Part II: insurer's liability. J Practical Psychiatry Psychiatry Behav Health 1996;2:315–318.

65. Appelbaum PS. Managed care and the next generation of mental health law. Psychiatr Services 1996;47:27–28.

66. American Psychiatric Association Committee on Confidentiality. Guidelines on confidentiality. Am J Psychiatry 1987;144:1522–1526.

67. Anonymous. Model law on confidentiality of health and social service records. Am J Psychiatry 1979;136:137–147.

68. Appelbaum PS, Meisel A. Therapists' obligations to report their patients' criminal acts. Bull Am Acad Psychiatry Law 1986;14:221–230.

69. Goldman MG, Gutheil TG. The misperceived duty to report patients' past crimes. Bull Am Acad Psychiatry Law 1994;22:407–410.

70. Faden R, Beauchamp T. A history and theory of informed consent. New York: Oxford University Press, 1986.

71. Grisso T. Evaluating competencies. New York: Plenum Press, 1986.

72. Appelbaum PS, Grisso T. Assessing patients' capacities to consent to treatment. N Engl J Med 1988;319:1635–1638.

73. Grisso T, Appelbaum PS. Comparison of

standards for assessing patients' capacities to make treatment decisions. Am J Psychiatry 1995;152:1033–1037.

74. American Psychiatric Association. Task force report: practice of electroconvulsive therapy. Washington, DC: American Psychiatric Association, 1990.

75. American Psychiatric Association. Task force report: consent to voluntary hospitalization. Washington, DC: American Psychiatric Association, 1992.

76. Zinermon v. Burch, 110 S.Ct 975 (1990).

77. Hoge SK. On being "too crazy" to sign into a mental hospital: the issue of consent to psychiatric hospitalization. Bull Am Acad Psychiatry Law 1994;22:431–450.

78. Appelbaum PS, Anfang SA. Civil commitment. In: Michels R, ed. Psychiatry. Philadelphia: Lippincott-Raven, 1997.

79. Lessard v. Schmidt, 349 F. Supp 1078 (ED Wisc. 1972).

80. Treffert DA. Dying with their rights on. Am J Psychiatry 1973;130:1041.

81. Hiday VA. Civil commitment: a review of empirical research. Behav Sci Law 1988;6:15–43.

82. Torrey EF, Kaplan RJ. A national survey of the use of outpatient commitment. Psychiatr Services 1995;46:778–784.

83. American Psychiatric Association. Involuntary commitment to outpatient treatment. Washington, DC: American Psychiatric Association, 1987.

84. Appelbaum PS. The right to refuse treatment with antipsychotic medication: retrospect and prospect. Am J Psychiatry 1988;145:413–419.

85. Appelbaum PS, Gutheil TG. Rotting with their rights on: constitutional theory and reality in drug refusal by psychiatric patients. Bull Am Acad Psychiatry Law 1979;7:306–310.

86. Gutheil TG, Bursztajn HJ. Clinician's guidelines for assessing and presenting subtle forms of patient incompetence in legal settings. Am J Psychiatry 1986;143:1020–1023.

87. Rogers v. Commissioner, 458 NE2d 308 (Mass 1983).

88. Resnick PJ. The psychiatrist in court. In: Michels R, ed. Psychiatry. Philadelphia: Lippincott, 1986.

89. Stone AA. Law, psychiatry and morality. Washington, DC: American Psychiatric Press, 1984.

90. Gutheil TG. Legal defense as ego defense: a special form of resistance to the therapeutic process. Psychiatr Q 1979;51:251–256.

91. Gutheil TG, Magraw R. Ambivalence, alliance and advocacy: misunderstood dualities in psychiatry and law. Bull Am Acad Psychiatry Law. 1984;12:51–58.

92. Goldstein RL. Psychiatrists in the hot seat: discrediting doctors by impeachment of their credibility. Bull Am Acad Psychiatry Law 1988;16:225–234.

93. Appelbaum PS. Almost a revolution: mental health law and the limits of change. New York: Oxford University Press, 1994.

Chapter 22

Treatment Guidelines and Algorithms in Acute Care Psychiatry

Carlos A. Zarate, Jr.

INTRODUCTION

The many advances in the areas of brain imaging, neurosciences, and genetics make it increasingly difficult to amass this information in a way that is both palatable and practical to clinicians. The field of neuropsychopharmacology has also been a part of this revolution. Many new psychotropic drugs will be available in the next few years; these newer agents appear to offer advantages over their predecessors both in terms of efficacy and side effect profile. Although these new and improved drugs are more than welcome, many psychiatrists may find it difficult to keep up with this vast knowledge and may feel overwhelmed with the multiplicity of choices. In addition, treaters may be uncertain as to which medication to use if the patient continues to fail to respond to treatment.

Not only are significant advances with drug therapies being made, but the settings in which treatment is being delivered is rapidly evolving as well. Guide-

lines and/or algorithms that summarize and present the available information in a practical and orderly way may be a partial solution to some of these problems. The principles of clinical conduct—variously known as practice guidelines, standards, protocols, or algorithms—have proliferated throughout medicine over the past decade. Institutional efforts to develop and promulgate guidelines for the evaluation and treatment of psychiatric disorders in adults are underway (1). This chapter reviews the concept and use of guidelines and algorithms, their similarities and differences, and their possible applications in the acute psychiatric care setting.

DEFINITION OF ALGORITHMS AND GUIDELINES

Algorithms differ from practice guidelines although they share some similarities. Guidelines consider a wide range of possibilities and are usually general; for the most part, their approach to treatment is practical and not theoretically influenced. Guidelines develop from the consensus of a group of experts in the field and an exhaustive review of the literature. One example is the guideline produced by the Agency for Health Care Policy and Research to assist primary care providers in the diagnosis and treatment of depressive disorders (2). In general, guidelines are systematically developed statements about health care for specific clinical conditions. They usually involve specific steps based on good research evidence resulting from multiple randomized, controlled trials. The American Psychiatric Association (APA) guidelines have adopted the method of rating the scientific literature based on the strength of evidence of treatment efficacy (3). The APA guidelines do not indicate the next step in treatment for a patient who continues to fail to respond, but instead offers alternative treatments at the same level.

Algorithms attempt to mimic real world practice by offering alternative choices at multiple levels, even if research evidence of efficacy is lacking. Clinicians typically encounter patients who fail to respond to the first-line therapy and thus commonly use treatments that have not been tested extensively in a controlled environment. An example would be a bipolar manic patient who failed to respond to monotherapy with lithium, valproate, or carbamazepine but who did respond to a combination of these medications. Treatment involving a combination of medications is commonly used in clinical practice; however, very little scientific data exist on the safety and efficacy of this strategy. Table 22.1 shows three levels of evidence used in guideline development.

Algorithms are rule-based deductive systems that operate with inputs, se-

Table 22.1. Types of Evidence

Good research-based evidence	Multiple randomized, controlled trials with substantial group opinion to support the guideline statement
Fair research-based evidence	At least one randomized, controlled trial with some group opinion to support the guideline statement
Minimal research-based evidence	Based primarily on group opinion but significant clinical experience

quences, timeframes, and outputs (4). An algorithm is a set of well-defined rules and processes used to solve a problem in a finite number of steps. They are commonly used and are the fundamental components for processing data. Algorithms consist of arranging data in a certain way, either as simple steps (i.e., sequenced rules) or branching (Fig 22.1). The "top-down" approach is one method of designing algorithms. This method starts at the top (the problem statement, which in this case may be the psychiatric diagnosis), then identifies the substrates to be carried out, and then repeatedly refines the individual steps until an algorithm with sufficient detail is obtained.

In the simple decision-making algorithm, A leads to B, and B leads to C. For example, I am hungry (A), leads me to get food (B), and then to eat (C). Although oversimplified, hunger is a complex biologic process, and this example illustrates the sequenced rules. In the parallel algorithm format, one choice may lead to different outcomes that are weighed equally and should be considered or tried before moving on. For instance, A may lead to A1, A2, or A3, and all these options should be considered before moving to B. In the previous example, A1 may be that I am

Simple decision making
or sequenced rules

Parallel or multidimensional decision making

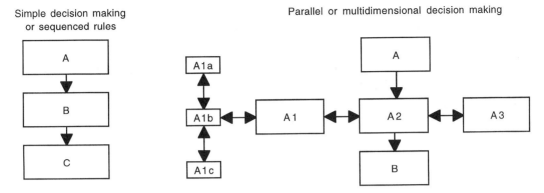

FIGURE 22.1.   Types of algorithms: simple and multidimensional.

also thirsty and I cannot eat until my thirst is quenched. The multidimensional decision-making process is more elaborate but realistically reflects the ultimate product. In the previous example, A1 branches out into another subdimension, A1a, A1b, and A1c. In the same example, A1a may be that I have no water, so I cannot eat until I drink water, but I cannot drink until I get water. One cannot move to B unless the subdimension A1 has been taken into account. This algorithm offers more options than the simple branch model and assures that the different alternatives offered have either been considered or tried before continuing with the decision tree. Other designs involving a yes-or-no format (used in computer programs to solve a problem) may be less practical because they would leave the clinician with too few choices. Algorithms now being developed for the medical field will most likely require a combination of the two models.

GUIDELINES VERSUS ALGORITHMS

The concept and use of guidelines and algorithms can be better understood by comparing the products resulting from the APA guideline for major depressive disorder (3) and any algorithm for the treatment of subtypes of unipolar depression (5). The APA guideline summarizes what is known about the disorder and offers a general overview of the treatment of the disorder. In addition, this guideline offers an initial choice in the pharmacologic treatment without offering many "next steps" should the patient fail to respond. In contrast, algorithms developed for the management of depression and its subtypes offer alternatives if the patient fails to respond. Whereas the focus and the goals of the APA guideline and the International Psychopharmacology Algorithm Project (IPAP) are somewhat different, they both provide useful and valuable information to help aid the clinician in treating a patient with a psychiatric disorder. One is not necessarily better than the other, and they complement each other although their goals are quite different. Only one of the six members who developed the algorithms for the treatment of unipolar depression participated in the development of APA guidelines for major depressive disorder. In the future development of both guidelines and algorithms for the diagnosis and treatment of psychiatric disorders, an effort toward integration is important.

Daily Setting

Algorithms are used in daily functions, including preparing for work, cleaning the house, completing a financial transaction, or boiling an egg. Although the majority of people are capable of boiling an egg, each does it differently. In general, each person develops his or her own algorithm of doing things. Occasionally, circumstances may lead to a variation from the usual method. In the following algorithm, steps for completing a financial transaction ($50 withdrawal) from an automatic teller machine (ATM) are:

1. Insert ATM card.
2. Follow instructions on ATM window.
3. Enter password.
4. Press withdrawal button.
5. Indicate $50.00 as the desired amount to withdraw.
6. Withdraw money, ATM card, and receipt.

To understand how these six steps describe an algorithm, each step must be well defined and the process must be completed in a finite number of steps. The three properties that describe an algorithm are that each step must be well defined (unambiguous), the process must stop in a finite number of steps, and the process must do what is claimed.

Medical Setting

In the past several years, different scientific disciplines (including medicine) have witnessed a revolution in the knowledge accumulated from technical advances. Clinicians who use this information may find it difficult to determine how, when, and in what circumstances this information should be applied. As a result, in recent years, interest in the development and use of algorithms has increased. A number of examples of algorithms used in medicine include making a diagnosis of deep venous thrombosis (6), matching residents to U.S. residency programs (7), computing data for statistical models for positron emission tomography and single-photon emission computed tomography (8), detecting psychiatric diagnoses in adults (9), and scheduling personnel (10).

Psychiatric Setting

The use of algorithms in psychiatry has been increasing over the past years, especially for diagnostic and therapeutic purposes. Formalized algorithms can be useful in promoting cost-effectiveness in the evaluation process. Minimal data beyond the first node of treatment algorithms are now available for treatment provided outside tertiary care centers. Initial treatment (first and second nodes) is usually heavily influenced by scientifically validated data. These initial treatment nodes are based on randomized, placebo-controlled trials. After the efficacy and tolerability of a specific treatment have been demonstrated, the information is generalized to other patient populations including children, the elderly, and the medically impaired. Unfortunately, in many instances, this scientific information may not apply to the real world. Patients participating in clinical trials are usually self-selected, compliant, in good physical health, and have few or no comorbid medical and psychiatric disorders.

Clinicians have developed a reasonable understanding of the efficacy, side effects, and mechanism of action of the psychotropic drugs. However, most of the literature presented in the textbooks on drug therapy for different psychiatric disorders are either in text or tabular form. Textbooks describe the number of studies to date, the design of the studies (open, double-blind), and comparison data (placebo or an active control drug) and summarize the different studies (in a type of meta-analysis) by stating that drug A was more, equally, or less effective than drug B and/or placebo. The tabular description of the efficacy and safety of a drug is usually available for the initial treatment but not for successive treatments if the patient develops side effects or fails to respond. After the first tiers of the treatment algorithms (or initial choices), little scientific data exist to justify the choice of the next best option. The subsequent steps in treating patients are usually empiric and are often referred to as the usual and customary practice or recommendations from experts in the field.

In recent years, efforts have been made to develop decision trees for the pharmacologic treatment of a variety of psychiatric disorders. Algorithms have been developed for the pharmacologic treatment of schizophrenia or chronic treatment-resistant psychosis (11–15), schizophrenia and comorbid disorders (16), subtypes of bipolar disorder (17–19), subtypes of unipolar major depression in adults (5, 20), depression in children (21), panic disorder (22), and obsessive-compulsive disorder (23).

Figure 22.2 exemplifies an algorithm for the treatment of bipolar mania; its format is similar to that used at the IPAP meeting (4). It is beyond the scope of this chapter to describe in detail all the different treatment choices offered. However, a general description of the development of an algorithm for the treatment of acute mania is provided. For this example, the input is the *Diagnostic and Statistical Manual*, 4th edition (DSM-IV) diagnosis of bipolar I disorder, currently in a manic episode (24). Based on the initial input, the decision tree is filled out from top to bottom, selecting the initial treatment of

choice. When several treatments are weighed equally, they can be specified and offered on the same level. After the initial choices have been selected, the next question is raised, "Following each treatment's failure, what would be the next logical treatment?" This would be pursued for as many levels as seem reasonable. At each step of the algorithm, lines are numbered. Each line may include one or more treatment interventions or possible outcomes that may be boxed as response, partial response, no response, or treatment limiting side effects. In some cases, depending on the outcome, other choices may be offered.

Figure 22.2 is a top-down algorithm. There are 11 lines, and each line may have an accompanying explanation about the options. They are rated as A, B, or C depending on the evidence to support the statement. In the example offered, line 1 specifies the diagnosis of DSM-IV bipolar I disorder, currently in a manic episode. If the patient does not have this diagnosis, the clinician must stop and not continue further with the decision tree. Line 2 classifies the patient as either having or not having psychotic features; if yes, the patient may require the addition of an antipsychotic drug in combination with the mood stabilizer. Line 3 offers one of the three mood stabilizers—lithium, valproate, or carbamazepine, with the option of combining them with a benzodiazepine (lorazepam or clonazepam). In general, one would give evidence A for lithium and valproate as initial choices for acute mania, and evidence B for carbamazepine. In the algorithm, decisions that are made early have better evidence support than decisions made at a later time. The APA guidelines on the treatment of bipolar disorder (25) generally focus on the initial steps to be taken for the management of mania (lines 1–4), but offer very few next

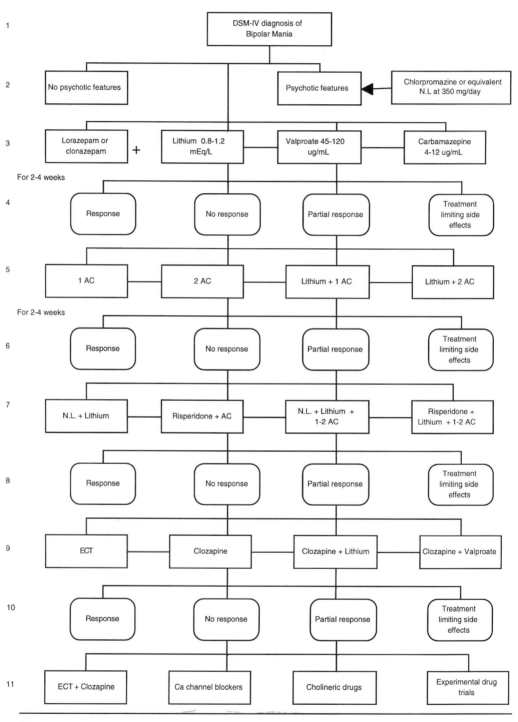

N.L. = neuroleptic drug; AC = anticonvulsant; ECT = electroconvulsive therapy

FIGURE 22.2.   Algorithm for the pharmacologic treatment of bipolar disorder.

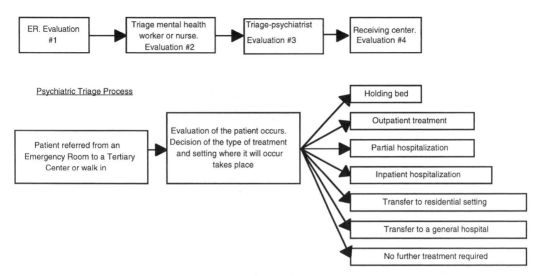

FIGURE 22.3.   The psychiatric triage process.

steps (in a systematized way) should the patient fail to respond. In contrast, the steps offered in this algorithm (lines 4–11) offer options for treatment failure.

The information present in algorithms may be enhanced by using the Delphi method (including being blind to each other's algorithms), systematically reviewing the literature, using a peer review process to develop algorithms, continually updating the algorithms with feedback from clinicians and researchers, and testing the algorithms on patients.

The Intake/Triage Process

Until recently, a patient seeking acute care generally had one of two choices: be hospitalized or be returned to the outpatient treaters. In many instances, patients may have been hospitalized when an alternative setting such as a holding bed, day treatment, residential treatment, or partial hospital would have sufficed. As a result, health-care delivery has been increasingly scrutinized in recent years. A search for ways to deliver the most effective care at the lowest cost is still underway. The triage system was created to decide the most appropriate treatment for the patient presenting for treatment. Triage is the screening and sorting of patients seeking acute care to determine which services are initially required and with what priority. The psychiatric triage entails a detailed psychiatric examination of the patient and the formulation of a treatment plan that addresses both the complaints for which the patient presented and the setting in which treatment will occur. For this system to work, an integrated and collaborative system must be designed (Fig. 22.3).

Patients may be referred in one of many ways, either by referral by an emergency department or as a walk-in with or without a scheduled appointment. The patient is evaluated by one or more clinicians, given a diagnostic interview, and at times given a series of laboratory tests. Before the development of triage, a patient would be subjected to any number of diagnostic interviews at different settings by different clinicians who would ask the same questions for the same complaint. These interviews would be conducted first in the emergency department by the doc-

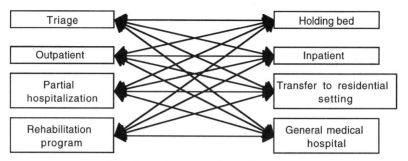

FIGURE 22.4.   The flow of a patient through a continuity of care model.

tor on call, second by the crisis team, third by the psychiatrist at the receiving facility, and fourth by the staff members on the unit. Figure 22.3 illustrates how a hospital might function without a triage system in place. By using an algorithmic approach, the system can be broken down into its components, examined, and designed more efficiently to avoid multiple psychiatric examinations, prevent unnecessary hospitalizations, reduce overall costs, and provide alternative treatment settings.

The triage system is only the initial phase of the mental health-care system. To function, it must be connected to alternative settings for the delivery of care. These different settings should be closely integrated to allow patients to move back and forth should the need arise.

Psychiatric treatment may occur in many settings. Figure 22.4 depicts a patient's typical movement through a health-care system. Problems with this flow may arise when different treaters are located at each of these settings, the treatment settings are not in close proximity, or the main treaters (psychopharmacologist or case manager) are not following the patient through the system. In other words, the algorithm in Figure 22.4 shows a system that attempts to prevent the fragmenting of care being delivered. Today, hospital systems are striving for a continuity of care model in which the patient may

go from one level of care to another, usually from a more-intensive to a less-intensive treatment setting. In this model, patients may be followed through the system by their treaters, who are familiar with the case, thus avoiding a duplication of services or "having to start over again" when moving among different levels of care.

Minimizing Adverse Drug Reactions

To minimize adverse drug reactions (26), The McLean Hospital Pharmacy and Therapeutics Committee recently reviewed the steps required from the time an order for medication is written to the time when the patient takes the prescribed dosage. Figure 22.5 shows approximately 14 steps in the prescription of a medication to a patient. An error may occur at any one of these steps, and this risk may increase exponentially if other factors are present (e.g., the number of medications, the length of stay, or frequent changeover of staff).

Using a computerized physician order entry system would shorten the number of steps required for prescribing a medication for an inpatient to seven, thus reducing the risk of a medication error. Furthermore, the computerized system may contain programs designed in algo-

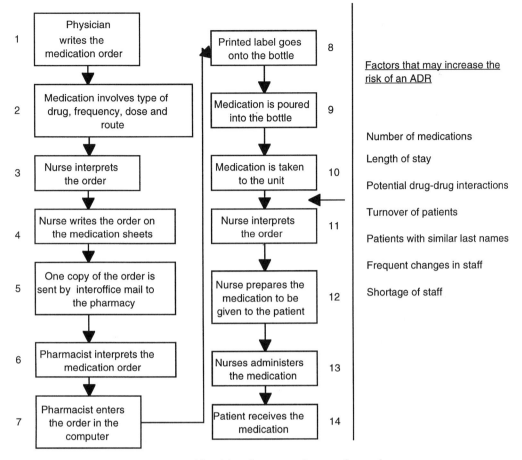

FIGURE 22.5.   Algorithm for preventing an adverse drug event.

rithmic form that alert the physician to potential drug-to-drug interactions, maximum recommended doses, dietary restrictions, and other critical information.

Cost Evaluation and Cost Control

Traditionally, most cost evaluation is focused at the top of algorithms. At the same time, there is an inordinate cost at the bottom of the algorithms with treatment-resistant illness. By examining how a system functions and dividing it into its basic components, more efficient and cost-ef-

fective systems can be developed. Cost-savings may result from using a pharmacologic algorithm (Fig. 22.2). For example, if a patient previously failed to respond to a drug or developed intolerable side effects, then one could save time and minimize repeating previously unsuccessful treatments by following the steps of the algorithm. In the same way, a patient's treatment could be standardized to prevent the initial selection of unorthodox strategies (perhaps costly), which might not be regarded as future alternatives should the patient continue to fail to respond. In the triage algorithm (Figs. 22.3 and 22.4), cost-savings would result from eliminating multiple psychiatric interviews of the same patient by different staff members. Finally, a more effective and less-costly system may occur if multiple steps were eliminated in the prescribing of a medication for a patient (Fig. 22.5). More intelligent and better designed systems could save costs and promote a better quality of care by minimizing the risk of medication error, avoiding unnecessary stress and multiple psychiatric interviews for patients, and reducing drug trials that are not likely to succeed.

Utilization Review/ Management

There is a growing interest in management guidelines or algorithms, both in professional organizations and in the managed care industry. Managed care companies continue to develop their own "algorithms" to aid in decision-making (e.g., questions regarding admission approval and continuation of treatment). Managed care companies are already using software to assist in the decision-making. Each company has developed guidelines or standards for approving or denying coverage for a specific treatment; unfortunately, these are not uniform. Administrators or managed care providers should not simply deny coverage for a service just because the care being provided has deviated from their "standard of care" as indicated by their guidelines or algorithms. If the algorithms are being developed by third-party payers without front-line experience, they may not take into account the multiple variables that influence the outcome of a patient. Using strict standards or rigid algorithms for deciding continued coverage for a service may have severe short-term and long-term detrimental effects for the patient. To best serve the needs of pa-

tients, the clinicians, hospital administrators, managed care administrators, and mental health policy planners must act conjointly to develop guidelines and algorithms for different groups of patients.

Algorithms as a Teaching Tool

Guidelines and algorithms should provide an incomparable learning tool for trainees. Using these pathways may offer trainees a view of how the experts think a problem through. Computerized algorithms could explain why one decision is recommended instead of another and could provide extensive and updated references. Many computer programs that use algorithms are specifically geared to psychiatric education. Interactive computerized programs are available for interviewing a psychiatric patient (25), using consultation psychiatry (27), providing accurate DSM-III-R psychiatric diagnoses (28), and using pharmacotherapy to treat psychotic patients (12). These technologies will help students to assimilate much more information in an interactive way. In other words, the availability of computerization, algorithms, and hypertext may ease and enhance the learning process.

IMPLICATIONS IN THE USE OF ALGORITHMS

Legal Implications

Guidelines should not be considered the standard of medical care. The practice guidelines developed by the APA for major depressive disorder, bipolar disorder in adults (3, 29), and the algorithms for the pharmacotherapy of psychiatric disorders (4) emphasize this point. Guidelines will not apply to every patient, nor will adherence to them ensure a positive outcome in every case. Consequently, algorithms should not be used as the "standard and recommended treatment" for legal or insurance purposes.

Research Applications/ Implications

Pharmacologic algorithms are ranked from the most effective treatment (demonstrated by multiple randomized, controlled trials) to the least tested treatment (minimal research evidence). In the example of the pharmacologic treatment of bipolar disorder (Fig. 22.2), each decision node is rated based on the research evidence to support the choice offered. Algorithms identify areas that have had either extensive or restricted research activity. Funding organizations can be urged to support those understudied areas of research as depicted by algorithms.

ADVANTAGES AND DISADVANTAGES

Algorithms are readily available and are inexpensive ancillary instruments for patient management. Decision-making pathways force a rigorous consideration of what is known about the area under consideration. Therefore, they are helpful in establishing the boundaries of current knowledge and outlining important areas for future research.

One disadvantage of guidelines and algorithms is that they can only be as good as the experts who develop them. Algorithms can never replace good clinical decision-making. In addition, they cannot be applied in every case, especially for unusual or complex patients. Instead, they can be used as tools and general guidelines in approaching a clinical problem.

Guidelines and algorithms can offer clinicians a method for making choices but cannot be used as a "cookbook" schema for medical decision-making.

CONCLUSIONS

The scientific basis for the information used in algorithms is constantly changing, and updated information about both new and older treatments appears frequently. Algorithms or "practice maps," decision trees, practice protocols, and practice guidelines are often developed with minimal peer review, by managed care companies, and without full consideration of the limits of algorithms. Algorithms are intended to be cognitive tools to assist in defining, but not limiting, the boundaries of the clinical decision-making process. It is critical that mental health professionals participate with managed care companies in the development of guidelines and algorithms so that the products suit the needs of patients, treaters, managed care companies, and mental health agencies.

REFERENCES

1. Board approves two new sets of practice guidelines. Psychiatric News 1995;30:5.
2. Depression Guideline Panel. Depression in primary care: volume 2. Treatment of major depression. Clinical practice guideline, number 5. Publication no. 93–0551. Rockville, MD: U.S. Department of Health and Human Services, Public Health Service, Agency for Health Care Policy and Research, AHCPR, 1993:April.
3. American Psychiatric Association. APA Practice guideline for major depressive disorders in adults. Am J Psychiatry 1993;150:1–26.
4. Jobson KO, Potter WZ. International psychopharmacology algorithm project report. Psychopharmacology 1995;31:457–507.
5. Nelson JC, Docherty JP, Henschen GM, et al. Algorithms for the treatment of subtypes of unipolar major depression. Psychopharmacol Bull 1995;31:475–482.
6. Burke B, Sostman HD, Carroll BA, et al. The

diagnostic approach to deep venous thrombosis. Which technique? Clin Chest Med 1995;16:253–268.

7. Peranson E, Randlett RR. The NRMP matching algorithm revisited: theory versus practice. National Resident Matching Program. Acad Med 1995;70:477–484.

8. Kay J. Statistical models for PET and SPECT data. Stat Methods Med Res 1994;3:5–21.

9. Pincus HA, Vettorello NE, McQueen LE, et al. Bridging the gap between psychiatry and primary care. The DSM-IV-PC. Psychosomatics 1995;36:328–335.

10. Bradley DJ, Martin JB. Continuous personnel scheduling algorithms: a literature review. J Soc Health Syst 1991;2:8–23.

11. Osser DN. A systematic approach to pharmacotherapy in patients with neuroleptic-resistant psychoses. Hosp Community Psychiatry 1989;40:921–927.

12. Bosworth T. Schizophrenia algorithms simplify clinical decisions. Prim Psychiatry 1994;1:16.

13. Zarate CA Jr, Cole JO. An Algorithmic approach to the treatment of schizophrenia. Psychiatr Ann 1994;24:333–340.

14. Zarate CA Jr. Broadening treatment perspectives. Algorithms for the maintenance treatment of schizophrenia. Prim Psychiatry 1995;2:20–25.

15. Zarate CA Jr, Cole JO, Pickar D, et al. Algorithms for the pharmacological treatment of schizophrenia. Psychopharmacol Bull 1995;31:461–467.

16. Zarate CA Jr. Broadening treatment perspectives. Algorithms for the diagnosis and management of schizophrenia and comorbid disorders. Prim Psychiatry 1995;2:26–39.

17. Gerner RH, Stanton A. Algorithm for patient management of acute manic states: lithium, valproate, or carbamazepine? J Clin Psychopharmacol 1992;12(Suppl):57–63.

18. Calabrese JR, Woyshville MJ. A medication algorithm for treatment of bipolar rapid cycling? J Clin Psychiatry 1995;56(Suppl 3):11–18.

19. Suppes T, Calabrese JR, Mitchell PB, et al. Algorithms for the treatment of bipolar, manic-depressive illness. Psychopharmacol Bull 1995;31:469–474.

20. Debattista C, Schatzberg AF. An algorithm for the treatment of major depression and its subtypes. Psychiatr Ann 1994;24:341–347.

21. Johnston HF, Fruehling JJ. Using antidepressant medication in depressed children: an algorithm. Psychiatr Ann 1994;24:348–356.

22. Jobson KO, Davidson JRT, Lydiard RB, et al. Algorithm for the treatment of panic disorder with agoraphobia. Psychopharmacol Bull 1995;31:483–485.

23. Jefferson JW, Altemus M, Jenike MA, et al. Algorithm for the treatment of obsessive-compulsive disorder (OCD). Psychopharmacol Bull 1995;31:487–490.

24. American Psychiatric Association. Diagnostic and statistical manual of mental disorders. 4th ed. Washington, DC: American Psychiatric Association, 1994.

25. Bairnsfather L, Pernotto DA. Psychiatric interview series. Chapel Hill, NC; Health Sciences Consortium, 1989. Interactive video disc.

26. Continuous Quality Improvement Update. Teaming up to improve patient care quality. McLean This Week, March 24, 1995.

27. Jachna JS, Powsner SM, McIntyre PJ, et al. Teaching consultation psychiatry through computerized case simulation. Acad Psychiatry 1993;17:36–42.

28. First MB. Computer-assisted assessment of DSM-III-R diagnoses. Psychiatr Ann 1994;24:25–29.

29. American Psychiatric Association. APA practice guideline for treatment of patients with bipolar disorder. Am J Psychiatry 1994;151:1–36.

Chapter 23

The Salience of Neuroscience in the Education of Psychiatrists

Joseph T. Coyle

INTRODUCTION

The place of neuroscience in the training of psychiatric residents epitomizes the fundamental issue of the role of psychiatry in future medical care. Psychiatry is undergoing rapid and perhaps wrenching changes that are affecting the basic tenets of clinical practice. What makes this situation particularly difficult for many psychiatric educators is that these changes in conceptual approach are driven primarily by external forces, i.e., the reorganization of psychiatric care and the advances in its scientific underpinnings. This chapter presents a thesis that these two forces are ineluctably intertwined and presage more effective, efficient, and humane approaches to the diagnosis, treatment, and rehabilitation of individuals suffering from mental disorders.

REORGANIZATION OF PSYCHIATRIC CARE

Managed Care

The rapid development of managed care is dramatically altering the role of the psychiatrist in the diagnosis and treatment of mental disorders, the locus of this treatment, and the mechanisms for reimbursement for the care provided (1). Perhaps the most telling aspect of managed care's impact is its effect on length of stay of psychiatric patients in hospitals. For example, over a 10-year period at McLean Hospital, a not-for-profit psychiatric hospital affiliated with Harvard Medical School, the average length of stay has declined 85%, from more than 90 days to 13 days (2). This experience is not unique to McLean Hospital but affects psychiatric inpatient units nationwide, although some acute care facilities in general hospitals historically have had shorter lengths of stay than free-standing psychiatric hospitals. Nevertheless, acute psychiatric hospitalization is now measured in days, not in weeks, and many patients who would have been hospitalized in the past are now diverted to ambulatory treatment settings.

If psychiatrists are still providing ethical care, then extraordinary changes have occurred in the efficiency of inpatient care to permit this reduction in the duration of hospitalization. However, despite the remarkable advances in psychopharmacology, behavioral therapy, and focused psychotherapy, no single advance in treatment methods accounts for this precipitous decline in the duration of hospitalization. In reality, the explanation relates to fundamental changes in the strategies and goals of acute inpatient treatment brought about by managed care. In the past, inpatient treatment was primarily directed at "curing" the episode responsible for hospitalization, with an underlining assumption that intensity and duration of treatment would correlate in a meaningful way with outcome. The paucity of solid outcome data does not provide credence for this belief; rather, evidence suggests that lengthy hospitalization may be associated with poorer outcome at greater expense (3).

Currently, under managed care, the primary goal of inpatient treatment is symptom reduction to enable the patient to be discharged to a graded sequence of less-expensive and less-restricted care settings, including day hospital, therapeutic residential care, and/or intense outpatient treatment. Ironically, treatment strategies commonly associated with public sector psychiatry, developed in response to limits set by fixed state budgets and bed constraints, have now become increasingly prominent in the private sector. Thus, the segregation of treatment into completely separate loci—the inpatient unit or the psychotherapist's office—is progressively being replaced by an integrated system of care that requires efficient coordination of treatment modalities.

Future Role of Psychiatry

The practice of psychiatry undoubtedly will be affected by another perhaps related change. The choice of psychiatry as a clinical specialty is declining dramatically. Within the past 5 years, the number of U.S. medical school graduates who participated in the match for psychiatric residency training programs decreased by 40%. In 1996, fewer than 50% of the available openings in psychiatric training programs approved by the Residency Review Committee were filled through the match. The reasons for the decline are complex and are not restricted to psychiatry; for example, this decline has also occurred in neurology. Psychiatry and neurology are considered subspecialties that do not emphasize the training of primary care providers.

The threat of declining income, as psychological treatments are increasingly provided by less-costly allied mental health professionals such as psychologists, nurses, and social workers, may contribute to the decreasing attractiveness of psychiatry. Projected income is an important issue because the average medical student's debt burden has risen to nearly $60,000 at graduation (4). The decline in the number of psychiatrists implies a role shift, especially in the context of a managed care system. The model of the independent therapist providing individual psychological treatment to a small number of patients in an office setting has become economically impractical. The recent practice surveys by the American Psychiatric Association indicate that the average psychiatrist spends the majority of his or her time treating patients with major mental disorders (5, 6).

Medicare/Medicaid

Another change in health-care provision results from the growth of Medicare/Medicaid covering the treatment for the "public sector" psychiatric patient (i.e., the persistently and severely mentally ill). An increasingly open access to treatment in psychiatric programs in general hospitals and free-standing private psychiatric facilities reimbursed by Medicare/Medicaid is changing practice demographics. As a consequence, the most severely ill, who traditionally have been sequestered to inpatient and outpatient facilities directed by state departments of mental health, are now obtaining care in clinical settings that previously focused primarily on privately insured patients. For example, at McLean Hospital in Belmont, Massachusetts, Medicare/Medicaid patients constituted 8% of the 1400 admissions in 1985; they comprised nearly 70% of the 4400 admissions in 1995 (S Mirin, personal communication, 1996).

Health-care reform, now largely occurring at the state level, will erode further the distinction between the private and public sector and provide access to private providers for the persistently and severely mentally ill. This change should contribute to the destigmatization of severe mental illness and will likely improve the quality of care by eliminating what has been a two-tier system. However, as a consequence, many psychiatrists are being confronted by patients with much more severe psychopathology, which often has a neurobiologic basis and requires a sophisticated integration of pharmacologic, psychosocial, and rehabilitative treatments.

In the future, clinical practice for the psychiatrists will be radically different from the practice experienced by their supervisors a decade ago. The new practice will be characterized by patients with a higher degree of severity of mental illness, with fewer psychiatrists to provide care. Inpatient treatment will be restricted to the most severely ill and directed primarily at symptom reduction to permit movement to less-restricted forms of intense treatment. Reimbursement for treatment will place a premium on efficiency and efficacy; psychological and rehabilitative treatments will be performed largely by nonphysician mental health professionals, such as psychologists, social workers, and nurses. Residents must be prepared to work within these new realities of clinical practice.

SCIENTIFIC ADVANCES

The second force transforming psychiatry is the remarkable advances in the biologic sciences relevant to psychiatry, including molecular genetics, neuroscience, and brain imaging. These developments represent a powerful force that will counter the devaluation of psychiatric expertise in mental health care that arose from a broadly held belief that mental illness is separate and distinct from medical illness. The insidious distinction between medical and mental disorders has permitted the "carving out" of behavioral health from medical insurance coverage. Advances in biologic sciences do not provide simply a rationale for the medicalization of psychiatry. Rather, these advances suggest a unifying perspective for understanding the relationship between brain and behavior that precludes a distinction between mental and medical disorders and reifies the interdigitization of biologic, psychologic, and rehabilitative treatments for the mentally ill (see Chapter 1).

Because neuroscience relies so heavily on the methods of molecular biology, the two disciplines should no longer be viewed as completely separate and distinct in terms of understanding brain function in health and disease (7). As individual proteins are purified from the brain, sequenced, and cloned, they are mapped on the human genome. Furthermore, linkage studies—which permit the approximate localization on a specific human chromosome of mutant genes responsible for heritable disorders—inevitably lead to "chromosome walking strategies" to identify the mutant gene. Examples of the power of the chromosome walking strategy are the recent success in identifying the gene mutation responsible for Huntington's disease (which had previously been localized to chromosome 4 by linkage methods [8, 9]) and the identification of mutant genes on chromosomes 1 and 14 that are responsible for most cases of early onset Alzheimer's disease (AD). "Candidate genes" encode for proteins for which circumstantial evidence indicates their involvement in specific psychiatric disorders, such as dopamine receptors in schizophrenia. These genes can be studied to determine whether mutations or allelic variants cosegregate with the risk for the disorder in affected pedigrees.

In addition to these molecular genetic methods that emphasize reductionistic approaches, imaging technologies (including positron emission tomography [PET], single photon emission computed tomography [SPECT], and magnetic resonance imaging [MRI]) provide methods for assessing structure, function, and chemical characteristics of the living human brain (10). These noninvasive techniques provide powerful new insights into integrative and cognitive neuroscience of the human brain and illuminate functional and structural abnormalities in psychiatric illnesses, such as schizophrenia, affective disorders, and obsessive-compulsive disorder (OCD). Because imaging methods can monitor alterations of brain function as a consequence of treatment, they refute the Cartesian split between biologic and psychological interventions. For example, Baxter et al. (11) recently demonstrated with PET imaging that an effective pharmacologic intervention with fluoxetine or an effective behavioral treatment both corrected a metabolic defect observed in the right caudate in OCD patients.

Given this scientific revolution that provides new ways of understanding human behavior (both normal and pathologic) and the remarkable changes in clinical practice, the didactic content and the clinical experiences that comprise residency training in psychiatry must be evaluated critically. Thus, the issue is not simply adding lectures on neuroscience, but rather reformulating the role of the psychiatrist. The psychiatrist should be identified as the one individual in the mental health-care system with the breadth and depth of knowledge of the brain and behavior to lead the diagnostic and treatment team. Accordingly, the goals of residency education should be directed toward providing the knowledge base to prepare graduates to keep pace with the rapidly advancing scientific frontiers that affect diagnosis and treatment.

CURRICULUM

The following discussion touches on content areas that should be considered for inclusion in a curriculum that addresses the new role of the psychiatrist. Residency programs cannot assume that this information was covered adequately in medical school because of the uneven nature of neuroscience education. Furthermore, given the rapid growth of neuroscience as a discipline in the past decade, information acquired as a freshman in medical school is hardly current 6–8 years later. Finally, the goal of the curriculum should not be to impart a myriad of facts to transform the resident into an active and critical consumer of the scientific literature that provides the foundations for psychiatry. This literature is not restricted to basic science journals, but is increasingly represented in the primary psychiatric journals including the *Archives of General Psychiatry* and the *American Journal of Psychiatry*.

Molecular Biology

The revolution in molecular genetics is transforming all aspects of medicine. Within the past few years, remarkable advances have occurred including the identification of gene mutations responsible for hypercholesterolemia, colon cancer, neurofibromatosis, and amyotrophic lateral sclerosis. These discoveries have led to gene-based diagnostic methods and insights into novel treatments. Specific, disease-oriented studies conducted by independent investigators have been transformed by the Human Genome Project (12). This multinational, coordinated endeavor links scientists throughout the world by the goal of sequencing and mapping the entire human genome. Since the Human Genome Project was first formulated, the time projected to achieve this goal has shrunk progressively due to unforeseen technologic innovations; it will be accomplished within a decade.

Some in psychiatry and the neurosciences may feel that the Human Genome Project has little relevance to psychiatry, at least in the near future, because of the genetic complexity of the brain. However, the facts clearly dispute this contention. The human genome contains a finite number of genes, approximately 100,000. More importantly, approximately 60% (or 60,000) genes are dedicated to products expressed uniquely in the brain (7). If this knowledge is to be used in an informed way to aid in diagnosis and treatment of mental disorders and (most importantly) to help patients, psychiatrists must understand the genome as internists, pediatricians, and neurologists currently do.

Genetic risk factors have been implicated compellingly in a growing number of psychiatric disorders, including schizophrenia, bipolar disorder, OCD, attention deficit disorder, and autism (13). In most of these conditions, the evidence supports the conclusion that nongenetic factors—quite possibly developmental life events—contribute importantly to the risk of developing the disorder or affecting the severity of its manifestations. Accordingly, understanding the psychosocial determinants of psychiatric morbidity will contribute to this emerging area of knowledge. Psychiatric residents must become informed consumers of the genetics literature and understand the interactions between genetic vulnerabilities and life circumstances.

Residents should understand positional mapping, gene cloning, and the nature of genetic vulnerability. Positional mapping is a molecular strategy for identifying the localization on human chromosomes of genes responsible for heritable disorders or vulnerability to disorder (7). The most important ingredient for successful positional mapping is diagnostically well-characterized families or pedigrees, in which affected individuals can be identified with confidence.

A serious confounding variable in interpreting the results from positional mapping relates to the issue of genetic heterogeneity and is particularly relevant to psychiatry. If a disorder has more than one genetic cause (or a genetic and nongenetic cause), positional mapping in different pedigrees could identify (with high statistical confidence) quite separate chromosomal localizations of genes responsible for the condition. For example, current evidence implicates at least three separate and distinct genetic loci on chromosomes 1, 14, and 21 for mutant genes responsible for AD (14). Furthermore, at least two alleles (i.e., normal heritable gene variants) affect the vulnerability and age of onset of AD. Because many psychiatric disorders are common, with variable symptomatic expression and phenocopies, positional mapping is a daunting strategy. A second challenge is the likelihood that multiple genes contribute to certain psychiatric phenotypes. Recent evidence supports the hypothesis that interaction of several genes result in bipolar disorder in the extensive Old Order Amish pedigree (15). Fortunately, technical advances are permitting the solution of these genetic "simultaneous equations."

Gene cloning techniques have permitted the identification and chromosomal localization of a rapidly increasing number of gene products. This strategy turns the basic law of genetics—DNA makes messenger RNA (mRNA), which makes protein—on its head because the triplet sequence of bases or the codons that encode each amino acid are now known. Accordingly, as proteins are purified to homogeneity, the amino acid sequence of the protein can be determined readily with automated sequenators. With knowledge of the sequence of amino acids, the sequence of bases that encode for that protein in the mRNA and ultimately in the DNA can be predicted with reasonable fidelity. Because of the high degree of specificity with which complementary sequences of nucleotides

bind to each other, the mRNA encoding for the protein of interest can be identified in tissue extracts or in libraries of cloned mRNA from brain incorporated in a virus or other vectors. With this strategy, the gene encoding the protein can be identified and then mapped on the genome.

An example of the power of these techniques in elucidating a disorder of direct relevance to psychiatry is the recent advance in the understanding of AD. Because clinical studies indicated that the density of cortical senile plaques correlated with severity of dementia and because neurochemical studies indicated that the density of cortical senile plaques correlated with the cholinergic deficits (16), it became apparent that the abnormal protein that formed the core of the plaque, amyloid, might provide a molecular clue to the pathobiology of AD. Amyloid was purified to homogeneity from the brains of patients dying of AD, and the amino acid sequence of this polypeptide was determined. With molecular techniques, the mRNA for a much larger protein of 695 amino acids was identified that contained the sequence for amyloid. Subsequent studies revealed that a family of so-called amyloid precursor proteins (which are normally expressed in the brain and in other tissues) existed, and that amyloid represented a deviant breakdown product of these larger cell surface glycoproteins (17).

In parallel, positional mapping was performed on families exhibiting heritable forms of AD. Convergence occurred with the demonstration that single point mutations (base substitution) in the amyloid precursor protein gene accounted for the vulnerability to AD in certain of these pedigrees, albeit a small number (17). In other pedigrees, mutations of genes located on either chromosome 1 or 14 resulted in heritable vulnerability to early onset AD. Furthermore, in the case of

Down's syndrome, in which all individuals developed a pathology of AD by the fourth decade of life, accumulation of amyloid is due to a marked overexpression of amyloid precursor protein as a consequence of the presence of three copies of this gene with the triplication of chromosome 21 in Down's syndrome (18). In addition, variants of a chromosomal 19 gene that encode for apolipoprotein E affect vulnerability to late onset AD.

The inevitable identification of gene mutations and/or gene variants responsible for vulnerability to psychiatric disorders has clear implications for the psychiatrists of the future. First, such gene markers will greatly aid in the diagnostic process that informs treatment decisions. Second, gene markers will permit the identification within affected families of individuals who bear the genetic vulnerability before they are symptomatic. At a heuristic level, this information will help resolve one component of the simultaneous "nature/nurture" equation and will permit more informed studies on the role of developmental factors in transforming genetic vulnerability to psychopathology. Identification of individuals at genetic risk will lead to preventive interventions that use both medical and psychological strategies. For example, Beardslee et al. (19) tested the ability of a family intervention to reduce depression in children who are at high risk because they have affective disordered parents. Third, the identification of molecular variants bearing risk for psychiatric disorders will promote the development of more effective pharmacologic treatments as the neurobiologic consequences of these genes on the nervous system structure and function are understood. For example, several pharmaceutical companies are developing drugs that slow the accumulation of amyloid, which could be prescribed to those at genetic risk for AD to forestall its onset. A sophisticated understanding of gene variants and mapping will be necessary for informed counseling of patients and their families about the implications of heritable risk factors for specific psychiatric disorders.

Neuroscience

The accrual of new knowledge through neuroscience research is increasing at a rapid rate. The neuroscience perspective is interdisciplinary with the goal of linking together the multiple organizational levels of brain and behavior through molecular, neurochemical, neuroanatomical, and functional approaches. Areas of remarkable advance of direct relevance to psychiatry are developmental neurobiology (which delineates the mechanisms involved in the differentiation, organization, and environmental modification of the nervous system) and cognitive neuroscience (which elucidates the neuroanatomic and neuropsychologic underpinnings of sensory, motor, and cognitive functions of the human brain in health and disease). Nevertheless, the mechanisms of signal transduction, which refers to the array of processes that mediate communication within and between neurons, hold particular interest and relevance to psychiatry.

Psychiatry has played a major role in the early development of the field of signal transduction research through the studies initiated in the 1960s to understand the mechanisms of action of the first generation of psychotropic medications, including the neuroleptics, monoamine oxidase inhibitors, psychotomimetics like LSD, opiates, and the tricyclic antidepressants. Signal transduction holds particular interest because it sheds light on the molecular and cellular mechanisms of action of psychotropic medications. Most current psychotropic medications exert their effects by altering synaptic neurotransmission. Research on synaptic mechanisms is expanding along several fronts that have significant implications for diagnosis and treatment.

First, at the presynaptic level, substances that serve as neurotransmitters and/or neuromodulators in specific neuronal pathways continue to be identified and mapped. For example, glutamic acid is now recognized as the major excitatory neurotransmitter in the brain and is intimately involved in critical processes such as pain sensation, anxiety, memory, and psychosis (20). Cytokines, previously thought to be signaling peptides limited to the immune system, and an expanding number of neurotrophic growth factors have now been implicated in the action of psychotropic medications (21).

Second, molecular neurobiologic strategies are disclosing a much more complex array of receptor transduction processes that mediate the action of brain neurotransmitters/neuromodulators than could be appreciated by the more traditional physiologic/pharmacologic methods (22). For example, whereas traditional pharmacologic methods suggested two major types of dopamine receptor, molecular cloning strategies have revealed five separate genes that encode for dopamine receptors (23). Furthermore, posttranscriptional editing of the mRNA may result in additional alterations in pharmacologic and physiologic characteristics of the receptors encoded by a specific gene. The implications of this molecular heterogeneity of receptors for psychiatry are only beginning to be appreciated. For example, the dopamine D-4 receptor was found to have a high affinity for clozapine, an atypical neuroleptic devoid of extrapyramidal side effects. This finding is consistent with the relative dearth of this dopamine receptor subtype in the caudate and putamen and the much higher level of its expression in limbic structures (24). Allelic variants of the D-4 receptor have also been linked to extroversion (25, 26). These advances hold great promise for the identification and characterization of receptor mechanisms that are altered in neurologic and psychiatric disorders, thereby facilitating the development of more specific drugs that act at discrete receptor subpopulations.

The third emerging area of investigation is the elucidation of intracellular transduction pathways activated by specific receptors. By understanding the differences, commonalities, and points of intersection among intracellular responses resulting from activation of different receptors, it is likely that pharmacologic interventions that exploit alternative receptors using the same transduction system will emerge. Convincing evidence reveals that psychiatric disorders result from dysregulation of these intracellular pathways and that psychotropic drugs exert their therapeutic effects by modifying the intracellular response to neurotransmitters. For example, the mechanism of action for lithium salts appears to be a disruption of an intracellular transducer, the phosphoinositol system, which is linked to a number of neurotransmitter receptors including alpha adrenergic and muscarinic receptors (7).

Ultimately, receptor activation alters gene expression in the brain. Studies are now revealing the remarkable plasticity of neurons in response to changes in receptor activation, which in turn results in robust changes in the neuronal gene expression. The delayed therapeutic response to psychotropic drugs such as antidepressants may reflect this alteration of gene expression. The theoretical salience of these studies is in the closing of the circle between external life events, drug effects on gene expression, and ultimately the genetics of vulnerability to psychiatric disorder.

Brain Imaging

Traditionally, brain imaging has been divided along methodologic lines (i.e., MRI, PET, and SPECT). An alternative approach distinguishes imaging methods by the information generated, namely dynamic (functional) or static (structural). Through the development of more powerful magnets and improvements in computer programs for resolving data, MRI is providing increasingly fine resolution of brain structure with sensitivity of a millimeter or less. By exploiting computer-based algorithms for volumetric and planar analysis of defined brain structures, an increasing number of studies are demonstrating subtle, regionally specific, but highly significant alterations in brain structures in major psychiatric disorders. For example, temporal lobe atrophy has been correlated with thought disorder in schizophrenia (27). MRI also has the capability of visualizing certain chemical components of brain. Although not particularly sensitive, recent MRI spectroscopic studies have revealed measurable reductions of N-acetyl aspartate, a marker for neuronal integrity, in certain brain regions in patients with AD and schizophrenia (28). Both PET and SPECT, because of their reliance on radioactive ligands, permit the measurement of trace markers in the brain such as neurotransmitter receptors or neurotransmitter high affinity transporters. This technology has revealed elevation in the density of dopamine (D_2, D_3, and D_4) receptors in the caudate and putamen of untreated schizophrenic patients (29).

PET and SPECT permit the assessment of regional brain activity in specific disorders through the use of radiolabeled ligands that are metabolically active, distribute with blood flow, or reflect oxygen consumption. With Echo Planar MRI, a recent development, blood flow studies can be performed without the use of radioactive tracers because the technique relies on changes in hemoglobin oxygen saturation secondary to regional changes in neuronal activity. This new method permits repeated studies in adult patients and in children because of the absence of ionizing radiation. Increasingly, these functional studies are informed by neuropsychological hypotheses in which patients are presented with specific tasks that challenge their vulnerabilities, thereby magnifying differences from controls that may not be apparent at resting baseline. For example, the Wisconsin Card Sort Task, which engages frontal cortical neuronal systems, provides much more robust evidence of hypoactivity of the frontal cortex in schizophrenics than studies performed in resting state conditions (30). Similarly, exposure to an imagined contaminated article augments disturbed cingulate neuronal activity in patients suffering from OCD (31). Both MRI and SPECT are clinically available diagnostic tools.

Currently, brain imaging in psychiatry is largely restricted to clinical research. Studies have revealed a rather low yield of undiagnosed neurologic disorders in structural brain imaging of patients presenting with uncomplicated psychiatric disorders such as depression (32). However, functional brain imaging is revealing an expanding number of psychiatric disorders with reproducible discrete abnormalities of neuronal activity, such as hypofrontality in schizophrenia and hypermetabolism of the right caudate/cingulate in OCD. As treatment corrects the abnormal neuronal activity in OCD, it is not unreasonable to expect a future in which functional imaging and spectroscopy will assume a greater role in diagnosis and treatment monitoring. Thus, the psychiatric resident must be well informed about the evolving use of SPECT and MRI in cost-effective patient management in a capitated environment.

PSYCHODYNAMIC TRADITION OF PSYCHIATRY

A major misunderstanding about the ascendance of neuroscience in psychiatry is that it may render psychodynamic constructs and other psychologically based interventions obsolete. Although there is little question that the synaptic circuitry of the brain is shaped by experience, understanding how specific experiences affect synapses in the individual is still unclear. Psychodynamic theory has provided psychiatry with insights that should continue to be an important part of residency training. First, training in psychodynamic therapy, coupled with its extensive literature, provides the trainee with insights into the patient's personal narrative that disclose the meaning of psychiatric illness to the patient. Understanding the meaning of illness is essential in gaining access to the patient and developing a deeper sense of therapeutic empathy. This knowledge transforms the resident's concept of the patient from simply a constellation of symptoms that must be treated to a unique individual for whom the symptoms have personal meaning.

Secondly, psychodynamic theory provides the resident with an insight into the concept of transference, which relates to the issue of fundamental, unconscious interpersonal assumptions that both therapists and patients bring to the treatment arena. A thorough understanding of this transference permits the psychiatrist to see below the surface responses and to use this understanding to facilitate treatment. An appreciation of the meaning of illness and of the processes of transference can come only through well-supervised, long-term psychotherapeutic experiences with carefully selected patients.

As an outgrowth of the psychodynamic tradition, an expanding number of psychological interventions are being developed and subjected to experimental evaluation to determine their efficacy in specific clinical disorders (33). These treatments are directed at individuals, groups, or families and incorporate a variety of theoretical perspectives including psychodynamic theory, behavioral psychology, and systems theory. These treatments are problem oriented, disorder specific, and time limited. With the ascendance of managed care and the salience of cost-benefit considerations, both specificity and efficacy of psychologic treatments must be demonstrated before they can be considered reimbursable (34). Psychiatry can gain from controlled studies demonstrating that several psychological interventions, when coupled with pharmacologic treatments, are more effective in reducing relapse rates in severe mental disorders (including depression, schizophrenia, OCD, and panic disorder) than pharmacologic treatment alone (35). Because of the difficulties in developing expertise in all areas of psychological interventions, psychiatric residents should concentrate on acquiring a working knowledge of clinical applications of psychological treatments in the comprehensive treatment of patients. It is likely that ongoing research through the use of functional brain imaging to document plastic changes in the brains of patients receiving psychologic interventions will further undermine the distinction between somatic and psychologic treatments.

CONCLUSION

An integrative approach grounded in brain and behavioral research should be the organizing principle for psychiatric training and practice. This unified conceptual approach clearly maintains the identity of the psychiatrist as a physician and emphasizes a special expertise in understanding the basic mechanisms of behavior and human psychopathology. The psychiatrist is thus the individual in the health-care system who most effectively and efficiently can use all available methods and technologies to formulate diagnoses and coordinate the broad range of treatments. Psychiatry recognizes that the brain represents the interface between experience (individual, social, and cultural) and intrinsic vulnerabilities and assets. This conceptual unity eliminates the distinction between psychodynamic psychiatry and biologic psychiatry. Because this expertise requires both a medical education and the advanced training of residency, psychiatrists are clearly delineated from psychologists and social workers.

The current level of scientific understanding allows for the appreciation of the seamless continuity from life experience and brain signal processing to the genetic determinants of brain organization and function. Psychological experience cannot exist without the brain, and no gene functions in the absence of an environmental context. The challenge and excitement of neuroscience lie in the understanding of this complex interface between intrinsic features and developmental life experiences. Psychiatrists can justifiably stake their claim to this territory, which represents the basis of psychopathology. Finally, in addition to providing a knowledge base in the neuroscientific foundations of psychiatry and the technical developments (e.g., molecular genetics, brain imaging)

that inform and will continue to transform diagnosis and treatment in psychiatry, residents must be educated about their role in the evolving system of mental health care. Although economic realities may require psychiatry to cede direct patient care for many psychological and rehabilitative treatments, only psychiatrists knowledgeable about care systems will succeed in translating their expertise into effective diagnosis and treatment for their patients.

ACKNOWLEDGMENTS

This chapter is a modification of an article originally published in *Academic Psychiatry*. The secretarial assistance of Frances MacNeil is gratefully acknowledged.

REFERENCES

1. Dorwart RA. Managed mental health care: myths and realities in the 1990s. Hosp Community Psychiatry 1990;41:1087–1091.
2. Mirin SM. The changing face of mental health care: doing what's needed, doing what's right. Psychiatr Times 1993;10:29–31.
3. Kiesler CA, Sibulkin AE. Mental hospitalization: myths and facts about a national crisis. Beverly Hills, CA: Sage Publications, 1987.
4. Association of American Medical Colleges. American medical education; institutions, programs and issues. Washington, DC: AAMC, 1992.
5. Olfson M, Pincus HA, Dial TH. Professional practice patterns of US psychiatrists. Am J Psychiatry 1994;151:89–95.
6. Dorwart RA, Chartock LR, Dial T, et al. A national study of psychiatrists' professional activities. Am J Psychiatry 1991;149:1499–1505.
7. Hyman SE, Nestler EJ. The Molecular Foundations of Psychiatry. Washington, DC: APA, 1993.
8. Gusella JF, Wexler NS, Conneally PM, et al. A polymorphic DNA marker genetically linked to Huntington's disease. Nature 1983;306:234–238.
9. Huntington's Disease Collaborative Research Group. A novel gene containing a trinucleotide repeat that is expanded and unstable on Huntington's disease chromosomes. Cell 1993;72:971–983.

10. Institute of Medicine. Mapping the brain and its functions. Washington, DC: National Academy Press, 1993.

11. Baxter LR Jr, Schwartz JM, Bergman KS, et al. Caudate glucose metabolic rate changes with both drug and behavior therapy for obsessive compulsive disorder. Arch Gen Psychiatry 1992;49:681–689.

12. Cohen D, Chumokov I, Weissembach J. A first generation physical map of the human genome. Nature 1993;366:698–701.

13. Gershon ES, Cloninger CR. Genetic approaches to mental disorders. Washington, DC: APA, 1994.

14. Corder EH, Saunders AM, Strittmatter WJ, et al. Gene dose of apolipoprotein E type 4 allele and the risk of Alzheimer's disease in late onset families. Science 1993;261:921–923.

15. Ginns EI, Ott J, Egeland J, et al. A genome wide search for chromosomal loci linked to bipolar affective disorder in the old order Amish. Nature Genetics 1996;12:431–435.

16. Coyle JT, Price DL, DeLong MR. Alzheimer's disease: a disorder of cortical cholinergic innervation. Science 1983;219:1184–1190.

17. Kosick KS. Alzheimer's disease: a cell biological perspective. Science 1992;256:780–783.

18. Coyle JT, Oster-Granite ML, Reeves R, et al. Down syndrome and the trisomy 16 mouse: impact of gene imbalance on brain development and aging. In: McHugh PR, McKusick V, eds. Genes, brain and behavior. New York: Raven Press, 1991:85–99.

19. Beardslee WR, Wright E, Rothenberg PC, et al. Response of families to two preventive intervention strategies: long term differences and attitude change. J Am Acad Child Adolesc Psychiatry 1996;35:774–782.

20. Robinson MB, Coyle JT. Glutamate and related acidic excitatory neurotransmitters: from basic science to clinical application. FASEB J 1987;1:446–455.

21. Hyman S, Coyle JT. The neuroscientific foundations of psychiatry. In: Hales RE, Yudofsky SC, Talbot JA, eds. American psychiatric press textbook of psychiatry. 2nd ed. Washington, DC: APPI, 1994:1–33.

22. Duman RS, Viadya VA, Nbuya M, et al. Stress, antidepressant treatments and neurotrophic factors: molecular and cellular mechanisms. Neuroscientist 1995;1:351–360.

23. Baldessarini RJ, Tarazi FI. Brain dopamine receptors: a primer on their current status, basic and clinical. Harvard Rev Psychiatry 1996;3:301–325.

24. Seeman P, Guan HC, Van Tol HHM. Dopamine D4 receptors elevated in schizophrenia. Science 1993;365:441–445.

25. Ebstein RP, Novick RU, Preel B, et al. Dopamine D4 receptor (D4DR) exon III polymorphism associated with the human personality trait of novelty seeking. Nature Genetics 1996;12:78–80.

26. Benjamin J, Li L, Patterson C, et al. Population and familial association between D4 dopamine receptor gene and measures of novelty seeking. Nature Genetics 1996;12:81–84.

27. Shenton ME, Kikinis R, Jolesz FA, et al. Abnormalities of the left temporal lobe and thought disorder in schizophrenia: a quantitative magnetic resonance imaging study. N Engl J Med 1992;327:604–612.

28. Shiino A, Matsuda M, Morikawa S, et al. Proton magnetic resonance spectroscopy with dementia. Surg Neurol 1993;39:143–147.

29. Wong DF, Wagner HN Jr, Tune LE, et al. Positron emission tomography reveals elevated D_2 dopamine receptors in drug-naive schizophrenics. Science 1986;234:1558–1563.

30. Berman KF, Torrey EF, Danial JG, et al. Regional cerebral blood flow in monozygotic twins discordant and concordant for schizophrenia. Arch Gen Psychiatry 1992;49:996–1001.

31. Rauch SL, Jenike MA, Alpert NM, et al. Regional cerebral blood flow measured during symptom provocation in obsessive compulsive disorder using oxygen-15 carbon dioxide and positron emission tomography. Arch Gen Psychiatry 1994;51:62–70.

32. Rauch SL, Renshaw PF. Clinical neuroimaging in psychiatry. Harvard Rev Psychiatry 1995;2:121–132.

33. Falloon IRH, Boyd JL, McGill CW. Family management in the prevention of morbidity of schizophrenia: clinical outcome of two year longitudinal study. Arch Gen Psychiatry 1985;42:887–896.

34. Barber JP, Ellman J. Advances in short-term dynamic psychotherapy. Curr Opinion Psychiatry 1996;9:188–192.

35. Weissman MM, Markowitz JC. Interpersonal psychotherapy: current status. Arch Gen Psychiatry 1994;51:599–606.

Chapter 24

Training Residents in Psychodynamic Psychiatry

Glen O. Gabbard

INTRODUCTION

Psychiatry is the medical specialty involved in integrating the biologic and the psychosocial dimensions of the diagnosis and treatment of mental illness. In this regard, psychiatrists must be equally as conversant with neurotransmitters, psychopharmacologic agents, and the genetics of major psychiatric disorders as they are with individual meanings, family dynamics, and internal object relations. To avoid the twin perils of psychoanalytic and biologic reductionism, clinical psychiatrists must remember that "mind" and "brain" are ultimately inseparable. Patients should be thought of both in psychological and biologic terms to avoid fragmenting the patient and the treatment.

For organizational reasons, this chapter artificially separates the psychodynamic and neuroscience aspects of psychiatry residency training. In practice, however, they must be integrated continuously. Moreover, psychodynamic psychiatry should not be regarded as antibiologic. Psychodynamic and biologic approaches generally work synergistically to enhance treatment outcomes and preserve the patient's holistic experience.

For purposes of this chapter, psychodynamic psychiatry can be defined as "an approach to diagnosis and treatment characterized by a way of thinking about both patient and clinician that includes unconscious conflict, deficits and distortions of intrapsychic structures, and internal object relations" (1). As this definition stresses, dynamic psychiatry and dynamic psychotherapy are not one and the same. The psychodynamic viewpoint may apply in virtually any treatment setting, regardless of whether the psychiatrist is involved in prescribing medication, administrating hospital or partial hospital treatment, conducting behaviorally oriented sex therapy, or participating in other situations. A carefully considered psychodynamic understanding of a patient's ego strengths and weaknesses, self-structure, and internal object relations may lead a clinician to conclude that noninterpretive interventions are optimal.

This definition also indicates that the

psychodynamic clinician is guided by theory. Ego psychology, represented by "unconscious conflict," derives from classical Freudian theory. The intrapsychic struggle between drives or wishes fighting for expression are emphasized, along with the defenses that attempt to keep them in check. In part, symptoms are regarded as compromises between these opposing forces. In addition to conflict, psychodynamic theory embraces a deficit model in which the patient's self is arrested developmentally due to trauma, neglect, or other inadequate responses from parental or caretaking figures. This perspective is reflected most notably in self psychology.

Object relations theory is a another perspective that stresses the unconscious repetition of internalized patterns of relationships from childhood in the present with the clinician and others. Various clinicians approach the use of theory in different ways. Some clinicians favor the use of one theory that may be considered all-inclusive, whereas others strive to integrate aspects of all three theories. Still other clinicians adjust the theory to the patient, depending on the best fit for a specific clinical situation.

The previously mentioned definition of psychodynamic psychiatry also focuses on the concept that it involves a two-person field (i.e., both patient and clinician). The patient's transference arises in concert with the clinician's countertransference. Transference is the unconscious repetition of past experiences in the present, leading the patient to consider the doctor as if he or she were a figure from the patient's past. Clinicians bring their own subjectivity to the clinical interaction, and the real characteristics of the doctor always influence the patient's transference (2–4). Moreover, the clinician's perception of

the patient's transference is similarly affected by the clinician's own subjective unconscious conflicts and internalized object relations. Countertransference in clinicians is narrowly defined as a clinician's transference to the patient. In the broader sense, clinicians respond to the patient in the same way that other people do (i.e., the patient evokes specific reactions that reflect the patient's internal object world). In most cases, countertransference is an integration of both the narrow and broad definitions; it is based jointly on the reaction that the patient evokes in the clinician and the preexisting internal world of that clinician, serving as a "hook" to whatever the patient projects into the clinician (5).

LENGTH OF TREATMENT AND PSYCHODYNAMIC PSYCHIATRY

The education of psychiatric residents in the knowledge and techniques of psychodynamic psychiatry in an acute care setting requires an adjustment of the usual linkage between time and psychodynamic approaches. Because of the historical evolution of dynamic psychiatry from the principles of psychoanalysis, there has long been an assumption that psychodynamic interventions require a long-term setting. In the 1970s, this assumption was first challenged by the brief dynamic therapy movement in the United Kingdom and the United States. Malan (6) developed a technique referred to as focal psychotherapy, in which psychoanalytic techniques were applied in carefully selected patients to once-weekly therapy that lasted only a few months. A key in the selection of those patients involved their capacity to identify a central focus for the process. In Boston, Sifneos (7) successfully adapted psychoanalytic techniques to a treatment called brief anxiety-provoking therapy that generally lasted only 12–16 sessions. He also stressed the importance of a focus.

The adaptation of principles gleaned from psychoanalysis to brief dynamic therapy provides a useful model for the shift from extended inpatient treatment to the acute care setting. There is a rich tradition of long-term, psychoanalytically informed hospital treatment (8–14) that can be modified by defining a more circumscribed focus in the acute care setting without losing the fundamental principles involved. Although the therapeutic effect may not be as great in a brief intervention as in one that extends many months or years, the principles of more extended psychodynamic hospital treatment can be applied just as readily. Among those principles is the concept that the patient recreates his or her internal world in the treatment setting (8). Treaters assume the roles of internal object and self-representations as the patient attributes certain qualities to them and evokes responses similar to those internal representations through the process of projective identification. By this process, patients may evoke responses in certain staff members that cause them to be transformed into "bad objects" through direct interpersonal pressure from the patient, who acts so unpleasantly as to coerce "bad object" responses from others. Different staff members may be idealized and take on qualities of the "good object" because of the patient's interpersonal pressure for them to conform to this particular internal representation. Treatment staff members attempt to understand the patterns and identify them, rather than to simply react as others do. Over time, a cumulative therapeutic effect is developed from the ongoing interactions with acute care staff members.

DIDACTIC INSTRUCTION

To become a proficient practitioner of psychodynamic psychiatry requires mastery of a considerable body of knowledge. Some learning can be acquired in the clinical setting with careful supervision, whereas other knowledge must come from classroom instruction and seminars that cover psychoanalytic theory and practice. Some didactic grounding is necessary to understand fully the interactions with patients and other staff members in clinical settings. Ideally, didactic seminars should be held in the first or second postgraduate year and should emphasize the application of psychodynamic thinking to general psychiatric settings rather than to psychoanalytic psychotherapy specifically (which can come later in the curriculum). For this reason, the classroom instructor must be reasonably conversant with the application of psychodynamic theories in acute psychiatric settings. Residents who are facing crisis situations daily on their clinical assignments often consider irrelevant those instructors who are involved primarily in the practice of analysis or long-term psychoanalytic therapy.

A Core Curriculum

A didactic seminar on psychodynamic psychiatry would include the following elements: ego psychology, object relations theory, self psychology, psychodynamic interviewing and formulation, psychodynamics of groups and families, psychodynamic understanding of major Axis I and Axis II disorders, and psychodynamics of prescribing medication.

Ego Psychology

Residents should learn the tripartite structural theory of superego, ego, and id as well as the conflict models of the symptom pathogenesis. The concept of compromise formation should be emphasized, and considerable time should be devoted to an appreciation of defense mechanisms. In particular, residents should be taught to identify defenses that are manifested in a clinical situation and to understand how they may reflect the degree of psychological disturbance in the patient. In addition, an introduction to ego psychology should acquaint residents with ego functions and the nondefensive, adaptive aspects of the ego. Finally, the developmental concepts of ego psychology, particularly the psychosexual stages and the Oedipus constellation, should be covered in sufficient detail so that residents understand the classical view and the postmodern feminist revisions of psychoanalytic theory.

Object Relations Theory

Residents should be exposed to the basic theory of the Kleinians, the middle group of the British school of object relations (e.g., Winnicott and Fairbairn) and the modern relational theorists in the United States. Concepts such as splitting and projective identification should be explained, as should internalization, identification, and introjection. Residents should be acquainted with the developmental ideas of Bowlby, Mahler, and others that lend support to object relations theory.

Self Psychology

Residents should learn the essential self-object transferences (i.e., the mirror, twinship, and idealizing transferences) and the theoretical basis of self psychology. Although familiarity with Kohut's work is important, contemporary revisionists of self psychology, including the intersubjectivists, should also be discussed. Finally, the developmental basis of self psychology, particularly the work of Stern and other "infant-watchers," should be included.

Psychodynamic Interviewing and Formulation

This aspect of the seminar should emphasize the methods used by a psychodynamic clinician to create rapport with the patient and to elicit psychodynamically relevant material. Similarly, the process of hypothesis formation and the link between clinical data and the psychodynamic formulation should be illustrated. Residents should receive a clear message that emphasizes the link between the biologic and psychodynamic formulation.

Psychodynamics of Groups and Families

Acute care is generally provided in a group setting, and one distinguishing feature of the psychodynamic approach is its understanding of the group dynamics observed in the care delivery system. Individuals behave differently in groups than they do when they are alone. A study of group therapy principles and group dynamics that are activated will serve clinicians well in complicated institutional systems. Similarly, most patients are in some way embedded in a family system, and the psychodynamics that operate within family systems may be crucial to understanding why these patients do not comply with treatment, why they cannot use their family as a support system, and how the family may contribute to either prevention of relapse or exacerbation of symptoms. These basic concepts are essential in the training of an effective psychiatrist.

Psychodynamic Understanding of Major Axis I and Axis II Disorders

A review of the literature provides a dynamic understanding of psychopathologic entities commonly encountered in an acute care setting. To avoid a reductionistic perspective, residents should be taught to integrate the psychodynamic features of the illness with the descriptive features so that both are taken into account in treatment planning.

Psychodynamics of Prescribing Medication

Noncompliance with medication is perhaps one of the major reasons that patients are admitted to an acute care setting. The principles of transference, countertransference, and resistance provide a useful conceptual framework to determine why patients do not fill their prescriptions or take them as directed. Moreover, medications take on particular meanings to patients, and those meanings need to be understood to address successfully problems of noncompliance. For this topic, as in all subjects for didactic seminars, classroom instruction should be linked closely to clinical examples illustrating psychodynamic concepts. The following application of dynamic principles to noncompliance is a good illustration.

☐ C A S E   E X A M P L E

Ms. A was a 38-year-old woman with recurrent unipolar depression. Although she had been prescribed 50 mg of paroxetine daily, as both a therapeutic and a maintenance dose, she relapsed and was readmitted to a brief-stay hospital unit with suicidal ideation and symptoms of a major depressive episode. The resident, Dr. B, who had been following her as an outpatient, could not hide his irritation when he learned that she had stopped taking the medication. Dr. B asked Ms. A why she had discontinued the paroxetine. Ms. A replied that her depression got better so she saw no point in continuing to take the medication. Dr. B reminded her of his explanation that 90% of patients who had three depressive episodes (as she had) would have a fourth, and that the maintenance dose must be the same as the therapeutic dose.

Ms. A stared at Dr. B blankly. Dr. B asked, "Do you remember my telling you that?" Ms. A replied, "I think so." Dr. B replied, "Well, either you do or you don't remember." Ms. A then said, "Well, I have trouble swallowing pills." Dr. B asked, "Can you swallow food okay?" Ms. A replied that indeed she could. In a voice filled with exhortation, Dr. B then said to her, "Well, if you can swallow food, you can certainly swallow pills." Dr. B could barely hide his exasperation, and Ms. A finally blurted out, "I feel like I'm being scolded." Dr. B, caught off guard, said, "Well, I'm not trying to scold you, but I gave you real clear instructions and you didn't follow them."

Fortunately for Dr. B, his supervisor was on the unit and overheard this interaction. She asked if she could have a word with Dr. B and spoke with him in the chart room behind the nursing station. Dr. B's supervisor commented that he seemed fairly upset with Ms. A. Dr. B acknowledged that his frustration with her for not following through on his clear advice. Dr. B's supervisor reminded him of an important psychodynamic principle—that many patients are ambivalent about getting better or staying better and that an exploratory approach to understanding that ambivalence is probably more effective than a strong arm approach.

Dr. B went back to see Ms. A later in the day and apologized for his rather authoritarian stance. Ms. A told him, "You sounded exactly like my father. He always told me I didn't do anything right." Dr. B said that he did not mean to sound like her father, but he just wondered why she would not take a pill that would help her stay healthy. Ms. A replied, "I told you. I can't swallow it." Dr. B asked her then if there was anything else she could not swallow, specifically the idea of being depressed. Ms. A responded, "Well, when I get over depression, I want to be over and done with it and not keep taking medicine for it." Dr. B then explained, "But it's not over when it appears to be because it's a recurrent illness." Ms. A then said, "But it makes me feel like a chronic mental patient to have to take an antidepressant all the time. It's like I'm just as much of a screw-up as my dad always said I was."

When Dr. B next talked with his supervisor, it became clear that with only this small amount of data, certain psychodynamic themes emerged. To Ms. A, paroxetine meant that she was a "chronic mental patient." Having a major psychiatric disorder to her was a fulfillment of her father's lifelong criticism. It was a confirmation that she was fundamentally defective. Moreover, the supervisor pointed out how Ms. A had unconsciously recreated a relationship with her father in the transference to Dr. B. By not taking the medication, she evoked a response in Dr. B that was much like her father's. He became authoritarian and critical in his tone and tried to force her to do things differently than what she wanted. Hence, her ambivalence about getting better was in part a reluctance to let go of her relationship with her father to whom she was very attached. As Dr. B explored the situation with Ms. A, he discovered that she had never been able to form a mutually gratifying, intimate relationship with a man and continued to depend on her father as though she were still a child. The transference-countertransference dimensions involved in the noncompliance revealed a great deal about the patient's internal world and the meaning of the medication to her.

This case illustrates that resistance is more than a strictly intrapsychic phenomenon residing in the patient. To a large extent, Dr. B participated in the resistance by enacting the role of the father and thus reinforced the patient's reluctance to comply with the prescribed medication. In other situations, the clinician's contribution to the resistance, sometimes referred to as counterresistance, may stem from the clinician's unconscious ambivalence about the treatment being recommended.

ON-SITE SUPERVISION OF CLINICAL ASSIGNMENTS

As the above case illustrates, the fundamentals of psychodynamic psychiatry should be applied in a resident's clinical, on-site supervised setting. Supervisors who are facile with the application of psychodynamic thinking in the acute care setting can serve as role models. Ideally, the supervisor should work with the resident for accessibility in crises and for facilitating the learning experience in the setting. Modeling may also help bolster the resident's confidence and promote the professional identity development.

Supervision at the clinical site can demystify the process of clinical inference. Psychiatry residents frequently misunderstand that discerning unconscious themes in the patient's material is tantamount to mind-reading. Supervisors can explain that psychodynamic inferences about the unconscious are based on observable behavior and language and a good theoretical approach to the mind, rather than on telepathic powers. Group meetings in an acute care setting are particularly useful for teaching the process of inference, as the following case illustrates.

□ CASE EXAMPLE

Ms. C, a 26-year-old patient with borderline personality disorder, was being treated in a day hospital setting that included group meetings. She had attended the day hospital for 3 days and had said nothing in the group. On the third day, other patients began to confront her with the fact that she had said nothing about herself while they were openly revealing their problems. Ms. C looked at the floor and said in a sullen, quiet voice, "I don't want to talk." The other patients in the group pointed out to Ms. C that they had all talked about their problems and that she needed to do so as well. Ms. C simply remained silent. The patients began to escalate in their demands that she say something. She eventually said to the group members, "You wouldn't understand my problems anyway."

One of the other group members said, "That's fairly insulting." Ms. C responded, "So be insulted." Another patient in the group said, "How do you know we won't understand?" Ms. C responded, "I just know." Another borderline patient in the group confronted Ms. C in a sarcastic voice, "Maybe if you weren't such a bitch, then people could understand you." At that point, Ms. C stood up and shouted, "That's what always happens. People think I'm a bitch and want nothing to do with me," and she stormed out of the room, leaving the rest of the group members feeling guilty, angry, impotent, and useless.

In a supervisory session following this group meeting, the resident running the group and her supervisor were able to see a clear pattern of relatedness, largely unconscious to the patient, that led to many of her difficulties. The supervisor pointed out that Ms. C's having everyone think that she was a "bitch" was directly related to behaviors that others found obnoxious. The supervisor stressed that Ms. C's tendency to see herself as a victim of others was something that was actually unconsciously created by her verbal and nonverbal behavior. The supervisor made an extremely important clinical point. He explained that the psychodynamic perspective is geared to pointing out what the patient is actively doing, however unconsciously, to recreate situations from the past in the present. An understanding of the specific behaviors, attitudes, and interactions is potentially liberating for the patient, who can then develop a greater freedom of choice in considering how to interact with others in a way that can lead to different responses.

The supervisor's role as someone actively involved in the treatment setting is important in assisting the resident to understand staff dynamics and staff countertransference. In the same day hospital setting, Ms. C's case was discussed on the day after the group meeting in which she had stormed out. Mr. D, a nurse working on the unit, opened the discussion by saying that Ms. C was getting so much flak from other patients that she was not able to use the treatment. The social worker on the team observed to Mr. D, "It sounds like you're blaming the other patients rather than Ms. C." Mr. D replied, "Well, when she talks to me in a one-to-one situation, she is quite open about her issues, but I think the group is scapegoating her and won't let her bring up the issues in the group." At this point in the discussion, the resident commented to Mr. D that perhaps he did not appreciate fully how Ms. C's behavior was responsible for turning everyone against her. Mr. D responded that the resident was new to the situation and did not yet understand how vicious the group could be. In a rather didactic tone, he told the resident, "A basic principle of group dynamics is that people behave differently in groups than they do as individuals."

The resident felt put down by this comment, and other staff members jumped to his defense by telling Mr. D that he was being "taken in" by the patient. Mr. D continued to defend himself and argued that no one else understood the patient in the way that he did. Finally, the resident's supervisor made the observation that, to some extent, the staff dynamics were paralleling what was going on in the patient group. Mr. D had become the scape-goat in the same way that Ms. C was the day before. This comment put an end to the discussion, and the staff meeting began to discuss another patient.

Later in supervision, the resident's supervisor noted that he had perhaps sounded like Mr. D and was possibly perceived as talking down to the other staff members. He knew it was important to support the scapegoat when one particular staff member was getting heat from everyone, but he recognized that his style of doing it may have stifled further discussion. He went on to explain to the resident how the process of splitting operates in a milieu treating borderline patients. Whereas Ms. C had indeed confided in Mr. D, she had been sullen and withholding with everyone else—exactly as she was in the group meeting. For whatever reasons, Ms. C treated Mr. D as a "good object" who was special. Only he could understand the way she felt. He became her defender and rescuer with a zealous mission to plead her case to the other staff (all of whom felt like "bad objects") and to protect her against scapegoating in the patient group.

The resident's supervisor pointed out how the forces of splitting and projective identification operate in groups in the same way as they do in dyads. Ms. C became a convenient container for the projection of all the patients' unacceptable qualities. In particular, certain patients projectively disavowed and deposited aspects of themselves into Ms. C. Because their defensive projections were now embodied in Ms. C, she became the carrier of the group's resistance. As is often the case, an escalation of these dynamics led to her extrusion by the group as a means of "solving" the problem of embarrassment about confronting and revealing the problems that all of them experienced, to one degree or another.

Practicing in an acute care setting in the contemporary health-care climate is much like being at the center of a pressure cooker. Internal administrative pressures, along with external pressures from managed care companies, work to create an atmosphere in which a psychiatry resident's professional autonomy seems to be severely compromised. A supervisor can help a resident to deal with aspects of the practical management of the situation and can provide an opportunity to reflect on the meaning of these pressures to the resident, the patient, the patient's family, and the rest of the staff. The following case example illustrates this function of the supervisor.

□ **C ASE E XAMPLE**

Dr. E was a second postgraduate year resident who had admitted Mr. F, a 28-year-old patient with an Axis I diagnosis of major depression and an Axis II diagnosis of borderline personality disorder. The managed care reviewer approved 5 days of hospitalization. Dr. E replied that the patient was extremely suicidal and would probably not be ready to leave in 5 days. The managed care reviewer's retort was, "You're letting yourself be manipulated by a borderline. These patients make gestures and get others worried about them, but they rarely commit suicide. Leaving them in the hospital for a long time makes them so dependent that they'll never learn any autonomy. The best treatment is to get them out as quickly as possible."

Dr. E, who was a bit intimidated by the air of confidence conveyed by the reviewer, explained to the patient that he would have to leave within 5 days. Mr. F became extremely distraught and cried out, "How could they do that to me?" Dr. E, identifying with the patient, replied, "Managed care companies call the shots these days. The most important thing is to save money." The patient pleaded with Dr. E, "Don't they know I'm going to kill myself?" Dr. E replied, "This guy doesn't even believe you're really suicidal. Can you believe that?" The patient became extremely agitated and said, "Well, I might as well end it all. Nobody believes me. I can't get treatment. What's the point in going on?"

Dr. E was furious with the managed care reviewer and recounted to her supervisor the details of her discussion with the reviewer and her last interaction with the patient. The supervisor empathized with Dr. E and validated the reality of the situation. Five days was an extremely brief time for someone who is suicidal. He also wondered if Dr. E was acting out her anger at the situation by speaking with the patient about the reviewer in a highly pejorative tone. He suggested that one way to cement an alliance (although not an enduring alliance because it is based on enmity) with such a difficult patient was to externalize all potential anger and aggression between patient and doctor by projecting it into a managed care reviewer who provided a convenient repository for the negative feelings. In the acute care setting, the external reviewer is easily cast in the role of the "bad object" by both patient and treaters (15). Dr. E reflected on this dynamic and acknowledged that she was venting and hoping that the patient would talk to her family and threaten to sue the managed care firm. Such actions might put some pressure on the employer to do something about the situation.

As irritating as the reviewer's manner was, the supervisor pointed out to Dr. E that he was representing a particular perspective (i.e., the voice of reality). The patient's benefits were limited, and he would have to learn to cope with suicidal feelings without a lengthy hospitalization. Dr. E argued, "But he's chronically suicidal. No brief hospitalization is going to fix that." The supervisor retorted, "Exactly. So ultimately he has to find some way to deal with the suicidal feelings outside of a protected setting."

In the same way that managed care reviewers can occupy specific roles within the patient's or the resident's internal world, administrators who are trying to balance a budget can be cast as "bad objects" who are callous and indifferent to the needs of staff members, let alone the treatment needs of patients. They may also be seen as idealized rescuers who will develop magical solutions to complex problems. Supervisors must help residents learn to balance their interest in the patient with the fiscal concerns of both society and the institution in which they work. The feelings of frustration and despair when unable to provide the ideal treatment must be put in context. Residents must reflect on the meaning of those feelings to avoid enacting various countertransference urges with the patient.

CONCLUSIONS

The acute care setting can be chaotic. Psychiatric residents, along with all clinicians, are under pressure to make quick decisions. Patients need to be discharged. Dispositions need to be made on limited data. It is important to preserve a sense of meaning and space for reflection in the midst of this chaos.

The patient's unique psychological features must be appreciated and considered in treatment. Although the entire personality cannot be the subject of intensive scrutiny in a brief treatment, focal psychodynamic issues—if unattended—will subvert treatment. For example, in the earlier case of Ms. A, her resistance to taking an antidepressant was linked to key psychodynamic issues that, when understood and discussed, led to better collaboration and compliance. In the treatment of Ms. C, the focal issue was her interpersonal style and how it alienated social support. By making this ego-syntonic character trait more ego-dystonic for the patient (and minimizing the group's rejection of her), the treaters enabled Ms. C to improve her relationships and develop a more supportive network of persons in her life. In the case of Mr. F, his feelings of passivity, helplessness, and victimization at the hands of his employer's managed care company had to be confronted. The focal issue for his treatment was to help him gain a sense of active mastery over his chronic suicidal risk, allowing him to leave the hospital with a systematic outpatient therapy strategy to manage suicidal feelings.

The preservation of reflection and meaning in the training of psychiatry residents is not limited to the intrapsychic meaning for the patient. Residents constantly operate in systems in which psychodynamic principles can be applied to seemingly irrational group and institutional behavior to make it understandable. A capacity to derive meaning from the maze of human and institutional chaos ultimately provides the resident with a feeling of mastery that will enhance all forms of psychiatric practice, not just the provision of psychotherapy. Understanding group and individual behavior makes the irrational more rational, develops a focus for therapeutic efforts, enriches the daily humdrum, and offers gratification to those who pursue this path.

REFERENCES

1. Gabbard GO. Psychodynamic psychiatry in clinical practice. Washington, DC: American Psychiatric Press, 1994.
2. Gill MM. Psychoanalysis in transition: a personal view. Hillsdale, NJ: Analytic Press, 1994.
3. Hoffman IZ. The patient as interpreter of the analyst's experience. Contemp Psychoanal 1983;19:389–422.
4. Renik O. Analytic interaction: conceptualizing technique in light of the analyst's irreducible subjectivity. Psychoanal Q 1993;62:553–571.
5. Gabbard GO. Countertransference: the emerging common ground. Int J Psychoanal 1995;76:475–485.
6. Malan DH. The frontier of brief of psychotherapy: an example of the convergence of research and clinical practice. New York: Plenum, 1976.
7. Sifneos PE. Short-term psychotherapy and emotional crisis. Cambridge, MA: Harvard University Press, 1972.
8. Gabbard GO. A contemporary perspective on psychoanalytically informed hospital treatment. Hosp Community Psychiatry 1988;39:1291–1295.
9. Gabbard GO. Comparative indications for brief and extended hospitalization. In: Tasman A, Riba MB, eds. American psychiatric press review of psychiatry. Washington, DC: American Psychiatric Press, 1992;11:503–517.
10. Hilles L. Changing trends in the application of psychoanalytic principles to a psychiatric hospital. Bull Menninger Clin 1968;32:203–218.
11. Kernberg OF. Psychoanalytic object-relations theory, group processes and administration: toward an integrative theory of hospital treatment. Ann Psychoanal 1973;1:363–388.
12. Menninger WC. The Menninger Hospital's guide to the order sheet (1939). Bull Menninger Clin 1982;46:1–112.
13. Schlesinger HJ, Holzman PS. The therapeutic aspects of the hospital milieu: prescribing an activities program. Bull Menninger Clin 1970;34:1–11.
14. Zee HJ. Purpose and structure of a psychoanalytic hospital. J Natl Assoc Private Psychiatr Hosp 1977;8:20–26.
15. Gabbard GO, Takahashi T, Davidson JE, et al. A psychodynamic perspective on the clinical impact of insurance review. Am J Psychiatry 1991;148:318–323.

Chapter 25

Ethical Issues in Acute Care

Jeremy A. Lazarus

INTRODUCTION

The changing health-care environment has created unprecedented challenges for medicine in general and psychiatry in particular. As the locus for short-term and more definitive treatment has shifted from inpatient to acute care settings, treatment innovations and their resultant uncertainties have created anxieties and optimism. The push for rapid assessment, briefer forms of treatment, intermittent treatment, and cost constraints creates increasing pressures on clinicians to provide treatment that is quick, safe, and ethical. The ethical challenges in this unprecedented set of circumstances relate to cost constraints and changes in the nature and patterns of treatment ushered in by managed care.

Medical ethics have their roots in the Hippocratic tradition. The American Medical Association's (AMA) Principles of Medical Ethics has shaped the ethical code for organized medicine, including psychiatry (1). The American Psychiatric Association (APA) has developed an an-

notated code based on the AMA principles (2). In addition, both the AMA and APA have collections of opinions that the respective organizations have promulgated to respond to specific ethical questions (3). However, both organizations recognize that their codes are not the only guides for resolving ethical questions.

A new form of medical ethics, bioethics, began in the second half of the 20th century (4) and now prevails in Western medicine. Four principles underlie modern bioethics: beneficence, autonomy, nonmaleficence (do no harm), and justice. These principles and the values they represent are often at odds with one another. For example, the long-standing values of medical paternalism and beneficence have been contested by proponents of patient autonomy and informed consent, especially since the 1960s. The value of nonmaleficence is under assault by proponents of physician participation in executions and physician-assisted euthanasia. In the 1990s, however, the primary concerns are the rising costs of health care and the extraordinary pressures to constrain costs. The dangers of economic rationing and maldistribution of health care have led to an ethical focus on the principle of justice: how can health-care dollars be spent fairly in our society (5)?

Although some medical ethicists continue to warn about the changing times (6), others are attempting to fashion a new world of medical ethics (7). Similarly, as some psychiatrists retain a tradition of patient advocacy (8), others are forging an expanded ethic of distributive justice to fit the new world of managed care (9). However, as these theoretical discussions continue, the mental health marketplace has caused outright upheaval in the delivery of services. The market demand for cost-effective treatment in the least restrictive environment has been adopted in position papers and policy documents by both the AMA and APA. Despite demands for scientifically valid outcome studies on which to base professional decision-making, the paucity of empiric evidence on cost-effective treatments casts the current marketplace revolution in a highly experimental mode, without conclusive data and with few controls on the power of economics (10).

ETHICAL DILEMMAS IN ACUTE CARE SETTINGS

Informed Consent

The ethical movement toward patient autonomy began in the 1960s in parallel with the civil rights movement, women's issues, gay rights, and the Vietnam war. Traditional medical paternalism, or "doctor knows best," was replaced by informed patient consent and the ideal of a doctor-patient partnership in medical decision-making. Doctor-patient informed consent is now complicated by the presence of sev-

eral other parties, including benefit managers, utilization reviewers, case managers, and at times Employee Assistance Programs and employers. In fact, many treatments require the concurrence of specific agents other than the doctor-patient dyad for medically necessary care to be reimbursed (hence, to occur).

The acute care setting, in particular, raises several thorny problems of informed consent. In acute care, many patients may be unable to participate fully in a meaningful discussion of the benefits and risks of treatment as well as different treatment options and their costs. Emergency treatment must often be provided while available benefits, membership in insurance plans, and other important information is not immediately available. Clinically, well-managed acute care requires a continuum of care delivered at the least restrictive level. Patients will frequently be moved quickly along that continuum, which can make for a daily tempo of informed consent in the context of discontinuity of clinician-patient relationships. Optimally, one clinician/administrator (case manager) who can follow the patient along the continuum can simplify accountability for informed consent and minimize disruptions in clinical relationships. Optimal conditions, however, often cannot be achieved by clinical care.

□ C A S E   E X A M P L E

A 55-year-old woman was hospitalized six times for severe depression, each time responding effectively to antidepressants. The gravity of her illness and the lag time in her response to antidepressants previously necessitated 6–8 weeks of hospitalization. Before her current admission, her employer's insurance carrier engaged a carve-out behavioral health-care company and established a case rate arrangement (a lump sum payment per admission to the hospital regardless of length of stay). At the time of the current admission, the case manager from the carve-out company (with consultation with the company's medical director) recommended a course of electroconvulsive therapy (ECT). The patient and her family were advised of this recommendation by the hospital psychiatrist and were told that ECT might improve her depression more rapidly.

Questions

Should the hospital psychiatrist have included in the informed consent discussion the manner of payment for the hospitalization? What is the ethical obligation of the hospital psychiatrist if the patient refuses ECT?

Discussion

The hospital psychiatrist had an obligation to include in the informed consent any factors that might directly or indirectly influence the recommendation for ECT. If the patient refused the treatment, the physician should have respected the patient's wishes unless it was an emergency and life-saving treatment.

Disclosure

The ethical principle of honesty derives from the expectation of trust that the vulnerable patient must hold in the provider of health care. Although the beneficent and paternalistic physician would not disclose information that he or she thought harmful to patients, current informed consent strives for complete and open communication (full disclosure) between physician and patient. The only exception might be a decision to withhold information that is likely to cause extreme harm.

Disclosure in the acute care setting includes providing patients with information about treatment options, administrative policies or practices that might interfere with the provision of medically necessary treatment, and any potential financial conflict of interest by the physician or healthcare system. In the current marketplace, in which providers and systems are financially "at risk" for the provision of services, disclosure is demanded because a conflict may exist between the provision of service and the financial bottom line. For example, in capitation arrangements, the provision of less service is financially beneficial to the system or the provider. Acute care systems must work with payers to maximize disclosure at the time the subscriber (future patient) contracts for insurance benefits. Success in subscriber education would relieve the delivery system of some ethical need to disclose.

Similar to informed consent, decisions concerning the timing of disclosure must be made with the patient's clinical condition in mind. Disclosure at inopportune times might interfere with the building of a therapeutic or treatment alliance; consequently, the principles of beneficence and nonmaleficence would need to be considered.

☐ **CASE EXAMPLE**

A 24-year-old married woman was admitted to an intensive psychiatric outpatient service. She was acutely depressed, with suicidal ideation but without an active plan. Her husband recently left her, and her usually supportive parents were out of the country on a 3-week cruise. Her insurance only provided limited outpatient treatment after the acute episode. The psychiatrist had to decide the clinical wisdom of disclosing this insurance information within the first few days of treatment. He decided to postpone discussion with the patient until her condition was stabilized, medications were begun, and engagement of other external supports could be achieved.

Question

Was this ethical?

Discussion

Yes. The psychiatrist's decision to withhold important information about benefit treatment restrictions until the patient's condition was more stable satisfied the principle of beneficence. The concern that full disclosure might be intrusive and potentially harmful to her stabilization satisfied the principle of nonmaleficence.

□ C ASE E XAMPLE

A 40-year-old man with major depression was admitted to an inpatient psychiatric unit after a suicide attempt. Although his condition stabilized after 7 days, he continued to have suicidal ideation. The psychiatric hospital and psychiatrist were working under a case rate (a fixed, total dollar amount no matter how many days the patient was hospitalized) for his hospitalization. The psychiatrist advised discharge to the patient, but the patient requested additional days in the hospital. The psychiatrist knew that the patient was not informed of the case rate arrangement either before or since the time of admission.

Questions

Should the psychiatrist (and hospital) inform the patient of the payment arrangement during the discussions about potential discharge? Would not doing so be unethical?

Discussion

The answer to both questions was yes. Because the financial arrangement could create a conflict of interest for the psychiatrist and hospital, disclosure was crucial. The patient must be fully informed on how clinical decisions might be influenced by the financial interests of the treaters. This was especially important if the patient did not concur with the level of care recommended. If an adverse event were to occur after discharge, substantial potential for both legal and ethical consequences existed if the financial conflict of interest was not disclosed.

Conflicts of Interest

Both providers and health-care systems delivering acute services can have conflicts of interest in the treatment of patients. These conflicts may be financial or may include multiple obligations of the provider(s) of service. Financial conflicts are most clear when providers or systems are at risk financially because the provision of services must be achieved within a fixed budget. The potential conflict is between the patient's clinical needs and the financial needs of the provider(s); the risk is to underutilize services.

Multiple obligations (often termed double agentry) of the treating clinician may pit the interests of the patient against the interests of the provider and the system. For example, for-profit and nonprofit systems have limited amounts of funding to provide free care. The limits placed on the amount, type, and length of treatment that can be offered without jeopardizing the financial integrity of the system may influence the provider's clinical approach toward the patient.

When a provider within an acute care

system recognizes such conflicts, they should be discussed or disclosed to the patient. When the conflict may result in limitations on treatment, whether medically necessary or not, disclosure is the essential ethical course to follow. The patient is given proper notice of the potential for conflict and can consider how the provider or care system mitigates those conflicts in a fair and ethical manner.

□ **C**ASE **E**XAMPLE

A psychiatric team in a general hospital emergency department provided triage for psychiatric hospitalization. The hospital employed the team and received a capitated payment to cover a population of patients who might require care.

Question

Should the psychiatric team and/or hospital inform patients in the course of evaluation of the hospital's arrangement?

Discussion

Theoretically yes. However, as noted before, the emotional state of the patient should also influence what is said and when. Ideally, patients should be informed at the time of their enrollment of the financial arrangements the payer has established with professionals, hospitals, or other systems of care. Enrollment education (disclosure) would obviate ethically cumbersome disclosure during an acute illness.

□ **C**ASE **E**XAMPLE

A psychiatrist who worked as a salaried employee in an HMO was told that the HMO was experiencing cash flow problems. Services would be even more closely monitored and year-end bonuses were in jeopardy. The psychiatrist recognized that he had become more rigid about the number of outpatient visits he set up with patients.

Question

Should he have informed the patients that he was aware of the budgetary issues within the HMO and that his potential bonus might have affected his decisions?

Discussion

Yes. A psychiatrist aware of corporate and personal financial conflicts should begin a discussion with patients so that they are aware of this potential. The conflict may not necessarily affect treatment but should be disclosed. Honest discussion may enhance the patient's trust in both the psychiatrist and the health-care system. Also, if the psychiatrist feels a dual obligation to the patient and to the financial survival of the HMO, the conflict should be disclosed.

Confidentiality

As acute treatment has expanded from the inpatient setting to outpatient acute care settings, concerns about confidentiality have resurfaced as major ethical issues. The number of clinical and administrative personnel with access to psychiatric charts and clinical information has skyrocketed. Protocols should be developed to assure that the rules protecting patient information are followed to maintain the strictest confidentiality in treatment settings.

Behavioral health-care companies and other managed systems of care are often involved in managing or reviewing acute care treatment. Managed care organizations usually have confidentiality protocols, but acute settings are obligated to protect patient confidentiality and can provide information only with a direct understanding by and signed release from the patient. Reviewers, case managers, administrators, and others who request information about patients must be clearly identified, and a contemporaneous release must be obtained from the patient. Blanket releases of information obtained from patients before treatment are not sufficient.

Accrediting bodies such as the Joint Commission on Healthcare Organizations and state mental and public health agencies have examined inpatient charts. More recently, however, because of expanded ambulatory care, greater focus is being placed on the partial hospital setting. For this reason, the same protections and protocols should be developed for Medicare records in every level of care. When a release of information has not been obtained, a redacted version of the chart may be used for accrediting purposes. Redacted charts should ensure that no identifying information about the patient or other individuals is present.

□ **CASE EXAMPLE**

A 35-year-old woman was treated in a partial hospital setting for bipolar disorder. One of the precipitants for her current illness and treatment was the breakup of a relationship with her boss (her employer) who also provided health insurance for her. Her chart was obtained by an auditor hired by her employer to review the company's health insurance. Although the patient's name was redacted, the boss's name was not deleted from the chart. When the auditor discovered the information, he mentioned it to the boss, who became enraged. The auditor then told the patient, who filed a complaint against the treating psychiatrist.

Question

Was the psychiatrist unethical?

Discussion

Possibly. In an ideal world, the psychiatrist should have reviewed the chart personally (perhaps with the patient) before its review by the auditor. Recognizing how cumbersome and unrealistic this would be, protocols should be established to guard against such system failures.

Patient Advocacy

The ethical position statements of the medical and psychiatric professional associations clearly identify advocacy for the individual patient as a foremost principle (1,2). Yet acute care systems often contract for responsibility for the mental health-care needs of a "population" of patients. When a fixed (prepaid) budget exists, a system of care will need to allocate or prioritize patient care expenditures. Like public systems that operate on an annual fixed budget, private (profit and nonprofit) behavioral health-care systems may not be able to provide all the care that may be medically desirable or perhaps even medically necessary. Although reinsurance can reduce financial loss, it operates only in catastrophic cases and would not be pertinent in day-to-day decisions.

If an acute care system has an allocation or rationing plan of care, it is ethically incumbent on the organization to inform consumers (patients) of the nature of its payment arrangement, unless the payer has already done so. Individual clinicians within a care system always have an ethical obligation to advocate for their individual patients. Systems must provide fair and impartial mechanisms to appeal utilization management decisions (e.g., engaging financially disinterested third parties or peer review committees). Risk-based systems of care will increasingly need to acknowledge the potential for disputes over needed treatment. Methods provided for resolving these conflicts must be considered trustworthy by today's increasingly educated and concerned health-care consumers.

Some systems of care have been designed to incorporate the ethical principle of justice. For example, some delivery systems provide more services to the severely mentally ill or charge this group a lower copayment. The Oregon health-care system allocates financial aid for the state's Medicaid and uninsured population based on a priority list of all health-care services. Just distribution of services can be problematic in managed care systems that underfund or otherwise unfairly allocate mental health and substance abuse services relative to other medical services.

Acute care systems may also be a part of a fully integrated health-care system. In these cases, clear obligations to the fiscal integrity of the overall system pertain. When an integrated model of care has a potential effect on patient care, there is an ethical obligation to disclose to patients, in an understandable manner, the patient's exposure. The underlying ethical principles of informed consent, full disclosure, and honesty should guide the conduct of the health-care system's management team. If possible, the burden for disclosure should be borne by the administrator of the system, not by the clinician. At times, however, only the clinician (especially in a psychiatric setting) may be able to discuss sensitively and appropriately these issues to a patient.

□ **C ASE E XAMPLE**

A psychiatrist was treating a 40-year-old man in outpatient psychotherapy. The patient was insured by a company that had a capitated arrangement with the hospital system that employed the psychiatrist. The psychiatrist asked the management of the care system for more intensive (outpatient) services during a period of clinical crisis for the patient. The initial utilization reviewer and psychiatric second-level reviewer declined the request.

Question

What should the psychiatrist have done?

Discussion

The psychiatrist had an ethical and medicolegal duty to appeal the management's utilization decision by all available appeal mechanisms. If the decision was based on budgetary considerations (allocated services or rationing), the patient should be informed of that fact in the decision-making process. In the ideal world of full disclosure of conflicts of interest (previously discussed), the patient would already have been informed of the health-care system's conflict of interest.

□ **C ASE E XAMPLE**

The same psychiatrist in the previous example becomes aware that the criteria for treatment appeared to vary by different contractual arrangements that the care system has with its payers.

Question

Did the psychiatrist have an ethical obligation to share that knowledge? If so, with whom?

Discussion

The psychiatrist had an ethical obligation to protest a system of care he or she believed to be unjust. If the psychiatrist believed that participation in the care system would lead to improvements resulting in the ethical acceptability of the system, he or she should continue to participate ethically. Each psychiatrist must decide individually the time and the degree of ethical dissatisfaction that would warrant terminating from a system of care and/or informing the care system's management and any involved patients.

RELATIONSHIPS AMONG MENTAL HEALTH PROFESSIONALS

The acute care of patients frequently requires multiple caregivers or teams of professionals to provide adequate treatment. Teams that traditionally were used in inpatient settings are now being used in the continuum of acute care (i.e., partial hospital and intensive outpatient treatment programs). Coordinating care to ensure quality is of paramount importance. Each mental health professional can provide services relative to their training and licensure; trainees can do so with necessary supervision. No provider should be asked or allowed to provide services that are beyond his or her licensure or capabilities unless adequate supervisory safeguards are in place. Psychiatrists should not delegate to nonmedical personnel decisions that require medical judgment. Conversely, psychiatrists should not perform tasks for which they have not been adequately trained or for which they do not have the appropriate credentials (e.g., psychological testing).

Adequate time and appropriate compensation should be available to allow multiple professionals involved in a patient's treatment to collaborate on their respective roles. Impediments to collaboration may lead to lapses in care, discontinuity, and other quality problems with potential adverse effects on patients. To the extent that systems of care do not support and encourage collaboration, significant ethical problems for the providers in that system can occur.

Many managed behavioral health-care companies provide internal case management when a patient has multiple providers. The providers should be given an opportunity to discuss their respective parts of the treatment and to assert what they believe to be medically necessary care. As noted above, time and compensation should be supported to avoid disincentives for collaboration.

Acute care systems must have adequate psychiatric and medical backup and oversight for the proper care of acute patients. Many of these patients have dual psychiatric diagnoses or medical comorbidity; some may require intensive medical interventions. For quality treatment to occur, adequate time for communication must be given to all health-care professionals involved in treatment. As part of a care system's quality improvement efforts, key care indicators should be measured, written and other forms of necessary clinical communication should be monitored, trends should be followed, and interventions should be developed when care or communication appears to be compromised.

Interference in the Doctor-Patient Relationship

Acute treatment often involves multiple caregivers to ensure patient safety and to provide intensity and quality of service.

Personnel who are not clinically involved in the care may still play a role (e.g., utilization review, case management, and other administrative duties). Unlike the traditional private practice setting, a team approach to treatment may define the psychiatrist's role more narrowly. Unless primary care physicians have additional training and assume greater risk, psychiatrists will most likely continue to see patients who are more severely mentally ill and patients who require complex pharmacologic consultation and treatment. To the extent that psychiatrists and managed care organizations are willing to accept a marginal or minimal role for psychiatrists, they will not be the captain of the ship; the team may have leadership but would lack medical leadership. This reduced role will most likely cause frustration and at times despair for most psychiatrists. Frustration for psychiatrists may be compounded by uncompensated time for case review. The potential for conflicted interactions among professionals without clear leadership and a specific dispute resolution system leaves all professionals and patients in vulnerable positions.

□ **C**ASE **E**XAMPLE

The case manager in an acute care system suggested to the treating psychiatrist that a 34-year-old patient with bipolar illness was ready for discharge to a less intensive level of care. Although the psychiatrist did not believe that the patient's condition was well stabilized, he agreed with the suggestion of the case manager.

Question

Was this ethical?

Discussion

No. The psychiatrist should have expressed his medical opinion to the case manager. The psychiatrist would be ethically and legally responsible if an adverse event occurred and it was determined that the psychiatrist did not exercise his professional judgment and appeal for the care he considered appropriate.

□ **C**ASE **E**XAMPLE

In the example above, the case manager (after receiving approval from the treating psychiatrist) discussed the case with the utilization review coordinator at the patient's insurance company. The utilization review coordinator suggested that even the level of care suggested by the case manager did not meet the level of care criteria of the insurance company. The case manager informed the treating psychiatrist.

Question

Was there any additional ethical obligation on the part of the case manager and the psychiatrist in this situation?

Discussion

Yes. The acute care system should have available all the level of care criteria and treatment protocols of managed care or insurance companies with whom they have contracted. Open criteria and protocols would provide important information for appeal of utilization review decisions and would allow appropriate documentation of differences of opinion. Documentation would be helpful if further appeals were needed and would help to protect both the acute care system and psychiatrist from ethical or legal action.

QUALITY TREATMENT

Acute care professionals and administrators must hold quality and compassionate treatment as the underlying principle shaping their actions. Current cost pressures will test the resolve of any care system and the patience and perseverance of professionals. Without a clear and firm view of what constitutes quality treatment, systems of care and professionals working within them will place themselves at both ethical and legal risk. Although few absolute written standards of care exist, practice guidelines for many psychiatric illnesses have been developed and approved by the APA. Some managed care systems use or refer to these guidelines, whereas others have developed their own. When a managed care company has developed guidelines that differ from those of professional organizations, the managed care organization should be prepared to defend itself on scientific grounds. Likewise, acute care systems and professionals within them should be able to refer to the guidelines of their professions as the basis for treatment decisions. When a treatment cannot be rendered based on cost constraints or benefit limits rather than medical guidelines, the denial of care should be discussed with the patient in an open and honest manner and be properly documented.

CONCLUSION

Acute care systems can work to achieve effective treatment at the lowest or most reasonable cost and can aim to provide easy and appropriate access to levels of care consistent with the needs of patients. Treatment within acute care systems must be competent, compassionate, and comprehensive. A system with a full continuum of care will allow for comprehensive treatment and minimize discontinuity among treatment professionals. As long as the focus is on scientifically established quality of care, there is every reason to believe that acute care systems and their professional staff members will uphold the highest ethics of medicine, psychiatry, and the other health professions.

REFERENCES

1. American Medical Association Council on Ethical and Judicial Affairs. Code of Medical Ethics Current Opinions, with annotations. 1994.
2. American Psychiatric Association. The principles of medical ethics with annotations especially applicable to psychiatry. Washington, DC: 1995.
3. American Psychiatric Association. Opinions of the ethics committee on the principles of medical ethics. Washington, DC: American Psychiatric Association, 1995.
4. Beauchamp TL, Childress JF. Principles of biomedical ethics. New York: Oxford University Press, 1994.
5. Daniels N. Just health care. Cambridge, MA: Cambridge University Press, 1985.
6. Pellegrino ED. The metamorphosis of medical ethics: a 30-year retrospective. JAMA 1993;269:1158–1162.
7. Morreim EH. Balancing act: the new medical ethics of medicine's new economics. Dordrecht, The Netherlands: Kluwer Academic Publishers, 1991.
8. Lazarus JA, Sharfstein SS. Changes in the economics and ethics of health and mental health care. In: Annual review of psychiatry. Washington, DC: American Psychiatric Press, 1994;13:389–413.
9. Sabin J, Daniels N. Determining medical necessity in Mental health practice. Hastings Cent Rep 1994;24:5–14.
10. Sharfstein SS. Assessing the outcome of managing costs: an exploratory approach. In: Mirin S, ed. Psychiatric treatment: advances in outcome research. Washington, DC: American Psychiatric Press, 1991.

Chapter 26

Assessing Quality of Care in Clinical Practice

Barbara Dickey and Lloyd I. Sederer

INTRODUCTION

Dramatic changes in how care is organized and financed have led to a reexamination of the processes and outcomes of treatment, especially inpatient treatment. What effect has this transformation in organization, financing, and delivery had on the quality of health care? Consumers and physicians worry that restrictions on treatment may diminish the quality of care. Conversely, payers and health system administrators view the transformation as an opportunity to manage resources and improve the quality of care efficiently. Quality is an important issue to all parties, yet it is difficult to obtain information about the level and appropriate measures of quality or the participants responsible for setting standards (1).

Traditional quality assurance programs are retrospective in design and do not meet today's standards for ensuring and improving quality (2). These evaluations were performed internally by hospital quality assurance committees and externally by peer review organizations. In the ab-

sence of validated criteria or outcome measures to assess quality, clinical activity was evaluated largely on the basis of structural criteria (e.g., facility and staffing characteristics) and reviews by professional peers. Although the Health Care Financing Agency was charged with linking the quality of care to the wise use of resources, this mandate was not matched by any authority to assess, much less constrain, how hospital resources were used. Utilization review was almost entirely retrospective and thus was unlikely to affect the appropriateness of care or the resources used during hospitalization.

Remarkably, the effectiveness of quality assurance programs has received little empiric scrutiny. In a 1988 review of quality assurance in mental health care, Zusman (3) observed that although an "overwhelming consensus" supported the idea that quality assurance activities improved the quality of care, no studies have actually demonstrated this improvement. Nevertheless, quality assurance programs have called attention to quality of care issues, spurred the development of criteria to assess quality, and legitimized peer review.

The convergence of two independent national events, the health-care reform debate and the growth of industrial quality control systems, has created an opportunity to improve quality in a time of diminishing resources. The highly competitive health-care environment is demanding more of physicians and other medical personnel at a time when every effort is being made to reduce expenditures (4). President Clinton's health-care debate sparked discussions about the relationship between quality of care and the cost of care: would constraints on health-care spending compromise quality? At the same time this debate was raging, the business world was accelerating the implementation in postwar Japan of a philosophy of management developed by Deming and Juran (5, 6). At the heart of this philosophy is consumer satisfaction, i.e., every employee must be engaged in efforts to continuously improve the company product or service. This management philosophy assumes that pleasing the customer translates into commercial success. Customers who are pleased with the value of the product or service will remain loyal customers. The link between Deming's continuous quality improvement (CQI) and the quality movement in health care lies in promoting the policy of managed competition between systems of care (4). Deming's answer to competition (satisfying the customer) and his view of organizational problems (systems, not people were to blame) fit this new way of thinking about heathcare delivery.

This chapter reflects Deming's belief that data should drive the quality improvement process. It is also shaped by the work of Donabedian (7), a physician who has devoted his career to the study and application of quality of care assessment. This chapter describes the critical influence of these two approaches on current developments in quality improvement. At first glance, these methods may appear to be separate or parallel activities; however, they are actually variations on the same theme, sharing similar methodology. Each successive chapter section will build on the preceding section. The first section on profiling describes a generic approach to data gathering and analyses; the next discusses report cards, a specific type of profiling intended for public use. The last section offers illustrations of CQI activities based on profiling that can be implemented in a hospital or health-care system.

The provision of measurable quality in psychiatric services, especially acute care, has never been more essential. The professional covenant to care for the patient must be upheld if the challenge of cost control is to be met with professional integrity. In this chapter, the conceptual underpinnings of quality will be translated into user-friendly methods for quality assessment that can be used effectively in clinical practice.

DONABEDIAN AND THE FOUNDATION OF ASSESSMENTS OF QUALITY

Avedis Donabedian, who has influenced the field of quality assessment perhaps more than any other scholar, still holds center stage after more than 25 years of scholarship (7). His work is conceptually and methodologically the most well developed and has become the standard for the design of quality of care research. He assumes that the highest quality of care is that which minimizes the risks and maximizes the benefits. Consequently, he first identifies benefits and risks to the patient as the primary factors in any assessment of quality. Second, he adds the dimension of volume of treatment over time to the definition. He argues that the risks and benefits associated with volume are not linear. At a certain point in time, a given volume of treatment results in maximum benefit; after that point, increases in treatment are not matched by equal increments of benefit. When volume of treatment is converted into costs, the net benefit to the patient is the sum of benefits minus risks and costs. This particular way of thinking about quality means that inefficiencies and unnecessary services reduce benefits.

Donabedian also developed a tripartite framework of the structure, the process, and the outcomes of health-care delivery that comprise quality of care (Fig. 26.1). This conceptual model can be applied to a study of the care of an individual or an entire health-care system. Structure refers to the characteristics of the delivery system (community, organizational, and provider characteristics) and the patient population (clinical and demographic characteristics). Process is the specification of procedures or treatment modalities provided to the patient. Process has two facets: the interpersonal aspects of care (i.e., the quality of the relationship between clinician and patient) and the technical aspects of care (e.g., the accuracy of diagnosis and the appropriateness of treatment). Outcomes

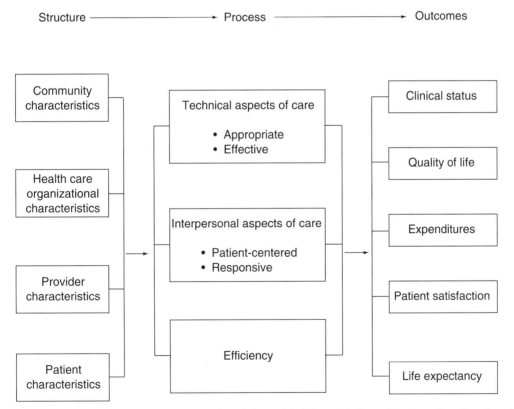

FIGURE 26.1.   Donabedian's conceptual model (modified from McGlynn EA. Domains of study and methodological challenges. In: Sederer LI, Dickey B, eds. Outcomes assessment in clinical practice. Baltimore: Williams & Wilkins, 1996).

of care include clinical and functional status, quality of life, expenditures, patient satisfaction, and life expectancy.

To avoid confusion about the meaning of concepts related to quality (such as criteria, standards, norms, and guidelines), Donabedian's nomenclature will be used. Criteria and standards are at the heart of efforts both to assess the quality of care and to manage resources (8). A criterion defines an aspect of care that can be counted, measured, or assessed in the course of evaluating interpersonal or technical quality. Criteria are drawn from the literature and from professional experience. To be useful, a criterion must have a range of values that can be interpreted as better or worse. A standard is the desired achievable performance for a given criterion, typically with a specified minimal level of acceptable performance. For example, a criterion for assessing the process of psychiatric hospitalization is the performance of a mental status examination. A standard would require all hospitalized patients to undergo such an evaluation. An acceptable level of performance might be the completion of mental status examinations in 95% of admitted patients.

Norms are statistically derived from the observations of a specific practice for a group of patients (such as inpatient episode length of stay). Norms are a referent in terms of performance and are typically presented as the mean and standard deviation. Data that fall above or below a range of scores around the mean (e.g., greater than 2 standard deviations) are outliers and might warrant peer review. Norms are sometimes called benchmarks in the context of CQI activities (see below).

Donabedian's concepts permit the complex interactions of health care to be operationalized into discrete variables for studying the cost-effectiveness of specific treatments, the efficiency of integrated delivery systems, and the equitable distribution of health-care resources among population subgroups. Building on Donabedian's theoretical framework over the past two decades, Brook and Lohr (9) have developed an operational model to evaluate the effectiveness, efficiency, and equity of health care and have applied their model to the study of medical care. More recently, two studies have described the benefits of Donabedian's approach in the context of evaluating the quality of mental health care (10, 11).

Donabedian and other analysts of quality, such as the Institute of Medicine, have emphasized the importance of multiple perspectives in quality assessment (12). The views of clinicians, third-party payers, consumers, and society all have a place in evaluating quality because each group has a unique perspective on what constitutes quality. Clinicians want to provide their patients with the best possible care, weighing the benefits and risks of each treatment. Payers, attempting to allocate limited health-care dollars judiciously, must focus on the costs of treatment decisions. Consumers seek the best care that is consistent with their preferences and lifestyles and want to be treated with dignity and respect. The societal perspective—shaped by the disciplines of public health, sociology, and economics—emphasizes the provision of adequate health care to the entire population within the cost constraints imposed by public and private payers (13).

PROFILING

Profiling is an analytical technique based on epidemiologic methods applied to health-care practice and patient outcomes (14). Unlike utilization management, which is primarily concerned with case-by-case assessment of medical necessity, profiling summarizes aggregate data that characterize populations served by health plans, institutions, or clinician groups. Profiling provides information about the accessibility of services, processes of care, clinical and functional outcomes, patient satisfaction, and costs (15). The findings from profiling can be traced to Donabedian's framework of structures, processes, and outcomes of care. Criteria exist for some of these aspects of care; in the absence of criteria, profiling can be based on statistical norms used to identify practices that diverge significantly from those that are typical.

A recent report of profiling, reported by Nelson et al. (16), concerns a quality improvement program initiated by a managed behavioral health-care organization. First, patient satisfaction with clinic services was assessed for a statewide network of clinics. Profiles developed from these data suggested wide variation in satisfaction from one clinic to another. Factor analysis was used to identify the aspects of care that best predicted overall satisfaction and to suggest specific areas for improvement. Second, the same clinics were profiled on their ability to meet treatment guidelines established by the managed care company. Results of the study found that clinics with high patient satisfaction rates were the same clinics that were providing treatment within the target guidelines. This finding was used to disseminate a Best Practice Project, led by the clinic with the best profile on both satisfaction and efficiency.

Another example of the use of profiling was recently reported in the *Boston Globe* (April 2, 1996), which rated HMOs on two dimensions—quality and satisfaction of beneficiaries. Quality was measured as the proportion of beneficiaries that were screened for cholesterol or the proportion who underwent mammography or had childhood immunizations. Seven plans were compared with each other, not against an industry or national benchmark, and the ratings were published along with the ratings of beneficiary satisfaction.

REPORT CARDS: ACCOUNTABILITY TO PURCHASERS OF CARE

Report cards are a brief, standardized form of profiling used to make comparisons among providers, health-care systems, and insurance plans. As a special case of profiling, these report cards are intended to be public information. Like all forms of profiling, they are at an early stage of development despite considerable attention in the media during the health-care reform debates of 1994 (17, 18). President Clinton's Health Security Plan included provisions for health plans to collect and report information about their quality of care. These report cards were to be used to hold plans accountable to purchasers of care and to consumers when choosing a plan. Below are four examples.

The first example was developed by The National Committee on Quality Assurance. This committee, composed of health plan administrators, physicians, and purchasers of health care, published a standardized list of performance measures called the Health Plan Employer Data and Information Set (HEDIS) (19). Like the other report cards described below, HEDIS relies primarily on measures of process that tended to be collected for other administrative purposes. The only indicator for mental health care is the percentage of inpatient admissions for depression that are followed by an outpatient visit within 30 days of discharge.

A second example was based on the concerns of corporate purchasers of care. The Foundation for Accountability (FACT) is a new foundation that aims to measure the value of employer-purchased health care. Charter members of FACT are GTE, Xerox, and Digital, with other large corporations supporting an accountable system of quality care. FACT developed a guidebook for performance measures and assesses the following five key conditions: asthma, breast cancer, diabetes, low back pain, and depression. The five domains identified for measurement are functioning, clinical outcomes, satisfaction, care processes, and cost.

Two more examples of report cards focused on mental health exclusively. One was created by a task force of consumers, researchers, and state mental health policy makers, appointed by the federally supported Mental Health Statistics Improvement Project (20). The task force described the report card as oriented toward consumers, based on value, concerned with serious mental illness, and conscious of cost and burden. Each domain is organized into three sections— the concern to mental health consumers, the indicator of that concern, and the measurement method to be used. The domains and their measurement are summarized in Appendix 26A.

The American Managed Behavioral Healthcare Association developed Performance Measures for Managed Behavioral Healthcare Programs (PERMS) as standards for voluntary data reporting (21) (Appendix 26B). The PERMS consists of three domains—access to care, patient satisfaction, and quality and appropriateness of care. Access to care included diagnosis-specific rates of use, such as hospital bed days per 1000 covered lives. Satisfaction is based on responses to a short questionnaire applied to a sample of treated patients. Quality and appropriateness are evaluated by measuring the following rates: treatment failure following substance abuse detoxification, outpatient

treatment 30 days after discharge, quarterly medication visits by psychiatrists for individuals with schizophrenia, inclusion of family members in the treatment of children, and time-limited treatment of adjustment disorders.

IMPROVING PROFILING AND REPORT CARDS

To be useful, profiles and report cards need to be improved in several ways (18). Donabedian's framework for assessing quality includes both process and outcome dimensions, but to date measures of process are far more likely to be collected. This is not surprising because these data are far more easily obtained. However, availability is not the same as utility. Many of these process measures, when used alone, cannot provide comparison data (e.g., good or bad, better or worse). Process measures must be reported together with clinical and functional outcomes to achieve the goals of treatment, i.e., evaluating the maintenance of health and ameliorating illness. Norm-based statistical analyses can identify practices that are outliers, relative to the average, but their significance remains unclear. For example, a profile might specify the number of psychotherapy sessions provided per patient and compare visit rates among providers. However, there is little agreement on the optimal number of sessions for a given disorder.

The addition of patient outcome data would be a necessary but not sufficient step toward improving comparisons of quality of care. Outcome data first must be adjusted for differences in the beneficiaries of health care. The variation among patient populations, demographics (case mix), and severity of illness (risk adjustment) must be considered if profiling is to be used in a meaningful way. Differences in patient characteristics, such as age, sex, and socioeconomic status, may result in significant variation in use of services and outcomes. Even more important, clinical factors such as differences in diagnosis, severity of illness, and comorbidity among patient populations can lead to different patterns of care and outcomes. Failure to account for case mix and risk factors can result in erroneous conclusions about the quality of care (22, 23). Data on demographic characteristics are usually available (if sometimes inadequate); however, methods for measuring the severity of illness have been difficult to construct (24).

The lack of availability and quality of data are other limitations. Many report cards are based on administrative (claims) data, i.e., basic demographic and diagnostic information collected by managed care organizations, insurance plans, and healthcare systems. Although administrative data are increasingly used to determine rates of use and patterns of care, limited clinical information of uncertain accuracy is provided, and only services covered by a specific plan or system are recorded. Benefit claims are susceptible to biases in the coding of clinical data in response to reimbursement pressures (17, 24). Moreover, available data may not be representative of the patient and provider populations being profiled. Finally, data from private insurance claims are often proprietary and rarely available to researchers, consumer groups, or purchasers of care. These data are the basis of indicators that measure administrative rather than clinical performance and focus on process rather than outcome.

The highly competitive nature of the health-care environment today makes reporting systems, especially those that are made public, potentially a high-risk venture. The possibility of the publication of relatively unfavorable scores on indicators of quality may lead an institution or health plan to protect itself from this exposure. High-risk patients may be referred elsewhere, or institutions may focus on ensuring that the types of care specific to the report card indicators are adequate to receive high marks and neglect other aspects of quality. Individual providers are at greatest risk. Reports of an individual performance could ruin a career if the results are not carefully adjusted for patient severity of illness. In psychiatry, however, such adjustments are in an early stage of development.

Evidence obtained from other medical specialties suggests that these potential limitations may be minimized and that report cards, as intended, will improve the quality of care. For example, the public reporting of mortality data specific to certain surgical procedures in New York state has had a positive effect in the reduction of mortality rates, although the number of high-risk patients increased by 73% (24).

CQI

Profiling data can be used within mental health-care organizations to improve the quality of care. The concept of data-based monitoring of the processes of care is integral to CQI, an industrial quality-control model that has become increasingly influential in medicine as services are consolidated into large systems of care (5, 6). CQI (or total quality management [TQM]) is based on assumptions that health-care services are provided within a system; members at all levels of the system are focused on improving the quality of the "product" delivered to the "customer." Data analysis is used to identify systemic problems, and improvement comes from participation in the CQI process at every level within the system. In contrast to one-time audits, CQI is intended to promote ongoing improvement.

Psychiatric hospitals and other health-care organizations are turning to CQI to improve services and increase efficiency (25). In keeping with the CQI approach, Nelson et al. (26) have proposed that profiling data be presented as instrument panels rather than report cards. Although report cards evaluate performance on selected aspects of care, they are static and retrospective, much like pupil report cards in school. Hospital administrators and clinical directors need more immediate feedback to improve their performance. The instrument panel, used for frequent systematic reporting, is designed to scan visual representation of performance quickly and to identify deviations from the expected profile. (An example of an instrument panel is provided below.) Availability of feedback can lead to immediate action to restore practice to meet institutional standards. This is important for hospital administrators or unit managers who need this information for real-time monitoring, planning, and ongoing improvement in the quality of care (26).

Patient satisfaction is increasingly recognized as essential to the evaluation of the quality of mental health care (27–29). Research indicates that satisfaction is also related to the perceived competence of the provider, the amount and clarity of information given, and the accessibility and convenience of care (30). Moreover, recognition of the consumer's perspective (rather than the provider's) has been urged by payers, patients, and advocates. As instruments for patient evaluations of care are refined and standardized, comparisons of patient satisfaction among hospitals and systems will be possible (30). One study demonstrated that differences among systems of ambulatory care (health maintenance organization, group practice, and solo or single-specialty practice) could be detected using a nine-item quality-of-care rating scale completed by patients (31).

Undoubtedly, market forces will lead to increased attention to patient satisfaction. Physician shopping, health plan disenrollment, complaints, and compliance with treatment have all been linked to dissatisfaction with the quality of care (32).

CQI in Clinical Practice

CQI offers clinical managers the opportunity to integrate structural, process, and outcome data into a dynamic information system for guiding clinical practice. Within the CQI principles of identifying problems, designing interventions, and measuring success, profiling systems can be designed to enhance care and outcomes. McLean Hospital in Belmont, Massachusetts, has developed such a system. Instrument panel reports are prepared on a regular schedule. A summary of each clinical unit's performance is provided based on the following sets of indicators: the clinical outcomes of care, as self-reported by patients using the BASIS-32 measure (see below); the interpersonal excellence of care, as measured by patients completing the Perceptions of Care; the percentage of admissions that result in readmissions within 30 days; and the quantification of adverse events, such as medication errors, seclusion and restraint, and patient and staff accidents. The goal of this system is to maximize outcomes and the interpersonal aspects of care while minimizing readmissions and adverse events.

Outcomes of Care: BASIS-32

The BASIS-32 was designed to assess outcome of mental health treatment from the patient's point of view (33, 34). It is a brief but comprehensive measure of self-reported difficulty in the major symptom and functioning domains that lead to the need for acute psychiatric and substance abuse treatment. The wording of the items is based on patients' responses to questions related to the reasons for their hospitalization. BASIS-32 has five subscales: relation to self and others, daily living skills, depression and anxiety, impulsive and addictive behavior, and psychosis (Appendix 26C). At McLean, the automated version is used to permit the measure to be scored and reported in the graphic format for the immediate use of the clinical staff.

Interpersonal Excellence: Perceptions of Care

Patients are the best informants of the interpersonal quality of their care. The patient's perspective provides less direct information about technical aspects of care (e.g., the accuracy of the diagnosis) but allows patients to comment on the nature of their relationship with the staff members and physician. The Perceptions of Care (PoC) measure, also developed at McLean Hospital, is included in the patient discharge planning packet. The PoC asks patients to rate specific aspects of the staff-patient relationship, specific aspects of staff-patient communication, coordination of care, outcome of care, and overall quality of care (Appendix 26D).

This 18-item scale provides specific information about patient interactions with staff members so that specific problems can be identified and actions can be taken to reduce the problem areas. For example, patient reports of poor information about hospital policies and procedures provided to them by their clinical team can immediately translate into CQI staff education efforts. Open-ended comments are also elicited, and patients are asked to name staff members that have been especially helpful. Based on the results, staff members are asked to devise unit-based initiatives to enhance the quality of care in areas that need improvement.

Readmissions Within 30 Days

This measure, similar to the HEDIS 2.5 measure, assesses the level of readmissions within 30 days, an indicator that can clearly be interpreted as a poor rather than a good outcome. The reasons for the returns are not so easily determined without additional information. Readmission might signify poor quality of clinical care on the inpatient unit, poor discharge planning, poor adherence to a good discharge plan, or in some cases a completely unavoidable situation.

A CQI team at McLean Hospital studied the readmission level in one unit and coupled the data with information from the same patients about their outcomes and perceptions of care. The resulting analyses led staff members to identify high-risk patients and design a special relapse prevention program as a targeted intervention in addition to their usual follow-up care. Continued monitoring of the same data over the next few months indicated that the intervention was associated with a lower readmission rate.

Adverse Events

The level of adverse events is another indicator used regularly to assess the quality of clinical practice. Adverse events have been defined as frequency and amount of seclusion and restraint, staff and patient injuries, medication errors, patient assaults, escapes, self-inflicted injury, and patient and family complaints. These events are reported quarterly.

Reporting Results

McLean Hospital uses two reporting mechanisms. McLean Reports is a report card that is widely distributed to the mental health community. It provides information on the four main indicators of

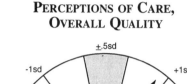

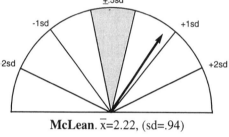

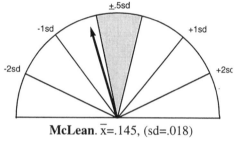

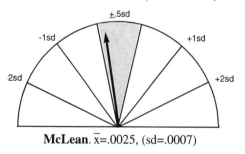

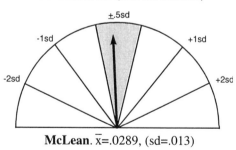

FIGURE 26.2.   An instrument panel developed by McLean Hospital.

performance (BASIS-32 outcomes, perceptions of care, readmission rates, and adverse events). A second reporting mechanism is used internally. Four times a year, the medical and nursing directors of each clinical program receive an instrument panel report that evaluates their program (relative to the hospital as a whole) on the following four measures of quality: clinical outcomes, interpersonal aspects of care, readmission within 30 days, and selected adverse events. These data are provided to staff members in a timely manner and focus on CQI projects.

As an example of the McLean instrument panel, Figure 26.2 depicts 6 of 12 indicators of quality reported on a regular basis and illustrates how a large amount of data can be simply summarized in graphic format.

The McLean report card approach to CQI is still in development. Case mix and risk adjustment of the data were performed during special studies, but the data shown in Figure 26.2 have not been adjusted. In addition to developing risk-adjusted data reporting, future plans for the report card include incorporating measures of efficiency. The cost of care is vitally important to prospective purchasers and should be included with other measures of quality. As pressure to reduce costs rises, concerns about quality also rise; clinicians must be able to carefully monitor the benefits, risks, and volume of treatment. It is essential to recognize when too little care (low volume) compromises quality or when unnecessary care (high volume) attenuates value if patients and payers are to be assured of obtaining the best quality of care with the utmost efficiency.

CONCLUSION

Methods already exist to assess the quality of care in clinical practice, but three steps must be taken before an organization can develop a data-based CQI plan. First, the organization must have a hospital information system that supports the CQI efforts. Second, trained personnel must be dedicated to the tasks involved. Third, the clinical leadership must develop an environment that encourages this activity. Despite the many difficulties that cost-containment presents, this era of change offers unparalleled opportunities to demonstrate the value of mental health treatment.

GLOSSARY OF TERMS

Continuous Quality Improvement

Continuous quality improvement (CQI) is an industrial quality control model that has become increasingly influential in medicine. CQI (or total quality management [TQM]) rests on assumptions that health-care services are provided within a system, that members at all levels of the system are focusing on improving the quality of the "product" delivered to the "customer," that data analysis is identifying systemic problems, and that improvement comes from participating in the CQI process at every level within the system.

Criterion

The discrete, clearly definable, predetermined phenomenon that one counts or measures to assess quality of care. Criteria are sometimes referred to as indicators.

Norms

The general rule about what constitutes goodness with respect to each criterion or phenomenon. For example, that the presence of a criterion is better than its absence, or that a larger quantity is better than a smaller one. Norms are sometimes defined as the usual observed performance.

Outcomes

Outcomes are the measurable results of patient care and can contribute to our judgment about quality of care.

Process

Process refers to the technical and interpersonal aspects of treatment. Its measurement also contributes to our judgment of quality of care.

Profiling

Profiling is an analytical technique based on epidemiologic methods applied to health-care practice and patient outcomes. Profiling summarizes aggregate data that characterize populations served by health plans, institutions, or clinician groups.

Quality of Care

Quality is a judgment about the technical and interpersonal aspects of treatment for an episode of care. Technical care consists of the application of medical science and technology in a manner that maximizes benefits without increasing risks. Interpersonal care relates to the management of the relationship between clinicians and patients and the extent to which these relationships meet the values, norms, and expectations of both parties.

Report Card

Report cards are a brief, standardized form of profiling used to make comparisons among providers, health-care systems, and insurance plans. As a special case of profiling, these report cards are intended to be public information.

Standard

Standard constitutes an acceptable or optimal goodness, or range of acceptable variation, with regard to each phenomenon under study.

Structure

Structure of care, one of three aspects of quality of care, refers to the characteristics of institutions and providers as well as to the demographic and clinical attributes of the patients served.

ACKNOWLEDGMENTS

The authors thank Susan V. Eisen, Richard Hermann, and LouAnn Muir-Hutchinson for their contributions to our thinking about this subject.

REFERENCES

1. Palmer RH. Considerations in defining quality of health care. In: Palmer RH, Donabedian A, Povar GJ, eds. Striving for quality in health care: an inquiry into policy and practice. Ann Arbor, MI: Health Administration Press, 1980.
2. Povar GJ. What does quality mean? Critical ethical issues for quality assurance. In: Palmer RH, Donabedian A, Povar GJ, eds. Striving for quality in health care: an inquiry into policy and practice. Ann Arbor, MI: Health Administration Press, 1980.
3. Zusman J. Quality assurance in mental health care. Hosp Community Psychiatry 1988;39:1286–1290.
4. Enthoven AC. The history and principles of managed competition. Health Aff 1993; 12(Suppl):24–48.
5. Deming WE. Out of the crisis. Cambridge: MIT, Center for Advanced Engineering Study, 1986.
6. Juran JM. Juran on planning for quality. New York: Free Press, 1988.
7. Donabedian A. Explorations in quality assessment and monitoring: the definition of quality and approaches to its assessment. Ann Arbor, MI: Health Administration Press, 1980;1.
8. Donabedian A. Explorations in quality assessment and monitoring: the criteria and standards of quality. Ann Arbor, MI: Health Administration Press, 1982;2.
9. Brook RH, Lohr KN. Efficacy, effectiveness, variations, and quality: boundary crossing research. Medical Care 1985;23:710–722.
10. McGlynn EA, Norquist GS, Wells KB, et al. Quality-of-care research in mental health: responding to the challenge. Inquiry 1988;25:157–170.
11. Wells KB, Astrachan BM, Tischler GL, et al. Issues and approaches in evaluating managed mental health care. Milbank Q 1995;73:57–75.
12. Lohr KN, ed. Medicare: a strategy for quality assurance: source and methods. Washington, DC: National Academy Press, 1990.
13. Cochrane AL. Effectiveness and efficiency: random reflections on health services. Nuffield Provincial Hospitals Trust, 1972.
14. Keller RB. Physicians and profiling. Group Pract J 1992;41:63–67.
15. Brand DA, Quam L, Leatherman S. Data needs of profiling systems. Physician payment review commission. Conference on Profiling, No. 92–2. Washington, DC: PPRC, 1992.
16. Nelson DC, Hartman E, Ojemann PG, et al.

Outcomes measurement and management with a large Medicaid population: a public-private collaboration. Behav Health Care 1995;4:31–37.

17. Epstein A. Performance reports on quality: prototypes, problems and prospects. N Engl J Med 1995;333:57–62.

18. United States Accounting Office. Health care reform: report cards are useful but significant issues need to be addressed. Publication GAO/HEHS-94–219. Washington, DC: General Accounting Office, 1994.

19. Report card pilot project: technical report. Washington, DC: The National Committee for Quality Assurance, 1994.

20. Mental Health Component of a Health Plan Report Card. MHSIP task force on design of the mental health component of a health plan report card under national health care reform. Washington, DC: Center for Mental Health Services, 1994.

21. American Managed Behavioral Healthcare Association. PERMS 1.0 performance measures for managed behavioral healthcare programs. Washington, DC: Quality Improvement and Clinical Services Committee of the American Managed Behavioral Healthcare Association, July 1995.

22. Iezzoni LI, Restuccia JD, Schwartz M, et al. The utility of severity of illness information in assessing the quality of hospital care. The role of the clinical trajectory. Med Care 1992;30:428–444.

23. Chassin MR, Hannan EL, De Bunono BA. Benefits and hazards of reporting medical outcomes publicly. N Engl J Med 1996;334:394–398.

24. Iezzoni LI. Data sources and implications: administrative data bases. In: Iezzoni LI, ed. Risk adjustment for measuring health care outcomes. Ann Arbor, MI: Health Administration Press, 1994.

25. Waxman HM. Using outcomes assessment for quality improvement. In: Sederer LI, Dickey B, eds. Outcomes assessment in clinical practice. Baltimore: Williams & Wilkins, 1996.

26. Nelson EC, Batalden PB, Plume SK, et al. Report cards or instrument panels: who needs what? J Qual Improv 1995;21:155–165.

27. Kalman TP. An overview of patient satisfaction with psychiatric treatment. Hosp Community Psychiatry 1983;34:48–54.

28. Larsen D, Attkisson C, Hargreaves W, et al. Assessment of client/patient satisfaction: development of a general scale. Eval Prog Planning 1979;2:197–207.

29. Lebow J. Consumer satisfaction with mental health treatment. Psychol Bull 1982;91:244–259.

30. Cleary PD, McNeil BH. Patient satisfaction as an indicator of quality care. Inquiry 1988;25:173–192.

31. Rubin HR, Gandek B, Rogers WH, et al. Patients' ratings of outpatient visits in different practice settings: results from the Medical Outcomes Study. JAMA 1993;270:835–840.

32. Ware JE, Davies AR. Behavioral consequences of consumer dissatisfaction with medical care. Eval Prog Planning 1983;6:291–297.

33. Eisen SV, Dill DL, Grob MC. Reliability and validity of a brief patient-report instrument for psychiatric outcome evaluation. Hosp Community Psychiatry 1994;45:242–247.

34. Eisen SV. Assessment of subjective distress by patients' self-report versus structured interview. Psychol Rep 1995;76:35–39.

Appendix 26A

Consumer-Oriented Mental Health Report Card

Final Report of the MHSIP Task Force, April 1996

ACCESS

Quick and Convenient Entry Into Services

Concern: Entry into mental health services is quick, easy and convenient.

Rationale: Quick, convenient entry into the healthcare system is a critical aspect of the accessibility of services. Delays can result in inappropriate care or an exacerbation of distress. If a person's problem is related to behavioral health, the time it takes to have contact with a mental health professional, rather than a professional with some other expertise, is a critical component of appropriate treatment.

Access 1: *The average length of time from request for services to the first face-to-face meeting with a mental health professional.*

Measure: The total time between request for services and the first face-to-face contact with a mental health professional for new admissions during the year, divided by the total number of new admissions.

Notes: This will be reported separately for emergent and non-emergent situations, and will also be reported separately for the following groups: children and adolescents with serious emotional disturbances, children and adolescents with other emotional disturbances, adults with serious mental illnesses, adults with other mental illnesses, and adults with a dual diagnosis of a mental illness and substance use disorder.[1]

An emergent situation is defined as one in which a person is in imminent danger to self or others or has a grave disability as a result of mental illness. A mental health professional is defined as a psychiatrist, psychologist, social worker, psychiatric nurse practitioner, marriage and family therapist, provider with specialty certi-

---

[1]This category may have to be broken down further into adults with *serious* mental illnesses and substance use disorders and adults with *other* mental illnesses and substance use disorders.

fication in mental health counseling from the National Board of Certified Counselors.

Source: Enrollment/encounter data.

Access 2:   *The percentage of consumers for whom the location of services is convenient.*

Measure: Consumer response to a survey question regarding location:
- The location of services was convenient (parking, public transportation, distance, etc.).

Note: The response format for all items on the consumer survey is a 5-point continuous scale from strongly agree to strongly disagree. The indicators based on this instrument are computed as the percentage of recipients who respond strongly agree or agree (or for those items that are reverse coded, those that respond strong disagree or disagree).

Source: Consumer survey.

Access 3:   *The percentage of consumers for whom appointment times are convenient.*

Measure: Consumer responses to a survey question regarding convenience:
- Services were available at times that were good for me.

Source: Consumer survey.

Access 4:   *The percentage of consumers who report that physicians, mental health therapists, or case managers can be reached easily.*

Measure: Consumer response to a survey question regarding provider availability:
- Staff returned my call within 24 hours.

Source: Consumer survey.

A Full Range of Service Options

Concern: A full range of mental health service options is available.

Rationale: The indicators below clearly do not reflect the full range of service options. They are indirect indicators of the extent to which a mental health system is (1) responsive to service needs articulated by enrollees, and (2) able to deliver on its actual or implied promises. However, if resources expended on services important to consumers, including consumer-run services and services in natural settings, are increasing (or are relatively high), this would reflect that a full range of services is probably in place.

Access 5:   *The average resources expended on mental health services.*

Measure: The total amount of direct service expenditures on mental health services in one year, divided by the total number of full-time enrollees who received at least one mental health service.

Note: This will be computed separately for the following groups: Children and adolescents with serious emotional disturbances, children and adolescents with other emotional disturbances, adults with serious mental illnesses, adults with other mental illnesses, and adults with a dual diagnosis of a mental illness and substance use disorder.

Source: Enrollment/encounter data; cost/expenditure data.

Access 6:   *The proportion of resources expended on mental health services that are consumer-run.*

Measure: The total amount of expenditures on consumer-run mental health services in one year, divided by expenditures on mental health services.

Source: Enrollment/encounter data; cost/expenditure data.

Access 7:   *The proportion of resources expended on mental health services provided in a natural setting (home, school, and work).*

Measure: For child and adolescent enrollees only: the total amount of direct service expenditures on mental health services that are provided in the child's home in one year, divided by the total amount of direct service expenditures for children and adolescents.

Source: Enrollment/encounter data; cost/expenditure data.

Access 8:   *The percentage of consumers for whom services are readily available.*

Measure: Consumer response to survey questions regarding availability:
   ◆ I was unable to get the services I thought I needed.
   ◆ I was able to see a psychiatrist when I wanted to.
   ◆ Staff were willing to see me as often as I felt it was necessary.

Source: Consumer survey.

Cultural and Linguistic Access

Concern: Enrollees have access to a primary mental health provider who meets their needs in terms of ethnicity, language, culture, age and disability.

Rationale: This concern identifies the degree to which cultural and linguistic barriers might affect access to services. The consumer survey item is a direct measure of this concern. A comparison of utilization rates across population groups is an indirect measure of a potential problem in this area. If compatibility is an obstacle, the problem group would be expected to have a higher rate of one and only one visit (which suggests dropouts), and a lower rate of one or more visits, compared to other groups. Of course, there are other possible interpretations for this type of outcome, and some effort should be made to assess potential differences among clients that might account for variations in service use.

Access 9:   *The percentage of consumers who report that staff are sensitive to their ethnicity, language, culture, and age.*

Measure: Consumer response to a survey question regarding staff sensitivity:
   ◆ Staff were not sensitive to my cultural/ethnic background.

Source: Consumer survey.

Access 10: *The percentage of people served in a year who had only one mental health contact.*

Measures: (a) For each of the following age, sex and ethnic groupings: the total number of enrollees receiving one mental health service in the past year, divided by the total number of enrollees.
Age: 0–21, 22–64, 65+
Sex: Male, female
Ethnicity: (I) White, African-American, Asian, other
              (II) Hispanic, non-Hispanic

(b) For the same age, sex, and ethnic groupings: the total number of enrollees receiving *one and only one* mental health service in the past year, divided by the total number or enrollees receiving *one or more* mental health services in the same year.

Source: Enrollment/encounter data.

Access 11: *The percentage of people receiving Supplemental Security Income (SSI) or Social Security Disability Insurance (SSDI) benefits who received services.*

Measure: For enrollees who are also enrolled in SSI or SSDI: the total number of people receiving at least one mental health service in the past year, divided by the total count of this group.

Source: Enrollment/encounter data.

Financial Barriers

Concern: The out-of-pocket costs to enrollees do not discourage the use of necessary mental health services.

Rationale: Access barriers may be caused by system characteristics, including the cost of services. A consumer's inability to pay for care should not limit access to needed services.

Access 12: *The percentage of consumers for whom cost is an obstacle to service utilization.*

Measure: Consumer response to a survey question regarding financial barriers:
 ◆ I was unable to get some services I wanted because I could not pay for them.

Source: Consumer survey.

APPROPRIATENESS

Voluntary Participation in Services

Concern: People using mental health services do so voluntarily and in collaboration with service providers. The use of involuntary mental health intervention is minimized.

Rationale: Involuntary mental health interventions are usually counterproductive and often lead to lasting trauma. They erode the consumer's ability to make decisions and to act responsibly, and they are antithetical to fostering cooperative, trusting relationships between consumers and health professionals. Involuntary treatment may create or exacerbate problems or signs of illness (e.g., paranoia), and it may have the unintended effect of creating resistance to mental health interventions in general.

The proportion of recipients who report actively participating in their service plans is an indirect measure of the extent to which treatment and services are voluntary. The proportion of enrollees who report feeling coerced into treatment or services is an indirect measure of the extent to which treatment and services are involuntary. The proportion of involuntary admissions for psychiatric inpatient treatment is an explicit measure of the extent to which treatment and services are involuntary.

Appro. 1:   *The percentage of consumers who actively participate in decisions concerning their treatment.*

Measure: Consumer response to survey questions regarding treatment:
- I, not staff, decided my treatment goals.
- I felt comfortable asking questions about my treatment and medication.

Source: Consumer survey.

Appro. 2:   *The percentage of consumers who feel coerced into treatment options or services.*

Measure: Consumer response to survey questions regarding treatment:
- Staff behaved as if I cannot choose what is best for me.
- I felt free to complain.

Source: Consumer survey.

Appro. 3:   *The percentage of admissions for psychiatric inpatient treatment that are involuntary.*

Measure: The total number of inpatient admissions in which a recipient is admitted involuntarily, divided by the total number of inpatient admissions in a 12-month period.

Source: Enrollment/encounter data.
[Alternative: If not available on information systems, include the following on the consumer report items form:
During the past 12 months, were you admitted to a psychiatric hospital when you did not want to go?   Yes____ No____]

Services That Promote Recovery

Concern: The mental health provider or system offers services that promote the process of recovery.

Rationale: There is an emerging distinction between services that address the acute symptoms of mental illnesses and those that promote long-term recovery. Services that promote recovery include psychiatric and psychosocial rehabilitation services that help people manage their illnesses and participate in their communities. Services that are focused on recovery should be an important component of any plan that serves people with serious mental illnesses.

Appro. 4:   *The proportion of resources expended on services that promote recovery.*

Measure: The total amount of unduplicated expenditures in one year on psychiatric and/or psychosocial rehabilitation services (e.g., housing support, vocational services/supported employment, consumer-run services, family education, etc.) for adult enrollees with serious mental illnesses, divided by the total amount of expenditures for mental health services. (This excludes case management services).

Source: Enrollment/encounter data.

Appro. 5:   *The percentage of consumers who receive services that support recovery.*

Measure: The response of consumers with serious mental illness to survey questions regarding services that promote recovery:
  ◆ Staff here believe that I can grow, change, and recover.
  ◆ Staff encouraged me to take responsibility for how I live my life.
  ◆ Staff helped me obtain the information I needed so that I could take charge of managing my illness.
  ◆ I was encouraged to use consumer-run programs (support groups, drop-in centers, crisis phone lines, etc.).

Source: Consumer survey.

Services that Maximize Continuity of Care

Concern: The mental health provider or system maximizes continuity of care.

Rationale: Disruptions in the provision of care are generally considered to be harmful. Three types of continuity are represented below. The first two, requiring prompt follow-up of inpatient or emergency care with outpatient services, are important to avoid the recurrence of acute symptoms and to move the process of recovery forward. The third assumes that any change in therapist, regardless of the cause, will impede recovery because of the need to start over with a new provider.

Appro. 6:   *The percentage of people discharged from inpatient services who receive ambulatory services within 7 days.*

Measure: The total number of discharges from psychiatric inpatient care during the past year that were followed by at least one outpatient (non-emergency) care visit within 7 days, divided by the total number of all discharges from psychiatric inpatient care during the past year.

Source: Enrollment/encounter data.

Appro. 7:   *The percentage of people discharged from emergency care who receive ambulatory services within 3 days.*

Measure: The total number of emergency psychiatric encounters during the past year that were followed by at least one outpatient (non-emergency) care visit within 3 days, divided by the total number of all emergency psychiatric encounters during the past year.

Source: Enrollment/encounter data.

Appro. 8:   *The percentage of service recipients who had a change in principal mental healthcare provider during the year or term of treatment.*

Measure: The total number of service recipients who had a change in principal mental healthcare provider during the year or term of treatment, divided by all mental health service recipients during the year.

Source: Enrollment/encounter data.

Consumer Involvement in Policy Development, Planning, and Quality Assurance Activities

Concern: People using mental health services have meaningful involvement in program policy, planning, evaluation, quality assurance, and service delivery.

Rationale: The indicator below provides a measure of consumer and family member involvement based on the structure and staffing patterns of the health plan. Meaningful involvement in the design, implementation, and delivery of behavioral health care services requires active participation by consumers and family members.

Appro. 9:   *The percentage of enrollees who are adult consumers and family members who serve on planning and development groups or hold paid staff positions in the health plan.*

Measures: (a) The total number of full-time staff positions (either direct care or administrative) that are occupied by consumers of mental health services, divided by the total number of full-time direct care and/or administrative staff.

(b) The amount of the mental health budget expended on peer advocates, divided by the total mental health budget.

(c) The total number of mental health consumers on planning, evaluation, and Total Quality Management teams, divided by the total membership of these groups.

(d) The total number of family members on planning, evaluation, and Total Quality Management teams, divided by the total membership of these groups.

Note: For purposes of these measures, consumers are defined as enrollees who have received or are currently receiving mental health services.

These measures assume that the provider's database includes measures of administrative structure, such as the number of planning committee members and paid staff who are identified consumers.

Source: Enrollment/encounter data.
[Alternative: If information is not available on information systems, include the following on the consumer report items form:
Does the agency providing you mental health services include consumers on its:

Advisory committees?	Yes____ No____ Don't know____	
Planning groups?	Yes____ No____ Don't know____	
Evaluation groups?	Yes____ No____ Don't know____	
Quality improvement teams?	Yes____ No____ Don't know____]	

Adequate Information to Make Informed Choices

Concern: Service recipients receive information that enables them to make informed choices about services.

Rationale: The participation of service recipients in treatment decisions contributes to positive outcomes. In order to enhance consumers' inclusion in the therapeutic process, they must have the information necessary to make informed choices about their care.

Appro. 10:   *The percentage of consumers who receive adequate information to make informed choices.*

Measure: Consumer response to survey questions regarding adequate information:
- I felt comfortable asking questions about my treatment and medication.
- I was given information about my rights.
- Staff told me what side effects to watch for.

Source: Consumer survey.

Application of Best-Practice Guidelines

Concern: Services are delivered, where possible, in accordance with known and accepted best-practice guidelines.

Rationale: Given the large number of people who have major depression, and the fact that APA guidelines exist for the treatment of this illness, the percentage of consumers receiving treatment that does not follow these guidelines becomes very meaningful.

Appro. 11:   *The percentage of service recipients whose treatment follows accepted, best-practice guidelines.*

Measure: The total number of adults with a diagnosis of depression who received medication at the range specified by American Psychiatric Association (APA) guidelines, divided by the total number of adults with the same diagnosis who were prescribed medication.

Source: Enrollment/encounter data; patient records.

OUTCOMES

Physical Health[2]

Increased Access to General Healthcare

Concern: Mental health service recipients have equal access (relative to the general population) to effective, general healthcare.

Rationale: Studies indicate that people with mental illnesses have poor access to general healthcare. This often compounds their mental health problems and makes recovery difficult. Although having an annual physical is not equivalent to adequate medical care, it is a minimal indication that the physical health needs of these individuals are being addressed.

Differential mortality due to medical causes may serve as a red flag, indicating that people with serious mental illnesses are not getting the same degree of aggressive, effective medical care as the general population. Restriction of the age range to 35 to 50 years avoids confounding effects of aging. Suicides are excluded because rates are expected to differ, and differential rates would therefore not be an indication of differential medical care. Higher death rates due to suicide among people with psychiatric disabilities should be separated from higher death rates due to medical problems. Since accident-related deaths might mask some suicides, such deaths are also excluded.

---

[2]The outcomes listed follow the World Health Organization typology of physical health, psychological health, level of independence, and social relationships.

Outcomes 1: *The percentage of people with mental illnesses who are connected to primary care.*

Measure: The total number of people with mental illnesses who received a physical exam during the past 12 months, divided by the total number of adult service recipients who received a physical exam during the past 12 months.

Note: This will be computed separately for the following groups: children and adolescents with serious emotional disturbances, children and adolescents with other emotional disturbances, adults with serious mental illnesses, adults with other mental illnesses, and adults with a dual diagnosis of a mental illness and substance use disorder.

Source: Enrollment/encounter data; patient records. [Alternative: If not available on information systems, include the following on the consumer report items form: Have you had a physical exam in the last 12 months? Yes____ No____]

Outcomes 2: *The differential evidence of mortality due to medical causes for service recipients who have/do not have serious mental illnesses.*

Measure: The total number of mental health service recipients between the ages of 35 and 50 who died during the last 12 months by specific cause (excluding suicide and accidents), compared with the same measure for non-mental health service recipients.

Source: Enrollment encounter data; patient records (both should include the cause of death for all enrollees).

Minimal Negative Outcomes from Treatment

Concern: Service recipients experience minimal, adverse iatrogenic effects.

Rationale: Tardive dyskinesia is considered to be among the most serious negative side effects resulting from prolonged use of neuroleptic medications. This disorder can cause irreversible neurological symptoms and may complicate treatment of disorders like schizophrenia, which are usually accompanied by problems with social isolation. Clinical studies have found elderly patients to be a particularly high risk. Since this disorder is caused by medications commonly used to treat severe psychotic symptoms, it qualifies as an important iatrogenic effect.

Outcomes 3: *The average level of involuntary movements resulting from the use of psychotropic medications for specified service recipient groups.*

Measure: For consumers with a history of taking neuroleptic medication, the average change score from an initial evaluation, compared to subsequent evaluations taken at annual intervals, using the Abnormal Involuntary Movement Scale (AIMS).

Notes: The initial evaluation (baseline score) is obtained three months after beginning neuroleptic medications, or, for individuals who have been taking neuroleptic medications for at least three months, at the time of program enrollment.

For purposes of this measure, the baseline score will consist of the sum of each of the first seven scale items: Facial and Oral Movements (four items), Extremity Movements (two items), and Trunk Movements (one item).

Source: The AIMS.

Psychological Health

Reduced Psychological Distress

Concern: The level of psychological distress from symptoms is minimized.

Rationale: Symptom level is distinct from symptom distress. Currently, symptom level is assessed by the mental health service provider, while symptom distress is usually reported by the consumer. For this reason, level of distress was selected to represent most closely whether an individual's symptoms are relieved following treatment. There may be individuals for whom self-reported psychological distress may not be an appropriate measure (e.g., children, people receiving involuntary treatment).

Outcomes 4:   *The percentage of consumers who experience a decreased level of psychological distress.*

Measures: The proportion of adults with mental illnesses who report a decreased level of psychological distress at selected intervals after admission for mental health treatment, according to the symptom distress scale:

(a) During the past 7 days, about how much were you distressed or bothered by:
- nervousness or shakiness inside
- being suddenly scared for no reason
- feeling fearful
- feeling tense or keyed up
- spells of terror or panic
- feeling so restless you couldn't sit still
- heavy feeling in arms or legs
- feeling afraid to go out of your home alone
- feeling of worthlessness
- feeling lonely even when you are with people
- feeling weak in parts of your body
- feeling blue
- feeling lonely
- feeling no interest in things
- feeling afraid in open spaces or on the streets

Notes: The response format is a 5-point continuous scale from not at all to extremely. Adults with serious mental illnesses, adults with other mental illnesses, and adults with a dual diagnosis of a mental illness and a substance use disorder will be asked to complete the symptom distress instrument at admission, following three months of mental health services, every 12 months thereafter, and at discharge.

    For purposes of this measure, admission is defined as the point at which an individual enters a mental health program to receive services for a current mental health episode. This would not include admission to a facility due to organizational changes in the system.

(b) The proportion of children and adolescents for whom there is a decreased level on the Child and Adolescent Functional Assessment Scale (CAFAS) Moods/Emotion subscale.

Note: This will be measured for children and adolescents with serious emotional disturbances and children and adolescents with other emotional disturbances.

Source: (a) Symptom distress scale (clinician administered), adapted from the SCL-90 and BSI.

(b) CAFAS for children and adolescents.

Increased Sense of Personhood

Concern: Service recipients experience an increased sense of personhood.

Rationale: Personhood is emerging as a critical concept and goal in the treatment of serious mental illnesses. It subsumes dignity, self-respect, self-mastery, self-esteem, and self-worth. The Rosenberg Self-Esteem Scale is a surrogate measure of this concept, but its fundamental nature should be reflected in any set of mental health outcomes being proposed.

Outcomes 5:   *The percentage of consumers who experience an increased sense of self-respect and dignity.*

Measure: The proportion of service recipients with serious mental illnesses who report an increase in sense of self-esteem based on the Rosenberg Self-Esteem Scale (11 items):

   ◆ I feel that I am a person of worth, at least on an equal basis with others.
   ◆ I feel that I have a number of good qualities.
   ◆ All in all, I am inclined to feel that I am a failure. (reverse coded)
   ◆ I am able to do things as well as most other people.
   ◆ I feel that I do not have much to be proud of. (reverse coded)
   ◆ I take a positive attitude toward myself.
   ◆ On the whole, I am satisfied with myself.
   ◆ I wish I could have more respect for myself. (reverse coded)
   ◆ I certainly feel useless at times. (reverse coded)
   ◆ At times, I think that I am no good at all. (reverse coded)
   ◆ There is really no way I can solve some of the problems I have. (reverse coded)

Note: This scale assumes at least two points of measurement, and rates of change are typically slow. It will, therefore, be necessary to repeat this measure at two predetermined intervals over a one-year period.

Source: Consumer response to the Rosenberg Self-Esteem Scale.

Level of Independence

Reduced Impairment from Substance Abuse

Concern: Enrollees experience minimal impairment from use of substances.

Rationale: Increased functioning is an important objective for people with mental disorders. This concern focuses on level of functioning related to alcohol or drug use.

Outcomes 6:   *The average level of impairment in service recipients with substance abuse problems.*

(a) The rate of all adults receiving services in the mental health system who are identified with substance use "greater than or equal to 3" on the Clinical Alcohol and Drug Use Scale.

(b) The proportion of children and adolescents for whom there is a decreased level on the CAFAS Substance Abuse subscale.

Source: (a) Clinical Alcohol and Drug Use Scale (clinician administered) for adults.

(b) CAFAS for children and adolescents.

Increase in Productive Activity

Concern: Enrollees experience minimal interference with productive activity, such as work, school, or volunteer activities, as a result of alcohol, drugs, and/or mental disorders.

Rationale: The economic loss resulting from alcohol, drug, and mental disorders is substantial. For the working population, as well as for their employers and other payers, a frequent and important goal of treatment is to maintain productivity. School attendance is an important aspect of role functioning for school-age children and adolescents. Attendance is a coarse but minimal measure of school functioning. Productive activity is an important component of role functioning and is typically assessed in health services outcomes research. The final indicator in this concern, taken from a widely used, consumer self-report measure of health status, taps a broader domain of productive activity than employment, and thus applies to a wider population of adults.

Outcomes 7: *The proportion of people with serious mental illnesses involved in competitive employment.*

Measure: Annual percentage figures based on positive consumer response to each of two questions:
- During the past three months, have you worked at any time for at least minimum wage?
- If so, did you do this work for any amount of time at least four weeks in a row?

Note: Because people with serious mental illnesses often begin work gradually and/or have an intermittent work history, a broad definition of employment is necessary. A narrow definition would exclude those who are just beginning their working life, or those who have been working recently but are currently unemployed. As more consumers become employed in competitive situations, the operational definition might be narrowed, or an indicator reflecting change in employment activity might be added.

Source: Consumer report items form.

Outcomes 8: *The average change in days of work lost.*

Measure: The response of employed adults with other mental illnesses to the following question:
- During the last four weeks, how many days did you miss work?

Note: The number of days lost as reported at follow-up is subtracted from days lost as reported at intake; this change score is averaged across respondents.

Source: Consumer report items form at entry into services and again at three months or at termination, whichever comes first.

Outcomes 9:   *The increase in the level of school performance.*

Measure: The proportion of children and adolescents for whom there is an increase after three months on the CAFAS School Performance subscale.

Source: CAFAS for children and adolescents.

Outcomes 10:   *The extent to which alcohol, drugs, or mental problems interfere with productive activity.*

Measure: The response of individuals without serious mental illnesses to the following question from the SF-36 scale:
During the past four weeks, have you had any of the following problems with your work or other regular daily activities as a result of any emotional problems (such as feeling depressed or anxious)?
- Cut down on the amount of time you spent on work or other activities?
- Accomplished less than you would like?
- Didn't do work or other activities as carefully as usual?

Source: Consumer report items form.

Capacity for Independent Community Living

Concern: Enrollees function in community settings with optimal independence from formal service systems.

Rationale: Independent community living is a goal frequently endorsed by people with serious mental illnesses. Though housing status is affected by a wide variety of factors, systems that address and support independent community living are expected to show higher ratios on this measure than systems that do not. Improvement in a consumer's housing situation is an indirect measure of the degree to which a mental health provider or system promotes independent community living for people with serious mental illnesses. Maintaining children successfully and safely at home is a valued outcome for both children and their families. In addition, at-home treatment typically is less expensive than out-of-home placements.

Outcomes 11:   *The percentage of children with serious emotional disturbances placed outside the home for at least one month during the year.*

Measure: The total number of children with serious emotional disturbances placed in any setting outside of the home for at least one month over the period of one year, divided by the total number of children with serious emotional disturbances served by the plan during the same year.

Source: Enrollment/encounter data.

Outcomes 12:   *The percentage of adults with serious mental illnesses living in residences they own or lease.*

Measure: At the time of annual reporting, the total number of adults with serious mental illnesses currently living in residences they own or lease, divided by the total number of adults with serious mental illnesses currently being served by the plan.

Source: Enrollment/encounter data.

Outcomes 13:   *The percentage of consumers whose housing situations improve as a direct result of treatment.*

Measure: The response of consumers with serious mental illnesses to a survey question regarding housing:
- As a direct result of services I received, my housing situation has improved.

Source: Consumer survey.

Increase in Independent Functioning

Concern: Service recipients experience increased independent functioning.

Rationale: Mental health services are expected to improve a person's ability to respond to problems, crises, and everyday situations they encounter.

Outcomes 14:   *The percentage of consumers who experience an increased level of functioning.*

Measures: (a) For children and adolescents, results of CAFAS.
(b) For adults, consumer response to survey questions regarding independent living:
As a direct result of services I received:
- I deal more effectively with daily problems.
- I am better able to control my life.
- I am better able to deal with crisis.
- I have become more effective in getting what I need.
- I can deal better with people and situations that used to be a problem for me.

Source: (a) CAFAS for children and adolescents
(b) Consumer survey for adults.

Reduced Involvement in the Criminal Justice System

Concern: People with mental illnesses should experience reduced involvement in the criminal justice system.

Rationale: An increasing number of people with mental illnesses are involved, often inappropriately, with the criminal justice system. This is even more likely to happen when budget cuts make it difficult to access appropriate services. Although this item may not be reported accurately by consumers, the possibility of matching mental health and criminal justice system records was considered too onerous.

Outcomes 15:   *The percentage of people who were in jail last year.*

Measures: (a) The total number of adults with serious mental illnesses who report spending some time in jail during the past year, divided by the total number of adults with serious mental illnesses served during the past year.
(b) The change in proportion of children and adolescents involved with the legal system as reported on the CAFAS.

Source: (a) Consumer reports items form.
(b) CAFAS for children and adolescents.

Participation in Self-Help Activities

Concern: Recipients take an active role in managing their own illnesses.

Rationale: Participation in self-help activities helps consumers better manage illness or disability. Such activities include informal interaction with fellow consumers, regular participation in self-help or support groups, and individual reading and self-education. The Task Force recognizes the importance of self-help activities and the significant role a mental health provider or system can play in promoting and supporting such endeavors.

Outcomes 16: *The percentage of consumers who are involved in self-help activities.*

Measure: Consumer response to questions regarding their participation in self-help activities:

♦ Do you participate in a self-help group or support group? (For example, AA, NA, depression support group, family support group, etc.)
Yes_____ No_____
♦ Does your plan provide you with written information about mental illness?
Yes_____ No_____
♦ Do you share information about mental illness with others?
Yes_____ No_____

Source: Consumer report items form.

Minimal Recurrence of Problems

Concern: People experiencing an episode of acute psychiatric illness receive care that reduces the likelihood of a recurrence within a short period of time.

Rationale: Given the increasingly limited use of psychiatric inpatient care, hospitalization most likely indicates an acute episode of illness. An important goal of mental health treatment is to minimize such episodes. Avoiding the recurrence of acute illness within 30 days of discharge is an important benchmark of effective mental health treatment.

Outcomes 17: *The percentage of inpatient readmissions that occur within 30 days of discharge.*

Measure: The total number of admissions to psychiatric inpatient care that occurred within 30 days of a discharge from psychiatric inpatient care during the past year, divided by the total number of all discharges from psychiatric inpatient care during the past year.

Source: Enrollment/encounter data.

Positive Changes (in Areas for Which Treatment is Sought)

Concern: Services result in positive changes in problems as defined by consumers.

Rationale: People seek help with their illness to get relief from symptoms or to better handle certain aspects of their everyday lives. This indicator measures whether the desired outcome has been achieved.

Outcomes 18:   *The percentage of consumers who report positive changes in the problems for which they sought help.*

Measure: Consumer response to the following question:
                   You came to our program with certain problems. How are those problems now?

Source: Consumer report items form.

Social Relationships

Increased Natural Supports and Social Integration

Concern: Service recipients experience increased natural supports and social integration.

Rationale: An individual's ability to have friends and a support network separate from the mental health system is critical to reducing dependence on case managers, therapists, and other care providers. In times of crisis, individuals may first seek assistance from friends, relatives, and other community members if these contacts have been developed.

Outcomes 19:   *The percentage of consumers who experience increased activities with family, friends, neighbors, or social groups.*

Measures: (a) For adults, consumer response to the following questions from the SF-36 scale:
                   ◆ During the past four weeks, to what extent has your physical health, emotional problem, and/or psychiatric disability interfered with your social activities with family, friends, neighbors, or groups?
                   ◆ During the past four weeks, how much of the time has your physical health or emotional problems interfered with your social activities (like visiting with friends, relatives, etc.)?

Note: The response format is a 5-item continuous scale from not at all to extremely for the first question, and from none of the time to all of the time for the second question.
                   (b) Also for adults, consumer response to the following survey questions regarding support and integration:

As a result of services I received:

- I am getting along better with my family.
- I do better in social situations.
- I do better with my leisure time.

(c) For children and adolescents, caregiver responses to the CAFAS and change in the CAFAS Behavior Toward Others subscale.

Source: (a) SF-36 items for adults.

(b) Consumer survey for adults.

(c) CAFAS for children and adolescents.

PREVENTION

Recent research on preventing mental disorders has set aside an earlier framework based on primary, secondary, and tertiary prevention in favor of one defined in terms of universal, selective, indicated preventive interventions.[3] These are described in brief below.

Universal preventive measures are those that can apply to the general public. Examples include information about mental health risk factors, stress management and moderation in use of alcohol and other drugs.

Selective preventive measures are directed toward apparently healthy individuals who are at elevated risk for developing mental disorders because of factors that include age, hazardous social setting, or an experience such as bereavement.

Indicated preventive measures are directed toward those individuals who show signs of increased risk for developing mental disorders; e.g., people engaged in high-risk use of alcohol, or children with school behavior problems who live in high-risk family setting.

Although the long-term goal of prevention is a reduction in the incidence of mental disorders (i.e., reduction in the occurrence of new cases), short-term strategies aim to reduce those risk factors that make certain individuals more likely than others to develop a mental disorder. Particular preventive interventions are typically focused on a single developmental stage, but prevention activities as a whole are relevant throughout the life cycle.

Research on the prevention of mental disorders is still in its infancy. It is too early to identify specific screening activities that will highlight risk factors for which effective interventions are known. Nonetheless, because early evidence indicates that many preventive efforts are useful, they should be incorporated in any comprehensive mental health treatment program. Currently, such activities can be monitored by determining how much a mental health provider or system spends on disseminating universal preventive information, and by the degree to which its members participate in selective and indicated intervention.

Apart from efforts to prevent illness, those activities that promote wellness (e.g., programs to enhance self-esteem) may be fundamental to preserving mental health. However, in the absence of empirical knowledge about their effectiveness, the Task Force has not incorporated health promotion activities in the formal evaluation of provider performance. To the extent that future research demonstrates their relevance, they should be included.

---

[3]Institute of Medicine (Patricia J Mrazek and Robert J. Haggerty, Editors.) *Reducing Risks for Mental Disorders: Frontiers for Preventive Intervention Research.* Washington, DC: National Academy Press, 1994.

Information Provided to Reduce the Risk of Developing Mental Disorders

Concern: Enrollees are provided information that helps lower their risk of developing mental and/or substance use disorders.

Rationale: The indicator below focuses on the degree to which health plans provide information designed to help enrollees make informed choices about their behavior. Such interventions are typically universal.

Prevent 1: *Expenditures per enrollee on dissemination of preventive information.*

Measure: Expenses incurred in developing and disseminating information about stress, depression, family communication, substance use, associated risk factors, and availability of support or educational groups or other structured interventions for people at risk, divided by all enrollees in the plan.

Notes: To measure this effort, mental health providers must track costs for these activities. Where such information is not available, acceptable methods for providing valid estimates will have to be specified.

Source: Administrative information systems/reports.

Interventions Designed to Reduce the Risk of Developing Mental Disorders

Concern: Individuals at risk are provided specific programs that enable them to reduce their risk of developing mental disorders.

Rationale: The indicator below addresses the degree to which health plans take explicit steps to reduce the risk of developing mental disorders among people with known risk factors.

Prevent 2: *The percentage of enrollees participating in selected or indicated preventive programs.*

Measure: The total number of enrollees with identified risk factors who are enrolled during a one-year period in mutual help and other support programs; programs for people with job loss, bereavement, and subclinical depressive symptoms; and skill and other developmental programs for youth at risk of substance abuse or childhood behavior problems, divided by the total number of enrollees during the same one-year period.

Note: To measure this activity, providers would have to track enrollment in these interventions. Typically, these activities are not covered healthcare services and are, therefore, not included in encounter data. Although including them in shadow data systems might be ideal, alternative data sources would include an ad-hoc survey of providers within a plan or a survey of enrollees.

Source: Administrative information systems/reports.

Appendix 26B

PERMS 1.0:

Performance Measures for Managed Behavioral Healthcare Programs Produced by the Quality Improvement and Clinical Services Committee of the American Managed Behavioral Healthcare Association, July 1995[1]

The Measures

I. ACCESS TO CARE

  A. Utilization-Based Indicators:

    1. Overall Penetration Rate

    The percentage of enrollees who have a MH or CD claim for a face-to-face visit within a one-year period of time. If the exact number of enrollees is unknown (i.e., no premium billing), employers will be asked to provide a number which converts the number of contracts into the number of covered lives. If employers are unable to provide such a number, a dependent to enrollee ratio of 2.3 will be assumed for calculating the number of covered lives.

    2. Overall Penetration Rate by Age and Diagnostic Category

[1]Copies of this report can be obtained by contacting: AMBHA, 700 Thirteenth Street, NW, Suite 950, Washington, DC 20005.

3. **Penetration Rate by Treatment Setting, Age and Diagnostic Category**
4. **Penetration Rate by Clinician Type**

   The percentage of enrollees with a MH or CD claim within a one-year period for a face-to face visit by the following types of clinicians:

   a. M.D. psychiatrist
   b. Ph.D. psychologist
   c. Master's level clinician (LCSW, Nurse, Psychologist)

5. **Outpatient Utilization**

   a. The average number of outpatient visits per patient who utilizes outpatient services by age and diagnostic category in a twelve month period.
   b. Outpatient visits per thousand covered lives by age and diagnostic category in a twelve month period.

6. **Inpatient Utilization**

   a. Inpatient discharges per thousand by age and diagnostic category in a twelve month period.
   b. Average length of stay by age and diagnostic category in a twelve month period.
   c. Inpatient days per thousand by age and diagnostic category in a twelve month period.

7. **Intensive Alternatives to Inpatient Care**

   Patient encounters per thousand for intensive alternatives to inpatient care by age and diagnostic category in a twelve month period.

8. **Cost Data for Severely and Persistently Mentally Ill**

   For patients with a psychotic or bipolar diagnosis only (ICD-9 codes 295, 296.4, 296.5, 296.6, 296.7, 296.8., 296.9, 298, and 299):

   a. The amount of their inpatient expenses[2] divided by the total amount of their expenses in a one-year period.
   b. The amount of their outpatient expenses divided by the total amount of their expenses in a one-year period.
   c. The amount of their intensive alternatives to inpatient care expenses[3] divided by the total amount of their expenses in a one-year period.
   d. The amount of their residential expenses[4] divided by the total amount of their expenses in a one-year period.

   Note: Utilization and expenses should be annualized using the following type of formula for patients who are not in the system for a full twelve months:

   $$\frac{\text{Expenditure}}{\text{\# enrolled months}} \times 12$$

   This indicator is intended to show the composition of expenses for a group of individuals with severe and persistent mental illness. A mix of treatment settings would be desirable in this case, as opposed to all inpatient or all outpatient care.

B. **Structural Indicators:**

   1. **Call Abandonment Rate**

      Percent of calls abandoned < 5 percent.

   2. **On-Hold Time**

      Percent of calls on hold < 30 seconds.

---

[2]Inpatient care is defined as a 24-hour stay in a facility licensed for acute hospital care.
[3]Intensive alternatives to inpatient care include partial, day, evening, and intensive outpatient programs.
[4]Residential care is defined as a 24-hour stay in a facility licensed for subacute or residential care.

3. Call Answer Time

Percent of calls answered in less than 5 rings.

II. CONSUMER SATISFACTION

A. Access

1. Satisfaction with Time Interval to 1st Appointment.

B. Intake

1. Degree of Satisfaction with Intake Worker.

C. Clinical Care

1. Degree of Satisfaction with Therapist.

2. Willingness to Recommend Therapist/Program.

D. Outcome

1. Self-Assessment of Outcome.

E. Global Satisfaction

1. Rating of Overall Satisfaction.

III. QUALITY OF CARE

A. Effectiveness

1. Ambulatory Follow up After Hospitalization for Major Affective Disorder

Given a discharge from inpatient treatment for adults with Major Affective Disorder, there is evidence of follow-up outpatient treatment within 30 days of hospital discharge. A measure of delivery system effectiveness in ensuring continuity of care.

2. Treatment Failure—Substance Abuse

The proportion of cases with a substance abuse detoxification service within 90 days of a detoxification service in programs with a substance abuse rehabilitation benefit. A measure of system ineffectiveness.

B. Efficiency

1. Continuity of Care—Mental Health

Given a psychiatric inpatient discharge, the proportional distribution of cases in four follow-up status categories in a period of 30 days following discharge. These categories are: (1) no follow-up, (2) follow-up contact, (3) contact plus readmission to a psychiatric inpatient unit and (4) readmission only. A measure of system utilization of the continuum of care for mental health patients.

2. Continuity of Care—Substance Abuse/Detoxification

Given an inpatient substance abuse detoxification discharge, the proportional distribution of cases in four follow-up status categories in a period of 30 days following discharge. These categories are: (1) no follow-up, (2) follow-up contact, (3) contact plus readmission to a substance abuse detoxification program and (4) readmission only. A measure of system utilization of the continuum of care for substance abuse patients.

C. Appropriateness

1. Availability of Medication Management—Schizophrenia

Given any one case with a diagnosis of schizophrenia during a calendar year, then also an activity (claim, authorization or encounter) for at least four visits for medication management or brief visit with psychiatrist.

2. Family Visit for Children 12 and under

Given any ambulatory treatment activity (claim, authorization, or encounter) for a child aged 12 years and younger, then also an activity (claim, authorization, or encounter) for a family visit.

3. **Appropriate Utilization of Resources—Adjustment Disorder**
   Given individual outpatient treatment for adults with adjustment disorder, the proportion with 10 or fewer visits.

Appendix 26C

BASIS-32™

Behavior and Symptom Identification Scale

NAME _____ I.D.# _____ Date _____

INSTRUCTIONS

Below is a list of problems and areas of life functioning in which some people experience difficulties. Using the scale below, WRITE IN THE BOX THE NUMBER that best describes THE DEGREE OF DIFFICULTY YOU HAVE BEEN EXPERIENCING IN EACH AREA DURING THE PAST WEEK.

> 0   no difficulty
> 1   a little
> 2   moderate
> 3   quite a bit
> 4   extreme

Please respond to each item. Do not leave any blank. If there is an area that you consider to be inapplicable, indicate that it is NO DIFFICULTY ("0").

Example

To what extent are you experiencing
difficulty in the area of <u>FRIENDSHIPS</u>: | 2 |

TO WHAT EXTENT ARE YOU EXPERIENCING
DIFFICULTY IN THE AREA OF:

1. MANAGING DAY-TO-DAY LIFE (e.g., getting
   places on time, handling money, making
   every day decisions)   ☐

2. HOUSEHOLD RESPONSIBILITIES (e.g., shopping, cooking, laundry, keeping room
   clean, other chores)   ☐

3. WORK (e.g., completing tasks, performance
   level, finding/keeping a job)   ☐

4. SCHOOL (e.g., academic performance,
   completing assignments, attendance)   ☐

WRITE THE NUMBER IN THE BOX

0 no difficulty
1 a little
2 moderate
3 quite a bit
4 extreme

TO WHAT EXTENT ARE YOU EXPERIENCING
DIFFICULTY IN THE AREA OF:

5. LEISURE TIME OR RECREATIONAL ACTIVITIES ☐

6. ADJUSTING TO MAJOR LIFE STRESSES (e.g., separation, divorce, moving, new job, new school, a death) ☐

7. RELATIONSHIPS WITH FAMILY MEMBERS ☐

8. GETTING ALONG WITH PEOPLE OUTSIDE OF THE FAMILY ☐

9. ISOLATION OR FEELINGS OF LONELINESS ☐

10. BEING ABLE TO FEEL CLOSE TO OTHERS ☐

11. BEING REALISTIC ABOUT YOURSELF OR OTHERS ☐

12. RECOGNIZING AND EXPRESSING EMOTIONS APPROPRIATELY ☐

13. DEVELOPING INDEPENDENCE, AUTONOMY ☐

14. GOALS OR DIRECTION IN LIFE ☐

15. LACK OF SELF-CONFIDENCE, FEELING BAD ABOUT YOURSELF ☐

16. APATHY, LACK OF INTEREST IN THINGS ☐

17. DEPRESSION, HOPELESSNESS ☐

18. SUICIDAL FEELINGS OR BEHAVIOR ☐

19. PHYSICAL SYMPTOMS (e.g., headaches, aches & pains, sleep disturbance, stomach aches, dizziness) ☐

WRITE THE NUMBER IN THE BOX

0   no difficulty
1   a little
2   moderate
3   quite a bit
4   extreme

TO WHAT EXTENT ARE YOU EXPERIENCING
DIFFICULTY IN THE AREA OF:

20. FEAR, ANXIETY OR PANIC ☐

21. CONFUSION, CONCENTRATION, MEMORY ☐

22. DISTURBING OR UNREAL THOUGHTS OR BELIEFS ☐

23. HEARING VOICES, SEEING THINGS ☐

24. MANIC, BIZARRE BEHAVIOR ☐

25. MOOD SWINGS, UNSTABLE MOODS ☐

26. UNCONTROLLABLE, COMPULSIVE BEHAVIOR
     (e.g., eating disorder, hand-washing,
     hurting yourself)   ☐
     SPECIFY_____

27. SEXUAL ACTIVITY OR PREOCCUPATION ☐

28. DRINKING ALCOHOLIC BEVERAGES ☐

29. TAKING ILLEGAL DRUGS, MISUSING DRUGS ☐

30. CONTROLLING TEMPER, OUTBURSTS OF ANGER
     VIOLENCE   ☐

31. IMPULSIVE, ILLEGAL OR RECKLESS BEHAVIOR ☐

32. FEELING SATISFACTION WITH YOUR LIFE ☐

Appendix 26D

Perceptions of Care

We would like to know your views about the mental health
services you received at this facility. We will use this
information to improve our quality of care.
We would like you to rate some things about your treatment
program in terms of whether they were
(1) Excellent (2) Very good (3) Good (4) Fair (5) Poor

Thank you very much. Your perceptions of care are very
important to us.

	EXCEL-LENT	VERY GOOD	GOOD	FAIR	POOR	DOES NOT APPLY
1. APPROPRIATENESS OF PROGRAM: how well the program you were in fit your needs	①	②	③	④	⑤	⑥
2. EXPLANATION OF RULES AND POLICIES: how well the rules and policies of the program were explained to you	①	②	③	④	⑤	⑥
3. INFORMATION ABOUT YOUR RIGHTS: amount of information you received about your rights as a patient	①	②	③	④	⑤	⑥
4. INFORMATION YOU WERE GIVEN: how clear and complete the explanations were about tests, treatment, and what to expect.	①	②	③	④	⑤	⑥
5. EASE OF GETTING INFORMATION: willingness of staff to answer your questions	①	②	③	④	⑤	⑥
6. CONSISTENCY OF THE INFORMATION YOU RECEIVED FROM STAFF	①	②	③	④	⑤	⑥
7. TEAMWORK AMONG STAFF WHO TREATED YOU	①	②	③	④	⑤	⑥
8. TIME STAFF SPENT WITH YOU	①	②	③	④	⑤	⑥
9. RECOGNITION OF YOUR OPINIONS: asking what you think and giving you choices	①	②	③	④	⑤	⑥
10. CONSIDERATION OF YOUR NEEDS: willingness of staff to be flexible in meeting your needs	①	②	③	④	⑤	⑥
11. CLINICAL STAFF'S UNDERSTANDING OF WHAT YOU THOUGHT WAS IMPORTANT	①	②	③	④	⑤	⑥
12. RESPECT AND DIGNITY SHOWN TO YOU	①	②	③	④	⑤	⑥
13. CONFIDENCE AND TRUST YOU FELT TOWARDS THE STAFF	①	②	③	④	⑤	⑥
14. COURTESY AND FRIENDLINESS OF STAFF	①	②	③	④	⑤	⑥
15. DISCHARGE INSTRUCTIONS: how clearly and completely you were told what to do and what to expect after leaving the program	①	②	③	④	⑤	⑥
16. COORDINATION OF CARE AFTER DISCHARGE: staff efforts to provide for your needs after leaving the program	①	②	③	④	⑤	⑥
17. OVERALL QUALITY OF CARE AND SERVICES YOU RECEIVED	①	②	③	④	⑤	⑥
18. THE OUTCOME OF YOUR CARE: how much you were helped by the care you received	①	②	③	④	⑤	⑥

Chapter 27

Professional Satisfaction and Compensation

Lloyd I. Sederer and Margaret T. Lee

PROFESSIONAL SATISFACTION

For the past decade a battle has been waged over the introduction of managed care into psychiatric practice. Initially efforts were made to forestall its advance and later to standardize and professionalize its practices. Today joint ventures between managed care and academia, hospitals, health systems, and practitioners are common occurrences.

Managed care has profoundly changed the locus of decision-making and control of professional practice. Choice over who cares for patients and how this occurs has been relocated from patients and clinicians to insurance corporations and managed care intermediaries.

As a consequence, psychiatrists and other mental health professionals find themselves explaining what they are doing to nameless and often lesser trained, but authoritative, individuals at the end of a telephone line thousands of miles away. To paraphrase an aphorism, psychiatrists who can no longer get what they want (for their patients and themselves) must try to get what they need. Professional satisfaction ranks high among their needs.

During the 1980s, three converging forces in the United States created the conditions for the phenomenal growth of managed health care through prepaid delivery systems and utilization review organizations (1–4). First, the absolute costs of health care grew remarkably, far in excess of the growth of the economy, yet did not provide insurance coverage for a significant proportion of the citizens. Second, the oversupply and maldistribution of physicians and hospitals fostered inefficiency, administrative waste, and unnecessary demand. Third, two decades of regulatory efforts failed to contain costs or to achieve an emerging national policy. Managed care or its heir, managed competition, promised to harness the healthcare industry and obtain the financial and clinical yield that payers (business and government) and consumers demanded. A redefinition of health care as an industry with products, distribution channels, and cost efficiencies further supported

543

managed care, which sold itself on the basis of managing costs, organizing distribution channels (the providers), and enhancing the quality and value of health care.

Identifiable trends in psychiatry were noted simultaneously. A national mail survey by the American Psychiatric Association (APA) revealed three principal trends: specialization, feminization (more women entering the field), and organizational diversification (5). Organizational diversification referred to a decline in the proportion of psychiatrists who identified private, office-based practice as their primary work setting. Notably, the proportion of psychiatrists reporting their primary work setting as an organization also increased. The growth of health maintenance organizations (HMOs), private psychiatric hospitals, and psychiatric units in general hospitals provided the opportunities for organizational diversification (6–9). Academic psychiatric departments were experiencing the advent of managed care, which extended the change from offices to university settings (10, 11). A half century of office-based and academic psychiatric practice was on the wane. The professional lives of psychiatrists, along with their sources of satisfaction, were changing.

The first section of this chapter reviews professional satisfaction in clinical situations largely extrinsic to psychiatry and also reports on satisfaction as it pertains to psychiatry. Although professional satisfaction can be a significant predictor of patient satisfaction and outcome, effective use of resources, continuity of care, and job performance, this subject seems to have received short shrift in the professional literature. The same can be said for the unprecedented influence of market dynamics in health care through the use of incentive compensation, which has re-

ceived only summary treatment. The second section of this chapter examines professional compensation and, in particular, certain models that have been proposed to explain physician behavior in response to payment systems.

Physician Satisfaction

Organizational and industrial researchers define satisfaction as an affective state "associated with the perceived difference between what is expected as a fair and reasonable return . . . and what is experienced . . . " (12). Hence, discrepancies between expectation and reality determine degrees of satisfaction or dissatisfaction. Because of the paucity of material on psychiatrist satisfaction, this chapter will first examine the literature on physician satisfaction and then consider publications relating to psychiatrists.

Aspects of Professional Satisfaction

Before the late 1970s, few empiric studies of satisfaction could be found beyond those examining factory or industrial personnel. Managed care did not exist, and psychiatrist satisfaction was not a topic of inquiry. However, in subsequent years, several studies were conducted that demonstrated methodologies for assessing professional satisfaction and an interest in studying satisfaction in organized systems of care.

In 1978, Stamps et al. (13) developed a seven-item scale by sampling physicians, nurses, and support staff in a private ambulatory group practice. Using factor analysis, the study identified pay, autonomy, task requirement, administration, interaction (social contacts), professional status, and the doctor-nurse relationship as the principal variables by which to study satisfaction.

To assess the satisfaction of physicians practicing in organized settings in the 1980s, Lichtenstein (14) developed a seven-faceted measure consisting of satisfaction with resources, self-directed autonomy (e.g., influence on pace of work and on organizational decisions), other-directed autonomy (e.g., alter practice to suit organization, answer to nonphysicians), patient relationships, professional relationships, status, and pay.

In a study of Canadian physicians practicing under national health insurance in the late 1980s, Kravitz et al. (15) used factor analysis to suggest the following four indices of satisfaction: quality of care, the rewards of practice (psychological and material, e.g., status, prestige, opportunities for advancement, income), patients, and practice environment (15). By the 1990s, for good reasons, the job satisfaction of physicians had become a subject of empiric investigation as we shall see below.

Professional Satisfaction and Its Effect on Patient Satisfaction and Clinical Outcome

To date, two studies conducted in the mid-1980s, one on physicians and one on nurses, may be the only available research that highlights the clinical and economic importance of professional satisfaction. Linn et al. (16) studied 16 internal medicine group practices in teaching hospitals. Those sites with more satisfied medical staff (and housestaff) were associated with more satisfied patients. High satisfaction scores for both physicians and patients indicated a consistent correlation with greater continuity of care, lower patient no-show rates, better use of ancillary staff (hence more efficient use of physician time), and more reasonable charges for follow-up visits.

The aesthetic environments of the practice settings were not associated with either patient or physician satisfaction.

Weisman and Nathanson (17) examined the job satisfaction of nurses in 77 family planning clinics using the two dependent variables of the satisfaction of teen-age patients with contraceptive services and their subsequent compliance with contraceptive prescriptions. The nursing staff's satisfaction was the best predictor of patient satisfaction, which in turn predicted patient use of the prescriptions provided. Although compliance was vulnerable to other variables, this study helped to establish that professional satisfaction can affect patient outcome.

Variables Affecting Physician Satisfaction

A number of studies have examined the variables affecting physician satisfaction. In the early 1980s, a study of academic and clinical faculty in a teaching hospital found both groups to be satisfied with their health status and life satisfaction but demonstrated differences in job satisfaction (18). Mean scores for the total sample indicated that physicians in both groups were most satisfied with the diversity of their patients, patient care, and educational stimulation. They were least satisfied with promotional opportunities, resources available, their role in making organizational decisions, and their ability to remain knowledgeable and current.

A small, cross-section of community physicians in the Midwest in the later 1980s was sampled by Reames and Dunstone (19) to identify problems, satisfaction, and problem-solving. This group of physicians cited the following principal problems: loss of control over decision-making and referral, threat of malpractice, ethical dilemmas facing physicians in

HMOs, and reduced income. However, those physicians who remained satisfied despite these problems attributed their happiness to personal, attitudinal adjustments rather than to success at the "business of medicine."

In a survey published in 1993, Lewis et al. (20) demonstrated that physicians who are highly satisfied with their work report higher satisfaction in marriage and less psychiatric symptomatology.

A number of studies of physicians reported dissatisfaction with various aspects of organizational employment; dissatisfaction was correlated with turnover, which could induce low morale and impair performance (21–28). Other studies have specifically examined the satisfaction of physicians in organized settings and under managed care. Lichtenstein (14) measured physician satisfaction in highly bureaucratic, prison health programs. His findings demonstrated that satisfaction was not a unitary phenomenon and that different facets of satisfaction such as status, pay, resources, and relationships should be considered to best understand and improve physician satisfaction. Kravitz et al. (15) studied physicians practicing under the Ontario Health Insurance Plan. Less satisfaction was associated with younger age, lower income, and the perception that it is difficult to be fairly reimbursed. Those physicians who were least satisfied were most likely to have participated in the 1986 Ontario province doctors' strike. In general, although the majority of physicians were satisfied, their greatest dissatisfaction was with their inability to make administrative decisions and to "manipulate the system for the benefit of their patients." (15).

Schulz et al. (29) concluded that—the bureaucratization of medicine notwithstanding—the satisfaction of primary care physicians was high in a setting in which 85% of all physicians were members of a single, closed panel HMO. They noted that " . . . physicians' expectations were found to be more negative than their experiences" (29). Perceived clinical freedom was a strong predictor of satisfaction. Both primary care physicians and specialists were generally satisfied. Importantly, the HMO was organized and controlled by the physicians, which suggests that management control may be important to physician satisfaction (30).

Baker and Cantor (31), in analyzing data from a survey of 4257 physicians younger than 45 years of age, concluded that managed care has not had the "deleterious impact" on medical practice that has been forecasted by its critics. Managed care was associated with lower levels of perceived autonomy in patient selection and allocation of time but was associated with higher levels of perceived autonomy in using inpatient care, tests, and procedures. HMO physicians were as satisfied as other physicians, although HMO specialists were more satisfied than generalists. Managed care was not associated with regrets among physicians for having chosen their field of medicine. The authors note, however, that the effect of a greater managed care influence might alter their findings.

Stamps and Cruz (32), in a text on physician satisfaction, provided an extensive review of the literature. Their findings supported earlier studies indicating that doctor-patient relationships are important to realizing professional satisfaction. They also found that the efficiency of and satisfaction with care provided by physicians is more important than the number of patients seen. In short, good doctor-patient relationships and effective, efficient work are more important than the amount of work required.

Psychiatrist Satisfaction

This review of physician satisfaction has been provided because remarkably few empiric studies exist to document psychiatrist satisfaction. The APA conducted two surveys of psychiatrists and peer reviewers in 1981 and 1982 to assess prevailing attitudes about peer review (33, 34). Although managed care is currently substituting networks and capitation for peer review as the primary means of managing care, the findings are notable. The first survey respondents reported that peer review verified claims, reduced abuse, and provided for the needs of the insurance companies (and, by inference, not those of patients or doctors). However, 61% of respondents rated peer review as favorable, 20% as neutral, and 19% as unfavorable. The second APA survey was limited to reviewers and concluded that those psychiatrists who were knowledgeable and involved in review were the most enthusiastic about this form of managed care.

The work by Schulz et al. (29) is the only other study that mentioned psychiatrists' attitudes about and satisfaction with managed care. This study of a highly managed HMO community in the Midwest revealed that the satisfaction of psychiatrists was the lowest of all specialty practices. Slightly more than half of these respondents were dissatisfied with their income, autonomy, and overall career in this HMO environment.

If professional satisfaction is a significant predictor of patient satisfaction and outcome, effective use of resources, continuity of care, and job performance and turnover, then too little attention has been paid to psychiatrist satisfaction. This subject will grow in interest and importance as the price wars in health care subside, as quality grows as an objective, and as professional satisfaction is more clearly linked to patient satisfaction (including retention in managed care plans) and clinical outcome.

Recommendations

Based on this review of the literature and ongoing discussion, the following organizational goals are recommended for psychiatrists working within systems of care. First, opportunities should be created and maintained for the development of collegial relationships. Second, systems of care should adequately compensate psychiatrists for the work they provide. Although the need for physicians may decrease as some claim, those who can work effectively within systems of care will still be in demand. Third, every effort should be made to minimize the amount of time physicians are expected to devote to the day-to-day, business administration of the practice. This may be seen as diminishing what is called the "hassle factor." Fourth, psychiatrists should be able to operate with the clinical autonomy that they identify as in the best interests of their patients and should be able to influence the organization in the proper allocation of resources for patient care. Fifth, disruption of physician networks should be minimized. Good patient care has traditionally been accomplished through physician referrals to trusted colleagues. If psychiatrists are to function in an integrated fashion with primary care physicians, and if psychiatry is not to be segregated from the rest of medicine, physician networks must be sustained. Sixth, every effort must be made to demonstrate that treatment works (35). A psychiatrist's experience of personal integrity and feeling of self-worth are tied to the provision of quality care. Unless psychiatrists believe that they are providing good care, they will have difficulty meeting internal standards of self-worth and self-respect.

PROFESSIONAL COMPENSATION

As physicians are organized into and paid by organized networks of care, many questions arise regarding compensation. These questions can be answered by considering the underlying motivation of physicians. Three models have been proposed to explain physicians' responses to payment systems (36). The fact that no distinction has been made between physicians and psychiatrists, and that no other mental health professionals have been included, reflects the limited discussion of this subject in the literature.

Profit Maximization Model

In the first model, physicians are likened to business entrepreneurs who characteristically behave in a manner that maximizes their profit. Although a simplistic view of behavior, the model is useful because it permits consideration of the purely financial incentives affecting physicians. Under this model (assuming reasonably ethical behavior), an increase in the demand for services will result in higher profits for physicians. Consequently, if volume (demand) is uncontrolled, the Medicare fee schedule would not limit costs, the Medicare fee schedule would not limit costs, because total Medicare costs are the product of price and volume.

Target Income Model

A specific income target is the physician's objective in this model. Instead of maximizing income, physicians seek both an income goal (target) and clear, desirable limits on their time and effort. The quality of the practice environment is another consideration and includes the lifestyle or academic interests of the physician. In this model, which allows for practice design, physicians can have greater influence on their hours, on-call schedules, and caseloads. Academic activity (e.g., teaching, research), which is generally less financially rewarding than patient care, is also congruent with this model. Unlike the profit maximization model, the target model considers the role of conscience in physician behavior by recognizing the physician's concerns about the social consequences of creating or decreasing demand to enhance their income (37).

Patient Agency Model

The economic forces driving physician behavior are minimized by this model. Although naive (given what is widely accepted about the power of financial incentives), this model contributes to an understanding of physician behavior under managed systems of care. By this model, physicians can act as clinical agents, market and competitive agents, social agents, and economic agents, all as variants of patient agency.

As a clinical agent, the physician's preeminent concern is the health of each patient (38). The clinical agent model is based on the traditional medical ethic of caring for the individual patient, which is articulated in the Hippocratic oath and is theoretically independent of the physician's financial needs or the needs of the community at large. As a market and competitive agent, the physician is engaged in setting prices and shaping demand according to assumptions about informed patient preferences. As social agent, the physician identifies his or her critical role in seeking to optimize the welfare of a community of individuals. For example, physicians working in public health and those involved in systems of care in which financing is blended with care delivery (e.g., HMOs) are accustomed to the concept of social agency. The care of a population in need, rather than the individual patient, is highlighted by this model. Finally, as economic agent, the physician is guided by the patient's (not the physician's) financial resources (38–40).

These models do not address medical decision-making (which is derived from clinical assessment) and biases developed during training. On the contrary, these models attempt to predict the behavior of physicians in financial systems to forecast service delivery and to guide policy makers in developing systems of professional compensation.

Allying Clinical, Organizational, and Financial Goals

A hotly debated issue among professionals and administrators in the organized clinical delivery system is how to harness the power of professional compensation to optimize the effectiveness and efficiency of care. To date, no uniform consensus exists and no distinct model has gained hegemony; however, certain lessons have emerged from the cauldron of experience.

First, financial incentives do work. The introduction of the concept of incentive pay among clinical professionals is relatively novel (41, 42). Two decades of experience in which clinicians are paid a fixed salary has taught that sustaining productivity, engaging clinicians in cost-conscious care, and aligning professional and administrative goals (e.g., efficiency, documentation) is difficult to achieve. As a consequence, physician-hospital organizations have evolved with significant incentives for physicians in order to meet competitive goals of today's medical marketplace (43, 44). In all their variants (which reflect differing degrees of integration between the hospital system and the clinical staff), one common denominator exists—the financial successes or failures of the joint enterprise are shared by both parties. With clinician oversupply (especially in urban settings), aggressive downward pressure on the price of medical care, and the power of networks over patient referrals, clinicians are forming groups and/or partnerships with hospital systems. Financial incentives will increasingly be used to enhance the performance and productivity of clinical staff.

Second, financial incentives alone are limited motivators (45–49). Professionals (including physicians) rank achievement, recognition, responsibility, the work itself, collegiality, and growth higher than financial reward. Lifestyle and academic interests, noted earlier in the section on satisfaction, also play an important role in motivation. Moreover, reward systems based exclusively on money can breed unnecessary competition and distrust among staff.

Third, financial incentives raise critical ethical issues (50, 51). The traditional medical ethic, dating back to Hippocrates, obligates the physician to place the individual patient first and foremost and forbids exploitation of the doctor-patient relationship. In managed systems of care with clinicians as partners in the financial outcome, the clinician's role—or imperative—is to allocate resources (money) efficiently across a population of patients. Advocacy becomes allocation, to paraphrase Mechanic (52), and allocation is becoming a euphemism for rationing.

Fourth, we live in a litigious society. As one pundit put it, "Americans would rather sue than queue." Legally, corporations (like insurance or managed care organizations) bear contractual liability, whereas clinicians bear professional liability (53). Contracts mandate accountability for matters such as access and payment. Professionals, however, are accountable for patients and outcomes. Clinicians cannot escape their responsibility for patients, nor should they. However, with financial incentives influencing their decisions, their exposure to claims of negligence or conflict of interest can only grow.

Fifth, an erosion of the trust that patients and society have had in physicians has lessened the status and satisfaction of physicians. Financial incentives (especially profit from limiting care in prepaid managed systems) may further erode this essential trust. Patients increasingly acting as consumers will have to have a voice in incentive payment to protect their interests!

In solving the problems of professional satisfaction and allying the goals of clinicians, payers, and institutions, the power of money cannot be ignored. How this power will be used is uncertain; however, one can be sure that it will be affected by the morals and ethics of psychiatry and medicine as well as the forces of legal and consumer action.

ACKNOWLEDGMENTS

The authors thank Drs. Helen Batten, Barbara Dickey, Richard Hermann, Connie Horgan, and Grant Ritter for their contributions to this manuscript.

REFERENCES

1. Sharfstein SS, Biegel A, eds. The new economics and psychiatric Care. Washington, DC: American Psychiatric Press, 1985.
2. Sederer LI, St. Clair RL. Managed health care and the Massachusetts experience. Am J Psychiatry 1989;146:1142–1148.
3. Fink PJ. Psychiatrists' roles in managed care programs. Hosp Community Psychiatry 1993;44:723–724.
4. Sederer LI. Psychiatrists and the new managed systems of care. In: Sharfstein SS, Lazarus JA, eds. The role of psychiatrists in new managed systems of care. Washington, DC: American Psychiatric Press, 1996.
5. Dorwart RA, Chartock LR, Dial TD, et al. A national study of psychiatrists' professional activities. Am J Psychiatry 1992;149:1499–1505.
6. Astrachan BM, Astrachan JH. Economics of practice and inpatient care. Gen Hosp Psychiatry 1989;11:313–319.
7. Olfson M, Klerman GL, Pincus HA. The roles of psychiatrists in organized outpatient mental health settings. Am J Psychiatry 1993;150:625–631.
8. Annual Report of the Professional Liability Insurance Program. Washington, DC: American Psychiatric Association, 1992–1993.
9. Dorwart RA, Schlesinger M. Privatization of psychiatric services. Am J Psychiatry 1988;145:543–555.
10. Moffic HS, Krieg K, Prosen H. Managed care and academic psychiatry. J Ment Health Admin 1993;20:172–177.
11. Brenneis CB. The skewing of psychiatry. Acad Psychiatry 1994;18:71–80.
12. Locke EA. The nature and causes of satisfaction. In: Dunnette MD, ed. Handbook of industrial and organizational psychology. Chicago: Rand-McNally, 1976.
13. Stamps PL, Piedmont EB, Slavitt DB, et al. Measurement of work satisfaction among health professionals. Medical Care 1978;16:337–352.
14. Lichtenstein R. Measuring the job satisfaction of physicians in organized settings. Med Care 1984;22:56–68.
15. Kravitz RL, Linn LS, Shapiro MF. Physician satisfaction under the Ontario health insurance plan. Med Care 1990;28:502–512.
16. Linn LS, Brook RH, Clark VA, et al. Physician and patient satisfaction as factors related to the organization of internal medicine group practices. Med Care 1985;23:1171–1178.
17. Weisman CS, Nathanson CA. Professional satisfaction and client outcomes. Med Care 1985;23:1179–1192.
18. Linn LS, Yager J, Cope D, et al. Health status, job satisfaction, job stress, and life satisfaction among academic and clinical faculty. JAMA 1985;254:2775–2782.
19. Reames HR, Dunstone DC. Professional satisfaction in physicians. Arch Int Med 1989;149:1951–1956.
20. Lewis JM, Barnhart FD, Howard BL, et al. Work satisfaction in the lives of physicians. Tex Med 1993;89:54–61.
21. Ben-David J. The professional role of the physician in bureaucratized medicine: a study in role-conflict. Hum Relations 1958;11:255–274.

22. McElrath DC. Perspectives and participation of physicians in prepaid group practice. Am Soc Rev 1961;26:596–607.

23. Ross A Jr. A report on physician termination in group practice. Med Group Management 1969;16:15–21.

24. Likert R. New pattern of management. New York: McGraw-Hill, 1961.

25. Mechanic D. General medical practice: some comparisons between the work of primary care physicians in the United States and England and Wales. Med Care 1972;10:402–420.

26. Mechanic D. The organization of medical practice and practice orientations among physicians in prepaid and non-prepaid primary care settings. Med Care 1975;13:189–204.

27. Porter LW, Steers RM. Organizational, work and personal factors in employee turnover and absenteeism. Psychol Bull 1973;80:151–176.

28. Prybil LD. Characteristics, career patterns and opinions of physicians who practice in large multispecialty groups. Med Group Management 1974;21:22.

29. Schulz R, Girard C, Scheckler WE. Physician satisfaction in a managed care environment. J Fam Pract 1992;34:298–304.

30. Barr JK, Steinberg MK. Professional participation in organizational decision making: physicians in HMO's. J Community Health 1983;8:160–173.

31. Baker LC, Cantor JC. Physician satisfaction under managed care. Health Aff 1993;(Suppl):258–270.

32. Stamps PL, Cruz NTB. Issues in physician satisfaction. New Perspectives. Ann Arbor, MI: Health Administration Press, 1994.

33. American Psychiatric Association's Peer Review Committee. APA Peer Review Survey, 1982 (Unpublished).

34. American Psychiatric Association's Peer Review Committee. APA Peer Review Survey, 1983 (Unpublished).

35. Sederer LI, Dickey B. Outcomes assessment in clinical practice. Baltimore: Williams & Wilkins, 1995.

36. Pauly MV, Eisenberg JM, Radany MH, et al. Paying physicians: options for controlling cost, volume and intensity of services. Ann Arbor, MI: Health Administration Press, 1992.

37. McGuire TG, Pauly, MV. Physicians' response to fee changes with multiple payors. J Health Economics 1991;10:385–410.

38. Eisenberg JM. Doctors, decisions and the cost of medical care: the reasons for doctors' practice patterns and ways to change them. Ann Arbor, MI: Health Administration Press, 1986.

39. Eisenberg JM, Williams SV. Cost containment and changing physicians' practice behavior: can the fox learn to guard the chicken coop? JAMA 1981;246:2195–2201.

40. Long MJ, Cummings KM, Frisof KB. The role of perceived price in physicians' demand for diagnostic tests. Med Care 1983;21:243–250.

41. Anders G. More managed health care systems use incentive pay to reward best doctors. Wall Street Journal January 25, 1993:B1–B2.

42. Pagoaga J, Williams JB. Dynamic pay initiatives. Hosp Health Networks 1993;67:22–29.

43. Ernst & Young. Hospital physician integration: results of a national survey. Cleveland, OH: 1993.

44. Goldstein D. Organizing physician equity alliances for aggressive growth and capitation. Group Pract J 1995;May/June:12–22.

45. Herzberg F. One more time. How do you motivate employees? Harvard Business Review 1968;46:53–62.

46. Kohn A. Why incentive plans cannot work. Harvard Business Review 1993;71:54–63.

47. Patton A. Why incentive plans fail. Harvard Business Review 1972;50:36–44.

48. Todd JS. Problems with incentives. JAMA 1990;264:1294–1295.

49. Wachtel TJ, Stein MD. Fee-for-time system: a conceptual framework for an incentive-neutral method of physician payment. JAMA 1993;270:1226–1229.

50. Lazarus JA, Sharfstein SS. Changes in the economics and ethics of health and mental health care. In: Oldham JM, Riba MB, eds. American Psychiatric Press review of psychiatry. Washington, DC: American Psychiatric Press, 1994;13:389–413.

51. Wolf SM. Health care reform and the future of physician ethics. Hastings Cent Rep 1994;24:28–41.

52. Mechanic D. From advocacy to allocation: the evolving American health care system. New York: Free Press, 1986.

53. Sederer, LI. Judicial and legislative responses to cost containment. Am J Psychiatry 1992:149:1157–1161.

Index

Note: Page numbers followed by "f" indicate figures; page numbers followed by "t" indicate tabular material.

Abreaction, for posttraumatic stress disorder, 204–205
Abuse
  history of, in depression, 94
  survivors of, 215
    childhood, 206–208
Access to care
  in Mental Health Statistics Improvement Project report card
    cultural and linguistic access, 518–519
    financial barriers and, 519
    full range of service options, 517–518
    quick and convenient entry into services, 516–517
  in Performance Measures for Managed Behavioral Healthcare Programs report card, 534–536
Accountability. *See also* Authority
  of case manager, 328–329
  organizational structure and, 329
  to purchasers of care
    report card quality assessment and, 507–508
  questions in, 328
Acetylmethadol, L-α, for maintenance treatment of heroin abuse, 239
Acknowledgement, of role of trauma, 206–207
ACT. *See* Assertive Community Treatment (ACT)
AD. *See* Alzheimer's disease (AD)
Addictive disorders. *See* Substance use disorder(s)
ADHD. *See*. Attention-deficit hyperactivity disorder (ADHD)
Adolescents
  disruptive behavior in. *See* Disruptive behavior, in children and adolescents

medications frequently administered to, 278t
suicide and. *See* Suicidal behavior, in children and adolescents
α-Adrenergic antagonism, with monoamine oxidase inhibitors, 101
Advocacy
  in case management, 326–327
    versus allocation of care, 549
    hospital or system fiscal conflict with, 498–499
    rationing of care and, 498–499
Affective disorders. *See* Mood disorders
Aggressive behavior. *See also* Violence
  interventions for, 36
  management of
    in private office and institutional settings, 36
Agitated patient
  psychosis in, 69
  toxicology screen of, 69
Agitation, in demented elderly, 265
Agitation and violence, 67–70. *See also* Violence
  associated diagnoses, 68
  definition of, 67
  demographics of, 68
  diagnosis of, 67–68
  history in, 68
Agnosia, in Alzheimer's disease, 261
Agoraphobia, panic disorder versus, 125
AIDS/HIV-infected patients, confidentiality and, 424–425, 445
Akathisia
  beta-adrenergic blockers for, 182
  drug-induced, 126
  with fluoxetine, 102
  neuroleptic-induced, 178t
  suicide risk in, 22

Alcohol abuse
  case example: child of alcoholic, 358
  depression in, 87, 89
  detoxification in, 236
  focal psychotherapy for, case example of, 361
  intoxication in, 234
  maintenance treatment of, 236–237
  obsessive-compulsive disorder in, 125
  panic disorder in, 124–125
  suicide risk in, 17, 20
  withdrawal from, 234, 235t, 236
    bipolar disorder relapse and, 148
    clinical signs in, 234, 235t, 236
Alcoholics Anonymous (AA), 241, 243
Algorithm(s)
  advantages and disadvantages of, 467
  for adverse drug reaction prevention, 464–465,
      465f
  for continuity of care, 464f
  for cost evaluation and control, 465–466
  in daily setting, 460
  definition of, 458
  Delphi method and, 463
  guidelines versus, 459
  for intake and triage process, 463–464, 464f
  legal implications with, 466–476
  in managed care, 466
  in medical setting, 460
  multidimensional, 459
  for pharmacologic treatment, 461, 463
    example in bipolar mania, 461, 462f, 463
    versus tabular safety and efficacy profile, 461
  in psychiatric setting, 460–463
  for psychiatric triage, 464f
  research applications and implications of, 467
  simple, 458–459
  as teaching tool, 466
  types of, 459f
  in utilization review, 466
Alopecia, with divalproex, 154
Allocation of care, justice in, 499
Alprazolam, for panic disorder, 132
Alzheimer's disease (AD). *See also* Vascular de-
      mentia
  versus dementia syndrome of depression,
      262–263
  descriptive diagnosis of, 261–262
  epidemiology of, 261
  heritable forms of
    positional mapping and, 474–475
  versus Parkinson's subcortical dementia, 262
  psychotic symptoms in, 262
  versus vascular dementia, 262
Amine hypothesis, for depression, 90
Amnesia
  dissociative, 199
  diagnosis of, 196
Amoxapine, 99
  dose range for, 97t
  side effects of, 100t

Anaclitic depression, 93
Anger
  in major depressive disorder, 110
  in schizophrenia, 172
  in substance-related disorders, 229
Anoxia, mental status changes in, 55t
Anticholinergic side effects
  of heterocyclic antidepressants
    in elderly, 256
  of neuroleptics, 179
Anticipatory anxiety, panic disorder and, 128
Anticonvulsants. *See also* Carbamazepine; Dival-
      proex sodium; Valproic acid
  for posttraumatic stress disorder, 208
Antidepressant(s)
  augmentation of, 97–98, 105
  for behavioral disorders
    in demented elderly, 265
  for borderline personality disorder, 302–303
  commonly prescribed, 97t
  for depressed suicidal patient, 24
  dose ranges of, 97t
    in elderly, 256t
  heterocyclics, 98
  lithium versus, 98
  monoamine oxidase inhibitors, 98
  for panic disorder, 132–133
  for posttraumatic stress disorder, 209
  response rate to, 105
  for schizophrenia with comorbid depression,
      182
  sedating versus nonsedating, 106–107
  selective serotonin reuptake inhibitors, 97t,
      100–104, 133–134
  for self-destructive behavior, 38
  sexual dysfunction with, 105
  side effect profiles of, 100t
    in elderly, 256t
  tricyclics, 98
  for violence, 38
Antihistamines, for borderline personality disor-
      der, 302
Antipsychotic(s), 175–182
  for borderline personality disorder, 302
  clozapine, 179–180
  drug interactions with, 180–181
  experimental, 181–182
  for hostility, 37
  long-acting depot, 179
  neuroleptics, 175–179
  novel, 179–180
  for schizophrenia, 175–182
  for violence, 37
Antisocial personality disorder (APD), 312–318
  alliance in
    difficulty in, 316
  chronicity of, 318
  countertransference and, 317
  course and prognosis of, 318
  definition of, 312–313

diagnosis of
  descriptive, 313–314
  DSM-IV criteria for, 313, 314
differential diagnosis of, 314
ego defense and character style in, 314
family support in, 317
family therapy in, 317–318
formulation of problem in, 314
level of care for
  assessment and transfer in, 315
psychopharmacologic management of, 316
versus psychosis, 314
psychotherapy for
  problems in, 317
secondary gain in, 315
versus substance abuse, 314
suicide risk in, 20–21
therapeutic milieu for, 318
violence in
  toward family and significant others, 317,
    318
Anxiety
  in major depression, 106
  as symptom of medical disorder, 126
Anxiety disorder(s)
  definition of, 123–124
  descriptive and differential diagnosis of, 125–126
  generalized anxiety disorder, 125
  obsessive-compulsive disorder. *See* Obsessive-
    compulsive disorder (OCD)
  panic disorder. *See* Panic disorder (PD)
  pharmacologic management of, 131–132
  treatment of, 131
Anxiety-provoking therapy, 483
Anxiolytic agents, for schizophrenia, 182
APD. *See* Antisocial personality disorder (APD)
Appropriateness of care
  Mental Health Statistics Improvement Project
    report card
    adequate information to make informed
      choices, 522–523
    application of best-practice guidelines, 523
    consumer involvement in policy develop-
      ment, planning, quality assurance activi-
      ties, 522
    services that maximize continuity of care,
      521
    services that promote recovery, 520–521
    voluntary participation in services, 519–520
Assault, risk assessment for, 38–39
Assertive Community Treatment (ACT)
  case management in, 325
  cost reduction with, 334
  description and characteristics of, 333
  reduction of psychiatric hospitalization with,
    333–334
Assessment
  diagnoses in, 5–7
  ego defenses in, 7–10
  focal problems in, 12–13

formulation of case in, 10–12
four questions in, 3–13
stressors in, 10–12
Attention-deficit hyperactivity disorder (ADHD).
    See also Disruptive behavior
  bipolar disorder versus, 146
  stimulants for, 290
Auditory hallucinations, violence and, 32, 35
Authority. *See also* Accountability
  of case manager, 328–329
Autonomy, 493
Avoidant behavior, in panic disorder, 124
Axis I diagnoses
  definition of, 5
  psychodynamic understanding of, 485
Axis II diagnoses
  personality disorders versus ego defenses, 5–6
  psychodynamic understanding of, 485

BASIS-32 (Behavior and Symptom Identification
    Scale), 538–540
Battering, victims of, 42
Behavioral disturbances, in dementia, 263
Bender-Gestalt test, in differential diagnosis of
    depression, 96
Beneficence, 493
Benzodiazepines
  for aggressive behavior, 38
  for alcohol detoxification, 236
  for borderline personality disorder, 302, 303
  for delirium, 72
  in demented elderly, 265
  interaction of
    with electroconvulsive therapy, 108
  for mania, 157
  with neuroleptics, 177
  for panic disorder, 132
    discontinuation of, 133
  for posttraumatic stress disorder, 209
  in substance use disorders
    with coexisting psychiatric disorders, 244
  for violence, 38
Bereavement, versus depression, 87
Beta-blockers, for violence reduction in antisocial
    personality disorder, 316
Bioethics, underlying principles of, 493–494
Biopsychosocial assessment
  change in
    necessary, 360, 361
    readiness for, 360–361
  components of, 358, 359f
  DSM-IV diagnosis and operational diagnosis
    in, 361
  limiting factor identification in, 358, 360–361
  patient's mythology in, 358
  resource identification in, 358
Biopsychosocial model
  disease orientation in, 4
  psychological perspective in, 4
  social perspective in, 4

Bipolar disorder
  carbamazepine for, 154–155
  course and prognosis of, 160–161, 161f
  dissociative disorders versus, 200
  divalproex for, 152–154
  family support, education, intervention in,
      150–151
  incidence of, 146
  lithium for, 151–152
  mania in. *See* Mania
  medication noncompliance in
      case example of crisis triage, 53
  multi-disciplinary treatment plan for,
      144f–145f
  noncompliance in, 150
  psychopharmacologic management of, 151–154
      maintenance, 155, 157
  substance use disorders in, 143, 160, 161
  suicide rate in, 113
  therapeutic alliance in, 149, 150
  therapeutic milieu in, 151
  treatment of
      practice guidelines for, 156f
      sample plan for, 144f–145f
Bipolar Disorder I
  prevalence rates for, 143
Bipolar Disorder II
  characterization of, 87
      classification of, 142
      DSM-IV criteria for, 142
      longitudinal pattern of, 142–143
  prevalence rates for, 143
Bleuler, E., schizophrenia and, 167–168
Blood dyscrasias, with divalproex, 154
Borderline personality disorder (BPD), 293–312
  antidepressants for, 302–303
  antipsychotics for, 302
  benzodiazepines for, 303
  biological evaluation and, 298
  case example in residency training
      projective identification in, 488–489
      psychodynamic approach to, 487–489
      splitting in, 488
      staff dynamics and countertransference in,
          488
  comorbidity and, 295–296
  controversies in care of, 309–312
      diagnostic issues, 310
      hospitalization, 310–311
      limit-setting versus permissiveness, 311
      medications, 311–312
      psychoeducation, 311
      psychotherapy, 312
      under- versus over-diagnosis, 310
  course and prognosis of, 312
  definition of, 293
  dependency and regression risk with hospital-
      ization for, 311–312
  diagnosis of
      descriptive, 294

  DSM-IV criteria for, 293–294
  dialectical behavior therapy for, 306
  differential diagnosis of, 294–296
  ego defenses and character style in, 296
  epidemiology of, 294
  family education about, 307–308
  family intervention in, 308, 350
  family support in, 308
  focal problems in, 296–298
      goals and, 296–297
      precipitants of, 298
      stressors, 297–298
      suicide risk reduction, 297
      transference, 297
  following childhood traumatization, 201
  inpatient units for
      locked, 300
      unlocked, 300
  level of care in
      suicide risk assessment for, 298–299
      transfers in, 308
  medicolegal issues in, 309
  mood stabilizers for, 303
  outpatient treatment of, 301
  problem formulation in, 296
  psychopharmacologic management of, 302–303
      response to, 302
  psychotherapy for
      acute versus follow-up, 305–306
      contraindications to, 312
      group, 306
  regression and dependency in, 301, 308
  relapse prevention in, 297–298
  residential programs for, 300
  shelters for, 301
  suicide risk in, 20
  therapeutic milieu for, 303–304
      hierarchy of priorities in, 304
      limit-setting in, 304–305
      rules and regulations in, 304
  treatment of
      control versus understanding of behavior in,
          301
      goal of, 301
      treatment team in, 306–307
BPD. *See* Borderline personality disorder (BPD)
Brain imaging
  functional information generation in, 477
  in mania, 149
  in psychiatrists' new role, 471, 472
  in residency training curriculum, 477–478
  in schizophrenia, 174–175
Brief reactive psychoses, versus posttraumatic
      flashbacks or dissociative state switches,
      200
Buprenorphine, for opioid detoxification
Bupropion
  dose range with, 97t
  in elderly, 257
  side effects of, 100

Buspirone
  in attention-deficit/hyperactivity disorder, 316
  in fluoxetine augmentation, 134

CAGE interview, in substance-related disorder
    diagnosis, 226
Carbamazepine
  for alcohol withdrawal syndrome, 148
  for borderline personality disorder, 25, 303
  for depression, 98
  in elderly, 258, 258t
  for hostility, 38
  for mania, 154–155, 157
  for schizophrenia, 182
  side effects of, 155
Cardiotoxicity, of heterocyclic antidepressants, in
    elderly, 256–257
Cardiovascular disease, depression in, 89–90
Case formulation
  precipitating event in, 10
  psychological purpose or function of sympto-
    matology in, 11
  stressors in, 10
Case management, 323–335. *See also specific model,*
    e.g., Assertive Community Treatment
    (ACT)
  activities in, 325t
  advocacy in, 326–327
  brokering for services in, 326
  case manager in
    accountability and authority of, 328–329
  coordination in, 327
  in crisis intervention, 59
    case example of, 59
  definition of, 324
  direct service in, 327–328
  effects of
    on costs of care, 334–335
    on psychiatric hospitalization, 333–334
  functions of, 323–324
  integration of private and public sector in,
    323–324
  linkage in, 326
  models in mental health care
    Assertive Community Treatment, 333
    generalist, 331–332
    intensive case, 332
    personal strengths, 331
  needs assessment in, 325–326
  outreach in, 325
  patient identification in, 324–325
  planning in, 327
  in posttraumatic stress and dissociative disor-
    ders, 211
  role of case manager in, 324–328
  task areas of psychiatric practice and, 329t,
    329–331
    medical, 329–330
    social control, 330–331
    social welfare, 331

Case record
  altering, 423
  clinical functions of
    archival, 416
    documentary, 417
    education, 418
    justificatory, 417–418
    planning, 416–417
    research, 418
    utilization, 418
  legal aspects of, 418–419
    consent forms for special procedures,
      422–423
    forensically significant events in, 422
    judgment calls and thinking aloud,
      421–422
    legal status paper, 422
    malpractice prevention versus good practice,
      419
    process-progress distinction in, 419–420
    professional tone in, 420
    reference to other patients and staff mem-
      bers, 420
  special considerations for, 415–416
Catatonic schizophrenia, 169
  electroconvulsive therapy for, 182
CBT. *See* Cognitive behavioral therapy (CBT)
Central nervous system, neuroleptic effect on,
    178t, 179
Cerebral disorder, agitation and violence in, 68
Change
  cognitive with electroconvulsive therapy, 109
  inability to, case example of grieving, 364
  necessary, 360, 361
  readiness for, 360–361
  rehearsal for, 370–371
  stages of, 363–364, 364f, 365t
Character diagnosis, levels of pathology in, 8–9
Child abuse. *See also* Childhood traumatization
  sexual, 196–197
  survivors of, 206–208
Childhood traumatization. *See also* Children;
    Traumatization
  borderline symptomatology following, 201
  chronic disempowerment from, 215
  course and prognosis of, 214–215
  dissociative defense in, 198–199
  dissociative disorders following, 196
  ego defenses and character style following,
    201–202
  psychotic symptomatology following, 200
  self-hate following, 201–202
  survivors of
    acknowledgment of role of trauma in, 206–207
    acute care model for, 206–208
    expression of feelings in, 207
    functioning normally in, 207
    relationship establishment in, 207–208
    self-care in, 205–206
    symptom control in, 206

Children. *See also* Childhood traumatization
    disruptive behavior in. *See* Disruptive behavior, in children and adolescents
    home-based care for. *See* Family and Home Consultation Service program
    medications frequently administered to, 278t
    suicide and. *See* Suicidal behavior, in children and adolescents
Chlordiazepoxide, for alcohol detoxification, 236
Chlorpromazine, drug interactions with, 180
Circadian rhythm, depression and, 92
Civil liberties
    commitment and involuntary treatment and, 185–186
    involuntary evaluation of patient, 41
Clonazepam
    for panic disorder, 132
    for posttraumatic symptoms in dissociative identity disorder, 208
Clonidine, for attention-deficit/hyperactivity disorder, 288
Clozapine
    candidates for, 179, 180
    in demented elderly, 265
    drug interactions with, 180–181
    for mania, 158
    for schizophrenia, 179–180
        late-onset, 268
    side effects of, 180
    for suicidal schizophrenic patient, 25
Cocaine use disorder
    epidemiology of, 224
    inpatient versus outpatient care in, 243
Cognitive behavioral therapy (CBT)
    group
        description of, 379–380
        effectiveness of, 380
        uses of, 380
    for obsessive-compulsive disorder, 135
    for panic disorder, 134
    in posttraumatic stress and dissociative disorders, 211–212
Cognitive deficits, in Alzheimer's disease, 262
Cognitive therapy, for depression, 93
Competency
    to accept treatment, 448
    assessment of, 448
    components of, 447–449
    to consent to hospitalization, 450
    general by court adjudication, 449
    implications of incompetence assessment, 450
    of involuntarily committed patient, 448
    specific, outside legal jurisdiction, 449
Compliance. *See* Medication noncompliance
Conduct disorders. *See* Disruptive behavior
Confidentiality
    AIDS/HIV patients and, 424–425, 445
    circle of confidentiality and information sharing, 444
    consent to release information and, 423–424

definition of, 444
exceptions to
    in commitment and guardianship hearings, 453
    disclosure of information to third-party payers, 444–445
    in emergency situation, 425, 444
    guardian of incompetent patient, 425, 444
    HIV-positive patient, 445
    to protect from harm from patient, 425
    special reporting requirements, 425
    in substance abuse disorders, 231
    extension of, 424
    in group psychotherapy, 384–385
    information sharing and, 424
    mandatory reporting requirements and, 445–446
    patient release of information and, 498
    versus privilege, 445
    receipt of information from concerned outsiders
    redacted charts for, 498
    sharing of information issues and, 424
Conflicts of interest
    clinician obligation to patient and to system, 496–497
    disclosure to patient, 497
Congenital disorders, mental status changes in, 55t
Consent. *See also* Informed consent
    for release of information, 423–424
    substituted, 449
Consent forms, inclusion in case record, 422–423
Consultation, in family, home-based care, 399
Consumer satisfaction
    in continuous quality improvement theory, 504
    in Performance Measures for Managed Behavioral Healthcare Programs report card, 536
    in quality assessment, 506
Continuity of care, algorithm for, 464f
Continuous quality improvement (CQI) (total quality management [TQM])
    in clinical practice, 510
        adverse event reporting in, 511
        outcomes of care in: BASIS-32, 510–511, 538–540
        Perceptions of Care measure in, 511
        readmissions within 30 days, 511
        results reporting, 511–513, 512f
    definition of, 513
    Deming, W.E. and, 504
    description of, 509–510
    origin of, 504
    patient satisfaction philosophy in, 504
    psychiatric hospitals and healthcare use of, 510
Contracts
    with borderline personality disorder patients, 299
    clinician-suicidal patient, 23, 77–78

in family and home-based care program, 401
Cost reduction, ethical issues and, 494
Cotherapy
  relationship in, 409–410
  training for, 410
Countertransference
  with antisocial personality disorder, 317
  with borderline personality disorder, 307
  with crisis recidivist, 61–62
  definition of, 482
  with depressed and suicidal patients, 110–111
  in interaction with legal system, 453
  in suicide risk evaluation, 17
CQI. *See* Continuous quality improvement (CQI)
    (total quality management [TQM])
Crisis, family use of acute care for, 340–341
Crisis intervention. *See also* Emergency care;
    Triage
  alliance from patient's perspective, 56–57
  crisis definition in, 55–56
  definition of, 56
  disposition in, 58–61
    case management, 59
    day or evening care programs, 59
    hospital, 60–61
    intensive outpatient, 58–59
    observation or holding beds, 60
    outpatient care, 58
    partial hospitalization, 59–60
    residential respite care, 60
  emergency and evaluation services in
    cost controversies, 62–63
  in Family and Home Consultation Service pro-
      gram, 392–393
  goals of, 56
  levels of care and, 58t
  medical illness of patient in, 50–51
  medication in, 56
  negotiation of formulation and plan, 57–58
    case example of, 57–58
  patient strengths in, 56
  status of attachments in, 56–57
  tasks of, 56
Criterion, in quality assessment, 506, 513
Culture
  access to care and, 518–519
  violence and, 32
Cyclothymia, versus depression, 87
Cytochrome P450IID6 isoenzyme inhibition, in
    selective serotonin
      reuptake inhibitor-drug interactions,
      103–104

Dangerousness
  duty to protect versus confidentiality and, 425
  risk of harm to self or others
    level of care and, 96
Day programs
  for crisis intervention, 59
  for psychotic disorders in elderly, 268

for schizophrenia
    late-onset, 268
DDNOS. *See* Dissociative disorder not otherwise
    specified (DDNOS)
Defense mechanisms. *See* Ego defenses (defense
    mechanisms)
  in borderline personality disorder, 296
  versus personality disorders, 5–6
  violence and, 32
Degenerative disease
  dementia from, 260t
  mental status changes in, 55t
Delirium
  agitation and assaultiveness in, 68, 69
  assessment of, 71
  case example of, 73
  causes of, 71
  clinical features of, 72
  definition of, 71
  versus dementia, 262
  drug-induced, 71
  evaluation for, 72
  populations at risk, 71–72
  psychopharmacologic management of, 72–73
  withdrawal
    clinical features of, 235t
Delirium tremens, 234
Delusional disorder
  course and prognosis of
    in late-onset, 268
  in elderly, 266–267
    versus dementia or delirium, 267
    descriptive diagnosis of, 266–267
    epidemiology of, 266
  schizophrenia versus, 171
Dementia. *See also* Alzheimer's disease (AD); Vas-
    cular dementia
  behavioral disturbances in, 263, 264, 265
  causes of, 260t
  coexisting major depression and, 254
  course and prognosis of, 265–266
  descriptive diagnosis of, 261–262
  differential diagnosis of, 262–263
  ego defenses and character style and, 263
  epidemiology of, 261
  focal problems in, 263–264
  formulation of problem in, 263
  in late-onset psychosis, 268
  psychopharmacologic management of, 264–265
Dementia praecox, 167
Dementia syndrome of depression (pseudodepres-
    sion), 262–263
Deming, W.E., continuous quality improvement,
    504
Denial, in antisocial personality disorder, 314
Dependency
  in borderline personality disorder, 301, 308
  in major depressive disorder, 110
Depersonalization disorder, diagnosis of, 196–197
Depot neuroleptics, 179

Depression, 83–113. *See also* Major depressive disorder (MDD)
  adoption studies and, 91–92
  age and, 86
  alliance and psychotherapeutic management of, 109–111
  anxiety in, 106
  behavioral model of, 93
  biologic hypotheses for
    amine deficiency, 90
    circadian rhythm, 92
    genetic, 91–92
    neuroendocrinologic, 92
    neurotransmitter disturbances, 91
    receptor sensitivity hypothesis, 91
  in bipolar II disorder, 87
  combination therapy for, 98
  controversies in treatment of, 112–113
  course and prognosis in, 113
  definition of, 83–84
  delusional
    combination antidepressant-neuroleptic therapy for, 99
    in elderly, 258
    late-onset, 260
    versus schizophrenia, 87
  diagnosis of, 85
    laboratory and radiologic studies in, 89t, 95
  differential diagnosis of, 86–87
  DSM-IV subtypes of, 84
  early life separation and, 93
  ego defenses and character style in, 90
  electroconvulsive therapy for, 98, 99, 112
  epidemiology of, 85
  family support, education, intervention in, 111–112
  focal therapy for
    rehearsal for change in, 370–371
  gender and, 86
  genetic risk for, 111–112
  history in, 94–95
  incidence of, 85
  late-onset
    course and prognosis of, 259–261
    with dementia, 254
    differential diagnosis of, 254
    epidemiology of, 253–254
    focal problems in, 255
    formulation of problem in, 254–255
    medical causes of, 250t
    personality traits and disorders and, 254
    psychopharmacologic management of, 255–258
    psychotherapy for, 259
    safety and, 254
  level of care in, 96
  managed care and rapid turnover in, 112–113
  marital status and, 86
  mental status changes in, 55t
  neuroendrocrine studies in, 95

neurotic. *See* Dysthymia (neurotic depression)
  physical examination in, 95
  polypharmacy for, 112
  postpartum, 84
  prevalence of, 85–86
  psychological models of, 92–93
  psychological testing in, 96
  psychopharmacologic management of, 96–103. *See also* Antidepressant(s)
    history of, 96–97
  psychotic, 87
    suicide risk in, 24
    treatment of, 24–25
  race and, 86
  recurrent, 113
  retroflexed rage hypothesis of, 92–93
  safety and, 94
  secondary to medical conditions, 88t, 89–90
  secondary to medical illness, 86
  signs and symptoms of, 83–84
  sleep studies in, 96
  social models of, 93–94
  socioeconomic status and, 86
  in substance-related disorders, 229
  suicidal
    family intervention for, 347
  suicide in, 113
DES. *See* Dissociative Experience Scale (DES)
Desipramine, for panic disorder, 32
Dexamethasone suppression test (DST), in depression, 95
Dextroamphetamine
  for attention-deficit/hyperactivity disorder, 288
  in children and adolescents, 278t
  in elderly, 258
Diabetes mellitus
  anxiety in, 126
  depression in, 89
Diagnosis(es)
  Axis I, 6–7
    major depressive disorder case example, 6–7
  Axis II, 5–6
  descriptive
    definition of, 5
  differential
    definition of, 5
  DSM-IV axes in, 5–6
Dialectical behavior therapy, for borderline personality disorder, 306
DID. *See* Dissociative identity disorder (DID)
Disclosure
  beneficence and nonmaleficence in, 495, 496
  case example of, 495–496
  content of, 495
  of potential effect of care model on patient, 498–499
Disruptive behavior
  antidepressant therapy for, 289–290
  biologic evaluation of, 297
  in children and adolescents, 283–290

child with versus having a problem, 288–289
definition of, 283–284
descriptive diagnosis of, 284–285
ego defenses and character style in, 285
epidemiology of, 284
family support and, 289
integration of care and, 290
contributing factors in
biologic, 285, 286
developmental, 285
family, 285, 286
school and peer, 286
treatment, 286
controversies in care of, 289–290
focal problem definition in, 286–287
level of care
selection of, 287
transfers in, 287–288
pharmacologic management of, 288
psychotherapeutic management of, 288–289
Dissociation
in antisocial personality disorder, 314
definition of, 198
Dissociative disorder not otherwise specified
(DDNOS)
definition of, 199
diagnosis of, 196
Dissociative disorder(s)
biologic evaluation of, 204
biologic processes in, 203
borderline personality disorder versus, 295
comorbidity in, 209–210
course and prognosis of, 214–215
definition of, 195
depersonalization disorder, 196–197
descriptive diagnosis of, 198–199
diagnosis of, 196–197
dissociative amnesia, 196
dissociative fugue, 196
dissociative identity disorder, 197
DSM-IV categories of, 196
family support, education, intervention in, 212
focal problems in, 203
formulation of problem in, 202–203
grounding techniques for symptom control in,
206
level of care for, 204
memory controversy in, 212–214. *See also*
Memory, of traumatic events
psychopharmacologic management of, 208
Dissociative Experience Scale (DES), 198
Dissociative identity disorder (DID)
definition of, 199
diagnosis of, 197
epidemiology of, 198
Disulfiram (Antabuse), in alcohol abuse treatment, 236
Divalproex sodium
for bipolar depression, 98
liver toxicity of, 153–154

monitoring for, 154
for mania, 152
comparison with lithium, 152–153, 157
oral loading technique with, 153
plus lithium
for mania, 157, 158
prophylactic, 157
safety of, 153
side effects of, 153, 154
Documentation
of aggressive or violent patient, 40–41
in borderline personality disorder cases, 309
of clinical judgment at decision points, 421
of mandated report, 446
of patients' capacity to participate in treatment,
421
purpose of, 417
risk-benefit analysis in, 421
suicide and homicide evaluation questions, 40f
Donabedian, A.
model of quality assessment
benefits and risks in, 505
description of, 504–505, 505f
expansions of, 506
influence of, 504
nomenclature in, 506
outcomes in, 505–506
perspectives in, multiple, 506
process in, 505
volume of treatment over time in, 505
Drives, regulation and control of, 7
DST. *See* Dexamethasone suppression test (DST)
Dysthymia (neurotic depression), 85
versus depression, 87
Dystonia, neuroleptic-induced, 178t

Eating disorders, in child abuse victims, 200
ECA studies. *See* Epidemiologic Catchment Area
(ECA) studies
ECT. *See* Electroconvulsive therapy (ECT)
Ego defenses and character diagnosis, 7–9
case example of, 9–10
Ego defenses (defense mechanisms)
definition of, 7
functions of, 7–8
levels of, 8
Ego psychology, in residency training, 484
Electrocardiogram, for lithium therapy, 151
Electroconvulsive therapy (ECT)
administration of, 108
adverse effects of, 109
in children and adolescents, 281
for depressed suicidal patient, 24
for depression
atypical, 98
controversy over, 112
psychotic, 99
drug interaction with, 108–109
in elderly
candidates for, 258–259

Electroconvulsive therapy (ECT)—*continued*
    complications of, 259
    indications for, 107
    informed consent for, 108
    for maintenance
        in elderly, 259
    as maintenance therapy, 155
    for mania, 155
    mechanism of action of, 108
    medical evaluation for, 108
    prediction of response with, 107–108
    response rate to, 107
    safety of, 108
Electroencephalogram
    in elderly, 252
    in schizophrenia
        indications for, 174
Emergency care. *See also* Crisis intervention;
        Triage
    contributing medical illness in, 50–51, 55t
    essential questions in, 48
    evaluation in, 48–53
    formulation of problem, 51–52
        case example of, 52–53
        in context of illness, 51
        dynamics of, 52
        patient's perspective in, 52
        relationships status in, 51
    suicide risk assessment in, 49–50
    symptom presentation in, 49
    violence assessment in, 50
Enactment of problem, in family, home-based
        care, 400
Encounter group, 376–377
Endocrine disorders, depression from, late-onset,
        250t
Environmental change, in etiology of decompen-
        sation, 202
Epidemiologic Catchment Area (ECA) Study
    mania in, 143
    violence and mental illness in, 30
Ethical dilemma(s)
    confidentiality, 497–498
    conflicts of interest, 496–497
    disclosure, 495–496
    doctor-patient relationship
        team member interference in, 500
    informed consent
        case example of, 494–495
        discontinuity of patient-physician relation-
            ships in, 494
        involvement of non-physician parties in, 494
    patient advocacy, 498–500
    quality treatment
        practice guidelines versus cost constraints,
            502
    relationships among mental health profession-
        als, 500–501
Ethical issue(s), 493–502
Evening care, in crisis intervention, 59

Expectations, patient, explicit and implicit,
        366–367
Exposure treatment, for obsessive-compulsive dis-
        order, 135
Expressed emotion, in families of schizophrenics,
        338–339
Extrusion, in family intervention, 1402

FACT. *See* Foundation for Accountability
        (FACT)
False memory (pseudomemory), 213–214
Family
    alliance with, 341
    of elderly patient
        therapeutic alliance with, 249
    evaluation of, 341
    extrusion of one member by another, 340
    medication involvement of, 346
    as patient, 338–339, 340
    psychodynamics of, 484–485
    psychoeducation of, 341, 342, 346
        need for, 346
    of schizophrenic patient
        psychoeducation of, 184
Family and Home Consultation Service program,
        391–401
    age distribution of clients in, 392t
    case management in, 393
    case mix in
        diagnostic, 395, 395t
    components of, 396–404
    cotherapy relationship in, 409–410
    crisis intervention and prevention in, 392–393
    cultural issues in, 410
    description of, 392–394
    development of, 393
    diagnostic case mix for 1995, 395, 395t
    family evaluation in, 397–398, 397–399
        of expectations, 398
        family therapy techniques in, 399
        genogram in, 398
        interview techniques in, 399
        of mental status, 398
        mental status and safety of identified client,
            398
        of safety concerns, 398
        safety issues in, 398
        of treatment history, 398
        treatment history in, 398
        for treatment plan development, 398–399
        treatment plan development and, 398–399
    family team approach in, 392
    first session, 399–400
        assessment of safety of family and identified
            patient, 400–401
        contracting, 401
        enactment or observation of problem, 400
        joining in, 400
        problem definition in, 400
        redefinition of problem in systems terms, 401

hospitalization reduction in, 395
intensive family therapy in, 393
provision, frequency, response interval of services, 396
psychiatrist role in, 394
referral to
  case example of, 397
  contacting family, 396–387
  issues in, 397
  receiving of, 396
  sources of, 396
referrals in, 394, 395
results of, 394–395
safety issue in, 394
service frequency and response intervals in, 396
service locations in, 393
short-term intervention parameters in
  case example, 405–407
  outcomes of, 405
  shift from blaming to responsibility, 405
  shift from linear- to systems-thinking, 404–405
systems consultation in, 401–404
  case example of, 402–404
  focus of, 402
  goals of, 401–402
  leader for, 402
  opening and closing of, 402
  professionals in, 401
team-client cotherapy model in, 393
therapeutic positioning in
  case example of, 408–409
  constructivist approach and, 407–408
  genograms in, 398, 408
  patterns of crisis and, 407
  structural issues in family and, 407
training cotherapists in, 410
treatment duration in, 395
  reduction of, 394, 395
Family history. *See also* Genograms
in depression, 94
Family intervention, 337–352
acute, working model of
  community-based support groups in, 351
  empiric studies of, 349–350
  in nonpsychotic psychiatric illness, 350—351
  recommendation guidelines for, 347–349
  summary of, 348t
    definition of, 346–347
  treatment controversies in, 351–352
acute team function in, 339–340
in affective disorders, 349–350
common goals in, 342–344
comparison of individual and family-oriented treatment, 337–338, 338t
effect on medication, 352
effectiveness, 352
evaluation in, 341
family and
  in western and nonwestern cultures, 337–338

family as patient in, 338–339, 340
family use of acute care and, 340–341
family-relevant functions in, 339–340
goals in
  acceptance of illness and understanding of episode, 342–343
  acceptance of need for continued treatment, 344
  controversies about, 351
  elucidation of stressful family interactions, 343–344
  identification of episode stressors, 343
  identification of potential stressors in, 343
  negotiation of, 341–342
  planning strategies with future stressors, 344
history of family treatment, 337–338
in hospital setting, 349
in outpatient settings, 350
process of, 341
psychodynamics of, 484–485
role in treatment, 351
Feedback
in group therapy, 376–377
in interpersonal group therapy, 380
  exercises in, 381
  psychotic patient and, 381
Feelings, expression of in trauma-related disorders, 207
Fenfluramine, for obsessive-compulsive disorder, 134
Fluoxetine
for antisocial personality disorder, 316
for borderline personality disorder, 303
dose range for, 97t
for obsessive-compulsive disorder, 134
  buspirone augmentation and, 134
for panic disorder, 133
pharmacokinetic profile of, 103t
side effects of, 100t, 102
Fluvoxamine, plus neuroleptic, for obsessive-compulsive disorder, 134
Focal conflicts
focal problem versus, 12
  case examples of, 12–13
Focal problems
versus focal conflict, 12
  case examples of, 12–13
Focal psychotherapy, 355–373. *See also* Psychodynamic psychotherapy
biopsychosocial assessment in, 358–362
versus brief, 356
catalyzing change in, 364, 365t, 366
change in
  stages of, 363–364, 364f
context in, 358
definition of, 356
diagnosis versus operational diagnosis in, 356–357
duration of, 371–372
event and adaptive effort in, 356

Focal psychotherapy—*continued*
    case examples of, 356–357
    future of, 372–373
    intermittent, 372
    longitudinal perspective in, 357–358
    medical necessity for, 355–356, 361
    open-ended, 372
    paradigm for, 359f
    for person with problem versus the problem, 357–358
    phases of
        developing focus in, 368–370
        establishing helping relationship in, 366–367
        motive and resistance in, 366
        reframing in, 367–368
        rehearsing for change, 370–371
        trial and error in, 371–372
    psychoanalytic techniques in, 482–483
    questions in, 356–363
        what next?, 362–363
        what now?, 357–362
        why now?, 356–357
    for restoration of normalcy in, 355–356
    suicide and
        attempted, 356–357
        successful, 357
Focus of therapy
    case examples of
        disruptive behavior and dangerousness, 370
        relapse of recovering alcoholic, 369
    commitment to, 368–369
    definition of, 368
        from systems perspective, 369–370
    versus duration, 368
Foundation for Accountability (FACT), assessment of employer-purchased health care, 507–508
Fugue
    dissociative, 199
    diagnosis of, 196

Gabapentin, plus divalproex or lithium, for mania, 158
Gene markers
    in diagnosis and treatment decisions, 475
    in identification of individual's genetic vulnerability, 475
Generalist (broker) model of case management
    description of, 331
    effectiveness of, 331–332
    reduction of inpatient care and, 334
Genetic disorders, dementia from, 260t
Genetic heritability
    in depression
        family education and, 111–112
    in obsessive-compulsive disorder, 127
    in panic disorder, 127
    in schizophrenia
        family counseling and, 184
    in substance-related disorders, 223

Genetic hypothesis, for depression, 91–92
Genograms, in family, home-based care, 398, 408
Geriatric patient, 249–270
    assessment of, 349
    biologic evaluation of, 251–252
    controversies in psychiatry and, 269–270
    dementing disorders in, 261–266
    electroconvulsive therapy for
        in delusional depression, 258
    informed consent and, 269
    levels of care assessment for, 252–253
    mood disorders in, 253–261
    psychiatric interview of, 249, 250
    psychopharmacologic management of
        medical evaluation for, 255
        pharmacodynamics and neurotransmission and, 256
        pharmacokinetics of psychotropic drugs and, 255–256
    psychotic disorders in, 266–268
    radiologic evaluation of, 252
    suicide and, 269–270
Global Deterioration Scale, in Alzheimer's disease, 265–266
Grand mal seizures, bupropion-induced, 101
Group psychotherapy, 375–388
    acute care models of, 377–382
        interpersonal, 380–381
        psychodynamic, 381–382
        skills development, 378–380
    group as microcosm of inpatient unit, 387
    history of, 375–377
    with hospitalized patients, 377
    inpatient population and, 382–386
        assignment to group, 383–384
        diversity of, 382–383
        frequency of sessions in, 383
        goals for, 385–386
        methods and, 386
        patient preparation for, 383
        safety and, 384–385
        selection of, 385
        team groups and, 383–384
    inpatient treatment team and, 386
        case managers and, 387
        dialogue with group leaders, 387
        negative model and, 387
    insight-oriented
        psychotic patients and, 377
    interpersonal, 380–381
    levels of groups for, 383
    task-oriented and social skills training, 377
    team groups in, 383–384
    therapeutic alliance in, 385–386
    therapist role in, 383
    treatment team and, 386–387
    value of, 388
Group therapy, in posttraumatic stress and dissociative disorders, 211–212
Groups, psychodynamics of, 484–485

Guanfacine, for attention-deficit/hyperactivity disorder, 288
Guardianship, court hearings and patient confidentiality, 453
Guidelines
    versus algorithm(s), 459
    definition of, 457–458
    development of, 458, 458t
    disadvantages of, 467
    standard of care versus, 466–467
    as teaching tool, 466
Guns, suicide risk and, 22

Haldol, for aggressive, psychotic men, 37
Haloperidol
    in acute psychosis in primary care, 75
    for borderline personality disorder, 25
    for delirium, 72
HCAs. *See* Heterocyclic antidepressants (HCAs)
Health Plan Employer Data Information Set (HEDIS), performance measures of National Committee on Quality Assurance, 507
HEDIS. *See* Health Plan Employer Data Information Set (HEDIS)
Hepatotoxicity
    of disulfiram, 236
    of divalproex, 153–154
Heroin
    dependence on, prevalence of, 224
    methadone replacement of, 239
Heterocyclic antidepressants (HCAs), 99, 101
    cardiotoxicity of
        in elderly, 256–257
    commonly prescribed, 97t
    dose ranges for, 97t
    in elderly, 256–257
Histamine receptor blockade, with monoamine oxidase inhibitors, 101
Home-based care, 391–410. *See also* Family and Home Consultation Service program
Homicidal behavior, child, case example of, 285
Homicide risk, in substance-related disorders, 230
Hospitalization
    in borderline personality disorder
        dependency and regression in, 311–312
    case management effects on, 333–334
    in crisis intervention, 60–61
    involuntary
        evidence of dangerousness to self or others, 451
        for grave inability to care for self, 451
        historic basis of, 450–451
        procedures and standards for, 451
    partial
        in crisis intervention, 59–60
        for psychotic disorders in elderly, 268
        for psychotic elderly patient, 268
        for schizophrenia, late-onset, 268
        for substance use disorders, 241–242

reduction with Assertive Community Treatment, 333–334
    of suicidal patient
        voluntary and involuntary, 23, 24
    of violent patient, 42
    voluntary, 450
Hostility. *See also* Violence
    medication management of, 36–38
Human Genome Project, 473
Human potential movement, group psychotherapy and, 376
Hyperthyroidism, anxiety in, 126
Hypomania, DSM-IV criteria for, 142
Hypothalamic effects, of neuroleptics, 179
Hypothalamic-pituitary-adrenal (HPA) axis, disturbance of, in depression, 95

Imipramine, for panic disorder, 32
Incompetency (patient)
    assessment of, 448
    confidentiality and, 425, 444
Infectious disease
    dementia from, 260t
    depression in, 88t, 250t
    mental status changes in, 55t
    in substance-related disorders, 231
Informed consent
    competency and, 447–448
    for disulfiram use, 236
    of elderly patient
        decision-making capacity and, 269
    for electroconvulsive therapy, 108
    exceptions to
        in emergencies, 448
        incompetent patient, 449
        patient's right to waive, 449
        therapeutic privilege, 448–449
    history of, 446–447
    information in, 447
    voluntariness in, 447
Insomnia
    in depression
        antidepressants and, 106–107
    from selective serotonin reuptake inhibitors, 106–107
Instrument panel reports
    McLean Hospital instrument panel, 512f, 512–513
    in profiling, 510
Intensive case management
    cost reduction with, 334–335
    description of, 332
    examples of, 332
    reduction of inpatient care and, 334
Interpersonal group psychotherapy
    exercises in, 381
    feedback in, 380–381
    role of, 380
    types of, 380–381

Interpersonal relationships, in etiology of schizophrenia, 171
Interview techniques
  in family, home-based care, 399
  psychodynamic, 484
Intoxication, mental status changes in, 55t
Involuntary commitment and treatment
  civil liberties issue and, 185–186
  court hearings and patient confidentiality,
    453
  ethical concerns in
    with children and adolescents, 283
Isolation, as escape from stress or threat, 202–203

Joining, in family, home-based care, 400
Justice, 493
  in allocation of care, 499

Kindling
  in bipolar disorder, 148
  in mood disorders, 289–290
Korsakoff's psychosis, 234–235
Kraepelin, E.
  dementia praecox versus bipolar disorder and,
    167
  and paraphrenia or late-onset schizophrenia,
    266

Lamotrigine, for mania, 158
Language deficits, in Alzheimer's disease, 261
Legal issue(s). *See also specific, e.g., Confidentiality*
  confidentiality, 231, 423–425, 444–446
  interaction with legal system and, 452–453
  malpractice, 431–442
  managed care and liability, 442–443
  patients' rights, 446–452
Legal system-psychiatrist interaction
  psychiatrist as witness, 453
  transference and countertransference issues in,
    453
  understanding adversarial process of system,
    452
Limit-setting, with borderline personality disorder patient, 304–305, 308, 311
Lithium
  administration of, 151–152
  antimanic effects of, 151
  in antisocial personality disorder, 316
  for borderline personality disorder, 303
  drug interactions with, 152
  in elderly, 257
    monitoring of, 257–258
  for hostility, 38
  interaction of
    with electroconvulsive therapy, 108
  for mania, 151–152
  monitoring of, 152, 257–258
  neuropsychological impairment with, 152
  plus antidepressants, 105
  plus carbamazepine

  for mania, 158
  prophylactic, 157
  for schizophrenia, 182
Loss, depression and, 93–94

Magnetic resonance imaging (MRI), functional
  information with, 477
Major depressive disorder (MDD)
  case example of, 6–7
  classification of, 85
  dysthymia and, 85
  in elderly. *See* Depression, late-onset
  with melancholia, 85
  with obsessive-compulsive disorder, 125
  with panic disorder, 124
  with psychosis, 84
  psychotherapeutic approaches in, 109–110
  suicide risk in, 19
  therapeutic alliance in, 110
  in women, 94
Malpractice, 431–442
  in borderline personality disorder cases, 309
  elements in, 431–433
    breach of standard, 432–433
    damages, 433
    direct causation, 433
    duty of provider (negligence), 432
  grounds for, 434
    abandonment versus termination, 440
    for dangerousness, 438–439
    medication/somatic treatments, 435–437
    misdiagnosis, 437–438
    sexual misconduct, 439
    suicide, 434–436
  prevalence in psychiatry, 433
  prevention of
    clinical consultation in, 440–441
    legal consultation in, 441
    patient-doctor relationship/alliance in, 442
    records and documentation in, 441–442
  risk for, 433–434
  type, frequency, success of claims, 433–434
Managed care
  algorithms and guidelines in, 466
  changes in professional practice, 543
  confidentiality in, 497–498
  in depression treatment, 112–113
  effect of
    duration of hospitalization, 469–470
    on psychiatric care, 469–470
    on schizophrenia management, 187
    on strategies and goals in acute care, 470
  growth of, forces for, 543
  health care redefined as industry and, 543–544
  level of care for mania and, 148
  liability in, 442
    patient rights and withholding of benefits in-
      formation, 443–443
  malpractice claim areas in, 442–443
  pressures from

case example in residency training, 489–490
Mandatory reporting requirements, 446
 documentation of mandated report, 446
Mania, 141–162
 brain imaging in, 149
 controversies in
  divalproex versus lithium, 159
  life-long maintenance, 159–160
 definition of
  DSM-IV, 141, 142
  historical, 141
 diagnosis of, 141–143
 differential diagnosis of, 146, 148
 divalproex versus lithium for, 157
 electroconvulsive therapy for, 155
 electroencephalogram in, 149
 epidemiology of
  in elderly, 253–254
 level of care in, 158–159
  assessing, 149
 pharmacologic management of
  algorithm for, 156f, 157–158
  changes in, 157
 predictors of relapse and recovery in, 160–161,
  161f
 prevalence of, 143, 146
 psychiatric and medical examination in, 149
 symptoms of manic episode and, 142
 toxicology screen in, 149
 treatment of, 149–158
MAOIs. *See* Monoamine oxidase inhibitors
  (MAOIs)
Maprotiline, 99
 dose range for, 97t
 side effects of, 100t
MAST. *See* Michigan Alcohol Screening Test
  (MAST)
McCabe v. City of Lynn-Federal District Court
  of Massachusetts, violence assessment
  and, 41
MDD. *See* Major depressive disorder (MDD)
Meaning of illness, psychodynamic theory and,
  478
Medical ethics. *See also* Bioethics
 historical perspective on, 493
 physician as clinical agent, 548
Medical necessity
 DSM-IV diagnosis for, 361
 frames of reference for, 355–356
Medical record. *See* Case record
Medicare, and professional compensation, 548
Medicare/Medicaid, effect on psychiatric practice,
  471
Medication psychoeducation
 for compliance, 150
 for family of borderline personality patient,
  307–308
Medication groups, in acute care, 378
Medication noncompliance
 in bipolar disorder, case example of, 360

family intervention for, 348–349
 psychodynamics of
  case example of, 486
  resistance in, 486
  transference and countertransference in, 485
 in schizophrenia, 188
Medicolegal issues, in borderline personality disorder, 309
Melancholia, psychodynamic formulation in
  Abraham and Freud, 92–93
Melatonin, mood disorders and, 92
Memory
 malleability of, 213
 pseudomemory versus, 213–214
  creation of, 213
  suggestion and, 213–214
 of traumatic events
  fragmentary, 214
  hyperamnesia and, 214
  nonintegration of, 212–213
  validity of, 212
Mental Health Statistics Improvement Project
  (MHSIP) report card, 508, 516–533
 access to care in, 516–529
 appropriateness of care in, 519–523
 level of independence in
  capacity for independent community living,
   528–529
  increase in independent functioning, 529
  increase in productive activity, 527–528
  minimal recurrence of problems, 530–531
  participation in self-help activities, 530
  positive changes, 531
  reduced impairment from substance abuse,
   526–527
  reduced involvement in criminal justice system, 529–530
 outcomes in
  level of independence, 526–531
  physical health, 523–524
  psychological health, 525–526
 prevention in, 532–533
  information to reduce risk of developing
   mental disorders, 533
  interventions to reduce risk of developing
   mental disorders, 533
  measures for, 532
  research in, 532
  wellness promotion in, 532
 social relationships in, 531–532
Mental status changes
 life-threatening causes of, 54t
 medication-induced, 55t
Mental status examination
 of agitated patient, 69
 in depression, 95
 of elderly patient, 251
 in emergency care, 49
 in violence assessment, 35
Metabolic abnormalities, depression in, 88t

Metabolic disorders
  dementia from, 260t
  depression from, late-onset, 250t
Methadone hydrochloride
  for maintenance treatment of heroin addiction, 239
  for opioid detoxification, 238
Methylphenidate (Ritalin)
  for attention-deficit/hyperactivity disorder, 288
  in children and adolescents, 278t
  in elderly, 258
Michigan Alcohol Screening Test (MAST), in substance-related disorder diagnosis, 226, 228
Milieu-based group psychotherapy. *See* Group psychotherapy
Mini-Mental Status Examination
  in depression, 95
  of elderly patient, 251
Molecular biology
  gene cloning and identification of gene products, 474
  gene markers in, 475
  genetic heterogeneity and, 473–474
  Human Genome Project and, 473
  interaction of genetic risk and life events, 473
  positional mapping in, 473–474
  relevance in Alzheimer's disease, 474–475
Monoamine oxidase inhibitors (MAOIs)
  for borderline personality disorder, 303
  commonly prescribed, 97t
  dose range for, 97t
  in elderly, 257
  interactions with
    drug, 101
    electroconvulsive therapy, 108
    food, 101
    selective serotonin reuptake inhibitors, 104
  mechanisms of action of, 101
  for panic disorder, 133
  side effects of, 100t
Mood disorders. *See also* Depression; Major depressive disorder (MDD); Mania
  bipolar II disorder, 87
  borderline personality disorder versus, 295
  epidemiology of
    in elderly, 253–254
  posttraumatic stress disorder versus, 199–200
  suicide risk in, 19
Mood stabilizers
  for borderline personality disorder, 303
  in elderly, 257–258, 258t
  for hostility, 38
  for violence, 38
Morel, B.A., dementia praecox and, 167
MRI. *See* Magnetic resonance imaging (MRI)
Muscarinic receptor blockade, with monoamine oxidase inhibitors, 101

Naltrexone

adverse effects of, 236–237
  in alcohol abuse treatment, 236–237
  for maintenance treatment of opioid abuse, 239
National Comorbidity Survey (NCS)
  of mania, 143
  violence and mental illness in, 30
Nefazodone
  for depression, 98
  dose range for, 97t, 104–105
  drug interactions with, 105
  for panic disorder, 133
  side effects of, 104
Neoplastic disease
  dementia from, 260t
  depression in, 88t
  mental status changes in, 55t
Neurohormonal hypotheses, for depression, 92
Neuroimaging, in schizophrenia, indications for, 174–175
Neuroleptic malignant syndrome, 178t
Neuroleptics, 175–179
  administration of
    rapid neuroleptization versus routine, standard dose, 177
    route in, 177
    schedule for, 177
  adverse effects of, 178t, 179
  akathisia and
    suicidal ideation with, 22
  in demented elderly
    for behavioral and psychotic symptoms, 264–265
  dosage of, 177
  efficacy of, 175–176
  for hostility, 37
  plus benzodiazepines, 177
  for posttraumatic stress disorder, 209
  in pregnancy and lactation, 179
  for schizophrenia, late-onset, 267–268
  selection guidelines for, 176–177
  side effects of
    in elderly, 264–265
Neurologic disorders
  delirium in, 71
  depression from, late-onset, 250t
  depression in, 88t
Neuroscience
  developmental neurobiology in, 475, 476
  receptor activation, 476
  signal transduction in, 475–476
Neurotransmitters, disturbances of, in depression, 90–91
Nicotine withdrawal, and aggression in psychotic patients, 173
Noncompliance
  in bipolar disorder, 150
  of elderly with psychosis, 267
  in schizophrenia, 173
    late-onset, 268

Nonmaleficence, 493–494

Norm, in quality assessment, 506, 513

Nutritional diseases, in substance-related disorders, 231

Object relations, 7
  psychodynamic perspective on, 9
Object relations theory, 482
  in residency training, 484
Observation
  in family, home-based care, 400
  inpatient in crisis intervention, 60
Obsessive-compulsive disorder (OCD)
  alliance, psychotherapeutic management, family involvement in, 134–136
  cognitive behavioral therapy for, 135
  cognitive loss of control in, 124
  combination treatment of, 136
  comorbidity and, 125
  definition of, 123–124
  epidemiology of, 125
  family intervention in, 350
  level of care in, 130–131
  neuropsychiatric components of, 127
  versus other anxiety disorders, 126–127
  pharmacologic management of, 131, 133–134
  psychodynamic, interpersonal components of, 128
  race and gender in, 125
Obsessive-compulsive personality disorder (OCPD)
  psychodynamic, interpersonal components of, 128–129
  psychodynamic treatment of, 136
  treatment controversies in
    behavioral versus pharmacologic therapy for, 136–137
    long-term risks, 137
OCD. *See* Obsessive-compulsive disorder (OCD)
Olanzapine
  for mania, 158
  for schizophrenia, 181
Opioid use disorder
  detoxification in, 238
  epidemiology of, 224
  intoxication with, 237
  maintenance treatment of, 238–239
  withdrawal from, 235t, 237–238
Oppositional defiant disorder. *See* Disruptive behavior
Outcome(s)
  data for profiling and report cards, 508–509
  in Donabedian model of quality assurance, 505f, 505–506
  in Donabedian quality assessment model, 505–506
  physical health
    increased access to general healthcare, 523–524

minimal negative outcomes from treatment, 524
  psychological health
    increased sense of personhood, 526
    reduced psychological distress, 525–526
Outpatient care
  in crisis intervention, 58
  intensive, 58–59
Overdose
  with opioids, 237
  with sedative-hypnotic medications, 237
Oxazepam, for alcohol detoxification, 236

Panic attack
  definition of, 124
  somatic loss of control in, 124
Panic control treatment, for panic disorder, 134
Panic disorder (PD)
  case example of crisis in, 129
  cognitive behavioral therapy for, 134–135
  comorbidity with, 124–125
  definition of, 123–124
  epidemiology of, 124–125
  formulation of, 129
  level of care in, 130–131
  neuropsychiatric components of, 127
  versus other anxiety disorders, 126
  pharmacologic management of, 131, 132–133
  psychodynamic, interpersonal components of, 127–128
  psychodynamic treatment of, 135
  suicide risk in, 17, 19–20
  treatment controversies in
    behavioral verus pharmacologic therapy for, 136–137
    long-term risks, 137
Parkinsonism, neuroleptic-induced, 178t
Parkinson's disease, dementia in, 262
Paroxetine
  dose range for, 97t, 102
  for panic disorder, 133
  pharmacokinetic profile of, 103t
  side effects of, 102–103
Patients' rights, 446–452. *See also specific, e.g., Informed consent*
  acceptance or refusal of treatment, 451–452
  admission
    consent to, 450
    involuntary, 450–451
  informed consent, 446–450
Payers, in quality assessment, 506
Perceptions of Care (PoC) measure, 541
Performance Measures for Managed Behavioral Healthcare Programs (PERMS) report card, 508, 534–537
  access to care in
    structural indicators of, 535–536
    utilization indicators of, 534–535
  consumer satisfaction in, 536
  quality of care in, 536–537

Personal strengths model (Kansas model) of case
        management
    central features of, 332
    comparison with generalist and ACT models,
        332
    reduction of inpatient care and, 334
Personality changes, in Alzheimer's disease,
        261–262
Personality disorders. *See also* Antisocial personal-
        ity disorder (APD); Borderline personal-
        ity disorder (BPD)
    agitation and violence in, 68
    with depressive features, 87
    family intervention in, 350
Personality traits and type, depression and, 90
Phenothiazines, drug interactions with, 180
Physician satisfaction. *See also* Psychiatrist satis-
        faction
    definition of satisfaction and, 544
    studies of
        aspects of, 544–545
        effect on patient satisfaction and clinical out-
            come, 545
        in organized settings
        variables affecting, 545–546
Polypharmacy, for depression, controversial,
        112
Polysomnography, in depression diagnosis, 96
Positional mapping, of genes for heritable disor-
        ders, 473–474
Positron emission tomography (PET)
    in elderly, 252
    functional information with, 477
Posttraumatic stress disorder (PTSD)
    from abusive relationship
        rehearsal for change in, 371
    addictive activity, 202
    alliance and psychotherapeutic management in,
        209–212
    biologic evaluation of, 204
    biologic processes in, 203
    in combat veterans, 195
        treatment of, 204–205
    comorbidity in, 199, 209–210
    course and prognosis of, 214
    definition of, 195
    descriptive diagnosis of
        characteristics and symptoms of, 199
    diagnosis of, 196
    differential diagnosis of, 199–200
    DSM-IV criteria for, 196
    dysfunctional isolation in, 202, 203
    epidemiology of, 197–198
    family support, education, intervention in, 212
    focal problems in, 203
    formulation of problem, 202
    gender and, 197–198
    grounding techniques for symptom control in,
        206
    group therapy in, 211–212

        individual therapy and case management in,
            211
        level of care for, 204
        lifetime prevalence of, 197
        nursing practice in, 209–210
        psychopharmacologic management of, 208–209
        self-destructive or suicidal behaviors, 202
Primary care emergency(ies). *See also specific, e.g.,*
        Agitated and violent patient
    acute delirium, 71–73
    acute psychosis, 73–76
    agitated and violent patient, 67–70
    suicidal patient, 76–79
Privilege
    patient
        versus confidentiality, 445
        exceptions to, 445
    therapeutic, 448–449
Problem-solving groups, 378–379
Process, in Donabedian model of quality assur-
        ance, 505, 505f
Process measures, for profiling and report cards,
        508
Process notes, progress notes versus, 418–420
Professional compensation
    allying clinical, organizational, financial goals,
        549–550
    incentive pay in
        advocacy versus allocation of care with,
            549
        competition and distrust with, 549
        conflict of interest and negligence with,
            549–550
        for staff performance and productivity, 549
    models for
        patient agency, 548–549
        profit maximization, 548
        target income, 548
    in optimization of effectiveness and efficiency
        of care, 549
Professional satisfaction, 543–547
    managed care effect on, 543–544
    of physician, 544–546
    of psychiatrist, 547
    recommendations for, 546
Profiling
    definition of, 514
    description of, 506–507
    examples of, 507
    improvements for
        outcome data, 508–509
        process measures, 508
    instrument panel reports in, 510, 512f
    limitations in, 509
    report cards in, 507–508
    versus utilization management, 506–507
Progress notes versus process notes, 418–420
Projection, in antisocial personality disorder,
        314
Protective custody, for violent patient, 42–43

Pseudodepression. *See* Dementia syndrome of depression (pseudodepression)
Psychiatric emergency services
cost of, 62–63
outcome research in, 63
Psychiatric practice
managed care effect on, 469–470
traditional versus emerging, 362t, 362–363
Psychiatrist
interaction with legal system, 452–453
new role of
brain imaging and, 471, 472
income reduction/cost-saving factors in,
479
Medicare/Medicaid and, 471
molecular genetics and, 471, 472
neuroscience and, 471, 472
scientific advances and, 471–472
shrinking residency programs and, 470
role in team treatment, 500–501
satisfaction of and trends in psychiatry, 544
Psychiatry
new role of. *See also* Residency training
psychodynamic. *See* Psychodynamic psychiatry
psychodynamic therapy
residency training in, 478
Psychodynamic group therapy
group as subgroup of psychiatric program, 381,
382
integration of object relations and systems theory in, 381
therapist's role in, 381–382
Psychodynamic psychiatry. *See also* Focal psychotherapy
applications of, 478
brief dynamic therapy and, 483
conflict in, 482
definition of, 481–482
duration of treatment and, 482–483
meaning of illness in, 478
versus psychodynamic psychotherapy, 481
residency training in, 483–486
core curriculum in, 483–486
ego psychology in, 484
interviewing and formulation in, 484
object relations theory in, 484
psychodynamic understanding of Axis I and
Axis II disorders, 485
psychodynamics of groups and families in,
484–485
psychodynamics of medication prescribing
in, 485
case example, 486
self psychology in, 484
transference in, 478, 482
Psychodynamic theory
applications of, 478
in residency training, 478
Psychoeducation
in acute family intervention, 348t

of borderline personality disorder patient, 311
of family, 341, 342
Psychosis. *See also* Psychotic disorders
acute episode
family intervention for, 347
brief reactive, 200
causes of
life-threatening, 73
medical, 73–74
psychiatric, 74
definition of, 73
in primary care
determination of treatment setting for, 75
evaluation of, 74–75
primary in psychiatric disorder, 74, 76
psychopharmacologic management of, 75
safety and, 74, 75
secondary in medical condition, 73–74, 76
Psychotherapy. *See* Focal psychotherapy; Group
psychotherapy
Psychotic disorders. *See also* Psychosis
antisocial personality disorder versus, 314
borderline personality disorder versus, 295
in elderly
day programs and partial hospitalization for,
268
psychopharmacologic management of,
267–268
epidemiology of
in elderly, 266–268
multi-disciplinary treatment plan for,
144f–145f
schizophrenia versus, 171
substance-induced
schizophrenia versus, 171
PTSD. *See* Posttraumatic stress disorder (PTSD)

Quality assessment
continuous quality improvement theory in, 504,
509–513
Donabedian model for, 504–506, 505f
profiling in, 506–507
report cards for accountability to purchaser,
507–508
Quality assurance programs, traditional, 503
Quality control, case record in, 418
Quality of care
definition of, 514
in Performance Measures for Managed Behavioral Healthcare Programs report card
appropriateness in, 536–537
effectiveness in, 536
efficiency in, 536
Quetiapine
for mania, 158
for schizophrenia, 181

Rabbit syndrome, neuroleptic-induced, 178t
Rationing of care, 498–499
Reality testing, 7

Referral
    in Family and Home Consultation Service program, 394, 395–397
    of suicidal patient, 77, 78
Reframing
    case example of, 368
    in focal psychotherapy, 367–368
    patient and clinician roles in, 367
Reimbursement and coverage restrictions
    conflicts of interest
        clinical versus provider, 496–497
    disclosure and, 495–496
    informed consent and, 494–495
Relationships
    establishment of by trauma survivors, 207–208
    of patient in crisis, 51
Report card(s)
    definition of, 514
    Foundation for Accountability, 507–508
    Health Plan Employer Data Information Set, 507
    improvements for
        outcome data, 508–509
        process measures, 508
    limitations of, 509
    McLean Hospital, 512–513
    Mental Health Statistics Improvement Project, 508, 516–533
    Performance Measures for Managed Behavioral Healthcare Programs, 508, 534–537
Residency training, 473–479
    curriculum in. *See also specific component, e.g., Brain imaging*
        brain imaging in, 477–478
        goal of, 472–473
        molecular biology in, 473–475
        neuroscience in, 475–477
    in psychodynamic psychiatry, 481–491. *See also* Psychodynamic
        psychiatry, residency training in
        application of with on-site supervision, case examples, 486–490
        role modeling in, 487
Residential treatment
    for borderline personality disorder, 300
    respite in crisis intervention, 60
    for substance use disorder, 242
Rheumatologic disorders, depression in, 89
Right to refuse treatment, 451–452
Risk-benefit analysis, in documentation, 421
Risperidone
    in adolescents, 37
    dose for adult men, 37
    for hostility, 37
    for mania, 158
    for posttraumatic stress disorder, 209
    for schizophrenia, 179, 180
        late-onset, 268
Role playing, in problem-solving groups, 379

SADS, Schedule for Affective Disorder and Schizophrenia (SADS)
SAFER (self-care, symptom control, acknowledgment, functioning, expression, relationships), 205–207
Safety
    of demented patients, 263, 264
    depression and, 94
    of elderly patient, 252
    in family, home-based care, 400–401
    in group psychotherapy, 384–385
    in home-based care, 394, 398
    inpatient versus home-based care and, 391
    in primary care setting
        agitated and violent patient, 68
        delirious patient and, 72
        psychotic patient and, 74, 75
Samarateens, in suicide prevention, 282
Satisfaction
    consumer (patient), 504, 506, 536
    physician, 543–547
    psychiatrist, 544
Schedule for Affective Disorder and Schizophrenia (SADS), in mania, 143
Schizoaffective disorder
    bipolar disorder versus, 146
    case example of crisis intervention in, 57–58
    versus depression, 87
    schizophrenia versus, 171
Schizophrenia, 167–188
    age at onset, 187
    aggressiveness in, 172, 173
    alliance and psychotherapeutic management of
        antiregressive, 182–183
        hope in, 183
    antidepressants in, 182
    antipsychotic agents for, 175–182
        representative, 176t
    anxiolytic agents for, 182
    beta-adrenergic blockers in, 182
    bipolar disorder versus, 146
    civil liberties and, 185–186
    clozapine for, 25, 179–180
    controversies in care of, 185–188
    course and prognosis of, 187
        predictors of, 188
    definition of, 167–168
        DSM-IV, 168
    depression in, 87
    diagnostic criteria for
        Bleuler, 167–168
        DSM-IV, 168–169
        Schneiderian first rank symptoms, 168
    differential diagnosis of
        medical and substance-induced conditions versus, 170t
    ego defenses and character style in, 171–172
    electroconvulsive therapy for, 182
    electroencephalogram in, 174
    environmental assessment and, 172

epidemiology of, 169
family support, education, intervention in,
  183–184
focal problem in, 172–173
formulation of, 172
group therapy for, 185
historical perspective and, 167–168
history in, 174
identity problems in, 172
imaging in, 174
laboratory tests in, 174
late-onset, 266
  day programs for, 268
  ego defenses and character style in, 267
  neuroleptics for, 267–268
  partial hospitalization for, 268
level of care in
  assessing, 175
managed care and, 187
mood stabilizers for, 182
paranoid
  case example of home-based care in,
    405–407, 408–409
pharmacotherapy and, 186
physical examination in, 174
psychopharmacologic management of,
  175–182
psychosocial rehabilitation for, 185
psychotherapy and, 186–187
  group, 378
relapse in
  alcohol and drug use in, 173
  medication noncompliance in, 173
risk factors and rates for, 169
substance use and, 187
subtypes of
  catatonic, 169
  disorganized, 171
  paranoid, 169, 171
  undifferentiated, 171
suicidal behavior in, 172
suicide risk in, 17, 20, 188
violence in, 30
Schizophreniform disorder, schizophrenia versus,
  171
Schizotypal patients, 171–172
Schizotypal personality disorder, family intervention in, 350
Schneider, K., phenomenology of schizophrenia,
  168
Secrecy, in borderline personality disorder, 307
Sedative-hypnotic use disorder
  epidemiology of, 224
  intoxication with, 237
  overdose of, 237
  withdrawal from, 235t, 237
Selective serotonin reuptake inhibitors (SSRIs),
  101–103
  in children and adolescents
    frequently used, 278t

commonly prescribed, 97t
for depressed suicidal patient, 24
differences among, 103
dose ranges for, 97t, 102
in elderly, 256t, 257
interaction of
  with drugs, 103–104
  with electroconvulsive therapy, 108
  with monoamine oxidase inhibitors, 104
  with tricyclic antidepressants, 104
for obsessive-compulsive disorder, 133–134
for panic disorder, 133
pharmacokinetic profiles of, 103, 103t
plus clomipramine
  for obsessive-compulsive disorder, 134
side effects of, 102–103
for violent, self-destructive behavior, 38
Self psychology, in residency training, 484
Self-care, in childhood traumatization treatment,
  205–206
Self-destructive behavior
  level of care and, 96
  selective serotonin reuptake inhibitors for,
    38
Self-esteem
  loss of
    in depression, 83, 93
    in panic disorder, 128
Self-hate, in child abuse victim, 201–202
Self-mutilation
  in childhood trauma victims, 205–206, 208
  impulse for
    emergency department case example,
      52–53
Separation anxiety, panic disorder and, 127–128
Sertindole
  for mania, 158
  for schizophrenia, 181
Sertraline
  dose range for, 97t
  for panic disorder, 133
  pharmacokinetic profile of, 103t
  side effects of, 100t, 102
Sexual abuse
  childhood, 196–197
    treatment of survivors and, 206–208
  helping relationship in
    case example of adolescent, 366–367
Sexual dysfunction, with antidepressants, medication strategies for, 105
Signal transduction
  identification of neurotransmitters and neuro-
    modulators in, 476
  intracellular pathways activated by specific re-
    ceptors, 476–477
  receptor transduction processes in, 476
  relevance to psychotropic drug mechanism of
    action, 475–476
  research in
    historical development of, 475

Single photon emission computed tomography (SPECT)
  in elderly, 252
  functional information with, 477
Skills development group(s)
  educational, 378
  problem-solving, 378–379
  structure and task orientation of, 378
Sleep disturbance, in posttraumatic stress disorder, 209
Social phobia, panic disorder versus, 125–126
Social skills groups, 379
Solpidem, for posttraumatic stress disorder, 209
Speech and language disturbance, assessment in elderly, 251
Splitting, in borderline personality disorder, 307
SSRIs. *See* Selective serotonin reuptake inhibitors (SSRIs)
Standard
  definition of, 514
  in quality assessment, 506, 514
Standard of care, 466–467
Stimulants
  for attention-deficit hyperactivity disorder (ADHD), 278t, 288, 290
    concurrent with antisocial personality disorder, 316
  in children and adolescents
    frequently used, 278t
Stressors
  in depression, 94
  in dissociative and posttraumatic stress disorders, 202
  in family intervention
    identification of current, 343
    identification of potential, 343
    management or minimization of future, 344
  in formulation of case, 10
    case example of, 10–12
  impact on panic- and obsessive-compulsive disorders, 129, 130
  in late-onset schizophrenia, 267
  in schizophrenia, 172
Structure
  definition of, 514
  in Donabedian model of quality assurance, 505, 505f
Substance abuse. *See also* Substance use disorder(s)
  DSM-IV criteria for, 222
Substance dependence. *See also* Substance use disorder(s)
  definition of, 221
Substance use, in schizophrenia, 173, 187
Substance use disorder(s), 221–245. *See also specific substance, e.g., Alcohol*
  abuse and, 222
  agitation and violence with, 68
  alcohol, 223, 234, 236–237, 243
  anger and, 229

antisocial personality disorder versus, 314
  bipolar disorder recovery and relapse and, 148, 160, 161
  borderline personality disorder versus, 294
  case example of home-based care for, 397
  in child abuse victims, 200
  cocaine, 224, 239–240, 243
  course and prognosis of, 244–245
  denial in, 228
  dependence and, 221
  depression and, 229–230
  depression in, 87, 89
  descriptive diagnosis of, 225
  diagnosis
    variables assessment in, 225
  diagnosis of, 221–223
    masking of symptoms in, 225
    screening measures for, 226, 228
    substance-associated diagnoses and, 226, 227t
    toxicology testing in, 225–226
  DSM-IV criteria for, 221–222
  epidemiology of, 223–224
  family intervention in, 350–351
  family therapy in, 241
  focal problems in, 230
  formulation of problem, 229
  gender and, 223
  group therapy for, 240–241
  inpatient versus outpatient care in, 243–244
  legal issues in, 231
  level of care in, 242–243
    criteria for, 233, 233t
  medical problems in, 230–231
  mental status evaluation in, 232
  motivation for recovery from, 228–229
  neurologic examination in, 233
  nonalcoholic
    risk factors for, 224
  opioids, 224, 237–239
  physical examination in, 232
  polysubstance dependence, 223
  populations at risk, 223
  populations with, 222–223
  psychiatric comorbidity and, 226, 227t
    medications for, 239–240, 244
  psychopharmacologic management of, 234–239
  remission in, 222
    definition of, 222
  sedative-hypnotics, 224, 237
  self-help groups for, 241
  social environment and, 231
  suicide risk in, 17, 20
  therapeutic alliance in, 240
  therapeutic milieu and, 241–242
  toxicology screens in, 232
  treatment milieu
    controversies in, 243–244
    indications for inpatient, 242–243
    partial hospitalization, 241–242

residential, 242
violence risk in, 230
withdrawal syndromes in
    clinical features of, 235t
Suicidal behavior
    in children and adolescents, 277–290
        alliance and psychotherapeutic management
            of, 281–282
        antidepressants and, 281
        in children and adolescents
            in children and adolescents
                evaluation in, 281
                toxicologic screen in, 281
            reduction of suicide risk in, 280
        contributing factors in, 279–280
        controversies in care of, 282–283
        course and prognosis of, 283
        definition of, 277
        diagnosis of, 277–278, 279
        ego defense and character style in, 279
        electroconvulsive therapy and, 281
        epidemiology of, 278
        family and, 281–282
        involuntary treatment of, 283
        levels of care in, 281
        plan for safety and, 282
        preventive interventions for, 283
        public education and, 282–283
        risk factors for, 278, 279
        Samariteens and, 282
    versus parasuicidal behavior, 299
Suicidal ideation
    level of care and, 96
    suicide and, 16–17
Suicidal patient
    alliance with, 23
    contracts with, 23
    hospitalization of
        partial, 23
        voluntary and involuntary, 23, 24
    in primary care
        assessment of, 76–77
        attempt or intent to commit, 77
        contract for safety in, 77–79
        referral of, 77, 78
        suicidal ideation and, 77
        telephone handling of, 78
    psychopharmacologic intervention for, 24
Suicide. *See also* Suicidal patient
    age and, 15
    attempted
        family intervention for, 347–348
    in borderline personality disorder
        rate of, 312
    case histories of focal psychotherapy and
        in attempted, 356–357
        in successful, 357
    in children and adolescents, 21
    in elderly
        in depression, 254

epidemiology of, 269–270
patients at risk for, 16–17
populations at risk for, 49–50
prediction problem and, 16
predictors of, 50
prevalence of, 15
rate of
    in bipolar depression, 113
    in unipolar depression, 113
risk assessment for
    countertransference in, 17
    goals of patient evaluation in, 18–19
    patient interview in, 17–19
risk factors for
    access to lethal means, 22
    age, 21
    akathisia, 22
    alcohol and substance abuse, 20
    family history, 22
    gender, 21
    health, 21–22
    history of attempts and threats, 21
    occupational, 21
    psychiatric disorders, 19–21
    social, 21
    terminal illness, 22
suicidal ideation and, 16–17
threatened
    case example of home-based care for, 397
        consultation in, 402–404
    in women versus men, 15–16
Suicide risk
    in alcohol and substance abuse, 20
        treatment of, 25
    in antisocial personality disorder, 315
        treatment of, 20–21
    assessment of
        for patient in crisis, 49–50
        in violence assessment, 35
    in borderline personality disorder, 20–21, 307
        assessment of, 298–299
        concurrent substance abuse and, 299–300
        depression and, 299–300
        psychopharmacologic treatment of, 25–26
    in depression
        psychotic, 24
    in elderly, 270
    in schizophrenia, 20, 25, 188
        treatment and, 25
    in substance-related disorders, 20, 25, 230
Support groups
    Alcoholics Anonymous, 241, 243
    for families, 351
Systems consultation, in family, home-based care.
    See under Family and Home Consulta-
    tion Service program

Tarasoff v. Regents of the University of Califor-
    nia-California Supreme Court, violence
    assessment and, 41

Tardive dyskinesia, neuroleptic-induced, 178t
TCAs. *See* Tricyclic antidepressants (TCAs)
Termination of treatment
    versus abandonment, 440
    in antisocial personality disorder, 318
    of violent patient, 70
Tetrahydroaminoacridine (THA, tacrine) (Co-
        gex), for dementia, 264
Therapeutic community, 376
Thiamine, intravenous, in alcohol use disorder,
        236
Thioridazine, drug interactions with, 180–181
Thioxetine, for borderline personality disorder,
        25
Thought processes, 7
Thyroid hormone (T_3), in combination with anti-
        depressants, 105
Thyrotropin-releasing hormone (TRH) stimula-
        tion test, in depression, 89t, 95
Total quality management (TQM). *See* Continu-
        ous quality improvement (CQI) (total
        quality improvement [TQM])
Training in Community Living (TCL) Program.
        See also Assertive Community Training
        (ACT)
    origin and adaptation of, 333
Transference
    definition of, 482
    in interaction with legal system, 453
    in psychodynamic psychiatry, 478, 482
    psychodynamic theory and, 478
Traumatic injury, mental status changes in, 55t
Traumatization. *See also* Childhood traumatization
    disruptive behavior following, 285
    dissociative disorders following, 196
    posttraumatic stress disorder following, 195
Trazodone, 101
    dose range for, 97t
    in elderly, 257
    for posttraumatic stress disorder, 209
    side effects, 100t
Treatment
    consent to, 451
    durable power of attorney and, 452
    of incompetent patient, 452
    right to refuse, 451–452
    role of guardian of incompetent patient in, 452
Triage. *See also* Crisis intervention; Emergency care
    acuity assessment in, 53
    definition of, 463
    in emergency department or psychiatric hospi-
        tal, 53
    life-threatening causes of crisis, 54t
    medical clearance in, 53–54
    patient referral in, 463–464
    process of psychiatric, 463–464
        algorithm for, 464f
    of special populations, 61–62
Tricyclic antidepressants (TCAs)
    for borderline personality disorder, 302–303

    in children and adolescents
        frequently used, 278t
    commonly prescribed, 97t
    dose ranges for, 97t, 99
    interaction of
        with electroconvulsive therapy, 108
    overdose of, 99, 107
    selective serotonin reuptake inhibitor interac-
        tion with, 104

Utilization review
    algorithms in, 466
    case record in, 418
    quality of care and, 503

Valproic acid
    for borderline personality disorder, 303
    in elderly, 258, 258t
    for hostility, 38
    for schizophrenia, 182
Vascular dementia. *See also* Alzheimer's disease (AD)
    versus Alzheimer's disease, 262
    epidemiology of, 261
    vascular pathologies in, 260t
Venlafaxine, 100
    for depression, 98
    dose range for, 104
    in elderly, 257
    for panic disorder, 133
    side effects of, 100t, 104
Violence. *See also* Aggressive behavior; Agitation
        and violence; Hostility; Violent patient
    antidepressants for, 38
    antipsychotics for, 37
    in antisocial personality disorder
        medication reduction of, 316
        risk of, 315
    assaultive
        physical, 29, 30
        risk assessment for, 38–39
        sexual, 29
        weapons in, 39
    assessment of
        legal issues in, 41
        medical evaluation in, 35
        measured, 34–35
        patient presentation in, 33, 50
        physical signs of, 50
        rapid, 34
        signs in, 34
        toxicology screens in, 35
        weapons concerns in, 33–34
    assistance for assaulted staff members, 39–40
    avoidance of high risk situations, 39
    benzodiazepines for, 38
    case example of home-based care in, 397
    clinical studies of, 30–32
    correlation with mental illness, 30
    cultural norms and, 32
    definition, assumptions and comparisons of, 31

documentation of, 40–41
domestic
    case example of home-based care for, 397
    pregnancy and, 32
epidemiology of, 29–30
in family, home-based care
    case example of, 405–407, 408–409
in family of origin, 32
juveniles and, 31
mental illness and, 30, 31
mood stabilizers for, 38
murder, 29–30
perpetrators of, 30, 31–32
prediction of
    demographic variables in, 32–33
    validity of, 33
prevention of
    staff training for, 39
psychopharmacologic management of, 36–38
risk evaluation and, 34–35
at risk populations, 31–32, 230
serotonin deficit and, 33
signs of, 343, 50, 68t
staff and trainee experience with, 38–40
in US versus Canada, 31
victims of, 31–32
women and, 31
Violent patient
hospitalization of, 42
management of
    in institutional setting, 36
    in private office setting, 35–36

outpatient treatment of, 42
primary care assessment of, 68–69
    signs of impending attack, 68t
primary care management of
    handling of threats in, 70
    weapon management in, 69
protective custody for, 42–43
treatment of
    family members and, 41–42
    home setting and, 41–42
    insurance and managed care effect on, 41
    termination of, 70

Wandering behavior, in demented elderly, 263, 264
Weapons
    in assessment of violence, 33–34
    in emergency departments, 38–39
Weight gain, with divalproex, 154
Wernicke's encephalopathy, 234, 236
Werther phenomenon, suicide and, 282–283
Withdrawal syndrome(s)
    alcohol, 148, 234, 236
    clinical features of, 235t
    nicotine, 173
    opioid, 237–238
    sedative-hypnotic, 237
WWHHHHIMPS
    mnemonic for life-threatening causes of mental
        status changes, 54t

Ziprasidone, for schizophrenia, 181–182

An Important Quality Control Tool for Your Practice from the Authors of *Acute Care Psychiatry*

OUTCOMES ASSESSMENT IN CLINICAL PRACTICE

Edited by
Lloyd I. Sederer, MD and Barbara Dickey, PhD

"Over the last twenty years, psychiatry has undergone more profound changes than any other area of medicine...it is essential that the field of psychiatry develop objective methods to assess the outcome and quality of mental health and substance abuse care."

—from the forward by
Joseph T. Coyle, MD

Eben S. Draper Professor of Psychiatry and of Neuroscience
Chair of the Consolidated Department of Psychiatry
Harvard Medical School

With psychiatrists taking a more active role in outcomes assessment, this practical, comprehensive resource is an essential tool for developing guidelines for your practice. This valuable reference provides:

- an overview of outcome assessment
- methods for using outcome assessment in clinical practice
- detailed information of a variety of instruments used in measuring outcomes
- expectations for the future

Outcomes Assessment in Clinical Practice is a distinctive manual on 18 different outcomes instruments. The contributors give thorough descriptions of each instrument, including key references and a profile of the instrument's application. More detail is given on the:

- target population for the instrument
- procedures for data collection
- language and cultural diversity
- psychometric properties
- utility of the instrument
- strengths and weaknesses of each instrument

Be prepared to manage your practice in the rapidly changing world of psychiatry well into the next century. Order today. 1996/384 pages/8 illustrations/07630-2

Preview this book for a full month. If you're not completely satisfied, return it at no further obligation (US and Canada only).

Phone orders accepted 24 hours a day, 7 days a week (US only).
From the US—Call: 1-800-638-0672 • Fax: 1-800-447-8438
From Canada—Call: 1-800-665-1165 • Fax: 1-800-665-0103
From outside the US and Canada—Call: 410-528-4223
From the UK and Europe—Call: 44 (171) 385-2357
From Southeast Asia—Call: (852) 2610-2339

INTERNET
E-mail: custserv@wwilkins.com
Home page: http://www.wwilkins.com

Williams & Wilkins
A WAVERLY COMPANY

Printed in US   1- 97